Contemporary Problems in Personnel:
Readings for the Seventies

W. Clay Hamner
Frank L. Schmidt
Michigan State Unive

St. Clair Press
3 East Huron Street
Chicago 60611

To Patti and Betty

Contemporary Problems in Personnel
Copyright © 1974 by St. Clair Press
All rights reserved. Printed in the United States of America.
No part of this publication may be reproduced, stored in a retrieval
system, or transmitted in any form or by any means,
electronic, mechanical, photocopying, recording, or otherwise, without the
prior written permission of the publisher.

Library of Congress Catalog Card Number 73-93871
ISBN 0-914292-01-3

Cover design by H. B. Smith

St. Clair Press
3 East Huron Street
Chicago, Illinois 60611

Preface

Managers are faced today with increasingly difficult and complex personnel decisions. New and sometimes exotic methods and approaches to personnel problems have appeared; these require examination and evaluation. Government rules and requirements have proliferated; these must be understood and met. This book is designed to help the reader understand the complexity of the problems and to suggest workable solutions.

This book is suitable for use as a text in introductory or intermediate courses in personnel. It can also be used to supplement or update other texts in the areas of personnel and labor relations. For those who teach a course in organizational behavior, industrial psychology, or human relations, this would be an ideal choice as a supplementary text to provide examples of orginal source writings and practical "real-world" applications without duplicating material covered in traditional organizational texts.

Our selection of topics to be covered and of individual readings was guided by two goals. First, the book should cover the broad range of personnel problems—not merely those traditionally assigned to the personnel function and not merely those encountered only in certain kinds of organizations or at certain organizational levels. In this we feel we have succeeded. Second, the book should cover topics of *current* interest—rather than rehash issues that are ancient history. With few exceptions, readings are drawn from the 1970-74 time period. This feature should allow the instructor who has a favorite text which is a little dated to continue to use that text, while employing this book as a supplement.

Many individuals have contributed to the successful completion of this book. We cannot list all their names here, but we particularly want to thank Herbert Heneman, III, for his advice and suggestions on the original manuscript. We also wish to thank our secretary, Ms. Marie Dumeney, for her outstanding work and her tolerance for our inconsistent democratic style of leadership.

W. Clay Hamner
Frank L. Schmidt

Contents

Modern Personnel: A Blending of the Needs of the Individual with the Needs of the Organization

Personnel as a discipline today is concerned with the application of psychological research and research methods to the problems of human resource utilization in organizational settings. As we move through the 1970s, the personnel function has taken on a much broader role in both private and public organizations. It is our intention in this first chapter to provide the reader with an appreciation of this broader role and to emphasize to the reader the reason why an understanding of the topics presented in this book will enhance his or her managerial talents.

In the early 1960s, Dunnette and Bass reflected a growing concern among academicians and businessmen alike that personnel management as it is presented in business schools and practiced in organizations was intent on pursuing a pattern of increasing stagnation and, therefore, a student receiving a degree in personnel administration as taught in the 1960s was not going to be equipped to face the business and industrial needs of the future. In order for personnel to survive as a discipline, it had to have less dependency on the industrial engineer and management historian and more emphasis on creativity, disciplined thinking and the appropriate use of the analytical tools and techniques of behavioral science. Dunnette and Bass, while often being overly critical,[1] seem to be right in suggesting that the personnel manager must become a behavioral scientist and be able not only to identify problems, but also to possess the tools necessary to solve these problems.

In a later article, Johnson (1971) says that changes coming in the 1970s will demand changes in the duties and responsibilities of the personnel administrator. In order to become, as he must, the director of human resources, the personnel major should have a well-grounded background in organizational behavior and applied psychology. Johnson says that the reason this background is needed is because of the added responsibility and demands placed on the personnel manager from inside and outside the organization. The personnel manager must have both upward as well as downward influence in the organization and must be able to advise top management on "people" programs (see the article by Hamner, chap. 6, for examples), and represent the employees of the organization. Johnson emphasizes the necessity for the possession of both statistical and accounting skills by personnel directors.

Examples of why personnel managers must be more skilled and assume more responsibility than ever before are also presented in Dunn and Stephens. They review the restrictions placed on personnel decisions by the federal government in the passage of the National Labor Relations Act (1935), Civil Rights Act (1964), Equal Pay

Act (1963) an the Occupational Safety and Health Act (1970). Decisions made by personnel managers in the area of hiring, training and development, compensation, record-keeping, and task design must now be subject to rigorous standards in order to be within the regulations set by federal and state agencies. The readings in this book attempt to introduce the reader to the tools necessary to meet the restrictions placed on them by federal and state agencies. Readings presented in chapters 2, 9, and 10 are especially relevant in this area.

Like the private sector, personnel departments in the public sector in the late 1960s and early 1970s found themselves dated and unable to meet the new demands being placed on them by their employees and the agencies they served. In order to help these agencies, the federal government passed the Intergovernmental Personnel Act in 1970. In our fourth reading, Robertson explores the meaning of this act and explains how it gives assistance to federal, state, and local governments to strengthen, update and increase the status of their personnel departments for more effective governmental administration.

While it is now a changing and growing field of prime importance which will play a vital role in the success of the organization of the future, the field of personnel as an academic subject in the 1960s, as described by Dunnette and Bass, was failing to attract future academicians. Carroll describes three studies which indicated a declining interest in personnel management as a major by graduate students and an increased interest in behavioral science majors (organizational psychology and organizational behavior). While many of the criticisms by the students were valid in the past, with the changes in the field occurring (as described in the first four readings), criticisms by students that the field is not quantitative enough, that it lacks a humanistic approach or that "even people of low academic ability" can succeed are no longer valid.

It is interesting to note that the students in the Carroll sample chose a major in organizational psychology or organizational behavior over that of personnel. In the last article in this first chapter, Bass outlines the reason why one cannot separate personnel issues from questions concerning the psychology of behavior. He points out that you cannot separate the two fields when he says, "The personnel specialist no longer can hide behind his validity coefficients, test blanks and training manuals. In turn, the organization scientist cannot remain assured of the generality of results from his surveys, field studies, and rational analysis" (Bass, 1968, p. 366).

Students at both graduate and undergraduate levels who are majoring in management, organizational behavior industrial or organizational psychology, or labor and industrial relations should not approach their major as being either behavioral science or applied personnel—it must be a blending of both. Students who have an interest in personnel should not shy away from courses in statistics, applied quantitative analysis, accounting or courses with a behavior science flavor. Students who are in doubt as to what courses should be taken to prepare for the personnel function of the future should visit personnel departments in several major firms to see what background would best prepare them for the job they seek. It is our opinion, based on our own experiences with personnel departments and our conversations with college recruiters, that companies that say they can take any college major and train him in personnel work are out of step with reality. Personnel is not a "seat of the pants" operation; it is, rather, a profession that holds more respect and status in the organization today than ever before.

In summary, this first chapter attempts to set the stage for the reader of this book. We have attempted in it to give the rationale for our belief that personnel is critical as a subject and to give an understanding of the importance of each article selected. Students who gain a thorough grasp of the topics covered in this book should have no trouble with advanced courses in personnel and related courses.

Note

1. See T. Patten, "Criticism and Comment" *Industrial Relations*, vol. 3, 1964, pp. 109-18, for a reply to the Dunnette and Bass paper.

Behavioral Scientists and Personnel Management

MARVIN D. DUNNETTE
BERNARD M. BASS

The search for the philosopher's stone which would transmute base metals into gold occupied alchemists for hundreds of years. Although they were concentrating on the wrong problem, many of the alchemists' techniques and much of their lore served eventually as the basis for the budding science of chemistry.

Like alchemists, personnel managers have concentrated on the wrong problem, trying one technique after the other in a long search for a psychological touchstone to solve all the human problems of industry. Meanwhile, particularly during the last decade, the behavioral sciences have developed principles and techniques which have proved immediately applicable and useful to the art of management. These developments are long overdue; they are occurring after more than a century of philosophizing and experimenting with various concepts of work, employment, management, and manpower marketing.

Prescientific management, in the Smith-Ricardo-Marx tradition, regarded work as a commodity to be bought at the lowest price and sold at the highest, with the worker an interchangeable part to be maintained at minimum cost in the production process. Taylorism, which followed, focused on rationalizing work, the workplace, and incentives in order to maximize output and induce workers to exert maximum effort in return for material gain. Paternalism, the precursor of the human relations school, sought to win employee loyalty either through crude bribery or more subtle and sophisticated manipulation. Faulty logic, coupled with false assumptions about the nature of man, resulted in generations of unnecessary conflict, rule-making and rule-breaking, dissatisfaction, and curtailed production.

Modern personnel management includes vestiges of each of these approaches in the programs it seeks to promote as its raison d'être. The tendency to regard labor as a commodity is reflected in the continuing practice of paying wage earners by the hour rather than on a salaried basis. Taylorism is reflected in job simplification, specifica-

Reprinted by permission of the authors and the publisher from *Industrial Relations*, vol. 2 (May 1963), pp. 115-30.

tion, and specialization, when job enlargement might be more appropriate. Paternalism has resulted in hidden labor costs and infringe benefits as high as 40 percent of the total payroll, creating what Bendix has called the new industrial feudalism.

Toward a Science of Industrial Behavior

During the past decade, efforts to promote the scientific and objective study of human behavior in industry have successfully penetrated management practice. Paralleling this movement, many of the leading schools of business and industrial administration have shifted from the descriptive study of current personnel practices to the application of principles of the social sciences to the analysis of organization problems. Emphasis is placed on creativity, disciplined thinking, and the appropriate use of analytical tools for effective decision-making. The behavioral sciences are making rapid strides and are moving to a central position in the study of industrial behavior. Yet personnel management seems intent on pursuing a pattern of increasing stagnation and lack of significant innovation. As a result, behavioral scientists are being employed by businessmen not only to undertake research but also to apply their findings to the actual operation of the enterprise. Psychology, sociology, and related disciplines are responding to the call of a new and enlightened management. Personnel management, with its traditional practices, appears to be ill-equipped to face the business and industrial needs of the future.

If this indictment of personnel management is valid, it raises some disturbing questions and has some interesting implications for the future role of the behavioral sciences in industry. This article will be concerned, therefore, with the following important questions:

1. In what respects has personnel management defaulted in meeting businessmen's needs for innovation in handling the problems of human behavior in industry? Why has this occurred? Is it too late to do anything about it?

2. What has been the role of the behavioral sciences in relation to the human problems of industry? How have the behavioral sciences responded to the changing needs and emphases of modern business?

3. What will be the role of the behavioral scientist in the business organization of the future? What problems of human behavior may he be asked to help solve, and what will be his mode of attack?

4. What are the "development needs" of personnel management? What kind of manager will the personnel manager of the future be? What contributions will he be expected to make to the business enterprise? To what extent will he depend on behavioral science? What will he contribute to the development of the behavioral sciences?

5. Finally, how will human behavior problems of the business firm of the future be handled? How will personnel management and behavioral science interact and supplement one another?

The Failure of Personnel Management

Evidence of the failure of personnel management to adapt to the changing climate of business is widespread and well-documented. Drucker was one of the first to call attention to the shaky future of the profession. In 1954, he assigned to the personnel function such chores as housekeeping, filing, and firefighting and suggested that it was destined to become a cluster of unrelated functions such as accounting, office management, and the handling of administrative arrangements—in other words, a sort of staff office boy to the rest of the organization.[1] Odiorne also finds little reason for optimism.[2] He suggests that too many personnel officers still reflect the naiveté of the early twenties and that many still practice the rites of the profession as if nothing had changed since 1925. The personnel program in most companies is not central to the enterprise and, indeed, is rapidly coming to be regarded as a function entirely ancillary to the major purposes of the firm. Herbert Heneman has provided a most discerning and thorough analysis of the present problems and uncertain future of personnel procedures.[3] Personnel management, in his opinion, has been marked by shallowness, negativism, static concepts, and oversimplified approaches to complex problems. Instances of these limitations are not hard to find.:

1. The personnel interview continues to be the most widely used method for selecting employees, despite the fact that it is a costly, inefficient, and usually invalid procedure.[4] It is often used to the exclusion of far more thoroughly researched and validated procedures. Even when the interview is used in conjunction with other procedures, it is almost always treated as the final hurdle in the selection process. In fact, other selection methods (e.g., psychological tests) are often regarded simply as supplements to the interview.

The continued uncritical use of the personal interview offers a clear illustration of what is perhaps personnel management's prime problem—that is, the great resistance to carrying out fundamental research on its practices and techniques. Careful programs of research have been conducted to assess the validity of other selection techniques, and progress has been made toward specifying their validity under a variety of conditions. Until similar research has specified the conditions under which the interview does have predictive value, its continued use must be rationalized as a public relations device rather than as a personnel procedure. Even so, there are still many outspoken and ardent supporters of the personal interview, many of whom are wedded to the device as their raison d'être.

2. Typical management development programs clearly illustrate the shallow and oversimplified approaches denounced by Heneman. Again, in connection with such programs, personnel management displays overenchantment with gadgetry and techniques, ignoring the need for research on the enormously complex problems of human behavior in industry. As Taylor has pointed out, these gimmicks in management development programs range from role-playing and brainstorming to management by committee and so-called "new" techniques of conference leadership.[5] Many personnel men have been only too ready to pose as experts in the difficult science of human development and behavior change. They have used gimmicks to promote an *art* of management development, without first undertaking the solid scientific research required to develop the principles on which a sound program might be based. No wonder the programs, so widely promoted by personnel staff departments, have gone from "fad" to "old hat" in less than a decade. Widespread disillusionment with management development programs has contributed substantially to the demise of personnel management.

3. Negativism, shallowness and static concepts are particularly evident in wage and salary administration. On the basis of an exhaustive review of the literature of the last ten years on employee and executive compensation, Belcher concludes that wage and salary administrators have developed an array of programs but have given practically no attention to evaluation of their relative merit.[6] Salary administration functions

in far too many firms constitute either holding actions or, at best, practices of keeping up with (but not ahead of) the Joneses. The old-fashioned idea of using money as an incentive to effort has very nearly disappeared. Even at the level of executive compensation, personnel men are concerned with gimmicks, procedures, and techniques to the near exclusion of principles of human motivation. An accounting philosophy and idle speculation about "programs" pervades their thinking.

It is extremely unfortunate that many early personnel men were "burned" when they tried to institute compensation schemes which conflicted with nonmonetary drives (e.g., social motives).[7] The salary and wage administration functions of many firms have, as a result, become shrouded in a veil of secrecy, and the possibility of innovation in the use of money as an incentive to effort, in conjunction with fundamental knowledge concerning employee motivation, seems remote. Thus, even though it has been abundantly shown that money is an effective incentive when used in combination with other motivating principles, most personnel managers lack the spirit of innovation and research mindedness necessary to work out effective combinations of money and other types of motivation.

4. Most personnel training programs, according to Bowles, are merely acts of wishful thinking on the part of the training directors responsible for them.[8] The principles of human learning spelled out so well by McGhee and Thayer are rarely given heed in industrial training efforts.[9] Indeed, if our public school systems carried out their educational functions in the manner of the typical industrial training program, the wailing and anguish of critics could probably be heard from here to the moon. In contrast to the situation in education, the lack of carefully designed training evaluation studies in industry is startling.[10] Personnel men apparently are unwilling to test the usefulness of training procedures by conducting periodic, experimentally designed audits of their programs.

Other writers have commented on the problems of personnel management in this country, Canada, and Western Europe.[11] There seems to be substantial agreement that classic personnel procedures have everywhere been found wanting. As a group, personnel managers have been too easily content with their "servicing" jobs. Early successes based on systematic applications of certain techniques and skills (e.g., recruitment practices, accounting systems for wage and salary payments, counseling, and "human relations" programs) apparently promoted a premature freezing of procedures. Generally, personnel men are content to follow the dictates of a technique-bound profession and have resisted opportunities to study problems involving human behavior in industry from a scientific point of view.

We believe that personnel management, as presently constituted, must yield its position to broader and more innovative behavioral sciences, which are proving capable of fulfilling management's needs for research as well as for the application of research results to the solution of problems of human behavior in industry.

Crisis in the Behavioral Sciences?

Clearly the behavioral sciences have not yet entirely come of age. In fact, they too nearly fell by the wayside as a result of premature crystallizing of techniques and procedures. For example, during the early and middle fifties, industrial psychologists were frequently criticized, usually justifiably, for a tendency to distort business problems to fit their pet measurement and testing procedures rather than to study actual human problems in business in order to develop novel approaches to their solution. As late as the fall of 1958, in his presidential address before the Division of Industrial Psychology of the American Psychological Association, Lawshe called attention to such practices and criticized industrial psychologists for them.[12] In a sense, the fifties constituted years of crisis for industrial psychology. In its applications to industry and business was it slated to become merely an occasionally useful adjunct characterized by sets of mechanistic tests, global case studies, and *a posteriori* reasoning? Or could it respond imaginatively to the growth of industry and the enlightenment of a new type of management seeking novel solutions to old problems?

The seeds of crisis were felt by many industrial psychologists early in the postwar years. Some of the more imaginative ones began to alter their ways and to develop more diversified approaches to business problems. However, the majority simply let the business world move by, as Leavitt has suggested:

> . . . classical industrial psychology is maybe a little bit under the weather. Its practitioners are apt to be . . . conflicted. If they have stuck to the pure and true—to test construction and job evaluation—they are finding themselves relegated to peripheral technicians' roles; at once outside the mainstream of the organization and also outside the mainstream of psychology. They have had a piece of bad luck too; the bad luck of allying themselves with the once promising young profession of personnel management. If not . . . moribund, that profession turned out to be at least disappointingly stodgy and unimaginative.[13]

In other words, industrial psychology, like its sister profession, personnel management, became technique-bound. The simple-minded paradigm of the classic selection model persisted for over half a century.[14] Psychologists played a large part in developing and promoting various wage and salary "plans," employee rating procedures, attitude scales, and an impressive array of other mechanically oriented devices. These pet techniques and psychological "instruments" became the stock in trade of the industrial psychologist. It is little wonder, then, that he fell into the habit of seeking or inventing problems to fit his methods, rather than devoting his time to the solution of actual business problems.

Moreover, the classical model of industrial engineering, designed to rationalize work and the workplace, has undoubtedly created more human problems in industry than it has solved. Here, too, the difficulty has been a too ready acceptance of simple procedures for the solution of complex problems. Indeed, industrial engineering appears to have been seized by a panacea complex and to have been incapable of coping effectively with the industrial employee as a human being.

While industrial psychology was often rendered sterile by a simple-minded reliance on shotgun data collected without any underlying rationale, its sister social sciences, such as industrial sociology and anthropology, suffered from a muddleheaded desire to explain the whole situation. Case studies, sometimes with samples consisting of a single subject, were often used as the basis for sweeping generalizations which, as Homans would put it, were interesting but not necessarily true.[15] The dependence on participant-observers or on limited data from interviews seriously biased conclusions. The reliability of observations was considered less important than whether the observations were consistent with a pronouncement by Durkheim or Pareto.

Even so, the insights and speculations of sociologists and anthropologists have changed our conceptions of worker motivation, of the significance of the work group, and of the discrepancy between prescription and description in the large organization.[16] The trend toward greater objectivity and reliability in sociology has been influenced by the work of Bales on small groups, Lazarsfeld and his co-workers, Guttman on attitude measurement, and many others.[17] Indeed, successful attempts have been made to reproduce in the laboratory certain societal phenomena, such as cycles of innovation and ritualization, which were previously merely a matter of speculation and crosscultural observation.[18] Moreover, reliable generalizations have been based on respectable numbers of observations, for example, in the examination of as many as 150 primitive cultures, using anthropological data.[19] Indeed, industrial sociology and anthropology have been transformed into a more general behavioral science of business. Weber's classic work on bureaucracy, formerly accepted as the sine qua non for understanding the large, formal business organization, now serves merely as an introduction to the subject.[20]

New Directions

These years of crisis for the behavioral sciences, painful though they were, did stimulate rapid growth and significant change. In addition to a small handful of industrial psychologists, other social scientists accepted the challenge of addressing themselves to the human problems of business.[21] By the mid-fifties, at least three new kinds of industrial behavioral science had emerged:

1. A science devoted to the purpose of assuring adequate recognition of human capabilities in the design of equipment and systems (predominantly military and weapons systems) came into being. Engineering psychologists, specializing in such work, are concerned with developing rules for designing equipment which can be operated efficiently by the *typical* human being. More broadly, they are concerned with identifying the sources of variation or error in any man-machine system. Thus, they use the knowledge and methods of experimental psychology, physiology, statistical methodology, and industrial engineering in attempting to solve complex equipment and systems-design problems.

2. As an unhappy alternative to the rather rigid and mechanistic approach of the classical industrial psychologist, there has been continuing widespread use of subjective and clinical procedures in connection with the human problems of business. Thus, executive counseling (with no discernible emphasis on research or evaluation) is enjoying a heyday, while projective techniques and depth interviewing are being widely used in personnel assessment programs. Since these methods are essentially unscientific, they cannot be subjected to objective tests. Even so, the therapeutic relationships established between executives and their counselors have often resulted in greater frankness among company managers, better adjustment to the pressures of modern-day business, and a more effective handling of interpersonal relationships in business. Although it is unlikely that clinical methods will persist in personnel assessment, there does appear to be sufficient evidence of improved human relationships to warrant the continued utilization of the clinician in industry.

3. The most promising development in the behavioral sciences takes the form of a merging of individual, experimental, and social psychology and the sociology of formal organizations, buttressed by computer technology, game theory, and related techniques. A vigorous new group of behavioral scientists is at the forefront with recent studies designed to gain an understanding of organizations and the human interactions which comprise them. This new discipline has been characterized by Leavitt as organizational psychology. Its nature, diversity, and high potential for successfully attacking the human problems of business are apparent from Leavitt's thumbnail description:

Organizational psychology occupies itself with the study of organizations and organizational processes. It is as much descriptive as normative; as much or more basic as applied; as much interested in developing theories of organizational behavior as ways of improving organizational practice. It is close on one of its boundaries to human relations psychology, especially the social-experimental part of that field. It is also touched with experimental psychology and the rapidly growing field of empirical sociology. Its other boundaries are quite different: predominantly economics and mathematics—the game theorists, the operations researchers, the computer people.[22]

Thus, it is clear that organizational psychology is a fortunate blending of the science of psychology, with its emphasis on the formulation and testing of general rules and principles, with more immediate day-by-day applications to the art of business management. Each branch serves and is served by the other in a fortunate symbiotic combination. The behavioral scientist of today is much less prone to display the inflexibility which has been characteristic of personnel management or of the technique-bound social sciences in the past. Instead he is alert to problems and research opportunities which can aid in the development of behavioral science while also improving the over-all effectiveness of business management.

Theories and Their Applications

The adaptions stimulated by the years of crisis in the behavioral sciences have resulted in a new industrial science—one well equipped to play a central role in the business management of the future. Already this new school of broadened and more comprehensive psychology has produced insights (both theoretical and empirical) which are having widespread impact on the business community. For example:

1. A revolution may well be under way in industrial training. At long last, experimental work in learning has been adapted to educational methods in the form of programmed instruction,[23] characterized by an effort to break instructional content down into highly organized, logical stages which demand a continuing active response from the trainee. After each response, the trainee receives "feedback" or knowledge on how he did. Thus he receives immediate reinforcement or reward for learning. In a pioneering study, Hughes compared the effectiveness of programmed instruction with that of conventional classroom instruction in training IBM customer engineers to learn the nomenclature of the IBM 7070 computer.[24] The group receiving programmed instruction required 27 percent less classroom time and showed a learning gain of 10 percent over that shown by the group in the conventional classroom situation. With such results as these, behavioral scientists are moving rapidly into the field of industrial training. The emphasis on motivation in programmed instruction and its use of important principles of learning, such as reinforcement, immediate knowledge of results, and attention to individual differences help to explain its role in providing a critical breakthrough for behavioral science in industry.

2. Business executives are being taught to become better decision-makers and to make more effective use of the abilities of other persons in solving complex business problems.[25] The methods were developed from the theoretical and methodological contributions made in group dynamics by Kurt Lewin. Beginning in the late forties, under the leadership of Leland Brandford, training sessions in "human relations" were held in Bethel, Maine, under a grant from the Carnegie Corporation. Lewin's theories

and group dynamics concepts received rigid testing for a number of years and were modified accordingly—a clear example of the testing of psychology's scientific insights in the rugged arena of actual application. The early programs tended to be somewhat "soft headed" and overly emphasized a namby-pamby kind of adjustment to other persons. Today, however, the most successful industrial programs provide simulated or contrived group-conflict situations, in which the participants become deeply involved and, with the help of instructors, gain insight into their own and others' problem-solving behavior. The goal, of course, is to train participants to be applied human scientists, who will approach problem situations according to systematic principles, carefully gathering and sifting all available information rather than relying on haphazard, rule-of-thumb, or simple habitual techniques, as has been the typical pattern in the past. Although the evidence is not yet in, the results so far seem far superior to those accruing from any previous effort to teach human-relations and/or problem-solving methods applicable to complex business problems.[26]

3. New approaches to problems of industrial selection have been suggested and tried out. Foremost among these has been the utility model elaborated by Cronbach and Gleser.[27] This approach emphasizes the desirability of computing the utility and/or cost associated with various kinds of selection outcomes.[28] Moreover, these authors suggest the use of a sequential program in the selection process. In other words, selection is based on a series of decisions related to the varying validities of different procedures for distinguishing among the applicants for various jobs. Personnel selection in the firm of the future is likely to be based on evidence supplied by careful behavioral research, rather than on a single technique (such as the interview), as it is in most firms today. As Dunnette has pointed out, the selection expert of the future.

> will not be blindly attempting to utilize identical methods for all his selection problems. Instead, he will be a sort of statistical clinician. He will have developed, through research, a wealth of evidence showing the patterns of validities for different techniques, candidates, jobs, and criteria. He will be a flexible operator, attentive always to the accumulating information on any given candidate, and ready to apply, at each stage, the tests and procedures shown to be optimal and most valid.[29]

4. Perhaps the most impressive and far-reaching contributions lie in the area of organizational theorizing and its implications for managerial and employee behavior in the firm of the future. A large and growing literature provides impressive evidence of the increasing interest in this approach.[30] Although the rash of activity in organizational psychology has as yet resulted in few applications to the actual art of managing,[31] it is precisely in this field that the interaction between management and the new industrial psychology are likely to be most evident and most productive.

Only a sampling has been provided of the contributions already made, and it is merely suggestive of the innovations to be expected from this rapidly expanding field in the years ahead. The years of crisis are essentially over; the shakeout has been accomplished. The evolution from technician, or academic observer, to educator-trainer and research specialist on human behavior in the industrial organization is well under way. Let us, therefore, speculate a bit concerning the developing role on the behavioral sciences in industry and the possible nature of their contributions to effective management in the future.

Optimizing the System

Current thinking in the behavioral sciences and in microeconomics suggests that any attempt to maximize some aspect of organizational output or to minimize some aspect of organizational input or waste is bound to end in less than the desired result somewhere else in the system. One can't have one's cake and eat it too—and the staff specialist in personnel must not only stop searching for the magic incantation or philosopher's stone but also cease to act as if he has already found it. Rather he must become an applied behavioral scientist, using the principles and methods of modern psychology, sociology, and economics to help management and workers optimize the total system that is the business organization.[32]

Experts in human affairs in industry must be trained in psychology, sociology, economics, and organization theory (note we do not say personnel management, as such) to know the relevant principles and methods that must be applied in seeking answers to certain types of managerial problems. These problems concern the interaction of inputs, outputs, and waste of (a) men and money or (b) men and materials.

For example, a typical question on which research might be conducted follows:

If we increase our management trainee budget, will we increase individual management growth and satisfaction, or increase waste of money and our inventory of unused talent? In his search for valid answers, the behavioral scientist must consider as interacting components: output (men) and input (money) with input (men) with waste (money) and waste (men).

Many important questions of this sort, for which solid research answers can be found, might be enumerated. For example, we suggest a sample of questions on which any respectable behavioral scientist of the future should be prepared to conduct appropriate research, applying appropriate methods and drawing on his knowledge of the literature:

1. What can we do to get people in an organization to say what they think, instead of merely saying what they think their bosses want to hear? How can the full range of ideas available in a group be brought to the surface? How do interpersonal relationships either facilitate or inhibit problem-solving effectiveness in business? How may group and personal interactions be capitalized upon to maximize organizational problem-solving effectiveness?

2. We have just discovered that our salesmen can't figure simple percentages. If they can't compute percentages, is it because they don't know how to divide, or what? Can we use some simple diagnostic tests to find out how widespread and serious the problem is? What kinds of self-training techniques are available for those needing them? If remedial action is inadequate, should salesmen use simple slide rules in front of their customers or do the figuring with them? Or, should all calculations be made at the office?

3. How do we use our computer facilities to increase feedback to employees? What kinds of information will contribute positively to the motivation of employees? What measures of results may be developed to enhance the learning and/or continued productive efforts of all employees—managerial as well as rank and file? May the measures be "computerized"? In what form may information be presented most effectively to employees?

4. What are the implications of the current and future racial composition of our employees on our over-all operations? Can we or should we maintain different policies

in different regions? Are our current selection tests as valid for our Negro as for our white applicants? What are the reactions of white jobholders in an occupational category in which Negroes begin to find employment? What about Negro supervisors and white subordinates?

5. Should our diversification of organization be along product, process, or geographical lines? What are the significant human factors to be considered here, as they interact with purely economic and engineering issues? What is likely to be the effect of the type of diversification on management development and organizational flexibility?

6. What effects may be expected from flattening the structure of our organizational hierarchy? What new managerial skills may be required? How will they be developed? What new controls may be necessary that are not required in a more vertically organized company? How will these be developed and implemented?

Currently, it is the Ph.D. in psychology or associated behavioral disciplines (not necessarily industrial psychology) who receives the education necessary for the "tough-minded" research demanded by an enlightened management. What other companies have done will not provide adequate answers to the really important questions—and too often the past education of the personnel manager has provided him with nothing more than the ability to follow where industrial engineers, industrial psychologists, or, much worse, industrial faddists have led.

In addition to an ability to search out answers, and to rephrase questions so that they are answerable, the behavioral scientist (formerly known as a personnel manager) will be able and eager to initiate new programs of research and training without waiting for the issues to arise. Thus, he may press for organizational gaming—developing specific games to meet particular needs in management and employee training and research through the stimulation of the system or subsystems. Or, he may, with top management, plan his own long-range educational program for such personnel needs as an executive training and replacement schedule.

Other important trends may be discerned. Like the Ph.D. in chemistry, who is beginning to be found in all types of positions in the chemical industry, the behavioral scientist of the future may more frequently become a member of line management.[33] This would be the opposite of the current tendency to rotate into personnel management from the line and would resemble the tendency for men who have advanced degrees in engineering to become executives.

The future research specialist in human factors may receive his education in behavioral science in schools of business administration as well as in departments of psychology, sociology, or related fields. He is also likely to have more training in associated areas, such as operations research, mathematics, and statistics. At the same time, he will tend to make more contributions to basic psychology and sociology, particularly in such areas as: human interaction, communications in organization, decision-making, emotional factors in learning, design of experiments, and bureaucracy. Indeed, the time may come when (as now occurs in certain branches of chemistry) a Ph.D. in psychology, sociology, or one of the other behavioral sciences commonly elects to join an industrial firm rather than remain at a university, so that he may have adequate facilities and opportunities to pursue his research interests.[34]

We believe, then, that the personnel man of the future will be an expert in the difficult and complex science of human behavior. What his formal label will be is not important, but his function will be that of a professional scientist and adviser, to whom problems of human behavior in business will be referred. The central role we anticipate for the behavioral sciences in the firm of the future is a far cry from the technique-bound services of present-day personnel management or from the myopic empiricism or global muddleheadedness of early social scientists. During the past decade, this new behavioral science of business practice began to develop. An enlightened management is calling for more industrial behavioral scientists such as we have described; our educational institutions should respond by training an increasing number of these personnel specialists of the future. It may be that they will be called neither personnel managers nor industrial psychologists. However, they will be uniquely equipped to handle the human problems arising out of our continuing efforts to optimize the organizational systems of the future.

Notes

1. P. F. Drucker, *The Practice of Management* (New York: Harper, 1954).

2. G. S. Odiorne, "Company Growth and Personnel Administration," *Personnel,* XXVII (January-February, 1960), 32-41.

3. H. G. Heneman, Jr., *Manpower Management: New Wrapping on Old Merchandise* (Minneapolis, Minn.: Industrial Relations Center, University of Minnesota, 1969).

4. See, for example, R. Wagner, "The Employment Interview: A Critical Summary," *Personnel Psychology,* II (1949), 17-46; G. W. England and D. G. Paterson, "Selection and Placement—the Past Ten Years," in H. G. Heneman, editor, *Employment Relations Research* (New York: Harper, 1960), pp. 43-72; M. D. Dunnette, "Personnel Management," *Annual Review of Psychology,* XIII (1962), 285-314.

5. E. K. Taylor, "Management Development at the Crossroads," *Personnel,* XXXVI (March-April, 1959), 8-23.

6. D. W. Belcher, "Employee and Executive Compensation," in Heneman, editor, *op. cit.,* pp. 73-131.

7. See, for example, Frances Torbert, "Making Incentives Work," *Harvard Business Review,* XXXVII (September-October, 1959), 81-92; William F. Whyte and others, *Money and Motivation* (New York: Harper, 1955); H. R. Northrup, "The Other Side of Incentives," *Personnel,* XXXVI (January-February, 1959), 32-41.

8. W. J. Bowles, "The Mismanagement of Supervisory Training," *Personnel,* XXXVIII (March-Aptil, 1961), 50-57.

9. William McGehee and Paul W. Thayer, *Training in Business and Industry* (New York: Wiley, 1961).

10. For excellent outlines of methods for evaluating training programs in industry, see D. L. Kirkpatrick, "Techniques for Evalutting Training Programs," *Journal of American Society of Training Directors* (1959-1960), pp. 13-14; L. K. Randall, "Evaluation: A Training Dilemma," *Journal of American Society of Training Directors,* XIV (1960), 29-35; T. A. Mahoney, *Building the Executive Team: A Guide to Management Development* (Englewood Cliffs, N.J.: Prentice-Hall, 1961).

11. D. B. Strother, "Personnel Management in Theory and Practice," *Personnel,* XXXVI (May-June, 1959), 63-71; J. D. Kyle, "Personnel Administration Must Embark on a Program of Rigorous Self Development," *Personnel and Industrial Relations Journal,* VIII (1961), 9-17; F. T. Malm, "The Development of Personnel Administration in Western Europe," *California Management Review,* III (Fall, 1960), 69-83.

12. C. H. Lawshe, "Of Management and Measurement," *American Psychologist,* XIV (1959), 290-294.

13. H. J. Leavitt, *Toward Organizational Psychology* (Pittsburgh, Pa.: Carnegie Institute of Technology, Graduate School of Business Administration, March, 1961).

14. That is, the classic test validation technique of dividing employees into "good" and "poor" groups and comparing their performance on a series of psychological tests. Although this is still a common technique of industrial psychologists, many more sophisticated approaches have been developed, these are discussed in a later section.

15. G. C. Homans, *The Human Group* (New York: Harcourt, Brace, 1959).

16. See F. J. Roethlesberger and W. J. Dickson, *Management and the Worker* (Cambridge, Mass.: Harvard University Press, 1943). See also, P. M. Blau and W. R. Scott, *Formal Organizations* (San Francisco: Chandler, 1962), for the best available summary of the literature on the sociology of organizations.

17. R. F. Bales, *Interaction Process Analyses* (Cambridge: Addison-Wesley Press, 1950); P. F. Lazarsfeld, *Latent Structure Analysis* (New York: Bureau of Applied Social Research, Columbia University, 1957); L. Guttman, "A Basis for Scaling Qualitative Data," *American Sociological Review*, IX (1944), 139-150.

18. R. L. Hamblin and J. A. Wiggins, *Ambiguity and the Rate of Social Adaptation*, Technical Report 1, ONR Contract N 811 (St. Louis, Mo.: Social Science Institute, Washington University, 1959).

19. S. H. Udy, Jr., *Organization of Work: A Comparative Analysis of Production Among Non-Industrial Peoples* (New Haven, Conn.: Human Relations Area File Press, 1959).

20. Max Weber, *The Theory of Social and Economic Organization*, translated by A. M. Henderson and T. Parsons (Glencoe, Ill.: Free Press, 1947).

21. See, for example, Leavitt, *op. cit,;* M. Haire, "Business Is Too Important to Be Studied Only by Economists," *American Psychologist*, XV (April, 1960), 271-273; M. Haire, "Problems Relevant to Business and Industry," *Psychological Bulletin*, LVI (May 1959), 169-194.

22. Leavitt, *op.cit.*

23. See, for example, McGehee and Thayer, *op. cit,;* A. A. Lunsdaine and R. Gleser, editors, *Teaching Machines and Programmed Learning: A Source Book* (Washington, D.C.: National Education Association, 1961); E. Galanter, editor, *Automatic Teaching: The State of the Art* (New York: Wiley, 1959); B. F. Skinner, "Teaching Machines," *Science*, CXXVIII (1958), 909-977.

24. J. L. Hughes, *The Effectiveness of Programmed Instruction: Experimental Findings for 7070 Training* (New York: International Business Machines, 1961).

25. See H. A. Shephard, "An Action Research Approach to Organizational Development." *Management Record*, XXII (June, 1960), 26-30; R. R. Blake and J. S. Mouton, "Group Dynamics in Decision Making: A Series," *Petroleum Refiner*, Vol. XXXIX (May-December, 1960); *Sensitivity Training: Curse or Cure* (New York: Industrial Relations Newsletter Special Report, March, 1962); C. H. Kepner and B. B. Tregoe, "Developing Decision Makers," *Harvard Business Review*, XXXVIII (September-October, 1960), 115-124.

26. See B. M. Bass, "The Management Training Laboratory—A Way to Improve Organizational Effectiveness," *Advertising Management*, XXV (1960), 11-15. For examples of evaluation studies of this approach to training, see R. S. Soar and N. C. Bowers, *Evaluation of Laboratory Human Relations Training for Classroom Teachers*, U.S. Office of Education Cooperative Research, Project No. 469, Vanderbilt University, 1962; and M. B. Miles, "Human Relations Training: Processes and Outcomes," *Journal of Counseling Psychology*, VII (1960), 301-306.

27. L. J. Cronbach and G. Gleser, *Psychological Tests and Personnel Decisions* (Urbana, Ill.: University of Illinois Press, 1957). See also S. R. Wallace, *What Price Selection* (Hartford, Conn.: Life Insurance Agency Management Association (1960).

V   28. For example, what is the cost to a firm of making a poor decision in selecting a salesman? Does the cost of a poor decision exceed the cost (recruiting, screening, etc.) of insuring a good decision? If it does not, it may well be argued that careful selection procedures are not warranted. This line of reasoning does not seem "new," but it is startling to observe the lack of attention given to utility and cost factors by the classic industrial psychologists.

29. Dunnette, *op. cit.*

30. A partial listing of significant contributions in the area of organizational psychology includes the following: James G. March and Herbert A. Simons, *Organizations* (New York: Wiley, 1959); Mason Haire, editor, *Modern Organization Theory* (New York: Wiley, 1959); G. B. Strother, editor, *Social Science Approaches to the Study of Business Behavior* (Homewood, Ill.: Dorsey Press, 1962); D. McGregor, *The Human Side of Enterprise* (New York: McGraw-Hill, 1960); B. M. Bass, *Leadership, Psychology and Organizational Behavior* (New York: Harper, 1960); Chris Argyris, *Understanding Organizational Behavior* (Homewood, Ill.: Dorsey Press,

1960); R. M. Stogdill, *Individual Behavior and Group Achievement* (New York: McGraw-Hill, Press, 1959); Rensis Likert, *New Patterns of Management* (New York: McGraw-Hill, 1960).

31. One outstanding example, however, has been reported to us by Dr. Arthur Kuriloff, Vice President, Manager of Performance and Development, Non-Linear Systems, Del Mar, California. Twenty-four months ago, the firm undertook a complete organizational change in accordance with the principles of McGregor's Theory Y and according to the functional alignments suggested by Drucker. It is noteworthy that the firm is still in business and over-all productivity per employee has increased by a factor of 31 percent, the highest ever achieved in the 10-year history of the firm—and the ceiling has not yet been reached.

32. We are indebted to Jack Dunlap for this idea.

33. There are, of course, already well-known examples of behavioral scientists serving as corporation presidents and members of top management in a variety of businesses and industries. But, we guess that the number is likely to increase.

34. Both G. E. and the Bell Laboratories now support experimental laboratories to conduct basic behavioral science research within their organization.

The Personnel Administrator
of the 1970s

ROSSALL J. JOHNSON

Stated in broad terms, personnel management as it is known today is too narrow and must be expanded to a point where the function requires that there be intervention in the day-to-day operations of an organization in order to protect the investment in human resources. In other words, a positive posture is needed.

To indicate a new role for the personnel manager, a change in name seems to be appropriate. Somewhat arbitrarily, the title of Director of Human Resources Management has been selected. This Director is not a Personnel Administrator with a new title, but an executive with training in information systems programming, budgeting, and organization theory, as well as the basis of psychology, sociology, and economics. Such a director can be thought of as a controller of human resources. There is an analogy in a way—the Controller of Finances is concerned with money aspects of an organization, while the Director of Human Resources Management is concerned with people. One should establish budgets for people and set up people reserves just as one must set up reserves of money. And finally there must be an evaluation for the use of people just as there is for money. The reason for drawing this analogy is that very few organizations give as much consideration to their investment in people as they do to their money investments.

It is becoming more and more apparent that the mobilization and allocation of human resources is of greater concern and import to organizations than the manage-

Reprinted by permission of the author and the publisher from *Personnel Journal*, vol. 50 (April 1971), no. 4, pp. 298-305, 309.

ment of financial and physical resources. There is no dispute that a business enterprise cannot get off the ground without financial backing and that for certain types of operations there is no business without the physical resources. But the prevailing thought should be that these resources are less valuable if they are misused, and it is people who will determine the fate of these resources.

The above, of course, is obvious and has been a well-known fact of life for some time. What is not so evident and what has been given less than adequate attention is the management of the people who are working with the money and the facilities. Much attention has been given to the structuring of the organizational pyramid, but little to the impact of individual development or change on the personnel.

A survey of some 70 companies in the Chicago area revealed that the planning of human resources is done only on a short range basis. Less than ten of these companies indicated plans for projecting people requirements for more than one or two years. There was little evidence that any of these companies had the necessary information for developing a long range manpower budget.

Traditionally, the personnel department has been viewed as a staff or service department, and traditionally, its role has been to engage in activities connected with:

Employment
Training
Wage and Salaries
Labor Relations
Various Fringe Activities
   Safety
   First Aid
   Recreation
   Insurance
   Cafeterias

The proposal here is not to do away with or neglect these areas but rather, to incorporate them into a model that will allow the people problems in industry to be considered in a more systematic way. This means that the area of personnel administration will be expanded and the *staff* orientation will be shifted to a control orientation.

Basically, the idea is to view people as a resource which must be managed with as much care as a corporation manages its funds. This means that there is a controller of people resources, and this also means that there is a people budget, a people audit, and control mechanisms to ensure that the people are being used as budgeted. Here the similarity stops because people are not dollars, and where dollar A equals dollar B, person A does not equal person B. The control mechanism must recognize individual rights and differences. It is at this point that the complexities of human resources management begin to become evident.

To examine this problem a simple over-all systemic approach will be introduced. Human resource management means that there is an appropriate selection of people who will implement the inputs into an organization so that the desired outputs result.

The following comments will start with the outputs, jump back to the inputs and then look at the implementation. Since basically there is a money input and a profit output, a program planning, and budget system would be appropriate.

Outputs

The desired output is reaching the organization objectives. In operational terms the objectives can be stated according to activities, markets, profits, product or service, that is, something that is operational in nature and something that the Director of Human Resources Management can interpret in terms of people requirements. The director is not taking a passive, advisory role in this planning stage; he is directing the thinking of management rather than sitting back and waiting for personnel requisitions to come in. He is not waiting; he is agitating. A key to the success of human resources management is that the attitudes of all executives be changed to expect the role of the human resources director to be control-oriented.

The director is first of all demanding *operational* objectives and then asking what talents are needed now and tomorrow so that the objectives can be met. He is also asking what changes need to be made in the organization structure now or in the future. This applies to an ongoing corporation or organization, where objectives change over a period of time. These objectives need to be clarified so that appropriate skills can be acquired, maintained, or developed. If the corporation is considering a change in objectives, the impact on the people budget should be reviewed *before* the decision is made. The emphasis on the phrase "before the decision is made" is another important point: in the past many corporations have completed a merger arrangement, shifted production facilities, opened new plants, etc., without considering the people problem. For instance, the lack of appropriate integration of the people in a number of mergers and acquisitions has been the cause of less than expected earnings and even resulted in failures to reach objectives. The Penn Central Railroad would be an example of an organization that failed to live up to its expectations because of the lack of integration of the two organizations.

The director of human resources must be in on the initial stages of most decisions. This means that his position must be at the vice-president level, and it also means that he should be an active member of the planning committee and in frequent consultation with the president. The director must be in a position to head off the dissipation of human resources and must be able to anticipate future demands for people talents. This requires the centralization of the function of human resources management. These are budgeting problems that should be in constant control. In summary then, the output of an organization is the target, and the shifting of the objective—gradual as it may be—is a necessary part of the control information. To reach these objectives, the inputs must be appropriate.

Inputs

One of the inputs required in a corporation is, of course, people activity. As indicated, the input must be appropriate if the output target is to be met. Here, again, there should be active participation on the part of the Human Resources Management department. It is at this stage that skills are being specified.

Not only should there be budget information for today, there must also be information for next year and the year after and for the next ten years. Unlike dollars and machines, people cannot be put into the bank or stored or sold for scrap or junked. People *now* make demands for security, and when a person is separated, a charge is made to the company. The separation cost may, in part, be in monetary terms such as increased premiums on unemployment insurance, or separation pay, or it may be a cost in terms of negative reputation, so that the best workers do not apply for jobs with the corporation, or it may be a cost in terms of poor employee relations, or a cost in terms of work disruption. And it is conceivable that in the not too distant future it may be that an employee cannot be separated without government approval. With these kinds of costs and restrictions facing the corporation, the days of trial and error are limited, and corporations need to sharpen the skill of budgetary control over human resources now. It should be recognized however, that all human resources needs cannot be satisfied; thus a trade-off must be made, a trade-off in terms of efficiencies versus desired skills and knowledge.

The input is in terms of the skills needed for the output. But the determination of the needed skills is dependent not only on the output but what is available in the organization. The term *skill* has a very broad definition and means not only achievement but also potential, and it means both ability in a technical sense and in the interpersonal behavior sense. To determine what is available in an organization and what is needed requires a sophisticated information system that will allow intelligent evaluations and decisions. There is no question, for instance, that, when a human resource need arises, the present manpower inventory of an organization should be thoroughly and quickly searched and evaluated before turning to external sources.

Implementation

Up to this point there have been comments on the output and the input. The core of the problem lies in the way in which inputs of the organization are transferred into outputs. That is, implementation is the necessary link between the two.

Keeping in mind that the concern is with an on-going organization, it must be remembered that nothing stops and that decisions are made continuously, even though the executives may choose not to make a decision, for that in itself is a decision, and the organization continues with its progress either toward the objective or off in another direction. Because implementation is on-going and because there is no stopping point, control mechanisms are used to govern the disposition of money, so it is necessary to have a systematic allocation of human resources.

Financial budgets are based on estimates, usually of revenue and in terms of what is needed to get the job done. The human resource budget is no different except that a much longer time factor is involved. A one-year human resource budget is mandatory, while a ten-year projection is also vital to maintain high efficiency and position attitudes as well as organizational continuity.

One might question the realism of a ten-year budget. There is no doubt that such a long projection will be subject to considerable revision as time goes on, but this is true of all budgeting processes. While ten years was arbitrarily selected, for some industries an eight or twelve-year budget might be more appropriate. The basic purposes of the long-range budget are to bring about a rethinking of organizational goals, an analysis of the human resources, implications of current trends in technology and an evaluation of the present manpower inventory in terms of future requirements. If an organization is unable to establish a long-range budget, then there should be a questioning of the adequacies of the current information; probably the whole information system needs to be overhauled with new inputs supplementing or displacing old ones.

The recent economic downtrend is a case in point. While the extent of the business setback could not be predicted, the need to plan for such an eventuality should have been recognized. Many organizations are now trimming their people requirements so as to reduce costs. While some reduction in the work force may be a direct result of loss of sales, some of it was based on an edict from above: cut your personnel by 10 percent or 15 percent or some other set figure. No thought was given, no investigation was made as to the long-term impact. There was a need to cut costs, and the consequences of wholesale discharge are to be faced later. Unless an organization is on the verge of bankruptcy, such across-the-board reduction in personnel is a very costly approach to the problem. If there are excesses of personnel in various departments, it probably is not 10 percent in each section. Some may be overstaffed by 50 percent and others by 2 percent or 15 percent or even understaffed. One should ask: if a company has extra staff, why did it wait until financial problems developed before reducing the staff and why not do it in an orderly manner at the time the excesses arise? To ask the question in a different way: what have the various corporations done about the internal environment on a continuous basis so that external factors will have a reduced impact?

Is there an implication that these mass layoffs and panic cost-cutting procedures needn't have taken place? It would seem so. All too frequently management is pressured into emergency situations which may relieve the immediate crisis, but which, over an extended period, year in and year out, may cause heavy losses.

It is imperative that the human resources be controlled and that control be centralized so that consistency and flexibility are not lost. The human resources budget requires considerable information, and the gathering processes and interpreting of this information require the efforts of many people. This is not a nose counting operation; it is a planning, programming, and budgeting procedure that is stated in terms of the work requirement, when it is to be done, and what kinds of skills are required. But its complexities are many. Perhaps a broad outline of some of the information will indicate the job to be done.

There are at least seven areas where information is needed for the implementation of effective control and use of the human resources. They are:

1. Evolution of the Organization

An organization goes through an evolutionary process from its inception to a period of rapid growth, to a plateau, to a decline or another growth period. Each step in the evolutionary process means changes in personnel, changes in the decision making process, changes in information system or, broadly speaking, changes in the organization structure and procedures.

For instance, in a new organization the main thrust may be on selling of ideas and objectives and in establishing role relationships. Later, the selling of objectives may be routine and the roles may be well coordinated. Those who are the specialists in the management of human resources should be observing to see that the appropriate changes in thrust come about because of the evolutionary processes and that the organization adjusts to the changes in emphasis.

There are any number of examples of organizations which entered a market with specific quality of goods or services only to find that later, when an attempt was made to change the quality in order to be more competitive, some people in the organization evidently didn't understand the need to change with time and refused to adjust. Or perhaps the owner-manager makes decisions today with 5,000 employees in the same manner as he did when there were only 50. The human resources manager needs to stand to one side and observe this evolutionary process so that he may make the appropriate recommendations and decisions.

2. Flow of People

What are the causes of the flow of people through the organization and in and out of the organization? Death, illness, retirement, obsolescence, involuntary separation, advancement and transfer, and voluntary separation. How many of these can be predicted? Perhaps all except the last one—voluntary separation—and even this may be predicted at times.

Actuary figures will not pinpoint the specific individual who will die, but it will indicate how many probably will die before reaching retirement and how many will be incapacitated by illness. Do companies make use of this available information in estimating manpower needs in five years or ten years? Everyone knows when his boss is going to reach retirement age, but is good use made of retirement information when forecasting people needs? Few companies use such information.

Obsolescence is a tough one, but in some cases the signs are quite obvious if one is trained to look for them. Here the director of human resources and his staff can make a unique contribution since it should be part of their job to anticipate obsolescence before it arrives. Those employees with obsolete skills should be alerted to the condition well before the fact. Such timing allows for planned retraining or planned early retirement. When pinpointed early a valuable employee (valuable in terms of attitudes and reliability) may be transferred to another job.

Discharge—defined here as leaving the organization at the request of the organization—involuntary. It may be because of unacceptable performance or because of reduction of work-force, etc. Within certain time constraints this can be anticipated, but over an extended period of time it is an unanticipated change unless a pattern can be established. While it is acknowledged that there will be some involuntary separations, in most organizations there are far too many. Here is an area where the human resources department can be useful in reducing turnover.

Voluntary separation is frequently the cause of an unpredictable void in an organization. This is a costly type of separation because it not only leads to less efficient operations, but frequently results in the vacancy being quickly filled by an unqualified person who must be trained on the job by an individual who is not completely acquainted with the job.

There have been studies on the probability of an individual advancing in the organization and how long he can expect to remain in any one position. This type of information can be useful in career planning for selected individuals, and it can be helpful in determining problem areas in the developing system. Blind alleys in the flow of personnel can be opened up and favored avenues for advancement can be reexamined. Undesirable voluntary separations can be reduced by regulating the avenues to advancement.

3. Role Establishment

Role Establishment refers to a process where individuals understand role relationships so that behavior may be predicted more accurately. There may be a difference, for instance, in view of the role of an engineer. He may look upon himself as a professional person and, therefore, behaves in a "professional manner," while the production manager sees the engineer's role as that of "any other employee" and refuses to accept the professional role behavior. While this type of information does not directly affect the number of people in a budget, it does allow for the full utilization of those in the work force. This, then, is a new and important dimension that is part of the job of the people budget director—the human resources manager. He must be observant of those potential points of friction that will reduce the efficiency of the organization. This leads directly into the area of interrelationships.

4. Interrelationships

Manpower requirements are increased or decreased according to effectiveness of interrelationships. These relationships can be at the interpersonal level or interdepartmental or interdivisional level. For the sake of brevity, these can be classified as intra-organizational relationships. In the past, the effectiveness of such relationships was dealt with at the local level. However, the inefficiencies and frictions and even sabotage that results from inappropriate intra-organizational relationships are too expensive to tolerate over extended periods of time. If the human resources are to be utilized efficiently and the budget is to be held to minimum requirements, the director of human resources must pinpoint inappropriate relationships. This is especially important at the levels above the interpersonal level. It may mean a direct intervention by the director of human resources, but hopefully, a correction will be encouraged from within. In effect, the director has taken on the role of change agent.

5. Change and Time

Change frequently causes people to feel threatened. The director of human resources can reduce the feelings of insecurity if he is able to anticipate change and send out the appropriate information or establish programs to meet the changing conditions.

A time factor is involved because most changes can be anticipated. The need is to identify those things which are going to disturb people—perhaps a new automatic machine, a different technique in packaging, a computerized operation, or the dropping of a line of goods. All of these have a lead time before the change becomes a reality, and it is during this time that action should take place to relieve anxieties.

6. Evaluation and Reward

Evaluation should be considered an on-going process at different levels. The job of the director of human resources management is to see that it is a continuous process and that the various levels are evaluated. While productivity may be one factor in evaluation, the organizational effectiveness of a group of people should also be included. At the individual level, some form of equity theory should be incorporated so that the relationships between perceived contribution and reward can be balanced with "actual" contribution and reward. Much more information must be processed more efficiently so that evaluations have greater validity and acceptance and thus, rewards may be more equitable.

7. Will to Work

Considerable research work has been carried out in the areas of the measurement of attitudes and the elucidation of motivating factors. To date there has been only limited success in pinpointing causes for poor work performance. Close supervision has been found to have caused both high and low productivity. The authoritarian leader has been shown to be more efficient, while the democratic leader has happier subordinates. On the other hand, there have been unhappy but efficient subordinates under a democratic leader. The director of human resources must be in the main stream of information flow so that he can make an analysis and recommendations on the will to work.

Centralized Control and Auditing

Considerable stress has been placed on control of human resources in the implementation comments. The term "control" is one of the words that is frowned upon by rights groups because it implies using workers as puppets. Here the term "control" is used to imply that people are operating in an organization with set objectives and that their talents are utilized to meet these objectives. At the same time, the organization has obligations to the individual in terms of compensation, job satisfaction, etc. Supposedly, there is a mutual advantage which can only be attained when controls are instituted.

Organizations are dynamic systems where the characteristics are continually changing. Because of the dynamic aspects, fixed rules and regulations, fixed policies and procedures, as well as the organization structure are outdated rather quickly. Some one person should be responsible for noting the conditions which have an impact on the human resources and then "recommend" changes that should be made.

The term "recommend" may imply a passive role, but the intent here is to indicate that the changes recommended will be adopted in most instances because the director is responsible for the management of the human resources.

It is the thesis here that the total human resources be controlled through a central point via the vehicle of the human resources programming, planning, and budgeting. In addition, it is recommended that the director of human resources management be given a major role in guiding the structuring of the organization and control of the people aspects.

There is a fine line to be walked by the director of human resources in this dominant role, for it is all too easy for him to undermine superior-subordinate relationships. There is no intention of disrupting the rapport of supervisors with subordinates. It is anticipated that the control mechanisms would strengthen the ties by the very fact that there is consistency, there is planning, there is increased flow of pertinent information, and there is more appropriate selection and training of supervisors. The director of human resources is one man with a staff, and he is in no position to know of or contend with all of the interpersonal contacts. This is not his function. His job is to see to it that through the placement of people, the flow of information, and the development programs, dysfunctional interpersonal and intra-organizational interactions are reduced. The supervisor is still the key to appropriate management of the human resources.

The inputs of people into an organizational effort are so critical that they must be controlled in a positive way and from a central point. It is no longer an acceptable practice to allow the supervisors, department heads, or division vice-presidents to set independent policy or make independent decisions concerning the disposition of people.

While the trend is toward decentralization in industry, the purse strings in financial management are held in the home office. The management of human resources should be under even greater control because of the long range implications. Not only should the human resources "purse strings" be centralized, but some basic policies should be adhered to in all parts of the organization.

Human Resources Audit

The audit of human resources management should be an integral and on-going function of the centralized control mechanism. This type of audit opens up a new facet to the control of the use of people. Some examples of the function may clarify the position.

First, there is the routine part which checks budgeted personnel against actual. As indicated before, this is not a numbers game but an audit of talents, skills, and potential. The computer can be very useful in maintaining a continuous audit of this type. There is also the evaluation of new employees in terms of the ability to handle the position they have been hired to fill, and also in terms of potential to be useful employees five years from now and ten years from now.

There are more complex issues to audit. For instance, the effectiveness of an organization is determined in part by an understanding by everyone of the objectives and goals. When there are multiple goals or objectives, there is a need to weight them. Question: Do all employees weight them the same? How do you motivate people toward the same goals or objectives and at the same time, how do you get them to give the same weights?

Simple example: What are the objectives of the fire department?

1. To put out fires
2. To reduce property damage
3. To save lives
4. To prevent fires

Do all firemen weight these the same? Which has the top priority?

The area of interpersonal or intraorganizational conflict should be subjected to audit. One should start with the assumption that not all conflict can be avoided and also that some conflict may be desirable. The problem then comes down to judging what is desirable and/or unavoidable conflict. While the fine differences may not be definable, there are conflicts which are so gross that there is no question but that the conflict is detrimental to the organization. It is these situations where the director of human resources can use his office to reduce or eliminate the friction. . . .

The basis for human resources decisions should also be incorporated into the audit process. The guiding question is: are the people decisions based on an open or closed system of information? "Closed system of information" means that only a limited amount of information within the organization is available as a basis for the decision. "Open system" means that both internal and external sources of unrestricted information are referred to. Generally speaking, the tendency is to use the closed system, and frequently this is acceptable. But when the open system should be used and is not used, some very poor decisions can result.

An example: Take a situation where a supervisor comes to work intoxicated and as a result creates a number of embarrassing incidents. The policy is quite clear in this company on dealing with inebriated employees. (1) The employee shall immediately be sent home. (2) The employee should not report back to work until a disposition has been made of his case and the penalty established. (3) Reporting for work in an intoxicated condition is considered sufficient grounds for immediate discharge.

A closed system approach could easily occur in the above situation, and in all probability the supervisor would be discharged. An open system approach might reveal that the supervisor:

1. Had been with the company for thirty years with no record of intoxication.
2. Is two years away from retirement.
3. Is physically deteriorating to the point where he is approaching senility.
4. A tragedy in his personal life had occurred prior to the date of his offense.

Now, after additional information is available, one might ask if a decision other than discharge should be made. Although the above type of incident may be appropriately handled right now in many organizations, there is a nagging question of, "Do we catch all of the closed system type of decisions which should have been based on an open system type of information?'' It is up to the director of human resources management to audit this and to see that adequate information is used as a basis for people decisions.

To sum it up, the role of the personnel director must be expanded; his image must be changed. The staff position of personnel director as an advisor to line personnel should be set aside and in its place there should be a director of human resources who guards the people investment through centralized control and inspection. The director of human resources management must report directly to the chief executive officer and be a party to all planning from the beginning.

The chief occupation of the director of human resources, then, is to:

1. Establish and manage a human resources planning, programming, and budgeting mechanism and auditing system.

2. Review and revise the information system so that adequate decision information is available.

3. Identify critical people areas and critical people problems.

4. Interpret events and situations in terms of impact on human resources.

5. Analyze the effectiveness of the organization today, recommend action, and plan for tomorrow.

Such a director needs to have expertise in the planning, programming, budgeting systems approach, and he must be capable of establishing an appropriate information system and control mechanism. Basic to the job is a working knowledge of organization theory, psychology, sociology, and economics. A professional with these qualifications is a necessity. Conditions of the 1970s will not allow anything else.

Federal Laws Affecting Personnel Management

J. D. DUNN
E. C. STEPHENS

Many of the restrictions on the employer's action of hiring employees . . . will be reviewed briefly here [first]; other restrictions will be discussed more fully.

National Labor Relations Act

The National Labor Relations Act (NLRA) of 1935 (commonly called the Wagner Act), as amended by later acts, declares it to be an unfair labor practice for an employer to discriminate in regard to hire or tenure of employment in order to encourage or discourage membership in any labor organization.[1] The usual violation of this provision is to refuse to hire a person whom the employer suspects or knows is a member of a labor union. One of the earliest cases establishing the legality of this interpretation was in 1941, when the Supreme Court upheld the National Labor Relations Board's (NLRB) ruling that the Phelps Dodge Copper Corporation violated the NLRA by refusing to hire two employees who had been on strike against the company. The Court held that the NLRA required that hiring of employees be conducted on a nondiscriminatory basis with respect to membership in a labor union.[2]

A refusal to hire a person because he is not a member of a union is also an unfair labor practice.[3] However, an employer can make an agreement to hire employees through a union hiring hall on an exclusive basis if the union contract specifies that the hiring hall will make referrals to the employer without regard to whether or not the person is a member of the union.[4]

Fair Employment Practices law

The Civil Rights Act of 1964 included a provision (Title VII) which established an Equal Employment Opportunity Commission (EEOC), whose purpose is to ensure that employers do not discriminate against employees or individuals with respect to such factors as race, color, religion, sex, or national origin. Section 703(a) states: "It shall be an unlawful employment practice for an employer—(1) to fail or refuse to hire or to discharge any individual, or otherwise to discriminate against any individual with respect to his compensation, terms, conditions, or privileges of employment, because of such individual's race, color, religion, sex, or national origin. . . ." This restriction applies to any employer whose business affects commerce and who has at least 25 employees. As of June 12, 1968, the factor of age was added as an additional restriction on hiring practices of employers.

The power to investigate alleged illegal practices is in the hands of the Equal Employment Opportunity Commission, a five-member board which hears complaints from individuals who believe they have been discriminated against. If the EEOC thinks the complaint is valid, it investigates the charge, and if it appears to be true, the EEOC tries to eliminate the alleged unlawful practice by informal methods of conferences, conciliation, and persuasion. The EEOC has been successful in about 50 percent of its cases in persuading the employer to comply with the law. [Editor's note: The Equal Employment Opportunity Act of 1972 has expanded the power of the EEOC. See the article by W. Brown, III in chap. 9, "The Equal Opportunity Act of 1972."] If compliance is not forthcoming, the individual may file a civil suit in court; however, such suits occur in only about 10 percent of the cases. The main reason more suits are not filed is the inability of the individual to finance such a suit.[5] . . .

Not only legislation, but also the purchasing power of the federal government is used to achieve desired purposes. In an effort to increase the employment of minority workers on construction projects, the Labor Department in 1969 announced that contractors bidding on federal construction contracts of $500,000 or more must present a plan showing that sufficient numbers of minority group employees would be hired to meet a quota or goal set by the Labor Department. This requirement for affirmative action was first used in the Philadelphia area; hence the name "Philadelphia Plan." This plan was called illegal and unworkable by both the labor unions and contractors. In early 1970 contractors in the Philadelphia area were trying to block enforcement of the plan by court action against the Labor Department. Labor unions were stressing the adoption of voluntary plans which they had negotiated in Chicago and Pittsburgh, and the Secretary of Labor was threatening to use "Philadelphia Plans" in other cities if labor unions stalled in setting up voluntary hiring procedures.[6]

The Civil Rights Act of 1964 has been used to restrict the use of tests in the employment function. . . . Many states have laws similar to the Civil Rights Act pertaining to the employment of minority group persons. As of January 1969, 37 states had fair employment practices acts. Of these, 22 limit inquiries as to the ethnic background of applicants; such information is also not allowed on the employee's personnel records after employment. The EEOC at first forbade such information but later discovered this information was very useful for determining whether the employer was complying with the purpose and intent of the law. The EEOC suggests that employee records by race are to be kept, but they should be separate from the individual's personnel file.[7]

Training and Development

The training and development function is perhaps the least restricted by federal legislation; however, it is affected by several laws. The Civil Rights Act applies to this function with respect to the selection of persons for a training program: you cannot refuse admission to a training program solely on the basis of a person's race, color, etc.

The law which is most directly concerned with the training function is the act of August 11, 1937, which established the National Apprenticeship Program. The Federal Committee on Apprenticeship, composed of an equal number of representatives from employers and unions, recommends the provisions which govern apprenticeship programs. These provisions cover such items as age, selection procedure, schedule of work experiences of the apprentice, a program of organized instruction on technical subjects, a schedule of wages, and other items.

The Manpower Development and Training Act of 1962 affects the person responsible for the training function only if his organization decides to seek federal funds under this act in order to set up training programs for training or retraining youths of 16 and older who cannot find employment owing to lack of skills or inadequate educational background.

Under the Economic Opportunity Act of 1964, employers may obtain federal assistance for training disadvantaged youths or the hard-core unemployed through contracts with the Manpower Administration for training programs. Job Opportunities in the Business Sector (JOBS), a program started in early 1968, has accounted for many of the training programs conducted by business firms under the Economic Opportunity Act.

Labor Relations

The personnel function of labor relations is affected by several federal laws; a fairly comprehensive coverage of this legislation is sufficient material for one or more college courses, and therefore only the highlights can be covered. . . .

Anti-injunction Act of 1932

In 1932 Congress passed the Anti-injunction Act (commonly called the Norris-LaGuardia for its sponsors) to limit the use of injunctions against unions and to deny the enforcement of yellow-dog contracts in federal courts. The act declares the policy of the United States is that the worker shall have "full freedom of association, self-organization, and designation of representatives of his own choosing to negotiate the terms and conditions of his employment." Federal courts are prohibited from issuing injunctions against certain activities of employees engaged in a labor dispute; injunctions may be issued for certain purposes only after hearings and certain qualifications are met. Prior to this act, many employers secured injunctions against a union whenever it appeared the union was about to engage in a strike against the firm.

National Labor Relations Act, as amended

The major labor law affecting personnel management is the National Labor Relations Act of 1935 (Wagner Act). Passed at a time of employer hostility toward labor unions, the act declares the policy of the United States is to encourage the practice and procedure of collective bargaining, to protect the right of employees' self-organization, and the right to choose representatives for the purpose of negotiating the terms and conditions of their employment. The act applies to employers in or affecting commerce, but it excludes employers covered by the Railway Labor Act of 1926,[8] government employees (at all levels, federal, state, and local), and agricultural laborers.

The NLRA established the National Labor Relations Board (NLRB), whose duty it is to enforce the law. In 1947, after a long battle, Congress passed the Labor-Management Relations Act (Taft-Hartley) over the veto of President Truman. The purpose of this act was to amend the NLRA; the major changes were the addition of union unfair labor practices, the right of employees to refrain from union activity, the outlawing of the closed shop, enlarging the employer's right of speech, and modifications with respect to elections and bargaining unit determinations. The NLRB was increased in size to five members, and a General Counsel was added, whose function is to investigate charges that the act has been violated and to prosecute such charges before the NLRB. The Taft-Hartley Act also provides a procedure for employers to sue unions for damages resulting from secondary boycotts, and strikes for unlawful purposes. Both parties may sue for breach of contract. The act also establishes a procedure for dealing with national emergency strikes.

Rights of Employees. The basic rights of employees are found in Section 7, which as amended in 1947 reads:

> Employees shall have the right to self-organization, to form, join, or assist labor organizations, to bargain collectively through representatives of their own choosing, and to engage in other concerted activities for the purpose of collective bargaining or other mutual aid or protection, and shall also have the right to refrain from any or all of such activities. . . .

The activities protected by section 7 involve the organizing and maintaining of a labor union, but other concerted actions such as the circulation of a petition requesting a wage increase are also protected. The act gives the NLRB the power to remedy or prevent unfair labor practices on the part of both employers and labor unions.

Employer Unfair Labor Practices. Section 8 (a) states that it is an unfair labor practice for an employer to:

> (1) Interfere with, restrain, or coerce employees in the exercise of the right guaranteed in Section 7.

Examples of interference: threatening to fire employees if they join a union, threatening to move or close the plant if the union wins an election, questioning employees about their union activities if such questioning restrains or coerces them, spying on union meetings, and granting wage increases at a time which defeats employees in their attempt at self-organization.

> (2) To dominate or interfere with the formation or administration of any labor organization or contribute financial or other support to it: *Provided,* that subject to rules and regulations made and published by the Board pursuant to Section 6, an employer shall not be prohibited from permitting employees to confer with him during working hours without loss of time or pay.

This section is designed to prevent an employer from dominating the union to the extent that it becomes a company union and does not reflect the desires of the employees. Examples of illegal conduct under this section include the employer helping to organize the union, putting pressure on employees to join a union, or playing favorites if two or more unions are attempting to organize his employees.

> (3) By discrimination in regard to hire or tenure of employment or any term or condition of employment to encourage or discourage membership in any labor organization: . . .

The rest of the section allows the union shop and provides that the employer shall not discriminate against any employee for nonmembership in a labor organization if he believes that the employee was denied membership for reasons other than failure to tender dues and initiation fees.

An 8 (a) (3) charge is the most common of all unfair labor practice charges against employers; in fiscal year 1967, 66.3 percent of all cases filed against employers included 8 (a) (3) charges.[9] Examples of this type of unfair labor practices include demoting or discharging an employee for union activities, refusal to reinstate an employee to a vacant job because he took part in a lawful strike, and refusal to hire a qualified applicant because he belongs to a union, or does not belong, or belongs to one union instead of another. This section does not interfere with the employer's right to hire or fire, unless the motive is antiunion.[10] The employer can legally fire strikers who are guilty of misconduct on the picket line or other illegal activities during a strike.[11]

> (4) To discharge or otherwise discriminate against an employee because he has filed charges or given testimony under this Act.

Any action by the employer which would violate section 8 (a) (3) would also violate 8 (a) (4) if the employee had given testimony or filed charges; this includes a discriminatory transfer to a lesser job or forced resignation.

> (5) To refuse to bargain collectively with the representatives of his employees, subject to the provisions of section 9 (a).

Section 8 (d) defines the duties of the parties with respect to collective bargaining as:

> For the purposes of this section, to bargain collectively is the performance of the mutual obligation of the employer and the representative of the employees to

meet at reasonable times and confer in good faith with respect to wages, hours and other terms and conditions of employment, or the negotiation of an agreement, or any question arising thereunder, and the execution of a written contract incorporating any agreement reached if requested by either party, but such obligation does not compel either party to agree to a proposal or require the making of a concession. . . .

Subjects for Collective Bargaining. Subjects which have been declared to be mandatory topics of bargaining include wages, hours, overtime, and work requirements; the practice and procedures with respect to discipline, demotion, promotion, discharge, recall, layoffs, transfers, suspension, health and safety practices, grievances, vacations and holidays, union security, leaves of absence, and reinstatement of strikers. Some subjects are not considered to be legal topics of bargaining; these include the closed shop, pay for work not to be performed, and preferential hiring. Certain subjects are legal but not mandatory subjects of bargaining; these include such items as the organization of the business, the type of products, and the size of the management staff. At one time the topic of subcontracting of work was a permissible subject, but not mandatory; however, the Supreme Court declared that if the subcontracting affected the work of the bargaining unit employees, the employer must notify the union and discuss this decision with the union, if it wants such discussion.[12]

Union Unfair Labor Practices. Section 8 (b) of the act declares that it is unfair labor practice for unions to engage in certain activities: (1) to restrain or coerce employees in the exercise of their rights under section 7, (2) to cause or attempt to cause an employer to discriminate against an employee in an effort to encourage or discourage union membership, (3) to refuse to bargain with an employer, (4) to engage in secondary boycotts and certain types of strikes and picketing, (5) to charge excessive or discriminatory union fees, (6) to exact pay for services not to be performed, and (7) certain types of recognition picketing.

Labor-Management Reporting and Disclosure Act of 1959
   This law was passed after congressional hearings uncovered many examples of breach of trust, corruption, and disregard of the rights of union members by union officials. The purpose of the act was to protect union members from abuse by union officials who were misusing their power. The main parts of the act have to do with the rights of union members and the conduct of union affairs; however, certain provisions affect the personnel function of employers, and the act contained some amendments to the NLRA. An employer must report any payment or loan of money or other item of value to an officer of a union, including stewards. He must also report any payment made to any of his employees if such payment was for the employee's services of encouraging or discouraging other employees with respect to their right to organize and bargain collectively. Any expenditure for the purpose of directly or indirectly interfering or restraining employees in their exercise of their right of collective bargaining must be reported, as any payment to a labor relations consultant for the same purpose must be.

Compensation

   The compensation function is affected by several federal laws, and the failure to comply with the law may result in a substantial financial burden on the firm. For example, on January 13, 1970, the U.S. Court of Appeals, Third Circuit, handed down a decision against the Wheaton Glass Company involving an order of over $250,000 in back wages, plus requiring a 21½-cent increase in the hourly wage of some 230 women employees. The suit was brought against the company under the 1963 Equal Pay Act. As of January 1970, the Labor Department had secured some $1.5 million in back wages under the act and secured wage increases for some 6,322 women employees.[13] The Wheaton case illustrates some of the dangers of operating without a knowledge of legislation affecting personnel management functions. The federal laws affecting the compensation function are quite complicated with respect to the exact determination of whether an employer is subject to the law and whether an employee is covered by the provisions of the acts. Of the several federal laws dealing with compensation, the main one is the Fair Labor Standards Act.

Fair Labor Standards Act

The Fair Labor Standards Act was passed in 1938 to establish minimum wages, maximum hours, overtime pay, and child labor standards. In 1939 an estimated 12.6 million employees were covered by the act, or about 23 percent of the civilian labor force. Owing to the growth in the covered firms and additional firms being brought under the act by various changes, at the end of 1966 the number of covered employees had risen to 41.4 million, about 54 percent of the labor force. The 1966 amendment added some 9.1 million workers, most of whom were employed in retail and service establishments which were brought under the act.

The original minimum wage was 25 cents per hour in 1938, and it was scheduled to rise to 40 cents by 1945. In 1949 the minimum wage was increased to 75 cents per hour, effective on January 25, 1950. A second amendment in 1955 increased the wage to $1.00 per hour as of March 1, 1956. Again in 1961 Congress raised the wage to $1.15 as of September 1, 1961, and $1.25 as of September 1, 1963. By 1966 Congress saw fit to increase the wage to $1.40, effective February 1, 1967, and $1.60 in 1968. For newly covered employees, the minimum wage was set at $1 per hour as of February 1, 1967; thereafter, each year it rose by 15 cents per hour until it reached $1.60 on February 1, 1971.

The act set up a maximum workweek, with time and a half to be paid for any hours worked beyond the maximum. The maximum was 44 hours per week until October 23, 1940, and 40 hours after that date. The maximum has remained 40 hours since then, as has the time and a half to be paid for overtime.

Coverage of Employees before 1966. Employees who were covered by the act before 1966, and who remain covered, include those in the following three categories:

1. Employees engaged individually in interstate or foreign commerce.

2. Employees engaged in the production of goods for interstate or foreign commerce, including closely related processes and occupations directly essential to such production.

3. Other employees employed in certain large enterprises having some employees engaged as above or handling, selling, or working on goods that have moved in interstate or foreign commerce.[14]

Employees Covered after 1966. The 1966 amendments added additional workers by including some establishments which were not covered and reducing the volume of sales for retail establishments to be covered. In general, these changes were:

1. Employees employed in the following enterprises who are not engaged in any previously covered employment are covered on and after February 1, 1967 if there are, in the activities of the enterprise, employees engaged in interstate or foreign commerce or in the production of goods for such commerce, including employees handling, selling or otherwise working on goods that have been moved in or produced for such commerce by any person, and if—

a. The enterprise has an annual gross volume of sales made or business done, exclusive of certain excise taxes, of at least $500,000 ($250,000 beginning February 1, 1969) or

b. The enterprise is engaged in the business of construction or reconstruction (regardless of dollar volume), or

c. The enterprise is engaged in laundering, cleaning, or repairing clothing or fabric (regardless of dollar volume), or

d. The enterprise is engaged in the operation of a hospital (except a Federal Government hospital), nursing home, or school (whether public, private, or nonprofit and regardless of dollar volume).

The act provided that none of the above enterprises will include any establishment which has as its only regular employees, the owner, his spouse, parents or children, or other members of the owner's immediate family.

2. The elimination and revision of various exemptions by the 1966 amendments have extended the application of the minimum wage provisions and overtime provisions to certain workers, and have changed the exemption status of other employees.[15]

The 1966 amendments also brought agricultural workers under the protection of the law if the farm on which the person worked employed at least 500 man-days of labor per year. Employees engaged only in farm work (and not specifically exempt) are to be paid at least $1.15 per hour beginning February 1, 1968, and $1.30 per hour beginning February 1, 1969. Such employees are not subject to the overtime provisions of the act.

Exemptions. Section 13 provides for exemptions from various parts of the act. Employees ". . . employed in a bona fide executive, administrative, or professional capacity . . . or in the capacity of outside salesmen . . ." are exempt from both the wages and hours provision of the act. This is the most common exemption. Other exemptions include employees of certain seasonal amusement establishments; fishing and seafood offshore processing; learners, apprentices, or other employees exempted by order of the Secretary of Labor; certain local newspapers; motion-picture theaters; and a few others. Some employees are exempt from the overtime requirements only. These include employees of interstate motor carriers; employers regulated by the Interstate Commerce Commission or the Railway Labor Act; offshore seafood processors; and several similar exemptions.

Equal Pay. The Equal Pay Act of 1963 amended the Fair Labor Standards Act to require that men and women on the same job or performing equal work must receive equal pay. Section 6 (d) (1) of the act provides that no employer shall discriminate by paying ". . . wages to employees in such establishments at a rate less than the rate at which he pays wages to employees of the opposite sex in such establishment for equal work on jobs the performance of which requires equal skill, effort, and responsibility, and which are performed under similar working conditions . . ." unless such payment is made on the basis of seniority, piece rates, merit system, or some factor other than sex.

Age Discrimination. The Age Discrimination in Employment Act of 1967 makes it an illegal act for an employer to discriminate against a person as to compensation, terms, conditions, or privileges of employment because of age. An employer cannot reduce the wages of any of his employees in order to comply with the act; thus if he paid an older worker a lower wage than a young worker, he must raise the older worker's wage (assuming both employees have the same duties, etc.).

Child Labor. Section 12 outlines the child labor provisions of the act. In general, the minimum age for most employment under the act is 16 years, although for employment in hazardous occupations (as defined by the Secretary of Labor), 18 years is the minimum. Fourteen years is the minimum age for employment outside of school hours in a variety of occupations for a limited number of hours per day.

Records. Employers must keep records on wages, hours, and other topics. No particular form is required, but the following information must be kept if the employee is subject to the hours and wages provisions of the act:

Name, home address and birth date if under 19.
Sex and occupation.
Hour and day when workweek begins.
Regular hourly pay rate for any week when overtime is worked.
Hours worked each workday and total hours worked each workweek.
Total daily or weekly straight-time earnings.
Total overtime pay for the workweek.
Deductions or additions to wages.
Total wages paid each pay period.
Date of payment and pay period covered.[16]

Enforcement of the Act. The person primarily charged with the enforcement of the act is the Secretary of Labor. He is responsible for securing an injunction against any employer who violates the act, or upon request from an employee he will file suit for back pay. The employee may personally sue his employer under the act for back wages, and an additional sum up to the amount of back wages as damages, plus attorney's fees and court costs. Investigators from the Wage and Hour Division of the Department of Labor may investigate and gather data about wages, hours, or other conditions of employment in any establishment covered by the act.

The Department of Labor prepares bulletins and other types of written information about the various parts of the act. Information can also be obtained from the many field offices of the Wage and Hour Public Contracts Division.

Walsh-Healey Public Contracts Act

The Public Contracts Act of 1936 sets labor standards for work done on government contracts exceeding $10,000 for materials, supplies, and similar items. The Secretary of Labor is to determine the prevailing minimum wages being paid in the industry, usually after a public hearing. This wage then becomes the minimum for workers engaged in the performance of a contract let under the act. Overtime commences after eight hours in one day, or 40 hours in one week. Time and a half must be paid for all overtime, which must be figured on the daily or weekly basis, whichever provides the most compensation.

Davis-Bacon Act

The Davis-Bacon Act of 1931 provides that the Assistant Secretary of Labor will determine the prevailing wage which must then be paid to laborers and mechanics in the construction, repair, or alteration of public buildings or public works. These wage rates must be written into the construction or repair contract, and the contractor must post a schedule of the rates at the work site. The contractor must also provide the prevailing fringe benefits or add an equivalent amount to the wages. Wages must be paid at least once per week and must be the full amount owed.

Welfare and Pension Plans Disclosure Act

This act was passed in 1958 and amended in 1962 to give the Secretary of Labor more power to enforce the law. The act applies generally to any employee pension or welfare plan, fund, or program established by or maintained by employers engaged in commerce, or by unions, or both. Pension plans are defined as any type of retirement plans, and welfare plans include medical, surgical, accident, sickness, and similar types of plans. The administrator of the plan must make a report available to the plan's members and file a report with the Department of Labor each year. Persons administering the plan and in a position to cause a loss through fraud or dishonesty must be bonded.

There are several other minor federal laws pertaining to the compensation of employees. Information about these can be obtained from the offices of the Labor Department or from the publications of one of the reporting services, such as Commerce Clearing House and the Bureau of National Affairs.

Health and Safety

Although health and safety are not always considered a personnel function, the personnel department is quite often given the responsibility for the organization's activities pertaining to them. Therefore, the federal laws affecting these activities are discussed [here].

In 1969, there were only eight laws and one Executive order dealing with safety on the national level; however, these held the Secretary of Labor responsible for safeguarding the 37.5 million workers covered by these laws. The small number of laws should not be interpreted as an indication that the federal government is not concerned about the safety and health of the labor force. Over 1,000 bills pertaining to safety were introduced into the first session of the Ninety-first Congress. One law passed in this area was the Coal Mine Health and Safety Act, which was signed into law December 30, 1969. This was a comprehensive law, updating the Federal Coal Mine Safety Act of 1952. The new law provides for compensation for victims of coal miner's "black lung" disease. It also contains strict safety standards designed to prevent coal mine disasters.

The Walsh-Healey Act provides that work covered by this act may not be performed under conditions which are unsanitary or hazardous or dangerous. Compliance with state laws is evidence of intent to comply but not conclusive evidence that the law is being followed. On May 20, 1969, the federal government set permissible occupation noise exposure levels under this act.[17]

In 1965, the Secretary of Labor established an advisory committee on safety. Following the committee's recommendation, the Secretary established a policy that the Department of Labor would adopt safety standards developed by voluntary groups such as the National Safety Council. The Nixon administration also took this approach by establishing a policy in May 1969, permitting adoption of standards set by consensus of various safety groups.[18]

The Construction Health and Safety Act was passed by Congress and signed into law on August 8, 1969, as Public Law 91-54. When first introduced into Congress, the act was to set safety standards for the building and construction trades in all federally financed or assisted construction projects. As finally passed, the act calls for the Secretary of Labor to consult with a nine-member advisory committee made up of members from construction contractors, workers, and members of the public and then set minimum safety and health standards.[19] In late 1970, Congress passed the Occupational Safety and Health Act, which made the Secretary of Labor responsible for setting safety and health standards applicable to the specific hazards in industries. Many of the bills which were introduced into Congress were quite comprehensive and would have put the federal government into the business of regulating the health and safety standards of nearly all business firms in the country. The majority of health and safety laws are state laws but may soon be superseded by a federal law.

Summary

[We have] discussed briefly some of the federal laws affecting the personnel man-

TABLE 1
FEDERAL LAWS AFFECTING PERSONNEL MANAGEMENT

Federal law, year passed, and common name in parentheses	Employment	Training and development	Labor relations	Compensation	Safety and health
Act of March 3, 1931 (Davis-Bacon)	..	..	..	x	
Anti-injunction Act of 1932 (Norris-LaGuardia)	..	..	x		
National Labor Relations Act, 1935 (Wagner Act)	x	x	x	x	
Public Contracts Act of 1936 (Walsh-Healey)	..	..	..	x	x
Fair Labor Standards Act of 1938 (Federal Wage and Hour Law)	..	..	..	x	
Labor-Management Relations Act, 1947 (Taft-Hartley Act)	x	x	x	x	
Federal Coal Mine Act of 1952	..	..	..	..	x
Welfare and Pension Plans Disclosure Act of 1958	..	..	x	x	
Labor-Management Reporting and Disclosure Act of 1959 (Landrum-Griffin)	..	..	x	x	
Manpower Development and Training Act of 1962	..	x			
Equal Pay Act of 1963	..	..	..	x	
Civil Rights Act of 1964	x	x	x	x	
Coal Mine Health and Safety Act, 1969	..	..	..	..	x
Occupational Safety and Health Act, 1970	..	..	..	..	x

agement functions. Anyone responsible for these functions in an organization covered by these acts should inform himself of the laws to avoid the penalties provided for in many of them. Much information can be obtained from the agencies of the government responsible for the enforcement of the law; another source is the reporting services mentioned earlier.

Table 1 provides a summary look at the federal legislation which has been discussed [here]. The list is in chronological order, and the personnel function(s) each law affects is indicated.

Notes

1. Section 8(a) (3).
2. 213 U.S. 177.
3. Cantrall Co., 96 NLRB 786.
4. Teamsters, Local 357 *v.* NLRB, 365 U.S. 667.
5. "Discrimination System Is Cumbersome—Brown," *Action,* vol. VI, no. 1, February 1970, p. 31. For specific information regarding the legal assistance an individual may receive, see 42 U.S. Code Annotated, sec. 2000 E-5.
6. "Unions Open Fire on Nixon over Jobs, Civil Rights," *U.S. News and World Report,* Mar. 9, 1970, p 69.
7. Herbert Garfinkel and Michael D. Cahn, "Racial-Religious Designations, Preferential Hiring and Fair Employment Practices Commissions," *Labor Law Journal,* vol. XX, no. 6, June 1969, pp. 357-372.
8. The Railway Labor Act applies to employers in the railroad and the airline industries. Its provisions are somewhat similar to the NLRA.
9. National Labor Relations Board, *Thirty-second Annual Report,* 1968, p. 218.
10. NLRB *v.* Jones and Laughlin Steel Corporation, 301 U.S. 1.
11. NLRB *v.* Fansteel Metallurgical Corp., 306 U.S. 240.
12. Fibreboard Paper Products *v.* NLRB, 379 U.S. 203.
13. "Landmark Court Decision for Women's Job Rights Hailed by Labor Department Official," *Retail Clerks Advocate,* vol. LXIII, no. 2, February 1970, p. 20.
14. U.S. Department of Labor, *Handy Reference Guide to the Fair Labor Standards Act,* 1968, p. 3.
15. *Ibid.,* p. 5.
16. *Ibid.,* p. 11.
17. Paragraph 50-204.10, *Federal Register,* vol. XXXVI, no. 96, part II, May 20, 1969, p. 7948.
18. Patrick F. Cestron, "Should the Federal Government Develop Safety Standards?" *National Safety News,* vol. Cl, no. 2, February 1970, p. 43.
19. AFL-CIO, *Labor Looks at Congress, 1969,* American Federation of Labor-Congress of Industrial Organizations, Washington, 1970, p. 48.

Intergovernmental Personnel Act:
The First Year

JOSEPH M. ROBERTSON

With the passage of the Intergovernmental Personnel Act of 1970, and its approval by the President on January 5, 1971, sound personnel management was reaffirmed as a vital element in effective governmental administration. The IPA established as public policy:

"That . . . a national interest exists in a high caliber of public service in State and local governments,

"That the quality of public service at all levels of government can be improved by the development of systems of personnel administration consistent with . . . merit principles, and

"That Federal financial and technical assistance to State and local governments for strengthening their personnel administration in a manner consistent with these principles is in the national interest."

The IPA is truly a landmark in federal legislation. Chairman Robert E. Hampton of the U.S. Civil Service Commission described it as "the first comprehensive statute designed to strengthen the personnel resources of state and local governments." It offers a unique opportunity to state and local governments for upgrading their manpower resources and improving the delivery of services to the public.

The need for legislation like the IPA became evident during the 1960s. Population growth and shifts, rapid technological changes, and the requirements of our increasingly complex and interdependent society began to place enormous demands upon State and local governments. Numerous studies showed that the needs of these governmental jurisdictions for well-qualified personnel would outstrip the supply, particularly in the critical professional, technical, and administrative occupations. Any failure of government to resolve our complex domestic problems could well result in diminishing confidence in our Federal system.

The need for a comprehensive approach to personnel management assistance was met by the IPA. The focus of the IPA program is on helping the chief executives of State and local jurisdictions raise the quality of public service by improving the competence of personnel and the quality of personnel systems. The Act includes provisions:

Emphasizing intergovernmental cooperation and the creation of a true partnership among all three levels of government;

Encouraging innovation and diversity on the part of State and local governments in the design and management of their systems;

Authorizing Federal financial and technical assistance to state and local governments for improving their personnel systems;

Authorizing grants for training state and local personnel and for establishing government service fellowships, and authorizing the admission of this personnel to Federal training programs;

Establishing for the U.S. Civil Service Commission a leadership role in the coor-

From *Personnel Administration,* May-June 1972. Reprinted by permission of the International Personnel Management Association.

dination of personnel management and training assistance available to state and local governments;

Transferring to the U.S. Civil Service Commission major responsibility for setting and administering merit system standards for Federal grant programs;

Providing for the temporary assignment of personnel between Federal agencies and state and local governments and institutions of higher education;

Establishing an Advisory Council on Intergovernmental Personnel Policy.

The first priority facing the U.S. Civil Service Commission was to establish an organization for administering the provisions of the Act. The Bureau of Intergovernmental Personnel Programs was established in Washington, with Intergovernmental Personnel Programs Divisions in all ten of the Commission's regional offices. The staff of the Office of State Merit Systems in the Department of Health, Education, and Welfare which had been responsible for administering Federal merit system standards and providing technical assistance in personnel management to state and local governments, was transferred to the Civil Service Commission.

The Commission's Intergovernmental Personnel Programs staff includes persons with experience in state and local governments and educational institutions, as well as specialists recruited from the U.S. Civil Service Commission and other Federal agencies. The Bureau has about 60 persons on its staff, while an additional 100 persons are working in the regional IPP divisions.

An early decision was made to decentralize the administration of the IPA. A key role is played in its administration by the Commission's regional directors and the regional IPP divisions. Priorities for personnel management improvement are determined by states and localities according to their particular needs.

The IPA grant program has begun as a relatively modest one—$12.5 million in fiscal year 1972. From the beginning, however, it has been our intention to exploit every provision of the Act as a vital part of the New Federalism. Although the basic purpose of the IPA grant program is to assist state and local governments in improving personnel administration, other extremely important aspects are fostering intergovernmental cooperation and improving the coordination of all Federal grant programs affecting state and local government employees and personnel management.

Program Accomplishments

Since the first IPA grant in October 1971, the Commission has made 115 grants totaling $7.6 million. Of that amount, 59 percent has been for personnel administration improvement projects, 40 percent for training, and less than 1 percent for government service fellowships. A few examples of grant projects now in operation may illustrate the wide scope of activity being supported.

In many states and localities the personnel function has historically been fragmented. Consequently, among the personnel management improvement projects, the most frequent area of concern is establishing or strengthening a central personnel agency. In Douglas County, Nebraska, for example, a central personnel program and agency is being established for the first time with the assistance of IPA grant funds.

A second area of widespread interest is the instituting or updating of personnel classification and compensation systems. For example, Shreveport, Louisiana, is updating the basic classification and pay structure for classified city employees.

Review and improvement of examining policies and methods, including the validation of tests and improving equal employment opportunity systems, is a third major area of project activity. The grant to the Commonwealth of Virginia, for example, includes funds to validate and revise civil service tests for both the state and local governments.

Examples of other personnel administration improvement programs currently being given assistance include projects to design and install automated personnel reporting systems, to develop affirmative equal opportunity employment programs, and to utilize modern manpower planning and management methods.

The training projects that have been funded under the IPA cover the wide range of administrative, managerial, and technical skills necessary in a modern public service. In addition to the core areas of management, executive development, and supervision, jurisdictions have been placing heavy emphasis on training in labor-management relations.

Not all activity in labor-management relations is in training, however. In Massachusetts, IPA funds are lending support to a pilot program to improve the speed of handling arbitration cases involving local governments. The program is being carried out by the state government and the American Arbitration Association with the cooperation of local governments and unions.

The IPA provides that elected and appointed officials, as well as career civil servants, may participate in projects funded under the Act. An association of parish officers in Louisiana took advantage of this provision in obtaining a grant to train newly elected parish officers in governmental administrative techniques. The Act also provides for the participation of the legislative and judicial branches of governments, as well as executive. Under this authority, a group of legislative auditors in Alaska is receiving instruction in modern auditing techniques. . . .

A Look into the Future

This first year has seen the IPA off to a good start. All provisions of the Act —grants, mobility, technical assistance, and training—are being utilized. Perhaps most significant is the high degree of consultation and cooperation between state and local governments in meeting their needs.

Although it is a good start, it is just a beginning. Many important challenges await us in the year ahead. Among these is the need to expand and improve our communications system, so that information about the IPA and its programs will reach all those who stand to benefit from it. Federal, state and local officials need to exchange information about personnel management improvement problems and projects, so that maximum benefits will be realized from the IPA.

We must also implement, fully, the Commission's responsibility under the Act for coordinating Federal grants, technical assistance, and training in personnel administration. This will help avoid duplication of effort and, even more importantly, help states and localities explore all possible avenues of assistance in meeting their personnel management needs.

As we assess the results of the first year's personnel improvement and training grants, we are keeping an eye focused on increasing effective utilization of available resources in meeting current and projected needs. For fiscal year 1973, the President's budget proposes significant increases in funds for administering IPA programs, including an 80 percent increase in grant funds. This would raise the level of funding for IPA grants by $10 million to a total of $22.5 million.

It has been a satisfying and challenging first year. The value of the efforts of state and local officials and the public interest organizations in identifying their priority needs and in supporting and using the authorities for assistance provided by the IPA cannot be overestimated. We look forward to their continued interest and cooperation.

Perhaps the major challenge we face is to be able to respond effectively to the expectations which have been generated by the first year of operations under the IPA. This is not an easy task, but the spirit of intergovernmental cooperation and partnership which we have seen during this first year is a most encouraging sign. By working with other public jurisdictions and interested organizations, we can help make public personnel administration based on merit principles responsive to current needs at all levels of government.

Graduate Student Attitudes Toward Personnel Management and the Future Development of the Field

STEPHEN J. CARROLL

Last year we had a general discussion of some things we ought to talk about in the future in this Manpower Management Division.[1] At that time I indicated that one problem to discuss might be the declining interest in the personnel management field by doctoral students. I pointed out that in the Behavioral Science Division of the Department of Business Administration at the University of Maryland, we have two major fields. These are organizational theory and behavior, and personnel and labor relations. I indicated that every single one of the 18 doctoral students we had up to that point in time chose to major in organizational theory and behavior rather than in personnel and labor relations. This is in spite of the fact that we have had what we feel is some strength in the personnel management area.

This greater interest of our students in what we call the organization theory and organizational behavioral area might be just unique to our own students. However, a study by Benjamin Schneider of the University of Maryland also showed a lack of interest in traditional personnel management subjects by students entering industrial behavioral science programs in business schools and psychology departments. In this study which was published in the Winter 1971 issue of *Professional Psychology*, Professor Schneider mailed questionnaires to 101 students entering graduate applied behavioral science programs in psychology departments and business schools at 20 of the leading universities with such programs. He received replies from 34 students entering such programs in psychology departments and from 25 students entering such programs in business schools. Schneider found that the average level of interest in organizational behavior topics was significantly higher than for the personnel manage-

Reprinted by permission of the author and the publisher from *Academy of Management Proceedings, 1972.*

ment topics for the business school behavioral science students. For example, the average business behavioral science graduate student had quite a lot of interest in the organizational behavior topics and only "some " interest in the personnel management topics. Of the personnel management topics, there was interest only in personnel selection and management development.

Another study by John Campbell of the University of Minnesota also published in the Winter, 1971 issue of *Professional Psychology* indicates that there are more courses in organizational behavior than in personnel administration in 32 graduate schools of business administration and that the number of behavioral oriented Ph.D.'s has increased significantly in business schools in recent years, and the trend in dissertation topics is in the organizational behavior area.

To find out more about this apparent lack of interest in personnel management subjects at the University of Maryland, I administered part of Schneider's questionnaire and an open-ended questionnaire to graduate sutdents in the Department of Business Administration of the University of Maryland. In the adaptation of the Schneider questionnaire, both M.B.A. and D.B.A. students indicated their current level of interest in a number of organizational behavior and personnel management topics. The open-ended questionnaire was given only to behavioral science doctoral students and elicited the reasons for the student's choice of a major field, their attitudes and expectations concerning the field of personnel management and their suggestions for improving the field.

What did I find from these two surveys? First, like Schneider I found a much stronger interest in organizational theory and behavior topics than in personnel management and labor relations topics among our behavioral science doctoral students. Personnel selection and labor relations were the only personnel management subjects which elicited much interest from these students. Among the M.B.A. candidates, however, there was about an equal interest in topics from the organizational theory and behavior and the personnel and labor relations areas. This was true of behavioral science M.B.A.'s and M.B.A.'s from other major fields.

In the open-ended questionnaire, the doctoral students reported the following perceptions of the field of personnel management:

1. Personnel management is a dull field. The material is too dry. The textbooks are boring.

2. In personnel management, there is too much emphasis on procedures and techniques and not enough emphasis on basic behavioral science theory. The personnel management courses require too much memorization of unimportant facts and methods. The fields of personnel and labor relations are too descriptive or legalistic.

3. The field of personnel management does not have high status in the business school. It is not challenging enough. It does not require much knowledge of quantitative techniques. Individuals of low ability can succeed in the area.

4. The field of personnel management is a low status field in the industry. Personnel managers are low paid and are not involved in important decisions of the organization. Also, many personnel managers lack knowledge of research and how to use modern techniques such as the computer and quantitative methods.

5. Personnel management is too applied. It does not deal with basic scientific knowledge like organizational theory and behavior. It is concerned about minor questions.

6. Personnel management is not sufficiently humanistic. Everything is done from the perspective of the organization and not from the worker's. In personnel you just try to get the worker to do more work for the same amount of money.

In spite of these criticisms, the doctoral students did believe the manpower field was important and would become increasingly so with greater government and industrial concern about the utilization of human resources. They indicated that they believe that the field of selection and labor relations would be especially critical in the future.

What suggestions did our doctoral students have?

1. The textbooks in the field should be rewritten so as to emphasize problems rather than procedures. Also, much more basic behavioral science theory must be integrated with the text material.

2. Professors must be hired to teach manpower management courses who have behavioral science backgrounds. There should be less reliance on lawyers and economists.

3. Manpower management courses and textbooks should take a more humanistic or worker-centered perspective.

4. More support and interest must be shown in the manpower management area. Conferences might be organized which establish research priorities. Contests may be set up for the best book or the best article in manpower management. Sessions might be organized in which innovative teachers in manpower management can provide suggestions to other teachers.

5. There should be greater use of "mathematical" and "systems" approaches in the field of manpower management where applicable.

It should be remembered that these comments are from doctoral students in organizational theory and behavior who also minor in personnel administration and labor relations. They are students who do have some knowledge of the manpower management field and who chose the organizational theory and organizational behavior field as their primary interest.

This survey of our behavioral science doctoral students was obviously very limited, but the data collected is congruent with other indications of some lack of interest in the field of personnel management on the part of doctoral students and faculty members. For example, the findings were similar to those of Schneider described earlier which were collected in a more comprehensive survey of graduate students. In addition, there is the obvious fact that the Manpower Management division is one of the smallest divisions in the Academy of Management and furthermore the number of papers submitted to this division and the average number of individuals attending its sessions is far less than for the Division of Organizational Behavior.

I, for one, think that these data are a cause for concern. A decline of interest among doctoral students in the field of manpower management would mean less research and still fewer students majoring in the field in the future. Certainly, our present doctoral students at the University of Maryland, when they become full-time faculty members, are not going to communicate much enthusiasm for the manpower management field to their doctoral students.

The field of manpower management needs a new perspective and a new orientation. [Elsewhere] Elmer Burack describes such a new perspective. One aspect of this newer approach is an increased emphasis on organizational manpower planning and career development. Under this newer perspective, organizational members are not looked upon as individuals hired only to carry out the tasks in simplified and rationally designed jobs but as valuable human resources capable of considerable development and growth under proper organizational conditions. In this approach there is an attempt to design the organization to fit the individual unlike the traditional personnel management approach which basically involves bribing the individual to adjust to the rationally designed organization. The new approach is a more "humanistic" approach since it considers what contributes to the welfare of the individual as well as to the objectives of the organization. There is an effort to better integrate the goals of the individual and the organization through the use of job enrichment, assessment centers, individual development programs and so on. The term "opportunity center" used by Burack in his paper is quite indicative of this new perspective in personnel management.

Under this newer perspective, traditional personnel procedures are used in a different way. Tests are used for purposes of counseling and placement and not just to screen out individuals who need jobs. Performance evaluation techniques are used to provide the feedback needed for growth and development rather than to coerce organizational members to work harder.

This newer approach in personnel management or human resource management does meet many of the objections to traditional personnel management voiced by behavioral science graduate students described previously. Personnel management becomes not only "management centered" but "employee centered" as well. The newer approach requires more training and more knowledge than the traditional approach. Operating personnel managers must have more knowledge from the behavioral sciences than they presently do. They must make much greater use of modern planning and "systems" techniques. They must become more familiar with the computer and modern data processing methods. All this should contribute to an enhancement of the status of the field of personnel management at the academic and the operating management level. These changes could contribute to increasing the appeal of personnel management to higher quality students. This newer approach to personnel management also is more congruent with modern societal expectations on the utilization of human resources. As Max Wortman [has pointed out elsewhere], there is greater public concern today for the disadvantaged, the undermotivated, the unemployed, and the underemployed. Wortman recommends the adoption of a concept of manpower which would involve career planning, guidance, and development throughout every citizen's life. Career counseling in corporations and other organizations would be just a part of this total approach. This approach would also support the quota system of employee selection that some feel we are moving toward. [Editors note: Quota hiring systems for minority and other population subgroups are, however, illegal under the Civil Rights Act of 1964—at least technically. See the article by Daniel Seligman, "How 'Equal Opportunity' Turned into Employment Quotas," in chap. 9 for a fuller discussion of this issue.]

In summary then, there is some evidence that traditional personnel management, as it is usually taught and usually described in textbooks, is viewed in a negative manner by graduate students and newer faculty members. This perspective of personnel management is creating some problems now for the field, and if it continues will create even greater difficulties in the future. There are, however, some indications of a growing interest in a newer approach or perspective. Burack and Wortman have discussed the advantages of adopting a career planning, guidance, and development approach for personnel management. This should lead to a better utilization of our human resources, and this means better management. This newer approach might also be expected to increase interest in the field by graduate students and faculty members and to increase the importance of the personnel function in operating organizations and in society itself.

Note

1. For sources on studies referenced, write Professor S. J. Carroll, Graduate School of Business, Univ. of Maryland, College Park, Md.

Interface Between Personnel and Organizational Psychology

BERNARD M. BASS

Among the Inca farmers, work was regarded as an end in itself, a ritualistic form of religious worship. But work that was not ceremonial lacked sense and meaning. Work and worship were inseparable (Von Hagen, 1957). Nevertheless, more often in nonindustrialized societies, work was done merely to subsist. Better yet, it was delegated to women or slaves. The Tibetan concentrated on his prayer wheel; the Talmudist on studying the Law; the Balinese on art; the Athenian on citizenship; and the Iroquois on military honors. Success, wellbeing, security, and prestige depended not on one's job but on contemplative zeal, scholarship, artistic efforts, oratory, or bravery in battle.

On the other hand, in modern industrialized society, as among the Incas, work is becoming the center of life. Twenty years may be spent preparing to enter the world of work. As much as half of each working day will be spent at work or commuting to and from it. Success in life, sense of well-being, sense of accomplishment, security, and prestige all will be tied to what work is done. Likewise, work will determine one's standard of living and economic well-being. Therefore it should come as no surprise to find that in our "work-intoxicated" society there are few considerations about employment recruiting, testing, hiring, training, job design, and other personnel problems that can be divorced from their setting within a larger context of social forces, organization, and society.

More generally, as Porter (1966) noted in his recent annual review chapter on personnel management, few issues in personnel psychology can be completely examined without attention to what usually are thought to be problems of organizational psychology. It may be profitable at this time to look at some of the more lively issues that lie at the interface between the two fields. Let us examine some organizational questions that appear when dealing with what usually are the concern of technicians in personnel psychology. To do this, I will focus briefly on recruiting, the application

Reprinted by permission of the author and the publisher from the *Journal of Applied Psychology,* vol. 52 (1968), pp. 81-88. Copyright 1968 by the American Psychological Association.

blank, testing, interviewing, training, and job design. Following this I will reverse the examination and look briefly at some significant personnel questions, questions of individual differences, which usually are the concern of organizational technicians.

Personnel Issues Involving Organizational Questions

Recruiting

In one large sales organization, approximately 3 percent of those applicants for jobs as salesmen were hired if they had been attracted to apply for the jobs through newspaper ads. On the other hand, 14 percent of those who had made application because of friends' suggestions or who had been recommended to the sales agency by friends were hired. Unfortunately, analyses of the merit ratings a year afterwards of those hired found that those who had been recruited through newspaper ads were in the fiftieth percentile in merit while those who had been introduced to the organization through friends were likely to be found below the twentieth percentile in merit. What had been revealed was quite simple to a technician. Different selection ratios were operating. Those recruited by newspaper advertisements were screened more carefully; proportionately fewer were hired. Those recommended by friends were screened less thoroughly; proportionately more were hired. The same phenomenon was seen quite differently by the social psychologist. For him, interviewers were showing too much acceptance of applicants simply because they had been sent for consideration for employment by friends.

There has been surprisingly little research on the social psychology of applicant sources. Yet, personnel technicians are aware of the overriding importance to the utility of a selection program of the selection ratio as well as the importance of the quality and quantity of recruits who apply for testing. There is little systematic evidence of the many biases involved in decisions about where to recruit and whom to recruit for testing. For example, in academia, we seldom try for a low selection ratio. Rather, we solicit applications for academic jobs from only the most prestigeful sources, neglecting the utilities of uncovering a larger number of recruits. The problem is complicated further when the recruits gravitate toward or away from certain occupations and organizations because of extraneous factors. Consider how difficult it is to hire Negro engineers when the problem is compounded by the difficulties in encouraging Negroes to prepare for careers in engineering, since traditionally it has been so difficult for them to enter such a career.

Application blank

In a sales selection program, serendipity revealed two *dynamic items* on an application blank (dynamic application questions concern the interplay between applicant and organization). When combined, these two items yielded a phenomenal validity of .70 against subsequent merit ratings. Hindsight made it relatively easy to understand why these two items were such powerful predictors of subsequent job performance. These items were: "Is it all right to contact your boss?" and "How soon can you start work?" Applicants who subsequently were meritorious on the job gave an unqualified "yes" in answer to the first question. It was perfectly all right to contact their boss. Applicants who did not turn out well on the job either said "no" or "yes, but. . . ." Those who turned into poor performers were ready to start work immediately, while those who insisted on at least two weeks notice were likely to be better salesmen, subsequently. Probably, what was being assessed by these dynamic items was the sense of responsibility and sense of security of applicants.

The increasing attention we are giving to biographical information blanks points to a likelihood of focusing more fully on the social and organizational history of the applicant, for so much of what is contained in biographical information is of this form. Consider some of the factors which emerged in Cassen's (1966) factor analyses of biographical information blank items in three cultures: upward mobility, family attitudes, achievement by conforming, interpersonal relations, etc.

Testing

There has been a merger of interest of social and personnel psychologists concerning attitudes toward work. There seems to be no simple response to the question. "Why men work?" Much research suggests quite strongly that what may be rewarding for the task-oriented worker may be punishing to the interaction-oriented worker (Bass, 1967b). Noncognitive dimensions of particular importance for selection and placement testing lie close to work itself or to organizational considerations. Heretofore, to a considerable degree, personality and motivation assessment have developed within counseling and clinical psychology and have been lifted bodily for application to industry. There has been more concern about neuroticism than there has been for need for achievement, yet there is likely to be more payoff from concentrating on the latter. Even in the case of hospitalized mental patients, it seems more prognostic in vocational rehabilitation efforts for them to know about how task oriented they are than how neurotic they are (Distefano and Pryer, 1964).

There has been little further exploration so far of some intriguing evidence that ability and aptitude tests tend to be more predictive of early success in organizations while interest and personality factors tend only to become useful for prediction of criteria where the criteria are measured much later in the applicant's subsequent career. This proposition as well as others which are being generated about the dynamic nature of criteria cannot help but result in a more sophisticated approach to forecasting using psychometric measurements.

Early in the history of industrial psychology, the miniature test was devised for selection purposes. Replicas of the real-life job were constructed and performance evaluated in these simulated situations. Now we see much more use of such simulations of organizations for assessment purposes. Such simulations can be accomplished through the "in-basket" technique, leaderless discussions, business games, organizational design problems, and the like. [Editor's note: The assessment center technique discussed by William Byham in his article "The Assessment Center as an Aid in Management Development" and by A. I. Kraut in his "A Hard Look at Management Assessment Centers and their Future" in chap. 2 represents a highly successful example of this approach.] To date, there has been relatively little exploration of the possibilities of creating for assessment purposes relatively simple games, each representing important organizational dilemmas with which to confront applicants who are seeking careers in those organizations.

Culture fair testing is still another critical issue lying between personnel and social psychology. Is culture fair testing even theoretically possible if past behavior is the best predictor of future behavior? Is it possible to rule out cultural influences in testing without eliminating the validity of the tests? To what extent does previous organizational history play a role in test responses? How different is the applicant of today who grows up in a school system where the administration of objective tests is an almost weekly routine from the applicant of the last generation for whom objective testing was more of a novelty?

As long as there is a basic mistrust between the applicant and the organization, we will live in a situation where the sensible applicant attempts to distort and fake his results on noncognitive tests. In what ways could sufficient trust be promoted between applicant and organization to increase the applicant's desire to give honest responses rather than socially desirable ones, or responses which he judges to be ideal or like those of his boss or like those that would land him the job?

Still another issue in testing which may involve public and organizational policy questions deals with the selection ratio and how it is set.

In one northeastern state, the Human Relations Commission suggests that cut-off scores should be no higher than necessary to screen out unqualified applicants. The company which exploits the selection ratio by recruiting more applicants and setting higher cut-off scores does so at the expense of discouraging applicants who score reasonably well on the test in question. Which is more important: more efficient use of screening devices by the company or avoiding the discouragement of average applicants?

Interviewing

Studies of the bases upon which interviewers make their decisions are beginning to appear more frequently. They may point ultimately to an interview which is a situational test, a replica of an organizational problem where performance can be evaluated completely objectively, primarily by attention to the process by which the interviewee copes with the interviewer. This most promising approach to interviewing treats it primarily as "the social psychology of two-person interaction." Thus Yonge (1956) permitted the interviewer considerable latitude as far as the content of the interview was concerned, but had him rate the interview process itself, specifically to assess the social skill and motivation demonstrated during this process by the interviewee.

The interview presents a particular challenge to the personnel and social psychologist, for no matter what can or cannot be demonstrated about its utility as an assessment device, it is almost universal in use for selection purposes. Above and beyond consideration of the interview as needed for transmittal of information about the job and organization to the interviewee and for helping the interviewee develop realistic expectations about the job for which he is applying, the typical employer still feels the need for face-to-face contact with the applicant before making the employment decision. Yet, it may be that even where the interviewer has been found to add validity to the assessment predictions above and beyond what could be done by statistical integration alone, such results may be handled more adequately in the future by better statistics. For instance, more attention to modifier variables may be required. Actually, modifiers may be merely symptoms of curvilinearity in the predictors. Under such circumstances, a Bayesian solution will always yield more accurate decisions, and in the last analysis will match the regression decisions when the data is linear (Clampett, 1966). At best, Sawyer's (1966) comprehensive review of research on methods for combining assessments strongly indicates that predictive efficiency is increased when interviewer judgments are mechanically combined or synthesized with test data to yield final predictions in contrast to following the usual practice of having interviewers make clinical judgments about the job applicant from his test scores and interview performance.

The problem and its solutions therefore may be stated as follows: no matter what, interviews will be held with applicants. To insure that the interviews do as little damage as possible to the accuracy of the entire selection process, it may be best to increase the number of recruits who are tested, thereby reducing the selection ratio and at the same time increasing the likelihood that all those who passed the first test screen, and as a consequence receive interviews, are all fairly good prospects for the job in question. At the same time, the interviewer's judgments should be treated like additional measurements to be combined statistically with test data available on the applicant to provide a final prediction for him. This required change in practice is an organizational question since the interviewer's role is reduced in importance. Resistance is likely particularly if the interviewer has considerable status or experience but in its resolution may lie the major portion of the utility of a selection program.

Training

Commenting on the fads and fashions in training is like commenting about the weather and what can be done about it. Nevertheless, organizational matters are vital in the decisions of training programs to be introduced, continued, or abandoned. Let me enumerate some well-known training problems at the interface of personnel and organizational psychology.

1. Trainers have discovered to their chagrin that it is one thing to maintain an effective program which meets its training objectives, but it is another to create a training program which both meets its objectives and obtains the approval of the trainees. Unfortunately, evaluation and continuation of the program are more likely to rest upon the latter rather than the former.

2. Familiar also is the organizational problem associated with the returning trainee. Fleishman (1953) provided sufficient evidence that whether or not the effects of the training program made their appearance on the job 6 months after training depended primarily on the attitudes of the boss and the climate of the organization to which the trainee returned.

3. The professional and the manager need to see themselves engaged in "life-long learning" to avoid obsolescence. The organization can help considerably to maintain expectations that its members must continue to keep up with the new developments.

4. To a considerable extent much more attention may need to be paid to a basic conflict between management trainer and management trainee. Managers see themselves performing a complex art whereas one may be trying to teach them simple science. A recent unpublished experiment by Alex Bavelas is relevant here and illustrates the tremendous difficulties involved in the training of people under these circumstances. One subject learns to discriminate the slide photos of healthy and sick cellular tissue through appropriate reinforcement of his responses. A second subject receives the same reinforcement schedule regardless of what responses he makes. The first subject forms a few simple hypotheses about what differentiates photos of a healthy and a sick cell; the second subject forms a complex set of hypotheses since his reinforcements have not been associated in any simple way with his different responses. Unfortunately, when the two subjects discuss the matter, the one with the complex art of judgment is more confident, more resistant to change, and less readily influenced than the other subject with the simple hypotheses.

Job design

As the organization introduces automation, there is a flattening of the distribution of skill demands on newly created jobs and the remaining old ones. More routine jobs as well as more skilled jobs emerge while those at intermediate levels of skill demand are abolished. One can only vaguely foresee the creation of less-fluid worker castes, the unskilled, and the elite, unless some effort is made to intervene with designs for more functional intermediate-level jobs. For instance, electronic data processing (EDP) has created the elite programming job. It has also created the unskilled job of pressing bent IBM cards which are returned by mail.

At the level of the manager, there seem to be two diametrically opposed predictions about how EDP is changing the organization of the future and the jobs within it. On the one hand Leavitt and Whisler (1958) see greater centralization decreasing responsibilities accorded middle managers; others see the reverse. Selection and training of future middle managers need to take account of EDP, but how to do so in the face of the uncertain effects of EDP is a dilemma we face at this time. Individual differences play an important role here. For instance, younger men at the same level in the organization see that their own jobs are changing as a consequence of EDP much more so than do older men at the same level of management (Vaughan and Porat, 1967).

Compensation

For too long the questions concerning equitable compensation have been left in the hands of organizational rationalists. We are just beginning to see the full extent of individual differences in attitudes toward compensation. For instance, in a simulation we use for training mangers, the managers must award salary increases to 10 engineers each of whom differs in merit and in other attributes. Each has a job somewhat different than those of the others who are to be assigned salary increases. Wide differences appear in the average increases recommended. North Europeans seem to feel that 4-6 percent is equitable, while South Europeans may push for as high as 36 percent. Obviously, differences in the rate of inflation in the economies of the different countries in question are of consequence. But just as important are the attitudes toward technicians and engineers that vary greatly from one country to the next. In this same exercise, American, British, and Irish managers generally seem unmoved by the possibility of losing good men to competition and do not feel that counteroffers should be the basis for salary increases. In fact, they sometimes tend to punish men who receive offers from other firms. Contrarily, Flemings, Norwegians, Italians, Indians, and Latin-Americans tend to be more prone to award relatively large increases to men with counteroffers. Even among managers from the same firm, we can see some opting for extremely complex differentials while others insist that regardless of merit or job or seniority, all engineers ought to receive the exact salary increase (Bass, 1967a).

Criteria of individual performance

Concern for an employee's performance in a firm must be viewed in terms of his firm's objectives. For example, Smith sells more merchandise faster than Jones, but Smith's customers complain more about their purchases. Smith brings in more new, nonrepeat busines, but Jones has more steady, satisfied customers. Who is the better salesman? The answer depends on the firm's goals, on what it values most. Smith is the better salesman if the firm is concerned most about its current share of the market. Jones is the better salesman if the firm is concerned about its long-term standing in the market.

We must understand something about how to assess organizational worth if we are to appreciate how individual personnel differ in their contributions to it. Individual differences in the proficiency of executives, for instance, can only be made meaningful if we understand the purposes of their jobs. This in turn entails determining the purposes of the department's divisions and ultimately the purpose of their enterprise

(Fiske, 1951). Assessing the adequacy of the performance of a manager can be tricky business indeed. As Shartle (1956) pointed out, one may discover 10 years too late that an executive who contributed the most to the firm had been discharged.

Organizational Issues Involving Personnel Questions

We have seen that the problems of recruiting, application forms, testing, interviewing, training, job design, and compensation, all ordinarily the primary interest of the personnel psychologist, are likely to contain social issues of interest to organizational psychologists, as well. Now let us reverse roles and look at some problems which usually are the concern of organizational technicians which nevertheless contain significant personnel questions as well: supervision, communications, conflict resolution, team composition, and organization design.

Supervision

For 25 years, there has been major interest by social psychologists in the utility of democratic or permissive rather than directive supervision. But evidence is continuing to accumulate that what type of supervision works best is often a matter of individual and cultural differences. In a number of studies, more directive approaches are favored by subordinates. Indeed, much direction is more often expected in many locales. For instance, in a recent pilot study completed in Spain, those who acted as subordinates were much more favorably disposed toward supervisors who attempted to persuade them rather than who attempted to share the decisions with them, for, they said, a supervisor who does not try to influence his subordinates fails to accord the subordinates the dignity to which they are accustomed by showing that he really does not have sufficient interest to bringing them over to his position. Numerous studies in the United States suggest that those who are highly authoritarian prefer in turn to submit to authority rather than to operate in an environment with opportunities for sharing decisions with their superiors. In turn, they expect to make decisions for their own subordinates (Bass, 1965).

Communications

In a similar vein, two-way communication is thought more effective as well as more satisfying than one-way communication. Yet, a group of Japanese frustrated an American management trainer who was trying to demonstrate the differences and relatively greater values of two-way communication. Among the Japanese, with whom he was working, the ease of communicating a pattern of rectangles one-way was somewhat greater for the task which was imposed, and as a consequence there was considerable confusion on the part of the students who were ostensibly being taught and shown the value of two-way over one-way communication. We have had similar experiences with engineering students who if they are communicating the pattern of rectangles to others with a great deal of background in mechanical drawing and blueprint reading, may communicate faster and more effectively one-way than two-way. Given individuals with common codes, one-way communication can be more effective and more satisfying than two-way communication.

Conflict resolution

Some zero-sum games where one party wins only under the condition that the other party loses are situations where conflict resolution is impossible for almost anybody. In some mixed-motive games, resolution will or will not occur, depending on who is playing the game. If one is able to compete with a generous opponent, it is possible to fleece him. If one himself is nurturant, speedy and highly satisfying resolutions can be achieved (Loomis, 1959). There would seem to be considerable payoff in the study of the interaction of person and structural conditions in various types of negotiating situations. Thus, Bass (1966) found that task-oriented negotiators were most likely to achieve settlements of high quality in contrast to settlements reached by less task-oriented negotiators.

Team composition

We are beginning to understand the personal ingredients in the assembly of members of a group required to achieve particular outcomes. For example, evidence accumulated so far suggests if we put together a number of highly task-oriented members, we are likely to generate a great deal of socioemotional conflict, although at the same time the chances are reasonably good that plenty of work will get done. At the same time if we mix together a group of primarily interaction-oriented personnel, the likelihood is that the group will be most satisfying to the members, there will be much play, but relatively little work will be accomplished (Bass, 1967b).

Organizational design

To conclude, let us look at what rational organizational designers would suggest as inviolate principles of organizational design and at the same time note the very opposite points of view voiced by behavioralists.

The rationalists would say that an organization should be designed so that someone is responsible for supervising all essential activities. The behavioralists would be primarily concerned with creating structures where leadership was shared.

The rationalists would argue that responsibility for specific acts should not be duplicated or overlapping. The behavioralists would feel that overlapping had much merit, providing opportunities for cross-training, backup, and increasing the reliability of the system of interacting workers.

The rationalists would argue for job simplification; the behavioralists would push for the reverse, job enlargement.

The rationalists would insist that responsibilities should be written, clear, and understood by job occupants. The behavioralists would argue that each person brings to a job somewhat different potentials and should be given freedom and flexibility to develop his own particular way of doing the job to make the most of the situation in which he finds himself.

The rationalists would argue that authority to make decisions should be commensurate with responsibility for those decisions. The behavioralists would state that authority cannot be assigned but rather goes with ability and esteem as an individual among associates. Furthermore, they would note that the rationalists' principle of authority primarily makes it easy for some people to shirk responsibility and also increases staff-line conflict.

The rationalists would want authority to be delegated so that decisions take place as close as possible to the point of action. The behavioralists would insist that the rationalists do not mean what they say, for to accomplish this goal they would accept the behavioralists' position that individuals should be responsible for decisions which affect themselves, whereas, in fact, the rationalists design organizations so that such decisions are lodged with the superiors of the individuals who must execute those decisions.

The rationalists have fixed notions about span of control; the behavioralists feel that the span of control creates as many problems as it solves. For example, the smaller the span of control in an organization the taller will be its structure resulting in greater separation of the top of the organization from the bottom. More possibilities will arise for filtering communications that must be transmitted through the organization. There will be greater differences between the goals of those at the top from those at the bottom of the hierarchy. Rather than concern themselves about span of control, the behavioralists would be much more interested in the opportunities for feedback between subordinate and superior; span of control could be much greater where feedback was accurate and easy.

The rationalists insist on a chain of command; the behavioralists say the chain of command is often a fiction interfering with the flow of communication that is needed by the organization, a flow which may be horizontal, diagonal, and in forms quite different than assumed by the rationalists. For example, the relation between the foreman and an assembly-line worker has been likened to that between a travel consultant and his client. The "real boss" in the situation is the machine (Bass, 1965).

Optimum organizational designs are likely to be found somewhere between rationalist emphasis on predictability and accountability through impersonal structure and behavioralist concern for interpersonal trust and interpersonal confidence as the bases of organizational stability and growth. Again, one can only agree that organizational design must attend to what has been learned about intrapersonal as well as interpersonal dynamics. Where the optimum lies between the rationalist's and the behavioralist's positions depends on the capabilities, training, and involvement of the personnel in the system. The fully programmed rationalist's organization is closer to the optimum when personnel capability, training, and involvement are low (and the rationalist's organization is likely to keep personnel involvement low). When personnel potential is high, the behavioralist's model becomes more feasible.

The personnel specialist no longer can hide behind his validity coefficients, test blanks, and training manuals. In turn, the organization scientist cannot remain assured of the generality of results from his surveys, field studies, and rational analyses. Models for organizational and personnel research need to take into account sources of variance due to jobs and organizational environment, sources due to individual characteristics, and, most important of all, sources due to the peculiar interactions of individuals and environments.

References

Bass, B. M. *Organizational Psychology.* Boston: Allyn and Bacon, 1965.

Bass, B. M. Effects on the subsequent performance of negotiators of studying issues or planning strategies alone or in groups. *Psychological Monographs,* 1966, vol. 80, no. 6, whole no. 614.

Bass, B. M. Combining management training and research. *Training Directors Journal,* 1967, vol. 21, no. 4, 2-7. (a)

Bass, B. M. Social behavior and the orientation inventory: A review. *Psychological Bulletin,* 1967, vol. 68, 260-292. (b)

Cassens, F. W. "Cross-cultural Dimensions of Executive Life History Antecedents." Unpublished doctoral dissertation, Louisiana State University, 1966.

Clampett, H. A., Jr. Psychological predictions based on Bayesian probabilities. *Technical Report No. 11,* March 1966, University of Pittsburgh, Contract Nonr 624, no. 14.

Distefano, M. K., Jr., and Pryer, M. W. Task-orientation, persistence, and anxiety of mental hospital patients with high and low motivation. *Psychological Reports,* 1964, vol. 14, no. 18.

Fiske, D. W. Values, theory and the criterion problem. *Personnel Psychology,* 1951, vol. 4, 93-98.

Fleishman, E. A. Leadership climate, human relations training, and supervisory behavior. *Personnel Psychology,* 1953, vol. 6, 205-222.

Leavitt, H. J., and Whisler, T. L. Management in the 1980's. *Harvard Business Review,* 1958, vol. 36, 41-48.

Loomis, J. L. Communication, the development of trust, and cooperative behavior. *Human Relations,* 1959, vol. 12, 305-315.

Porter, L. W. Personnel management. *Annual Review of Psychology,* 1966, vol. l7, 395-422.

Sawyer, J. Measurement and prediction, clinical and statistical. *Psychological Bulletin,* 1966, vol. 66, 178-200.

Shartle, C. L. *Executive Performance and Leadership.* Englewood Cliffs, N.J.: Prentice-Hall, 1956.

Vaughan, J. A., and Porat, A. M. Managerial reaction to computers. *Banking,* 1967, vol. 59, no. 10, 119-122.

Von Hagen, V. W. *Realm of the Incas.* New York: Mentor, 1957.

Yonge, K. A. The value of the interview: An orientation and a pilot study. *Journal of Applied Psychology,* 1956, vol. 40, 25-31.

CHAPTER 2

Techniques of Selection: Interviews, Testing, Assessment Centers, and Work Sampling

The basis of all selection and placement work is the bedrock fact of human differences. Obviously, if individuals were all identical in abilities, skills, traits, and potentialities, personnel selection would be unnecessary and superfluous. It would not matter who was assigned to which job. Tyler presents rather dramatic evidence that differences between individuals are a universal phenomenon, extending from man down the hierarchy of life to even the single-cell organisms. She indicates that scientific personnel selection is indeed based on a solid foundation.

But even if we understand the magnitude of human differences and succeed in developing accurate methods of assessing them, in many real-life situations individuals with the desired "profile" of characteristics may not be available, either from inside or outside the organization, when organizational needs require them. Thus, the need for manpower planning—for a built-in organizational system which anticipates future needs for individuals with various trait and potential profiles. In his brief article, Megginson explains why manpower planning is important not only to the organization but also to the nation. He presents the general objectives of this function, including a brief introduction to the new and important area of human resource accounting.

Over the years, industrial psychologists have developed a number of procedures and techniques that can be used to accurately identify and measure the traits and abilities needed for success on different jobs. Such measurements can then be used in selection and placement decisions. Korman's article provides a step-by-step discussion of these techniques, pointing out their limitations as well as their strengths.

Finally, the article by Wickert again broadens the scope of the discussion. Using decision-theory principles, he shows that selection techniques of any kind—tests, recommendations, the interview, or whatever—cannot be evaluated in isolation. The value of each depends on its contribution to the accuracy and utility of the overall personnel decision process—and on its cost to the organization.

In summary, individual differences are universal and ineradicable. They must not only be recognized, they must be taken into account in organizational planning, via manpower planning. Industrial psychology has provided organizations with procedures for the determination and measurement of work related traits and dimensions, and decision theory contributes a conceptual framework for the evaluation of such measurements.

The interview is a virtually universally used selection technique. In his article,

Miner points out that it is indeed useful for many of the purposes for which it is employed, but its major purpose in most selection settings is probably to predict future job performance, and for this purpose it is usually invalid. Starting with this basic fact, Carlson, Thayer, Mayfield and Peterson describe a program of research carried out on the interview by one organization. The results of this research led to changes in the way the interview was used and a new training program for interviewers. From a more general point of view, this article illustrates how behavioral science research can lead directly to improvements in personnel operations.

It is essential in any discussion of personnel testing, especially at the introductory level, to work from a clear definition of just what a psychological test is. Misconceptions and erroneous ideas are extremely common in this area. Anastasi's definition goes a long way toward clarification: a psychological test—any psychological test—is simply a sample of behavior used to predict future behavior. Within the context of this simple but accurate definition, she provides a lucid discussion of the psychometric concepts of standardization, test difficulty, reliability, and validity. Her article thus provides a basis for understanding of the other readings in this section of this chapter.

But is personnel testing really worthwhile in terms of payoff to the organization? This is an important question, of course. The Schmidt and Hoffman study is included here primarily because it provides an answer. This study shows that even with a lower-level job the savings resulting from the use of a valid selection instrument can be substantial. (Although the instrument used is a weighted application blank and not a test, the principles are identical.) We are aware that this reading is more difficult than most in the book, but the major points should be clear even to the student who does not understand the technical details. Besides demonstrating the potential economic value of a valid selection instrument, the study illustrates a number of concepts in personnel. For example:

1. The processes of validation and cross-validation, as discussed by Korman in section A of this chapter.

2. The evaluation and use of statistical models of utility in personnel.

3. Application of cost-accounting techniques to personnel problems.

Additional development of point 3 above can be found in articles by Megginson (chap. 2, section A), Ruch (chap. 2, section C), Caplan (chap. 5), Brummet, et al. (chap. 5), and Jeswald (chap. 7). In our judgment, this general area, often referred to as human resource accounting, will become increasingly important in the future.

Perhaps the major development in the past decade in personnel selection, however, has been the increasing concern on the part of government about the racial and ethnic fairness of commonly used selection techniques. Although this concern extends to nontest techniques such as the interview and the background check, the major focus—rightly or wrongly—has been on personnel tests. In his article, Ruch explores the meaning of the 1971 landmark Duke Power Supreme Court case for personnel selection. His focus is on job-relatedness or validity requirements imposed by the 1964 Civil Rights Act as interpreted by the U.S. Equal Employment Opportunity Commission. In the last article in section C of this chapter, we see that there is an additional legal requirement which must be met before a selection technique can be considered to be fair.

Government requirements that selection procedures must be demonstrated to be job-related has created a heavy demand by business organizations for outside consultants with the training and skills necessary to carry out validation studies. In order to protect organizations from charlatans and the unqualified, the Professional Affairs Committee of division 14 of the American Psychological Association (the division of

Industrial and Organizational Psychology) has drawn up a set of guidelines for the selection of validation consultants, which we here reprint. (Thus, the ubiquitous selection problem extends even into the selection of selection researchers. An interesting tongue-in-cheeck question here is whether or not these selection procedures meet EEOC legal requirements.)

Much of the discussion of the fairness of employment tests and other selection procedures has centered on the question of possible racial differences in validity. In this context, validity is defined as the correlation between test scores and job success. Is it possible that personnel selection procedures that are valid for the majority are typically invalid for minority group members? Boehm's review of the research indicates that the answer is probably No. Backing up Boehm's review, a more recent study (Schmidt, F. L., Berner, J. G. and Hunter, J. E. Racial differences in validity of employment tests: Reality or illusion? *Journal of Applied Psychology,* 1973, *58,* 5-9), has shown that, when differences between blacks and whites in size of group studied are taken into account, employment tests are apparently valid for one race but not the other no more often than would be expected on the basis of chance alone. This finding indicates that there is perhaps no such thing as racial differences in test validity. But, as we shall see later, equal validity in both races is not enough to insure that a selection procedure is fair and legal.

Gael and Grant's short but somewhat complex study is an excellent example of what must be done to meet Equal Employment Opportunity Commission requirements for test validation. The reader should be careful to note that Gael and Grant go beyond merely showing that their test composite has approximately equal validity coefficients in the black and white groups. They also show that the test scores do not underpredict the average level of black job performance. That is, they demonstrate a lack of unfair prediction bias. For complex statistical reasons, a test may show equal validity coefficients for both races but still underestimate actual minority group job performance.

To add further complexity to this issue, there are definitions of test bias other than the one used by Gael and Grant, and these other definitions sometimes lead to different conclusions about the fairness of a test, interview or other procedure (cf. Schmidt, F. L. and Hunter, J. E. Racial and ethnic bias in psychological tests: divergent implications of two definitions of test bias. *American Psychologist,* 1974, *29,* in press). These statistical and measurement intricacies serve to emphasize the need for outside professional aid in validation research and, therefore, indirectly refer back to the guidelines on consultant selection presented earlier in this chapter.

Next to government intervention designed to insure selection fairness, the most important development in personnel selection in the past decade or so is probably the rise of assessment centers. In reading the articles by Byham and Kraut, keep in mind Anastasi's definition (chap. 2, section C) of a psychological or personnel test as a sample of behavior used to predict future behavior. It is obvious that most assessment center exercises are behavior samples from the universe of managerial behaviors. (Section E of this chapter is devoted to the principles of work sampling and performance testing.) Because of this, Byham can state that they have content validity and thus meet EEOC validation requirements (see the Ruch article in section C of this chapter). In addition, many validity studies have been carried out using the principles described by Korman (section A of this chapter), and these indicate that assessment center evaluations show substantial correlations with subsequent managerial success.

As both Byham and Kraut point out, the assessment center is a development as well as a selection technique (see chap. 4), and is often developed and used in combination with training programs.

In recent years, there has been somewhat of a trend away from aptitude tests (which supposedly measure basic potential and have connotations of fixedness) to achievement tests (which attempt to measure currently developed skills and knowledges and which suggest the possibility of individual improvement in the areas measured). The relevance of the content of most achievement tests is more obvious to most testees, and, thus, the test is more likely to be accepted as fair. In addition, achievement tests often have obvious content validity. They are less likely to be challenged by EEOC or OFCC (Office of Federal Contract Compliance), and they may actually be better predictors of future performance than aptitude measures.

One of the principal differences betweeen aptitude and achievement tests is that the behavior measured by achievement tests is more similar to the behavior actually required on the job. Wernimont and Campbell suggest that this should be a basic principle of performance prediction: make the behaviors sampled by the predictor or test as similar as possible to the job behaviors to be predicted. Their article thus points in the direction of work-sample or performance tests. Campion's study then provides a description of the successful construction and use of a work-sample selection test. Performance tests similar to Campion's are now being used by the New Jersey, New York, and Michigan Civil Service Commissions. One of the present writers is currently conducting research on performance testing supported by the U.S. Department of Labor. In the judgment of both of the present writers, performance testing of this sort will become increasingly important in the future—not only because of its greater acceptability to employees and the general public, but also because it will prove to be more valid.

Variability among Individuals—A Universal Phenomenon

LEONA E. TYLER

This [article] is about *human* differences. But before we examine these human differences in detail, it may be instructive to consider briefly what we know about variability in other forms of animal life. Ordinary observation demonstrates again and again that one animal of a species differs in many ways—in behavior as well as appearance—from other animals of the same species. Dog-lovers never tire of stories about some dog's unusual intelligence, resourcefulness, or devotion. Farmers recognize and deal appropriately with temperamental differences in cows. Horses differ in intellectual achievements as well as running speed.

As experimental psychologists have observed animals in their laboratories, a body of scientific knowledge about individual differences has accumulated. It can be concluded with some certainty that individual variability characterizes all species—from the highest to the lowest.

It is not surprising that monkeys differ in behavioral characteristics. Any zoo visitor can observe this for himself. A study by Fjeld (1934) contributes some quantitative evidence as to just how marked the differences between individual monkeys are in a kind of problem-solving capacity somewhat analogous to what we call intelligence in human beings. Figure 1 shows the sort of performance required.

To get the food box open, each animal was required to depress one or more of the plates in the floor. In Problem 1, the easiest problem, all he had to do was to depress Plate 1 and the door would open. In Problem 2, he must depress Plates 1 and 2 in turn, then the door opened; in Problem 3, Plates 1, 2, and 3. Problem 4 required him to depress 1, 2, and 3, reverse his direction, and step on 2 again. In Problem 7 the order was Plate 1, 2, 3, 2, 1, 2, 3. Out of a group of fifteen rhesus monkeys who served as subjects through the whole experiment, one was unable to learn more than 2 problems, whereas one learned 22. The rest varied all the way from 3 to 13. A similar study by Koch (1935) on Cebus monkeys gave similar results with somewhat less variability in performance from animal to animal.

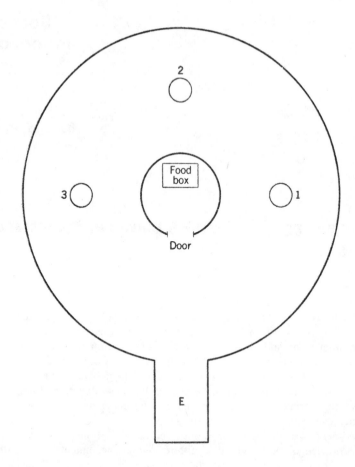

Figure 1. Design of Problem Box Used in Fjeld Experiment (Fjeld, 1934)

A good demonstration of individual differences in cats is a study by Warren (1961). What he required each animal to do in order to obtain food in this kind of experiment was to choose one of two small objects presented to him simultaneously. The "right" object was distinguished from the "wrong" one in different ways in different experiments. In some experiments, it was the *position* that mattered—for example, the left-hand one was always correct. In other experiments it was the shape of the object that was the clue, and the animal had to notice whether it was a square, triangle, circle, trapezoid, or some other geometrical form. The problem was made more difficult for the animal by arranging things in such a way that he must take *size*, as well as position or shape, into consideration. Thus in the position experiments, he was rewarded for choosing the left-hand object when the stimuli were small and for choosing the right-hand object when the stimuli were large. In the shape discrimination experiments, he was to choose one of the pair (e.g., square) when the stimuli were large and the other (e.g., semicircle) when the stimuli were small. It was the task of each cat to discover through a series of trials just what he was expected to do. Once he "caught on" he would choose correctly every time.

It turned out that discriminations on the basis of shape were more difficult than discriminations on the basis of position, but that there were very large differences between animals. The most "brilliant" of the 21 cats Warren tested required only 54 trials to solve the shape-size problem. The "dullest" one required 760 trials. The others ranged somewhere in between.

Because rats have been a favorite kind of experimental subject in psychological laboratories, a considerable amount of information about individual differences in this species has accumulated. They differ widely in maze-running ability (Tryon, 1942), and in temperamental traits such as wildness (C. S. Hall, 1951). Geier, Levin, and Tolman (1941) carried out an elaborate study in which they identified four different traits upon which their rat subjects differed from one another, two of them "intellectual" traits and two "emotional" or "motivational" traits.

What is more surprising than these findings, however, is the report by J. Hirsch that there are individual differences in the behavior of fruit flies (Hirsch, 1962). The object of Hirsch's research program has been to find out more about the genetic bases of behavior. . . . But it is worth noting here that individual differences have been demonstrated in what biologists call *taxes,* such as phototaxes and geotaxes—the tendency to approach or to withdraw from light, and the tendency to move upward (against gravity) or to move downward (with gravity). Figure 2 shows graphically the percentages of trials on which different individuals in one experimental population moved *up* in an ingeniously contrived geotactic maze (Hirsch, 1959). Its resemblance to the kind of distribution we often obtain from testing human subjects is obvious.

But individual differences in behavior have been found in species lower than the fruit fly, even in one-celled animals. There is evidence, for instance, that protozoa show changes in behavior with continued experience in a situation, a form of learning that seems to be an elementary sort of conditioned response. Razran (1933) reported that whereas the average protozoon took 138.5 trials to "learn" this, the range from

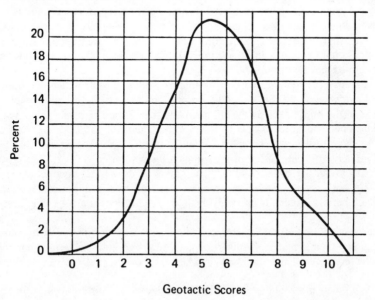

Figure 2. Distribution of Geotactic Scores for Male Fruit Flies in a Particular Breeding Population (Hirsch, J., 1959)

fastest to slowest was from 79 to 284 trials. Some experiments by French (1940), using paramecia as subjects, supplied evidence on two other traits or characteristics. One is the tendency to form groups. By an ingenious method, French separated the "groupers" from the "free-swimmers," kept them separate and in clear water for a half hour, and then put them back into separate food solutions to see if the grouping tendency persisted. It did, to a striking extent. Similar experiments were run to see whether tendencies to enter or not to enter solutions in which a small amount of some foreign chemical had been placed would persist. Again, differences turned out to be fairly large in some of the experiments and statistically significant in all.

Examples based on many other types of performance in many other species might be given, but enough have probably been cited to convince the student of human psychology that variation in mental characteristics is far from being an exclusively human phenomenon. Such studies are important for us in that they suggest that differences are universal and usually ineradicable. If this is the case we must learn to understand them, accept them, and use them in the building of our common society.

Human Characteristics in Which Differences Have Been Measured

Many types of measurement have been made on human beings. First, it is obvious to all of us that human individuals are not the same in size and shape. We have learned to expect and to make at least some provision for this kind of variation, though the army still sometimes has trouble fitting out the new recruit whose shoes are size 13, and women find that both the 8's and the 46's are sometimes hard to obtain at dress shops. Much first-rate work has been done in the field of anthropometric measurements. Not only gross height and weight, but the exact sizes of most of the individual parts of the body have been measured. Second, measurements have been made of the physiological processes, or the way various organ systems of the body function. Basal metabolism, the amount of calcium, sugar, acid, and hemoglobin in the blood, respiratory rate, pulse rate, and concentrations of acid and of urea in the urine are physiological characteristics in which individuals have been found to show definite, measurable differences.

The extensive research work of Williams (1956) has provided an impressive amount of evidence about this variability in physical and physiological characteristics. The organs of the body, such as the stomach and the heart, differ markedly in size and shape. The chemical composition of the various fluids of the body show a similar variability. Take saliva, for example (Williams, 1956, p. 59). The amount of uric acid secreted in saliva by nine different individual subjects varied from 2.5 μg. per ml. in one case to 150 μg. per ml. in another. The amino acids, serine, glycine, alanine, and lysine, were not present at all in some cases but occurred in appreciable amounts in others. Each person's saliva is probably as unique as his appearance, voice, or disposition.

In successive chapters, Williams summarizes evidence with regard to individual differences in enzymic patterns, endocrine activities, excretion patterns, pharmacological manifestations, and nutrition, all of which he considers to be genetically determined. . . .

There is even more abundant evidence for individual differences in all sorts of psychological characteristics. There is much variability with regard to motor capacities, such as reaction time, speed of tapping, steadiness, and swiftness of blow.

Individuals differ markedly in sensory and perceptual characteristics such as keenness of vision, hearing, and sense of smell. Some are better than others at analyzing and remembering complex patterns of lines, colors, or sounds. Differences in intelligence and the more narrowly defined intellectual processes, such as memory, judgment, and problem solving, have been demonstrated in hundreds of surveys at all age levels. Among persons who have had equal amounts of schooling there are wide discrepancies in how much they know. People differ in aptitudes and talents, in interests, values, and attitudes, in personality assets and liabilities. In short, research on human beings corroborates the conclusion from animal studies—individual differences in measurable characteristics constitute a universal phenomenon. . . .

References

Fjeld, H. A., "The Limits of Learning in the Rhesus Monkeys," *Genet. Psychol. Monogr.,* 1934, 15, 369-537.

French, J. W., "Individual Differences Paramecium," *J. Comp. Psychol.,* 1940, 30, 451-456.

Geir, F. M., Levin, M. and Tolman, E. C., "Individual Differences in Emotionality, Hypothesis Formation, Vicarious Trial and Error and Visual Discrimination Learning in Rats," *Comp. Psychol. Monogr.,* 1941, 17, No. 3.

Hall, C. S., Individual Differences. In C. P. Stone, *Comparative Psychology* (3rd edition), Englewood Cliffs, New Jersey: Prentice-Hall, 1951.

Hirsch, J., "Individual Differences in Behavior and Their Genetic Basis. In E. L. Bliss (Ed.), *Roots of Behavior,* New York: Hoeber-Harper, 1962, Ch. 1.

Koch, A. M., "The Limits of Learning Ability in Cebus Monkeys," *Genet. Psychol. Monogr.,* 1935, 17, 164-234.

Razran, G. H. S., "Conditional Responses in Animals Other Than Dogs." *Psychol. Bull.,* 1933, 30, 261-324.

Tryon, R. C. Individual Differences. In F. A. Moss (Ed.), *Comparative Psychology* (rev. edition), Englewood Cliffs, New Jersey: Prentice-Hall, 1942, Ch. 13.

Warren, J. M., "Individual Differences in Discrimination Learning by Cats," *J. Genet. Psychol.,* 1961, 98, 89-93.

Williams, R. J., *Biochemical Individuality,* New York: Wiley, 1956.

Manpower Planning and Forecasting

L. C. MEGGINSON

A basic aspiration of most owners and managers is to perpetuate the organization with which they are involved. To achieve this objective, the chief executive officer must find a successor to himself, and qualified people must be selected to fill the

Reprinted with permission from Megginson, *Personnel: A Behavioral Approach* (rev. ed.; Homewood, Ill.: Richard D. Irwin, Inc.), pp. 197-203.

vacancies that periodically occur throughout all levels of the organization. Thus, it is probably an understatement to say that an organization's manpower planning function constitutes one of its most important personnel responsibilities. The results obtained from recruiting, selecting, placing, training, developing, and motivating employees, depend directly for their success upon the effectiveness of the planning and forecasting phase of manpower development.

However, because of the systems concept, manpower planning cannot be studied in isolation, organizational planning and manpower planning are interrelated and interacting. Organizational planning, by its nature, takes precedence over, and provides direction to, manpower planning. The latter, in turn, can be most effectively done within the framework of properly structured organizational relationships and predetermined positions.

Futhermore, if the concept of organizational development is to be utilized by a firm, meaningful plans for providing structural units with sufficient qualified personnel cannot even be established, much less implemented, unless anticipated organizational requirements have been established. These requirements, in turn, are based upon the dynamic concept of an outgoing organizational flow.[1] Finally, to be most effective, manpower planning must be considered as an integrated approach to organizational development, with plans being formulated and implemented at all levels, and in all units, of the enterprise. . . .

Why Manpower Planning Is Important

The paramount problem in manpower planning is searching for individuals with the potential for development, for if the prospective employee is capable and is not hired, he does not enter the promotional stream of employees from which supervisory and managerial employees are obtained. If he is incapable and hired anyway, he enters the upward-flowing stream and may become an incapable manager through the inexorable workings of the seniority system.

Although a work team is a group in action, it is composed of a number of individual members with unique personalities. The only way to strengthen the group is to improve the caliber of individuals hired, for it is impossible to improve the collective group except through improving the abilities of its component members.

Importance to the Nation

A principal reason for the economic supremacy of the United States has been its fortunate selection and development of employees to staff its business enterprises. It has been tacitly assumed that this supply of personnel would automatically be replenished, both quantitatively and qualitatively, as the need arose, thus assuring a continuous supply of producers and leaders to meet the ever-increasing demands made upon the nation's productive capacity. It is becoming increasingly apparent that this is not a valid assumption, as it becomes evident that producers and leaders are in scarce supply. One of the great limitations placed upon our productive capability is the lack of an available supply of adequately trained and developed personnel for the rapidly expanding activities associated with technological advancement.

The economic slack in the early 1970s has served to hide this tendency. Now, though, with industry, commerce, and government expanding their activities, personnel officers are discovering that men in the prime working ages with the right skills and experience are increasingly hard to find. If the United States is to remain preeminent in the economic realm, it must somehow perpetuate the supply of managerial, technical, and skilled employees to meet the growing needs for increased productivity and social responsibility.

Importance to Organizations

National interest in effective planning is equaled by the concern of individual organizations. The judicious recruitment and hiring of a sufficient number of qualified individuals is significant in that these individuals provide the basic productive resource of which an organization is composed. They furnish the source for present and future managerial talent in the organization, since most organizations follow the policy of promoting from within. Only when there are capable employees in the lower levels are there potential managers to promote into the higher organizational echelons.

Although automation is making progress, people are still needed to run the companies. The future of business organizations depends upon these employees, the work they perform, and the ideas they contribute toward improving operations. People remain the greatest asset; though all companies can buy the same materials and equipment, people make the difference in what that equipment produces.

Although effective employment is important to all organizations, it is especially important to expanding companies. It is axiomatic that these enterprises continually look for the one resource for which there is no substitute, namely "talent," or personnel with the mental ability, creativity, and initiative needed for meeting the requirements of these growing concerns. Previously, the need for these talents focused on the research and development function, but now this type of talent is just as urgently needed in production, sales, finance, and every other organizational area. This need is not confined to the company's top echelons, for such personnel are required at every level where the capacity for independent action spells the difference between success and failure.

The main function of a manager is to assemble individuals into a productive organization. Through selective employment, employee cooperation, and coordination of managerial and employee efforts, productive activity can be accomplished. The "pragmatic test of practicality" is that the successful manager is able to assemble a productive organization while the unsuccessful one is not.

Manpower Planning Objectives

Organizations can no longer rely upon finding talented manpower just when they need it. Systematic steps must be taken in order to assure that a reservoir of talent is available when vacancies occur. Consequently, planning and searching for qualified talent must be continuous. Therefore, the overall objectives of manpower planning are to: relate human resource needs to the overall activity of the enterprise; make long-range estimations of the firm's specific and general needs; and maximize the return on investment in human resources.

Relating Human Resources to Enterprise Needs

The human resources of a business are an integral part of all of its activities. It should be recognized that development of those resources is dependent upon other organizational resources; consequently, selecting, developing, and utilizing human resources must be considered as one integrated process designed to incorporate both present and future needs of the firm. Therefore, organizational goals should be clearly defined and established so that selection can be based upon finding personnel capable of realizing those goals.

As an organization grows and develops, its need for manpower with special skills, knowledge, and expertise [increases]. Usually, this increasing need tends to coincide with a shortage of such personnel because of the lead time needed to educate and train people to use the new technology. Thus, long-range manpower plans are needed to adjust to this imbalance. Also, other planning activities become involved.[2]

The cost of recruiting this short-supply, high-talent personnel then poses a problem. So, wages and benefit systems require planning in order to provide internal consistency and external competitiveness.

The problem of integrating this elite group into the organizational framework of statuses and emotional webs must be planned for. The training and development of these personnel, as well as the upgrading of present employees pose a related problem.

The efficient matching of people and jobs, as well as the removal of barriers to flexibility in moving people within the firm, create related problems. The introduction of new technologies and managerial techniques enhance the need for planning how to use the talents, enthusiasm, and dedication of less talented people so their objectives, as well as those of the firm, will be achieved.

Finally, the problems associated with motivating all these individuals need planning for in order to encourage high productivity and employee satisfaction.

Estimating Long-range Manpower Needs

While most forward-looking managers now recognize the crucial importance of maintaining a pool of talented personnel, there is no agreement on how best to develop a reserve of this resource. It is becoming increasingly clear that the adjustment of the work force on an immediate need basis has certain weaknesses. Among these weaknesses are: hurried and indiscriminate selection, which prevents a thorough survey of available talent; a rapidly accumulating backlog of work; and inadequate training of new employees.

There is frequently an excessive demand for immediately available personnel during certain periods of the business cycle, during emergency periods, and in areas with a shortage of personnel. In such cases, an otherwise unacceptable candidate will often be employed in order just to have someone to fill the position. Conversely, when the company has a sufficiently high reputation, or when there is an abundant supply of workers relative to the demands, a company may "hoard" personnel in anticipation of future needs.

Even though there is no uniformity in defining manpower planning or in determining how to create a "pool" of qualified personnel, there is general unanimity concerning the problems manpower planning is concerned with. These objectives can be classified as: planning future manpower needs as a whole, that is, ascertaining how many people from both a qualitative and a quantitative point of view will the firm need in order to operate its business in future periods; planning the future manpower balance within the firm, or establishing how many of those presently employed by the organization will stay with it in future periods; planning for those recruiting and selecting activities required to provide the enterprise with the required personnel, and in case manpower needs are smaller than the present manpower balance within the firm; planning for laying off of the manpower surplus.[3]

In estimating long-range needs, a distinction needs to be made between planning and forecasting. Forecasting implies a passive process, whereas, planning involves not only forecasting but other active decisions regarding manpower requirements and how they can be met.

A company's manpower needs are influenced by external, as well as internal, factors. Among others, the external factors consist of the political situation, the nation's level of production as indicated by the GNP, the level of overall technological development, actions of competing companies, and the development of substitute products and changed uses of the firm's own products.

Manpower planning is basically derived out of other plans. Manpower needs are not autonomous, so planning for these needs must take into account various other internal factors which will influence manpower requirements. Some of those factors are expected sales, production plans, and labor productivity.

Maximizing Return on Investment in Human Resources

A new concept in manpower planning is developing whereby the human resources are treated as capital assets in much the same way that plant and equipment are presently treated. In essence, this system attempts through an accounting model to measure the cost of the resources, what it would cost to replace the resources, and what their value would be based upon their potential earning ability.

This new system emphasizes that man is a unique entity requiring individualized consideration. Thus, managers are becoming more concerned with *accounting for the human resources,* both in terms of the cost involved and in terms of general information to be used in long-range manpower planning and for decision-making purposes. The new system would supply management with a management audit to forecast requirements, to acquire the necessary human resources, and then to develop the human asset to its optimum capacity.

If employees were viewed as a capital asset, several changes would probably occur in the management of the resource. Higher management would insist upon recruiting and selecting the best people; more emphasis would be placed upon the completion of human development programs; greater devotion would be given to an individual's developmental activities; and time and consideration would be given to matching employees with jobs in order to ensure that they were placed in challenging positions which would effectively utilize their capabilities. The aim of the firm would be to ensure a maximum return on investment on their human resources.[4] In attempting to achieve this goal, managers would strive to expand the span of responsibility of employees who would be construed to represent major investments even when formal positions of advancement are not available. Management would also become more selective in making its initial investments in human resources.

This form of accounting could provide management with an additional indicator of an employee's potential growth before advancement is made in his position. This system would focus attention on the employee as a valuable *investment* which enhances earning power rather than as an *operating expense* which acts to drain the organization's financial resources.

Paradoxically, accounting for man as a capital asset should restore the personality of each individual and pave the way to more humanistic treatment of employees. Greater attention would be given to an individual's selection, development, placement, advancement, motivation, and redevelopment. Finally, the dangers of overextending an individual, underutilizing his talents, and allowing for managerial obsolescence, would probably be avoided.

The basic premise underlying this new system is that the analytical and conceptual frameworks designed for the management of physical and financial assets can be applied to the management of human resources.[5] Also, any decision based only upon the physical and financial considerations and which ignores the value of the key personnel factor is likely to lead the executive to a nonoptimal conclusion.

The personnel manager is prone to "deal" his way through a series of familiar activities without questioning how the cost of his actions compares with the value derived from them. Often, he is unable to have projects accepted by higher management because he cannot provide them with a practical and cost-oriented value judgment. As the function of the personnel manager focuses on the most important and valuable asset of an organization, and while this element is seemingly subjective and highly intangible, the personnel man must be value conscious, and this leads to the need to quantify his actions. Thus, *human value accounting* has unlimited possibilities for making future decisions and evaluating past commitments.

According to the vice president of personnel and public affairs, Caterpillar Tractor Company, his firm spent $8.5 million for personnel training and development in 1966.[6] He proposed that in this day of electronic data processing there must be some way to "quantify" the personnel function in an accounting fashion by measuring its value in relation to its cost.

The R. G. Barry Corporation has conducted an experiment in accounting for human resources whereby it uses the process for human resource planning and reporting.[7] Investment in human resources is contained in a pro forma balance sheet and income statement in an effort to capitalize the company's cost of acquisition, development, maintenance, and utilization of its human resources. While the system in no way attempts to reflect adequately the underlying value of the human resources, a cost analysis approach does present a beginning point from which other systems can be developed. . . .

Notes

1. George Steiner, "Rise of the Corporate Planner," *Harvard Business Review,* Vol. 48, No. 5 (September-October, 1970), pp. 133-39.

2. Frank H. Cassell, "Manpower Planning: The Basic Policies," *Personnel,* Vol. 42, No. 6 (November-December, 1965), pp. 55-61.

3. Burckhardt Wenzel, "Planning for Manpower Utilization," *The Personnel Administrator,* Vol. 15, No. 3 (May-June, 1970), pp. 36-40.

4. Robert Wright, "Managing Man as a Capital Asset," *Personnel Journal,* Vol. 49, No. 4 (April, 1970), pp. 290-98.

5. James S. Hekimian and Curtis H. Jones, "Put People on Your Balance Sheet," *Harvard Business Review,* Vol. 45, No. 1 (January-February, 1967), pp. 105-13.

6. Roger T. Kelley, "Accounting in Personnel Administration," *Industrial Relations,* Vol. 7, No. 2 (February, 1968), pp. 24-28.

7. William C. Pyle, "Human Resource Accounting," *Financial Analysts Journal,* Vol. 26, No. 5 (September-October, 1970), pp. 69-78.

Personnel Selection:
The Basic Models

A. K. KORMAN

The Traditional Personnel Selection Model:
Predictive Validity

The major contributions which industrial psychology has made to the personnel selection process have been in two areas. One has been the development of psychological measures which predict job performance and which are available to the employing company prior to the time of hiring or rejecting, while the second has concerned itself with the development of appropriate methodologies for evaluating whether or not a given predictor is actually operating effectively, i.e., whether it is predicting the behavior which it should be predicting. Information relating to these two questions has then generally been reported to management, to be used by them in their judgment and decision making in the way they see most fit. . . .

Step 1—The Job Analysis

The traditional personnel selection model has as its first step the study of the characteristics and required behaviors of the job for which the selection process is being undertaken. It is obvious, of course, that one must have some understanding of the nature of the job that one wishes to select for, since not to know this would reduce all selection to a purely random, chance basis. The procedure for finding out this information (which also has value for various other organizational functions such as training, job transfer, and performance appraisal) is known as a "job analysis," and it consists, usually, of a description of the various behaviors, characteristics, and abilities required of the occupant of that job. The ways in which this information is obtained varies with the company, the job, the occupant, etc., but in essence there are two major procedures.

One way is to ask the current job occupant to describe what he does, either subjectively or along some defined dimensions. This method has some advantages. It elicits worker cooperation by bringing him in on the decision making and possibly enhances his self-esteem (with consequent implications for performance) at the same time. A second advantage is, of course, that the job occupant probably knows the job better than anybody else. At the same time, however, there is the disadvantage that the job occupant will probably be most motivated to distort, either consciously or unconsciously, his description in a favored direction. Furthermore, there is another disadvantage to this procedure in that the occupant may not be psychologically, educationally, or emotionally equipped to write an accurate description of his job duties.

Similar advantages and disadvantages attach themselves to the other major job analysis method, that of "observation." Analyzing a job by observation has the advantage of eliminating "faking" to a great extent since an observer should generally be more objective. Furthermore, the observer will also usually be a "qualified" recorder.

However, the first advantage could be illusory in that the job occupant may fake his performance, either consciously or subconsciously, if someone is watching him. In addition, a second possible disadvantage is that this procedure is completely inappropriate for mental "thinking" jobs and for jobs which involve a long period of time before a specific job activity is finished. (The analogy here is between the division manager who might be working on a decentralization plan taking five years as opposed to the mechanical repetitive job.) Since these "long-cycle" types of jobs are becoming increasingly the norm in our society, we might expect to see a decrease in the method of "observation" in job analysis as time goes on.

Besides the advantages and disadvantages of each of these procedures, there are problems in job analysis which are common to both (and, in fact, to any observational system involving the rating of such social objects as jobs and people, as we shall point out in our later discussion on performance appraisal methods). One set of these problems has been called the "judgment" errors and can be summarized as follows:

1. *The "halo" error:* This is the tendency to allow one characteristic of a rating object to dominate ratings along other dimensions of the object being rated. An example of this is when we are more likely to attribute intellectual qualities to a person who wears glasses than a person who does not.

2. *The "central tendency" error:* This is the tendency to rate all rating objects around the "middle" or mean of a rating continuum and not to use the extremes.

3. *The "leniency" error:* This is the tendency to rate all social objects in a relatively favorable manner and not to attribute negative aspects to them.

While there are other kinds of judgment errors besides these, these are probably the most important. How one overcomes them is a different problem, however, and about this there is little agreement. In fact there are some who argue that these may not be errors at all and that one of the only reasons they are considered as such is due to the stubborn refusal of psychologists to admit that (1) some kinds of human behavior may not be distributed according to the normal bell-shaped curve (i.e., in some cases, all people might be "good") and (2) some people may actually have all their characteristics integrally a function of their main characteristic (i.e., the halo error is not an error). This seems an extreme position to take, however. Suffice to say for our purposes here that these behaviors are probably "errors" in the traditional sense but their importance and possible remedial actions will probably vary according to the given situation. . . .

A second problem of perhaps more serious import in job analysis is how one incorporates into a description of a job's characteristics some recognition of the fact that jobs are becoming increasingly of the type whereby the behaviors that are engaged in cannot be specified in advance but result from the characteristics of the person who happens to fulfill the role at that particular time. For example, let us look at the differences between a management role and the role of a sewing-machine operator in a dress factory. It is much simpler to specify in advance what the behavior of the latter should be than the former. In fact, it is probably very much the case that the essence of the managerial role is success in the ability to handle problems which cannot be specified or "programmed" in advance. While this difference in potential specificity of roles was always a problem for job analysts, its signficance is increasing greatly because more jobs in our automated society are becoming increasingly like that of the manager and increasingly less like that of the sewing-machine operator.

It should be emphasized that we are not suggesting that we do away with the job analysis as an aid in the selection (and other manpower utilization) program. This is clearly an impossibility, since the alternative is chaos. However, it is to suggest that this is a significant problem which must be taken into account in future job analysis research.

Step 2–Hypothesis Development

The second step in the traditional model is derived from the job analysis, with this step consisting, essentially, of hypothesis generation as to the kinds of individuals who would be most likely to fit the behavioral demands of the job. This step can be a subjective one based on a subjective appraisal on the job analysis information. Hence, it can be highly dependent on the cognitive characteristics of the person developing the hypotheses. Unfortunately, we know little about the kinds of people who would be particularly good at this type of thing. Such recognition of this situation is, undoubtedly, one of the reasons the more common procedure in job analysis has been to describe jobs in terms of more objective psychological dimensions and then to verify such descriptions by either (1) testing job occupants with unambiguous tests of these dimensions or (2) getting qualified interjudge agreement as to the importance of the dimensions for the given job. Due to the difficulty of getting tests which are unambiguous measures of simple psychological dimensions, particularly in nonability areas, the latter verification procedure is the more common one today.

A good example of the kinds of dimensions by which jobs may be described and compared to one another in terms of the requirements they call for is seen in Table 1. This summarizes some recent work by McCormick and his co-workers (cf. McCormick, Cunningham, and Gordon, 1967). Since these dimensions can be used in varying quantities to describe a variety of different jobs, it is obvious that this project has great potential for assisting in such personnel activities as selection, job promotions, transfers, training, etc.

TABLE 1
DIMENSIONS OF JOB BEHAVIOR AND EXAMPLES

1. *Decision making and communication activities:*
   Develops budgets; supervises management personnel; verbal presentations; forecasts needs; variety of communications; personnel decisions
2. *Hierarchical person-to-person interaction:*
   Instructs; supervises students, trainees, patients, subordinates, etc.; issues directives; schedules work of others; interchanges information with prospective employees, students, or trainees
3. *Skilled physical activities:*
   Skill of hand tool usage; number of hand tools used; finger manipulation; estimates size
4. *Mental vs. physical activities:*
   Positive loadings—deals with data; interprets information; intelligence; uses mathematics; clerical tasks
   Negative loadings—manual force; moves objects by hand; deals with things
5. *Responsible personal contact:*
   Persuades; interchanges information with customers, clients, patients, etc.; distractions from people seeking or giving information
6. *General physical activities:*
   Adjustment to the vertical; climbing; balancing; general physical coordination
7. *Unpleasant vs. pleasant working conditions:*
   Uncomfortable atmosphere; unclean environment
8. *Decisions affecting people:*
   Personnel decisions (promotions, transfers, hiring, etc.)

9. *Varied intellectual vs. structured activities:*
Positive loadings—interpretation of information; intelligence; usage of mathematics; occupation prestige
Negative loadings—high job structure; repetitiveness; deals with things

10. *Supervisory activities:*
Supervises others; issues directives; number of people supervised

11. *Man-machine control activities:*
Control operations; monitors work process; interpretation of information; responsible for physical assets

12. *Planning and decision making:*
Uniqueness of decisions; time span of decisions; forecasts needs; develops methods

13. *Skilled manual activities:*
Skill of hand tool usage; finger manipulation; number of hand tools used

14. *Intellectual vs. physical activities*
Positive loadings—"thinking" (vs. "doing"); occupation prestige
Negative loadings—activity domain—things; repetitiveness; job structure

15. *Body-balancing activities:*
Adjustment to the vertical; balancing; climbing

16. *Physical vs. sedentary activities:*
Positive loadings—standing; general force; manual force
Negative loadings—activity domain—data

17. *Clerical activities:*
Clerical tasks (filing, typing, shorthand, etc.)

18. *Knee-bending activities:*
Crawling; kneeling; stooping

19. *Informative communications:*
Giving information; instructing; issuing directives; verbal communications

20. *Communication of data:*
Reporting; activity domain—data; interchange of information; written communication

21. *Persuasive communications:*
Persuading; verbal presentations; negotiating

22. *Public contact activites:*
Publicizing; information interchange with public

23. *White- vs. blue-collar situations:*
Positive loadings—wearing presentable clothing; social obligations; occupational prestige
Negative loadings—receiving hourly and/or overtime pay; receives close supervision

24. *Job security vs. performance-dependent income:*
Positive loadings—job security; occupational prestige
Negative loadings—receives tips; commissions, hourly pay, and/or overtime pay

25. *Apparel: Optional vs. work clothes:*
Positive loading—wears special working clothes
Negative loading—dress left to incumbent's discretion

26. *Apparel: Formal vs. optional:*
Positive loadings—wears presentable clothing; social obligations; occupational prestige
Negative loading—dress left to incumbent's discretion

27. *Apparel: Specific uniform:*
Wears specific uniform

28. *Hourly pay vs. salary:*
. Positive loading—regular salary
Negative loading—hourly pay; overtime pay

29. *Annoying environment:*
Noise; uncomfortable atmosphere; poor illumination; cramped work space

Source: E. J. McCormick, J. W. Cunningham, C. G. Gordon: Job dimensions based on factorial analyses of worker-oriented job variables. *Personnel Psychology,* 1967, *20,* 417-30.

Step 3—Predictor Development

Once the relevant psychological and behavior variables have been hypothesized, it is time for the third step. This consists of deciding how one is to measure individual differences in job applicants on the relevant variables. The most important problem is that it is important that one choose a measure which actually measures the relevant psychological variable which one is proposing as being demanded by the job. The reasons for this are simple. If the chosen measure is not an actual measure of the relevant variable, two possible problems develop, depending on whether or not the measure is actually related to job performance. First, we may reject a good hypothesis as to the cause of good job performance in a given job and not know it. Hence, whatever else we eventually learn about the job in terms of selection and training, such knowledge must always be incomplete, perhaps seriously so. Suppose, however, that the "mistake" works; i.e., suppose we have hypothesized "sociability" as an important variable but have measured "anxiety" by mistake (without knowing it) and "anxiety" does actually predict job performance. It does not matter, the "practical" man says, that it does not measure what it is supposed to measure, since it predicts job performance and hence can be used for selection. The answer to this is that this is a wasteful, shortsighted, uneconomical attitude. One reason that is so can be seen if we assume that the relevant important psychological variable is "sociability" (when it is really "anxiety"). First, of all the recommendations for managerial action in training, development, appraisal, and promotion which would follow from such a successful prediction would be based on a mistaken, erroneous belief. A second reason this attitude is an impractical one relates to the fact that jobs do change, and sometimes a variable which used to predict performance no longer does. Hence, if we find that our measure of sociability (which is really anxiety) no longer predicts job performance, we shall start looking for new predictors eliminating sociability, although a good measure of sociability might now be a good predictor on the changed job.

How does one decide, then, when a measure is actually a measure of the desired variable? The best process for this is a procedure known as "construct validity," consisting basically of looking at all the relationships which the proposed measure of the variable has with other measured variables and then deciding whether or not these observed relationships are consistent with what they should be if the measure was really measuring what it says it is. (The judgment is, of course, a subjective one and hence must be a result of the knowledge and skills of the person making the judgment.) . . .

It should be noted that the process of establishing the construct validity of an instrument is a never-ending one and that we must continually be concerned with obtaining new information on the construct validity of our instrument since the more we know about it, the more we can have confidence that we are actually measuring what we claim we are measuring. In this sense, then, the development of the construct validity of an instrument is similar to the testing of the utility of a theory. In both cases, however, as we have emphasized throughout this [article], great practical benefits ensue.

What kinds of predictors are typically chosen? As indicated above, . . . the development of measures of characteristics that will be good predictors of performance has been a primary concern of industrial psychologists with the result that a wide variety of different measures may be used. Briefly, we may summarize them into the following categories (others besides these are possible):

1. *Ability tests:* These consist of measures of verbal and other abilities. . . .
2. *Objective personality tests:* These are measures of personality characteristics

which have a relatively structured format; i.e., the individual respondent describes himself along dimensions defined by the test constructor rather than along dimensions defined by himself.

3. *Projective personality tests:* These are measures of personality characteristics which have an unstructured format and which allow the individual to respond along any dimension which he wishes and which he constructs.

4. *Objective life-history items:* These consist of questions concerning relatively objective characteristics of a person's school, work, and personal background; the rationale for these is that they are measures of various attitudinal and personal characteristics of the individual which are not measured by other means.

5. *Interviews and other judgmental assessments:* These consist of judgments by various individuals as to the extent to which the individual possesses the behavioral characteristics which are felt to be necessary for adequate job performance.

Which of these are the best? . . . This is a multidimensional question, with the answer depending on the criteria used, the occupations involved, various ethical problems, theoretical measurement problems, etc. To some extent, it is even a meaningless question since such a question implies that one may have a choice in the given situation. Yet, this may not be the case.

For example, the best predictors of job performance have consistently been ability tests. However, just as consistently, it has also been shown that their predictive effectiveness will reach only a certain point and that it is necessary to use personality test variables if one wishes to predict performance more accurately above this point, even though personality tests are generally not as effective predictors as ability tests (Guion and Gottier, 1965).

For these reasons, then, our later procedure will be not to bother to make any comparative claims as to the relative fruitfulness of these kinds of measures, since all have their uses in given situations and all must be improved to the greatest extent possible. Their usefulness depends on the given prediction situation and the given prediction problem, and they must be evaluated as such, a procedure which constitutes the basis for our discussion here. . . .

Step 4–Administration of Predictors to Applicant Sample

Once the measures of the relevant behaviors have been decided upon, they are administered to the applicants for the job in question. However, the measures are *not* used as a basis for selection at this time. Rather, the applicants are then selected for the job in question on the basis of whatever procedures for this process are existing at that time. The scores on the hypothesized predictor measures are filed away at this time, to be utilized in connection with step 5.

The reasoning behind this procedure can be explained quite simply. Thus, if we use the hypothesized measure as a basis for hiring, then we shall never know what the job performance would have been of those individuals with the predictor scores who were not hired. That is, if the company were to take in only those with high scores, then we would not know the eventual performance of those with low scores and vice versa. The problem is, of course, that the unselected group might have been better in job performance than the selected; something we could not know unless we gave them the opportunity.

Step 5–Relate Predictor Test Scores to Measure of Job Performance

After the applicants have been hired and been on the job for a long enough period of time to get some meaningful measure of differences in job performance, the first critical point in this process is reached. This is to relate scores on the predictor variable to the measure of job performance, i.e., the criterion.

There are two major problems which are of concern here. First, what measures of relationship should be used, and what are the advantages and disadvantages of each of these measures? Second, how shall we interpret the results found in terms of their practical significance for organizational action? These are the questions we shall attempt to answer here, discussing both where we have only *one* predictor variable for each applicant and where we have more than one predictor variable for each person.

1. The correlation coefficient. Undoubtedly, the most popular method for describing the relationship between two variables that has been utilized in personnel selection research has been the correlation coefficient, or *r*, . . . The reasons for this are several. First, there is the element of familiarity, i.e., most industrial psychologists are quite familiar with it, having studied it as part of their graduate training. Second, it is a convenient way of summarizing a relationship into one general descriptive term. Hence, when we say that a correlation is .60, it is agreed that this means something different than when we say a correlation is .10 or − .35. A third reason for the great utilization of the correlation coefficient is that there is a considerable amount of theory developed around it, theory concerned with how much confidence we can have in certain obtained results, given certain assumptions. Thus, because the theory concerning the correlation coefficient is well developed, we are able to specify, given certain assumptions, the likelihood that our results are not due to "chance" or "unstable" factors and we can also estimate the degree to which our specifications will be in error. Related to both this reason and the second is a fourth advantage of using the correlation coefficient as a measure of a relationship and that is that the actual *r* obtained is directly convertible into a measure of predictive accuracy, the purpose of the whole selection mechanism process. . . .

These advantages hold whether we are concerned with the situation when we have only one predictor variable for each applicant or, the far more common case, when we are concerned with more than one predictor in a given selection situation. In the latter situation, the correlation coefficient which is used is called the multiple correlation coefficient, as opposed to the "simple *r*," the measure used in the case where there is only one predictor variable. The two can be distinguished in this way:

1. For the case of one predictor—one criterion, we correlate the two variables X (the predictor) and Y (the criterion) using the appropriate formula.[1]

2. For the case of multiple predictors—one criterion, the procedure can be outlined conceptually as follows:[2]

    a. Assume four predictor variables, X_1, X_2, X_3, and X_4, and one criterion variable Y.

    b. All the predictor variables are correlated with the criterion variable and with each other.

    c. Each predictor variable is then weighted by a statistical procedure according to the degree of its intercorrelations with the criterion and with the other predictor variables; the higher the correlation with the criterion and the lower the correlation with the other predictors, the greater the weight that specific variable has for predicting that criterion.

    d. The absolute sum of these weights are then converted, again statistically, into a correlation coefficient called the multiple *r* which is then interpretable along the *same* scale as the regular *r*. In other words it has the same range from −1.00 to +1.00, an *r* of 0.00 means no relationship between the two variables, and so on. In this case, of course, the X or predictor variable is not a single variable, but a weighted composite of the four predictor variables, with each individual's score on this composite being the average of his scores on each of the predictor variables, corrected by the weight for the variables. An example of this procedure is given in Figure 3.

The last statement does point to one difference between the simple and multiple r which the reader should keep in mind and which does limit to an extent the general equating of the two we have made here. This difference results because the weighting system used in developing the multiple correlation is based on *maximizing* the correlation between the predictors and criterion and all variables are weighted on this basis, whether the scores that are being weighted are based on real, valid differences between people or on chance, accidental influences on the scores. The problem is that these chance, accidental scores are counted only if they add to the level of the correlation coefficient. They are *not* counted if they decrease this level; rather, they are ignored. It is for this reason that the multiple r has a general tendency to be too high, given the nature of the scores involved. Hence, it is even more necessary in the case where the multiple r is used that the step we have called "cross-validation," which we shall discuss later, be employed. . . . [Editor's note: Because chance does to some extent affect the computed weights, the multiple correlation technique of combining tests into a composite is often no more effective—and sometimes less effective—than simply adding up scores on the different tests with no weighting. See Frank Schmidt, "The Relative Efficiency of Regression and Simple Unit Predictor Weights in Applied Differential Psychology." *Educational and Psychological Measurement*, 1971, 31, 699-714. This is especially true when there is a small sample involved. See W. Clay Hamner, "The importance of Sample Size, Cut-off Techniques, and Cross-validation in Multiple Regression Analysis, *Proceedings, Midwest American Institute for Decision Sciences* meeting, East Lansing, Michigan, April, 1973.]

Perhaps the only way of . . . approaching some kind of meaningful judgment as to whether a given correlation is of practical significance is to view it in terms of the specifics of a given situation since it is these specifics which may play an important part in determining whether or not to use selection instruments at all. . . .

Let us assume that we do not have any selection instruments at all and we hire all people who apply for each job; that is, we predict that *all* will succeed. The number of mistakes in prediction we shall make are as follows:

Situation A = 10% (the base rate of success is 90%)
Situation B = 55% (the base rate of success is 45%)
Situation C = 90% (the base rate of success is 10%)

Hence, if a test is to be of practical usefulness, its correlation coefficient must be higher in situation A than in situation B and much higher than in Situation C, since our accuracy of prediction is so much higher in the former than the latter without the use of any selection instruments at all. (It is for this reason that selection instruments are often utilized in managerial and high-level selection which would be considered to be too low to be of practical usefulness when dealing with lower-level employees.) This, then, is one factor which enables us to interpret when a correlation coefficient is practically useful.

A second factor of significance is the selection ratio. Consider the situation where we need select only 1 of 100 applicants for a job, as opposed to one where we must select 50 of 100. Since in the first case we can take only the best, a selection instrument does not have to be very accurate in increasing our ability to predict job behavior over chance levels. It only has to be a little bit better than chance in order to help us in picking out the best person for the job. On the other hand, this is not the case in the latter situation, where we must pick out 50 and where, hence, the selection instrument must be high in validity to be useful. The former case is called a "low selection ratio" situation and the latter, of course, a "high selection ratio" situation.

These two factors, then, the "base rate of success" (or "difficulty level" of the job) and the selection ratio in the given situation, are the major guides we have in determining the practical usefulness of a given selection instrument for any given selection question. . . .

a

	Number with this score	Approximate odds of success
	14,682	9 in 10
	15,286	9 in 10
	24,367	8 in 10
	30,066	8 in 10
	31,091	7 in 10
	22,827	6 in 10
	11,471	4 in 10
	2,239	3 in 10
	904	2 in 10

b

	Number scoring in this range	Approximate odds of staying with firm 1½ years or more
	18	9 in 10
	20	6 in 10
	21	4 in 10
	24	1 in 10

Figure 1. Examples of simple cut-off systems relating test scores to job behavior. (a) Chart showing relation between pilot aptitude score and successful completion of pilot training ("Psychological Activities in Training Command AAF," *Psychological Bulletin*, 1945, *42*, (b) Chart showing relation between biographical "score" and length of service for female office employees ("Development of a Weighted Application Blank to Aid in the Selection of Office Employees," *Research Report No. 7*, Personnel Research, 3M Co., 1956). (Source: M. D. Dunnette and W. Kirchner: *Psychology Applied to Business and Industry*. New York: Appleton-Century-Crofts, 1965.)

2. Simple and multiple cut-off systems. To overcome some of the weaknesses of the correlation coefficient as a way of describing the relationship between the hypothesized predictors of job behavior and actual job behavior, an increasing number of psychologists have suggested the use of simple and multiple cut-off systems. These, in essence, are expectancy charts and/or tables which depict the level of job performance which is to be expected from any given level of predictor scores; cut-offs can then be developed both for simple and multiple predictors which will maximize the level of performance. . . .

Although the cut-off methods do not provide convenient summary figures for describing the obtained relationships, a look at this chart indicates the obvious advantages which account for its increasing usage. It is clear and easy to interpret, thus overcoming the resistance to the correlation coefficient as a medium of communication which is frequently found among nonpsychologically trained people. A second advantage is perhaps a more technically important one in that it can be keyed to any type of relationship, linear or curvilinear, better than the correlation coefficient. Consider the example given in Figure 2.

Predictor X	Criterion Y
10	25
9	25
8	25
7	25
Acceptable performance	Unacceptable performance
6	20
5	18
4	16
3	14

Figure 2.

If we were to compute the correlation coefficient between these variables, it would probably not be a high one due to the lack of variation in criterion performance for all those with predictor scores of 7 or above. Hence, we might discard this predictor if we were using correlation analysis. On the other hand, if we were using a cut-off system, we would have perfect prediction if we selected all those with predictor scores of 7 or more and rejected those with scores of 6 or less.

The comparative discussion is somewhat analogous but does get more complex when we talk about situations where there are multiple predictors. To review our previous comments, the reader will recall that in the multiple r situation the various predictor variables are weighted in terms of their relationships to the criterion. In essence, each individual is then assigned a score based on his scores on the predictor variables, corrected by the weights for each variable. Consider Figure 3, taken from our example in Figure 1.

One aspect which is immediately apparent and which is crucial to our discussion is that there is a variety of ways by which a person may derive a given X score on the composite variable. Hence, person A gets a score of 62 by being high on variables 2 and 3, even though he is only medium on variable 1. On the other hand, individual E is high on variable 1 but he is considerably lower on variables 2 and 3. In other words, E has "compensated" for being low on variable 2 by being higher on variable 1. This principle of "compensation" and of there being alternative ways to derive high predictor scores is the essence of the multiple correlation system.

Suppose, now, that we wanted to use a multiple cut-off system. How would this operate? Using the same sample, suppose we found that the following cut-offs for each of the variables led to the highest level of predicted performance:

Cut-off Levels

Variable X_1 = 9 or more

Variable X_2 = 6 or more

Variable X_3 = 3 or more

According to these levels, using our previous examples, the following decisions would be made:

Individual A = Hire

Individual B = Reject

Individual C = Reject

Individual D = Hire

Individual E = Hire

Hence, we see that requiring each individual to be above a given level on all predictors, as in the multiple cut-off system, leads to different decisions than when we allow a person to compensate for being low on one predictor by being extra high on the other.

Which system is a better one? There is, of course, no simple answer to this. It depends on the situation. In some prediction situations it would seem that we can safely allow compensation and use the multiple *r* method, given the other advantages we have previously mentioned. However, it is also apparent that cut-offs may be necessary on some variables in that a low score on that given predictor cannot be compensated for by high scores on any other predictor. An example of this concerns the necessity of visual acuity for being a dentist. Unless the dentist has a high level of visual acuity, any other ability of his, verbal, manipulative, or otherwise, is not likely to be of use or value to him.

Hence, perhaps the best approach to use in the multiple predictor situation is a combination of the multiple cut-off and multiple correlation methods. The first step would be to use the multiple cut-off method for those variables where a minimum level is considered necessary and select people on that basis. After this is done, the multiple *r* method should be used with the remaining predictors in order to select from those remaining after the initial cut-off is made.

Step 6–Cross-validation

The next step in the traditional personnel selection model depends on whether or not the results in step 5 look promising. Assuming that they do, the next step is to *repeat the entire procedure,* utilizing the same job, same measure of performance, same kinds of applicants, etc. The reason for this kind of procedure relates to the essentially conservative nature of the scientific endeavor in that it is felt that despite proper precautions of the type we have discussed, it is always conceivable that a single obtained result, no matter how positive the relationship, could always occur on the basis of chance factors alone. Hence, to have greater confidence in the results, one should always replicate or repeat the study. This is the purpose of the cross-validation step.

Unfortunately, it is often the case that the results of step 5 are not promising enough to continue to the cross-validation attempt. In this case, there is nothing else to do according to the traditional personnel selection model but start all over again.

Step 7–Recommendation for Selection

Finally, the last step in the procedure, assuming that step 6 works out, is to make recommendations for selection. The essential problem here is to develop a procedure as to the kinds of scores which will be acceptable for selection and to set up guidelines for the administration of such recommendations. . . .

Predictors					Variables	
	X_1	X_2	X_3	X_4	Composite predictor	
Individual weights	3	2	1	0	score (i.e., the X vari-able in the multiple	Level necessary for hiring
Applicants					correlation equation)	decision = 55
A	10	12	8	9	62	Hire
B	6	7	15	9	47	Reject
C	13	3	11	15	56	Hire
D	9	6	8	4	47	Reject
E	13	10	3	8	62	Hire

Figure 3.

The Concurrent Validity Model

The first major revision to be made in the traditional personnel selection model is, in some respects, not a revision at all, since its historical antecedents are at least as old. In addition, it is probably more commonly used in the industrial situation than is the traditional selection model. The reason for this is that its major purpose is to eliminate what is practically the most frustrating aspect of the traditional model, the delay between the administration of the predictor measures and the collection of job behavior measures. In essence, the concurrent validity model differs from the traditional model (which we call "predictive validity") in that it utilizes present, already working groups on employees as test groups upon which to determine whether given variables are related to job performance. In other words the procedure is very much the same as the traditional approach except that the hypothesized predictors of successful job performance are administered to those already on the job for whom job performance data are immediately available. If the expected relationships occur and are replicated in a cross-validation relationship and so on, then the measures are recommended for administrative use in selection procedures.

There is little doubt that it is because this procedure overcomes the time problem inherent in the traditional model that it became the most popular method for developing selection instruments in industrial situations. Yet, there are some who feel that despite this enormous benefit of the concurrent validity model, this advantage, when weighed in the balance, does not compensate for the very serious disadvantages entailed, disadvantages which include almost all of those in the traditional model plus several that are unique to it alone. These additional disadvantages, we shall see, are so serious that some have argued the concurrent validity procedure should be used only as a hypothesis generator, not as a hypothesis tester (Guion, 1965).

[Now], this procedure also makes the following crucial assumptions:

1. The motivational determinants of responding to a possible selection instrument such as personality tests, attitude questionnaires, etc., are the same for those already on the job as for those applying for the job.

2. Scores on a potential predictor of job behavior are not related in any systematic manner to experience on the job.

It is quite obvious that these are two very important assumptions, violations of which would destroy the validity of this whole procedure. How often are they violated? There is little systematic evidence available, but it would appear that this would depend to a great extent on the instruments being studied. For example, there are studies on record where various kinds of leadership attitudes have been studied via a concurrent validity procedure and then recommended for administrative use in selection. It seems hard to believe that attitudes in this area are not reflecting organizational experience to a great extent. Similarly, when a person with union security is asked about his motivational characteristics, it is hard to believe that the psychological determinants of his answers are similar to those of a person who has been out of work for several months.

There is a third problem associated with the concurrent validity procedure, and that is a technical one. Consider the situation where an organization has a job category involving 40 positions but which now has 5 available openings. Who are the 35 currently on the job? Technically, they are a subgroup of those who were originally hired for that position, differing from the 5 who left in that they remained on the job. Now if we assume, that in general, the person who stays on the job or who is not fired is more competent than the one who quits or is fired, then the 35 now on the job would, in general, show less variation in job performance than the original unrestricted group of 40. If this were so, then it would be harder to find any correlation between predictor and job performance, since a correlation measures the similarity in variation between two variables and one of the variables does not have much variation. This, in turn, would depress the level of the correlation to a level perhaps lower than it would be if we had used it in a predictive validity situation. . . .

References

Dunnette, M. and Kirchner, W., *Psychology Applied to Business and Industry,* New York: Appleton, 1965.

Ghiselle, E. and Brown, C., *Personnel and Industrial Psychology,* 2nd edition, New York: McGraw-Hill, 1955.

Guion, R. M., *Personnel Testing.* New York: McGraw-Hill, 1965.

Guion, R. and Gottier, R. F., "Validity of Personnel Measures in Personnel Selection," *Personnel Psychology,* 1965, 18, 135-64.

McCormick, E. J., Cunningham, J. W. and Gordon, C. E., "Job Dimensions Based on Factorial Analysis of Worker-Oriented Variables," *Personnel Psychology,* 1967, 20, 417-430.

Decision Theory and Personnel Testing, Selection, and Utilization

FREDERIC R. WICKERT

Until recently little thought was generally given by test users to the question of how tests could best serve in making decisions. Instead, tests were thought of primarily as measuring instruments. Test theory concerned itself with the accuracy with which tests measured. It was found, for example, that a well-made test of achievement in mathematics or an intelligence test would usually measure rather accurately. However, personality tests, especially when they were tried out for the first time after just having been constructed (even when the best known principles of test construction were utilized), sometimes gave surprisingly inaccurate, inconsistent measurements. After numbers of experiences of this kind, it is little wonder that psychologists became preoccupied with accuracy of measurement.

According to decision theory, the purpose of tests is to help administrators and teachers make decisions about people rather than give the test psychologist the satisfaction of having made the most accurate possible measurement. The usefulness of accurate measurement is recognized under decision theory, but at the same time the value of a test is seen to depend on many qualities in addition to its accuracy. These other qualities include the relevance of the measurement to the particular decision being made and the loss resulting from an erroneous decision. Even more important may be the fact that the decision maker is both reminded of the possible courses of action available to him and helped in choosing from among them. With respect to the making of personnel selection decisions, for example, the decision maker can see the relative v lue of such alternative courses of action as getting a little but highly accurate test information, or getting more but less accurate test information.

Some Definitions and Terms from Decision Theory

Certain familiar words take on new meanings in decision theory. A definition of such words will serve as a good introduction to decision theory as applied to occupational selection.

Let us begin with the word *treatment*. A decision in personnel work concerns what is to be done, that is, what treatment to give one or more persons. Should an individual be hired or rejected, for what job should he be trained, to what counselling or therapy or educational course should he be assigned? The word treatment takes on a broad meaning. "Every personnel decision involves assigning each individual to an appropriate treatment." The number of individuals and the number of treatments available in any one decision problem may be large or small.

Next, three terms often encountered in personnel work—*selection, classification,* and *placement*—can be more sharply defined in the light of decision theory, and especially in the light of the concept of treatment as just defined.

In a *selection decision* an institution decides to accept some persons (give them

Adapted from *Educational and Occupational Selection in West Africa,* edited by A. Taylor and published by Oxford University Press.

the acceptance treatment) and to reject others (give them the rejection treatment). Hiring or not hiring candidates for employment, or admitting or turning away persons who have applied for admittance to a school would be examples of selection.

In *classification*, the decision is made regarding which one of many possible, dissimilar assignments (or treatments) an individual is given. An applicant at a store may be assigned to a clerical job, or to selling in the store, or to receiving incoming goods, or to guarding the store after hours, etc.

When persons are assigned to different levels of treatment rather than to quite different types of treatment, a *placement* decision is said to have been made. An ex ample of placement would be the sectioning of students into several classes according to their ability to learn as determined by a general intelligence test.

One should differentiate between the two-category placement treatment: for example, sectioning students into two classes according to their ability to learn as determined by a general intelligence test; and the selection-rejection treatment, for example, admitting some candidates into a school and rejecting the others on the basis of scores on a test, possibly again a general intelligence test. In placement, the persons remain within the institution; in selection, one group enters or remains in the institution while the other group has no further association with the institution. It will be seen from time to time farther on in this paper that the decision theory implications differ appreciably for the non-selection as compared with the selection problem.

Personnel decision matters, whether they are concerned with selection or classification or placement, may be characterized on still another basis, namely, the presence of certain common constraints on the kind of decision that can be made. Two broad types of constraints on personnel decisions are encountered: (1) the number of treatments per man, and (2) the number of men per treatment. Mostly each man is assigned to a single treatment: one job, one training program, or one diagnosis. When a man is assigned to more than one treatment, these treatments are usually interrelated. For example, a university student may be enrolled in three related subjects in any one trimester. In this case the personnel decision problem becomes one of finding for the individual the best pattern of treatments among those available.

On the other hand, the number of men per treatment may be constrained by a quota. The quota may be absolute or relative. An absolute quota is set when a definite number of vacancies has been established. For example, the establishment may provide for three clerks. A relative quota is set when a certain proportion of the group being considered is assigned to a treatment. Examples would be hiring a set percentage of applicants, or releasing a set percentage of soldiers from further military service, or promoting a set percentage of civil servants in a given year.

Strategy is another term frequently encountered in discussions of decision theory. A strategy is defined as a rule for arriving at a decision. One possible classification of strategies is into sequential as compared with non-sequential strategies. A sequential strategy involves not making an irrevocable assignment of an individual to a treatment. Instead, information is gathered during each stage of an individual's treatment and this information in turn is used to help form a decision about what his next treatment will be. For instance, an employee may be assigned to a job, that is, a terminal treatment, after just one test has been given to him; or he may be given additional tests, that is, assigned to additional treatments to get more information about him. These "tests" may include not only the usual psychological tests but such treatments as job tryouts, or psychotherapy, or counselling, or training, or even sending him at the institution's expense to get more education. We shall see later that sequential strategies are often better from a decision-making point of view than non-sequential ones.

It is obvious that we are continually making decisions as we go about our day-to-day work of occupational and educational selection and administration, but seldom do we go to the trouble of stating our strategy. Cronbach and Gleser (1965) point out that strategies can be made explicit—often laid out in tabular form. When this is done, the decision maker has revealed possibilities of which he may have been previously unaware.

Two related terms, the last ones to which we are formally introduced in this discussion of decision theory, are *outcome* and *payoff.* The outcome of a strategy consists of the consequences of a decision to assign a person to a given treatment. Further, any specific outcome is expressed in terms of some criterion (or set of criteria). In a textile mill, for example, the outcome of hiring an individual could be measured in terms of such criteria as his hourly production, how much trouble he was to supervise, how much material he wasted, the amount of time the machines he was assigned to tend were idle, the amount of training time to achieve some expected standard of production, etc.

There are some difficulties with decision theory at this point. Almost never is the decision maker able to anticipate the outcome for each person under each possible treatment. At best, he can only predict the probability distribution of the outcomes. Empirical results from previous cases are needed to determine how the information about a person is related to the criterion.

But outcomes alone are not enough. We need to go beyond outcome to payoff. An evaluated outcome is called a payoff. For example, it is clear that in the case of a factory operative the higher the proportion of perfect objects he produces, the more valuable he is. Cronbach and Gleser cite a hypothetical case in which a 2 percent rise in quality from 94 percent to 96 percent might be of great value because this rise might be just enough to permit the factory management to eliminate routine inspection altogether, but a gain of 2 percent from 74 percent to 76 percent might mean relatively little because complete inspection of the whole output would still be required. In other words, gain on the criterion measure may not be a linear function.

A strategy may be evaluated by considering its payoff, and two or more strategies can be evaluated by comparing their respective payoffs. It is important that the cost of a test or other information-producing procedure be expressed in monetary or utility units and deducted from the expected payoff in each instance.

Insights into Occupational Selection Provided by Decision Theory

Now that we have some notion of what decision theory is and we understand some of its main concepts and terms, we shall turn to a few of the insights from decision theory regarding occupational selection. To a certain extent these are quite technical, but every attempt will be made to present these implications in as non-technical a manner as possible. Here, as previously, much of what is said is a paraphrase of the Cronbach-Gleser argument.

The first of the insights from decision theory to consider concerns comparing a "fixed" with an "adaptive" treatment following a given selection procedure. In fixed-treatment selection individuals are chosen for one specified treatment which cannot be modified. In adaptive-treatment selection, the treatment is modified depending on the improved quality of the people selected. A good selection procedure becomes much more valuable when it is followed by a treatment which takes advantage of the improved quality of the persons selected. All too often following the installation of more effective educational selection procedures in a school system, the level of instruction remains the same. Decision theory indicates that improved educational selection will give greatest benefit when the methods of instruction are adjusted by introducing whatever pace and procedures are most appropriate for students of the quality selected. Most test theory to date has limited itself to fixed treatments and may have underrated the contribution better personnel procedures could make. The utility from selected persons is always greater with adaptive treatment than with fixed treatment as long as the selection method has some validity and the adaptations are appropriate.

The optimal strategy in any personnel situation would be a complex mixture of adaptation and selection. Decision theory asks in each instance in which selection and adaptation are manipulated that the payoff functions for the several possible arrangements be determined empirically. Only then can one make appropriate decisons.

Before dismissing all this as impractical, we should consider some of the truly important implications of the above reasoning for the making of personnel decisions in industry and government. The traditional sequence in personnel research that has been designed to bring about a better quality of personnel decisions has been first to establish a job and an associated training procedure, and then to look for tests or other selection procedures which would weed out applicants likely to perform poorly. Under decision theory there would be no reason to regard the job organization or the training procedure as being independent of the selection procedure. All three are regarded as variables on the same level. Personnel research should seek to identify the best combination of tests, training method, and job organization, as well as such other possible significant factors as the incentive plan and other motivational factors. The initial recruitment methods and sources might also be useful to include as variables.

A closer look at the relation between two of these personnel variables, job organization and selection, will serve to exemplify the power of the decision theory approach. In recent years in highly industrialized countries two new professions, job simplification expert and human engineer, have come into existence. Frequently these experts seek to organize the job so that any unselected man can do the work. The greater their success, the less the value of occupational selection. The tester is competing with the treatment simplifier, whose methods may be the more economical because his changes may be relatively permanent, while the tester must evaluate new employees forever. However, if the tester and the job simplifier were to cooperate and use decision theory, they should be able to arrive at a better combination of treatments.

All too often managers of institutions throughout the world stress occupational selection as a method for solving their personnel problems. They assume that their problems of managing people will be minimal if they can somehow limit the people in their organization to those who are already able, intelligent, well trained, and easily satisfied. Unfortunately, not enough such people exist. Managers must take into their organizations mostly imperfect people like the majority of us. The processes of training people, carefully organizing their jobs, and skillfully motivating imperfect people may be more difficult, expensive, and time-consuming for managers, but it is frequently more realistic to stress these processes rather than selection. Such stress may well yield a greater payoff. Some experts on developing areas of the world like West Africa, where adequate numbers of experienced, well-trained people are rarely available, recommend that more effort and money be put into training and motivating people and less into selection. According to decision theory, however, all these personnel activities are profitable. It is the best combination that has to be worked out in each case.

A second set of insights of decision theory are those associated with sequential testing. Efficiency of testing is often improved by a sequential scheme which allows the decision maker to continue testing whenever he is in doubt about accepting or rejecting an individual. The mathematical statistics of sequential testing was first worked out in the field of industrial inspection in manûfacturing. The striking similarity, from a statistical point of view, between industrial inspection and personnel selection was discovered later. Sequential testing is useful because it costs something to gather information. Obviously it would always be better to administer the full series of tests to every person if observations cost nothing. But testing does cost. Theoretical considerations suggest that sequential procedures can provide a given level of accuracy of decisions with about half the amount of testing required by non-sequential procedures.

It will be realized that sequential procedures can be applied within a test as well as within a group of tests. Instead of having all persons taking a test take all the items in a standardized way as in the past, each person answers questions only until the required decision can be made about him.

Another set of insights of decision theory relates to further improving the efficiency of testing. The personnel director who is concerned with selecting men for different assignments must decide under what conditions tests can make the greatest contribution. In the past he might have selected those tests with the highest validity, that is, those tests with the greatest measured accuracy in predicting success on the criterion. In the light of decision theory, however, he now knows that the importance of an assignment can justify using a test of low validity. "Tests for important decisions which fall far short of the ideal predictor may be much more worth using (and improving) than tests which give excellent guidance in making minor decisions."

Another variable to work with in improving testing efficiency is the length of the test. In traditional test theory it was long ago determined that the longer a test (within very broad limits), provided it had some validity to start with, the greater validity of the test. But decision theory has begun to suggest ways to determine the optimal length of a test, that is, that point beyond which "increases in cost outweigh benefits from greater validity."

The benefits of greater validity might also be sacrificed for a greater variety of test information. Variety of information is especially likely to be of value when, for example, test scores are to be used to select for many different jobs from among the same pool of applicants—in other words, situations in which multiple decisions have to be made. To get a greater variety of information in a given, usually limited amount of testing time, personnel men in the United States are increasingly turning to batteries made up of several relatively short tests not closely related to each other in what they test. One of these test batteries has been developed by the U.S. government and is enjoying wide usage. It is called the General Aptitude Test Battery.

One last type of insight of decision theory we consider here has to do with the implications of decision theory for several types of tests. The first of these types of tests we might consider are the general ability tests, that is, those measures of academic and intellectual ability widely used to predict performance in schools and on the job. Decision theory shows such tests to have certain hitherto not clearly formulated advantages and disadvantages. On the advantage side of the ledger the criteria or outcomes which the general ability test predicts are usually of the highest importance, and we have seen earlier that the importance of a decision frequently constitutes adequate grounds to accept a test of lower validity. Also, decision theory indicates that a test which contributes to many decisions may be more valuable than a test which contributes to few or but one decision. The general ability test does contribute to many decisions. The intelligence test score of a secondary school student may tell teachers of several subjects whether or not the student is under-achieving, what range of occupations the student might appropriately consider, whether or not to think of going on to the university, etc.

The disadvantages of general ability tests, as revealed by decision theory, turn out to be quite damaging, despite their advantages. If valid decisions can be made using information at hand or cheaply available, any test should be judged by the increase in validity it offers. But because the general ability test deals with qualities required in a wide range of performances, information on those qualities can be obtained from past performances. In England, for example, Professor Vernon has reported that success in grammar school has been very closely predicted from primary school ratings, and that the best general ability tests added almost nothing, even though the measured validity of the general ability tests was high. What may well be more useful might be tests which have lower validity but which might contribute to decisions where substitute information is not so readily available, e.g., tests on motivational patterns, emotional functioning interests, and the like. Consider briefly the use of general ability tests in doing occupational counselling with university students in the United States. The common problem in this situation is the choice of a curriculum. Since general ability tests predict success in about all curricula to about the same degree, they provide no useful information toward the decision regarding which curriculum to follow. What is needed are differential predictors. The same weakness of general ability tests applies. to the classification of military personnel.

Another weakness of general ability tests becomes apparent from a point made earlier in this paper. In the world of work, job simplification experts may so simplify work that men, unselected with respect to general ability, could do the work readily. Under such circumstances selection by general ability test would add little. Even at university level the elimination through careful planning of intellectual hurdles, which are irrelevant to a person's later performance, could reduce the importance of selection on general intellectual characteristics. It can be concluded that general ability tests have their strengths and weaknesses, and that their use in the future could better be associated with the kind of decisions to which they were expected to contribute.

The second and last type of test for which we are to consider the implications of decision theory are called *wide-band* procedures, a term from the information theory recently developed for the study of electronic communication systems. Band-width, or greater coverage, is obtained only at the cost of lowered fidelity or dependability. For any decision problem there is optimum band-width, although in conventional selection theory it has been assumed that it is always desirable to maximize dependability. Important wide-band procedures include (1) the interview, as used in guidance, counselling, and therapy, and in both educational and occupational selection, and (2) the projective techniques. These tend to be unsatisfactory when judged by conventional standards of predictive efficiency and dependability. Nevertheless, they continue to be widely used. One may infer from decision theory that their value lies in arriving at reversible, or investigatory, rather than terminal decisions. They are especially useful in situations where sequential procedures can be used. "A sequential process makes ideal use of fallible data, trusting them only to the extent that they deserve." The wide-band procedures are especially useful for directing the decision-maker's subsequent observations so that he finds what is pertinent. Consequently these wide-band procedures have the value of the wide-ranging, initial survey. Following the survey, the decision-maker can turn to the more dependable, narrow-band procedures to use in order to arrive at a reasonably dependable terminal decision.

Section B
The Interview
as a Selection Technique

The Selection Interview

JOHN A. MINER

. . . Although it should be evident that interview procedures are widely used for a variety of purposes, the primary concern here is with specific applications in the evaluation of human inputs to a business organization. Thus, applications in such areas as marketing research, employee counseling, managment appraisal, attitude surveys, and so on will receive very little attention.

Even within the input context, the interview serves a number of purposes. It is much more than a selection device. Probably this is why it has survived and even thrived in the face of extended attacks by industrial psychologists and others and of considerable evidence that as commonly used it is often not a very effective selection technique.

There are, in fact a number of requirements connected with the input process that at present cannot be accomplished in any other way, although telephone and written communication might be substituted in certain instances. Interviews are used as often to sell the company and thus recruit candidates for employment as to select. A single interview frequently involves both selection and recruiting aspects. Furthermore, terms of employment characteristically are negotiated in the interview situation, and an important public relations function is performed. Rejected applicants are particularly likely to leave with very negative attitudes toward the company, if they have not talked with a responsible representative.

Even when the focus is directly on the selection process, the interview appears to possess certain unique values, which may account for its continued widespread use. For one thing, the great flexibility of the technique, which can contribute to limited validity in some selection situations, may represent a major asset at other times. The interview is the method *par excellence* for filling in the gaps between other selection techniques—gaps that could not have been foreseen until the other techniques were actually applied. Responses on the application blank may make it clear that further information regarding the circumstances surrounding certain previous employment and separation decisions is needed. An interview can be of considerable help in providing such information.

It is also clear that the interview is widely used to determine whether an applicant is the type of person who can be expected to fit in and get along in the particular firm. Its use with reference to such organizational maintenance considerations is probably much more widespread than its use in predicting productivity. This is not to imply that other selection techniques cannot be used to predict maintenance criteria, but that, for various reasons, they often are not given the same emphasis as the interview. Something about the process of personal judgment produces a strong feeling of validity, even when validity is not present. It is not surprising, therefore, that many companies place heavy emphasis on interviewing when attempting to predict whether a man will be a source of conflict, will have a negative impact on others, or will be an extremely unhappy employee.

Finally, there are situations, especially when managerial and professional positions are involved, where the interview is the only major selection technique that realistically can be used. When a man who already has a good job, who gives every evidence of being a good prospect, and who does not have a strong initial incentive to make a move is faced with extensive psychological testing, a physical exam, and an application blank (above and beyond the resume he has already submitted), he may shy away. If this seems likely, it is often wiser to rely on the interview, reference checks, and the like, in spite of their shortcomings, than to face the prospect of losing the man entirely.

What Is Known about the Selection Interview

A great deal has been written regarding the techniques of interviewing for various purposes (1, 3, 5, 6). Much of this, however, derives from the expertise and opinion of specific individuals. What is really known, in the sense that it is based on studies using selection models . . . and on other scientific research procedures, is considerably less.

The discussion here will be restricted to that which is known in this scientific sense. Unfortunately, when this is done, a great deal is left to the discretion of the individual interviewer. Yet there is little point in continuing to perpetuate much of the existing lore, which in many instances has been developed out of situations far removed from the company employment office, and which may therefore be quite erroneous when applied to a selection interview in the business world.

Consistency of Interviewer Judgments

There is considerable evidence that, although an interviewer will himself exhibit consistency in successive evaluations of the same individual, different interviewers are likely to come to quite disparate conclusions (7). When two employment interviewers utilize their idiosyncratic interview procedures on the same applicant, the probability is that they will come to different decisions. They normally will elicit information on different matters, and even when the topics covered do overlap, one man will weigh the applicant's responses in a way that varies considerably from that employed by the other.

These problems can be overcome. Interviewers can be trained to follow similar patterns in their questioning and to evaluate responses using the same standards. When more structured interview techniques are used, when the questions asked are standardized and responses are recorded systematically, the consistency of the judgmental process increases markedly. Within limits, it does not matter which interviewer is used; the results tend to be similar. Unfortunately, however, structuring of a kind that will increase the consistency of judgments appears to be the exception rather than the rule in most personnel offices. Where strong reliance is placed on the interview, the final selection decision often depends as much on which interviewer is used as on the characteristics of the applicant. On the other hand, agreement does not guarantee accuracy of prediction; there can be great consistency in picking the wrong people.

Accuracy of Interview Information

Studies aimed at determining the accuracy of statements regarding work history made in the interview indicate that reporting errors may occur. In one instance, when a check was made with employers, information given by the interviewees regarding job titles was found to be invalid in 24 percent of the cases. Job duties were incorrectly reported by 10 percent, and pay by 22 percent (11). In general, the tendency was to upgrade rather than downgrade prior work experience.

Other research suggests that, in most employment situations, interview distortion is probably not so prevalent as the preceding figures suggest (9). Yet, in any given instance an interviewer may be faced with an applicant who deliberately, or perhaps unconsciously, falsifies his report. The tendency is for the man to make his record look better than it is. It can be assumed, also, that many applicants will avoid discussing previous instances of ineffective work performance. Where valid data are essential, it is usually desirable to check interview statements against outside sources.

Accuracy of Interviewer Judgments

The inevitable conclusion derived from a number of investigations is that interview judgments, as they are usually made in the employment situation, are not closely related to independent measures of the characteristics judged nor to measures of success on the job. In an over-all sense, the evidence regarding the validity of the selection interview yields a distinctly disappointing picture (7).

There are conditions under which the interview exhibits considerable strength as a selection device, and there are some characteristics capable of being judged more effectively than others. Studies dealing with the relationship between interview estimates of intelligence and test scores indicate that the interview can be quite valid in this area. In addition, the interview would appear to have good potential as a predictor of self-confidence, the effectiveness with which a man can express himself, certain types of attitudes, sociability, and a variety of mental abilities. Such characteristics as dependability, creativity, honesty, and loyalty seem more difficult to estimate correctly in the normal interview situation.

The evidence regarding the value of the interview as a selection procedure is certainly not all negative. Where the interview approach is planned in advance and a relatively structured format is followed, so that much the same questions are asked of all interviewees, relatively good validities have been obtained against job performance criteria (4, 12). The results of one such study, which utilized the concurrent model, are presented in Table 1. Clearly these interview judgments constitute quite adequate predictors in certain instances. Others among the attitude estimates are considerably less effective.

In another series of studies, rather sizable predictive validities were reported for over-all interviewer estimates of suitability for employment, when a highly structured, patterned interview approach was followed (8). When validated against duration of employment for the 587 people who left the company within an eighteen-month period, the interviews yielded a correlation of .43. The men rated higher initially in the employment interview stayed longer. The 407 employees who were still on the job eighteen months after hiring were rated for performance effectiveness by their superiors, and the results were compared with the earlier interview judgments. A predictive validity coefficient of .68 was obtained. Subsequent studies using the same patterned interview format produced correlations with success criteria consistently in the .60's.

TABLE 1

CORRELATIONS BETWEEN ATTITUDE EVALUATIONS FROM INTERVIEWS AND
SUPERVISORS' PERFORMANCE RATINGS

Attitudes	*Group 1* *(N = 12)*	*Group 2* *(N = 14)*
Formulation of goal	.14	.60
Strength of job interest	—.13	.40
Strength of general interests	.42	.85
Self-regard	.67	.63
Acquisitive perseverance	—.13	—.30
All five attitudes combined	.45	.71
Formulation of goal, strength of general interests, and self-regard combined	.54	.66

Source: Adapted from K.A. Yonge, "The Value of the Interview: An Orientation and a Pilot Study," *Journal of Applied Psychology*, Vol. 40 (1956), p. 29.

It is evident that when the selection interview is used in a relatively standardized manner and individualized interviewer approaches and biases are controlled, the interview can be quite effective. Under such standardized conditions, the interview takes on certain characteristics of the application blank or a psychological test. It becomes in many respects an oral version of the common written selection procedures, although still with greater flexibility. There is nothing in what has been said to imply that less structured (and less directive) interviews may not yield equally good validities under certain circumstances and with certain interviewers, but without further research it is not possible to specify exactly what these requisite conditions are.

The McGill University Studies

Certain other conclusions regarding the decision-making process in the interview are derived from a series of studies carried out at McGill University over a 10-year period (10). As a result of this research, it is now clear that in the actual employment situation most interviewers tend to make an accept-reject decision early in the interview. They do not wait until all the information is in. Rather, a bias is developed and stabilized shortly after the discussion starts. This bias serves to color the remainder of the interview and is not usually reversed.

Second, interviewers are much more influenced by unfavorable than by favorable data. If any shift in viewpoint occurs during the interview, it is much more likely to be in the direction of rejection. Apparently, selection interviewers tend to maintain rather clear-cut conceptions regarding the role requirements of the jobs for which they are interviewing. They compare candidates against these stereotypes in the sense of looking for deviant characteristics, and thus for negative evidence with regard to hiring. Positive evidence is given much less weight.

These findings suggest certain guidelines for maximizing the effectiveness of employment interviewing. For one thing, if it is intended that the interview should make a *unique* contribution to the selection process, the interviewing ought to be done with relatively little foreknowledge of the candidate. Contrary to common practice, application blanks, test scores, and the like should be withheld until after the initial selection interview. Personal history data should be obtained directly from the candidate in oral form even if written versions are available. This approach will serve to delay decision-making in the interview with the result that information obtained during the latter part of the discussion can be effectively utilized in reaching a judgment. If data are needed to fill in the gaps between the various selection techniques, these can be obtained from a second interview. Thus, the interview as an independent selection tool should be clearly differentiated from the interview as a means of following up on leads provided by other devices. The interviewer should be clear in his own mind as to which objective he is seeking.

When the interview is used as an independent procedure, information obtained from the various sources should be combined and evaluated subsequently to reach a final selection decision, rather than during the interview proper. When the interview is used to supplement application blank, medical history, and psychological test data, it should be as an information-gathering device only, not as an ideally constituted selection procedure. In neither case should it assume the proportions of a final arbiter superseding all other techniques and sources of information.

Types of Employment Interviews

It is evident that the content of the selection interview may be varied. Different interviewers may ask different questions, concentrate on different parts of the man's prior experience, and attempt to develop estimates of different characteristics. It is also true, however, that the basic technique or procedure may be varied.

Patterned, or Structured, Interviews

The patterned, or structured, interview already has been noted in connection with the discussions of the consistency and accuracy of interviewer judgments. Often a detailed form is used, with the specific questions to be asked noted and space provided for the answers. The form is completed either during the interview or immediately afterward, from memory. In other cases, only the areas to be covered are established in advance, the order of coverage and actual question wording being left to the interviewer. Either way the more structured approach offers distinct advantages over the usual procedure, where different interviewers may go off in completely different directions depending on their own and the candidate's predilections. On the other hand, it should be recognized that information loss may occur because of a lack of flexibility.

Nondirective Procedures

The nondirective approach derives originally from psychotherapy and counseling. It permits the person being interviewed considerable leeway in determining the topics to be covered. The basic role of the interviewer is to reflect the feelings of the other person and to restate or repeat key words and phrases. This tends to elicit more detailed information from the interviewee, especially with reference to his emotional reactions, attitudes, and opinions. Because the candidate actually controls the content of the interview, this procedure may take the discussion far afield. It frequently yields a great deal of information about the prior experiences, early family life, and interpersonal relationships of the individual, but much of this often has no clear relationship to the employment decision. For this reason, the nondirective technique is usually mixed with a more directive, questioning approach when it is used in the selection interview.

Multiple and Group Interviews

Another procedure, which has proved to yield good validity (7), involves the use of more than one interviewer. Either the candidate spends time talking to several different people separately or he meets with a panel or board whose members alternate in asking him questions. This latter approach can easily be integrated into a patterned or structured format, and when this is done the resulting decisions and evaluations appear to maximize prediction of subsequent performance. Normally, the group evaluation is derived after discussion among the various interviewers, but independent estimates can be obtained from each man, and these then are averaged to achieve a final decision. The major disadvantage of any multiple interviewer procedure, of course, is that it can become very costly in terms of the total number of man-hours required. For this reason, it is usually reserved for use in selecting people for the higher level positions.

Stress Interviews

The stress approach achieved some acceptance in the business world after World War II as a result of its use during the war to select men for espionage work with the Office of Strategic Services. As used in industry, this procedure usually involves the induction of failure stress. The interviewer rather suddenly becomes quite aggressive, belittles the candidate, and throws him on the defensive. Reactions to this type of treatment are then observed.

Because it utilizes a sample of present behavior to formulate predictions, rather than focusing on past behavior, the stress interview is in many ways more a situational test than a selection interview. It has the disadvantage that rejected candidates who are subjected to this process can leave with a very negative image of the company, and even those whom the company may wish to hire can become so embittered that they will not accept an offer. This does not happen often, and usually a subsequent explanation can eradicate any bad feelings. When the fact that there is little positive evidence on the predictive power of the stress interview is added to these considerations, it seems very difficult to justify its use under normal circumstances. The selection situation itself appears to be anxiety-provoking enough for most people.

The Interview and Selection Models

It seems absolutely essential, if a company is to make effective use of the selection interview, for the interviewer to receive some systematic feedback on the validity of his decisions. In order to accomplish this, written evaluations of each candidate must be recorded at the conclusion of the interview. These interview ratings can then be compared at a later date with criterion information provided by the man's immediate superior or derived from some other source. In this way, the interviewer can modify his technique over time to maximize his predictive validity (2).

This approach suffers in that no follow-up can be made on those applicants who are not hired. However, in most companies, personnel recommendations are not followed religiously. For various reasons, those recommended for rejection are hired on occasion. In addition, other selection procedures may outweigh an original negative interview impression. Thus, there will be individuals in the follow-up group who have received rather low ratings, although the preponderant number will have had generally favorable evaluations in the interview.

One should not expect perfect success from these studies, of course. Yet, an interview should contribute something above what might be obtained by chance alone, and from the use of other techniques. Also, if a standardized interview form is used, individual questions can be analyzed to see if they discriminate between effective and ineffective employees. If certain questions appear not to be contributing to the predictive process, others can be substituted and evaluated in a similar manner.

References

1. Bellows, R. M., and M. F. Estep, *Employment Psychology: The Interview*. New York: Holt, Rinehart & Winston, 1961.

2. England, G. W., and D. G. Paterson, "Selection and Placement—The Past Ten Years," in H. G. Heneman *et al.* (eds.), *Employment Relations Research*. New York: Harper & Row, 1960, pp. 43-72.

3. Fear, R. A., *The Evaluation Interview*. New York: McGraw-Hill, 1958.

4. Ghiselli, E. E., "The Validity of a Personnel Interview," *Personnel Psychology*, Vol. 19 (1966), 389-394.

5. Kahn, R. L., and G. F. Cannell, *The Dynamics of Interviewing*. New York: Wiley, 1957.

6. Lopez, F. M., *Personnel Interviewing–Theory and Practice*. McGraw-Hill, 1965.

7. Mayfield, E. C., "The Selection Interview—A Re-evaluation of Published Research," *Personnel Psychology*, Vol. 17 (1964), 239-260.

8. McMurry, R. N., "Validating the Patterned Interview," *Personnel*, Vol. 23 (1947), 263-272.

9. Tiffin, J., and E. J. McCormick, *Industrial Psychology*, 5tn ed., Englewood Cliffs, N.J.: Prentice-Hall, 1965.

10. Webster, E. C., *Decision-Making in the Employment Interview*. Montreal, Can.: Industrial Relations Centre, McGill Univ., 1964.

11. Weiss, D. J., and R. V. Dawis, "An Objective Validation of Factual Interview Data,"*Journal of Applied Psychology*, Vol. 44 (1960), 381-385.

12. Yonge, K. A. "The Value of the Interview: An Orientation and a Pilot Study," *Journal of Applied Psychology*, Vol. 49 (1956), 25-31.

Improvements in
The Selection Interview

ROBERT E. CARLSON
PAUL W. THAYER
EUGENE C. MAYFIELD
DONALD A. PETERSON

The effectiveness and utility of the selection interview has again been seriously questioned as a result of several comprehensive reviews of the research literature.[1] Not one of these classic summary reviews of the interview research literature arrived at conclusions that could be classed as optimistic when viewed from an applied standpoint. Yet none of this is new information. As early as 1915, the validity of the selection interview was empirically questioned.[1] Despite the fact that it is common knowledge that the selection interview probably contributes little in the way of validity to the selection decision, it continues to be used. It is clear that no amount of additional evidence on the lack of validity will alter the role of the interview in selection. Future research should obviously be directed at understanding the mechanism of the interview and improving interview technology. As Schwab has stated, "Companies are not likely to abandon the use of the employment interview, nor is it necessarily desirable that they do so. But it is grossly premature to sit back comfortably and assume that employment interviews are satisfactory. It is even too early to dash off unsupported recommendations for their improvement. A great deal of research work remains, research which companies must be willing to sponsor before we can count the interview as a prime weapon in our selection arsenal."[3] This was essentially the conclusion that the Life Insurance Agency Management Association reached some six years ago. In addition, the life insurance industry, through LIAMA, took action and sponsored basic research on the selection interview.

The research reported here is an attempt to improve the use of the selection interview in the life insurance industry. The role of the interview in selection presented a particularly difficult problem for the life insurance industry where each agency manager is responsible for many of the traditional personnel management functions. In addition, these agencies are scattered across the U.S. and Canada and make centralizing the selection process difficult. In order to strengthen the role of the selection interview in each manager's selection system, LIAMA has been doing basic research on the selection interview for the past six years.

The research reported here is part of a long-run research program concerned with how interviewers make employment decisions. Its purpose is to try to determine the limits of an interviewer's capability in extending his judgment into the future. This summary covers the early studies in a program of research to develop interim tools and the training necessary to make the selection interview a useful selection instrument.

The first step in the interview research program was to observe and record numerous interviews, to interview in depth the interviewers on their decision process, to conduct group decision conferences where the interviewers discussed their percep-

Reprinted by permission of the authors and the publisher from *Personnel Journal*, vol. 50 (April 1971), no. 4, pp. 268-75, 317.

tion of their decision process for a given taped interview, and to examine the published research on the selection interview. Based upon this information, a model of the selection interview was constructed that specified as many of the influences operating during the interview as could be determined. Initially, there appeared to be four main classes of influences operating to affect/limit the decision of the interviewer. They were:

- The physical and psychological properties of the interviewee
- The physical and psychological properties of the interviewer
- The situation/environment in which the interviewer works
- The task or type of judgment the interviewer must make

The research strategy has been to systematically manipulate and control the variables specified in the model, trying to eliminate variables that do not have any influence, trying to assess the magnitude of those variables that have an influence, and adding variables that other research has shown to be promising. The first section of this article will describe some of the research findings; the second section will describe some of the materials that have been developed; and the third section will describe the interviewer training that has been developed.

What Are Some Findings?

Structured vs. Unstructured Interviews

One question that has often been asked is, "What kind of interview is best?" What interview style—structured, where the interviewer follows a set procedure; or unstructured, where the interviewer has no set procedure and where he follows the interviewee's lead—results in more effective decisions? In this study, live interviews were used. Each interviewee was interviewed three times. Interviewers used the following three types of interviewing strategies: structured, where the interviewer asked questions only from an interview guide; semistructured, where the interviewer followed an interview guide, but could ask questions about any other areas he wished; and unstructured, where the interviewer had no interview guide and could do as he wished. The basic question involved was the consistency with which people interviewing the same interviewee could agree with each other. If the interviewers' judgments were not consistent—one interviewer saying the applicant was good and the other saying he was bad—no valid prediction of job performance could be made from interview data. Agreement among interviewers is essential if one is to say that the procedure used has the potential for validity.

The results indicated that only the structured interview generated information that enabled interviewers to agree with each other. Under structured conditions, the interviewer knew what to ask and what to do with the information he received. Moreover, the interviewer applied the same frame of reference to each applicant, since he covered the same areas for each. In the less-structured interviews, the managers received additional information, but it seemed to be unorganized and made their evaluation task more difficult. Thus, a highly-structured interview has the greatest potential for valid selection.[4]

Effect of Interviewer Experience

In the past it had been assumed that one way to become an effective interviewer was through experience. In fact, it has been hypothesized that interviewers who have had the same amount of experience would evaluate a job applicant similarly.[5] To determine whether this was indeed the case, a study was done that involved managers who had conducted differing numbers of interviews over the same period. Managers were then compared who had similar as well as differing concentrations of interviewing experience. It was found that when evaluating the same recruits, interviewers with similar experiences did not agree with each other to any greater degree than did interviewers with differing experiences. It was concluded that interviewers benefit very little from day-to-day interviewing experience and apparently the conditions necessary for learning are not present in the day-to-day interviewer's job situation.[6] This implied that systematic training is needed, with some feedback mechanism built into the selection procedure, to enable interviewers to learn from their experiences; the job performance predictions made by the interviewer must be compared with how the recruit actually performs on the job.

Situational Pressures

One of the situational variables studied was how pressure for results affected the evaluation of a new recruit. One large group of managers was told to assume that they were behind their recruiting quota, that it was October, and that the home office had just called. Another group was ahead of quota; for a third group, no quota situation existed. All three groups of managers evaluated descriptions of the same job applicants. It was found that being behind recruiting quota impaired the judgment of those managers. They evaluated the same recruits as actually having greater potential and said they would hire more of them than did the other two groups of managers.[7]

One more highly significant question was raised: Are all managers, regardless of experience, equally vulnerable to this kind of pressure? Managers were asked how frequently they conducted interviews. Regardless of how long the person had been a manager, those who had had a high rate of interviewing experience—many interviews in a given period of time—were less susceptible to pressures than were those with a low interviewing rate. The interviewers with less interviewing experience relied more on subjective information and reached a decision with less information. It was concluded that one way to overcome this problem of lack of concentrated interviewing experience was through the general use of a standardized interview procedure and intensive training in its use.

Standard of Comparison

Another condition studied was the standards managers applied in evaluating recruits. It was found, for example, that if a manager evaluated a candidate who was just average after evaluating three or four very unfavorable candidates in a row, the average one would be evaluated very favorably.[8] When managers were evaluating more than one recruit at a time, they used other recruits as a standard.[9] Each recruit was compared to all other recruits. Thus, managers did not have an absolute standard —who they thought looked good was partly determined by the persons with whom they were comparing the recruit. This indicated that some system was necessary to aid a manager in evaluating a recruit. The same system should be applicable to each recruit. This implied that some standardized evaluation system was necessary to reduce the large amount of information developed from an interview to a manageable number of constant dimensions.

Effect of Appearance

Some of the early studies utilized photographs to try to determine how much of an effect appearance had on the manager's decision. A favorably rated photograph was paired with a favorably rated personal history description and also with an unfavorably rated personal history. It was found that appearance had its greatest effect on the interviewer's final rating when it complemented the personal history information.[10] Even when appearance and personal history information were the same (both favorable or both unfavorable), the personal history information was given twice as much weight as appearance. However, the relationship is not a simple one and only emphasized the need for a more complete system to aid the manager in selection decision-making.

Effect of Interview Information on Valid Test Results

In many selection situations, valid selection tests are used in conjunction with the interview data in arriving at a selection decision. Two recent studies have investigated how the emphasis placed on valid test results (*Aptitude Index Battery*) is altered by the more subjective interview data. Managers do place great emphasis on the AIB knowing that the score does generate a valid prediction.

However, how much weight is given to the score depends on other conditions; e.g., a low-scoring applicant is judged better if preceded by a number of poor applicants, unfavorable information is given much greater weight if it is uncovered just prior to ending the interview, etc. This finding suggested that what is needed is some system that places the interview information and other selection information in their proper perspective.[11]

Interview Accuracy

A recent study tried to determine how accurately managers can recall what an applicant says during an interview. Prior to the interview the managers were given the interview guide, pencils, and paper, and were told to perform as if *they* were conducting the interview. A 20-minute video tape of a selection interview was played for a group of 40 managers. Following the video tape presentation, the managers were given a 20-question test. All questions were straightforward and factual. Some managers missed none, while some missed as many as 15 out of 20 items. The average number was 10 wrong. In a short 20-minute interview, half the managers could not report accurately on the information produced during the interview! On the other hand, those managers who had been following the interview guide and taking notes were quite accurate on the test; note-taking in conjunction with a guide appears to be essential.

Given that interviewers differed in the accuracy with which they were able to report what they heard, the next question appeared to be "How does this affect their evaluation?" In general it was found that those interviewers who were least accurate in their recollections rated the interviewee higher and with less variability, while the more accurate interviewers rated the interviewee average or lower and with greater variability. Thus, those interviewers who did not have the factual information at their disposal assumed that the interview was generally favorable and rated the interviewee more favorable in all areas. Those interviewers who were able to reproduce more of the factual information rated the interviewee lower and recognized his intra-individual differences by using more of the rating scale. This implied that the less accurate interviewers selected a "halo strategy" when evaluating the interviewee, while the more accurate interviewers used an individual differences strategy. Whether this is peculiar to the individual interviewer or due to the fact that the interviewer did or didn't have accurate information at his disposal is, of course, unanswerable from this data.

Can Interviewers Predict?

The ultimate purpose of the selection interview is to collect factual and attitudinal information that will enable the interviewer to make accurate and valid job behavior predictions for the interviewee. The interviewer does this by recording the factual information for an applicant, evaluating the meaning of the information in terms of what the interviewee will be able to do on the job in question, and extending these evaluations into the future in the form of job behavior predictions. The question is, "How reliably can a group of interviewers make predictions for a given interviewee?" Without high inter-interviewer agreement, the potential for interview validity is limited to a few interviewers and cannot be found in the interview process itself.

In this study, a combination of movies and audio tapes were played simulating an interview. In addition, each of the 42 manager-interviewers was given a detailed written summary of the interview. The total interview lasted almost three hours and covered the interviewee's work history, work experience, education and military experience, life insurance holdings, attitude toward the life insurance career, family life, financial soundness, social life and social mobility, and future goals and aspirations. After hearing and seeing the interview and after studying a 20-page written summary, each interviewer was asked to make a decision either to continue the selection process or to terminate negotiations. In addition, each interviewer was asked to make a list of all the factual information he considered while making his decision. Also, the interviewer was to rate the interviewee in 31 different areas. The ratings were descriptive of the interviewee's past accomplishments, such as his job success pattern, the quantity and quality of his education, his family situation, financial knowledge and soundness, etc. Finally, the interviewers were asked to make job behavior predictions in 28 different job specific activities such as, Could he use the telephone for business purposes? Could he make cold calls? Would he keep records? Would he take direction? What about his market?

The interviewers agreed quite well with each other on which facts they reportedly considered in making their employment decision. Almost 70 percent of the factual statements were recorded by all the interviewers. The remaining 30 percent of the factual statements were specific to interviewers. This tended to confirm a hypothesis of Mayfield and Carlson where they postulate that the stereotypes held by interviewers consist of general as well as specific content.[12] It was concluded that interviewers do record and use similar factual information with agreement.

The interviewers agreed less well with each other on the evaluation or value placed on the facts. The median inter-interviewer correlation was .62, with a low of .07 and a high of .82. This means that the interviewers still agreed reasonably well on the evaluation—good vs. bad—quality of the information they received. They would make similar selection-rejection decisions.

The job behavior predictions of the interviewers, however, were not nearly as high in agreement. The median inter-interviewer correlation was .33 with a low of —.21 and a high of .67. This means that the interviewers do not agree with each other on how well the interviewee will perform the job of a life insurance agent in 28 different areas. In addition, those predictions that required the interviewer to extend his judgment further into the future had significantly greater inter-interviewer variability than did those predictions that could be verified in a shorter period of time. Thus, interviewers can agree more with each other's predictions if the job behavior is of a more immediate nature.

These findings imply that although interviewers probably use much the same information in making a decision, they will evaluate it somewhat differently. Furthermore, the interviewers are not able to agree on how well the individual will perform on the job.

Thus, it was concluded that interviewers evaluate essentially similar things in an applicant; they agree reasonably well whether an applicant's past record is good or bad, but they cannot agree on good or bad for what. Yet here, and only here, is where the clinical function of the interviewer is difficult to replace with a scoring system. In being able to make accurate and valid job behavior predictions, the interview can pay for itself in terms of planning an applicant's early job training and as a mechanism whereby a supervisor can learn early how to manage an applicant. In order for the interviewer to be able to make accurate and valid job behavior predictions, it follows that he must have a feedback system whereby he can learn from his past experiences. Only through accurate feedback in language similar to the behavior predictions can the interviewer learn to make job behavior predictions. The results further imply that the interviewer must be equipped with a complete selection system that coordinates all the selection steps and provides the interviewer with as relevant and complete information as possible when he makes job behavior predictions.

Conclusions

These early studies in LIAMA's interview research program provided little in the way of optimism for the traditional approach to the selection interview. However, this research did indicate specific areas where improvements in selection and interview technology could be made. It did indicate where interim improvements could be tried and evaluated while the long-term research on the interview continued.

Two major applied implications may be derived from the interview research to date. First, the selection interview should be made an integral part of an over-all selection procedure, and to accomplish this, new and additional materials are needed. The new materials should include a broad-gauge, comprehensive, structured interview guide; standardized evaluation and prediction forms that aid the interviewer in summarizing information from all steps in the selection process; and an evaluation system that provides feedback to the interviewer in language similar to the preemployment job behavior predictions he must make. The second major applied implication is that an intensive training program for interviewers is necessary if interviewers are to initially learn enough in common to increase the probability of obtaining general validity from the selection interview. Thus, the early studies have provided specific information that has been used to change the way selection is carried out in the insurance industry.

Implementation: Development of a Selection Process

As a result of and based upon the early interview research, LIAMA constructed the *Agent Selection Kit*. This is a complete agent selection procedure to be used by agency branch managers and general agents in the field. Selection begins when the agency head secures the name of a prospective recruit and ends when the new agent has been selling for six months or when negotiations or employment is terminated. Because research demonstrated the necessity of formally taking into consideration each step in the selection process, each step in the procedure is carefully placed to maximize the potential of succeeding and following steps. The *Agent Selection Kit* introduced the following new ideas to the insurance industry:

(1) *Selection should more properly be viewed as manpower development.* The *Agent Selection Kit* is a completely integrated process, more properly described as

manpower development; it goes beyond just selection. The assumption is that if industry is really going to have an appreciable effect on the manpower problem, it will have to think of recruiting, selection, training, and supervision as parts of a total manpower development process and not as entities by themselves. Quantity and quality of recruiting have an impact on selection—selection affects training—training capabilities, in turn, should affect selection. Unless viewed as a continuous, dependent process, maximum use cannot be made of the information the tools provide. If viewed as a complete process, the information gained from each step is carried forward to make future steps and the final decision more powerful.

(2) *Organizational differences must be taken into consideration in selection.* Because the *Agent Selection Kit* is a complete selection process, it can be modified to meet company and agency differences. By clearly spelling out the philosophy and principles behind the steps in the *Agent Selection Kit,* the company and the agency head are able to evaluate what is being gained or lost by altering the steps in selection. Further, because the agency head is forced to make job behavior predictions, he can begin to consider each recruit in terms of his particular agency needs, style, and strengths. Agency differences as well as individual differences enter into the employment decision in a systematic manner.

(3) *A career with any company should be entered into based on realistic job expectations.*[13] The company should know what the job recruit expects from his association with the company. Under such a condition, the manager can make a manpower development decision that properly considers selection, early training, motivation, and supervision practices of the applicant in question. The job recruit should know what the company expects of him, how the company is going to help him accomplish these goals, and the difficulties and benefits he may encounter in undertaking the job. With such knowledge, the recruit can make more than a job decision. He can make a career decision. The creation of realistic expectations further implies that the employment decision be one of "mutual consent." Professional management of the future will not be able to rely on a slanted job presentation to attract recruits to a career in hopes that one or two applicants will succeed. Manpower development decisions will replace selection decisions. The *Agent Selection Kit* is built around the concept of "mutual consent" with respect to a career decision. There are already indications that the recruit of the future will respond to a "mutual exploration" theme, where together he and the manager will examine the individual's future in an industry. The *Agent Selection Kit* provides a systematic fact-finding procedure that appeals to the recruit.

(4) *The selection interview should proceed according to a highly-structured format.* The *Agent Selection Kit* contains two self-contained structured interview guides. The first interview guide is to be used with applicants who have had extensive prior work history and concentrates on this work experience. The alternate interview guide is to be used with applicants just completing their education or military experiences and without any work experience. In addition, both interview guides cover the recruit's education, military experience, attitude toward insurance and toward the insurance agent's job, family commitments, finances, social mobility, social life, and future goals and aspirations. The interview guides present the initial series of questions and several alternative probes. Experience and pretesting have indicated that recruits are receptive to a structured approach and that interviewers can learn to use the guides after brief, but intensive, training.

(5) *Employment decisions should be based on predictions of future job behavior.* The *Agent Selection Kit* considers decision-making from the point of view of a prediction of future behavior, rather than from vague, over-all impressions of potential or

character. The manager manages the agent's activity, use of the telephone, record-keeping, prospecting, etc. The *Agent Selection Kit* enables the manager to make predictions about such job behaviors.

(6) *The manager should be able to learn from and correct his selection system.* The *Agent Selection Kit* procedure contains a built-in "feedback system" that enables the manager to learn from and correct his selection process. LIAMA interview research has shown that managers do not learn from the traditional approach to selection interviewing. To correct this, the *Agent Selection Kit* includes an Agent Performance Rating Form that the manager uses to compare to his final decision ratings. Discrepancies between his prediction and results point to areas in his selection and early training process that need extra effort.

Implementation: Training in Selection and Interviewing

To ensure at least uniform initial introduction to the material, LIAMA designed a three-day skill-building workshop. Three general training objectives and 16 specific behavioral objectives served as guides in setting up the training program. The first general goal was to develop in each trainee *knowledge* of selection and interview techniques; the second goal was to create favorable *attitudes* in the managers toward selection and self-confidence in their ability to conduct a technically good selection interview; and third, to develop *skill* in actually using the selection and interview materials. As a result of participating in the training, the agency heads are to actually be better at selection and interviewing than they were prior to training, to know they are better, and to be able to immediately use the new material with some skill. Thus, the goals of the training are to change attitudes as well as to develop knowledge and skill. These specifications dictated that the workshops be built around small-sized classes, class participation, and practice with standardized case material and controlled feedback.

To accomplish the goals of the training program, the first step in the workshop is to help the agency manager to understand and accept the principles behind the steps in the selection process. This helps to make the trainees receptive to discarding their current approach to selection and to accepting the new approach. Once the agency head accepts the logic of the principles on which the *Agent Selection Kit* is based, the next step is to get the trainee to recognize and question how he is currently conducting his selection process. This is accomplished through the use of edited tapes that demonstrate some of the effects of violating the selection principles. At the end of this first phase of the training, the agency heads are receptive to a new procedure and are aware of what a good procedure should contain.

The skill training that follows is designed to make the agency head more proficient in the use of the interview and evaluation procedures. The interview technique training includes taped examples, practice, and critique. The final evaluation practice sessions are extremely important to agency heads. Here the manager is asked to combine information from all the selection methods he has utilized—the interview, reference checks, credit reports, interview with the wife, precontract training, etc. The manager practices making job behavior predictions in areas such as use of the telephone, night work, markets, prospecting activities, etc. For the first time, managers recognize that they will not be managing the recruit's character or how impressive he looks, but rather they recognize that they must manage his work activities. Managers begin to recognize that selection should try to predict the recruit's performance in these activities.

During the workshops, the participants' attitudes swing from skepticism to receptivity, from impatience with the training detail to complete acceptance. These swings in attitude are built into the schedule, since early experimental workshops showed that they were necessary to modify and solidify managers' attitudes.

The managers leave their workshop with greater knowledge, with a skill that is well along in development, and with much greater self-confidence in their selection and early training procedure that they can put into practice immediately.

The Future

The *Agent Selection Kit* was introduced to LIAMA's 300-plus member companies in 1969. By mid-1970, 40 major life insurance companies had introduced it to their general agents and managers. Obviously, at this time it is much too early to evaluate its effectiveness. However, it is currently being evaluated as part of LIAMA's research program on the selection interview. In addition, it also provides a natural field setting for further pure research on the selection interview. Thus, LIAMA's research on the interview is an example of pure research generating an improved product, which, in turn, furthers the pure research effort.

Notes

1. See, for example, R. Wagner, "The Employment Interview: A Critical Summary,' *Personnel Psychology*, Vol. 2 (1949), pp. 17-46.

G. W. England and D. G. Paterson, "Selection and Placement—The Past Ten Years," in H. G. Henneman, Jr., et al. (Editors), *Employment Relations Research: A Summary and Appraisal*, New York: Harper, 1960, pp. 43-72.

E. C. Mayfield, "The Selection Interview: A Reevaluation of Published Research." *Personnel Psychology*, Vol. 17 (1964), pp. 239-260.

L. Ulrich and D. Trumbo, "The Selection Interview Since 1949," *Psychological Bulletin*, Vol. 63 (1965), pp. 100-116.

2. W. D. Scott, "The Scientific Selection of Salesmen," *Advertising and Selling*, Vol. 25 (1915), pp. 5-6 and 94-96.

3. D. P. Schwab, "Why Interview? A Critique," *Personnel Journal*, Vol. 48, No. 2 (1969), p. 129.

4. R. E. Carlson, D. P. Schwab, and H. G. Henneman III. "Agreement Among Selection Interview Styles," *Journal of Industrial Psychology*, Vol. 5, No. 1 (1970), pp. 8-17.

5. P. M. Rowe, "Individual Differences in Assessment Decisions," Unpublished doctoral thesis, McGill University, 1960.

6. R. E. Carlson, "Selection Interview Decisions: The Effect of Interviewer Experience, Relative Quota Situation, and Applicant Sample on Interviewer Decisions," *Personnel Psychology*, Vol. 20 (1967), pp. 259-280.

7. Ibid.

8. R. E. Carlson, "Effects of Applicant Sample on Ratings of Valid Information in an Employment Setting," *Journal of Applied Psychology*, Vol. 54 (1970), pp. 217-222.

9. R. E. Carlson, "Selection Interview Decisions: The Effect of Mode of Applicant Presentation on Some Outcome Measures," *Personnel Psychology*, Vol. 21 (1968), pp.193-207.

10. R. E. Carlson, "The Relative Influence of Appearance and Factual Written Information on an Interviewer's Final Rating," *Journal of Applied Psychology*, Vol. 51 (1967), pp. 461-468.

11. R. E. Carlson, "The Effect of Interview Information in Altering Valid Impressions," *Journal of Applied Psychology*, In Press.

12. E. C. Mayfield and R. E. Carlson, "Selection Interview Decisions: First Results from a Long-Term Research Project," *Personnel Psychology*, Vol. 19 (1966), pp. 41-53.

13. Life Insurance Agency Management Association, *"Realistic" Job Expectations and Survival*, Research Report 1964-2 (File 432).

Nature and Use
of Psychological Tests

ANNE ANASTASI

. . . Although the general public may still associate psychological tests most closely with "IQ tests" and with tests designed to detect emotional disorders, these tests represent only a small proportion of the available types of instruments. The major categories of psychological tests [are] tests of general intellectual level, traditionally called intelligence tests: tests of separate abilities, including multiple aptitude batteries, tests of special aptitudes, and achievement tests; and personality tests, concerned with measures of emotional and motivational traits, interpersonal behavior, interests, attitudes, and other nonintellectual characteristics.

In the face of such diversity in nature and purpose, what are the common differentiating characteristics of psychological tests? How do psychological tests differ from other methods of gathering information about individuals? The answer is to be found in certain fundamental features of both the construction and use of tests. It is with these features that the present [article] is concerned.

What Is a Psychological Test?

A psychological test is essentially an objective and standardized measure of a sample of behavior. Psychological tests are like tests in any other science, insofar as observations are made on a small but carefully chosen *sample* of an individual's behavior. In this respect, the psychologist proceeds in much the same way as the chemist who tests a patient's blood or a community's water supply by analyzing one or more samples of it. If the psychologist wishes to test the extent of a child's vocabulary, a clerk's ability to perform arithmetic computations, or a pilot's eye-hand coordination, he examines their performance with a representative set of words, arithmetic problems, or motor tests. Whether or not the test adequately covers the behavior under consideration obviously depends on the number and nature of items in the sample. For example, an arithmetic test consisting of only five problems, or one including only multiplication items, would be a poor measure of the individual's computational skill. A vocabulary test composed entirely of baseball terms would hardly provide a dependable estimate of a child's total range of vocabulary.

The *diagnostic* or *predictive value* of a psychological test depends on the degree to which it serves as an indicator of a relatively broad and significant area of behavior. Measurement of the behavior sample directly covered by the test is rarely, if ever, the goal of psychological testing. The child's knowledge of a particular list of 50 words is not, in itself, of great interest. Nor is the job applicant's performance on a specific set of 20 arithmetic problems of much importance. If, however, it can be demonstrated that there is a close correspondence between the child's knowledge of the word list and his total mastery of vocabulary, or between the applicant's score on the arithmetic problems and his computational performance on the job, then the tests are serving their purpose.

It should be noted in this connection that the test items need not resemble closely the behavior the test is to predict. It is only necessary that an empirical correspondence be demonstrated between the two. The degree of similarity between the test sample and the predicted behavior may vary widely. At one extreme, the test may coincide completely with a part of the behavior to be predicted. An example might be a foreign vocabulary test in which the students are examined on 20 of the 50 new words they have studied; another example is provided by the road test taken prior to obtaining a driver's license. A lesser degree of similarity is illustrated by many vocational aptitude tests administered prior to job training, in which there is only a moderate resemblance between the tasks performed on the job and those incorporated in the test. At the other extreme one finds projective personality tests such as the Rorschach inkblot test, in which an attempt is made to predict from the subject's associations to inkblots how he will react to other people, to emotionally toned stimuli, and to other complex, every-day-life situations. Despite their superficial differences, all these tests consist of samples of the individual's behavior. And each must prove its worth by an empirically demonstrated correspondence between the subject's performance on the test and in other situations.

Whether the term "diagnosis" or the term "prediction" is employed in this connection also represents a minor distinction. Prediction commonly connotes a temporal estimate, the individual's future performance on a job, for example, being forecast from his present test performance. In a broader sense, however, even the diagnosis of present condition, such as mental retardation or emotional disorder, implies a prediction of what the individual will do in situations other than the present test. It is logically simpler to consider all tests as behavior samples from which predictions regarding other behavior can be made. Different types of tests can then be characterized as variants of this basic pattern.

Another point that should be considered at the outset pertains to the concept of *capacity*. It is entirely possible, for example, to devise a test for predicting how well an individual can learn French before he has even begun the study of French. Such a test would involve a sample of the types of behavior required to learn the new language, but would in itself presuppose no knowledge of French. It could then be said that this test measures the individual's "capacity" or "potentiality" for learning French. Such terms should, however, be used with caution in reference to psychological tests. Only in the sense that a present behavior sample can be used as an indicator of other, future behavior can we speak of a test measuring "capacity." No psychological test can do more than measure behavior. Whether such behavior can serve as an effective index of other behavior can be determined only by empirical try-out.

Standardization

It will be recalled that in the initial definition a psychological test was described as a standardized measure. Standardization implies *uniformity of procedure* in administering and scoring the test. If the scores obtained by different individuals are to be comparable, testing conditions must obviously be the same for all. Such a requirement is only a special application of the need for controlled conditions in all scientific observations. In a test situation, the single independent variable is usually the individual being tested.

In order to secure uniformity of testing conditions, the test constructor provides detailed directions for administering each newly developed test. The formulation of such directions is a major part of the standardization of a new test. Such standardization extends to the exact materials employed, time limits, oral instructions to subjects, preliminary demonstrations, ways of handling queries from subjects, and every other detail of the testing situation. Many other, more subtle factors may influence the subject's performance on certain tests. Thus, in giving instructions or presenting problems orally, consideration must be given to the rate of speaking, tone of voice, inflection, pauses, and facial expression. In a test involving the detection of absurdities, for example, the correct answer may be given away by smiling or pausing when the crucial word is read. . . .

Another important step in the standardization of a test is the establishment of *norms*. Without norms, test scores cannot be interpreted. Psychological tests have no predetermined standards of passing or failing. An individual's score can be evaluated only by comparing it with the scores obtained by others. As its name implies, a norm is the normal or average performance. Thus, if normal eight-year-old children complete 12 out of 50 problems correctly on a particular arithmetic reasoning test, then the eight-year-old norm on this test corresponds to a score of 12. The latter is known as the raw score on the test. It may be expressed as number of correct items, time required to complete a task, number of errors, or some other objective measure appropriate to the content of the test. Such a raw score is meaningless until evaluated in terms of a suitable set of norms.

In the process of standardizing a test, it must be administered to a large, representative sample of the type of subjects for whom it is designed. This group, known as the standardization sample, serves to establish the norms. Such norms indicate not only the average performance but also the relative frequency of varying degrees of deviation above and below the average. It is thus possible to evaluate different degrees of superiority and inferiority. . . .

It might also be noted that norms are established for personality tests in essentially the same way as for aptitude tests. The norm on a personality test is not necessarily the most desirable or "ideal" performance, any more than a perfect or errorless score is the norm on an aptitude test. On both types of tests, the norm corresponds to the performance of typical or average individuals. On dominance-submission tests, for example, the norm falls at an intermediate point representing the degree of dominance or submission manifested by the average individual. Similarly, in an emotional adjustment inventory, the norm does not ordinarily correspond to a complete absence of unfavorable or maladaptive responses, since a few such responses occur in the majority of "normal" individuals in the standardization sample. It is thus apparent that psychological tests, of whatever type, are based on empirically established norms.

Objective Measurement Of Difficulty

Reference to the definition of a psychological test with which this discussion opened will show that such a test was characterized as an objective as well as a standardized measure. In what specific ways are such tests objective? Some aspects of the objectivity of psychological tests have already been touched on in the discussion of standardization. Thus, the administration, scoring, and interpretation of scores are objective insofar as they are independent of the subjective judgment of the individual examiner. Any one individual should theoretically obtain the identical score on a test regardless of who happens to be his examiner. This is not entirely so, of course, since perfect standardization and objectivity have not been attained in practice. But at least such objectivity is the goal of test construction and has been achieved to a reasonably high degree in most tests.

There are other major ways in which psychological tests can be properly described as objective. The determination of the difficulty level of an item or of a whole test, and the measurement of test reliability and validity, are based on objective, empirical procedures. The concepts of reliability and validity will be considered in subsequent sections. We shall turn our attention first to the concept of difficulty.

When Binet and Simon prepared their original, 1905 scale for the measurement of intelligence, they arranged the 30 items of the scale in order of increasing difficulty. Such difficulty, it will be recalled, was determined by trying out the items on 50 normal and a few mentally retarded children. The items correctly solved by the largest number of children were, *ipso facto*, taken to be the easiest; those passed by relatively few children were regarded as more difficult items. By this procedure, an empirical order difficulty was established. This early example typifies the objective measurement of difficulty level, which is now common practice in psychological test construction.

Not only the arrangement but also the selection of items for inclusion in a test can be determined by the proportion of subjects in the trial samples who pass each item. Thus, if there is a bunching of items at the easy or difficult end of the scale, some items can be discarded. Similarly, if items are sparse in certain portions of the difficulty range, new items can be added to fill the gaps. . . .

The difficulty level of the test as a whole is, of course, directly dependent on the difficulty of the items that make up the test. A comprehensive check of the difficulty of the total test for the population for which it is designed is provided by the distribution of total scores. If the standardization sample is a representative cross section of such a population, then it is generally expected that the scores will fall roughly into a *normal distribution curve*. In other words, there should be a clustering of individuals near the center of the range and a gradual tapering off as the extremes are approached. A theoretical normal curve, with all irregularities eliminated, is shown in Figure 1. In plotting such a frequency distribution, scores are indicated on the baseline, and frequencies, or number of persons obtaining each score, on the vertical axis. A smooth curve like the one illustrated is closely approximated when very large samples are tested.

Let us suppose, however, that the obtained distribution curve is not normal but clearly skewed, as illustrated in Figures 2A and 2B. The first of these distributions, with a piling of scores at the low end, suggests that the test has too high a floor for the group under consideration, lacking a sufficient number of easy items to discriminate properly at the lower end of the range. The result is that persons who would normally scatter over a considerable range obtain zero or near-zero scores on this test. A peak at the low end of the scale is therefore obtained. This artificial piling of scores is illustrated schematically in Figure 3, in which a normally distributed group yields a skewed distribution on a particular test. The opposite skewness is illustrated in Figure 2B, with the scores piled up at the upper end, a finding that suggests insufficient test ceiling. Administering a test designed for the general population to selected samples of college or graduate students will usually yield such a skewed distribution, a number of students obtaining nearly perfect scores. With such a test, it is impossible to measure individual differences among the more able subjects in the group. If more difficult items had been included in the test, some individuals would undoubtedly have scored higher than the present test permits.

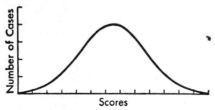

Figure 1. A Normal Distribution Curve

When the standardization sample yields a markedly nonnormal distribution on a test, the difficulty level of the test is ordinarily modified until a normal curve is approximated. Depending on the type of deviation from normality that appears, easier or more difficult items may be added, other items eliminated or modified, the position of items in the scale altered, or the scoring weights assigned to certain responses revised.

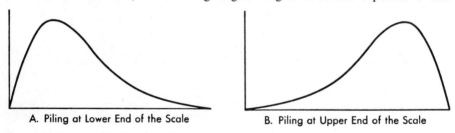

A. Piling at Lower End of the Scale   B. Piling at Upper End of the Scale

Figure 2. Skewed Distribution Curves

Such adjustments are continued until the distribution becomes at least roughly normal. Under these conditions, the most likely score, obtained by the largest number of subjects, usually corresponds to about 50 percent correct items. To the laymen who is unfamiliar with the methods of psychological test construction, a 50 percent score may seem shockingly low. It is sometimes objected, on this basis, that the examiner has set too low a standard of passing on the test. Or the inference is drawn that the group tested is a particularly poor one. Both conclusions, of course, are totally meaningless when viewed in the light of the procedures followed in developing psychological tests. Such tests are deliberately constructed and specifically modified so as to yield a mean score of approximately 50 percent correct. Only in this way can the maximum differentiation between individuals at all ability levels be obtained with the test. With a mean of approximately 50 percent correct items, there is the maximum opportunity for a normal distribution, with individual scores spreading widely at both extremes.[1]

Reliability

How good is this test? Does it really work? These questions could—and occasionally do—result in long hours of futile discussion. Subjective opinions, hunches, and personal biases may lead, on the one hand, to extravagant claims regarding what a particular test can accomplish and, on the other hand, to stubborn rejection. The only way in which questions such as these can be conclusively answered is by empirical trial. The *objective evaluation* of psychological tests involves primarily the determination of the reliability and the validity of the test in specified situations.

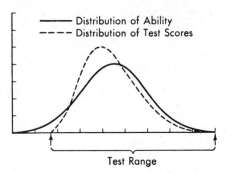

Figure 3. Skewness Resulting from Insufficient "Test Floor"

As used in psychometrics, the term reliability always means consistency. Test reliability is the consistency of scores obtained by the same persons when retested with the identical test or with an equivalent form of the test. If a child receives an IQ of 110 on Monday and an IQ of 80 when retested on Friday, it is obvious that little or no confidence can be put in either score. Similarly, if in one set of 50 words an individual identifies 40 correctly, whereas in another, supposedly equivalent set he gets a score of only 20 right, then neither score can be taken as a dependable index of his verbal comprehension. To be sure, in both illustrations it is possible that only one of the two scores is in error, but this could be demonstrated only by further retests. From the given data, we can conclude only that both scores cannot be right. Whether one or neither is an adequate estimate of the individual's ability in vocabulary cannot be established without additional information.

Before a psychological test is released for general use, a thorough, objective check of its reliability must be carried out. . . . Reliability can be checked with reference to temporal fluctuations, the particular selection of items or behavior sample constituting the test, the role of different examiners or scorers, and other aspects of the testing situation. It is essential to specify the type of reliability and the method employed to determine it, because the same test may vary in these different aspects. The number and nature of individuals on whom reliability was checked should likewise be reported. With such information, the test user can predict whether the test will be about equally reliable for the group with which he expects to use it, or whether it is likely to be more reliable or less reliable.

Validity

Undoubtedly the most important question to be asked about any psychological test concerns its validity, i.e., the degree to which the test actually measures what it purports to measure. Validity provides a direct check on how well the test fulfills its function. The determination of validity usually requires independent, external *criteria* of whatever the test is designed to measure. For example, if a medical aptitude test is to be used in selecting promising applicants for medical school, ultimate success in medical school would be a criterion. In the process of validating such a test, it would be administered to a large group of students at the time of their admission to medical school. Some measure of performance in medical school would eventually be obtained for each student on the basis of grades, ratings by instructors, success or failure in completing training, and the like. Such a composite measure constitutes the criterion with which each student's initial test score is to be correlated. A high correlation, or *validity coefficient,* would signify that those individuals who scored high on the test had been relatively successful in medical school, whereas those scoring low on the test had done poorly in medical school. A low correlation would indicate little correspondence between test score and criterion measure and hence poor validity for the test. The validity coefficient enables us to determine how closely the criterion performance could have been predicted from the test scores.

In a similar manner, tests designed for other purposes can be validated against appropriate criteria. A vocational aptitude test, for example, can be validated against on-the-job success of a trial group of new employees. A pilot aptitude battery can be validated against achievement in flight training. Tests designed for broader and more varied uses are validated against a number of criteria and their validity can be established only by the gradual accumulation of data from many different kinds of investigations.

The reader may have noticed an apparent paradox in the concept of test validity. If it is necessary to follow up the subjects or in other ways to obtain independent measures of what the test is trying to predict, why not dispense with the test? The answer to this riddle is to be found in the distinction between the validation group on the one hand and the groups on which the test will eventually be employed for operational purposes on the other. Before the test is ready for use, its validity must be established on a representative sample of subjects. The scores of these persons are not themselves employed for operational purposes but serve only in the process of testing the test. If the test proves valid by this method, it can then be used on other samples in the absence of criterion measures.

It might still be argued that we would only need to wait for the criterion measure to mature, or become available, on *any* group in order to obtain the information that the test is trying to predict. But such a procedure would be so wasteful of time and energy as to be prohibitive in most instances. Thus, we could determine which applicants will succeed on a job or which students will satisfactorily complete college by admitting all who apply and waiting for subsequent developments! It is the very wastefulness of such a procedure that tests are designed to reduce. By means of tests, the individual's eventual performance in such situations can be predicted with a determinable margin of error. The more valid the test, of course, the smaller will be this margin of error. . . .

Validity tells us more than the degree to which the test is fulfilling its function. It actually tells us *what* the test is measuring. By examining the criterion data, together with the validity coefficients of the test, we can objectively determine what the test is measuring. It would thus be more accurate to define validity as the extent to which we know what the test measures. The interpretation of test scores would undoubtedly be clearer and less ambiguous if tests were regularly named in terms of the criteria against which they had been validated. A tendency in this direction can be recognized in such test labels as "scholastic aptitude test" and "personnel classification test" in place of the vague title "intelligence test."

Note

1. Actually, the normal curve provides finer discrimination at the ends than at the middle of the scale. Equal discrimination at all points of the scale would require a rectangular distribution. The normal curve, however, has an advantage if subsequent statistical analyses of scores are to be conducted, because many current statistical techniques assume approximate normality of distribution. For this and other reasons, it is likely that most tests designed for general use will continue to follow a normal-curve pattern for some time to come. In the construction of custom-made tests to serve clearly defined purposes, however, the form of the distribution of scores should depend on the type of discrimination desired.

An Empirical Comparison of Three Methods of Assessing the Utility of a Selection Device

FRANK L. SCHMIDT
BERNHARD HOFFMAN

The evaluation of benefit obtained from selection devices has been a problem of continuing interest in industrial psychology. Most attempts to evaluate benefit have focused on the validity coefficient, and at least five approaches to the interpretation of the selection coefficient have been advanced over the years. The oldest are $E(E = 1 - \sqrt{1 - r^2_{xy}})$, the "index of forecasting efficiency" and r^2_{xy}, the "coefficient of determination." E compares the standard error of scores predicted by means of the selection device to the standard error when there is no information on the individual and the overall mean is used as an estimator of his score; r^2_{xy} expresses the ratio of predicted variance in payoff to the total variance. According to both these interpretations, a high validity coefficient is necessary to obtain substantial benefit from a selection device. E describes a test correlating .50 with the criterion as predicting only 13 percent better than chance; r^2_{xy} describes the same test as accounting for 25 percent of the variance in the criterion.[1] Neither of these interpretations recognizes that the value of a test varies as a function of the parameters of the situation in which it is used. They are general interpretations of the correlation coefficient and have been shown to be inappropriate for interpretating the selection coefficient (Taylor and Russell, 1939; Brogden, 1946, Cronbach and Gleser, 1965, p. 31).

The well-known interpretation developed by Taylor and Russell (1939) which takes in account the selection ratio and the base rate (the percentage of applicants who would be "successful" without the test), yields a much more optimistic interpretation of the value of selection devices. This model indicates that even a test with a relatively low validity can substantially increase the percentage successful among those selected when the selection ratio (S.R.) is low. Brogden (1946), in a paper which has not re-

Reprinted by permission of the publisher from *Journal of Industrial and Organizational Psychology,* vol. 1 (1973), pp. 1-11.

ceived the attention it merits, showed that the validity coefficient itself is a direct index of selective efficiency. When the predictor and criterion are continuous and identical in distribution form, the regression of the criterion on the predictor is linear, and the selection ratio is held constant, a test with a validity of .50 can be expected to produce 50 percent of the gain that would result from a perfect selection device. Thus, if a perfect procedure would yield savings of $300,000 per year, a test with a validity of .50 would save $150,000 per year. The most recently advanced interpretation of the selection coefficient is the decision theory model of Cronbach and Gleser (1965). Their general utility equation (p. 24), when modified for the selection situation (p. 37), produces, like Brogden's interpretation, a direct linear relation between the validity coefficient and utility (S.R. held constant). The Cronbach and Gleser formulation, however, formally introduces the variable of cost of testing into the equation, while Brogden's (1946) formulation does not.[2] The reduction of the general decision theory utility equation to simplified equations applicable to the selection situation requires an assumption (i.e., normality of the distribution of payoffs) which may not always be met. When this assumption is not met the general equation can be expected to produce savings estimates somewhat different from those produced by the more restricted equations and the Brogden formulation which testing costs added.

The primary purpose of the present study is to compare actual savings resulting from use of a selection device to savings predicted from (a) the Taylor-Russell interpretation; (b) Brogden's interpretation; and (c) the general utility equation of decision theory. An additional purpose is the determination of the effect on utility estimates of substituting a theoretical (i.e., normal) probability distributions for the empirical distributions of test scores in interpretation (c). (The Taylor-Russell model assumes normality of distribution for predictor and underlying criterion variable; Brogden's model assumes they are identically, but not necessarily normally, distributed.) Tiffin and Vincent (1960) investigated this problem with respect to the Taylor-Russell tables and concluded that theoretical and empirical probabilities of success coincide remarkably well. A final purpose was to illustrate the magnitudes of utilities that can reasonably be expected from a selection instrument.

Method

The utility analysis was applied to a weighted application blank developed to predict turnover among nurses's aides. An analysis of turnover in the job during the years 1969-70 revealed that 75 percent of those who left the job did so in less than two years after being hired. Among those with more than two years seniority, turnover rates declined sharply, indicating that perhaps different psychological factors were involved. Accordingly, a random sample of application blanks of 85 long-term (over two years tenure) and 85 short-term (less than two years tenure) were selected for analysis. These blanks were divided into a validation group of 40 long-term and 40 short-term aides and a cross-validation group of 45 long-term and 45 short-term aides. A total of 16 items were found to discriminate significantly in the validation group. Application of variable weights produced a scale with a point-biserial r of .46 between tenure and total score. When applied to the cross-validation group, this correlation, surprisingly, showed a small increase (to .49) instead of the usual shrinkage. This association is predictive in nature, in as much as the application data used had been gathered from a few months to a number of years prior to gathering of criterion measures. Validities of this order of magnitude have not been infrequent for instruments of this sort in the prediction of turnover (Mosel and Wade, 1951; Kriedt and Gadel 1953; Dunnette and Maitzold, 1955; Kirchner and Dunnette, 1957; Fleishman and Berniger, 1961). The fact that the performance of this scale was nearly identical in the validation and cross-validation sample allowed the combining of these two groups for further computations. Overall validity in this combined group was .47.

Cost accounting techniques were used to estimate the loss incurred as a result of turnover. The cost of a single resignation was considered to be the total cost of hiring and fully training a replacement. According to hospital estimates, full proficiency was reached, on the average, after 20 weeks of training, with the cost to the hospital per day of training declining gradually to zero over this time period. A partial breakdown of costs follows:

Cost of hiring: (includes testing, checking references, interviewing, processing application, physical exam., and overhead) .... $ 50.78

Cost of training: wages (100%, 80%, 60%, 40%, and 20% of wage of $2.38 for 1st to 5th four-week periods, respectively) $1,085.28

Cost of training: fringe benefits (pension, health insurance, etc., over same 20-week period, prorated same as wages) .... $ 105.35

Administrative cost per trainee during training period (prorated same as wages) .... $ 576.00

Overhead during training period (prorated costs of light, heat, etc.) .... $ 34.00

Total cost to replace a nurse's aide $1,817.75

The total cost figure above applies only for aides who quit after the 5-week training period. For aides quitting prior to the end of this period, total cost is the cost of hiring a replacement and bringing her to the point in training at which her predecessor quit. It was found that 22.5 percent of the aides who quit within two years left before the end of training and that the average stay in this group was eight weeks. Taking this group into account, the adjusted average cost to replace an aide is .775 (1,817.75) + (1,079.95) or $1,651.75 (where $1,079.95 is the cost of hiring and training through the eighth week, computed as above).

A total of 380 nurse's aides were on the payroll as of the end of the 1969-70 time period. During this period there had been 209 resignations (55.0%) turnover; 75 percent, or 157, of these turnovers were aides with less than two years seniority. Considering this group only, the turnover rate was 41.39 percent for the two-year period. Total cost of turnover during this period, then, was 157 x $1,651.75, or $259,324.75. This figure also represents the maximum possible savings, that is, the savings that would be produced by use of a perfect selection device. The selection ratio in operation during 1969-70 was found to be .302. In addition, results that would have been associated with a S.R. of .50, holding number of applicants constant, were examined. With a S.R. of .50, 629 (instead of 380) aides would have been hired, expected number turning over would have been 260, and maximum savings would have been $429,190.55. The empirical probabilities of turnover within two years were .1565 and

.1876, respectively, for S.R.'s of .302 and .500, as compared with .4139 without the selection device. Assuming the hiring of 308 and 629 aides, empirical probabilities were used to calculate expected number of resignations over two years for S.R.'s of .302, .500, respectively. Cost of these resignations was then subtracted from the figures (above) for cost of turnover without the selection device to give an estimate of actual savings at each of the two selection ratios. Cost of administering and scoring the blank was determined to be $.50 per applicant, or $628.50 for the 1,257 applicants. This cost was the same at the two S.R.'s and was subtracted from savings estimates.

Application of Taylor-Russell Model

The Taylor-Russell model assumes normality of both predictor and underlying criterion variable, linearity of the regression of the criterion on the predictor, and a validity coefficient in the form of a Pearson-product moment correlation. Accordingly, the point biserial r of .47 was converted to a biserial coefficient to provide an estimate of the Pearson r under those circumstances. With a validity of .592, a base rate of .59, and a selection ratio of .302, the Taylor-Russell model yields, by interpolation, a prediction of 85.6 percent satisfactory. When the selection ratio is .50, this prediction is 78.6 percent satisfactory. 1.00 minus proportion predicted satisfactory is the estimated probability of turnover for each selection ratio. These probabilities were used to estimate savings in the same manner as was done in the direct computation of savings. Again, cost of administering the blank was subtracted from these estimates. These final savings estimates were compared to those derived empirically.

Application of Brogden's Model

This model assumes identical (but not normal) and continuous distributions for predictor and criterion scores and linearity of the regression of the criterion on the predictor, and so r_{bis} was again employed. Because Brogden's model assumes a constant S.R., care was taken to determine as accurately as possible the S.R. in effect during 1969-70. Having determined this S.R. (.302), it was possible to determine results, in terms of turnover, that would have obtained with a S.R. of .500, and thus to test the model at this S.R. also. According to Brogden's (1946) derivations, actual saving at any selection ratio is equal to r_{xy} times maximum savings. Accordingly, at both S.R.'s, .592 was multiplied by the computed maximum savings to provide an estimate of actual savings. Again, cost of testing was subtracted and the final savings estimates were compared to those computed empirically. In addition, the ratio of actual to maximum savings was examined at both S.R.'s; Brogden's model predicts that this ratio will equal the validity coefficient.

Application of the General Utility Equation from Decision Theory

This general equation makes no distributional assumptions about the variables involved, although certain equations derived from it for specific situations do (Cronbach and Gleser, 1965, p. 24 and 37). This equation, in a form convenient to the purposes of this study is as follows:

$$U = N \underset{xd}{\epsilon\epsilon} \, P_x \, P_{d/x_0} \, \epsilon \, P_{o/dx} \, V_o - NC,$$

where U = utility of the instrument in dollars, P_x = Probability of a given test score, $P_{d/x}$ = probability of the decision to hire given a specified test score, $P_{d/x}$ is 0 or 1. $P_{o/dx}$ = probability of an outcome (quitting) given a test score and the decision to hire, V_o = the value of an outcome in dollars, here a minus $1651.75, N = the number of applicants considered, C = the cost of administering and scoring a single test. It can be seen that it is the negative utility that is being computed. The equation as used here estimates the cost of a given decision strategy. This equation was applied twice—once using the empirical probability distributions for P_x and P_{o/d_x} and once using theoretical distributions for these variables derived from the normal curve tables.[3] Each analysis was carried out at both selection ratios, and the resulting cost estimates were subtracted from computed costs without the blank to yield an estimate of savings. These estimates were then compared to the empirically computed estimates.

Results and Discussion

The distributions of scores on the weighted blank for the long and short term aides are presented in Table 1. It can be seen that more than 1 SD separates the means. Table 2 illustrates the direct calculation of actual dollar savings expected from use of the weighted blank at each of the two S.R.'s. In addition to the two-year figures, yearly, monthly, and weekly savings estimates are presented. Table 3 presents, for both S.R.'s the final savings estimates derived from each of the validity interpretation models, their deviation from computed actual savings, and the percent error each deviation represents. At both S.R.'s the most accurate estimate is that made by the general decision theory equation using empirical probabilities. This should not be surprising. This model makes no distributional or other assumptions, and, in fact, is essentially conceptually identical to the direct computation of savings.

The other three models appear about equal in the accuracy of their savings estimates, although the Taylor-Russell model shows a slightly higher average percent error over the two S.R.'s because of a relatively large miss at S.R. = .50. For all three models the estimates are remarkably close, in view of the fact that some of the assumptions of each are not met. Brogden's model assumes the predictor and underlying criterion variable have identical distribution shapes and that the regression of the criterion on the predictor is linear. The combined distribution of predictor scores in Table 1 is probably close to normal, but it is highly doubtful that the underlying continuous dollar criterion is normally distributed. If its distribution form is not normal or near normal, the relation cannot be linear. The normality and linearity assumptions of the Taylor-Russell model are thus also probably unmet. The decision theory equation using theoretical probabilities assumes that the predictor distributions for long and short tenure aides are both normally distributed. Table 1 indicates that this assumption is not met. Both distributions are somewhat platykurtic (flat). In addition, the long tenure distribution is somewhat negatively skewed, while the short tenure distribution shows positive skewness. Despite these assumptional violations, estimates of savings produced by these models, with one exception, show less than 10 percent error. Brogden's model also predicts that the ratio of actual to maximum possible savings will equal the validity coefficient, here .592. This ratio is .622 and .545 at the S.R.'s .302 and .500, respectively. Again, the fit of the model to the data appears quite close despite violations of assumptions.

In view of the fact that these three models appear to be about equal in accuracy of savings estimates, which is to be preferred? When the S.R. and the base rate are unchanging, Brogden's model is probably the most convenient. To use it, one need only compute the validity coefficient and determine an estimate of maximum possible savings. When S.R.'s and base rates are subject to change, the Taylor-Russell approach would appear best suited. In addition to the validity coefficient and cost esti-

TABLE 1
DISTRIBUTION OF WEIGHTED APPLICATION BLANK SCORES

Score	Long Tenure		Short Tenure	
	F	%	F	%
42-44	7	8.23	1	1.17
39-41	13	15.29	0	.00
36-38	17	20.00	7	8.23
33-35	12	14.11	5	5.88
30.32	9	10.58	6	7.05
27-29	9	10.58	8	9.41
24-26	6	7.05	8	9.41
21-23	5	5.88	20	23.52
18-20	6	7.05	18	21.17
15-17	1	1.17	9	10.58
12-14	0	.00	3	3.52
<12	—	—	—	—
N	85	99.4	85	99.4
M	32.65		23.84	
SD	7.04		6.82	
Skewness	-.53		.51	
Kurtosis	-.63		-.63	

TABLE 2
CALCULATION OF ACTUAL DOLLAR SAVINGS EXPECTED FROM USE OF WEIGHTED APPLICATION BLANK AT TWO DIFFERENT SELECTION RATIOS

S.R. =.302

Number Hired...380
Number Leaving in 2 yrs. Without Blank=[(.4131) (380)]= 177
Expected Turnover with Blank=[(.1565)(380)]= 59

Reduction in Turnover= 98

Preliminary Saving Est. = (98)(1651.75) =   161,871.50
Cost of Testing = 1257 applicants x $.50 =   628.50
Final Savings Estimate = 161,243.00/2 yrs.
80,621.50/1 yr.
6,718.46/1 mo.
1,550.41/1 week

S.R. = .500

Number Hired...629
Number Leaving in 2 yrs. Without Blank =[(.4131)(629)]= 260
Expected Turnover with Blank = [(.1876)(629)] 118

Reduction in Turnover = 142

Preliminary Savings Est. = (142)(1651.75) = 234,548.50
Cost of Testing = 1257 applicants x $.50 =   628.50
233,920.00/2 yrs.
116,960.00/1 yr.
9,746.67/1 mo.
2,249.23/1 week

mates, this model requires determination of the S.R. and the base rate. Next in terms of ease of usage is the direct computation of savings, as illustrated in Table 2. In addition to the information required by the Taylor-Russell model, this approach requires computation of the empirical probability of the outcome of interest at the S.R. chosen. The general decision theory equation using empirical probabilities gives virtually identical estimates with much more work. And the decision theory equation with theoretical probabilities is even more difficult and time consuming to apply.

TABLE 3
COMPARISON OF DOLLAR SAVINGS ESTIMATES FROM TAYLOR-RUSSELL, BROGDEN, AND DECISION THEORY MODELS WITH ACTUAL SAVINGS AT TWO SELECTION RATIOS

Method	*S.R. =.302* Final Savings Estimate	Estimate-Actual	% Error
Taylor-Russell	167,850.00	6,607.00	4.09
Brogden	152,891.75	-8,351.25	5.17
Decision Theory (Empirical Probabilities)	162,729.58	1,486.58	.92
Decision Theory (Theoretical Probabilities)	171,772.18	10,529.18	6.53
Actual Savings	161,243.00		

Method	*S.R. = .500* Final Savings Estimate	Estimate-Actual	% Error
Taylor-Russell Model	207,492.00	−26,428.00	11.29
Brogden Model	253,452.30	19,532.30	8.32
Decision Theory (Empirical Probabilities)	237,769.82	3,849.82	1.64
Decision Theory (Theoretical Probabilities)	217,241.75	−16,678.25	7.12
Actual Savings	233,920.00		

It should be noted that the utility estimates in Tables 2 and 3 are all large enough to be quite significant from a practical point of view. These figures illustrate that, even in the case of a relatively low level job with modest hiring and training costs, the dollar savings that can be expected from introduction of a valid selection device are quite large. The potential of good selection practices for effecting utility to an organization appears to be too often overlooked—perhaps because such utilities are seldom calculated or reported in the literature. A certain lingering adherence to such inappropriate interpretations of the validity coefficient as r^2 and E could also be contributing to this state of affairs. Considering the biserial validity coefficient of .592, r^2 and E are .350 and .195, respectively, in this study. Should r^2 be misinterpreted as indicating a 35 percent reduction in turnover, calculated savings at S.R. = .302 would be $90,217.75, underestimating actual savings by $71,025.25. A value for E of .195 is interpreted as indicating prediction 19.5 percent above chance level. If this E were misinterpreted to mean a 19.5 percent reduction in turnover, estimated savings, again at SR = .302, would be computed as $46,443.34, an underestimate of actual savings by $114,829.66. It can be seen that when validities are in the .30's or .40's, interpretations of this sort may indicate utilities so low as to result in a decision not to employ the instrument when in fact the utility of the device is quite high.

A final comment pertinent to the specific variety of predictor used in this study is perhaps appropriate. Utilities can be maintained only as long as predictor validities are maintained; results from a number of studies indicate that the validities of weighted application blanks decline gradually over time as labor market conditions, manpower needs, and personnel policies change (Wernimont, 1962; Buel, 1964; Roach, 1971). Periodic monitoring and revalidation when needed is clearly required (Roach, 1970).

Notes

1. Despite this fact, r^2_{xy} as an interpretation of the selection coefficient still appears in at least one recent text (Korman, 1971) and is sometimes employed by critics of testing in an effort to argue that the benefit from testing is usually quite small (e.g., see Cooper and Sobel, 1969).

2. In a later paper (Brogden, 1949), Brogden treated in detail the relation of cost of testing and S.R. to utility.

3. The separate distributions for long- and short-term aides were normalized and proportions in each were corrected for differing population base rates (41% for short term and 59% for long term). Then for each two-point interval on the scale, P_x and $P_{o/dx}$ were computed.

References

Brogden, H. E. When testing pays off. *Personnel Psychology,* 1949, 2, 171-183.

Brogden, H. E. On the interpretation of the correlation coefficient as a measure of predictive efficiency. *Journal of Educational Psychology,* 1946, 37, 65-76.

Buel, W. D. Voluntary female clerical turnover: The concurrent and predictive validity of a weighted application blank. *Journal of Applied Psychology,* 1964, 48, 180-182.

Cooper, G. and Sobol, R. B. Seniority and testing under fair employment laws. *Harvard Law Review,* 1969, 82, 1598-1679.

Cronbach, L. J. and Gleser, Goldine C. *Psychological tests and personnel decisions.* Urbana: University of Illinois Press, 1965.

Curtis, E. W. and Alf, E. F. Validity, predictive efficiency, and practical significance of selection tests. *Journal of Applied Psychology,* 1969, 53, 327-337.

Dunnette, M. D., & Maitzold, J. Use of a weighted application in hiring seasonal employees. *Journal of Applied Psychology,* 1955, 39, 308-310.

Fleishman, E. A. & Berniger, J. One way to reduce office turnover. *Personnel,* 1961, 37, 63-69.

Kirchner, W. K. & Dunnette, M. D. Applying the weighted application blank technique to a variety of office jobs. *Journal of Applied Psychology,* 1957, 41, 206-208.

Korman, A. K. *Industrial and organizational psychology.* Prentice Hall, Inc., Englewood Cliffs: N.J., 1971.

Kriedt, P. H. & Gadel, M. S. Prediction of turnover among clerical workers. *Journal of Applied Psychology,* 1953, 37, 338-340.

Mosel, J. N. & Wade, R. R. A weighted application blank for reduction of turnover in department store sales clerks. *Personnel Psychology,* 1951, 4, 177-184.

Roach, D. E. Double cross-validation of a weighted application blank over time. *Journal of Applied Psychology,* 1971, 55, 157-160.

Taylor, H. C. and Russell, J. T. The relationship of validity coefficients to the practical effectiveness of tests in selection. *Journal of Applied Psychology,* 1939, 23, 565-578.

Tiffin, J. and Vincent, H. L. Comparisons of empirical and theoretical expectancies. *Personnel Psychology,* 1960, 13, 59-64.

Wernimont, P. F. Reevaluation of a weighted application blank for office personnel. *Journal of Applied Psychology,* 1962, 46, 417-419.

The Impact on Employment Procedures of the Supreme Court Decision in the Duke Power Case

FLOYD L. RUCH

There are three basic positions that employers have assumed with regard to the hiring of minorities, especially Blacks. Stated in the simplest terms, these are:

1. Hire none irrespective of their qualifications.
2. Hire minorities to fill a quota or meet a goal regardless of their qualifications.
3. Hire the best qualified applicant without regard to their race, religion or sex.

Evaluation of Hiring Practices

The first position is not only illegal but immoral, and it is poor business as well. It is immoral because it violates the individual's fundamental human right to be judged as a person; poor business practice because many competent minority group members can be found through affirmative action.

The law that makes position 1 illegal is clearly stated in Section 701 (a) of the Civil Rights Act of 1964. This section sets forth the fundamental obligations imposed on employers and declares it to be an unlawful practice:

1. To fail or refuse to hire or to discharge any individual or otherwise to discriminate against him with respect to his compensation, terms condition or privileges of employment—because of his race, color, religion, sex or national origin.

2. To limit, segregate or classify employees in any way that would deprive or tend to deprive any individual of employment opportunities or otherwise adversely affect his status as an employee—because of his race, color, religion, sex or national origin.

However, Title VII specifically states that there is no unlawful hiring practice: "Where the employer acts upon the results of a professionally developed ability test that is not designed or intended to be used to discriminate." The Supreme Court has more to say on this point. In the words of Chief Justice Burger who wrote the unanimous opinion in the Duke Case:

> The Act proscribes not only overt discrimination but also practices that are fair in form, but discriminatory in operation. The touchstone is business necessity. If an employment practice which operates to exclude Negroes cannot be shown to be related to job performance, the practice is prohibited.

It is within the power of the employer to find this law as interpreted by the Supreme Court to be a boon rather than a bugaboo. The law permits him to assume position 3, namely of hiring competent individuals without regard to their race, color, religion, sex or national origin. But, if he is not alert to his problem he will eventually be forced into position 2, for a time at least. Forced, that is, into a quota system of

Reprinted by permission of the author and the publisher from *Personnel Journal*, vol. 50 (October 1971), no. 4, pp. 777-83.

hiring. [Editor's note: See the article "How 'Equal Opportunity' Turned into Employment Quotas," by Daniel Seligman, in chap. 9.]

The Supreme Court opinion goes far to permit the employer to implement the third practice, namely to hire the most competent of available applicants without regard to their race, religion, national origin or sex. For at another point Chief Justice Burger says:

> *Nothing in the Act precludes the use of testing or measuring procedures; obviously they are useful. What Congress has forbidden is giving these devices and mechanisms controlling force unless they are demonstrating a reasonable measure of job performance. Congress has not commanded that the less qualified be preferred over the better qualified simply because of minority origins. Far from disparaging job qualifications as such, Congress has made such qualifications the controlling factor, so that race, religion, nationality and sex become irrelevant.*

The Burden of Proof

There can be no doubt that the burden of proof is on the employer to show that his hiring standard is job-related. This burden is the same for all hiring standards including psychological tests, personal interviews, scored and unscored application blanks, police and court records, and the findings of medical examinations.

The last sentence of Chief Justice Burger's opinion tells us loud and clear what the employer must do:

> *. . . Congress has placed on the employer the burden of showing that any given requirement must have a manifest relationship to the employment in question.*

This brings up the point of the kinds of proof of job relatedness that are acceptable under the law. The Supreme Court says that the EEOC Guidelines are entitled to great deference. The 1970 Guidelines have much to say on this very important point. They demand that employers using tests or other employment standards have available "data demonstrating that the test is predictive of, or significantly correlated with important elements of work behavior comprising or relevant to the job or jobs for which candidates are being evaluated,"

There is no doubt that data of this nature clearly showing the test to be job related will protect the employer against a false accusation of discrimination no matter how large the number or proportion of minority group applicants rejected. At the same time, the minority group member is protected from unfair discrimination.

Types of Validity

There are two basic types of procedure to show validity or job relatedness: *empirical* and *rational*.

Empirical validation procedures are required by the EEOC Guidelines, when feasible. There are two forms of *empirical validation, predictive* and *concurrent*.

In the *predictive validation* design all applicants are tested prior to employment but the scores are not used in making the employment decision. Later, the scores are correlated to a measure of training or job success, to see whether those with high scores do substantially better than those with low scores. This is the most elegant method scientifically, but in the past it was not always used in its purest form because many employers held it to be costly and slow. For the small employer it is not feasible. This procedure has been followed by the Southern California Gas Company and is now being used by State Farm Insurance Company to name just two companies with whom Psychological Services, Inc. is currently working.

In the *concurrent validation* design, present employees are tested and the job performance of those who score high is compared with that of those who score low, to see whether there are significant differences. This method has been widely used in the United States Employment Service.

The two *rational* methods of validation are permissible under the OFCC Testing Order and the EEOC Guidelines when *empirical validation* is not feasible. These are the methods of *content* and *construct* validity. Both require a thorough knowledge of job demands based on careful job analysis.

Content validity may be established by a systematic observation of the job and the test content to determine that the test contains a sampling of the knowledge, skills and other behaviors required for the successful performance of the job. Thus, a typing test is a valid measure to use in hiring stenographers, although it does not cover all of the domain of stenography. The same can be said for a shorthand test. Both, used together, give a more complete sampling.

The *construct validity* of a test is the extent to which it measures a "theoretical construct" or trait. Examples of such constructs are *verbal ability, space visualization* and *perceptual speed*. When careful job analysis shows that workers must read blueprints, a test of *space visualization* is valid as part of the employment procedure.

There are many life situations in which *content* and *construct* validities are the only ones available. A prime example is the selection of astronauts where these methods appear to have been quite effective. To rule out their use would seriously handicap the smaller employers whose work forces are not large enough to support the use of more elegant validation designs. Fortunately, Title VII, as interpreted by EEOC permits the use of these methods where *predictive* and *concurrent* validity studies are not feasible because of small number of employees on a particular job.

Five Recommendations for Immediate Action

Acting upon the following five recommendations will help the employer find qualified people within the constraints now imposed by law.

(1) Make a detailed analysis of *all* hiring and promotion standards that are now being used. Among the many questions the employer should ask himself in doing this are the following:

1. What proportion of applicants both minority and non-minority are being rejected at each stage of the hiring process?

The author knows of a case in which top management was highly dedicated to the concept of fair employment, but way down the line was a receptionist who turned back 50 percent of the applicants. When asked why, she replied: "Two reasons. I turn them away if I think they won't pass the tests or if I think the interviewer won't like them." Most of the applicants were Black. Nobody knows how many good prospects were lost.

2. The employer should ask of each hiring standard, "Why am I using this? What does it mean in terms of actual behavior on the job?"

A good example is the high school or college diploma requirement. Take the case where the owner-manager of a large bakery who was a great believer in higher educa-tion required that his route men all have college degrees. Sometimes he had to relax this standard and take high school graduates. An analysis of the job performance of both groups showed the college graduates to be inferior to the less educated driver-salesmen in actual sales produced. Obviously, this is a foolish and discriminatory stan-dard.

In the Duke Power Case, the Court ruled that coal handlers may not be required to be high school graduates.

Where the standard is not job-related and where it rejects a disproportionate number of Blacks, it should be discontinued. The employer loses nothing in doing so and can gain credit with EEOC for being a good guy.

(2) Accurate records of why each applicant was rejected should be kept. A gen-eral notaton of "not sufficiently well qualified" is not enough. Say why in such objec-tive terms that these reasons can be validated when sufficient cases are available.

(3) If a general intelligence test such as the Wonderlic or Otis is being used for hiring or promotion for jobs for which it has not been validated, this practice should be discontinued until a validation study on all of the jobs for which it is being used has been conducted. If the results of such a study are inadequate, abandon the practice and set up a more modern program.

The Wonderlic and Otis tests have been so misused that the EEOC is so set against them that evidence of validity will have to be overwhelming.

At the EEOC hearings held in Houston, Texas, in June of 1970, the following dialogue took place between EEOC Chairman Brown and Mr. LeRoy R. Johnston of the Gulf Oil Company:

Chairman Brown: Would you estimate the number of general intelligence tests?
Mr. Johnston: In the various departments, I would say three or four different types. Otis, Wonderlic and the Bennett test for arithmetic are being used and a number of that type of tests. We are in the process of validating all our tests.
Chairman Brown: Are you aware of the fact that this Commission has deter-mined that the Wonderlic test is discriminatory?
Mr. Johnston: No. I'm not aware of that. I have heard people suggest that. I didn't know you knew.
Chairman Brown: But we have, by *specific decision.*

Although the Otis and the Wonderlic can be valid for certain jobs, they have often been misused and have, therefore, invited close scrutiny by EEOC. It is important at this juncture to see why.

General intelligence testing as we know it today originated in the public schools of Paris, France, in the early 1900s. French educators were confronted with the problem of separating pupils who lagged behind their classmates into groups of those who were lazy and those who were dull. To resolve this problem, the Minister of Education set up a commission of which the psychologist Alfred Binet, a young professor of the then new science of psychology, was the most active. His test contained problems selected to be objectively scoreable. These problems stressed judgment and reasoning rather than rote memory. Follow-up studies showed clearly that such a test predicted an individual's ability to *learn school subjects.*

The advent of World War I confronted the United States with the huge task of mobilizing a large armed force in a country that was peaceful by tradition and ill pre-pared to face the German military might. Group tests were developed to speed the induction and classification of recruits. The Army Alpha Test of intelligence developed by Otis for this purpose was based on the same general philosophy as the original Binet.

Shortly after World War I, the famous Army Alpha Test was revised and restandardized by numerous psychologists, resulting in a wide variety of testing instruments available for use in business and industry. The two best known are, of course, the Otis and the Wonderlic. These are viewed critically by the EEOC for good reason.

The first tests of general intelligence, developed to predict academic success, were built around the concept that people are bright or dull in all aspects of intelligence. Research during the 20's and 30's however, proved that this is not the case. Using a complex statistical method known as factor analysis, L. L. Thurstone of the University of Chicago, demonstrated that there are seven varieties of intelligence. These are called unique abilities. For practical purposes we are mainly interested in five of them:

Verbal Factor (V), is the ability to absorb and disseminate information through the written and spoken word. A high level of this ability is the most identifying characteristic of top management as compared with the rank and file of employed people.

Numerical Factor (N), is the ability to perform mentally with speed and accuracy the four fundamental arithmetic operations of addition, subtraction, multiplication and division. It is in this type of ability that actuaries and accountants excel.

Reasoning Factor (R), is the ability to put facts together to form a general principle or to apply an already-formed general principle to a particular case. Here again is an ability in which top management stands very high relative to the general population.

Space (S), is the ability to visualize the relationships of objects to one another in space. It is particularly important in occupations such as design engineering or drafting, in which a three-dimensional object is described by a two-dimensional drawing. A high level of space ability is not required in most office work.

Perceptual Speed (P), is the ability to identify rapidly and accurately similarities and differences among familiar objects. The important thing about a perceptual speed test is that the problems solved are so simple that anybody could handle them if given enough time. The score on such a test reflects the speed and accuracy with which these simple problems can be handled by the individual being tested. Perceptual speed is extremely important in all clerical occupations and is also required by the manager who must process considerable amounts of paper.

When the United States mobilized for World War II, testing procedures based on factor analysis provided a much more effective kit of tools than was available in the old general intelligence types of test. One of the outstanding achievements of World War II was the testing program of the United States Army Air Force which employed factor-analyzed tests. The psychologists of the Air Force were so successful in selecting trainable pilots that an estimated saving of $1,000 in training costs per dollar spent in testing was made.

A properly chosen battery of tests measuring unique factors that are known to be related to the successful performance of a particular job will permit more accurate selection than is possible with the same amount of testing time required by a test of general intelligence. Studies on the Army Alpha, after which the Otis and the Wonderlic were patterned, reveal that these tests measure principally three factors—*verbal, reasoning,* and *number*—but omit other factors of great importance such as, *perceptual speed,* and *space.* Jobs differ in the demands they put upon people. People differ in their abilities to meet these demands. For example, a draftsman must be high in *number* and *space,* but he need not be high in *verbal.* A file clerk must be high in *perceptual speed* but need not be high in *space, verbal* or *reasoning.* An executive must be high in many factors, especially *verbal, numerical, reasoning* and *perceptual speed,* although he need not be high in *space* unless he is in some mechanical line.

General intelligence tests are dull tools because they contain elements unrelated to a particular job. For example, the *reasoning* factor in the Army Alpha, Otis and Wonderlic is not highly predictive of the job performance of a file clerk. The employer who uses tests that measure factors that are not job related is breaking the law.

Another disadvantage of the general intelligence test for selection is that two individuals receiving the same total score can earn this test score in very different ways. For example, one applicant may be high in *reasoning,* low in *number,* and average in *verbal.* The other may be high in *number,* average in *reasoning* and low in *verbal.* Which one will make the better figure clerk? Obviously the second one.

This is such an important point that it is worthwhile to look at another example. Draftsmen and secretaries are about equal in general intelligence as measured by test. But draftsmen are higher in *space* and *number* factors while secretaries are higher in *perceptual speed* and *verbal.*

(4) If you are not now testing, start to test new applicants with unique factor tests, but do not consider the test scores in hiring. After a significant number of cases have been hired and evaluated for job-performance criteria such as supervisor's ratings of quantity, quality, safety, judgment, learning speed, industry, etc., do a forward validation.

Failure to establish a job-related battery of validated hiring standards can eventually force the employer into a quota system.

The employer must bear in mind that the personal interview is subject to challenge if it rejects a disproportionate number of minorities unless it has been validated and found to be predictive of job success. Its results must be expressed quantitatively and validated.

(5) If applicants are being tested with factored tests and there is reason to believe that the tests in use will prove to be valid, a predictive validity study on present employees using their recorded scores should be conducted. This should be done for all jobs where numbers are sufficient.

If the results are not impressive enough to meet with EEOC approval, testing should be continued without using scores in hiring until a predictive validation study on the new hires with unrestricted range of test scores has been completed. The greater the range of scores, the higher the validity coefficients that will be obtained from job-related tests.

The procedure for setting test standards for already-employed candidates being considered for apprentice training may require a different approach because of the length of time that would be involved in waiting for the trainee to succeed or fail, that is, in waiting for the criterion to mature. In this case, test standards should be set by using the concurrent validation procedure on presently employed journeymen.

Economics of Testing

The savings resulting from a testing program can be very impressive. In a recent study, at the Southern California Gas Company, it was found that a testing program that accepts 50 percent of the applicants, reduced termination rates for typing clerks by 36 percent. In the case of crewmen, the same selection ratio reduced turnover by 28 percent. Being more selective produces an even greater reduction in turnover. These results are based on all hires found to be qualified on the basis of the employment interview alone. Obviously, testing improves the batting average over that which can be obtained by the interview alone.

What does this mean in dollars saved? A report entitled *Labor Turnover Handbook 1970*, recently released by Merchants and Manufacturers Association, gives the results of a survey in the Los Angeles area which indicates that the average cost of turnover of office and technical personnel is about $1,139 per person. This means that a company hiring 100 people a year will save 30 percent of $113,900 or $34,170 a year and this is a small company. If the employer is hiring 1,000 people a year, the estimated annual savings on turnover costs would be over a third of a million dollars. [See the preceding article in this chapter, "An Empirical Comparison of Three Methods of Assessing the Utility of a Selection Device," by Frank L. Schmidt and Bernhard Hoffman for another example of how personnel managers can save money by using appropriate selection techniques. E. H. Caplan, in his article, "A Behavioral View of Performance and Evaluation," in chap. 5, discusses the importance of costing human resources.]

But this is a small gain compared to the higher work output the employer will get by selecting the most competent applicants. These savings will pay several times over the costs of doing the necessary test validation.

Test validation can be fairly complicated and many employers will want professional help. They should contact the publishers of the tests they use or are thinking of using for help or for recommendation of a local expert. [Editor's note: In the next article in this chapter, "Proposed Guidelines for Choosing Consultants for Psychological Selection Validation Research and Implementation," the criteria by which personnel managers should select an expert to help with the validation of a testing program to meet the EEOC guidelines are discussed.]

What, then, is the impact of the Duke Power Case? It forces employers to evaluate more carefully all of their employment practices. This will result in dropping some old methods and trying new ones, in discarding invalid hiring standards and seeking valid ones. However, the required investment in research will pay off not only by satisfying government requirements, but also by increasing the ability to identify in advance those employees who will perform most effectively. It also protects the minority group member in his inalienable right to be treated as an individual.

Proposed Guidelines for Choosing Consultants for Psychological Selection Validation Research and Implementation

PROFESSIONAL AFFAIRS COMMITTEE
DIVISION 14
AMERICAN PSYCHOLOGICAL ASSOCIATION

The proper use of procedures in selection and placement of people in organizations is not only desirable, but in most instances, it is required by law. It is necessary that any selection device (tests, interviews, application forms, etc.) be used in a manner that does not select unfairly among individuals. In order to satisfy legal requirements in most situations, the selection tests or other procedures must be properly "validated." "Validation" is the term commonly employed to describe the determination of the value of personnel selection procedures.

Validation of psychological tests and other selection tools requires a high degree of specialized competency and experience which is not always available within organizations, particularly smaller ones. Nevertheless, it is necessary that all organizations meet the requirements of various state and federal laws and it is often necessary to seek the professional services of persons or firms qualified to validate selection procedures. The professional standards that individuals or firms should meet to qualify for test validation work are not well known outside of the professional community itself.

The Industrial and Organizational Division (Division 14) of the American Psychological Association (APA) has prepared the following guidelines to assist organizations in the determination of qualified individuals or firms seeking professional help in selection validation procedures. There is not a single simple standard upon which a judgment about qualification for selection validation can be made (e.g., special validation license, list of recommended or acceptable persons, etc.). Therefore, the standards are termed guidelines in recognition of the fact that the burden for deciding upon candidates for validation work rests within the organization seeking such services.

Some judgment must be exercised by the person or firm having to select a qualified selection validation consultant and, to some degree, the problem is no different than that of selecting a consultant of any kind. However, most consultants (individuals or firms) with sufficient competence and experience to perform psychological test validation would fulfill the requirements of the [following] guidelines.

Certification

Most states require that persons who offer psychological services to the public, including test validation, must be certified or licensed. Requirements vary state by state, but such certification or licensing should be considered as a minimum requirement. Proof of certification or licensing may be demanded because official documents

Reprinted by permission of the Professional Affairs Committee, Division 14, American Psychological Association.

are provided to persons having passed the examination and other requirements for state certification or licensing.

Professional Membership

Generally, persons engaged in test validation work belong to the American Psychological Association (APA). Membership in Division 14 of the American Psychological Association (Division of Industrial and Organizational Psychologists) is probable. Although membership in either the APA or Division 14 is not crucial, it indicates that the person subscribes to the principles and ethics of this professional organization. Thus, membership in the APA is strongly recommended.

Education

Most industrial and organizational psychologists hold the Ph.D. degree. Some competent persons do not, but in these cases, the experience of the person should be explored very carefully. A Bachelor's Degree is not sufficient.

Knowledge and Experience

A potential consultant should be able to provide evidence of similar work and experience in the area of test validation including, if possible, reprints or reports of his researches. In the case of test validation, a minimum requirement should be that the consultant demonstrate familiarity with existing federal and state laws and regulations that are applicable [e.g., Equal Employment Opportunity Commission (EEOC) and Office of Federal Contract Compliance (OFCC), etc.]. Similarly, the potential candidate should be familiar with the Standards for Educational and Psychological Tests and Manuals published by the APA.

In cases where individuals may not have had the time to build a repository of experience, then evidence of specific graduate training in Test and Measurement Theory and Practice should be sought (preferably from a transcript from an accredited college or university).

Recent Clients

The names of previous clients should be provided in order that they may be verified. Questions about the consultant's specific tasks performed, integrity, promptness, and fulfillment of obligations could be answered in this manner.

Claims Made

Normally, a competent professional will *not* make any claims for extraordinary results nor guarantee certain positive outcomes. Such claims, if made, should be grounds for discontinuing further consideration of the potential consultant. Exaggerated claims, whether made verbally or in a brochure, are unethical and would not be made by acceptable consultants. Further, the potential consultant should not be interested in selling or promoting a unique method or device that only he can perform. Acceptable procedures are available to all qualified professionals.

Fees

No generally agreed upon standard fee or fee rate is established. The nature of the task and experience of the person(s) will figure in determining the fee to be charged. The firm seeking the services of the consultant should negotiate a fee satisfactory to each party. However, the fee should be for services performed and, in no case, should be dependent upon provisions of some "positive" or "guaranteed" results.

Negro-White Differences in Validity of Employment and Training Selection Procedures: Summary of Research Evidence

VIRGINIA R. BOEHM

The possibility of different validities for Negroes and whites of employment tests and other employment and training selection devices has caused great concern during recent years. If the same procedures used in a selection situation demonstrate either significantly different validities for these groups or significant validity for one group but not the other, the implications are serious both from the viewpoint of those concerned with equal employment opportunity and the users of selection tests. This review examines the presently available empirical data on this topic, focusing on two kinds of situations—differential validity and single-group validity.

A situation where *differential validity* exists is here defined as one where: (*a*) There is a significant difference between the correlation coefficient of a selection device and a criterion obtained for one ethnic group and the correlation of the same device with the same criterion obtained for the other group. And (*b*) the validity coefficients are significantly different from zero for one or both groups.

A related but not identical situation is that where a given predictor exhibits validity significantly different from zero for one group only, and there is no significant difference between the two validity coefficients. This situation is here termed *single-group validity*.

As the area investigated is employment and job-training selection procedures, studies in conventional school settings are not considered, although industrial training

Reprinted by permission of the author and the publisher from the *Journal of Applied Psychology,* vol. 56 (1972), no. 1, pp. 33-39. Copyright 1972 by the American Psychological Association.

situations are included. Also excluded are studies where the samples of the two groups are drawn from different sources.

Thirteen studies that cover a variety of occupations and involve widely varying numbers of Ss are discussed here. They differ greatly in techniques used and methodological sophistication. Some of the studies used experimental tests, other studies used the actual predictors used in the selection process. In some, the criterion measures used were devised especially for the study. In others, the investigators used routine company ratings, termination indexes, or other measures. Among the 13 studies, 57 predictors and 38 criterion measures are used. Only the roughest comparison across studies is possible as they have in common only the elements for which they were selected, that is, at least one predictor and one criterion, with separate correlations for white and Negro Ss in a situation involving employment or training selection procedures.

Criterion-related Validity

Before the questions of differential or single-group validities can be dealt with, the data from these studies should be examined to assess the extent of any criterion-related validity for either or both groups. Table 1 lists the studies, the occupations involved, the number of Negro and white Ss, the number of predictors and criteria, the number of correlation coefficients computed for each ethnic group, and the number of those that were significant at the .05 level (in either direction) for either or both groups.

It would appear that complete lack of criterion-related validity is a serious problem in these studies. The majority (100 out of 160) of the predictor and criterion combinations used did not yield significant correlations for either ethnic group.

In several of these studies (Kirkpatrick, Ewen, Barrett, & Katzell, 1968, Studies 1 & 2; Lopez, 1966; Mitchell, Albright, & McMurry, 1968; Ruda & Albright, 1968; Tenopyr, 1967) at least some of the predictors in the studies had been used as part of the selection procedure for the occupation being investigated, with resultant restriction of range. The predictors in these studies were generally of low validity. Since only one study (Lopez, 1966) investigated restriction of range, it cannot be clearly determined to what extent low criterion-related validities can be attributed to this cause.

The use of tests or other predictors in selection prior to their validation for the occupation or training program, in addition to creating restriction of range problems of unknown severity for the investigator, tends to exclude a higher proportion of Negro than white applicants at the outset, as Negroes tend to score lower on many kinds of tests (Dreger & Miller, 1968; Moore & MacNaughton, 1966; Rosen, 1970; Wallace, Kissinger, & Reynolds, 1966). This exclusion appears to have happened in some cases (Kirkpatrick et al., 1968, Study 2; Mitchell et al., 1968; Ruda & Albright, 1968) so that methodological problems of range restriction are compounded by small Ns in the Negro group.

Other studies that did not use the experimental predictors as heavily weighted parts of the selection procedure demonstrated methodological improvements. In one study (Grant & Bray, 1970), the investigators were able to exert considerable control over the hiring process itself, assuring that substantial numbers of Negroes and whites who did not meet usual hiring standards were employed and included in the sample. They were therefore able to maximize the chances of equating the predictor means of the Negro and white samples, removing one source of variation that tends to compli-

TABLE 1

CRITERION-RELATED VALIDITY IN DIFFERENTIAL VALIDITY STUDIES

Investigator	Occupation	Ss		No. measure		Validity coefficient	
		White	Negro	Predictors	Criteria	Computed	p<.05 for either or both ethnic groups
Campbell, Pike, & Flaugher (1969); Flaugher, Campbell, & Pike, 1969; Pike, 1969	Medical technicians	297	168	8	1	8	8
Grant & Bray (1970)	Telephone craftsmen	219	211	8	1	8	8
Kirkpatrick, Ewen, Barrett, & Katzell (1968)							
Study 1	Clerical workers	100	26	5	6	30	1
Study 2	Clerical workers	39	33	7	4	28	6
Study 3a[1]	General maintenance	30	50	2	2	4	3
Study 3b[1]	Heavy vehicle operator	39	38	2	1	2	1
Lopez (1966)	Toll collectors	80	102	4	4	16	7
Mitchell, Albright, & McMurry (1968)	Semiskilled hourly workers	830	194	1	2	2	0
Ruda & Albright (1968)	Office personnel	176	67	2	1	2	2
Tenopyr (1967)[2]	Machine shop trainees	84	83	4	10	40	12
Wollowick Greenwood, & McNamara (1969)[3]	Administrative personnel	60	60	4	2	8	5
Wood (1969)	Psychiatric aides	544	222	1	3	3	1
United States Department of Labor (1969)[4]	Welders	59	57	9	1	9	6
Total						160	60

[1] These studies also included Spanish Americans not discussed here. Two other studies in the book by Kirkpatrick et al. (1968) are not included because the Negro and white samples were drawn from different sources, and one also involved a school setting.
[2] Twelve additional criterion measures used by Tenopyr (1967) were grades earned in each quarter of the training courses. The final grades are included here and the use of the quarter grades was felt to be unnecessary.
[3] The white subsample, matched with the Negro sample on total test scores, was used in this analysis.
[4] One American Indian is grouped with the Negro sample in the data analysis.

cate interpretation of these studies. The use of a task criterion also represented an improvement in that it removed a source of potential bias from the assessment procedure.

Wollowick, Greenwood, and McNamara (1969) attempted to control several sources of variation by matching the Negro sample with three white subsamples, one matched on total test score, one on supervisors' rating, and one on salary. While other kinds of controls, for example, tenure and education, could be investigated, this study is notable for the emphasis placed on the existence of secondary differences in *S* population that frequently interact with the primary difference.

The low validity obtained in many of these studies could also be viewed as a function of the criterion measures used. Campbell, Pike, & Flaugher (1969) compare both aptitude test scores and supervisors' ratings against the same criterion, a "Job Knowledge Test," so as to be able to examine not only the validity of the predictor tests but also the validity of supervisors' ratings. Their discovery that rating differences were related to both the supervisors' and the workers' ethnic group membership suggests a whole line of research that requires further exploration. In view of the fact that supervisory ratings of some form are by far the most common criteria used in validity studies (Bennett, 1969; Guion, 1965; Owens & Jewell, 1969), the potential implications of such a finding are great.

That there might be biasing factors in some of the ratings used in these studies is indicated by the fact that the obtained validities in the Campbell, Pike, and Flaugher (1969) study using the Job Knowledge Test were quite high, as were those in the research of Grant and Bray (1970) where a performance criterion. was also used.

Differential and Single-group Validities

Because the one instance where the correlations of a predictor and criterion, while insignificant for both groups were significantly different from each other, cannot properly be considered differential validity, this discussion of differential and single-group validities deals only with those 60 instances in Table 1 where the predictor concerned showed some significant criterion-related validity with one or both ethnic groups.

Table 2 divides the number of significant validity coefficients into those significant for Negroes only, whites only, and both. The last column contains the number of instances where the correlation coefficients are significantly different at the .05 level (two-tailed test) for Negroes and whites, according to the procedure outlined by Guilford (1965, pp. 189-190).

When differential validity is strictly defined as a significant difference in the Negro and white validity coefficients, there are seven occurrences out of the 60 instances where some validity was present for one or both ethnic groups. While this is a number slightly higher than would be expected if differential validity were a chance outcome, it does not indicate a widespread phenomenon, especially since three of these seven were from the Lopez (1966) study where the total group correlations were uncorrected and the subgroup ones corrected for restriction of range.

These instances and the more common event of single-group validity which occurs in 33 instances (6 of which overlap with the instances of differential validity) can be attributed to inadequate samples in many cases. None of the studies where the *N* of both Negro and white samples exceeded 100 (Campbell et al., 1969; Grant & Bray, 1970; Mitchell et al., 1968; Wood, 1969) contributed any instances of either differential or single-group validity.

There is also some indication that single-group validity, like absence of validity, may depend on the criterion involved. Table 2 indicates that of 60 instances where some validity was demonstrated, 27 involved significant validity coefficients for both groups, and 33 were cases of single-group validity (20 cases of validity for whites only, 13 cases of validity for Negroes only). Examination of the studies involved shows that in 22 of the 27 cases of overall validity, the criterion used was something other than a rating, ranking, or grade. On the other hand, 19 of the 33 instances of single-group validity involved some type of rating criteria.

TABLE 2
DIFFERENTIAL AND SINGLE-GROUP VALIDITIES FOR NEGROES AND WHITES

Investigator	No. validity coefficients significant for:			No. cases significantly different validity
	Both groups	White only	Negro only	
Campbell, Pike, & Flaugher (1969);				
Flaugher, Campbell, & Pike, 1969; Pike, 1969	8	0	0	0
Grant & Bray (1970)	8	0	0	0
Kirkpatrick, Ewen, Barrett, & Katzell (1968)				
Study 1	0	1	0	0
Study 2	0	4	2	1
Study 3a	0	0	3	1
Study 3b	1	0	0	0
Lopez (1966)[1]	2	4	1	3
Mitchell, Albright, & McMurry (1968)	0	0	0	0
Ruda & Albright (1968)	1	1	0	1
Tenopyr (1967)	5	5	2	0
Wollowick, Greenwood, & McNamara (1969)[2]	0	5	0	0
Wood (1969)	1	0	0	0
United States Department of Labor (1969)	1	0	5	1
Total	27	20	13	7

[1] This analysis uses the actual rating sample N rather than the applicant population N from the Lopez (1966) study.

[2] Wollowick et al. (1969) report three significantly different validities. However, these are not significant when a two-tailed test is used.

It would seem that when some objective measure of job performance or a complex behavioral measure such as termination, salary, etc., is used as a criterion, single-group validity is uncommon. It seems possible, however, that supervisors and instructors may in some instances rate Negro and white employees differently enough so that predictors valid for one group are not valid for the other when a rating criterion is used.

Other theoretically possible situations that might contribute to discrimination in selection tests (although not involving differential or single-group validity) have been described by Bartlett and O'Leary (1969, pp. 4-5). These situations could result when there is a mean difference between the Negroes and whites on either the predictor or the criterion, resulting in a validity coefficient for the combined sample smaller than that for either group.

In Table 3, those instances from Table 1 where total-group as well as single-group correlations are available are divided into three situations: (*a*) those where the combined validity coefficient is numerically less than that for either subgroup, (*b*) those where it is greater, and (*c*) situations where the combined validity coefficient is between or the same as the two ethnic group validities.

It is quite clear that combining the two groups is more likely to add to the overall validity than subtract from it. There are only 3 cases out of 120 where validity is decreased by combining the groups as opposed to 23 cases where it is increased. In over three-fourths of the cases, the combined validity coefficient is between that of the two groups, as would be expected if the Negroes and whites in the same occupation were considered two samples drawn from the same population.

TABLE 3
COMPARISON OF NEGRO, WHITE, AND TOTAL GROUP VALIDITY COEFFICIENTS

Investigator	Validity coefficient computed[1]	Instances where numerical value of the total group validity coefficient is:		
		Lower than either ethnic group	Higher than either ethnic group	Between the ethnic groups or equal
Grant & Bray (1970)	8	0	2	6
Kirkpatrick, Ewen, Barrett, & Katzell (1968)				
Study 1	30	0	0	30
Study 2	28	2	2	24
Ruda & Albright (1968)	2	0	0	2
Tenopyr (1967)	40	0	15	25
Wood (1969)	3	1	0	2
United States Department of Labor (1969)	9	0	4	5
Total	120	3	23	94

Note.—The Campbell, Pike, & Flaugher (1969); Mitchell, Albright, & McMurry (1968); and Wollowick, Greenwood, & McNamara (1969) studies do not provide validity coefficients for the total group. The data from Kirkpatrick, Ewen, Barrett, & Katzell (1968), Studies 3a and 3b, includes the Spanish-American *S*s in the total group correlations. Lopez (1966) presents correlations corrected for restriction of range for the ethnic groups and uncorrected for the total group. For these reasons, data from these studies are not included in this table.
  [1]Computed from Table 1.

Discussion

The concept of differential validity has received far more attention than the data would seem to justify. There appear to be at least five reasons for this. In the first place, the practical significance of even occasional incidents of differential validity can be severe. While the data would indicate that such cases are the exception, a routine check for differential validity should be made when the samples used in validity studies permit it.

Also, the initial published research study (Lopez, 1966) showed the strongest indications of differential validity yet obtained. As has been mentioned previously, however, the statistical procedures used in the Lopez study make interpretation and evaluation of the results difficult. But since it represented the first empirical evidence in this socially relevant area, the Lopez study received disproportionate attention.

Another reason for the popularity of the differential validity concept is the use of nonvalidated tests. Lack of relevance of selection procedures is a prime consideration of those concerned with equal employment opportunity (APA, 1969; Doppelt & Bennett, 1967; Enneis, 1969; Equal Employment Opportunity Commission, 1970). Judging from the studies reviewed here, the use of nonvalidated methods for selection is apparently not uncommon. A nonvalidated test often excludes a disproportionate number of Negroes for reasons unrelated to job performance, inviting the charge that the selection process is unfair to Negroes. Since the whites fare better, they have less reason to question the validity of the procedure. What results is that nonvalidity (or unknown validity) masquerades as differential validity.

Also, there has been a tendency not to differentiate between two situations that are statistically quite different, differential validity and single-group validity. Differential validity is very apt to involve single-group validity, but single-group validity, a much more common occurrence in the data available, usually does not involve significant group differences. Single-group validity may be related to inadequate sample size or to the use of a rating criterion. The determination as to which of these two elements is most closely linked to the phenomenon depends on further research as the studies to date which use larger samples also tend to use criteria other than ratings. Whether single-group validity is more than a methodological problem cannot be determined without further research. It is, in any case, a less serious problem than differential validity. Where differential validity is proof of unfairness, single-group validity is only lack of proof of fairness.

The fifth reason stems from the confusion of differential validity with differences in mean scores. Guion (1965) addressed himself to this point:

> A difference between group means is not competent evidence of unfair discrimination if that difference is also associated with performance on the criterion. That is, the very factors that depressed test performance may also depress trainability or speed of performance or whatever criterion is to be predicted [p. 492].

While there was very little differential validity found in the studies reviewed here, there were several cases of significant differences in both predictor and criterion, resulting in similar validities. In four studies (Campbell et al., 1969; Tenopyr, 1967; Wollowick et al., 1969; United States Department of Labor, 1969) whites scored significantly higher than Negroes both on most predictors and most criteria. Two of these studies (Tenopyr, 1967; United States Department of Labor, 1969) also demonstrated evidence of improved validity when the two groups were combined (see Table 3).

Such results reflect long-standing social practices that have disadvantaged the Negro over a period of generations. Factors such as competitiveness, time sense, adherence to instructions, conformity, etc. that could be hypothesized to aid an individual in satisfactory test performance could reasonably be expected to relate to job performance also. In these cases, both predictor and criterion reflect the norms of the prevailing culture. To the extent that the demands of the culture are consistent in the selection and work situations, the validities of selection procedures should be similar for Negroes and whites.

While nonvalidity (or unknown validity) appears to be common in the selection devices used in this research, it can be concluded that differential validity is a rare occurrence in the data currently available although there are a fairly large number of cases of single-group validity. However, more research is needed in this area as even the occasional instance of differential validity can have consequences both socially and practically undesirable. The work to date must be regarded as indicative rather than conclusive. Particularly needed is more careful attention given to criterion development.

The research indicates that the existence of subtle biases in rating-type criteria is a definite possibility that needs careful investigation.

References

American Psychological Association, Task Force on Employment Testing of Minority Groups. Job testing and the disadvantaged. *American Psychologist,* 1969, 24, 637-650.

Bartlett, C. J., & O'Leary, B. S. A differential prediction model to moderate the effects of heterogeneous groups in personnel selection and classification. *Personnel Psychology,* 1969, 22, 1-17.

Bennett, G. K. Factors affecting the value of validation studies. *Personnel Psychology,* 1969, 22, 265-268.

Campbell, J. T., Pike, L. W., & Flaugher, R. L. *Prediction of job performance for Negro and white medical technicians–A regression analysis of potential test bias: Predicting job knowledge scores from an aptitude battery.* (Educational Testing Service Rep. PR-69-6) Princeton, New Jersey: Educational Testing Service, 1969.

Doppelt, J. E., & Bennett, G. K. *Testing job applicants from disadvantaged groups.* (Test Service Bulletin No. 57) New York: Psychological Corporation, 1967.

Dreger, R. M., & Miller, K. S. Comparative psychological studies of Negroes and whites in the United States: 1959-1965. *Psychological Bulletin,* 1968, 70 (3, Pt. 2).

Enneis, W. H. Minority employment barriers from the EEOC viewpoint. Paper presented at the meeting of the American Psychological Association, Washington, D. C., September 1969.

Equal Employment Opportunity Commission. Guidelines on employment selection procedures. *Federal Register,* 1970, 35, 12333-12335.

Flaugher, R. L., Campbell, J. T., & Pike, L. W. *Prediction of job performance for Negro and white medical technicians– Ethnic Group membership as a moderator of supervisor's ratings.* (Educational Testing Service Rep. PR-69-5) Princeton, New Jersey: Educational Testing Service, 1969.

Grant, D. L., & Bray, D. W. Validation of employment tests for telephone company installation and repair occupations. *Journal of Applied Psychology,* 1970, 54, 7-14.

Guilford, J. P. *Fundamental statistics in psychology and education.* (4th ed.) New York: McGraw-Hill, 1965.

Guion, R. M. *Personnel testing.* New York: McGraw-Hill, 1965.

Kirkpatrick, J. J., Ewen, R. B., Barrett, R. S., & Katzell, R. A. *Testing and fair employment.* New York: New York University, 1968.

Lopez, F. M., Jr. Current problems in test performance of job applicants. *Personnel Psychology,* 1966, 19, 10-18.

Mitchell, M. D., Albright, L. E., & McMurry, F. D. Biracial validation of selection procedures in a large southern plant. *Proceedings of the 76th Annual Convention of the American Psychological Association,* 1968, 3 575-576. (Summary)

Moore, C. L., Jr., & MacNaughton, J. F. An exploratory investigation of ethnic differences within an industrial selection battery. Paper presented at the meeting of the American Psychological Association, New York, September 1966.

Owens, W. A., & Jewell, D. O. Personnel selection. *Annual Review of Psychology,* 1969, 20, 419-446.

Pike, L. W. *Prediction of job performance for Negro and white medical technicians –Development of the instrumentation.* (Educational Testing Service Rep. PR-69-4) Princeton, New Jersey: Educational Testing Service, 1969.

Rosen, D. B. *Employment testing and minority groups.* (New York State School of Industrial and Labor Relations Key Issues Series No. 6) Ithaca, New York: Cornell University, 1970.

Ruda, E., & Albright, L. E. Racial differences on selection instruments related to subsequent job performance. *Personnel Psychology,* 1968, 21, 31-41.

Tenopyr, M. L. Race and socioeconomic status as moderators in predicting machine-shop training success. Paper presented at the meeting of the American Psychological Association, Washington, D. C., September 1967.

Wallace, P., Kissinger, B., & Reynolds, B. Testing of minority group applicants for employment. Washington, D. C.: Office of Research and Reports, Equal Employment Opportunity Commission, 1966.

Wollowick, H. B., Greenwood, J. M., & McNamara, W. J. Psychological testing with a minority group population. *Proceedings of the 77th Annual Convention of the American Psychological Association,* 1969, 4, 609-610. (Summary)

Wood, M. T. Validation of a selection test against a turnover criterion for racial and sex subgroups of employees. Paper presented at the meeting of the Midwestern Psychological Association, Chicago, May 1969.

United States Department of Labor, Manpower Administration. *Development of USTES aptitude test battery for welder, production line (welding) 810.884.* (United States Training and Employment Service Tech. Rep. S-447) Washington, D. C.: United States Department of Labor, Manpower Administration, 1969.

Employment Test Validation for Minority and Non-minority Telephone Company Service Representatives

SIDNEY GAEL
DONALD L. GRANT

Employment test bias, as is the case with test utility, cannot be gauged unless the tests are related to meaningful job standards. The position that employment tests are biased against minority group members because they usually score lower than white applicants is untenable unless accompanied by a statement regarding job performance. Invariably, definitions and discussions of employment test bias or unfair discrimination refer to the important relationship between tests and job performance (e.g., Guion, 1966). . . .

The objectives of the present test validation study were to (*a*) determine which combination of tests already in use contribute significantly to the selection of job applicants with appropriate service representative (SR) potential, (*b*) ascertain the fairness of the selected tests to minority (black) as well as nonminority job applicants, and (*c*) formulate employment test standards for SRs that will be used nationwide.

Method

Job

A brief description of the SR job is contained in the Dictionary of Occupational Titles (United States Department of Labor, 1965) under Code 249.368. The SR is re-

Reprinted by permission of the author and the publisher from the *Journal of Applied Psychology,* vol. 56 (1972), no. 5, pp. 372-76. Copyright 1972 by the American Psychological Association.

quired to integrate a wide variety of customer contact, clerical, computational, and filing activities under the pace imposed by a steady influx of calls. Examples of the work performed are (*a*) taking orders for new telephone services, (*b*) explaining and adjusting telephone bills, (*c*) recording the details associated with equipment malfunctions and reporting problems to the maintenance organization, and (*d*) notifying customers that their payments are due and making payment arrangements. Throughout, the SR prepares, handles, and files a large amount of paperwork.

Sample

Applicants were first screened for the study in April 1968, and data collection continued until December 1969. Performance evaluations were obtained upon the conclusion of training for 107 minority and 193 nonminority SRs. The age range for the total sample was 18-47 yr., the average being 23 yr. Only 1 percent of the sample did not graduate from high school, while most had some education beyond high school, and 10 percent were college graduates. Two percent of the sample had no prior work experience, whereas the majority had worked for 2 or more yr. prior to accepting the SR job. Incidentally, the biographical items mentioned above were not related to performance as measured.

Predictors

A general learning ability test, five clerical aptitude tests, and a specially developed role-play interview were administered to study participants during the employment process. Specifically the tests were:

1. Bell System Qualification Test I (BSQT I) Short Form—an adaptation of the School and College Ability Test, Level 2, published by Educational Testing Service;

2. Spelling—40 multiple-choice items with one of three spellings correct;

3. Number Comparison—100 pairs of four- to nine-digit numbers;

4. Arithmetic—100 simple addition and subtraction examples;

5. Number Transcription—25 randomly arranged numbers and 25 names to be paired with the numbers;

6. Filing—15 randomly listed names to be inter-filed with 44 alphabetically arranged names; and

7. SR Aptitude (SRAT)—a role-playing interview modeled after tasks performed by SRs in telephone contacts with customers.

Unlike the BSQT I and the SRAT which require 30 and 45 min., respectively, the clerical tests are highly speeded with time limits ranging from 1½ min. for the Spelling test to 3½ min. for the Number Transcription test. Exclusive of directions, 87.5 min. were required to test each job applicant.

Employment offices were requested regarding the assignment of applicants to the study to obtain broad and comparable BSQT I score ranges for both ethnic groups.

Criteria

The guidelines followed in designing and developing the criterion instruments were to (*a*) measure both the acquisition and application of job knowledge as objectively as possible, and (*b*) obtain direct measures of task proficiency in a standardized situation. Accordingly, a pencil and paper achievement test, the Job Knowledge Review (JKR) and an individually administered work sample test, the Job Performance Review (JPR) were developed specifically for the study by a team of SR supervisors, SR trainers, and a psychologist. The JKR was composed of approximately 70 completion and 40 multiple-choice items covering every major aspect of the 8 wk. of training and was aimed at determining comprehension and retention of company policies and job procedures and practices. The JPR required about 75-90 min. for each administration and was composed of typical calls in which SRs engage, plus the concomitant clerical work.

When a class of SRs completed the JKR, one SR at a time was oriented to the JPR, a replica of the SR work position. The scene was set by a specially trained administrator who reviewed instructions and encouraged questions about the expected performance. Prior to leaving the SR on her own, the administrator set the wall clock at 8:55 a.m., and told the SR to get ready to begin a typical work day (the starting time, the date, and several other conditions were constant throughout to agree with the available records, etc.). The administrator then proceeded to an adjoining room where telephone calls to the SR originated. One administrator initiated the calls and acted as a customer while a second specially trained administrator listened to each customer contact and evaluated the SR's oral performance on a specially prepared rating form. Examples of oral behavior rated are the way the SR opened the contact with the customer, determined the primary reason the customer called, sold new equipment and services, quoted charges for different types of equipment, obtained credit information, and closed the contact.

Proficiency measures resulting from the JPR were: (*a*) record preparation (RP), the sum of the points accorded each part of a record prepared or completed (points were determined by comparing the records to a model set with points already assigned); (*b*) verbal contact (VC), the sum of the ratings of the verbal interaction with the "customer"; and (*c*) filing (F), the number of records *not* in the designated location when the JPR was terminated.

Criterion scores were standardized by city, and standard scores were combined to form a composite performance index (CPI) by the formula

$$CPI = Z_{JKR} + Z_{RP} + 2Z_{VC} - Z_F.$$

The Z_{VC} was doubled because of its judged importance to overall performance, and the Z_F was subtracted because the raw score was an error score.

Separate analyses were conducted for the black, white, and combined samples by city and across cities. Means and standard deviations were computed for each variable. All variables intercorrelated, and statistics for the ethnic groups compared. A multiple correlation between the employment tests and the CPI was calculated in accordance with the Wherry test selection method (Stead, Shartle, Otis, Ward, Osborne, Endler, Dvorak, Cooper, Bellows, & Colbe, 1940). The two most predictive tests were combined by simply adding the raw scores. Regression equations were obtained for the combined white and black samples, and the regression equations compared using a procedure outlined by Potthoff (1966). Finally, expectancy tables were prepared and employment standards derived.

Results

The predictor and criterion means; standard deviations; sample sizes for the combined, nonminority, and the minority samples; and the results of the comparisons between the nonminority and minority sample means are presented in Table 1. It was not possible within the data collection period to obtain the desired correspondence between the nonminority and minority sample BSQT I distributions. Though the BSQT I score ranges for the ethnic groups are comparable, the difference between the means is statistically significant, as are the differences between the arithmetic, filing, and number transcription test means. Criterion mean differences are significant for the JKR and the

TABLE 1
EMPLOYMENT TEST AND CRITERIA MEANS AND STANDARD DEVIATIONS

Variable	Nonminority sample			Minority sample			Minority vs. nonminority t
	$\bar{X}$	SD	N	$\bar{X}$	SD	N	
Employment tests							
BSQT I	307.3	11.3	193	299.4	11.0	106	5.88[3]
Arithmetic	57.3	18.1	186	53.1	15.7	103	2.06[1]
No. Comparison	49.7	17.2	186	51.2	11.0	103	.90
Filing	12.3	2.6	186	11.0	2.9	103	3.79[3]
No. Transcription	29.1	6.0	184	27.2	6.1	97	2.50[1]
Spelling	37.5	7.0	186	38.8	6.8	103	1.54
SR Aptitude	2.0	.51	184	2.0	.44	101	—
Composite	336.4	13.52	184	326.6	13.15	97	5.88[3]
Criteria							
JKR	.14	1.02	193	−.24	.91	107	3.33[3]
JPR							
F	−.08	1.02	193	.17	.93	107	2.17[1]
VC	.07	1.02	193	−.12	.94	107	1.63
RP	.08	1.02	193	−.13	1.07	107	1.66
CPI	.44	3.64	193	−.78	3.32	107	2.95[2]

Note.—Abbreviations: BSQT = Bell System Qualification Test, SR = service representative, JKR = Job Knowledge Review, JPR = Job Performance Review, F = filing, VC = verbal contact, RP = record preparation, CPI = composite performance index.

[1] $p < .05$.
[2] $p < .01$.
[3] $p < .001$.

JPR-F but not for the RP and the VC. The difference in overall performance as represented by the CPI is significant with the nonminority sample attaining higher scores than the minority sample.

Validity coefficients are shown in Table 2. Six of the seven employment tests are significantly related to the CPI for the total and the nonminority samples, and three tests are significantly related for the minority sample. The BSQT I, Number Transcription, and SRAT are significantly related to the CPI for both ethnic samples. The differences between the validity coefficients for the minority and nonminority samples, except for the Spelling test, are not statistically significant.

The best single predictor of overall performance for the total sample is the BSQT I. The Number Transcription and the SRAT were identified by the Wherry test selection method as the second and third tests to combine with the BSQT I. The respective shrunken multiple correlations are .37 and .40. None of the remaining tests contribute to the multiple correlation despite the fact that three of the four tests are individually predictive. The three employment tests selected by the Wherry method are the same three tests that are significantly related to the CPI for the total, minority, and nonminority samples. The SRAT, however, was not recommended for employment office use because its contribution to test variance and predictability were outweighed by practical administering and scoring considerations.

Test fairness or bias, a primary concern, was examined by comparing the slopes and intercepts of the minority and nonminority sample regression lines (Potthoff, 1966). The results of the comparisons, along with the composite test and criterion statistics, and the regression equations appear in Table 3. Regression line slopes and intercepts for the nonminority and minority samples are not significantly different, indicating that the composite predictor is unbiased.

Test standards were established by first selecting a proficiency level that distinquished the more from the less effective performers. Several managers responsible for SR performance concluded that the total sample CPI average was a reasonable point at which to make the distinction. Composite predictor distributions were plotted separately for the more effective and less effective SRs, and the intersection of the distributions was used to determine the test cutting score that would minimize employment decision errors (Blum & Naylor, 1968).

Inasmuch as the lower limit of the second quarter coincided with the previously determined cutting score, the top two composite test score quarters were combined to form a test qualified category. The third quarter is offered as an intermediate range from which applicants can be selected only under extended tight labor market conditions. Finally, the bottom quarter is the test unqualified range. Table 4 contains the test standards recommended for employment office use and the associated expectancies.

Though the validity coefficients with the CPI range from zero to moderate (.02—.33) and the shrunken multiple correlation (.37) is not especially high, the expectancies indicate that the composite predictor differentiated the more from the less effective performers for the minority, nonminority, and total samples. As expected, the largest percentages of more effective performers are found in the test qualified range, and as the test score ranges decline so do the percentages, except for a slight reversal for the minority sample. Additionally, the percentages of more effective performers in the test qualified range differ sharply from those in the intermediate and test unqualified ranges. Nearly two-thirds of the test qualified SRs for the total sample were more effective performers, but only a little more than one-third of the SRs in the intermediate and unqualified ranges were more effective performers. Of the 140 SRs obtain-

TABLE 2
VALIDITY COEFFICIENTS

Employment tests	JKR			JPR-F			JPR-RP			JPR-VC			CPI		
	Total	Non-minority	Minority	Total	Non-minority	Minority	Total	Non-minority	Minority	Total	Non-minority	Minority	Total	Non-minority	Minority
BSQT I	40²	39²	31²	11	11	02	23²	18²	28²	22²	27²	09	33²	33²	23¹
Arithmetic	18²	18¹	11	08	13	−09	11	10	10	17²	17¹	16	19²	20²	13
No. Comparison	02	03	01	04	03	08	05	02	16	01	02	08	04	02	13
Filing	23²	22²	15	12	09	10	10	09	07	10	09	06	18¹	16¹	13
No. Transcription	09	04	11	19²	19²	15	21²	22²	16	17²	18¹	12	23²	22²	20¹
Spelling	13¹	24¹	−04	16²	26²	00	09	12	05	12¹	18¹	03	17²	27²	02
SR Aptitude	13¹	13	14	09	05	20¹	13¹	19²	00	18¹	15¹	22¹	20²	18¹	24¹

Note.—The sample size for each correlation is a smaller *n* in Table 1 for the pair. Decimal points have been omitted, and the JPR-F score was reflected. Abbreviations: BSQT = Bell System Qualification Test, SR = service representative, JKR = Job Knowledge Review, JPR = Job Performance Review, F = filing, VC = verbal contact, RP = record preparation, CPI = composite performance index.
[1] *p* < .05.
[2] *p* < .01.

ing average and above average CPIs, 26 percent are minority SRs and 74 percent are nonminority SRs. Below average CPIs were obtained by 43 percent minority and 57 percent nonminority SRs. When minority and nonminority samples are considered separately, the percentages obtaining average and above average CPIs are 38 percent and 56 percent respectively.

TABLE 3
COMPOSITE PREDICTOR AND CRITERION MEANS AND STANDARD DEVIATIONS, REGRESSION EQUATIONS, AND COMPARISON OF REGRESSION LINES

Sample	Composite test		Composite criterion			Regression equation	Significance test	
	$\bar{X}$	S_x	$\bar{Y}$	S_y	r		Slope F	Intercept F
Total	333.0	14.08	.00	3.57	.375	$\hat{Y}=.0950X - 31.6350$		
Nonminority	336.4	13.52	.44	3.64	.386	$\hat{Y}=.1039X - 34.5119$	1.04	1.67
Minority	326.6	13.15	—.78	3.32	.283	$\hat{Y}=.0714X - 24.0992$		

Discussion

Tests, singly or in combination, can be said to be biased with respect to a population (specified by ethnic background, sex, age, etc.) if they are not predictive of performance for the population or inaccurately estimate performance of its members. The purpose of designing a test validation study in which the results are separately determined for identified populations is, therefore, to determine whether the tests involved are biased with respect to the populations studied.

The study described resulted in the selection of a combination of two tests which are reasonably free of the undesired bias for two ethnic populations, that is, minority (black) and nonminority applicants for SR positions in Bell System telephone com-

TABLE 4
EXPECTANCY TABLE FOR THE COMPOSITE PREDICTOR AND COMPOSITE CRITERION

Test category	Total sample[1]		Minority sample[2]	Non-Minority sample[3]
	Predictor composite range	% Average & above	% Average & above	% Average & above
Qualified	332 & above	63	59	64
Intermediate	323 331	40	25	48
Unqualified	322 & below	32	29	36
Total		50	38	56

[1] $N=281$.
[2] $N=97$.
[3] $N=184$.

panies. For both populations, scores on the combined tests are predictive of perform-ance, as measured, and estimate performance with relatively the same degree of accuracy. Generalizing the results to other populations (e.g., Spanish-surnamed Americans), to other performance criteria (e.g., supervisory ratings), and to other oc-cupations would, of course, be questionable. The results, however, do correspond with those achieved for other telephone company occupations (i.e., installation and repair [Grant & Bray, 1970] and toll operators [Gael & Grant, 1971]).

A major effort was devoted to the development of instruments that provide meas-ures of directly relevant job proficiency. Although the overall correlations with per-formance are not as high as might be desired, probably due to restrictions in range on the predictors and on the criterion, it was shown that the selected test combination identifies SRs who, on the average, will be able to learn and perform the work.

References

Blum, M. L., & Naylor, J. C. *Industrial psychology: Its theoretical and social foundations.* New York: Harper, 1968.

Gael, S., & Grant, D. L. Validation of a general learning ability test for selecting telephone operators. *Experimental Publication System, 1971, Issue No. 10.* (Preprint).

Grant, D. L., & Bray, D. W. Validation of employment tests for telephone company installa-tion and repair occupations. *Journal of Applied Psychology,* 1970, 54, 7-14.

Guion, R. M. Employment tests and discriminatory hiring. *Industrial Relations,* 1966, 5, 20-37.

Potthoff, R. F. Statistical aspects of the problem of biases in psychological tests. *Institute of Statistics Mimeo Service No. 479,* Chapel Hill, N.C.: University of North Carolina, 1966.

Stead, W. H., Shaptle, C. L., Otis, J. L., Ward, R. S., Osborne, H. F., Exdler, O. L., Dvorak, B. J., Cooper, J. H., Bellows, R. M., & Colbe, L. E. *Occupational counseling techni-ques.* New York: American Book, 1940.

United States Department of Labor. *Dictionary of occupational titles.* Washington, D.C.: United States Government Printing Office, 1965.

Section D
The Assessment Center
as a Selection Technique

The Assessment Center as an
Aid in Management Development

WILLIAM C. BYHAM

Assessment centers can aid an organization in the early identification of management potential and in the diagnosis of individual management development needs so that training and development effort can be invested most efficiently. Centers can also act as a powerful stimulant to management development, providing self-insight into problem areas and identifying possible development actions. In addition, the method can increase the accuracy of initial selection of potential managers or salesmen, which will give the management development practitioner better material with which to work. More than one hundred large and small organizations are presently using this relatively new method; some of these are AT&T, IBM, Standard Oil (Ohio), Sears Roebuck, Olin, Cummins Engine, Department of Agriculture, G.E., J. C. Penney, Ford, Steinberg's, Northern Electric, Kodak and Merrill Lynch, Pierce, Fenner and Smith. Hundreds more are actively implementing applications. Reasons for the increasing interest in the technique are three-fold:

1. Accuracy of the technique has been proven in studies conducted by AT&T, IBM, Sears Roebuck and Standard Oil (Ohio). Candidates chosen by the method have been found to be two to three times more likely to be successful at higher management levels than those promoted on the basis of supervisory judgement.

2. Time and money are saved by combining assessment and development in the same procedure. Participation in the program is an extremely powerful learning experience for both participants and the higher management assessors who observe and record the participants' behavior.

3. Management acceptance is high because the assessment center looks valid and makes sense to management. Management is impressed by the simulations of the challenges an employee will face as he or she moves up in management and by the fact that

line managers usually make the judgment of potential and management development needs.

Assessment centers differ greatly in length, cost, contents, staffing and administration, depending on the objectives of the center, the dimensions to be assessed and the employee population. Basically an assessment center is a formal procedure incorporating group and individual exercises for the identification of dimensions of managerial or sales success identified as important for a particular position or level of management. It differs from other techniques in that a number of individuals are processed at the same time, trained managers who are usually not in a direct supervisory capacity conduct and evaluate the assessment, and multiple exercises are used to evaluate behavior.

Typical Center

In a typical center aimed at identifying the potential of first-level managers for middle-level management positions, 12 participants are nominated by their immediate supervisors as having potential based on their current job performance. For two days, participants take part in exercises developed to expose behaviors deemed important in the particular organization. A participant may play a business game, complete an in-basket exercise, participate in two group discussions and in an individual exercise, and be interviewed. Six assessors observe the participants' behavior and take notes on special observation forms. After the two days of exercises, participants go back to their jobs and the assessors spend two more days comparing their observations and making a final evaluation of each participant. A summary report is developed on each participant, outlining his or her potential and defining development action appropriate for both the organization and the individual. (See Appendix A for a description of a typical two-day center.)

The level of candidate assessment usually dictates the length of the center. Centers for identifying potential in non-management candidates for foreman positions often last only one day while middle management and higher management centers can last as long as two and a half days.

Assessment centers are most popular and seem to be most valid when the position for which the individuals are being considered is quite different from their current positions, for instance, the promotion of salesmen or technicians into management or from direct supervision to middle management where he or she must manage through others. Because the new job requires different skills and abilities than the present job, it is difficult for managers to assess the candidates' managerial aptitude prior to promotion. Thus, many failures result. By simulating in an assessment center the problems and challenges of the level of management for which the individual is being considered, it is possible for management to determine the potential of the individual for the higher level position.

Early Identification

Because of the difficulty of determining supervisory skills in most non-management jobs, the greatest use of assessment centers is the identification of potential for first-level supervision. AT&T alone has assessed more than 70,000 candidates for the first-level management, and about one-half of the assessment center operations in the United States are aimed at identifying supervisory potential.

Another increasing use of assessment centers is in the *early* identification of potential. There are many situations in which management potential must be identified at an early stage so various administrative actions can be taken. For example, AT&T has a program of identifying management potential in blacks and women during their second year of employment so various compensatory training and development activities can be planned to speed them toward management. Another example is found in firms with a commission-sales salary structure which forces them to identify potential early in order to get the salesman on a track into management before high sales income makes movement impossible. Several organizations are using assessment centers for this purpose.

Increasingly, assessment centers are being used at higher levels of management; and it is in these applications that the full potential of centers for management development is achieved. There are numerous middle management assessment centers in operation and a few centers aimed at top management positions.

Individual Management Development Needs

Assessment center summary reports are not usually go—no-go documents. Rather they detail the strengths and weaknesses of participants on the dimensions the organization has previously identified as important to success. Examples of specific behavior at the center are provided as an aid to problem diagnosis and in the later feedback of performance to the participant. Frequently the manager/assessors will make specific developmental recommendations which are also included in the report. . . . This may go directly to management or to staff experts who add additional developmental suggestions based on the needs identified.

Most assessment centers above the bottom level of management have as their primary or strong secondary objective the building of individual development plans. This is not true at bottom-level management because many of those assessed at that level will not reach management; thus, an investment in diagnosing development needs is questionable. While some developmental diagnosis may be possible for those recommended for advancement, it is not generally a prime objective in such programs.

After a number of candidates have been processed, it is possible to use assessment data as an aid in allocating training and development expenditures and in planning new development programs. An extremely useful development needs audit can be obtained by summarizing the needs of a number of assessed participants. Common areas of need can be identified for special priority. Information from multiple assessments can also aid in designing new programs. For instance, Kodak recently developed a new pre-foreman training program based on its early assessment experience. Insights from assessments of candidates for the position of product service center manager by the J. C. Penney Company resulted in the development of a totally new development plan. So few technically-trained candidates were found to have the necessary management potential that the company decided to change its whole approach to filling the position and developed a program to give technical training to people of proven managerial competence.

Stimulation of Self-Development

Participation in an assessment center is a developmental experience. As can be quickly recognized, many assessment exercises such as the in-basket, management games and leaderless group discussions also are training exercises. Thus, to the extent that performance feedback is provided, participation in an assessment center is a developmental experience. In most centers above the lowest level of management, considerable performance feedback is provided during the assessment program. A good example of the kinds of feedback provided is the assessment center program of the Autolite Division of the Ford Motor Company. Participants take part in professionally led critiques of their performance in group activities, and they watch their performance in groups by means of videotape. After individually taking the in-basket for assessment purposes, they meet in small groups to share their decisions and actions with each other, to evaluate their reasoning and to broaden their repertory of responses.

Even without special feedback opportunities built in, there is a great deal of evidence that most participants gain in self-insight from participating in assessment exercises and that this insight is fairly accurate. The evidence comes from comparing participant responses on self-evaluation questionnaires given after exercises with assessor evaluations. Correlations of .6 and higher based on large samples from several organizations have been found.

While self-insight gained from taking part in assessment center exercises is important, it is secondary to the insights gained from receiving feedback of the assessor observations. Almost all assessment centers provide feedback to participants. The amount and detail of the feedback vary greatly but are largely related to organizational level. Higher-level participants get much more information than lower-level participants. Career counseling and planning discussions are often combined with assessor feedback for higher-level participants. Most feedback interviewing ends in a written commitment to action on the part of the participant and sometimes the organization.

Combined Assessment and Training

Still another important way the assessment center can stimulate development is to combine physically an assessment program with a training program. This is sometimes done because of the sheer economics of the combination. Junior Achievement Incorporated was able to put an assessment program into the beginning of an existing two-week training program with little loss in training impact. The Huyck Corporation recently completed a series of centers in which an entire level of upper middle management was assessed. Since it is an international company, this entailed bringing in participants from Australia, South America and Europe in addition to participants from throughout the United States. Rather than have the participants leave after two and a half days as would be normal, they followed the regular center activities with two and a half days of training exercises. The economics of travel and facilities was such that these additional days of training could be added at slight increase in expense.

But most important as an argument for combining or closely associating training and assessment is the "unfreezing" process that occurs with assessment. As indicated above, even without formal feedback from assessors, center participants are greatly sensitized to their own shortcomings and open to development ideas and training. A number of companies have recognized the advantages of integrating training and assessment because of this unfreezing process. Most have chosen to follow the assessment with training designed to correct common problems such as group efficiency, sensitivity to others, public speaking, management skills and decision making. The ideal situation is for assessor observations to be fed back during the training period to maximize development.

Assessor Training

An assessor in an assessment center benefits more than the participant in terms of direct training. Between assessor training and participation as an assessor in a center, the assessor benefits in the following ways:

1. Improvement in interviewing skills
2. Broadening of observation skills
3. Increased appreciation of group dynamics and leadership styles
4. New insights into behavior
5. Strengthening of management skills through repeated working with in-basket case problems and other simulations
6. Broadening of repertory of responses to problems
7. Establishment of normative standards by which to evaluate performance
8. Development of a more precise vocabulary with which to describe behavior

While many on-the-job uses can be made of these improved skills, perhaps the greatest impact is in performance appraisal interviewing. Extensive self-report data from assessors indicate a vast improvement in both accuracy and success of appraisal interviewing. Organizations such as G.E. feel so strongly about the many benefits from assessor training that they have increased the ratio of assessors to participants in their programs in order to expose more assessors to the experience.

Assessor training comes from a formal training program prior to the center, but principally from application of the procedures as an assessor in an assessment center. It is a unique opportunity for managers to focus on observing behavior without the normal interruptions associated with business. After observing the behavior, the assessors can compare their observations with those of other assessors and sometimes have the opportunity to repeat the observation via videotape recording. The procedures learned in assessor training are put into practice and thus stamped into the assessor's memory.

The principal focus of assessor training is usually on interviewing, observing behavior and handling the in-basket. All exercises in an assessment center usually call for some combination of these skills. In addition, practice on all the exercises to be observed in assessment centers is usually provided. Any number of assessors can be trained at once, with assessor training for as many as 25 individuals not uncommon. Many organizations starting assessment centers initially train large numbers of managers as assessors to establish a pool from which to draw assessors. This plan has a number of other benefits which include providing a large number of management people with a quick orientation to the program so that they can most effectively use the reports generated. It also allows the opportunity for a rough screening of the assessors so that the most skilled assessors can be used in the assessment center program.

In most centers run by large corporations, assessors serve only once. The exception is AT&T centers where assessors work on six-month assignments. In smaller companies assessors must, by necessity, be used more often. In all situations assessors must be trained, but naturally more training is committed to the person who will serve for 20 weeks than for one week. Training for new, short-service assessors usually takes from two to five days, depending upon the complexity of the center, the importance of the assessment decision and the importance management gives to assessor training. A few organizations have cut assessor training to the point that it is more orientation than training, but this is not advisable. Training is important both for accurate results and for the assessors themselves.

Assessor Level

Assessors are usually line managers two or more levels above the participants nominated by their supervisors for the task. Line managers are used because:

1. They are familiar with the jobs for which the participant is being assessed and can therefore better judge the participant's aptitude.

2. Participation as an assessor is a developmental experience.

3. The involvement of the line management greatly increases the acceptance of the program by other managers and by the participants themselves.

4. Exposure as an assessor increases familiarity with the program, assuring most effective use of the results.

Providing broad familiarity with an assessment program is an extremely important result. Take, for instance, the common situation found in the use of psychological test results by managers. Managers usually over-rely or under-rely on test results. They have difficulty determining the correct emphasis because they are not familiar with the tests, tester or intent of the program. While the same lack of understanding can happen relative to an assessment center report, the involvement of line managers both in the development of the program and as assessors in the program gives a much wider basis of understanding. When a manager who has been an assessor gets the assessment report, he knows the basis for the observations and judgments and can more accurately weigh them against data on job performance and other available information.

A few organizations mix line managers and personnel department or other staff people. This decision usually results from a difficulty recruiting assessors or as a means of decreasing assessor training (the trained staff people lead the line managers in completing forms, etc.).

Even less frequently are professional psychologists used as assessors. AT&T has made occasional use of academic psychologists hired for the summer as assessors in their research centers and in the evaluation of very high levels of management. A few other organizations have done similar experimentation with professional psychologists as assessors but have discontinued the process. The little research available indicates that professionals do no better than *trained* line managers in performing their tasks. While the professional psychologists may have some superior observational skills, this is probably negated by their lack of company knowledge. A few organizations use a single professional assessor to do certain kinds of testing and interpreting of results.

Validity and Relation to EEOC Guidelines

To insure that they are getting what they have paid for, practitioners have always been concerned with the validity of selection, appraisal and training techniques. Since the *Griggs et al. vs. Duke Power* Supreme Court Case (1971), which affirmed the guidelines on employee selection and promotion promulgated by the Equal Employment Opportunity Commission, organizations must be prepared to prove that their standards for selection and appraisal are job-related. [Editor's note: The article in this chapter by Floyd L. Ruch, "The Impact on Employment Procedures of the Supreme Court Decisions in the Duke Power Case," gives a detailed analysis of the implications of this case.] This includes assessment centers.

Assessment centers can be shown to be job-related through their content. To the extent the center's dimensions resulted from an accurate and complete job analysis and to the extent that the exercises and procedures used accurately measured the dimensions, the procedure is valid. Center exercises often are forms of job samples just as a typing test is a job sample of a typist's job and thus possess rational validity; they make sense. An in-basket exercise obviously meets most of the criteria for a job sample but so also does an exercise measuring group effectiveness if given to executives who must spend a great deal of their time in meetings. Perhaps because of the reasonableness of the assessment center method to both participants and observers, no known charges of discrimination resulting from applying the assessment center method have been filed anywhere in the United States.

To prove a center job-related through its content, particular care must be taken in establishing the dimensions through a complete job analysis and in choosing the proper exercises and procedures to be sure that the desired dimensions are brought out. Research relating dimensions to individual assessment center exercises conducted by Standard Oil (Ohio)[1] and AT&T[2] will help in the latter step.

The superior way of establishing job-relatedness is through statistically relating job criterion such as performance ratings or advancement in the organization with assessment center ratings. An organization adopting the assessment center method should set up procedures to collect data so such relationships can be investigated. In the meantime there is strong evidence from organizations more experienced with the method that the procedure is, in general, extremely valid. While validity in one organization does not necessarily mean the procedure is valid in another, the existence of these studies would be an important consideration in any court case involving assessment centers.

There are 22 published research studies attempting to evaluate the overall validity of assessment centers applications. Fifteen show positive results, six have such small samples as to show no results, and one study based on a very small sample indicates the assessment center process is not effective. While 15 positive studies may not seem like a massive research finding, it becomes more impressive when the extremely high quality and scientific rigor of many of the studies are considered and when the research is compared with research attempting to establish results of other management selection or development programs. Even given its recent adoption by most organizations as a management development tool, far more is known about the assessment center method than most other procedures with the exception of tests.

Pure Research Studies

Two excellent research studies have been conducted under conditions that meet the most rigorous experimental specifications. Both conducted by AT&T, they involve situations in which employees were processed through centers, the results not used in any way, and later progress and performance followed up. The first study involved 123 new college hires and 144 non-college first-level managers.[3] After a period of eight years, 82 percent of the college assessees and 75 percent of the noncollege assessees who reached middle-level management were accurately identified by the center. Equally important, 88 percent of the college assessees and 95 percent of the noncollege assessees who were never promoted out of the first-level management were identified. Thus the assessment center was found to be valid at choosing both "comers" and "losers." This study differs from all other studies to be discussed in that AT&T used, in the main, professional psychologists as assessors and supplemented the usual assessment exercises with a number of clinical techniques.

The second study rating the title of "pure research" was conducted to validate

AT&T's salesman selection assessment centers.[4] Seventy-eight newly-hired system salesmen were assessed right after being hired, but management had no access to the assessment data. Later on, an experienced field review team having no knowledge of assessment center reports observed the assessees during actual sales calls and rated their performance. The validity results were particularly impressive. The assessment panel predicted that nearly one-half of the assessees would not be acceptable, and only 24 percent of those gave acceptable sales calls compared to 68 percent of the "acceptable" group and 100 percent of the "more than acceptable" group. The correlation between the assessment panel global rating and the field review rating was .51, a substantial increase in prediction compared to the multiple correlation of .33 between four paper and pencil tests and the criteria. Also indicating the importance of the assessment center prediction was the finding that supervisor and trainer ratings were unrelated to job performance.

Operational Studies

Most of the large organizations that have operated centers for any significant length of time have some validity data on their ongoing centers. To various extents, these studies all suffer from methodological flaws caused by the fact that use was made of the data in the organization. To the extent that good performance in a center affected the criterion used, e.g., promotion, use of the criterion as a measure of validity is impaired. The extent of this contamination remains a mystery; but through various statistical and experimental design methods, most of the reported studies have minimized the effect.

Being the first to apply the technique, AT&T has also conducted the most impressive operational validity studies. An early study conducted by Michigan Bell compared an assessed group promoted to management with a group promoted before the assessment center program.[5] But unfortunately, the groups were not matched. Results revealed nearly twice as many high performance and potential men at first-level management in assessed as in non-assessed groups. Another study conducted by New England Bell Company compared "acceptable" and "non-acceptable" assessed groups consisting of craftsmen promoted to first-level management and first-level managers promoted to second level. The acceptable group was "definitely superior" to the non-acceptable group according to the researchers.[6] A large follow-up study,[7] using four other Bell companies, compared three groups (N = 223) of first-level candidates assessed "acceptable," "questionable" and "not acceptable" and subsequently promoted to management to non-assessed groups (N = 283) promoted before and after the assessment program. As in the other follow-up studies, this study was also limited to recently promoted managers in the assessed group; but unlike the other studies, by denoting a "not acceptable" assessed group of those promoted, the false negative rate could be determined. Moreover, by studying the two non-assessed groups, possible halo bias due to promotion before versus after the assessment center could be determined. An attempt was made to match assessed and non-assessed groups but it was not entirely successful.

While use of assessment centers obviously improved selection odds, it was by no means perfect as indicated by the fact that nearly 50 percent of those thought to be non-acceptable actually succeeded on the job. This research and most other research indicate that assessment centers are better at predicting ratings of management potential and actual advancement than performance at first level. This is probably caused by the increasing importance of the management component of jobs as individuals rise in an organization. It is this management component that is most commonly and accurately measured in an assessment center.

TABLE 1
SUMMARY OF THE FINDINGS

Assessed	% Rated Above Average in Job Performance in First Level Management	% Rated as Having High Management Potential	% Promoted
Acceptable	68	50	11
Questionable	65	40	5
Non-Acceptable	46	31	0

By far the most impressive AT&T study followed up 5,943 assessees as they advanced in management.[8] The criterion was advancement above first-level management, the level at which the assessment results were used and thus felt to be relatively clear of bias. Individuals assessed "more than acceptable" were twice as likely to be promoted two or more times than individuals assessed as "acceptable" and almost 10 times more likely than those rated "not acceptable." In addition it was found that the correlation of .461 was raised only minutely with the use of a mental ability test (r of .463).

Standard Oil (Ohio) validity studies include a managerial progress criterion and additionally includes 12 job performance ratings and a potential rating. The findings confirm the earlier AT&T findings of the moderate validity of a center in predicting managerial performance but its high validity coefficients substantially exceed those for performance ratings based upon the interview and projective tests.[9]

IBM Studies

IBM has conducted 11 studies of its assessment center programs. All show a positive relationship between center findings and various criteria of success with more than half of the 22 correlations being statistically significant.[10] One study [11] involved 94 lower and middle level managers. From job analyses of positions held, a criterion measure of progress (increase in management responsibility) was constructed and correlations of .37 were found between the progress criterion and the global assessment rating from the center. But interestingly it was found that if statistical methods were used in combining the judgments relative to the rating dimension, the correlation climbed to .62.

Another interesting study which was almost assuredly not contaminated involved sales managers demoted after becoming first-line managers.[12] Of 46 individuals assessed as having potential for higher management and subsequently promoted, 4 percent were demoted because of job failure. Of 71 individuals promoted in spite of the assessment center finding of low potential, 20 percent failed.

Extremely thorough and comprehensive research has been conducted by Sears Roebuck into the validity of its assessment centers. Both their center used for the initial selection of management trainees and their centers to assess management potential have been subjected to rigorous study which has shown most components of the center to be statistically related to various criteria of job success.[13]

Negative Studies

These are the principal studies established in the validity of the assessment centers. Other studies have either used such small samples or questionable methodology as not to warrant discussion.[14] The two studies which might be considered negative to assessment centers also suffer from a number of methodological problems. The first is not really a validity study as assessment centers were used as the criterion rather than job performance. This study[15] seems to indicate that a thorough study of a participant's personnel file and an interview will provide information comparable to the results of an assessment center. If true, such a finding would be a wonderful cost saving to organizations. Methodological and other factors relative to the study make generalizations difficult.

The only study indicating that assessment centers are less valid than normal assessment procedures was based on 37 participants in an assessment center conducted by the Caterpillar Tractor Company.[16] Two groups of recently promoted first-line supervisors were studied, including 37 subjects assessed in an assessment center program and 27 subjects assessed by traditional methods, which included a review of personnel files and personnel interviews with each candidate and his first-line supervisor. Using supervisor rating as a criterion, the study found that the assessed group was rated above average in performance slightly more often than the non-assessed group. But both were highly accurate.

A detailed analysis of all known validity studies relative to assessment centers can be found in "Validity of Assessment Centers" by Cohen, Moses and Byham (in press). With the exception of the two "pure" AT&T research projects, all the studies mentioned above are subject to various biases, statistical restrictions in range, etc., which are typical of practical operational programs. Yet, putting them all together, the impact seems clear. The assessment center is a superior method of predicting management potential—compared with methods such as supervisor appraisals and tests.

Differential Validity

An important consideration is whether, like some paper and pencil tests, assessment centers are biased against minority groups and women. There is no published research on this question, but unpublished studies indicate that the final judgment of a center is equally valid for whites and blacks. Performance on individual exercises is different, but this seems to be somehow taken into consideration by the assessors. The area is definitely in need of research. In the meantime, a number of organizations have adopted a policy that two or more blacks must be in a center or none at all. They feel that being the only black out of 12 participants might put the black at a disadvantage.

Even less information is available about possible discriminatory effects on women, apparently because center administrators have observed no problems in this area. Some organizations with large work forces of women have segregated centers by sex, but most have mixed the sexes with apparently no problem. Again this is an area much in need of research.

Problems in Assessment Centers

Two potential problems in using the assessment center method involve the employee who does not get nominated to the assessment center and the employee who attends and does poorly.

A philosophical weakness of most assessment center programs is the reliance on the supervisor to nominate employees for participation. Some high potential employees may never be nominated because qualities of aggressiveness, curiosity and intelligence that might make a person successful at higher levels of management are not always appreciated by lower-level supervision. To get around this problem, some companies use self-nomination or put everyone at a particular level of management through a program. Other organizations have experimented with nominations based on personnel department records indicating interest in advancement such as application for educational aid, etc., while IBM has investigated the use of tests to select people for attendance.[17]

Perhaps more of a concern to many managers is the attitudinal impact on those not nominated. Again no research evidence is available, but the feeling of "not getting to show what I can do" must be present in many individuals. Such feelings are not unique to assessment centers. The same feeling can be generated in those who are not tapped to attend any kind of managerial development program. Obviously anxiety is highest where the developmental program or assessment center is *the* stepping stone up in management. Self-nomination and other methods around the supervisor roadblock seem to be the only answer, but they can be expensive.

Typically the greatest concern of management is the individual who attends an assessment center and does poorly. As noted above, he usually recognizes his poor performance whether or not he receives a formal feedback. Will he look for another job where his chances are untainted by his poor assessment center performance? Research at three companies says no, while research at one says definitely yes—but maybe it is a way of clearing out the deadwood. It appears that organizations that have made a deliberate effort to avoid problems through expert handling of the feedback process and providing alternate methods of advancement (e.g., technical ladders) experience no problem. Most organizations go to great lengths to stress that the assessment center is only one portion of the assessment process—a supplement to regular appraisal and other information. They stress that the participant has an opportunity on the job to disprove any negative insights gained from assessment. If precautions are not taken, some increase in turnover of lower-rated participants can occur. Turnover may not actually be increased—just speeded. The assessment center process speeds the realization that promotion is questionable.

Anxiety

Anxiety at an assessment center can also be a problem. There is no doubt that the assessment process is stress-provoking and that the performance of a few participants is affected by the stress. The fact that the individual's performance may have been affected by stress is usually recognized by the assessors and taken into consideration in the final assessment judgment. Stress does not seem to be an important problem.

"Crown Princesses" or "Golden Boys" can emerge from an assessment center if the organization allows special treatment of successful participants in the program. This can be good or bad. It is natural for the outstanding participants in centers to get prime developmental experiences to prepare them for positions management sees in the future. This is not making a crown prince; it is just putting the company's money where it will reap the greatest dividends. But special treatment is wrong if the individual is given special consideration on his present job. A negative effect on the morale of other members in the unit can result if the individual is seen as being allowed to do less work because he is the "number one boy."

A frequently raised fear is that assessment centers will turn out more and more stereotyped versions of the particular organization's "organization man." The only data on this comes from IBM which found that far from being organization men, successful participants in assessment centers were less conforming and more independent. Because the assessment center method brings out a much broader range of data about the individual than is typical from interviews and other conventional means, decision-making is not restricted to the superficial characteristics often associated with an "organization man."

Costs

Costs vary dramatically among centers depending on the objectives of the center, number of participants and assessors, length, location and most of all what is figured in costs. Organizations have come up with cost figures for their programs ranging from $5.00 a head to $500. The figure, however, cannot be compared and may be vastly misleading because they include quite different elements. The cost of assessors' time (including training), participants' time, and administrators' time (including preparing for the center and writing reports) depends on the length of the center and the amount of training given assessors. Assessor and administrator commitment can be cut markedly if training is conducted separately from assessment or when the company reaches the situation that assessors are being repeated, thus requiring no additional training.

Costs of meals and facilities can be figured based on the organization's experience conducting training programs. Programs on company premises can cost as little as $50, while program at a resort can cost as much as $3,000 for 12 participants, six observers and one administrator.

Exercise costs depend on the length of the program and the nature of the exercises. They generally are between $100 and $200 for six participants. There is usually a one-time investment in reusable supplies which will run about $100. These costs assume all exercises are purchased commercially. In actual fact, many organizations develop at least one unique exercise for their center and some organizations prefer to have all unique exercises.

The remaining cost considerations are start-up costs. These costs depend upon the organization's needs for consulting help. Many organizations take information from articles such as this one, order exercises and start the assessment center. Other organizations send their potential assessment center administrators to workshops on assessor training. Many others use consultants to aid in planning, assessor training, administration of several pilot programs, the initial writing of assessment center reports and the planning of feedback interviews. Consultants can make their greatest contribution in planning a center and in assessor training.

Aid in Reaching a Decision

Attendance at an assessment center is the best way to get a real feel for the concept. Many organizations have arranged to have key managers attend a center run by another company as a way of selling the technique. Some organizations are happy to have guests, especially during the assessor discussion portion of the program. If this is not possible, showing videotape recordings of assessment centers in operation can accomplish nearly the same result. These are available from the author. Another effective means of acquainting managers with the methods is to put them through a representative exercise or two. Managers quickly see the potential value of the kinds of behaviors that are brought out.

Conclusions

Assessment centers are relatively new as aids in identifying and developing sales and management potential, but the method shows great promise. Many previous management development techniques and instruments have had great popular success but have waned when the spotlight of empirical research was trained on them. Their effectiveness could not be proved. Assessment centers, on the other hand, came out of a basic research study, AT&T's "Management Progress Study"; and research has continued on the method in almost every organization where it has been applied. Much more research is needed both on general validity and on specific exercises and procedures used; but based on the findings to-date, one must conclude that the method works. It also has the advantage of great acceptability to management. But it does not work equally well in all circumstances and should be used selectively. Nevertheless the method should be added to the repertory of tools available to the management development practitioner.

STEPS IN STARTING AN ASESSMENT CENTER

The following outline represents the principal steps in establishing an assessment center:

1. Determine objectives of program
2. Define dimensions to be assessed
3. Select exercises that will bring out the dimensions
4. Design assessor training and assessment center program
5. Announce program, inform participants and assessors, handle administrative detail
6. Train assessors
7. Conduct center
8. Write summary reports on participants
9. Feedback to participants a summary of performance at center and development actions
10. Evaluate center
11. Set up procedures to validate center against a criterion of job success

While the task of starting a center may appear large and extremely time-consuming, it need not be. Numerous organizations have started operating centers less than one month after management gave the go ahead. Like most techniques that have considerable rational appeal to management, there usually is great pressure to get the program going after it is approved.

Notes

1. Carleton, F. O., *Relationships Between Follow-up Evaluations and Information Developed in a Management Assessment Center*, Paper presented at the meetings of the American Psychological Assn. Convention, Miami Beach, Fla. 1970.

Finley, R. M., Jr., *An Evaluation of Behavior Predictions from Projective Tests Given in a Management Assessment Assessment Center*, Paper presented at the meetings of the American Psychological Assn. Convention, Miami Beach, Fla. 1970.

2. Bray, D. W., and Grant, D. L., "The Assessment Center in the Measurement of Potential for Business Management, *Psychological Monographs*, 1966, 80 (17, Whole No. 625).

3. Bray andGrant, ibid.

4. Bray, D. W., and Campbell, R.J., "Selection of Salesmen by Means of an Assessment Center," *Journal of Applied Psychology*, 1968, 52, 36-41.

5. Bray, D. W., "The Management Progress Study," *American Psychologist*, 1964, 19, pp. 419-420.

6. Campbell, R. J., and Bray, D. W., "Assessment Centers: An Aid in Management Selection," *Personnel Administration*, Mar.-Apr. 1967.

7. Campbell and Bray, ibid.

8. Moses, J. L., *Assessment Center Performance and Management Progress* (ATT), Paper presented as part of the symposium, "Validity of Assessment Centers," at the 79th Annual Convention of the American Psychological Assn., 1971.

9. Carleton, op. cit; Finley, op. cit.

10. Dodd, W. E., Summary of IBM Assessment Validations," Paper presented as part of the symposium, "Validity of Assessment Centers," at the 79th Annual Convention of the American Psychological Assn., 1971.

11. Wollowick, H. B., and McNamara, W. J., "Relationship of the Components of an Assessment Center to Management Success," *Journal of Applied Psychology*, 1969, 53, pp. 348-352.

12. Dodd, op. cit.

13. Bentz, V. Jon, *Validity of Sears Assessment Center Procedures*, Paper presented as part of the symposium, "Validity of Assessment Centers," at the 79th Annual Convention of the American Psychological Assn., 1971.

14. Bender, J. M., Calvert, O. L., and Jaffee, C. L., *Report on Supervision Selection Program*, Oak Ridge Gaseous Diffusion Plant, Union Carbide Corporation, Nuclear Div., Apr. 17, 1970 (K1789).

Schaffer, A. J., *Information about Assessment Center for ES&D Program Finalists*, Memorandum from Director, Personnel Div., National Office, Internal Revenue Service, Sept. 16, 1970.

Tennessee Valley Authority, *TVA's Experiment in the Assessment of Managerial Potential*, undated.

15. Hinrichs, J. R., "Comparison of 'Real life' Assessments of Management Potential with Situational Exercises, Paper-and-Pencil Ability Tests, and Personality Inventories," *Journal of Applied Psychology*, 1969, 53, pp. 425-433.

16. Bullard, J. F., *An Evaluation of the Assessment Center Approach to Selecting Supervisors*, mimeo report, Caterpillar Tractor Co., May 1969.

17. Dodd, W. E., and Kraut, A. I., *The Prediction of Management Assessment Center Performance from Earlier Measures of Personality and Sales Training Performance*, a preliminary report, 1970 (internal company report).

Appendix A

A Typical Two-Day Assessment Center

DAY 1

Orientation Meeting

Management Game—"Conglomerate." Forming different types of conglomerates is the goal with four-man teams of participants bartering companies to achieve their planned result. Teams set their own acquisition objectives and must plan and organize to meet them.

Background Interview—A 1½ hour interview conducted by an assessor.

Group Discussion—"Management Problems." Four short cases calling for various forms of management judgment are presented to groups of four participants. In one hour the group, acting as consultants, must resolve the cases and submit its recommendation in writing.

Individual Fact-Finding and Decision-Making Exercise—"The Research Budget." The participant is told that he has just taken over as division manager. He is given a brief description of an incident in which his predecessor has recently turned down a request for funds to continue a research project. The research director is appealing for a reversal of the decision. The participant is given 15 minutes to ask questions to dig out the facts in the case. Following this fact-finding period, he must present his decision orally with supporting reasoning and defend it under challenge.

DAY 2

In-Basket Exercise—"Section Manager's In-Basket." The contents of a section manager's in-basket are simulated. The participant is instructed to go through the contents, solving problems, answering questions, delegating, organizing, scheduling and planning, just as he might do if he were promoted suddenly to the position. An assessor reviews the contents of the completed in-basket and conducts a one-hour interview with the participant to gain further information.

Assigned Role Leaderless Group Discussion—"Compensation Committee." The Compensation Committee is meeting to allocate $8,000 in discretionary salary increases among six supervisory and managerial employees. Each member of the committee (participants) represents a department of the company and is instructed to "do the best he can" for the employee from his department.

Analysis, Presentation and Group Discussion: "The Pretzel Factory." This financial analysis problem has the participant role-play a consultant called in to advise Carl Flowers of the C. F. Pretzel Company on two problems: what to do about a division of the company that has continually lost money, and whether the corporation should expand. Participants are given data on the company and are asked to recommend appropriate courses of action. They make their recommendation in a seven-minute presentation after which they are formed into a group to come up with a single set of recommendations.

Final Announcements

DAYS 3 and 4

Assessors meet to share their observations on each participant and to arrive at summary evaluations relative to each dimension sought and overall potential and training needs.

A Hard Look at Management Assessment Centers and Their Future

ALLEN I. KRAUT

The assessment center technique was pioneered by Dr. Douglas Bray and his associates at American Telephone and Telegraph Company in the mid 1950s. In the last decade, it has spread in usage to many other companies, large and small. The heart of the technique is a series of situational exercises in which a dozen candidates for management take part while being observed systematically by several raters who are usually managers themselves. The exercises are simulated management tasks and include individual exercises such as an in-basket and group exercises such as a leaderless group discussion. In some assessment centers, personal interviews and psychological tests are also used.

One of the most common questions asked is whether the method is valid. The earliest and strongest evidence comes from the work done by Bray and Grant (1966) with several hundred new hires into AT & T who were assessed and then followed-up several years later, without the data being allowed to influence their careers in any way. The raters' predictions about who would move into middle management ranks were accurate at significantly above the chance level. Similar data have been reported by Wollowick and McNamara (1969) on some 94 men from service and administrative occupations who were assessed and showed subsequent success. In this case also, the higher-rated men moved significantly further.

A study Kraut and Scott (1972) recently completed of 437 salesmen who had gone through an assessment center from 1965 to 1970 followed up on the number who had been promoted by the end of 1970. The data had been used to promote these men to first-line management, but subsequent promotions seemed unlikely to be influenced by the assessment ratings and anecdotal evidence supports this assumption. As shown in table 1, among the men who went on to first-line management after assessment, those who were higher rated were more likely to move on to second promotions.

Even more dramatic evidence on the program's validity comes from the number of management demotions. We see that salesman who are poorly rated in the assessment center were more likely to fail as managers. Again, anecdotal evidence supports the belief that demotions were uninfluenced by assessment ratings. We must also remember that the low-rated salesmen were promoted after the assessment program and *despite* their low rating. If anything, this additional screening helped to select the best of the low-rated group.

These studies and many others lead one to conclude that assessment programs have validity in predicting those who will move ahead in an organization. Many of the studies have flaws, but there is a consistent pattern of apparent validity.

Acceptability

The apparent validity also exists at another level, that of face validity. In table 2

Reprinted by permission of the author and the publisher from *Personnel Journal*, vol. 51 (May 1972), no. 5, pp. 317-26.

we can see the distribution of over-all rating awarded to the salesmen in our study. A very substantial proportion are poorly rated even though all of these men were rated promotable as a condition of nomination to attend. Discriminations of those who are judged to have more or less management potential are certainly being made. We know from the work of Greenwood and McNamara (1967) that they are also made with satisfactory reliability (r's mostly in the .70s and .80s). Interviews reveal that management observers generally feel the program is valid, the exercises seem reasonable and they can make discriminations which are meaningful to them.

TABLE 1
MOBILITY OF ASSESSMENT CANDIDATES AFTER BECOMING
FIRST-LINE SALES MANAGERS

Original Assessment Rating (of Ultimate Potential)	No. Promoted to First-Line Manager	A % Promoted to Higher Levels	B % Demoted from First-Line Manager	
Executive Management	12	42	0	
				— 4
Higher Management	34	50	6	
Second-Line Management	50	30	14	14
First-Line Management	40	15	20	
				—20
Remain Non-Management	31	13	19	
Over-all	167	28	14	14
		$X^2 = 16.18$ $p<.01$	$X^2 = 5.82$ $p<.22$	$X^2 = 5.57$ $p<.07$

(From Kraut & Scott, 1972)

Face validity seems to extend to the participants themselves. This conclusion comes from data collected by the writer and several colleagues on similar assessment programs in several countries. Although the numbers of people in these studies are relatively small and the questions are not always worded identically, the major thrust of the evidence is clear. As shown in table 3, the assessees see the technique as really getting at the abilities important to being a manager.

This face validity on the part of most assessees goes even further. As shown in table 4, most of them also feel that this data would be useful in making promotional decisions in the selection of first-line managers.

Morality

Doubts about assessment centers have been thought of, but less often expressed, at another level—that of morality. Some people wonder whether assessment centers are morally proper. To judge the morality we must examine the consequences of the process and not merely the process itself. The consequences have to be compared against the effect of existing promotional systems. This comparison shows that assessment programs are more likely to encourage decision making about promotions to be made openly and objectively, with agreed upon standards, and based on relevant, systemically gathered data. Further, the explicitness of this method, contrasted with the relative invisibility of existing promotional systems, helps us to evaluate its appropriateness.

Doubts about the morality of assessment programs rest largely on a failure to critically examine current systems of promotional decision making. We must recognize that promotional decisions are continually being made, even in the absence of assessment centers, and usually on an inadequate basis. From what we know so far, the management assessment technique seems to be a morally superior technique.

TABLE 2

PROMOTION AND SEPARATION RATES OF SALES NON-MANAGEMENT CANDIDATES
ASSESSED FROM 1965 TO 1970

Original Assessment Rating (of Ultimate Potential)	A Distribution of Ratings		B % Promoted to First-Line Manager	C % Later Separated From Company
	No.	%		
Executive Management	14	3	86	0
Higher Management	57	13	60	5
Second-Line Management	114	26	44	5
First-Line Management	123	28	33	5
Remain Non-Management	129	30	24	3
Over-all	437	100	35	4
			$X^2 = 38.69$	
			$p < .001$	N.S.

(From Kraut & Scott, 1972)

The advantages of a formal assessment approach are also apparent if we compare it to typical promotional systems in most companies on a psychometric basis. The typical system, with heavy reliance on the immediate manager, is overshadowed on several counts. The assessment center technique offers evaluations from multiple raters, who tend to be objective and trained to make judgments of management skills, based on attentive observation of relevant standardized tasks, with all candidates being compared on a common yardstick.

Value Added

At another level of validity, one must ask how much an assessment program adds to existing promotional systems. After all, current systems operate fairly well, according to many executives. Again, some of the early AT & T studies present some of the best evidence.

Campbell and Bray (1967) compared 40 first-line managers promoted before an assessment program was installed to 40 managers assessed and then promoted. Nearly twice as many among the assessed group were rated higher on both management job performance and future potential. In this case, the assessment program seems to have had a strong positive effect.

In a later and larger AT & T study (also reported by Campbell and Bray, 1967), high rated managers were judged higher on job performance only slightly more often than men not assessed, or rated as not acceptable, as shown in table 5. However, considerably more were rated as having higher future potential. It may be that the performance of first-line managers in this company is heavily dependent on technical skills which the men carry into that level of management and that the power of the assessment center shows up primarily when they are considered for higher levels of management.

TABLE 3
ASSESSORS' OPINIONS: FACE VALIDITY

"To what extent do you believe the assessment program measures important qualitities required of (your company's) managers?"

		To a Very Great Extent	A Great Extent	To A Sufficient Extent	A Moderate Extent	Not Very Much	Not At All
United Kingdom	(11)	36%	55	N/A	9	0	0
Japan	(36)	47%	34	N/A	19	0	0
Germany I	(36)	11%	31	50	3	3	0

"Does It Appear To You That the Assessment Program Measures Many of the Important Qualities Required of Effective Managers?"

		Yes	No	No Opinion
U.S.A.	(138)	74%	18	8

TABLE 4
ASSESSEES' OPINION: USE FOR SELECTION
"To what extent do you believe assessment information could be used to help in the selection of employees for promotion to first-line management?"

		Very Good for This Purpose	Good	Fair	Poor	Very Poor
United Kingdom	(11)	73%	27	0	0	0
Japan	(36)	14%	69	14	3	0
Germany I	(36)	8%	53	30	6	3

"Do you believe the assessment program can give valid predictions about a person's ability and future success as a manager?"

		Yes. Very Good Statement	Yes, Useful Statement	Only Partly Useful	No, Only Partly Relevant	No, Nothing
Germany I	(60)	22%	51	25	2	0
Germany II	(70)	30%	62	7	1	0
					(Undecided)	

"Do you believe that assessment program information should be used to help in the selection and promotion of men to first-line management?"

		Yes	No	No Opinion
U.S.A.	(135)	47%	47	7

A study done by John Hinrichs (1969) in a large technology-based company suggests where the advantage of the assessment program may lie. He compared the assessment ratings on 47 men to the ratings independently given by two executives after a review of the men's personnel jackets. The two sets of ratings overlapped considerably ($r = .47$) but, as shown in table 6, the assessment ratings correlated significantly with an outside criterion of relative salary standing ($r = .37$) whereas the executive ratings were insignificantly correlated with the criterion ($r = .10$). The two sets of ratings also overlap considerably on the three major factors tapped by the assessment program except for one. This factor, based on observed interpersonal activity, is exactly what contributed the greatest amount of unique variance to the criterion, as well as to the over-all assessment itself. Incidentally, the interrater reliability of the two executives was only .56 compared to considerably higher reliabilities typically reported for the assessment program.

Impact on the Organization

When an organization sees this method as having value and installs it, what is the impact on the selection system? One fear is that it may undermine the first-line

TABLE 5
PERCENTAGE OF MEN DESIGNATED AS (A) ABOVE AVERAGE PERFORMERS
AND (B) HIGH POTENTIAL FOR ADVANCEMENT

	Total	High Performance	High Potential
Assessed Men			
Acceptable	136	68	50
Questionable	61	65	40
Not Acceptable	26	46	31
Men Not Assessed			
Promoted Since Pgm.	132	63	19
Promoted Before Pgm.	151	55	20

(From Campbell & Bray, 1967)

manager's position. But generally, a manager nominating a subordinate to an assessment center is in exactly the same position as before, namely, recommending his man to a higher level manager who is asked to choose between several eligible candidates. In most organizations without assessment programs, the manager's nominees are not automatically promoted. Thus, assessment data becomes an additional input for the higher level decision maker to use.

From another side, different critics may respond, "Doesn't this method serve merely to perpetuate the existing management system, breed conformity and fail to select the different kinds of talent needed for the future?" There may be some truth in this question. According to some research by Dodd and Kraut (1970), men nominated to attend assessment centers were more likely to be lower in independence and higher on conformity, as measured by the Gordon Survey of Interpersonal Values, than their peers who were not nominated. But these characteristics were unrelated to success in the assessment centers. Still, managers may have valid reasons for not nominating these particular non-conformists. Perhaps we should treat the manager's judgment as a moderator variable along with other measures which are useful predictors.

What techniques can be used to overcome blocks to the nomination of deserving candidates? The most obvious is to invite candidates to nominate themselves to attend the assessment centers. The self-nominations have been used by some companies with great success. We should also consider the use of nomination by peers, or promising test scores, or other unorthodox techniques which might foster greater opportunities to talented individuals.

TABLE 6
CORRELATION OF TWO PARALLEL EVALUATIONS OF MANAGEMENT
POTENTIAL TO OTHER CRITERION (N=47)

Criterion	*A* Over-all Assessment Rating	*B* Personnel Jacket Evaluation	Contribution Made to Criterion Controlling for Existing Data (Partial R_1 A • B)
Relative Salary Standing	.37[1]	.10	.37[1]
Assessment Factors:			
1. Activity	.78[1]	.49[1]	.72[1]
2. Administrative	.50[1]	.48[1]	.36[1]
3. Stress Resistance	.25	.26	.15

[1] p<.05
(From Hinricks, 1969)

How to select men who will be suitable for the demands of the future is a difficult challenge, although a surmountable one, if we have an idea of what kind of characteristics, behaviors and skills are required. Appropriate exercises could be developed. But there is not yet a clear consensus as to what the future demands will be or how soon they will be demanded. We can get some clues by looking at the trends within our own organizations and looking at trends in organizations generally, and making educated guesses about a few years from now. In the meantime, it seems sensible to select people who can function well in today's organization. It's also realistic to expect that these people are the most likely to be adaptable to the demands of tomorrow's organization.

Characteristics Measured

Having gotten the right people into the assessment center, we might ask if we are really measuring relevant characteristics. It seems likely that we are doing so only in part. Most assessment programs are not based on an empirical study of the manager's role, as might be done through careful job analysis or a critical incident study. At best, they are based largely on a review of the research literature and the judgment of executives in the organization as to what makes for an effective manager. At worst, they tend to be copies of programs in other companies. As a result, various programs differ widely in the characteristics they measure, although there is a good deal of overlap.

Assessment programs generally measure administrative skills and to a much greater degree they measure emergent leadership skills. By contrast, there are some important characteristics rarely captured by current programs. Perhaps it is too much to expect relatively short programs to tap the skills related to building trust, confidence and team work, but at least we must recognize this limitation. Also, we should recognize that many people may act like capable managers if placed in such a role, although they may not have the ascendancy to wrench such a position from other candidates. People generally may act somewhat differently when placed in situations where they are more familiar and confident of the existing conditions and also expect to live with the consequences of their actions. Fortunately, it seems that most assessment center observers are astute enough to make some necessary allowances. Still, if we think about measuring relevant skills via management assessment programs, we must admit there is a great deal of room for improvement.

A related question about measurement is whether people behave naturally in assessment situations. On the one hand, we are told that some people show up poorly in such situations either because they choke up or because the situation is merely artificial. On the other hand, we are also told that some people distort their real selves to look good. But these adept games players may not be equally good in real life. Again, the evidence on this issue is sparse. Of course, we can assume that most people put into an assessment situation will try to look as good as they can. It may be that the ability to discern and operate on the relevant dimensions of the assessee's role is the major clue as to how one will discern and operate on relevant dimensions if put into a managerial role.

To the extent that the assessment center exercises are properly built, they will be work samples of the managerial role. As such, we would expect that they predict fairly well the performance in the actual managerial role. Research done by Carleton (1970) on Sohio's assessment experience supports such an assumption. On a sample of 122 men, he compared assessment center ratings on thirteen behavioral characteristics to supervisory ratings of the same behaviors several years later, after the men were promoted to managerial jobs. He found moderately high levels of consistency (.30's and .40's). Apparently, behaviors in assessment centers are somewhat comparable to behavior in actual managerial situations. Obviously, more research on this point would be very desirable.

Impact on Careers

Critics sometimes ask if two days' observation is enough to decide a man's entire career. The question is a red herring in two ways. First, we must recognize and admit that many promotional decisions are currently made on much less than two days' observation. The results of a twenty-minute speech, a lunch time conversation or a brief field visit may be the basis for an executive's decision to promote one man over another. The assessment center may represent two days' more of observation than existed before.

Secondly, the results are not intended to cast a final die on any man's entire career. Certainly, they impact his next promotional move, but even here the effect of a low rating is not quite a "kiss of death." The promotion rates associated with various assessment rating in our salesmen's study are shown in table 1. Admittedly, a poor rating slows one down, but the promotion rates for the lowest rated group is still two-thirds of the average of the total group.

This table also answers the fears that such a program must create "crown princes." Overall, only a third of all those assessed had been promoted by the end of 1970. Certainly this is not enough for program attendance alone to be a sign of being a "crown prince." The table also dampens our fears that a high rating in the program will have a "golden boy" effect. A high rating in the program increases one's chances of moving ahead, but does not seem to guarantee it. Promotions seem to be influenced by other things as well and not necessarily assured by a high assessment rating.

Incidentally, the fear of overly impacting a man's career with the assessment judgment would be minimized, if the over-all assessment rating does not express a person's *ultimate* career potential. It should express simply how well qualified he is at the present time to move to the next level job. This judgment is likely to be more accurate, more acceptable and less abused. The data should also be discarded for any decision making purpose after two years or so.

Another negative effect of assessment programs is a possible demoralization of those who perform poorly. If this might lead to the loss of trained, competent people, it would be very undesirable. Table 2 shows the separation rates of salesmen who got different assessment ratings. The proportion of the bottom rated people does not differ significantly from the top rated people. If we judge by attrition rates, the program does not seem to demoralize.

Impact of Stress

Perhaps this criterion of negative impact is too long term. Some critics have raised the issue of short-term negative impacts. In particular, they ask if the programs are not too stressful. Certainly the exercises involve a fair amount of stress, although nothing like that associated with sensitivity training. And attempts are made in many programs to keep stress to an acceptable level. This is done variously by adjusting the difficulty level of exercises, thoroughly informing participants about the program in advance, inviting only those judged to be promotable, making it easier to decline a program invitation, and being sensitive and supportive with persons manifesting signs of anxiety.

More research needs to be done on the degree and effects of stress. In the meantime, we must recognize that stress is often a fundamental part of the manager's job. Reactions to reasonable amounts of stress are important data in evaluating suitability for management and are rated in most assessment programs.

Developmental Segments

Some recent innovations in assessment programs may sharply influence the participants' reactions to stress as well as to poor performance. Many such programs have added significant development portions to the assessment procedures. A typical development session will add two or three days' activities to an assessment program with a specific purpose of integrating the two segments. Like other development programs, it may utilize films, discussions and outside speakers. Unlike most other programs, it will typically include videotape playbacks of the assessment exercises and a personal interview providing feedback on one's assessment performance, during which time specific development plans will be sketched out.

Such programs capitalize on the unusually high motivation of the assessees to learn more about the management skills just tested. The assessees want very much to develop their communications and leadership skills, to understand group dynamics and so on. The developmental portion also permits individuals to decompress from the intensive climate of the preceding days in a supportive climate. Judging by observations made during this period, the result is for participants to have a more realistic and positive self-image before leaving. The extra days of training have the effect of visibly affirming the company's interest in them and its sincerity in regarding them as its most promising people. Since most of these people have, in fact, been judged promotable by their nominating managers and many of them will be promoted, the extra developmental session can also be seen as an especially meaningful course in premanagement training.

TABLE 7
ASSESSEES' OPINIONS: SELF-DEVELOPMENT

"How rate the program . . . for your self-development?"

A

United Kingdom (11) . . . "Value in giving you additional information?"

	Very Great Value	Great Value	Some Value	Not Very Valuable	Not At All
	18%	46	36	0	0

Japan (36) . . . "Effectiveness to promote self-development?"

	Very Effective	Effective	Moderate	Ineffective	Very Ineffective
	44%	50	6	0	0

Germany . . . "How do you feel about its usefulness for self-development?"

		Very Positive	Positive	Neither/ Nor	Bit Negative	Very Negative
Germany	(60)	36%	58	2	4	0
Germany II	(70)	37%	57	5	1	0

Some participants' reactions to these development programs are shown in table 7. Participants are quite favorable when asked about the effectiveness of programs in helping their self-development.

Another question, perhaps the most telling of all, asks if the participants would recommend a friend to attend the program. As shown in table 8, the number who say they would is rather impressive.

Development of Observers

The potential of the assessment center for furthering the development of participants is just starting to be fully appreciated and exploited. Even more promising is the potential in the assessment center for the development of the observers. These managers often gain greatly from their role in the center. In the future we may expect to see managers being sent to assessment centers as observers in lieu of other management development courses, specifically to become more astute in behavioral observation, group dynamics and problem solving. Even their observer training will be more explicitly geared to helping them develop as managers.

The research and experiences we have just reviewed answer only some of the questions we might ask. Yet the evidence seems persuasive that assessment centers are, indeed, a good solution to the difficult problem of management selection. Even though the technique might be abused and requires some improvements, there is enough value in the method to assure that it will be with us for some time. No doubt it will change. There will be changes in its form, its uses and its relationship to other organizational processes such as manpower planning and development. We can also expect to see it extended to new areas. We are already witnessing its use for the selection of salesmen, retail store management trainees, and the upgrading of women in industry.

TABLE 8
ASSESSEES' OPINIONS: PARTICIPATION

"Would you recommend to a good friend at about your level in the company that he volunteer to participate in an assessment programs?"

		Certainly	Probably	Undecided	Probably Not	Certainly Not
United Kingdom	(11)	82%	18	0	0	0
Germany I	(60)	53%	40	7	0	0
Germany II	(70)	59%	37	4	0	0
		To All Friends	To Some Friends	Not Strongly		Not At All
Japan	(36)	67%	27	6		0

Future Needs

Where do we go from here? We must keep asking questions about the assessment center technique and its impacts. For our answers, we should look to meaningful research to provide hard data. In the future we should look beyond simple-minded questions of validity to examine the broader effects of assessment programs. For example, our criteria of success should be expanded to include peer judgments and the ratings of subordinates about the assessees' managerial practices. We should look at the impact on participants' behavior, self-concepts and careers. We should look at the program's effectiveness for training observers to be better managers.

Also, our conduct of research should reflect the real world in which these techniques are being applied. From asking "is the technique good?" we should shift to asking "how much does this technique add to what we already have?" At the same time we must consider whether it isn't also time to apply our rigorous investigations and critical questions to other areas which may need them more urgently. For example, hasn't management development generally been taken on faith as being worthwhile, and isn't this an area of greater activity with large expenditures of time and money?

As for the assessment center technique itself, we can look forward to a continuation of critical questioning. This is healthy. We can also look forward to extensions and expansions of the method. If done right, this, too, is healthy. Any way you look at it, assessment centers are here to stay.

References

Bray, D. W., and Grant, D. L. The assessment center in the measurement of potential for business management. *Psychological Monographs,* 1966, 80 (17, Whole No. 625).

Campbell, R. J., and Bray, D. W. Assessment centers: an aid in management selection. *Personnel Administration,* 1967, 30, 6-13.

Carleton, F. O. Relationships between follow-up evaluations and information developed in a management assessment center. Paper presented at the American Psychological Association Convention, Miami Beach, Florida, 1970

Dodd, W. E., and Kraut, A. I. Will management assessment centers insure selection of the same old types? Paper presented at the American Psychological Association Convention, Miami Beach, Florida, 1970.

Greenwood, J. M., and McNamara, W. J. Interrater reliability in situational tests. *Journal of Applied Psychology,* 1967, 31, 101-106.

Hinrichs, J. R. Comparison of "real life" assessments of management potential with situational exercises, paper and pencil ability tests, and personality inventories. *Journal of Applied Psychology,* 1969, 53, 425-433.

Kraut, A. I., and Scott, G. The validity of an operational management assessment program. *Journal of Applied Psychology,* 1972.

Wollowick, H. B., and McNamara, W. J. Relationship of the components of an assessment center to management success. *Journal of Applied Psychology,* 1969, 53, 348-352.

Section E
Work Sampling
as a Selection Technique

Signs, Samples, and Criteria

PAUL F. WERNIMONT
JOHN P. CAMPBELL

Many writers (e.g., Dunnette, 1963; Ghiselli & Haire, 1960; Guion, 1965; Wallace, 1965) have expressed concern about the difficulties encountered in trying to predict job performance, and in establishing the validity of tests for this purpose. In general, their misgivings center around the low validities obtained and misapplications of the so-called "classic validity model." To help ameliorate these difficulties it is proposed here that the concept of validity be altered as it is now applied to predictive and concurrent situations and introduce the notion of "behavioral consistency." By consistency of behavior is meant little more than that familiar bit of conventional wisdom, "The best indicator of future performance is past performance." Surprisingly few data seem to exist to either support or refute this generalization. It deserves considerably more attention.

Some History

It is perhaps not too difficult to trace the steps by which applied psychologists arrived at their present situation. During both World War I and World War II general intelligence and aptitude tests were effectively applied to military personnel problems. Largely as the result of these successes, the techniques developed in the armed services were transported to the industrial situation and applied to the personnel problems of the business organization. From a concentration on global measures of mental ability, validation efforts branched out to include measures of specific aptitudes, interests, and personality dimensions. The process is perhaps most clearly illustrated by the efforts of the United States Employment Service to validate the General Aptitude Test Battery across a wide range of jobs and occupations. In general, testing seemed to be a quick, economical, and easy way of obtaining useful information which removed the necessity for putting an individual on the job and observing his performance over a trial period.

It was in the context of the above efforts that an unfortunate marriage occurred, namely, the union of the classic validity model with the use of tests as signs, or indicators, of predispositions to behave in certain ways (Cronbach, 1960, p. 457), rather than as samples of the characteristic behavior of individuals. An all too frequent procedure was to feed as many signs as possible into the classic validity framework in hopes that the model itself would somehow uncover something useful. The argument here is that it will be much more fruitful to focus on meaningful samples of behavior, rather than signs of predispositions, as predictors of later performance.

The Consistency Model

To further illustrate the point, consider a hypothetical prediction situation in which the following five measures are available:
1. Scores on a mental ability test;
2. School grade-point average (GPA);
3. Job-performance criterion at Time 1;
4. Job-performance criterion at Time 2;
5. Job-performance criterion at Time 3.
Obviously, a number of prediction opportunities are possible. Test scores could be correlated with GPA; school achievement could be correlated with first-year job success; or the test scores and GPA could be combined in some fashion and the composite used to predict first-, second-, or third-year job performance. All of these correlations would be labeled validity coefficients and all would conform to the classic validity model. It is less clear what label should be attached to the correlation between two different measures of job performance. Few would call it validity; many would probably refer to it as reliability. There seems to be a tendency among applied psychologists to withhold the term validity from correlations between measures of essentially the same behavior, even if they were obtained at two different points in time. That is, the subtleties of the concept of reliability and the ingredients of the classic validity model seem to have ingrained the notion that validity is a correlation between a predictor and a criterion and the two should somehow be dissimilar.

However, each of the 10 correlations that one could compute from the above situation represents the degree of common variation between the two variables, given the appropriateness of the linear correlation model. After all, that is what correlation is all about. In this sense there is no logical reason for saying that some of the coefficients represent validity and others reliability, although there certainly may be in other contexts. An implicit or explicit insistence on the predictor being "different" seems self-defeating. Rather one should really be trying to obtain measures that are as similar to the criterion or criteria as possible. This notion appears to be at least implicit in much of the work on prediction with biographical data where many of the items represent an attempt to assess previous achievement on similar types of activities. Behavior sampling is also the basis on which simulation exercises are built for use in managerial assessment programs.

At this point it should be emphasized that for the consistency notion to be consistent, the measures to be predicted must also be measures of behavior. For example, it would be something less than consistent to use a behavior sample to predict such criteria as salary progression, organizational level achieved, or subunit production. The individual does not always have substantial control over such variables, and, even with the more obvious biasing influences accounted for, they place a ceiling on the maximum predictive efficiency to be expected. Furthermore, they are several steps removed from actual job behavior. In this respect, the authors are very much in accord with Dunnette (1966) who argues strongly for the measurement of abservable job behavior in terms of its effect on meaningful dimensions of performance effectiveness. A . . . method for accomplishing this aim is the behavior retranslation technique of Smith and Kendall (1964). The applied psychologist should reaffirm his mandate and return to the measurement of behavior. Only then will one learn by what means, and to what extent, an individual has influenced his rate of promotion, salary increases, or work group's production.

In general terms, what might the selection or prediction procedure look like if one tried to apply a consistency model? First, a comprehensive study of the job would be made. The results of this effort would be in the form of dimensions of job performance well defined by a broad range of specific behavior incidents which in turn have been scaled with respect to their "criticalness" for effective or ineffective performance.

Next, a thorough search of each applicant's previous work experience and educational history would be carried out to determine if any of the relevant behaviors or outcomes have been required of him or have been exhibited in the past. Items and rating methods would be developed to facilitate judging the frequency of such behaviors, the intensity with which they were manifested, the similarity of their context to the job situation, and the likelihood that they will show up again. These judgments can then be related to similar judgments concerning significant and consistent aspects of an individual's job behavior.

Such a procedure places considerable emphasis on background data and is similar in form to the "selection by objectives" concept of Odiorne and Miller (1966). However, the aim is to be considerably more systematic and to focus on job behavior and not summary "objectives."

After the analysis of background data it might be found that the required job behaviors have not been a part of the applicant's past repertoire and it would be necessary to look for the likelihood of that job behavior in a variety of work-sample or simulation exercises. A number of such behavior measures are already being used in various management assessment programs.

Finally, individual performance measures of psychological variables would be given wider use where appropriate. For example, the Wechsler Adult Intelligence Scale (Wechsler, 1955) might be used to assess certain cognitive functions. Notice that such a measure is a step closer to actual performance sampling than are the usual kinds of group intelligence tests.

How does the above procedure compare to conventional practice? The authors hope they are not beating at a straw man if the usual selection procedure is described as follows. First, a thorough job analysis is made to discover the types of skills and abilities necessary for effective performance. This is similar to the consistency approach except that the objective seems to be to jump very quickly to a generalized statement of skills and abilities rather than remaining on the behavioral level. The conventional approach next entails a search for possible predictors to try out against possible criteria. Based on knowledge of the personnel selection and individual differences literature, personal experience, and "best guesses," some decisions are made concerning what predictors to include in the initial battery. It is the authors' contention that the classic validity model has forced an undue amount of attention on test and inventory measures at this stage. Witness the large amount of space devoted to a discussion of "test validation" in most books dealing with the selection problem. Again, signs seem to take precedence over samples. Lastly, one or more criterion measures are chosen. Too often the choice seems to be made with little reference to the previous job analysis and is based on a consideration of "objectivity" and relevance to the "ultimate" criterion. Unfortunately, even a slight misuse of these considerations can lead to criteria which are poorly understood. In contrast, working within the framework of a consistency model requires consideration of dimensions of actual job behavior.

It might be added that the above characterization of the conventional approach is meant to be somewhat idealized. Certain departures from the ideal might reinforce the use of signs to an even greater extent. For example, there is always the clear and present danger that the skill requirements will be stated in terms of "traits" (e.g., loyalty, resourcefulness, initiative) and thus lead even more directly to criteria and predictors which are oriented toward underlying predispositions.

Relationship to Other Issues

The consistency notion has direct relevance for a number of research issues that appear frequently in the selection and prediction literature. One important implication is that selection research should focus on individuals to a much greater extent than it has. That is, there should be more emphasis on intraindividual consistency of behavior. In their insightful discussion of the criterion problem, Ghiselli and Haire (1960) point out that intraindividual criterion performance sometimes varied appreciably over time, that is, is "dynamic." They give two examples of this phenomenon. However, after an exhaustive review of the literature, Ronan and Prien (1966) concluded that a general answer to the question, "Is job performance reliable?" is not really possible with present data. They go on to say that previous research has not adequately considered the relevant dimensions that contribute to job performance and very few studies have actually used the same criterion measure to assess performance at two or more points in time. In the absence of much knowledge concerning the stability of relevant job behaviors it seems a bit dangerous to apply the classic validation model and attempt to generalize from a one-time criterion measure to an appreciable time span of job behavior. Utilizing the consistency notion confronts the problem directly and forces a consideration of what job behaviors are recurring contributors to effective performance (and therefore predictable) and which are not.

In addition, the adoption of signs as predictors in the context of the classic model has undoubtedly been a major factor contributing to the lack of longitudinal research. It makes it far too easy to rely on concurrent studies, and an enormous amount of effort has been expended in that direction. Emphasis on behavior samples and behavior consistency requires that a good deal more attention be devoted to the former, along with very explicit consideration of the crucial parameters of a longitudinal study.

The moderator or subgrouping concept also seems an integral part of the consistency approach. The basic research aim is to find subgroups of people in a particular job family for whom behavior on a particular performance dimension is consistent. Subgrouping may be by individual or situational characteristics but the necessity is clear and inescapable. Only within such subgroups is longitudinal prediction possible.

Lastly, the process the authors are advocating demands a great deal in terms of being able to specify the contextual or situational factors that influence performance. It is extremely important to have some knowledge of the stimulus conditions under which the job behavior is emitted such that a more precise comparison to the predictor behavior sample can be made. Because of present difficulties in specifying the stimulus conditions in an organization (e.g., Sells, 1964), this may be the weakest link in the entire procedure. However, it is also a severe problem for any other prediction scheme, but is usually not made explicit.

It is important to note that the authors' notion of a consistency model does not rest on a simple deterministic philosophy and is not meant to preclude taking account of so-called "emergent" behaviors. Relative to "creativity," for example, the question becomes whether or not the individual has ever exhibited in similar contexts the particular kind of creative behavior under consideration. If a similar context never existed, the research must investigate creative performance and outputs obtained in a test situation which simulates the contextual limitations and requirements in the job situation.

An additional advantage of the consistency approach is that a number of old or persistent problems fortunately appear to dissipate, or at least become significantly diminished. Consider the following:

1. Faking and response sets—Since the emphasis would be on behavior samples and not on self-reports of attitudes, beliefs, and interests, these kinds of response bias would seem to be less of a problem.

2. Discrimination in testing—According to Doppelt and Bennett (1967) two general charges are often leveled at tests as being discriminatory devices:

(a) Lack of relevance—It is charged that test items are often not related to the work required on the job for which the applicant is being considered, and that even where relationships can be shown between test scores and job success there is no need to eliminate low-scoring disadvantaged people since they can be taught the necessary skills and knowledge in a training period after hiring.

(b) Unfairness of content—It is further maintained that most existing tests, especially verbal measures, emphasize middle-class concepts and information and are, therefore, unfair to those who have not been exposed to middle-class cultural and educational influences. Consequently, the low test scores which are earned are not indicative of the "true" abilities of the disadvantaged. Predictions of job success made from such scores are therefore held to be inaccurate.

The examination of past behaviors similar in nature to desired future behavior, along with their contextual ramifications, plus the added techniques of work samples and simulation devices encompassing desired future behavior, should markedly reduce both the real and imagined severity of problems of unfairness in prediction.

3. Invasion of privacy—The very nature of the consistency approach would seem to almost entirely eliminate this problem. The link between the preemployment or prepromotion behavior and job behavior is direct and obvious for all to see.

Concluding Comments

The preceding discussion is meant to be critical of the concepts of predictive and concurrent validity. Nothing that has been said here should be construed as an attack on construct validity, although Campbell (1960) has pointed out that reliability and validity are also frequently confused within this concept. Neither do the authors mean to give the impression that a full-scale application of the consistency model would be without difficulty. Using available criteria and signs of assumed underlying determinants within the framework of the classic model is certainly easier; however, for long-term gains and the eventual understanding of job performance, focusing on the measurement of *behavior* would almost certainly pay a higher return on investment.

Some time ago, Goodenough (1949) dichotomized this distinction by referring to signs versus samples as indicators of future behavior. Between Hull's (1928) early statement of test validities and Ghiselli's (1966) more recent review, almost all research and development efforts have been directed at signs. Relatively small benefits seem to have resulted. In contrast, some recent research efforts directed at samples seem to hold out more promise. The AT&T studies, which used ratings of behavior in simulated exercises (Bray & Grant, 1966), and the In-basket studies reported by Lopez (1965) are successful examples of employing behavior samples with management and administrative personnel. Frederiksen (1966) has reported considerable data contributing to the construct validity of the In-basket. In addition, Ghiselli (1966) has demonstrated that an interview rating based on discussion of specific aspects of an individual's previous work and educational history had reasonably high validity, even under very unfavorable circumstances. In a nonbusiness setting, Gordon (1967) found that a work sample yielded relatively high validities for predicting final selection into the Peace Corps and seemed to be largely independent of the tests that were also included as predictors.

Hopefully, these first few attempts are the beginning of a whole new technology of behavior sampling and measurement, in both real and simulated situations. If this technology can be realized and the consistencies of various relevant behavior dimensions mapped out, the selection literature can cease being apologetic and the prediction of performance will have begun to be understood.

References

Bray, D. W., & Grant, D. L. The assessment center in the measurement of potential for business management. *Psychological Monographs,* 1966, 80 (17, Whole No. 625).

Campbell, D. T. Recommendations for APA test standards regarding construct, trait, and discriminant validity. *American Psychologist,* 1960, 15, 546-553.

Cronbach, L. J. *Essentials of psychological testing* (2nd ed.) New York: Harper & Row, 1960.

Doppelt, J. P., & Bennett, G. K. Testing job applicants from disadvantaged groups. *Test Service Bulletin* (No. 57). New York: Psychological Corporation, 1967. Pp 1-5.

Dunnette, M. D. A modified model for test validation and research. *Journal of Applied Psychology,* 1963, 47, 317-323.

Dunnette, M. D. *Personnel selection and placement.* Belmont, Calif.: Wadsworth, 1966.

Frederiksen, N. Validation of a simulation technique. *Organizational Behavior and Human Performance,* 1966, 1, 87-109.

Ghiselli. E. E. *The validity of occupational aptitude tests.* New York: Wiley, 1966.

Ghiselli, E. E., & Haire, M. The validation of selection tests in the light of the dynamic character of criteria. *Personnel Psychology,* 1960, 13, 227-231.

Goodenough, F. *Mental testing: Its history, principles, and applications.* New York: Holt, Rinehart & Winston, 1949.

Gordon, L. V. Clinical, psychometric, and work sample approaches in the prediction of success in Peace Corps training. *Journal of Applied Psychology,* 1967, 51, 111-119.

Guion, R. M. Synthetic validity in a small company: A demonstration. *Personnel Psychology,* 1965, 18, 49-65.

Hull, C. L. *Aptitude testing.* New York: Harcourt, Brace & World, 1928.

Lopez, F. M., Jr. *Evaluating executive decision making: The In-basket technique.* New York: American Management Association, 1965.

Odiorne, G. S., & Miller, E. L. Selection by objectives: A new approach to managerial selection. *Management of Personnel Quarterly,* 1966, 3 (3), 2-10.

Ronan. W. W., & Prien, E. P. *Toward a criterion theory: A review and analysis of research and opinion.* Greensboro, N. C.: Richardson Foundation, 1966.

Sells, S. B. Toward a taxonomy of organizations. In W. W. Cooper, H. J. Leavitt, & W. W. Shelly, II (Eds.), *New perspectives in organization research,* New York: Wiley, 1964.

Smith, P. C., & Kendall, L. M. Retranslation of expectations: An approach to the construction of unambiguous anchors rating scales, *Journal of Applied Psychology,* 1963, 47, 149-155.

Wallace, S. R. Criteria for what? *American Psychologist,* 1965, 20, 411-417.

Weschler, D. *Manual for the Weschler Adult Intelligence Scale.* New York: Psychological Corporation, 1955.

Work Sampling for Personnel Selection

JAMES E. CAMPION

In a recent article Wernimont and Campbell (1968) proposed a new strategy for personnel selection. They argue that it would be beneficial in test validation to adopt a model that emphasizes samples of work behavior as predictors of future work behavior. Wernimont and Campbell prefer this behavioral consistency model to the classical model which focuses on the use of tests as signs of predispositions to behave in certain ways on the job. They assert that pursuing the behavioral consistency approach and making test content more relevant to work would have several immediate advantages, such as diminishing the problem of faking or response sets and reducing charges of discrimination and invasion of privacy in testing.

Initial applications in field settings have shown promise. For example, assessment center research (Bray & Campbell, 1968; Bray & Grant, 1966; Hinrichs, 1969) with simulation exercises has been successful in demonstrating the advantages of the consistency approach in selecting managers. Furthermore, Hinrichs (1970), in a controlled laboratory setting, found that the most precise predictors of proficiency in a rotary pursuit task were apparatus tests which closely resembled this psychomotor task.

These initial findings seem promising and suggest that the concept of behavioral consistency may have considerable applied value. However, before this concept can be translated into a useful strategy for the practitioner, additional work is needed to develop guidelines for constructing work sample measures. In particular, the lack of guidelines for behavioral sampling seems to be a major obstacle to wider use of the consistency approach. The present research was designed to examine the effectiveness of one sampling strategy. Specifically, a modified version of Smith and Kendall's (1963) retranslation method was used to provide a framework for behavioral sampling, and concurrent test validation data were used to determine the utility of this methodology.

Method

Sample Characteristics

The sample consisted of 34 males (32 Caucasian, 1 Negro, 1 Latin) maintenance

Reprinted by permission of the author and the publisher from the *Journal of Applied Psychology,* vol. 56 (1972), no. 1, pp. 40-44. Copyright 1972 by the American Psychological Association.

mechanics (Dictionary of Occupational Titles, Job Code 638.28) employed by a food processing company located in a large Southwestern city. Their ages varied between 23 and 47 yr., with an average age of 35.8 yr. Educational attainment varied between 10 and 16 yr., with an average level of 12.4 yr. Their job tenure varied between 9 and 139 mo. with an average of 32.3 mo.

Development of Work Sample

The development of the work sample measure required a thorough examination of the job. This information was obtained from several technical conferences with a group of job experts. These job experts were an industrial engineer, who was an assistant to the plant maintenance superintendent, and three foremen, who were responsible for supervising the work of the maintenance mechanics. These conferences progressed through several stages, each of which was designed to achieve a specific objective.

Stage 1. In the first stage the experts were requested to list all possible tasks that maintenance mechanics were required to perform in the company; and for each task they were asked to indicate frequency of performance and to evaluate its relative importance to the job.

Stage 2. In the second stage these experts, plus a member of the personnel department, were requested to provide another task listing based upon the previous work experiences of their maintenance mechanic applicants. All five members who participated in this conference were responsible for screening applicants for maintenance mechanic work.

Stage 3. In the third stage the objective was to delineate the crucial dimensions of work behavior for maintenance mechanics. A modified version of Smith and Kendall's (1963) retranslation technique was used. First, the group of experts listed the major dimensions of work behavior that they felt discriminated between effective and ineffective performance on the job. Second, each expert independently generated behavioral incidents to illustrate performance on each dimension. The procedures followed in this step adhere generally with the guidelines provided by Flanagan (1954) for use with his critical-incident technique. Following this, the experts pooled their information, discussed differences, and decided that there were two critical dimensions of work behavior for maintenance mechanics: use of tools, and accuracy of work. Speed of work also was suggested as a major factor of work behavior; however, the experts eliminated it due to a lack of agreement on choice of behavioral incidents to illustrate it.

Stage 4. In the next stage tasks were selected as possible work sample measures. It was important that the tasks selected were representative of the tasks performed by the maintenance mechanics in the plant, but they could not be unique to this plant. They also had to make them appropriate for the job applicants. These two requirements were satisfied by considering as possible job sample measures only those tasks which were common to the lists obtained in Stages 1 and 2. In addition, each job sample task had to meet two other requirements. Each task had to provide a situation where the opportunities were maximal for the examinee to exhibit behaviors relevant to use of tools and accuracy of work. Also, the behaviors elicited by the job sample tasks had to be the kind that a test administrator could reliably record.[1]

Based on the above criteria, four tasks were selected: installing pulleys and belts, disassembling and repairing a gearbox, installing and aligning a motor, and pressing a bushing into a sprocket and reaming it to fit a shaft.

Stage 5. In the final stage these four tasks were broken down into the steps logically required to complete them. Each step was then analyzed in detail, in order to determine the various approaches a job applicant might follow. The recordable behaviors associated with these approaches were specified and weights assigned to them based on their correctness as judged by the job experts. This resulted in a list of possible behaviors associated with each step in task performance, with every behavior assigned a weight for scoring purposes. Thus, the recording form was in a checklist format which required that the test administrator simply describe rather than evaluate the job applicant's behavior. The applicant's responses were later evaluated by adding the weights associated with the behaviors marked on the checklist.

Test instructions were written for the examiner to read. A set of tools and materials were selected that maximized the opportunity for the unqualified examinee to respond inappropriately. The tools and materials, the manner in which they were displayed, and the time given examinees to study them were standardized. All testing was done in the same test administration room, with only the examiner and examinee present. Four hours were allotted for test administration.

Example items and their corresponding weights are as follows:

Installing Pulleys and Belts

		Scoring weights
1.	Checks key before installing against:	
	——shaft	2
	——pulley	2
	——neither	0

Disassembling and Repairing a Gear Box

10.	Removes old bearing with:	
	——press and driver	3
	——bearing puller	2
	——gear puller	1
	——other	0

Installing and Aligning A Motor

1.	Measures radial misalignment with:	
	——dial indicator	10
	——straight edge	3
	——feel	1
	——visual or other	0

Pressing a Bushing Into Sprocket and Reaming to Fit a Shaft

4.	Checks internal diameter of bushing against shaft diameter:	
	——visually	1
	——hole gauge and micrometers	3
	——Vernier calipers	2
	——scale	1
	——does not check	0

Paper-and-Pencil Measures

Scores on a battery of paper-and-pencil tests were also available for all members of the validation sample. These tests were: the Test of Mechanical Comprehension, Form AA (published by the Psychological Corporation); the Wonderlic Personnel Test, Form D (published by E. F. Wonderlic); and the Short Employment Tests (published by the Psychological Corporation).

TABLE 1
MEANS, STANDARD DEVIATIONS, AND INTERCORRELATIONS
FOR CRITERIA MEASURES

Measure	$\bar{X}$	SD	Intercorrelations	
			Accuracy of work	Overall mechanical ability
Use of tools	51.6	13.3	.72	.67
Accuracy of work	51.3	13.7		.87
Overall mechanical ability	50.2	14.1		

The standard deviation on the Test of Mechanical Comprehension was restricted. This was due to the mechanics having been preselected, based upon their performance on this test. The cutting score was 44. The other tests were required of all employees but were ignored in selecting craft personnel.

Criteria

The criteria were collected employing the paired comparison method. The three foremen who had participated in the technical conferences as experts were asked to evaluate their subordinates on each of the following factors: use of tools, accuracy of work, and overall mechanical ability. Each mechanic was evaluated by the foreman who was most familiar with his work performance.

Data Collection Procedure

Concurrent validation data were collected in three stages. First, criteria information was obtained from the foremen. Second, performance on the paper-and-pencil measures was collected from personnel records. Last, the work sample test was administered to the 34 maintenance mechanics. A test administrator was hired from an outside consulting firm, in order to prevent contamination between predictor and criterion measures. The means, standard deviations, and intercorrelations for the criteria, paper-and-pencil tests, and the work sample measures are presented in Tables 1, 2, and 3, respectively.

TABLE 2
MEANS, STANDARD DEVIATIONS, AND INTERCORRELATIONS
FOR PAPER-AND-PENCIL MEASURES

Measure	$\bar{X}$	SD	Intercorrelations			
			Wonderlic Personnel Test	Short Employment Tests		
				Verbal	Numerical	aptitude
Test of Mechanical Comprehension (Form AA)	50.9	4.0	.56	.24	.15	.26
Wonderlic Personnel Test (Form D)	23.8	5.9		.62	.37	.50
Short Employment Tests:						
Verbal	23.6	9.5			.10	.22
Numerical	46.6	17.2				.62
Clerical aptitude	33.3	11.0				

Results

Examination of Table 4 indicates that the mechanics' performance on the work sample measure was in all instances significantly and positively related to their foreman's evaluations of their work performance, whereas, none of the 15 validity coefficients computed for the paper-and-pencil tests reached acceptable levels of statistical significance. As noted above, the validity coefficients for the Test of Mechanical Comprehension are difficult to interpret due to its being employed in selecting the mechanics in the validation sample. Normative data describing the standard deviation for a similar group of mechanics who had not been pre-selected on this test variable were not available. Consequently, the validity coefficients could not be corrected for restriction of range on the predictor.

Discussion

The approach developed here evolved from a need to solve a specific selection problem. The personnel decision was either to hire or reject. The applicants were being considered for only one position, and whether or not they were hired depended upon whether or not they possessed the appropriate work skills. It was assumed that the applicant population included persons with previous work experience that qualified them for the present job opening. A possible shortcoming of these findings is that the concurrent validities found for the experienced, employed mechanics may or may not accurately reflect predictive validity for less experienced applicants for mechanic work. This question can only be definitely answered with data obtained from predictive validation studies. However, as noted in Table 4, performance on the work sample measure and mechanic work experience were insignificantly correlated (—.27) for this sample.

TABLE 3

MEANS, STANDARD DEVIATIONS, AND INTERCORRELATIONS
FOR WORK SAMPLE MEASURES

Part	$\bar{X}$	SD	B	C	D	Total
			\multicolumn{3}{c}{Intercorrelations}	
A. Installing pulleys and belts	60.3	15.8	.25	.01	.16	.63
B. Disassembling and repairing a gearbox	62.9	12.9		.11	.27	.64
C. Installing and repairing a motor	71.1	11.2			.07	.42
D. Pressing a bushing into sprocket and reaming to fit a shaft	51.5	19.0				.70
Total	246.2	36.5				

The significant validity coefficients for the work sample measure support the Wernimont and Campbell (1968) assertions regarding the utility of the behavioral consistency approach. Furthermore, these positive findings suggest that the work sampling methodology developed here may provide useful guidelines for constructing work samples in other areas of personnel decision making.

For example, consider the situation where job applicants cannot be presumed to possess any of the prerequisite work skills for the job and, therefore, are first placed in training programs. Here, selection into training is usually based on general ability measures. This seems to be the correct strategy, for these instruments have been shown to work best for predicting training criteria in industrial settings (Brown & Ghiselli, 1952; Ghiselli, 1966). However, future decisions in the sequence concerning who should continue training or who should graduate from training may be more appropriately attacked within the behavioral consistency model. Fleishman's (1957, 1967) research on individual differences in learning is relevant here. This research has shown that ability requirements for task performance change over the training period. Particularly relevant is his finding that general ability measures predict performance during early stages of training, whereas, performance variance in the later stages is increasingly a function of habits and skills required in the task itself.

Consequently, the behavioral consistency approach has implications for sequential strategies of personnel decision making as well. Work sample measures for these decisions would be embedded in the training program. Whether the training is on the job or in the classroom, the goal would be to incorporate, early in training, exercises that maximize the opportunity for the trainees to exhibit behavior judged important for later job success. Thus, candidates with low probabilities of later success could be eliminated or rerouted to other training programs.

TABLE 4
CRITERION BETWEEN PREDICTOR AND CRITERION VARIABLES

Variable	Use of tools	Accuracy of work	Overall mechanical ability
Work sample[1]	.66[3]	.42[2]	.46[3]
Test of Mechanical Comprehension (Form AA)	.08	—.04	—.21
Wonderlic Personnel Test (Form D)	—.23	—.19	—.32
Short Employment Tests:			
Verbal	—.24	—.02	—.04
Numerical	.07	—.13	—.10
Clerical aptitude	—.03	—.19	—.09

[1] Performance on the work sample measure and mechanic work experience at this company were insignificantly correlated at —.27.

[2] $p < .05$.

[3] $p < .01$.

In summary, it seems that several aspects of personnel decision making could be affected by a strategy that used a behavioral consistency approach to determine a candidate's qualifications and/or deficiencies in hiring or promoting him.

REFERENCES

Bray, D. W., & Campbell, R. J. Selection of salesmen by means of an assessment center. *Journal of Applied Psychology,* 1968, 52, 36-41.

Bray, D. W., & Grant, D. L. The assessment center in the measurement of potential for business management. *Psychological Monographs,* 1966, 80 (17, Whole No. 625).

Brown, C. W., & Ghiselli, E. E. The relationship between the predictive power of aptitude tests for trainability and for job proficiency. *Journal of Applied Psychology,* 1952, 36, 370-377.

Flanagan, J. C. The critical incident technique. *Psychological Bulletin,* 1954, 51, 327-358.

Fleishman, E. A. A comparative study of aptitude patterns in unskilled and skilled psychomotor performance. *Journal of Applied Psychology,* 1957, 41, 263-272.

Fleishman, E. A. Individual differences and motor learning. In R. M. Gagne (Ed.), *Learning and individual differences*. Columbus, Ohio: Merrill, 1967.

Ghiselli, E. E. *The validity of aptitude tests*. New York: Wiley, 1966.

Hinrichs, J. R. Comparison of "real life" assessments of management potential with situational exercises, paper-and-pencil ability tests, and personality inventories. *Journal of Applied Psychology*, 1969, 53, 425-432.

Hinrichs, J. R. Ability correlates in learning a psycho-motor task. *Journal of Applied Psychology*, 1970, 54, 56-64.

Smith, P., & Kendall, L. N. Retranslation of expectations: An approach to the construction of unambiguous anchors for rating scales. *Journal of Applied Psychology*, 1963, 47, 149-155.

Wernimont, P. F., & Campbell, J. Signs, samples, and criteria. *Journal of Applied Psychology*, 1968, 52, 372-376.

Notes

1. Of course, reliability is essentially an empirical matter. Unfortunately, the author was not able to convince company officials that it would be worth the added expenses of retesting or of using two test administrators.

CHAPTER 3

The Importance of Training Methods

Once the personnel manager has selected his employees (see chap. 2), he must then choose training objectives and techniques which accurately match individual and organizational needs. A well-chosen training program can increase individual productivity and job satisfaction for the individual and the over-all effectiveness of the organization.

Yukl and Wexley (1971) have outlined several reasons for the popularity of formal training programs in most organizations today. First, personnel selection and placement do not usually provide organizations with new employees skillful enough to meet the demands of their job adequately. Second, experienced employees must be continually retrained because of changes in job content due to promotions, technology, and transfers. Third, management is aware that effective programs result in increased productivity, decreased absenteeism, reduced turnover, and greater work satisfaction. (We will have more to say about these topics in chaps. 6 and 7).

A wide range of training techniques is available to the personnel manager. The first reading in this chapter, the article by Campbell, Dunnette, Lawler, and Weick, compares the advantages and disadvantages of various formal training methods, including the lecture method, conference method, sensitivity training, laboratory education, and simulated methods of training. They also include a discussion about the advantages and disadvantages of using an on-the-job training program instead of a formal program.

In order to choose the most effective training method, one must have accurate information as to the relative effectiveness of different available training techniques for the learning problem at hand. In the second article in this chapter, Carroll, Paine, and Ivancevich compare training directors' evaluations of training methods with the results of research. Their conclusion is that training directors may not accurately evaluate the strengths and weakness of available approaches to training.

Training and Development: Methods and Techniques

JOHN P. CAMPBELL
MARVIN D. DUNNETTE
E. E. LAWLER
K. E. WEICK

The terms "training" and "development" are often given somewhat different meanings. They may be distinguished on the basis of either the subject matter involved or the level in the organization from which the participants are drawn. In the former instance training usually refers to rather specific, factual, and narrow-range content, while development implies a focus on general decision making and human relations skills. Relative to the latter distinction, development usually refers to activities provided for middle and upper management.

However, the two terms are used synonymously [here] and are meant to entail the following general properties and characteristics:

1. Management training and development is, first of all, a learning experience.
2. It is planned by the organization.
3. It occurs after the individual has joined the organization.
4. It is intended to further the organization's goals.

The first item implies that a relatively permanent change in the individual must be intended, whether it be an increased body of knowledge, new methods for solving problems, or more effective interactions with other people. Programs that are meant only to stimulate momentary feelings of goodwill, company zeal, or other marked but temporary behavior changes are not training programs. It is obvious that a considerable amount of learning relative to the managerial job is not consciously planned by the organization and that an individual learns a great deal, both good and bad, about managing before he joins the organization. However, these kinds of learning are excluded from our definition of management development for the following reason: Some of the areas most in need of research involve the *interaction* of the organization's training efforts both with the skills, knowledge, and attitudes that the individual brings to the job and with the unplanned kind of training that goes on between superior and subordinate and among coworkers. To include all these learning experiences under the rubric "management development" might obscure some of these very important joint influences.

Management development is thus a teaching activity planned and initiated by the organization. The word "planned" is not meant to imply negativistic things about manipulation or efforts toward eliciting conformity behavior, nor does it necessarily mean the planning must be done by the management hierarchy—in fact, it is usually delegated. Its aim is to further the goals of the organization by enhancing the managerial inputs which are in the form of abilities, skills, motives, and attitudes of individuals. However, participants in programs that fall within our definition of management development need not be managers. In fact, such training programs tend to break down into two general classes: those which are directed toward *preparing* nonmanagement people for future management responsibilities and those which are intended to improve the performance of individuals who are already functioning as managers (Miner, 1966). Although the development effort must have something to do with the organizational goals, the particular goals under consideration need not be restricted to narrow economic aims. Personal development for personal development's sake may indeed be a conscious objective of the organization.

Given the obvious and overwhelming importance of the managerial inputs to an organization and the tremendous amount of time and money that is spent on trying to enhance these inputs through training, it is little wonder that a considerable body of written literature has accumulated on the topic of management training and development. It is the purpose of [this paper] to examine and summarize, in some coherent fashion, [some of] this body of knowledge. Special attention will be paid to reports of research that try to evaluate whether or not the managerial inputs to the organization are indeed being enhanced by means of the various training and development efforts. On the basis of this look at "what is known" in the training area, some suggestions will be made as to what kinds of research and investigation must be carried out in the future to make management development as meaningful and fruitful as possible.

The professional literature seems to organize itself under four general headings:

1. Descriptions of the various programs and techniques

2. Discussions of the application of principles of learning and motivation to problems of training

3. Methodological articles on how the effects of training should be evaluated, including discussion of the necessity of various aspects of evaluation

4. Empirical or quasi-empirical studies of the effects of training on the attitudes, opinions, and job performance of managers. . . .

Training Techniques, or "How to Teach"

Management development and training methods seem to fall roughly into three different categories, which we shall label *information presentation techniques, simulation methods,* and *on-the-job practice.* Specific training methods will be discussed under each of these categories.

Information Presentation Techniques

These are devices which have as their aim the teaching of facts, concepts, attitudes, or skills without requiring simulated or actual practice on the job itself.

The lecture. This most traditional of teaching methods has taken its share of lumps from educators and industrial training personnel. McGehee and Thayer (1961) conclude that as usually employed, the lecture is of little value in industrial training. Its principal difficulties seem to be that no provision is made for individual differences on the part of the learners, the lecturer must be an outstanding teacher, it is very difficult for the learners to obtain feedback regarding how they are doing, and there is little opportunity for the learner to participate in the process. The lecture method is not without its friends, however. D. S. Brown (1960) argues that this technique is valuable because of its sheer information-giving ability, its wide acceptance, the fact that it is economical, and the opportunity it affords a master teacher to provide an inspirational model of scholarship for his students. Bennett (1956) makes the point that managers are an intelligent lot and lectures by recognized authorities are in keeping with the status and complexity of the managerial job. Both these writers agree, however, that the lecture must be used sparingly and with due regard for its shortcomings. Tiffen and McCormick (1965) also point out that the lecture might profitably be considered for the presentation of new material or when summarizing material developed by another instruction method.

The conference method. This technique is really the management development analog to the graduate school seminar. The emphasis is on small group discussion, and the leader provides guidance and feedback rather than instruction. Its usual objectives are to develop problem-solving and decision-making capabilities, present new and complex material, and modify attitudes. The keystone is active participation of the learner, primarily by means of verbal discussion with the other group members. The conference is almost always oriented toward discussion of specific problems or new areas of knowledge. The topics for discussion may be chosen by the leader or by the participants themselves (Buchanan & Ferguson, 1953). Each of the participants may also be given practice in leading conference sessions (Zelko, 1952). Along with the participative aspect, feedback to the participant regarding his performance and attitude is an extremely important part of the conference method. It may be provided by the leader, the other participants, or a trained observer. The conference technique was really one of the first products of the reaction against the lecture method and has served as the backbone of the "human relations" type of training. It is most often used to teach such things as effective communication, supervisory techniques, and general approaches to problem solving and decision making. The conference method is perhaps the most widely used managerial training technique (Yoder, 1962).

A serious constraint on this method is its restriction to small groups. However, a large group may be broken down into smaller groups called "buzz" groups (H. A. Boyd, 1952), which then operate as problem-solving or discussion groups and report back to the main body. This technique may be used to illustrate approaches to the same problem, or each group may be assigned a portion of the main topic.

Criticisms of the conference method as a training technique center around its inability to cover much substantive content in a reasonable length of time, the frequent lack of organization, and an emphasis on demonstrating verbosity rather than learning (Jennings, 1956).

Yet another embellishment of the buzz-group technique is the method of forced leadership training described by Jennings (1953a). In most buzz groups a natural leader usually emerges to guide the discussion and keep the conversation going. This individual is identified, and in the second training session the leaders from the first buzz groups are all placed together and new buzz-groups are formed, using individuals who did not act as leaders during the first session. Thus in the second buzz-group session an individual who has not previously acted as leader is almost forced to assume this role. The cycle of regrouping nonleaders into new buzz groups is repeated until as many as possible have been given practice in leading the group.

T (training) groups or sensitivity training. This is a difficult technique to describe in a few words or paragraphs, chiefly because there are now so many different variations with different characteristics and different goals. In general, the method is a direct descendant of the conference technique, with its emphasis on small groups and individual participation. However, in the *T* group as it orginally evolved, the subject matter for discussion is the actual behavior of the individuals in the group, or the "here and now." That is, the group members discuss why they said particular things, why they reacted in certain ways to what others said, and what they thought was actually going on in the group. They examine one another's ability to communicate, the defenses an individual throws up to protect his self-image, why some people seem to attack or reinforce others, why cliques or subgroups seem to form within the main group, and so on. This is accomplished by having the group members honestly and openly communicate as best they can what they are thinking and feeling relative to what they or someone else is saying or doing. For example, one individual may inform another that even though he is verbally expressing approval, his facial expression says the opposite. The other individual may then try to communicate what he was actually thinking and feeling as he was talking.

Perhaps the most succinct characterization of a *T* group is given by Shepard (1964, p. 379), who defines a *T* group in terms of a norm that must be shared by the members. It consists of a "joint commitment among interdependent persons to process 'analysis,' that is, to shared examination of their relationships in all aspects relevant to their independence."

Descriptive accounts of some specific *T* groups have been given by Schein and Bennis (1965); Klaw (1962); Kuriloff and Atkins (1967); Bradford, Gibb, and Benn (1964); and Tannenbaum, Weschler, and Massarik (1961). A basic ingredient of this technique seems to be a certain amount of frustration and conflict (Argyris, 1963), which occurs when an individual attempts to use his previous modes of operation in the *T* group and is brought up short by the other group members, who wonder aloud why he tries to project his particular self-image, why he gets defensive when questioned about certain things, or why he tries verbally to punish other participants.

Many of the variations in the *T* group method revolve around the role of the trainer. In most *T* groups the trainer acts as a resource person and as a behavior model for the other group members; that is, he expresses his own feelings openly and honestly, does not become defensive and withdrawn when critized, and exhibits an acceptance of the behavior of others. Beyond this, however, some trainers may try to be as nondirective as possible and let the group move along as it sees fit. Others may exhibit considerably more guidance and periodically attempt to point out to the group what is happening and offer an interpretation of what people are really saying to one another. Another kind of *T* group, referred to as the "instrumented group" (Blake & Mouton, 1962), operates without any trainer at all. The participants are provided with a set of rating scales with which they can rate themselves, the other group members, and the group itself on such things as openness, willingness to express feelings, ability to listen to other people, defensive behavior, and the formation of cliques. The positive ends of the scales implicitly define desirable behavior on the part of the group members, and over a series of ratings made during the life of the group the members tell themselves how they are progressing.

Although sensitivity training originally dealt only with behavior expressed in the group, more recent variants of the technique have introduced a specific problem-solving element, and the group members may examine their interpersonal skills as they affect efforts to work out a solution to a problem. This is frequently the technique used when all the people in the group are from one organization (Morton & Bass, 1964).

The type of group composition is another dimension along which groups can vary. They may be "stranger" groups made up of people from different organizations or "family" groups comprised of people from the same organization. In the latter case participants might be from the same level within a firm, or they might represent a vertical slice that includes a number of levels of responsibility.

Other variations of this basic technique include systematically introducing additional conflict in the group (Reed, 1966), to give the group members more practice in handling severe interpersonal stress, or running the group continuously for twenty-four or forty-eight hours instead of a few hours each day. Supposedly a process which normally stretches over a period of one to three weeks can be compressed into one or two days in this fashion and have even greater impact.

Very distinct from the weekend *T* groups, but still aimed at a compression of time, are the so-called micro *T* groups. With this method sessions are compressed into ten- or fifteen-minute intervals with brief lectures and problem-solving sessions interspersed.

Lastly, a procedure described by Tannenbaum and Bugental (1963) involves breaking the parent *T* group into smaller groups of four to six people or even into pairs. The pairs and smaller groups are intended to allow more interaction per person and provide additional feelings and impressions that the entire group can discuss when it meets together.

The objectives of this kind of training have been stated by many (Argyris, 1964b; Bradford et al., 1964; Schein & Bennis, 1965; Shepard, 1964; Tannenbaum et al., 1961) and in summary they seem to amount to the following:

1. To give the trainee an understanding of how and why he acts toward other people as he does and of the way in which he affects them
2. To provide some insights into why other people act the way they do
3. To teach the participants how to "listen," that is, actually hear what other people are saying rather than concentrating on a reply
4. To provide insights concerning how groups operate and what sorts of processes groups go through under certain conditions
5. To foster an increased tolerance and understanding of the behavior of others
6. To provide a setting in which an individual can try out new ways of interacting with people and receive feedback as to how these new ways affect them.

Which of these relative specific objectives is adopted by a particular training effort depends upon whether the general objective is to teach individual self-awareness and personal development or to enhance understanding of group processes for the sake of organizational effectiveness.

In addition, *T* groups that are made up of individuals from one organization usually have as their aim the release and subsequent understanding and acceptance of the repressed feelings on the part of superior and subordinate that often inhibit communication. They also usually strive for increased tolerance and understanding among the various levels of management and for the building of a cohesive "team" feeling. The implicit assumption in all this seems to be that if these objectives are met, the result will be improved managerial performance.

Laboratory education. Laboratory education is the label applied to a more complete program of training experiences in which some form of *T* group is the prime ingredient. The other ingredients may consist of short lectures, group exercises designed to illustrate problems in interpersonal or intergroup behavior, role-playing sessions, and the like. Specification of the content of the various elements, their duration, their participants, and their sequencing constitutes the training or laboratory "design." Designs may vary depending on the training needs and situational elements the planners feel to be crucial. The laboratory education practitioner responsible for guiding the program is often referred to in the literature as a "change agent."

The variations in the laboratory designs are numerous, and we shall attempt no summary.

Discussions may be found in Bradford et al. (1964), Schein and Bennis (1965), and almost any issue of the *Journal of Applied Behavioral Science.*

Systematic observation. A little-used technique, but one advocated by Crow (1953), involves having the individuals in the development program observe an experienced manager or management group in action by sitting in on management committee meetings or observing a manager's meeting with his staff. The learner is cast in a very passive role, but the material being presented is the "real thing" and is presumably relevant for the trainee. A potential drawback is that the relative importance of what is observed is left to the judgment of the trainee.

Closed-circuit television. Although this technique has found wide application in educational institutions, it has had very limited use in management training. A rather unique utilization of television in a large aircraft company was reported by Niven (1966). After a certain hour in the evening, the educational television station in the region scheduled no regular programs, and the company used this open time to present courses in supervision, industrial relations, etc., to its managers and supervisors. Achievement tests were given to all those who participated, which turned out to be several hundred people.

Programmed instruction. The programmed technique involves defining what is to be learned, breaking it down into its component elements, and deciding on the optimal sequence for the presentation and learning of these elements. The presentation may be by "teaching machine," programmed texbook, or some other device, but the essential ingredient in the procedure is that the learner must make an active response to each element (or "frame") such that his response reveals whether or not he has learned what he is supposed to have learned at that point. There is immediate feedback concerning whether the learner was right or wrong, and the entire procedure is automated, which allows each individual to proceed at his own rate. The sequencing of the elements and the proper feedback are provided by the machine or the programmed book.

There are two principal variants of the above procedure—the so-called linear technique, developed by Skinner (1954), and the branching technique, developed by Crowder (1960). With the linear method the objective is to lead the learner from the simple to the complex in such a way that he almost never makes an incorrect response. The branching technique adopts the notion that incorrect responses may be indicative of certain misconceptions, and subprograms are provided to explore and correct the reasons for an incorrect response. After completing a subprogram, the learner continues on with the main program.

The programmed technique has not been widely utilized in management training, although the situation may be changing. It has been used in one instance to teach motivational principles to managers in a photochemical firm (Lysaught, 1961). At the National Institute of Health a program (teaching machine) was used in an attempt to increase supervisory skill in scheduling appointments, conducting meetings, handling reports, and delegating responsibility (Prather, 1964). It would also seem to have possible merit for teaching factual material in such areas as accounting, finance, contract management, and the like.

The advantages that have been claimed for programmed instruction are that it recognizes individual differences by allowing each individual to set his own pace, requires that the learner be active, provides immediate knowledge of results, and forces the people doing the teaching to break down the topic into meaningful elements and then present these elements in a sequence conducive to optimal learning (Hilgard, 1961). Also, once a program is ready, it obviously has a great deal of operating flexibility.

Some disadvantages often pointed out are its high initial cost, the considerable amount of time required to develop and perfect a program, and the seductive nature of the hardware itself (teaching machines, computers, etc.). Pressey (1963) has forcefully warned that the glamour value of the technique may detract from the fundamental and very difficult task of defining what is to be learned, breaking the subject into its component elements, and sequencing their presentation in an optimal fashion.

Training by correspondence. This method was used in one company to teach principles of business administration and personnel management to supervisors located in over two thousand scattered offices around the country (Krist & Prange, 1957). An achievement test was given at the end of each section, and small study groups were encouraged at each office to discuss the individual lessons.

Motion pictures. A survey reported by Bobele, Maher, and Ferl (1964) showed that some firms do use films in management training, but primarily at the lower levels and usually for introducing new subject matter and stimulating discussion relative to human relations problems. One drawback of films, according to the survey, seems to be the entertainment stigma. A variant of the film presentation is the so-called interruption technique, in which a problem is presented or a situation partially portrayed and the participants are asked to respond to the problem or complete the situation.

Reading lists. Besides providing straight information, executive reading programs can be organized around regular discussion sessions (Hook, 1963), in which managers can exchange opinions and ideas about what they have been reading.

Simulation Methods

In this category are included the techniques in which the trainee is presented with a simulated or artificial representation of some aspect of an organization or industry and is required to react to it as if it were the real thing. In other words, these techniques require actual practice of the managerial role with varying degrees of realism, but the actions of the trainees have no effect on the operation of the organization.

The case method. With this technique certain aspects of the firm are simulated by describing the organizational conditions on paper. The trainees are then usually required to identify problems, offer solutions, and otherwise react to the paper organization which is presented. Cases vary a great deal in length and complexity, but the objective is to be as representative of the problems of the real organization as possible. Cases are usually presented to groups of trainees, and active participation in suggesting a solution is encouraged. This allows an individual to obtain feedback regarding his own suggestions and to learn from watching others approach the same problem. Critics of the case method point to its inability to teach general principles and the general lack of guided instruction concerning the inferences the trainees draw from discussion of the case. Advocates point out that self-discovery is more meaningful and that general principles generated by the trainees themselves are learned better and remembered longer. Of course, cases can also be used in conjunction with other training techniques for the purpose of illustrating and reinforcing general principles that have been previously presented in some more direct fashion.

A variant of the case method is the "demand" technique described by Potter and Strachan (1965). With this procedure the trainees are divided into small groups of three or four individuals, and each team is given an organizational problem to research and present to the entire group. The various solutions are then discussed and critiqued within the entire group.

The incident method. Closely related to the case method is the incident technique (Pigors & Pigors, 1955). With this procedure the trainees are given a sketchy outline of a particular incident which requires action on the part of the manager, and they have to ask questions of the trainer to get more information. When the trainees think they have enough information, they try to come up with a solution. At the conclusion of the session, the trainer reveals all the information that he has, and a solution based on complete information is compared with the solution based on the information the trainees obtained.

Role playing. Here the realism of the simulation is heightened by having trainees "act out" the roles of individuals who are described in the case. With this technique the focus is almost exclusively on the human relations aspect of management and supervision, and the trainee has the opportunity to work through the problem exactly as he would if he were on the job. The success of the method rests on the ability of the players actually to adopt the roles specified in the case problem and to react to the actions of the other players just as they would if they were in the work situation. If they are successful, the trainee can try out various solutions and judge their success. He can also receive feedback regarding his supervisory techniques, communication skills, and attitudes toward superiors and subordinates.

The method is time-consuming and expensive in that only a few people can play at a time. Some variants of the role-playing method designed to overcome this problem are described by Maier, Solem, and Maier (1957). One of these is the multiple role-playing procedure, in which a large group breaks down into smaller groups and the same problem is role-played within each group without a trainer. All the players then reassemble and discuss, with the trainer, what happened in their groups, what sort of solutions were suggested, what kinds of human relations problems emerged, and how they were handled. A less satisfactory solution is to have some members of the group role play the situation while the rest of the trainees act as observers and take part in the critique session later.

Another type of role-playing method is described by Speroff (1959). He calls it the "substitution method," and it consists of role playing a meeting between a superior and a subordinate or between a union and a management representative in such a way that one of the pair is kept constant but a number of different people take turns playing the other role. The relative successes and failures of each of the substitutes are then analyzed in a critique session.

Speroff (1954) has also described a technique that combines the notions of job rotation and role playing and allows every manager to continue in his job while attempting to learn about the operations and problems of other parts of the organization. For example, a production manager might be given a sales problem along with all the relevant information the sales organization possesses. He may then adopt the role of the sales manager and sit in on sales conferences, ask questions, and talk to various sales personnel. After a week or two, the production manager (still role playing the sales manager) meets with the appropriate sales people and role plays a problem-solving meeting, centered around the sales problem orignally given him. (At the end of each session all the participants join in a critique session.) The production manager may continue to role play the sales manager for a period of several months, and over the course of one to five years each manager role plays the jobs of managers from many different parts of the business.

Business games. The nature of the simulation in this method is considerably different from that in role playing or the case method. The business game attempts to represent the economic functioning of an industry, company, or organizational subunit. The game actually consists of a set of specified relationships or rules which are derived from economic theory and/or from detailed studies of the operations of relevant businesses and industries. These relationships describe how variation in the inputs to a firm (raw materials, capital, equipment, and people) coupled with variation in certain mediating factors (wage rates, price of finished product, advertising budget, amount spent on research and development, etc.) influences the firm's outputs (amount sold, profit, net worth, etc.). The trainees play the game by making decisions about what price to charge for products, how much to spend on advertising, how many people to hire, and so on. The quality of their decisions is reflected by the variation in the output variables. The objective may be to teach general decision-making skills or to convey information as to how a specific business or industry actually operates. In either case the trainee is also supposed to come away with a realization of the complex interrelationships between various parts of an organization and an appreciation for how the effects of a decision made in one department may be felt in another.

There are literally hundreds of business games in use today of varying shades of complexity and realism (Croft, Kibbee, & Nanus, 1961). Some require as many as several hundred operating decisions every period (K. J. Cohen, 1960) and incorporate a number of firms in competition with one another. Several players may make up a firm. With the larger games there must be a division of labor among the players, and this allows some of the supervisory and human relations aspects of management to come into play. One of the characteristics of the business game is that it may become extremely realistic for the players. The frequent use of a computer to calculate the effects of operating decisions on outputs adds to the status and glamour of this training method.

The business games in use tend to fall into two general categories: top management games and functional games. Top management games are those which attempt to simulate the major decision-making functions of the chief officers in an organization. Functional games are much narrower in scope and are intended to simulate the operations of specific functional areas in an organization such as production control, marketing, or finance.

Some of the criticisms that have been voiced are that games do not allow for the novel approach and may teach an overreliance on particular kinds of decisions unless they are a balanced representation of the real world. A great deal of reliance is placed on the validity of the simulations. For example, if the model used in the game incorporates an oversimplified relationship between research and development investment and profits, the participants may carry away the notion that a surefire way to increase profits is to divert more funds into developmental research. On the other hand, the game may be too realistic, and the trainees may play with such fervor that the training objectives fall by the wayside. The participants may also spend too much time trying to discover "gimmicks" in the model which can be exploited. Most of the users of business games recommend lengthy critique meetings at the end of each session to help avoid some of these pitfalls.

The task model. Keltner (1965) describes a technique which he claims combines the advantages of role playing and business games. Some complex but easily built physical object is constructed, and a group of trainees is assigned the task of duplicating the model, given the proper materials. Various communication arrangements are used, and only certain trainees are allowed to view the object. Difficulties in communication are discussed as they arise, and solutions are obtained through group discussion. The method may also be used to incorporate competition between teams of trainees, or a portion of the training group can be used as observers to train them to recognize emerging leadership patterns and the like.

The In-basket technique. As described by Frederiksen, Saunders, and Wand (1957) and Lopez (1965), this development method consists of presenting the trainee with a description of a managerial role he is to assume and an In-basket containing such things as customer complaints, correspondence, operating statements, requests for advice from subordinates, and the like. The In-basket materials are intended to resemble a realistic operating situation with a variety of problems of varying complexity. The trainee must work through the In-basket, making decisions and giving advice where called for. The heart of the training is in the follow-up discussions, which allow the trainer and trainees to evaluate and interpret what each man did.

    As is the case with business games, the objective seems to be primarily the teaching of decision-making skills, with little or no attention paid to learning new facts, human relations attitudes, or interpersonal skills.

    A variant of the In-basket technique which does tend to incorporate some of these other considerations is the Kepner-Tregoe approach (Kepner & Tregoe, 1960). Instead of one trainee working in isolation, four individuals operate together as members of one company. The training begins with each man seated at his desk faced with an In-basket of work. The four In-baskets are meant to simulate an interrelated set of organizational problems typical of those faced by any management group. The participants may call each other on the phone to obtain additional information relevant to their own problems, or they may meet together in a conference room. All these things take time, however, and in the evaluation of the session a premium is placed on obtaining the most relevant information as quickly as possible. Again, the heart of the training is in the critique session, and although a certain number of interactive elements are introduced, the main objective is still to teach problem-solving and decision-making skills.

    To incorporate still more realism into the In-basket format, Gibson (1961) suggests using a movie along with the In-basket. The film shows a vice-president who periodically interrupts the trainee's work on the In-basket to suggest additional problems that must be handled immediately. Supposedly this builds a realistic amount of tension into the situation.

On-the-job Training

    The methods within this category all incorporate the notion of practice—practice on the actual task to be performed, i.e., the managerial job itself.

Job rotation. This technique is by far the most long-term and expensive way to train management personnel, but many people argue that it is both a necessary and an effective development method (Koontz & O'Donnell, 1955). The main objective is to give the trainee factual knowledge about the operations of different parts of the organization and practice in the different management skills that are required. Learning is largely by trial and error, unless combined with some other technique, and this lack of guidance or structure is the focus of most of the criticism of the method. Wall (1963) suggests that for job rotation to be effective, managers must be given instruction in how to coach and give feedback to the trainer and that definite training goals should be set for each job assignment. The success of job rotation also depends on the job assignments' being actually different so that the trainee learns more than he would by spending all his time on the job for which he was actually selected.

As noted by Koontz and O'Donnell (1955), the general term "job rotation" obscures a number of variations in the method which may or may not be important for a particular organization. First of all, the trainee may be rotated through a series of *nonsupervisory* work situations so as to acquaint him with the range of activities actually undertaken by the firm. Although such a scheme allows the trainee to learn the "production" end of things, many of the training positions may not offer enough of a challenge to the management trainee and indeed may bear little relationship to the skills that will be eventually needed in the management position. It is not inconceivable that such a rotation plan would make the trainee a less effective manager than he would be otherwise. However, for certain types of managerial jobs this kind of training could be very valuable. Rotation among actual managerial positions is perhaps the most common variant and obviously entails something quite different from rotation among nonsupervisory jobs. This difference is illustrative of the argument over whether a potential manager should concentrate on learning administrative and supervisory skills or become proficient in the actual work he is going to manage. Koontz and O'Donnell also discuss rotation among "assistant to" or "acting" managerial positions. Such rotation plans obviously attempt to use actual job experience for training in administrative and supervisory skills, but with some of the risk removed. However, there is also a risk that some of the commitment and involvement of the trainee will be diminished and that much of the substance of the job to be learned will be withheld from him.

Committee assignments or junior executive boards. A more short-term and less comprehensive method involves having the trainees form committees, which then are given real organizational problems to tackle and solve (McCormack, 1938). Problems may be selected from a number of different functional areas, and the trainees may be required to do a considerable amount of information gathering before suggesting a solution. This method differs from the role-playing committee assignment in that the solutions given are the ones actually utilized by the organization.

On-the-job coaching. With this method the superior-subordinate relationship is also a teacher-learner relationship, and the superior acts very much like a tutor in an academic setting. Coaching may vary from being very systematic to being very unsystematic and informal. Regardless of the particular form it takes, most people would argue (e.g., Haire, 1965) that it is one of the prime responsibilities of a superior. However, others (e.g., Argyris, 1961) have pointed to the difficulty of the teacher-learner roles and to the fact that they require the learner to continually try new methods and the teacher to be tolerant of mistakes. These are activities which may not be rewarded by the organization, and the roles of the superior as a good manager and as a good coach may be in conflict.

Performance appraisal. One of the stated goals of performance appraisal usually found in most textbooks is to provide feedback to the subordinate concerning good and bad features of his performance. Presumably this will motivate the individual to improve his performance. As a development technique, appraisal provides an opportunity for the superior and subordinate to discuss means of improving the subordinate's performance. In this sense it is systematic coaching and is distinct from the use of appraisal to identify training needs which may then be approached using other training and development techniques.

Other specialized practice techniques. In addition to exposing trainees to operational and managerial problems in various parts of the organization, other on-the-job techniques seem aimed at more specific goals. For example, some firms (Wilson, 1965) provide opportunities for managers to serve as recruitment and selection interviewers of college graduates. The manager may operate by himself or with other managers on a selection committee. Another firm (P. B. Smith, 1964) has used its management trainees as interviewers to follow up on company-wide attitude surveys. The trainees are first given instruction and practice in nondirective interviewing techniques. Then after the survey results are complete, they conduct interviews with personnel in the departments which showed dissatisfaction in certain areas. The objectives are to find out whether the sources of the dissatisfaction are such that they can be remedied by the company and at the same time to train the prospective managers in this type of face-to-face interaction. The problems of establishing rapport and assuring the employees of his anonymity are obvious. Lastly, in order to train managers in public speaking and simultaneously serve the cause of company public relations, some organizations often set up speaking engagements for their managers and encourage them to give talks at professional meetings.

Training Content, or "What to Teach"

Up to this point we have been talking about techniques and methods in management training and development. When an organization decides to institute or alter a development program, the decision regarding which technique(s) to use is not the only decision that must be made. The decision about *what* to teach also looms large on the horizon and obviously should be made even before techniques are considered.

On their face at least, management training programs have been used to teach a bewildering variety of topics; however, for the sake of a meaningful organization, we have attempted to group them into five categories:

1. *Factual content.* Such a category would include everything from company rules and policies to courses in the humanities. Perhaps the most popular topics in this category are personnel management and business administration concepts. A somewhat novel body of knowledge is utilized by Miner (1965) in a carefully worked-out program to teach managers the causes of ineffective managerial performance and some means for overcoming them.

2. *Approaches and techniques for problem solving and decision making.* Examples of this sort of content are skill in adequately defining the problem of elements in the decision, an appreciation for the interrelatedness of decisions, the importance of planning or optimal sequencing of the steps in the decision-making process, and the realization that many problems do not have one best solution or any permanent solution. Attempts to teach creativity such as those by Parnes and his associates (Meadow & Parnes, 1959) and the means for effective group problem solving as discussed by Maier (1963) would also have to be included here. The creativity work tends to focus on the

individual's approach to obtaining solutions and stresses nonroutine, or "divergent," thinking. Maier's efforts, on the other hand, are aimed at teaching leaders and groups how to utilize more effectively the knowledge and contributions of the individual members to achieve a more effective combined solution.

3. *Attitudes.* Although extremely difficult to define, this sort of training content refers to such things as a positive regard for democratic leadership, consideration for the contributions of others, tolerance for other people's mistakes, and the like. It seems vital to many people that such attitudes go hand in glove with the teaching of human relations skills in order to avoid teaching a role that is only manipulative and not effective (Jennings, 1953b). Somewhat unique in this category is the training program developed and described by McClelland (1965), which attempts to instill in the trainees a high need for achievement. This program attempts to go somewhat beyond attitude change and actually tries to modify the individual's motivated structure.

4. *Interpersonal skills.* In this category fall such things as effective communication, how to listen to other individuals, and how to be an effective group member.

5. *Self-knowledge.* Knowledge concerning how one's behavior affects others and what other people think of one and a realistic perception of one's abilities and limitations should be included here. The state of one's physical health, as it may influence job effectiveness, is also relevant.

Modifiers

When one looks at the myriad training efforts described in the literature, the two dimensions of *"what* is taught" and *"how* it is taught" still do not satisfactorily describe all the variations in programs. There is an additional set of characteristics, which we shall label "modifiers," that various writers and investigators in the field sometimes view as important for training outcomes. Included here are such things as whether the training is on company time or individual time, the total time involved in the training (can the same learning be accomplished in less time?), and the locale of the training session, that is, whether the training is conducted inside or outside the plant. With regard to this latter modifier, the virtues of university versus company programs have often been argued (Anshen, 1954; Boudreaux & Megginson, 1964; Huneryager, 1961), and the prestige, teaching facilities, and isolation of the university setting are pointed to as either desirable or distracting elements. *T*-group advocates often speak of the "cultural island" as a necessary or unnecessary part of such training. Here the choice is between conducting the training sessions at a very isolated setting where little contact with the outside world is allowed and holding the program in-house. A great deal of discussion has also been centered around who does the training—the line, the staff, or some outside consultant. Here there are the obvious considerations of relative costs, trainer competence, and flexibility. However, the motivational considerations relative to both trainer and trainee are also often pointed out as having a direct bearing on deciding who trains. Many people argue that trainees respond much more favorably when the training is carried about by their own management and management has obviously assumed the responsibility (e.g., Blake & Mouton, 1966b).

In brief, these things we have called "modifiers" can be summed up in a few questions: Where should training take place? Who should train? How much time should be spent for training? Whose time?

Obviously, not all training and development programs utilize just one technique or are intended to teach one particular topic. The objectives and scope of a two-year job rotation program are not all comparable to those of a two-hour seminar on human relations employing role playing and the conference method. By arranging all these methods in an organized "list," we do not mean to imply that they are comparable in terms of the "domain of behavior" they seek to influence.

However, it is also true that many more than one combination of training method and modifier can be used for a particular training or development objective. For example, a programmed booklet may attempt to teach the same thing as a business game, or role playing may be used to reach the same objective as a *T* group. It is a truism to say that given a particular objective, different costs and different payoffs are associated with different combinations of techniques and modifying circumstances.

Perhaps it would be well for people interested in training and development to examine a number of possible combinations with a view toward systematically justifying, on the basis of theory and empirical findings, the pros and cons of each one. . . . Briggs (1966) suggests that there is an optimal combination of training method and "what is to be learned" and that it behooves educators, organizational training specialists, and learning theorists alike to get on with the job of finding out what these optimal combinations are.

Team Training

Up to now we have been talking about training and development efforts in the context of the individual trainee. Somewhat distinct from this orientation is the notion of team training (Blake, Mouton, & Blansfield, 1962; Boguslaw & Porter, 1962; Porter, 1964). Instead of developing individual managers, the emphasis is on training teams of managers. Blake et al. (1962) use the analogy of a baseball team to illustrate that individual training cannot do the whole job. The team must be trained as an interacting unit. Porter (1964) has pointed out that the skills, information, and attitudes obtained from team training revolve largely around problems of coordination and thus are not the same as what is learned in individual training. Viewed in this fashion, it would seem that for team training to be effective, a great deal of individual training must have gone before. That is, there must be individual skills and attitudes available for coordination in the team setting. On the other hand, it also seems reasonable that an individual must learn something about the various aspects of team performance before the crucial requirements for individual training become apparent. The two interact.

The literature regarding the use of team training for executive development is rather sparse. Not much has been said about possible training techniques, what is to be taught, or what the modifiers of such training are. However, some of the simulation methods seem especially appropriate for this kind of training. Porter (1964) describes the use of a simulated situation to train the entire work force in an air defense installation, including people with managerial responsibilities. The larger, more complex business games which allow a number of trainees to make up a firm and which require effective coordination among the trainees could be used for team training if the players making up a firm were a functioning management group in real life.

A very specialized method which, according to Blake, Mouton, Barnes, and Greiner (1964), does attempt to develop both individual and team or organizational skills is the Management Grid approach. The content is also quite specialized, and the initial objective is to teach a particular management style, referred to as the "9,9 style." Managerial style is conceived as having two dimensions—a concern for people and a concern for production—and Blake and Mouton (1964) have developed questionnaire-type measures to locate individual managers on these two dimensions (or grids). A 9,9 style describes a manager who has both a maximal concern for people and a maximal concern for production. The first steps in the training focus on the individual, and a modified *T*-group method is used to teach each participant how the other group members see his managerial style. Trainees are first familiarized with the grid language and theory. The group then proceeds to work through a series of exercises and case problems which allow each individual to exhibit his management style, and this behavior then becomes the object of *T*-group type of feedback. Participants supposedly develop skills which enable them accurately and candidly to reflect the management behavior of each individual. This process is intended to instill an appreciation for the human problems of production and move the trainees toward the 9,9 region of the grid.

After this initial phase, the trainees are supposed to go back to their functional groups and use what they have learned to move the entire team to 9,9 methods of operating. It is intended that the "openness" and "candor" learned in the first group carry over to the functional group, starting with the boss and his chief subordinates, and that they become a part of the daily work routine. Finally, attempts are made to extend the utility of the 9,9 approach beyond a particular work team by identifying actual sources of intergroup or interdepartment conflict and incorporating the 9,9 approach in intergroup problem-solving exercises. New attempts are also made to redefine problems and set goals for the organization as a whole. In order for these objectives to be realized, all the managers in an organization must take part in the training. Blake et al. (1964) thus conceive of their program as organizational development rather than management development. The same is true for certain advocates of laboratory education (Schein & Bennis, 1965).

It should be emphasized again that team training is meant to be something distinct, but not entirely independent, from individual training and that the success of the former depends to a degree on the success of the latter. The two obviously interact. As with the other training techniques, team training can potentially at least be directed at a number of content areas. For example, the "family" type of *T* group can be used to familiarize members of a management team with one another's methods of communication, self-images, etc. It is hoped that this will reduce some of the interpersonal barriers that dampen effective coordination. Notice that in such an instance the contribution of team training would be knowledge about the behavior of specific people, i.e., the people who work together in the job situation. The functional team must thus be trained intact. As another example, perhaps a business game could be used to teach team procedures for planning an organization's short-term and long-term goals. The team members could learn which individual functions best as a "critical evaluator," who is an "idea" man, etc., and then devise means for coordinating these specialized skills in future goal-setting tasks.

The interactions between the objectives of individual and team training are obviously complex, and not all aspects of these interactions are always relevant. However, the notion of team training as applied to the management development sphere deserves more attention than it has received.

References

Anshen, M. Executive development: In-company vs. university programs. *Harvard Business Review*, 1954, *32*, 83-91.

Argyris, C. Puzzle and perplexity in executive development. *Personnel Journal*, 1961, *39*, 463-465, 483.

Argyris, C. A brief description of laboratory education. *Training Directors Journal*, 1963, *17* (10), 4-8.

Argyris, C. T-groups for organizational effectiveness. *Harvard Business Review*, 1964, *42* (2), 60-74.

Bennett, W.E. The lecture as a management training technique. *Personnel*, 1956, *32*, 497-507.

Blake, R.R., & Mouton, J.S. The instrumental training laboratory. In I.R. Weschler & E.H. Schein (Eds.), *Issues in human relations training*. NTL Selected Readings Series, 1962, No. 5.

Blake, R.R., & Mouton, J.S. *The managerial grid*. Houston: Gulf, 1964.

Blake, R.R., & Mouton, J.S., & Blansfield, M.G. How executive team training can help you. *Journal of the American Society of Training Directors*, 1962, *16* (1), 3-11.

Bobele, H.K., Maher, C.R., & Ferl, R.A. Motion pictures in management development. *Training Directors Journal*, 1964, *18* (9), 34-38.

Boguslaw, R., & Porter, E.H. Team functions and training. In R.M. Gagne (ed.), *Psychological principles and systems development*. New York: Holt, 1962.

Boudreaux, E., & Megginson, L.C. A new concept in university sponsored executive development programs. *Training Directors Journal*, 1964, *18* (11), 31-41.

Boyd, H.A. The buzz technique in training. *Personnel*, 1952, *31*, 49-50.

Bradford, L.P., Gibb, J.R., & Benne, K.D. *T-group theory and laboratory method*. New York: Wiley, 1964.

Briggs, L.J. *A procedure for the design of multi-media instruction*. Palo Alto, Calif.: American Institutes for Research, 1966.

Brown, D.S. The lecture. *Journal of the American Society of Training Directors*, 1960, *14* (12), 17-22.

Buchanan, P.C., & Ferguson, C.K. Changing supervisory practices through training: A case study. *Personnel*, 1953, *30*, 218-230.

Cohen, K.J., et al. The Carnegie Tech management game. *Journal of Business*, 1960, *33*, 303-321.

Croft, C.J., Kibbee, J., & Nanus, B. *Management games*. New York: Reinhold, 1961.

Crow, R. Group training in higher management development. *Personnel*, 1953, *29*, 458-460.

Crowder, N.A. Automatic tutoring by intrinsic programming. In A.A. Lumdsdaine & P. Glaser (Eds.), *Teaching machines and programmed learning: A source book*. Washington: National Education Association, 1960.

Frederiksen, N., Saunders, D. R., & Wand, B. The in-basket test. *Psychological Monographs*, 1957, *71* (9, Whole No. 438).

Gibson, G.W. A new dimension for "in-basket" training. *Personnel*, 1961, *38*, 76-79.

Haire, M. The incentive character of pay. In R. Andrews (Ed.), *Managerial compensation*. Ann Arbor, Mich.: Foundation for Research in Human Behavior, 1965. Pg. 13-17.

Hilgard, E.R. What support from the psychology of learning? *NEA Journal*, November, 1961, *50*, 20-21.

Huneryager, S.G. Re-education for executives. *Personnel Administration*, 1961, *24* (1), 5-9.

Jennings, E.E. Advantages of forced leadership training. *Personnel*, 1953, *32*, 7-9. (a)

Jennings, E.E. Attitude training versus technique training. *Personnel*, 1953, *31*, 402-404. (b)

Jennings, E.E. Today's group training problems. *Personnel*, 1956, *35*, 94-97.

Keltner, J.W. The task-model as a training instrument. *Training Directors Journal*, 1965, *19* (9), 18-21.

Kepner, C.H., & Tregoe, B.B. Developing decision makers. *Harvard Business Review*, 1960, *38*, 115-124.

Klaw, S. Two weeks in a T-group. *Fortune*, 1961, *64*, 114-117.

Koontz, H., & O'Donnell, C. *Principles of management.* New York: McGraw-Hill, 1955.

Krist, P.C., & Prange, C.J. Training supervisors by mail: The Railway Express program. *Personnel,* 1957, *34,* 32-37.

Kuriloff, A.H., & Atkins, S. T-group for a work team. *Journal of Applied Behavioral Science,* 1966, *2,* 63-94.

Lopez, F.M., Jr. Evaluating executive decision making: The In-basket technique. American Management Association Research Study No. 75, 1966.

Lysaught, J.P. *Programmed learning: Evolving principles and industrial applications.* Ann Arbor, Mich.: Foundation for Research on Human Behavior, 1961.

Maier, N.R.F. *Problem-solving discussions and conferences: Leadership methods and skills.* New York: McGraw-Hill, 1963.

Maier, N.R.F., Solem, A., & Maier, A. *Supervisory and executive development.* New York: Wiley, 1957.

McClelland, D. Achievement motivation can be developed. *Harvard Business Review,* 1965, *43,* 6-24, 178.

McCormack, C. *Multiple management.* New York: Harper, 1938.

McGehee, W., & Thayer, P.W. *Training in business and industry.* New York: Wiley, 1961.

Meadow, A., & Parnes, S.J. Effects of "brainstorming" instructions on creative problem solving by trained and untrained members. *Journal of Educational Psychology,* 1959. *50,* 171-176.

Miner, J.B. Relationships between management appraisal ratings and promotions. Mimeographed paper, personal communication, 1966.

Morton, R.B., & Bass, B.M. The organizational training laboratory. *Journal of the American Society of Training Directors,* 1964, *18* (10), 2-15.

Niven, J.R. Personal communication, 1966.

Pigors, P., & Pigors, F. *The incident process: Case studies in management development.* Washington: Bureau of National Affairs, 1955.

Porter, L.W. *Organizational patterns of managerial job attitudes.* New York: American Foundation for Management Research, 1964.

Potter, C.J., & Strachan, G.D. Project training groups: A "demand" technique for middle managers. *Training Directors Journal,* 1965, *19* (9), 34-41.

Prather, R.L. Introduction to management by teaching machine. *Personnel Administration,* 1964, *27* (3), 26-31.

Pressey, S.L. Teaching machine (and learning theory) crisis. *Journal of Applied Psychology,* 1963, *47,* 1-6.

Reed, J.H. Two weeks of managed conflict at Bethel. *Training Development Journal,* 1966, *20,* 6-16.

Schein, E.H., & Bennis, W.G. *Personal and organizational change through group methods: The laboratory approach.* New York: Wiley, 1965.

Shepard, H.A. Explorations in observant participation. In L.P. Bradford, J.R. Gibb, & K.D. Benne, *T-group theory and laboratory method,* New York: Wiley, 1964.

Skinner, B.F. The science of learning and the art of teaching. *Harvard Educational Review,* 1954, *24,* 99-113.

Smith, P.B. Attitude changes associated with training human relations. *British Journal of Social and Clinical Psychology,* 1964, *3,* 104-113.

Speroff, B.J. Rotational role playing used to develop managers. *Personnel,* 1954, *33,* 49-50.

Speroff, B.J. The substitution method in role playing grievance handling. *Personnel,* 1959, *38,* 9-12.

Tannenbaum, R., Weschler, I.R., & Massarik, F. *Leadership and organization: A behavioral science approach.* New York: McGraw-Hill, 1961.

Tiffin, J., & McCormick, E.J. *Industrial psychology.* Englewood Cliffs, N.J.: Prentice-Hall, 1965.

Wall, R.G. Untangling the snarls in a job rotation program. *Personnel,* 1963, *42,* 59-65.

Wilson, A.T.M. Personal communication, 1964.

Yoder, D. *Personnel management and industrial relations.* (5th ed.) Englewood Cliffs, N.J.: Prentice-Hall, 1962.

Zelko, H.P. Conference leadership training: A plan for practice projects. *Personnel,* 1952, *29* (1), 37-42.

The Relative Effectiveness of Training Methods—Expert Opinion and Research

STEPHEN J. CARROLL, JR.
FRANK T. PAINE
JOHN J. IVANCEVICH

Programmed instruction, sensitivity training, computer games, television, and role playing have been widely used in training only in recent years. These newer techniques when added to the older methods of the lecture, conference method, movie films, and case study method provide the fields of training and education with a number of alternatives to use in a particular situation. While availability of resources in the form of money, time, and personnel do play a significant part in the choice of one training method or another, another important criterion must be the relative effectiveness of the training method being considered for a particular training objective.

The obvious approach for identifying the relative effectiveness of various training methods for particular training objectives would be to analyze the research data on the subject. An attempt by the authors to do this, however, identified many limitations in the research studies that were carried out and great variability in the amount of research carried out on particular training methods.

With the difficulties experienced in examining the research on the subject, the authors decided to focus on expert opinion. Therefore, a survey was conducted of the 200 training directors who worked for the companies with the largest numbers of employees as indicated on *Fortune's* list of the top 500 corporations. It was felt that the number of employees in a firm would be a rough indicator of the amount of training the organization carries out. Since the research data on the effectiveness of various training methods was available, it was also decided to compare the limited research available with the judgments of the training directors. This might provide some indication of the extent to which research results on training method are known to training directors. In comparing ratings of effectiveness of the training directors with research, primary emphasis was placed on research studies carried out with adults in the employment situation since this would be the group most familiar to the training directors. Of course, this involves a minority of research studies done in this area. Most research studies on the effectiveness of alternative training methods have been carried out with college students.

Reprinted by permission of the authors and the publisher from *Personnel Psychology,* vol. 25 (1972), pp. 495-509.

Method

Questionnaire

A questionnaire was constructed which asked respondents to indicate the relative effectiveness of nine different training methods for achieving each of six training objectives. In the questionnaire, each training method was considered one at a time for the six different training objectives. In the effectiveness rating, five alternative degrees of effectiveness were used and these were scored as follows: highly effective (5), quite effective (4), moderately effective (3), limited effectiveness (2), and not effective (1).

Sample and Analysis

Two hundred questionnaires were mailed to the training directors of the two hundred firms with the largest number of employees. A follow-up letter was also used. There was a final usable return from 117 of these training directors for a return rate of 59 percent.

The average effectiveness ratings of the various training methods for each of the six training objectives were calculated and compared to each other by means of a "*t*" test.

Training Methods and Training Objectives

The training methods compared by the training directors were: programmed instruction, case study, lecture method (with questions), conference or discussion method, role playing, sensitivity training (*t*-group), TV-Lecture (lecture given to large audience over TV), Movie films, Business Gaming (using computer or hand calculator).

The training objectives used in the study were: acquire knowledge, change in attitudes, participant acceptance, retention of what is learned, development of interpersonal skills, development of problem solving skills.

Results

The results of the study are presented in table 1. This table indicates the relative ranking of the nine training methods for each of the training objectives, the average effectiveness rating given for each training method for each objective, and whether the differences in average ratings between any two training methods are large enough to be statistically significant.

Acquisition of Knowledge

Table 1 indicates that the training directors rated programmed instruction highest of all training methods on effectiveness in the acquisition of knowledge. The lecture is ranked as least effective of all training methods. The mean ratings indicate the average respondent believes that programmed instruction is "quite effective" for acquiring knowledge and the lecture method has only limited effectiveness for this objective.

Research on the subject seems to support the high relative rating given to programmed instruction by the training directors for knowledge acquisition. In 20 studies which compared programmed instruction to conventional lecture and discussion in an industrial situation, it was found that immediate learning was at least 10 percent higher under programmed instruction in seven comparisons, and there was not a practical difference between the conventional and programmed instruction in 13 comparisons (Nash, Muczyk, and Vettori, 1971). In 18 studies where programmed instruction and

TABLE 1

RATINGS OF TRAINING DIRECTORS ON EFFECTIVENESS OF ALTERNATIVE TRAINING METHODS FOR VARIOUS TRAINING OBJECTIVES

Training Method	Knowledge Acquisition		Changing Attitudes		Problem-Solving Skills		Interpersonal Skills		Participant Acceptance		Knowledge Retention	
	Mean	Mean Rank	Mean	Mean Rank	Mean	Mean Rank	Mean	Mean Rank	Mean	Mean Rank	Mean	Mean Rank
Case Study	3.56[2]	2	3.43[4]	4	3.69[2]	1	3.02[4]	4	3.80[4]	2	3.48[5]	2
Conference (Discussion) Method	3.33[4]	3	3.54[4]	3	3.26[5]	4	3.21[4]	3	4.16[1]	1	3.32[6]	5
Lecture (with questions)	2.53	9	2.20	8	2.00	9	1.90	8	2.74	8	2.49	8
Business Games	3.00	6	2.73[6]	5	3.58[2]	2	2.50[3]	5	3.78[4]	3	3.26[6]	6
Movie Films	3.16[7]	4	2.50[6]	6	2.24[7]	7	2.19[7]	6	3.44[7]	5	2.67[8]	7
Programmed Instruction	4.03[1]	1	2.22[8]	7	2.56[6]	6	2.11[7]	7	3.28[7]	7	3.74[1]	1
Role Playing	2.93	7	3.56[4]	2	3.27[5]	3	3.68[2]	2	3.56[5]	4	3.37[6]	4
Sensitivity Training (*t* group)	2.77	8	3.96[1]	1	2.98[5]	5	3.95[2]	1	3.33[7]	6	3.44[6]	3
Television Lecture	3.10[7]	5	1.99	9	2.01	8	1.81	9	2.74	9	2.47	9

[1] More effective than methods ranked 2 to 9 for this objective at .01 level of significance.
[2] More effective than methods ranked 3 to 9 for this objective at .01 level of significance.
[3] More effective than methods ranked 4 to 9 for this objective at .01 level of significance.
[4] More effective than methods ranked 5 to 9 for this objective at .01 level of significance.
[5] More effective than methods ranked 6 to 9 for this objective at .01 level of significance.
[6] More effective than methods ranked 7 to 9 for this objective at .01 level of significance.
[7] More effective than methods ranked 8 to 9 for this objective at .01 level of significance.
[×] More effective than method ranked 9 for this objective at .01 level of significance.

conventional lecture and discussion methods used in an industrial situation were compared with respect to time required to reach a certain level of proficiency, programmed instruction was superior to conventional instruction in 14 comparisons and there were no practical differences in four studies (Nash, Muczyk, and Vettori, 1971). A very large number of studies conducted with students also support the findings that programmed instruction is probably more effective than conventional instruction on amount of time taken to learn the material or on amount of material learned (Nash, et al., 1971; Schramm, 1962a). Nash and his colleagues, however, have pointed out that most of the studies involving a comparison of programmed with conventional instruction have not used a well planned and well carried out conventional class as the basis for comparison (Nash, et al., 1971).

The very low rating given to the lecture method as compared to the discussion method by the training directors with respect to effectiveness for knowledge acquisition is not congruent with research results in a few studies carried out with adults and in many studies with students as subjects. For example, Richard Hill (1960), in a controlled study, compared three lecture classes of 233, 25, and 25 participants with twelve discussion classes made up of 22 to 28 members each and found no difference in amount learned. Andrew (1954) found a lecture approach superior to that of a discussion and a film for imparting mental health information. Four extensive reviews of the literature where the subjects were primarily college students all concluded that on the basis of research comparisons made, lecture and discussion methods are equally effective for the acquisition of knowledge (Buxton, 1956; Dietrick, 1960; Stovall, 1958; and Verner and Dickinson, 1967).

The training directors also rated the television lecture as more effective than the conventional lecture. No studies were found where adults in the employment situation were compared, but the training directors' ratings are not supported by research results with students as subjects which generally show no significant differences between television lecture courses and conventional lecture courses. For example, in 32 comparisons between television and conventionally taught college students there was no difference in 29 of the comparisons (Carpenter and Greenhill, 1958). In 28 comparisons between television and conventionally taught courses at Miami (Ohio) University, only four differences were significant at or beyond the .05 level and three of these favored the conventional (Klausmeier, 1961). Schramm (1962b) in summarizing 393 studies of the amount learned in television courses versus conventionally taught courses found that in 65 percent of the comparisons there were no differences, in 21 percent of the comparisons the television approach was more effective, and in 14 percent of the comparisons the participants in the television courses did worse.

The training directors indicated that movie films and the case method were superior to the lecture method for knowledge acquisition. In the Andrew study (1954) cited earlier, the lecture was superior to a film for imparting knowledge to adult subjects. In a well controlled study where a class taught by the case method was compared to a class taught by a lecture-discussion approach, the case study section scored significantly higher on achievement tests (Butler, 1967).

Changing Attitudes

Table 1 indicates that the training directors believe that, in a relative sense, sensitivity training is the most effective way to change attitudes. They also believe that role playing, the conference method, and the case study method are more effective in changing attitudes than management games, movie films, programmed instruction, lecture and TV. The scores given the various methods indicates that most of the training directors only consider the first four methods listed in the table as having any effectiveness in changing attitudes.

The training directors indicated that the discussion method was superior to the lecture method in changing attitudes. In two fairly well controlled studies where the lecture and discussion approaches were compared in situations involving attitude change among adults (prisoners and executives), the discussion approach was more effective (Butler, 1966 and Silber, 1962). In five controlled studies involving changes in behavior of adults, the discussion approach was more effective than the lecture method in changing behavior (Bond, 1956; Levine and Butler, 1952; Lewin, 1958). Some of these comparisons were not entirely fair to the lecture method, however, since in the discussion groups the participants were usually asked to commit themselves to future actions while the subjects in the lecture groups were not asked to do this. In spite of this, it does appear that the discussion approach is superior to the lecture in changing attitudes and behavior as the training directors indicated.

The training directors believe that role playing can be quite effective in changing attitudes. Several studies conducted among students do show that role playing can be effective in changing attitudes (Festinger and Carlsmith, 1959; Harvey and Beverly, 1961). Role playing seems especially effective if the subjects participating in the role playing situation are asked to take the point of view opposite to their own and to verbalize this opposite point of view to others (Culbertson, 1957; Janis and King, 1954; King and Janis, 1956; Janis and Mann, 1965).

The low rating on effectiveness given to movies and business games by the training directors may not be justified. A U.S. Army study among adults showed that attitudes could be changed by films and that at least half of the attitude changes found persisted for at least nine weeks (U.S. War Department, 1943). Another study found that participation in a business game by students significantly changed attitudes toward risk taking (Lewin and Weber, 1969). However, this is obviously a very specific type of attitude.

The training directors rated the case method as more effective than the lecture in changing attitudes. In the one study found which made such a comparison, attitudes did change significantly more in a section where the case study approach was used than in the section of the course taught by the lecture-discussion method (Butler, 1967).

Finally, the training directors believe that sensitivity training is fairly effective in changing attitudes. Four studies using control groups have been conducted with adults where an attempt was made to see if behavior was changed as a result of sensitivity training (Boyd and Ellis, 1968; Bunker, 1965; Miles, 1965; Underwood, 1965; and Valiquet, 1968). These studies did find behavioral changes as a result of sensitivity training. With respect to attitude rather than behavior change, two studies, using a "before-and-after" measure without controls and with student and adult participants, found attitude changes as a result of sensitivity training (Schutz and Allen, 1966; Smith, 1964). Although there were certain methodological deficiencies in these studies, on balance, the results do indicate that sensitivity training can result in at least short run behavioral and attitudinal change although such change may not be related to greater job effectiveness (Campbell and Dunnette, 1968).

Problem Solving

For purposes of developing effectiveness in problem solving skills, the training directors rated the case study method, business games, role playing, and the conference method as having some effectiveness. In addition, these methods were rated more effective than sensitivity training, programmed instruction, movie films, the TV lecture, and the conventional lecture. These results are listed in table 1.

The case study method was rated highest in effectiveness for this training objective by the training directors and certainly it is true that the case study is probably generally considered to be the primary means of developing problem solving skills. Unfortunately, the research on the effectiveness of the case study as a training approach is very limited. Only a few studies were found that involved more than an attempt to obtain testimonials from course participants. Fox (1963) found that about one third of the students exposed to case study analysis improved significantly in their ability to handle cases, about a third made moderate improvement and a third made no improvement. Solem (1960) found that both the case study method and role playing were effective in learning how to derive solutions to problems but felt role playing better taught participants about how to gain acceptance of solutions. There is more evidence on the effectiveness of role playing in developing problem solving skills. In addition to the study by Solem (1960), studies by (Maier, 1953), Maier and Maier (1957), Maier and Hoffman (1960a; 1960b) and Maier and Solem, 1952) indicate that problem solving skills can be improved for both students and managers with the use of role playing. Two studies (Parnes and Meadow, 1959; Cohen, Whitmyre, and Funk, 1960) found that training in brainstorming could improve problem solving ability. Brainstorming could be taught by means of role-playing.

The training directors also ranked business games as being an effective training method for developing problem solving skills. However, as with the case study method, there is little research or analysis. Dill and Doppelt (1963) conducted a student self-report study which indicated that the students did not seem to learn much about specific problem solving solutions or strategies that could be used in other situations. Raia (1966) found that experience with a business game did not improve the ability to handle cases. However, the comparison group used case material. McKenney (1962) found that students in sections with games plus lectures understood the interrelationship between organizational factors better than students in sections with cases plus lectures.

Interpersonal Skills

Table 1 indicates that the training directors see the sensitivity training and role playing as being the most effective of the training methods in developing Interpersonal skills and feel the conference or discussion method and the case study method also have some effectiveness for this objective. In general, business games, movies films, programmed instruction, and the conventional and TV lecture are not considered effective for the development of interpersonal skills.

Most of the research which has concerned itself with the effectiveness of training methods in developing interpersonal skills have been on sensitivity training. Six studies of sensitivity training indicate that participants in sensitivity training describe others in more interpersonal terms than people without such training (Campbell and Dunnette, 1968). However, research specifically measuring changes in perceptual accuracy of others as result of sensitivity training has been inconclusive.

Some research on the development of interpersonal skills has examined role playing. A study by Bolda and Lawshe (1962) showed that role playing can be effective in increasing sensitivity to employee motivations, if the participants were involved in the role play. Another study indicated role playing effective in improving interviewing skills (Van Schacck 1957). In addition, studies by Maier, 1953; Maier and Hoffman,

1960a; and Maier and Maier, 1957) indicate that role playing can be used to improve group leadership skills which are a form of interpersonal skills.

Participant Acceptance

As table 1 indicates, the training directors rated the conference or discussion method, the case study method, and the use of business games as being significantly more acceptable to training course participants than movie films, sensitivity training, programmed instruction, the conventional lecture method, and the television lecture. In absolute terms the training directors seem to believe that all the methods except for the conventional and TV lecture are effective for achieving the objective of participant acceptance.

Several studies on managerial acceptance of the lecture versus the discussion approach indicate a preference among managers for the lecture or more leader centered approach. (Anderson, 1959; Filley and Reighhard, 1965; House, 1962; Mann and Mann, 1959). Two other studies of managers and a study of adults found no difference in reactions or attitudes to the use of the lecture and discussion approaches (Hill, 1960; House, 1965).

The training directors also indicated that the television lecture rated low on participant acceptance. Reviews of research by Kumata (1956 and 1960; and Schramm, 1962a) indicate that television has fairly high acceptance among adults as a training method and with young children, and much lower acceptance among high school and college students.

The training directors rated business games as high on participant acceptance. Raia (1966) found that business students in sections of a course which used a business game did not differ in attitudes toward the course from students who had sections without the business game. Rowland, Gardner, and Nealey (1970) found only a few students participating in a business game felt the game was a valuable learning experience and attitudes toward the course were not improved as a result of the addition of the business game to it.

The training directors rated role playing as effective in participant acceptance. A series of studies in six organizations by Bolda and Lawshe (1962) indicated fair acceptance for role playing by managerial personnel. The training directors also rated the case study method as high on participant acceptance. A study by Fox, 1963; found that attitudes toward the case study method in the form of student testimonials were favorable. However, Castore (1951) found interest in cases dwindled after a period of exposure to them. The relatively higher rating given by the training directors to programmed instruction versus the lecture method is supported in a study conducted at IBM (Hughes and McNamara, 1961), and in a study by Neidt and Meredith (1966). It should be remembered, however, that several studies show that participant acceptance of a training approach is a function of their experience with it (Guetzkow, Kelly and McKeachie, 1954; Harris, 1960; and Hughes, 1963).

Retention of Knowledge

As table 1 indicates, the training directors rate programmed instruction, the case study method, sensitivity training, role playing, the conference method and business gaming as significantly more effective than movie films and conventional and television lectures. These latter three training methods are also rated in absolute terms as not being effective for retention of knowledge.

There has not been much research on this topic. The research that has been completed has been primarily with college students and shown no clear superiority for the lecture or discussion methods as compared with each other (Dietrick, 1960, Verner and Dickinson, 1967), for the movie film as compared with the lecture and discussion methods (Sodnovitch and Pophorn, 1961; VanderMeer, 1948; Verner and Dickinson, 1967), for the television lecture as compared to the conventional lecture or discussion approach (Kumata, 1960; Klausmeir, 1961), or for programmed instruction as compared to the conventional lecture or discussion methods (Nash, Muczyk, Vettori, 1971). The research reviews generally conclude that the amount of material retained is proportional to the amount learned (Dietrick, 1960; Verner and Dickinson, 1967).

Discussion

For most of the training objectives the training directors believed that about half of the training methods listed were effective and the other half not very effective for the training objective stated. Furthermore, the training methods considered effective for one objective were usually considered ineffective for another objective. This seems to indicate that the training directors are properly discriminating in their evaluations of the various alternative training methods. The training directors differ most from the research results in their ratings of effectiveness for the lecture method for various training objectives. In general the research shows that the lecture method has more effectiveness for acquiring knowledge, and for participant acceptance, than the training directors believe it has. It is not known why such a negative attitude toward the lecture method exists. Among reasons suggested for this bias against different forms of the lecture are: the current emphasis on "participation," the fact that nonspecialists can use the lecture method, but not other methods, the downgrading of the lecture method by advocates of other approaches, or unsatisfactory personal experiences with the lecture approach.

The training directors may err somewhat too much toward the positive side in the evaluations of programmed instruction. While it is an effective training method, it does not seem to be as superior as the training directors believe it is. (Nash, et al., 1971)

With respect to particular training objectives the training directors seem to be most different from the research on participant acceptance. The evidence to date certainly would indicate that the conference or discussion method, and the business games are not rated as high by participants as by the training directors. Also the lecture, conventional and TV lectures, and sensitivity training are rated higher than the training directors indicate.

The review of the literature reveals great gaps in knowledge about the effectiveness of various training methods. While a considerable amount of research has been conducted on sensitivity training, the conventional and TV lecture, and conference methods, little research has been conducted on the case study method, the business game and role playing. In addition, much more research needs to be focused on the personal and situational factors which moderate the effectiveness of alternative training methods.

In carrying out new research studies it is important that the alternative training methods being compared are subjected to a fair evaluation. As indicated previously, we and others, have noticed in several studies that although control groups were used and before and after measures were taken, fair comparisons were not always made between the alternative training methods studied.

References

Anderson, R. C. Learning in discussions: A resume of the authoritarian-democratic study. *Harvard Educational Review*, 1959, 29, 201-215.

Andrew, G. A study of the effectiveness of a workshop method for mental health education. *Mental Hygiene*, 1954, 38, 267-278.

Bolda, R. A. and Lawshe, C. H. Evaluation of role playing. *Personnel Administration*, 1962, 25, 40-42.

Bond, B. W. The group discussion-decision approach—An appraisal of its use in health education. *Dissertation Abstracts*, 1956, 16, 903.

Boyd, J. B. and Ellis, J. D. *Findings of research into senior management seminars*. Toronto: The Hydro-Electric Power Commission of Toronto, 1962. Cited by J. P. Campbell and M. D. Dunnette. Effectiveness of T-group experiences in managerial training and development. *Psychological Bulletin*, 1968, 70, 73-104.

Bunker, D. R. Individual applications of laboratory training. *Journal of Applied Behavioral Science*, 1965, 1, 131-148.

Butler, E. D. An experimental study of the case method in teaching the social foundations of education. *Dissertation Abstracts*, 1967, 27, 2912.

Butler, J. L. A study of the effectiveness of lecture versus conference teaching techniques in adult education. *Dissertation Abstracts*, 1966, 26, 3712.

Buxton, C. E. *College teaching: A psychologist's view*. New York: Harcourt-Brace, 1956.

Campbell, J. P. and Dunnette, M. D. Effectiveness of T-group experiences in managerial training and development. *Psychological Bulletin*, 1968, 70, 73-104.

Carpenter, C. R. and Greenhill, L. *An investigation of closed circuit television for teaching university courses*. Instructional Television Project Report #2, University Park, Pennsylvania. Penn. State University, 1958.

Castore, G. F. Attitudes of students toward the case method of instruction in a human relations course. *Journal of Educational Research*, 1951, 45, 201-213.

Cohen, D., Whitmyre, J. W., and Funk, W. H. Effect of group cohesiveness and training upon creative thinking. *Journal of Applied Psychology*, 1960, 44, 319-322.

Culbertson, F. Modification of an emotionally held attitude through role playing. *Journal of Abnormal and Social Psychology*, 1957, 54, 230-233.

Dietrick, D. C. Review of research, in R. J. Hill, *A comparative study of lecture and discussion methods*. Pasadena, California: The Fund for Adult Education, 1960, pp. 90-118.

Dill, W. R. and Doppelt, N. The acquisition of experience in a complex management game. *Management Science*, 1963, 10, 30-46.

Festinger, L. and Carlsmith, J. Cognitive consequences of forced compliance. *Journal of Abnormal and Social Psychology*, 1959, 58, 203-210.

Filley, A. C. and Reighard, F. H. *A preliminary survey of training attitudes and needs among actual and potential attendees at management institute programs*. Madison: University of Wisconsin, 1962, cited in R. J. House, Managerial reactions to two methods of management training. Personnel Psychology, 1965, 18, 311-319.

Fox, W. M. A measure of the effectiveness of the case method in teaching human relations. *Personnel Administration*, 1963, 26, 53-57.

Guetzkow, H., Kelly, E. L. and McKeachie, W. J. An experimental comparison of recitation, discussion, and tutorial methods in college teaching. *Journal of Educational Psychology*, 1954, 45, 193-207.

Harris, C. W. (Ed.) *Encyclopedia of educational research*. New York: Macmillan, 1960.

Harvey, O. and Beverly, G. Some personality correlates of concept change through role playing. *Journal of Abnormal and Social Psychology*, 1961, 63, 125-130.

Hill, R. A. *A comparative study of lecture and discussion methods*. Pasadena, Calif.: The Fund for Adult Education, 1960.

House, R. J. An experiment in the use of management training standards. *Journal of The Academy of Management*, 1962, 5, 76-81.

House, R. J. Managerial reactions to two methods of management training. Personnel Psychology, 1965, 18, 311-319.

Hughes, J. L. Effects of changes in programmed text format and reduction in classroom time on achievement and attitudes of industrial trainees. *Journal of Programmed Instruction*, 1963, 1, 143-55.

Hughes, J. L. and McNamara, W. J. A comparative study of programmed and conventional instruction in industry. *Journal of Applied Psychology*, 1961, 45, 225-231.

Janis, I. and King, B. The influence of role playing on opinion change. *Journal of Abnormal and Social Psychology*, 1954, 49, 211-218.

Janis, I. and Mann, L. Effectiveness of emotional role-playing in modifying smoking habits and attitudes. *Journal of Experimental Research in Personality*, 1965, 1, 84-90.

King, B. and Janis, I. Comparison of the effectiveness of improvised vs. non-improvised role playing in producing opinion changes. *Human Relations*, 1956, 9, 177-186.

Klausmeier, H. J. *Learning and human abilities*. New York: Harper and Bros., 1961.

Kumata, H. *An inventory of instructional television research*. Ann Arbor, Michigan: Educational Television and Radio Center, 1956.

Kumata, H. A decade of teaching by television. In W. Schramm, (Ed.), *The impact of educational television*. Urbana: University of Illinois Press, 1960, 176-192.

Levine, J. and Butler, J. Lecture vs. group decision in changing behavior. *Journal of Applied Psychology*, 1952, 36, 29-33.

Lewin, A. Y. and Weber, R. L. Management game teams in education and organization research: An experiment on risk taking. *Academy of Management Journal*, 1969, 12, 49-58.

Lewin, K. Group decision and social change. In E. E. Maccoby, T. M. Newcombe, E. L. Hartley, (Eds.), *Readings in social psychology*. New York: Henry Holt and Company, 1958, pp. 197-211.

McKenney, J. L. An evaluation of a business game in an MBA curriculum. *The Journal of Business*, 1962, 35, 278-286.

Maier, N. R. F. and Solem, A. R. The contribution of the discussion leader to the quality of group thinking. *Human Relations*, 1952, 3, 155-174.

Maier, N. R. F. An experimental test of the effect of training on discussion leadership. *Human Relations*, 1953, 6, 161-173.

Maier, N. R. F. and Maier, R. A. An experimental test of the effects of "developmental" vs. "free" discussions on the quality of group decisions. *Journal of Applied Psychology*, 1957, 41, 320-323.

Maier, N. R. F. and Hoffman, L. R. Quality of first and second solutions in group problem solving. *Journal of Applied Psychology*, 1960, 44, 278-283. (a)

Maier, N. R. F. and Hoffman, L. R. Using trained "developmental" discussion leaders to improve further the quality of group decisions. *Journal of Applied Psychology*, 1960, 44, 247-251. (b)

Mann, J. H. and Mann, C. H. The importance of group tasks in producing group-member personality and behavior change. *Human Relations*, 1959, 221, 75-80.

Margulies, S. and Eigen, L. D. *Applied programmed instruction*. New York: John Wiley and Sons, 1962.

Miles, M. B. Changes during and following laboratory training: A clinical-experimental study. *Journal of Applied Behavioral Science*, 1965, 1, 215-242.

Nash, A. N., Muczyk, J. P., and Vettori, F. L. The relative practical effectiveness of programmed instruction. Personnel Psychology, 1971, 397-418.

Neidt, C. O. and Meredith, T. Changes in attitudes of learners when programmed instruction is interpolated between two conventional instruction experiences. *Journal of Applied Psychology*, 1966, 50, 130-137.

Parnes, S. J. and Meadow, A. Effects of brainstorming instructions on creative problem solving by trained and untrained subjects. *Journal of Educational Psychology*, 1959, 50, 171-176.

Raia, A. P. A study of the educational value of management games. *The Journal of Business*, 1966, 39, 339-352.

Rowland, K. M., Gardner, D. M., and Nealey, S. M. Business gaming in education and research, in *Proceedings of the 13th Annual Midwest Management Conference Academy of Management,* Midwest Division, East Lansing, Michigan, April, 1970.

Schramm, W. *The research on programmed instruction: An annotated bibliography.* Stanford, Calif.: Institute for Communication Research, 1962. (a)

Schramm, W. What we know about learning from instructional television, in *Educational Television–The Next Ten Years,* Stanford: Stanford University Press, 1962, 52-74. (b)

Schutz, W. C. and Allen, V. L. The effects of a T-group laboratory on interpersonal behavior. *Journal of Applied Behavioral Science,* 1966, 2, 265-286.

Silber, M. B. A comparative study of three methods of effecting attitude change. *Dissertation Abstracts,* 1962, 22, 2488.

Smith, P. N. Attitude changes associated with training in human relations. *British Journal of Social and Clinical Psychology,* 1964, 3, 104-113.

Sodnovitch, J. M. and Pophorn, W. J. *Retention value of filmed science courses.* Kansas State College of Pittsburg, 1961.

Solem, A. R. Human relations training: Comparisons of case study and role playing. *Personnel Administration,* 1960, 23, 29-37.

Stovall, T. F. Lecture vs. discussion. *Phi Delta Kappan,* 1958, 39, 255-258.

Underwood, W. J. Evaluation of laboratory method training. *Training Directors Journal,* 1965, 19, 34-40.

U. S. War Department. *What the soldier thinks: A monthly digest of war department studies on the attitudes of American troops.* Army Services Forces, Morales Services Division, I, 1943, 13.

Valiquet, I. M. Contribution to the evaluation of a management development program. Unpublished master's thesis. Massachusetts Institute of Technology, 1964. Cited by J. P. Campbell and M. D. Dunnette. Effectiveness of T-group experiences in managerial training and development. *Psychological Bulletin,* 1968, 70, 73-104.

VanderMeer, A. W. *Relative effectiveness of exclusive film instruction, films plus study guides, and typical instructional methods. Progress Report #10.* Instructional Film Program. State College, Pennsylvania: Pennsylvania State College, 1948.

Van Schacck, H. Jr. Naturalistic role playing: A method of interview training for student personnel administrators. *Dissertation Abstracts,* 1957, 17, 801.

Verner, C. and Dickinson, G. The lecture, an analysis and review of research. *Adult Education,* 1967, 17, 85-100.

CHAPTER **4**

Development Problems: The Individual, the Organization, and the Career

One of the new emphases of the personnel administrator of the 1970s (see the Johnson reading in chap. 1) is consideration of the needs and desires of the individual when making job assignments. Along these same lines, the personnel manager must be able to project his human resource needs on a long-range basis. By examining the organization's needs for future manpower assignments, the personnel department can better help the new employee plan his career—not just his first job assignment.

More and more organizations are currently employing career development specialists to help the new and older employees alike plan their future with the organization. While a training program (as described in chap. 3) is designed to help the employee adjust to the organization at a specific point in time, career development is an ongoing program which is designed to help the employee best serve himself and the organization during his working life.

In the first reading in this chapter, Hall examines the careers of recent college graduates in organizational settings. He describes how the desires and values of new graduates affect the organization, and how the organization, in turn, affects the new graduate. Hall presents a model of career development which he recommends to the personnel administration as a method of increasing the young manager's commitment and improving the organizational climate.

A more traditional program for improving the manager's commitment to the organization has generally been found in the management development program. In chap. 3, Campbell, *et al.* state that a "training" program and a "development" program are usually distinguished on the basis of the subject matter (specific versus general) or the level in the organization from which the participants are drawn (nonmanagers versus managers). Burke, in the second reading in this chapter, compares a management development program with an organizational development program. He agrees with Campbell, *et al.* that a management development program is nothing more than an executive training program designed to modify attitudes and skills of managers. Such training programs are designed to help the managers understand the contingencies of reinforcement (see the Hamner article in chap. 6) and how he can perform in order to be rewarded.

Whereas management development focuses on the individual in the organization, organizational development, or O.D., begins with an examination of the current or-

ganizational culture—that is, norms, procedures and general climate of the organization. O.D. is a method of modifying the culture of the organization to take advantage
of human resources and to allow the organization to become proactive rather than
reactive to changes in the environment of the organizations.

While Burke compares and contrasts development at the individual and organizational level, our third reading by Beer and Huse describes how a systems approach
model of O.D. was successfully applied in an ongoing organization. Both the Burke
and the Beer and Huse articles point out that training, career development and management development programs are not incompatible with an O.D. program. Instead, they
should be viewed as a few of many tools used that can be in a formal O.D. program.

The Beer and Huse model assumes that an organization is an open system that
converts individual needs and expectations into outputs. Organizational outputs can be
increased by improving the quality of the inputs and by unleashing more of the potential inherent in the human resources. The adjustment of the organizational processes to
meet the needs of the environment and of the persons in it is one of the key objectives
of O.D. programs.

Generally, the organizational development program falls under the direct responsibility of the personnel director. For example, at General Motors, this program is
under the direction of the Vice-president of Personnel, Organization and Development,
and at Corning Glass Works under the direction of the Manager of Organizational
Research and Development. When we examine the status and importance of these two
departments (which are becoming more and more typical in large organizations) within
their respective organizations, we see many of the reasons why the readings in chapter
1 are appropriate—the personnel function is no longer the "whipping boy" of the typical organization but is now seen as a vital contributor to the productivity and
survival-potential of the organization.

Potential for Career Growth

DOUGLAS T. HALL

What Young People Want in Work

. . . Recent graduates want challenging work—work that is meaningful and
ability-stretching to them. Basically they want to have more of a sense of feeling competent in the work they do. Competence, the need to have an impact on one's personal
environment, is a critically important human need (White, 1959). This seems especially
strong in the present generation of young people.

Another valued feature is a more collaborative relationship with their superiors:
they want a lowering of the authority distance between them and the next man up,

From *Personnel Administration*, May-June 1971. Reprinted by permission of the International Personnel Management Association.

more opportunities to make their own personal choices, and an organizational climate that is more open and flexible. They also want an opportunity to get more psychologically involved in the work they are doing; they place increasing stress on intrinsic rather than extrinsic rewards for their work. Dissatisfaction about intrinsic work challenge is especially strong in the first year of work (Schein, 1968). There are many complaints about job rotation training programs, in which people are given special projects and are asked to do research on a limited problem. Very often they feel they are unable to get deeply enough into that one project to get a sense of being competent and a feeling that they are really learning something new; it may be a standard project that all new people are assigned to for two or three months, a training assignment that the company does not really take seriously. The new employees may also feel frustrated because they cannot go to the next step and be responsible for action that may grow out of their recommendations.

Difficulties Encountered

Often, however, the talk of wanting challenge and competence seems to be more rhetoric than reality. When one looks at what happens, what the new people actually do, they often seem to avoid precisely what they say they most desire.

There is a tendency to avoid sustained effort on one activity, even though there is much talk about wanting to get really involved in something. If the opportunity exists young people often do not take advantage of it. Related to this, although they talk of personal involvement and growth, one senses that they really do not push themselves to their limits. This is especially frustrating when one knows that these are impressively bright people. Perhaps one reason athletes tend to do well in business is that they are used to developing themselves—setting goals for themselves and getting into the disciplined process of pushing themselves to their limits. Unfortunately, many new recruits are so bright that they can perform fairly well on a minimum amount of effort. Then they tend to become apathetic because they rarely experience success by their own high standards.

Another frequent problem is a difficulty in committing oneself for too long to any one system. Very often, when young people talk about personal searching and discovering themselves, one gets the impression that they are actually avoiding committing themselves to anything permanent. They move from one job to another and from one system to another—whether the system is an organization, a group, or a family relationship.

In spite of their concern for challenge, new people often avoid some of what I see as the true challenges in work—facing up to authoritarian supervisors and trying to work with them, confronting differences, and resolving those differences. As Ondrack (1970) says, among people who score low on authoritarianism there is a tendency to give up on those who score high and say, "Okay, he's rigid, that's his bag. I can't fight it."

There is a tendency to avoid interpersonal conflicts, which is surprising because a lot of students are committed to the idea that there are very strong conflicts and problems existing in society, and that there is a need to use power and confrontation to produce social change. . . .

However, conflict can be one of the most important determinants of challenge in a job. Indeed, some returned Peace Corps volunteers have indicated that business—or work in other types of large organizations—is more challenging than anything they faced in the Peace Corps, because in business there is greater conflict and resistance to their ideas. It is relatively easy, they say, to go to a foreign country where everybody sees them as experts. However, when a person goes to work in business, people resist his ideas; he has to compete and sell his ideas to superiors skeptical of (and perhaps threatened by) the efforts of the young.

Another characteristic of recent graduates is a sense of impatience and confidence often based on moral imperatives that create an appearance of arrogance. These are people who are critical and concerned. They look as if they have all the answers, and this creates a sense of threat for older people in an organization. Unfortunately, it may be an impression that is quite a bit stronger than the young people themselves want to communicate.

A Syndrome of Unused Career Potential

One unfortunate overall result of these differences between young graduates and older members of organizations is the creation of a syndrome of unused potential, a syndrome which shows up in several different self-reinforcing effects.

Results from a number of different studies (Berlew and Hall, 1966; Schein, 1967; Hall and Lawler, 1969; Campbell, 1968) show clearly that challenge is very important to the way a person's career develops. In a way it is unfortunate that the word *challenge* has become a part of the rhetoric both for students criticizing organizations and for recruiters praising their organizations, because people tend to lose track of just how important it really is. A study of young managers (Berlew and Hall, 1966) followed people at American Telephone & Telegraph for five years and in another company for seven years. Performance was evaluated by their salary scale and ratings from their supervisors and other people, mainly in personnel, who were in a position to evaluate them.

The more challenging a man's job was in his first year with the organization, the more effective and successful he was even five or seven years later.

Unfortunately, the amount of challenge in initial jobs in most organizations is invariably low, despite the fact that it is very important. In a study of R & D organizations, there were only two companies out of twenty-two interviewed in which people described their first jobs as being moderately high or high on challenge (Hall and Lawler, 1969). There was only one company that had a conscious policy of making the first assignments difficult. Most companies felt that they should bring the person along slowly, starting him off on an easy project and cautiously adding more challenge only as the recruit proved his ability at each stage of escalation. This is a strategy to *measure* the person's ability by approaching it from below rather than by *stretching* it through high work goals and high standards of excellence!

A traditional problem is the expensive training which is invested in new employees before they can earn their pay. Increased challenge and less formal training would increase the utilization of new people from the very beginning, benefiting both the individual and the organization.

Another factor found to be related to performance was pressure on the person to do high quality work and to assume a degree of financial responsibility in his work (Hall and Lawler, 1970). In the R & D setting this pressure was often associated with accepting responsibility, getting new projects for the organization, and obtaining outside funding for the work. This may have required direct contact with customers rather than through the supervisor. Organizations in which people felt personal pressure for quality work and attaining the financial goals of the organization were found to be highly effective. But again, we rarely found evidence of quality pressure or evidence of professional people being given financial responsibility in their work.

Self-actualization Satisfied Least

A further problem was that the most important need for the researchers—self-actualization—was the least satisfied (Hall and Lawler, 1969). Further, we found that the longer researchers worked for an organization, the less important self-fulfillment was to them and the more important security was. Increasing tenure was also related to three significant changes in self-image: the people reported themselves as being less active, less strong, and less independent as tenure increased. The intriguing idea here was that there is theory (Argyris, 1957) that predicts just this kind of human decay with increasing length of service in organizations. Because of the conflict between the needs of growing individuals and the requirements for organizations for tight control and uniformity, people become less concerned about their own growth, and they become less independent, less strong, and less active as they spend more time in the organization.

Another finding (Hall and Lawler, 1969) that surprised the R & D managers in our feedback session with them concerned a communications gap—a disagreement between what the managers were doing and what their subordinates said the managers were doing. We asked everyone if the organization had a regular performance appraisal system and, if so, were the results discussed with the man appraised. In most of the organizations, the directors said, "Sure, we do it every six months."

We talked to the researchers. Not only did they generally report that the appraisals did not take place, but for some we had to explain what a performance appraisal system was!

Because the appraisal system seemed to be there when we talked to the directors and it was not there when we talked to the professionals, we called it the "vanishing performance appraisal." There was little feedback on how people were performing. We know that feedback is important for the learning and self-correction of any kind of system, and this resource was being lost to these R & D systems.

High Aspirations

Another aspect of the syndrome was a great sense on the part of the recent graduates that their important skills and abilities were not being used. New graduates possess high levels of training when they begin work. Indeed, the definition of education is to bring students to the frontiers of knowledge, the very latest techniques and theories. One purpose of a college or university is to perform the change function in society, and one way it does this is through the people they send out. In this sense, new graduates are societal change agents. They come into the organization with new techniques, and they want to apply them. They find this difficult first because they lack the skills of applying what they know and second, because the organization tends to resist innovation. This difficulty is compounded by the fact that people coming out of college build up a falsely high aspiration level about the extent to which they are going to be using their new skills.

One example of the unrealistic aspiration problem is a man I knew who had just finished his first year at the Harvard Business School. He was seriously hoping to begin as a vice president of finance for a respectably-sized organization. He was convinced that he had the ability to perform the job, and he was going to find it. Although he did not find it, he still felt that he *ought* to be a vice president in charge of finance. That attitude shows through; on the one hand it creates anger on the part of his superiors, and on the other hand it creates a certain amount of threat. In fact, developing this degree of confidence in students is one of the main socializing functions of many business schools.

Creating Challenge

Another problem is that the new recruit really does not know how to create his own challenge in a job. This is the fault of educational institutions. Very often people are accustomed to being *given* projects and *given* challenging work. They do not know how to take an unstructured and undefined situation and find something important in it, thereby defining the job for themselves. There is a contradiction: they want challenge, and independence, but they don't want to find challenge independently. They want it given to them by someone else. Research has shown that people tend to be rather passive about even major career decisions: the type of organizations they work for, whether they change jobs, and the type of jobs they accept (Roe and Baruch, 1967). Very often they respond to external challenge, demands, or changes more than they do to their own career blueprint. A person does not tend to chart a course for himself and decide that this is the time to make this move, and this is the time to make this other move, and this is how to get from point A to point B. Career choice is not really as much a conscious strategy as one might expect.

Sources of Threat

Young graduates often threaten their superiors (Schein, 1968) and this threat is probably a major contributor to the syndrome of unused potential. There are different reasons why superiors may be threatened by a new man. For one, training programs are often defined so that the new man is seen as someone special, a "bright young man," or a "crown prince." However, his supervisor may be in a terminal position. He may have worked all his life to reach his position, and now is confronted with a "young kid," who within a year, may be promoted above the position which the supervisor had taken his whole career to attain.

Another cause for threat is that new men are coming in right out of college and may know more about a special area than the superior does. This threat may apply more in technical work than in general management. This threat is compounded when the superior has had to spend a great deal of time doing administrative work which kept him from upgrading his technical knowledge.

High starting salaries cause problems, too. The young man today makes far more than the boss did when he started his career; in fact, the new man's salary probably comes painfully close to what the boss is making right now. Personal styles are also different—the young man is probably more likely to rock the boat, make waves, and create pressure for change. All of these personal threats created by young people can reinforce the syndrome of unused potential and actually make their later experiences less satisfying.

Negative Effect

The overall result of this syndrome is that in the early career years one finds great changes in the man's self-image, attitudes, aspirations and motivation—all generally in a negative direction. He is less optimistic about how he is going to succeed with the organization (Campbell, 1968). He sees himself as having less impact on the organization, and his values tend to conform more to those of the organization (Schein, 1967). Schein's research shows how the values of business students tend to move toward those of authority figures in whatever system they join. Among students in an MBA program, values tend to move toward the values of the faculty and, interestingly, away from those of businessmen. But when the MBA's start working, they move back again toward the managers' values and away from the faculty's values. Thus, as they become more integrated into their organization, a certain amount of change toward organizational values tends to occur, but one would hope that the new man would not also lose whatever creativity he might bring into the system.

Model for Career Growth

If there is some sort of self-perpetuating syndrome causing decay in the new man's self-image and career motivation, it is possible to reverse that process and find a way to increase his motivation and self-image.

One way of thinking about career growth is in terms of analogies with child development. It is generally agreed that the first year of a child's life is a critical period (Bowlby, 1951), and that the first year of a person's work experience seems equally critical (Berlew & Hall, 1966). We also know that there tend to be more changes in attitude and motivation in the career than in specific skills and ability (Campbell, 1968); i.e., post-college career development seems to be more a process of socialization and attitude change than a process of acquiring skill and competence.

If the first year is the critical period in developing attitudes, why not begin by giving the new person the kind of challenging job experience which will have a lasting effect?[1]

Every challenge can establish a self-motivated cycle of behavior. Hall and Nougaim (1968) found that young managers who were successful in their organization experienced greater satisfaction of their achievement and self-esteem needs than people who were less successful; also, in all managers there was a marked increase in the need for achievement over time, which seems appropriate for business managers.[2] Achievement is important in a business career, but achievement satisfaction increased only for successful people; it decreased for less successful people. The more successful men also became more involved in their work—they saw work as playing a more important role in their total lives at the end of five years in the organization than they did in their first. It is interesting that the people who were less successful did not become less involved; they stayed about equally involved. This is encouraging, because it may mean that if there is some sort of cycle, it may work more in the positive direction than in the negative. The encouraging thing for the people who are less successful is that they do not seem to decrease their involvement or to "drop out." At some later point they may move into more challenging jobs, experience some sort of success, and then become more involved. Therefore, the problems of unused potential may not be irreversible.

Conditions for Psychological Success

When one puts these ideas of success cycles together, one comes close to a concept developed by Kurt Lewin (1936) and applied by Chris Argyris (1964) to organizations, called *psychological success*. In experimental studies where people were working on attaining very specific tasks, a person would be asked to set a target or goal for himself and try to achieve it. Lewin measured their aspiration levels and then looked at what happened to the aspiration levels and self-esteem after either success or failure. After people were successful they generally tended to raise their level of aspiration and to experience greater self-esteem. The response to failure varied. If the person had an initially high sense of self-esteem, he tended to persist, not to lower his aspirations. The reaction to success also varied. If a person had a history of failure and had succeeded once, he often stopped while he was ahead.

The relationship between a career and the experiment seems clear; the difference is that with the career the time span is the person's entire life rather than a two-hour experimental session. But the similarities seem quite strong. One can get some clues to career growth by looking at the conditions that Lewin found were important to psychological success.

1. The person had to choose a challenging goal for himself, one that represented a challenging level of aspiration to him.

2. He had to set his goals independently; it had to be his own goal, not one imposed by somebody else.

3. The goal must be meaningful to him, central to his image of himself, so that if he succeeded he would see himself in a different light as a more competent person.

4. He had to attain the goal he sought.

In terms of the psychological success model, then, if people set challenging goals for themselves related to their careers, and if they work independently and attain them, they should experience a sense of success, and they should see themselves in a

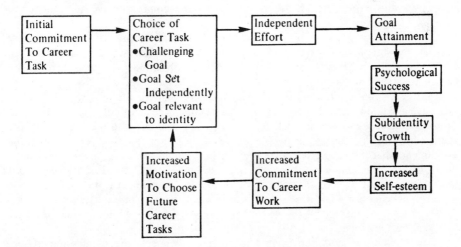

Figure 1. A Model of Career Growth Through Psychological Success. (From Douglas T. Hall. "A Theoretical Model of Career Subidentity Development in Organizational Settings," in *Organizational Behavior and Human Performance*, 1970).

different light. This success would then lead to self-identity growth. The experience of increased self-esteem may also generalize to their career identity, so that they would be more committed to their careers and be more likely to set additional career goals again at a later time.

This model is shown in Figure 1.

The success model is also similar to McGregor's (1960) description of management by objectives and target setting. McGregor was not talking specifically about a man's career, but it is easy to relate the two. Challenging goals, as used here, are similar to what McGregor talks about as an objective, a concrete measurable target that a man can work for and either attain or not attain over a particular time period. Then later to the extent that the person attains the goal, he becomes more involved in his career and also becomes a more effective member of his organization.

Changes Needed to Facilitate Growth

What kind of changes in the organization might be made to facilitate career development? Probably the very first would be changes in jobs. How does one change jobs to get people into a positive success cycle?

The First Assignment

The first step would be to analyze the initial jobs that new people are given in the organization. What happens to a young person when he walks in the door? If that first year is a critical period, when he is especially susceptible to learning new attitudes, what is happening to him during that important time? Is he just absorbing information and not really accomplishing important objectives? Is that time sort of an investment that the company feels required to make in him? Or is the first year a time when the company really expects to challenge him? Does the company have some concrete goals for him to reach?

The ironic fact seems to be that organizations look at the first year as a necessary evil: an investment they have to make in the person, until they can assign him an important project where he can make a valuable contribution. At the same time, the man is impatient for something that has meaning and challenge.

Both the organization and the individual want and need the new person to have challenge and good performance, but for understandable reasons both are frustrated. It is not easy to make jobs more challenging when one gets down to the specifics of the task. It may mean hiring fewer people so the organization can do a better job on the assignments that they are given. One organization found that its turnover was so high that it had to hire 120 men each year in order to have 20 at the end of the year. So it took a gamble and figured that perhaps this attrition was because the first-year jobs were so unchallenging. The next year it hired 30 people and worked hard on upgrading first-year jobs. At the end of the year 25 people were employed and giving far better first-year performances.

Another recommendation related to early challenge is the elimination of job-rotating training programs. The first job ought to be a realistic, permanent assignment and not one seen as special or part of a training program. This generates *job success* rather than a *succession of jobs*. Moving through different short-term jobs means men are observers of different parts of the organization, rather than fully-functioning participants. The term "rotation" literally means "going around in circles." Maybe that is one reason why young employees' self-perceptions tend to go down in the first year. The young person feels that he is not doing anything really worthwhile, that he is just being paid to sit around and observe. If he stays, this is going to have an adverse effect on his self-image—he is being paid a lot for doing little.

The Supervisor

Another consideration is the superior to whom a new man is assigned. Probably the boss has more impact on the definition of the job than any other factor. Therefore, if management is going to redesign jobs, it must also redesign bosses or train them to deal with a new man.

This was another realization of the previously-mentioned company that tried upgrading first-year jobs. It learned in the first year that it had to work with the bosses as well as new recruits. In the second year it put the supervisors through a long training program before new people came into the organization. Then, as part of the training program for the new people, the company also involved the superiors, so that each recruit and his boss went through the program as a team.

This type of learning helps a superior develop a sense of what we call "supportive autonomy" (Hall and Schneider, 1969), so he can tread the fine line between allowing a man independence (i.e., "sink or swim") on the one hand, and providing assistance with excessive control, on the other hand. The combination of autonomy and the supervisors' availability and willingness to work as a coach when the young person wants help may be the best combination for learning (Hall and Schneider, 1969; Pelz and Andrews, 1966).

Performance Review

Supervisors should also learn how to provide performance reviews. This very specific kind of skill is one that supervisors ought to be able to do quite well. If the new employee is left on his own to determine his performance, his conclusion may be based on highly distorted information. It is far better to have the feedback come through formal channels and get it straight rather than have the person get it through indirect and unreliable means, such as the supervisors' manner of saying hello on a certain morning.

An important need for supervisors in this area is to develop skills in confronting interpersonal problems. If the new person is given autonomy, and if the supervisor sees himself as a bit more of a helper than he may have originally, this suggests that some new problems may arise. The new man is going to make mistakes, and he and his supervisor are going to have to learn how to get through these problems and conflicts as a pair. Also, the supervisor has to learn to put on pressure at the appropriate times, when to exercise authority, and when to get tough. It is not only a matter of learning new values and attitudes about supervisory style, it is also a matter of translating these into specific interpersonal skills and knowing how to apply them at various times.

One way of achieving some of the necessary confrontation and problem-solving skills would be through a planned, structured exercise. A group of new employees could meet and draw up a statement describing their attitudes toward the organization, toward their supervisors, and toward their careers. Their supervisors would also meet as a group and draft a similar statement covering their attitudes toward the new men and their ideas of what the views of the new recruit are. These statements would then be used in diagnosing important career and organizational problems. The structured process and the group-level focus may make it less threatening to confront the problems and to work through to solutions than unstructured or one-to-one encounters may be.

The Recruit and His Goals

A third area of change concerns the organization's long-term plans for the new recruit. Perhaps most important would be the creation of a semi-annual work planning and review program, designed after the work of McGregor (1960) and the General Electric Company.

The purpose of such a program would be to establish collaborative goal-settings and more self-directed careers. However, the organization and the individual must be aware of and avoid the tendency for such programs to "vanish." Such a program should allow for individual differences in administrative and interpersonal skills, which have been found to be related to career success (Campbell, 1968). Its focus should be on developing these skills in terms of specific day-to-day behaviors which can be measured and changed by the person and his supervisor.

Another useful exercise would be for the new recruit and his supervisor to examine the company's goals (or the department's or work group's goals) in relation to the recruit's personal goals and desires. One issue would be the *valence* of the organization's goals to the recruit: can he identify with them? Are they important to him and how can they be made more important? The other issue is their *instrumentality*: does he see his efforts toward the organization's goals as also leading to his own satisfactions? If not, how could this connection be better established?

The organization must be aware of the emotional development taking place in the recruit in his early career years. Organizations, like universities, have tended to see personal growth as being independent of or irrelevant to the "really important" career development changes—new skills, abilities, and knowledge. The bulk of a man's career changes, however, are in the motivational and attitudinal area (Campbell, 1968). Since motivation and attitudes are related to performance and success (Hall, 1970), it is clear that organizations should see these personal changes as relevant to their interests. In particular, one never knows when, how, and what attitudes may be acquired by a new man. The change may result as much from the climate of the organization as from the work itself. Much personal stress may result from the need to achieve, and the relative lack of security in the first year with a new organization. It would also be useful to be alert for turning points which may help mark important career transitions—the first performance appraisal, the first completed project, or a particular transfer or promotion. Certain events may have symbolic value which make them far more important to the recruit than the organization or the supervisor may realize, and it is important to attempt to see the recruit's career as it appears to him.

Family Changes

Along with recognizing the career as emotional change and identity development, it is also important to recognize the impact of another important contributor to these changes—the family. Family changes, such as marriage, children, relocation, or the death of a relative often have profound effects on a person's identity, attitudes, and motivation. If these family changes happen to be congruent with career changes, the mutually reinforcing effects could be far more potent than the sum of the separate influences. An example of congruent family and career effects might be the way marriage and a significant promotion could both contribute to increased career involvement and personal responsibility. On the other hand, a problem in a critical family transition could greatly disrupt a person's adjustment to an equally important career change. An example here might be in-law problems in the new marriage and problems with the supervisor in the recent promotion which might both center on the issue of competence in relationships with older people or authority figures. The combination of similar problems around the same issues in two central areas of one's life could greatly compound any feeling of incompetence or low esteem which might result from either problem separately. This interaction of family and career issues is discussed in White (1952), Levinson (1968), and Cox (1970).

The Organization Reward Structure

The fourth arena for facilitating career development concerns characteristics of the organization itself. One important activity would be the examination of the organization's reward structure in relation to the new recruit's path-goal profiles. Is the company using rewards that are valued by the new recruit? Also, does the recruit know what kind of behavior leads to these rewards? An example of a mismatch here occurred in R & D labs, where the most common rewards were money (pay raises); however, the scientists did not really understand what they had to do to get a pay raise, and furthermore, there was evidence that intrinsic satisfactions, such as greater challenge or autonomy, meant more to them than money. As a result the companies were trapped in an upward spiral of salaries with little apparent change in employee satisfaction (Hall and Lawler, 1969). Therefore companies should: 1) attempt to design jobs so that efforts toward company goals also contribute to satisfying employees' needs, and 2) clarify the organization's reward structure so that executives and lower-level employees are in agreement about the kind of performance that is expected and rewarded. Again, an examination of these issues through a structured exercise involving senior managers and recent graduates would probably be fruitful.

Even before the recruit is hired these organizational expectations should be communicated to him, clearly and realistically. College students have become surprisingly accurate at diagnosing inflated or distorted recruiting information, and it usually backfires. This is especially important in view of the great sensitivity and value for openness found in today's students. Indeed, according to Schein (1969), students report that the areas companies stress the most in their recruiting literature are often those about which they are most defensive; therefore, what are promoted as their strongest points often betray their weakest. In the insurance industry, an experiment revealed that recruitment literature stressing both the pros and cons of selling life insurance attracted just as many new agents and resulted in lower turnover among the new employees and the concomitant high costs of training (LIAMA, 1966). Therefore to get and retain good people, "Tell it like it is."

Impact of Peer Group

Another part of the individual's organizational environment with high potential for career impact is his employee peer group. Most of the new member's informal learning is communicated by the peer group (Becker, Geer, Hughes and Strauss, 1961; Becker, Geer, and Strauss, 1969; Hall, 1969). The peer group can also provide important emotional support, coaching, and identification models to help the new recruit manage identity changes, difficult problems, and critical turning points (Hall, 1969; Schein, 1968). Peer group interaction is also associated with reduced turnover (Evan, 1963).

The peer group is often the employee's main emotional link to the organization; often he comes to value the organization only because of his regard for his peers. For example, much of the zeal and bravery of Marine troops is based on their devotion to their buddies rather than a general commitment to Marine Corps values. Therefore, an organization would do well to examine the nature of work group interaction patterns, norms, and values.

If these norms and values run counter to the organization's goals, a serious problem may exist, and an organizational diagnosis might be conducted to determine the probable reasons. If the work group culture is supportive (or perhaps neutral) *vis-a-vis* organizational goals, it would be useful to create structures which would encourage work-related peer interaction—such as weekly problem-solving sessions, an informal morning coffee break, team projects, or older "coaches" assigned to new men.

The important point here is that because the peer group is a potent force, there is a certain amount of risk attached to utilizing it. A group of employees can very accurately diagnose a "poor" organizational climate and can effectively transmit this awareness and quota-restricting pressures to new members. Thus, the peer group can be either strongly functional or strongly dysfunctional for organizational identification.

Conclusion

Perhaps one common element among most of these lever points for facilitating careers is that they have high potential value in either causing or curing problems. There is much in the way of energy and resources in both the new recruit and the organization he enters. In nature, when two systems in different states interact—as in a value gap or an electrical voltage differential—potential energy is available. By applying what we know about organizations and careers to the so-called generation gap, we may develop its potential rather than short circuit it.

Notes

1. Some companies have found that upgrading initial jobs has the unintended consequences of making subsequent jobs seem less exciting and stimulating. However, if the impact of the first job is more enduring than that of later work, the gains of initial challenge will outweigh the problems. What these companies' experiences have shown, however, is the systematic and interactive nature of jobs with careers and organizations: changing a person's job affects his attitude toward his subsequent jobs. To maintain the positive gains from improved initial jobs, the organization should also improve later jobs. Changing such a wide range of jobs, though, very quickly evolves into a full-blown program of organization development. The last section of this paper describes in more detail the connection between career development and organization development.

2. A business career is probably one of the best arenas for satisfying a person's achievement needs. Businesses have very concrete goals and one can easily measure his performance. Despite all the negative stereotypes about business careers, one cannot overlook how useful a setting they create for satisfying achievement needs.

References

Argyris, C. *Integrating the individual and the organization*. New York: Wiley, 1964.

Becker, H., Geer, Hughes, E., & Strauss, A. *Boys in white*. Chicago: University of Chicago Press, 1961.

Becker, H., Geer, B., & Strauss, A. *Making the grade*. Chicago: University of Chicago Press, 1969.

Behavioral Research Service. *A comparison of a work planning program with the annual performance appraisal interview approach*. Crotonville, N.Y.: General Electric Company, undated.

Berlew, D., & Hall, D. T. The socialization of managers: Effects of expectations on performance. *Administrative Science Quarterly*, 1966, 11, 207-223.

Bowlby, J. *Maternal care and mental health*. Geneva: World Health Organization, 1951.

Campbell, R. Career development: The young business manager. In J. R. Hackman (Chm.), Longitudinal approaches to career development. Symposium presented at the American Psychological Association, San Francisco, August 1968.

Cox, R. D. *Youth into maturity*. New York: Materials for Mental Health Center, 1970.

Evan, W. M. Peer-group interaction and organizational socialization. *American Sociological Review*, 1963, 28, 436-440.

Hall, D. T., The impact of peer interaction during an academic role transition. *Sociology of Education*, Spring 1969, 42, 118-140.

Hall, D. T. A theoretical model of career sub-identity development in organization settings. *Organizational Behavior and Human Performance*, 1970, in press.

Hall, D. T., & Lawler, E. E. III. Unused potential in research and development organizations. *Research Management*, 1969, 12, 339-354.

Hall, D. T., & Nougaim, K. An examination of Maslow's need hierarchy in an organizational setting. *Organizational Behavior and Human Performance*, 1968, 3, 12-35.

Hall, D. T., & Schneider, B. Work assignment characteristics and career development in the priesthood. In L. W. Porter (Chm.), Traditional bureaucratic organizations in a changing society. Symposium presented at the American Psychological Association, Washington, D. C., August 1969.

Levinson, D. J. A psychological study of the male mid-life decade. Unpublished research proposal, Department of Psychiatry, Yale University, 1968.

Lewin, K. The psychology of success and failure. *Occupations*, 1936, 14, 926-930.

L.I.A.M.A. *Recruitment, selection, training, and supervision in life insurance*. Hartford: Life Insurance Agency Management Association, 1966.

Maslow, A. *Motivation and personality*. New York: Harper, 1954.

McGregor, D. *The human side of enterprise*. New York: McGraw-Hill, 1960.

Ondrack, D. A. An examination of the generation gap: Attitudes toward authority. *Personnel Administration*, May-June 1971, Vol. 34, pp. 8-17.

Pelz, D. C., & Andrews, F. M. *Scientists in organizations*. New York: Wiley, 1966.

Roe, A., & Baruch, R. Occupational changes in the adult years. *Personnel Administration*, July-August 1967, 30, 26-32.

Schein, E. H. Attitude change during management education: A study of organizational influences on student attitudes. *Administrative Science Quarterly*, 1967, 11, 601-628.

Schein, E. H. The first job dilemma. *Psychology Today*, March 1968, 1, 27-37.

Schein, E. H. Personal change through interpersonal relationships. In W. Bennis, E. Schein, F. Steele, & D. Berlew (Eds.), *International dynamics*. (Rev. ed.) Homewood, Ill.: Dorsey, 1968, 333-369.

Schein, E. H. How graduates scare bosses. *Careers Today*, charter issue, 1968, 89-96.

Schein, E. H. The generation gap: Implications for education and management. Working paper #326-68, Massachusetts Institute of Technology, 1969.

Slater, P. *The pursuit of loneliness: American culture at the breaking point*. Boston: Beacon, 1970.

White, R. W. *Lives in progress*. New York: Holt, Rinehart, and Winston, 1952.

White, R. W. Motivation reconsidered: The concept of competence. *Psychological Review*, 1959, 66, 297-323.

A Comparison of Management Development and Organization Development

W. WARNER BURKE

The growth of organization development (OD) has been accompanied by a predictable confusion about its conceptualization and practice. Many people have conducted or have been involved in "pieces" of OD for several years. Others claim to have been "conducting OD" when, in fact, what they have been conducting is laboratory training for members of their organization. Still others, after hearing some explanation of organization development, will declare that they have heard nothing new, and that such events are everyday occurrences in their organization.

It is quite possible that none of these claims is unjustified, since OD does consist of a variety of activities including laboratory training. Persons who examine the way they conduct their everyday operation, especially in the area of human relations, may be behaving according to some principles and practices of organization development.

But OD is more than the conduct of training laboratories. It can be defined as a *planned process* of cultural change. This process consists of two phases: (a) diagnosis and (b) intervention. OD begins with a diagnosis of the current organizational culture, i.e., an identification of the norms, procedures, and general climate of the organization. This identification process becomes more diagnostic as a distinction is then made between those standards of behavior, procedures, and so on which seem to facilitate the organization's reaching its objectives (while meeting the needs of its members) from those which do not facilitate the attainment of its goals.[1] Following this diagnostic phase, interventions are planned to change those norms which are seen as barriers to effective individual and organizational functioning.

In summary, although persons may be involved in events that are properly labeled as OD technology, such activities are not considered *organization development* if they are not part of a planned effort at changing the organization's culture. [Editor's note: The article in chap. 6 by Hamner gives examples of current OD programs.]

Reprinted by special permission from *The Journal of Applied Behavioral Science*, vol. 7 (1971), no. 5, pp. 569-78, copyright 1971 by NTL Institute for Applied Behavioral Science.

Dimensions of Comparison

One way to clarify a relatively new concept, principle, or practice is to compare it with something more familiar. In this article, management development will serve as a counterpoint. This will be doubly useful, since OD is confused more with management development than with any other concept or practice.

Management development is practiced in various ways: managers are systematically shifted from one kind of job to another to learn different facets of organizational life; managers take psychological tests and then have sessions with a counselor who helps them interpret their test scores; managers receive clinical counseling by psychologists working in the role of management consultants. A more common practice, however, is to provide managers with education: managers attend company training programs, are sent away for several months to attend an "advanced executive" course at a school of business administration, or they enroll in brief training programs such as three-day workshops on management systems or one-week sensitivity training programs. This educational approach to management development will be used as the primary counterpoint in the comparison with OD. [Editor's note: Career development as discussed by Hall in the preceding article can be enhanced both by management development programs and OD programs.]

Several dimensions are critical to both of these developmental strategies for change in organizations. They are: *reasons for use, typical goals, interventions for producing change, time frame, staff requirements,* and *values.* In order to clarify OD and to pinpoint some of the practical concerns of this strategy for change, it will be contrasted with management development along each of these six dimensions. A summary of these comparisons is provided in Figure 1.

Reasons for Use

Leaders in organizations often turn to OD (provided they know about it) when there are difficult problems to be solved. As Beckhard (1969) says, somebody or something is "hurting" and there is a *felt need* to make some organizational changes in such areas as (a) organizational structures and roles, (b) intergroup conflict or collaboration, (c) methods of problem solving, and (d) the way the organization handles acquisitions and mergers, to name only a few.

A management development program may be established to deal with these same needs, but the orientation typically focuses more on individuals than on the organization. The needs are usually diagnosed as managers' lack of skill and expressed in this way: "Our managers need to be brought up to date on the latest thinking and techniques."

The primary reason for using OD is a need to improve some or all of the *systems* that constitute the total organization. The main reason for using some form of management development is a need to improve some aspect of the *manager.*

Typical Goals

To avoid repetition, the reader can refer to Figure 1 for a listing of goals for both OD and management development. Other sources for statements of OD objectives are NTL Institute's *News and Reports,* 1968, issue which covered "What is OD?" and the recent book by Beckhard (1969). Management development objectives have also been discussed elsewhere (Burr, 1967; French, 1970).

Management development is a program of developing managers who will be able to contribute more to their organization; OD is a continual process of developing social conditions so that the manager can make these contributions. Although the strategies have different objectives, they are complementary, not incompatible.

Interventions for Producing Change

In OD there are at least five major categories of interventions: team building, intergroup problem solving, data feedback, technostructure, and training. Team building is probably the cornerstone of OD and is utilized most often. Team building does not necessarily involve conducting a T Group with an organizational "family" unit, although this is one approach (Blake, Mouton, & Blansfield, 1962). Other forms concentrate on improving the "task work" of the team, e.g., goal-setting, decision-making, or problem-solving techniques (cf. Beckhard, 1969; Burke & Hornstein, in press; Schein, 1969).

Category	Organization Development	Management Development
Reasons for Use	Need to improve overall organizational effectiveness Typical examples of tough problems to be solved • Interunit conflict • Confusion stemming from recent management change • Loss of effectiveness due to inefficient organizational structure • Lack of teamwork	Need to improve overall effectiveness of manager Managers do not know company policy or philosophy Managers are void in certain skills Managers seem to be unable to act decisively
Typical Goals	To increase the effectiveness of the organization by— • Creating a sense of "ownership" of organization objectives throughout the work force • Planning and implementing changes more systematically • Facilitating more systematic problem solving on the job To reduce wasted energy and effort by creating conditions where conflict among people is managed openly rather than handled indirectly or unilaterally To improve the quality of decisions by establishing conditions where decisions are made on the basis of competence rather than organizational role or status To integrate the organization's objectives with the individual's goals by developing a reward system which supports achievement of the organization's mission as well as individual efforts toward personal development and achievement	To teach company values and philosophy To provide practice in management skills which lead to improved organizational effectiveness To increase ability to plan, coordinate, measure, and control efforts of company units To gain a better understanding of how the company functions to accomplish its goals

Category	Organization Development	Management Development

Interventions for Producing Change	Education and problem solving is on the job; learning while problem solving and solving problems while learning
	
	Following a diagnosis, utilization of one or more of the following techniques:
	• Team building
	• Training programs
	• Intergroup confrontations
	• Data feedback
	• Technostructural interventions
	  Change in organizational structure
	  Job enrichment
	  Change in physical environment
	  (social architecture)
		Sending of manager to some educational program
		Job rotation of managers
		Specialized training "packages'
		Courses and/or conferences
		Counseling
		Reading of books and articles

Time Frame	*Prolonged*	*Short, intense*
Staff Requirements	Diagnostician Catalyst Facilitator Consultant/Helper Knowledge and skill in the dynamics of planned change Experience in the laboratory method of learning	Teacher/Trainer Program Manager Designer of training programs Knowledge in the processes of human learning
Values	Humane and nonexploitative treatment of people in organizations Theory Y assumptions Collaboration Sharing of power Rationality of behavior Openness/candor/honesty Importance of surfacing and utilizing conflict Right of persons and organizations to seek a full realization of their potential Explicitness of values as a value in itself	Competition Belief that "education is progress" Belief that managers need challenging periodically Manager's right to have time for reflection and renewal Belief that individual should "fit" organization's needs Right of person to seek full realization of his potential

Figure 1. A Comparison of Organization Development and Management Development.

Intergroup problem-solving interventions are well known (Blake, Shepard, & Mouton, 1964; Harrison, 1967) and may be adapted to OD quite easily (Beckhard, 1969). These interventions may be quite useful when there is unproductive conflict between organizational units, such as sales and production in industry or administration and faculty in a university.

Data feedback as an intervention for change is discussed at some length in Hornstein, Bunker, Burke, Hornstein, and Lewicki (1971). The method which has had most use is the survey feedback procedure developed by Mann (1957). This procedure has as its primary component the analysis and discussion of self-generated data by members of overlapping organizational units.

Technostructural interventions refer to changes in the structure of an organization or of a person's job. An example of the latter is Herzberg's (1968) job enrichment technique; Trist's (1960) sociotechnical change (e.g., modifying work flow patterns) is an example of the former. Technostructural interventions may also include the modification of invironment: e.g., changing the physical arrangement of an office to affect human interaction patterns.[2]

Naturally, training can often be a useful OD intervention. The intervention may take the form of (a) skill training for all levels of management (e.g., conducting appraisal interviews); (b) more education in substantive areas (e.g., systems analysis); or (c) further education in organizational management in general (e.g., attending a 16-week "executive course" at a major university). In the OD context, a training program is most useful when it is designed to meet a *diagnosed need* in the organization. For more specific examples of this relationship, see Buchanan's (1962) discussion of the use of training laboratories in OD.

Training is probably the major subcategory of management development in use today. Other facets of management development include job rotation, counseling, and career development—but the major focus is on educating the manager. The major strategy for change in management development is to improve the manager's knowledge and skill and, to some extent, to modify his attitudes. The major strategy for change in OD is to change the organization's *culture* from one which deals with problems "as we have always done" to a culture which (a) takes full advantage of the human resources available, and (b) allows for a process to develop which will ensure that the organization can plan and implement needed change at all levels rather than having to "adjust" to change already in progress.

Time Frame

Since OD is a *process,* not a program, there is an implied timelessness. This implication is no accident. OD is a process of continual organizational renewal. The process is one of constantly examining the way the organizational systems are functioning and looking for ways of improving these functions. Management development, on the other hand, usually takes the form of some program which has a beginning and an end.

Staff Requirements

The primary areas in which an OD specialist should have competence—or the areas which should be represented in an internal OD department or group—are these:

Ability to diagnose problems of an organizational nature accurately

Ability to function as a facilitator or catalyst for groups in the organization

Understanding of and skill in the consultative process; the ability to give help which is useful

Understanding of the dynamics and realities of planned change

Skill and knowledge in experience-based learning methodology.

The specialist in management development should also have skill and knowledge in the technology of experience-based learning, in particular, and some understanding of human learning, in general. Other areas of competence which should be represented are (a) lecturing and various methods of training which are not necessarily experience based, (b) program management, (c) managerial counseling, and (d) career development.

Values

The major general value which OD represents is the humane and nonexploitative treatment of people in organizations. All other values of OD seem to relate, in one way or another, to this primary value of human dignity.

A listing of some of the more specific values of OD is found in Figure 1. Most of these are self-explanatory, but an elaboration of several is probably in order.

McGregor's motivational statements about man, which he labeled "Theory Y," are not only based on some psychological principles of human behavior but also imply certain values as well (e.g., man is not inherently lazy; he seeks rather than shuns responsibility).

While OD does not necessarily advocate the restructuring of all organizations according to the democratic process, a goal of power sharing (e.g., decentralizing decision making to the lowest point of relevant information in the organization) does have a value connotation. There is "something bad," OD practitioners believe, in a condition where *all* power is vested in one individual.

A value of surfacing conflict and dealing with it has always been a part of OD. This particular value is beginning to be modified from one of "it's good to resolve conflict" to one of "it's good to resolve conflict some of the time, but not always." Some OD practitioners have found that old conflicts they had once helped "to resolve" sometimes reappear, and that they either need to be reworked or that they can be recognized as unsolvable and therefore "lived with."

An interesting development in OD is the emphasis on making values themselves more explicit. Today many OD practitioners are advocating that organizations and their members be more explicit about the values they represent. This advocacy usually becomes operationalized when the practitioner is working with an organization in the area of goal setting or mission.

In management development there is still a value premium on competition. This emphasis may not be at the expense of collaboration, but the latter certainly takes a back seat. Managers are trained to beat their market competitors as part of the free enterprise system in our country. But this norm (value) of competition also extends internally to the managers' organizational team where it can frequently negate overall organizational effectiveness. To keep this competitive edge, management development practitioners believe that managers should be challenged periodically and that they should have a chance for reflection.

The last two values of management development mentioned in Figure 1 are somewhat contradictory, but they are found in some management development programs. Specifically, lip service is given to "*self*-actualization," but what the organization's authority figures really want is a better fit of the individual to the *organization's* goals and objectives. In organizations which are quite explicit about this latter value and norm, if the manager does not want to "fit," he can look for a job elsewhere. Other organizations give more than lip service to a manager's developing his potential by reinforcing efforts made in that direction.

While there are some value conflicts between OD and management development, or at least in the way management development is practiced in certain organizations, there is also overlap and compatibility (e.g., the right of a person [and an organization] to seek full realization of his [its] potential).

Concluding Comment

In an effort to clarify the nature of OD, a method of comparing it with a more common change strategy, management development, has been chosen. While this comparison technique may be useful for clarification, the method should not dictate the message. The two strategies for change are not incompatible. On the contrary, management development and OD are quite complementary. Management development should be one of several intervention techniques available to an OD effort.

Management development programs should *respond* to diagnosed needs in the organization. This is not to say that other OD interventions cannot be developed as a result of some management development program. Either strategy can develop from the other. The point is that an appropriate OD intervention, whether it be a management development program or a change in the organizational structure, is one which originates from study and diagnosis of current, relevant data.

References

Argyris, C. *Integrating the individual and the organization.* New York: Wiley, 1964.

Beckhard, R. *Organization development: Strategies and models.* Reading, Mass.: Addison-Wesley, 1969.

Blake, R. R., Mouton, Jane S., & Blansfield, M. G. The logic of team training. In I. R. Weschler and E. H. Schein (Eds.), *Issues in training.* Selected Readings Series, No. 5. Washington, D.C.: National Training Laboratories, associated with the National Education Association, 1962. Pp. 77-85.

Blake, R. R., Shepard, H. A., & Mouton, Jane S. *Managing inter-group conflict in industry,* Houston: Gulf, 1964.

Buchanan, P. C. Training laboratories in organization development. In I. R. Weschler and E. H. Schein (Eds.), *Issues in training.* Selected Reading Series, No. 5. Washington, D.C.: National Training Laboratories, associated with the National Education Association, 1962. Pp. 86-92.

Burke, W. W., & Hornstein, H. A. (Eds.) The Social technology of organization development. Washington D.C.: NTL Learning Resources Corporation, in press.

Burr, R. B. Management development. In R. L. Craig and L. R. Bittel (Eds.), *Training and development handbook.* New York: McGraw-Hill, 1967. Pp.363-395.

French, W. L. *The personnel management process* (Rev. Ed.). New York: Houghton Mifflin, 1970.

Harrison, R. Training designs for intergroup collaboration. *NTL Training News,* 1967, 11 (1), 1-3.

Herzberg, F. One more time: How do you motivate employees? *Harvard Bus. Rev.,* 1968, 46, 53-62.

Hornstein, H. A., Bunker, Barbara B., Burke, W. W., Hornstein, Marion G., & Lewicki, R. J. *Social intervention: A behavioral science approach.* New York: Free Press, 1971.

Mann, F. C. Studying and creating change: A means to understanding social organization. In C. M. Arensburg and W. Ellison Chalmers (Eds.), *Research in industrial human relations.* New York: Harper, 1957.

NTL Institute for Applied Behavioral Science. What is OD? *News and Reports,* 1968, 2 (3).

Schein, E. H. *Process consultation: Its role in organization development.* Reading, Mass.: Addiso-Wesley, 1969.

Steele, F. I. Organization development and sticks and stones. In H. A. Hornstein, Barbara B. Bunker, W. W. Burke, Marion G. Hornstein, and R. J. Lewicki. *Social intervention: A behavioral science approach.* New York: Free Press, 1971.

Trist, E. L. *Socio-technical systems.* London: Tavistock Institute of Human Relations, 1960.

Notes

1. This general objective of OD, a stronger integration of the goals of the organization with those of individual members, has been discussed by Argyris (1964) and outlined in NTL Institute's *News and Reports* issue on "What is OD?"—1968, 2 (3).

2. See Steele's (1971) discussion of this approach, which is sometimes referred to as social architecture.

A Systems Approach to Organization Development

MICHAEL BEER
EDGAR F. HUSE

. . . This article is written to provide the reader with an understanding of the systems organizational model that guided our efforts as change agents; to describe the varied approaches used for organizational change; and to describe the results and what we have learned about the process of change and its prospects in large, complex organizations. Rather than consigning the conclusions to the end, we shall underscore our major findings as we proceed through the sections of the case study.

The organizational development program took place in a plant designing and manufacturing complex instruments for medical and laboratory use.

Through the efforts of the personnel supervisor, enough interest existed initially for our holding a series of seminars which contrasted traditional approaches with newer approaches based on behavioral research findings and theory. Although these seminars never succeeded in getting an explicit decision on the pattern of management that would prevail in the plant (indeed, as will be discussed later, there was considerable resistance to "theory"), they did start to unfreeze the managerial group (which was steeped in the tradition of the parent organization) sufficiently to commit themselves to "trying" some new approaches on a very limited basis. This constituted much less than commitment to a new pattern of management, but it did open the door to experimentation and examination.

Overworked Theories

A number of practitioners of OD stress the importance of top management commitment to OD if such a program is to be successful. As one author puts it, "Without such support, we have found no program of this kind can ever succeed. . . . First, we worked with top managers to help them fully understand. . . . This proved vital, not only in helping their understanding of the concepts but also in earning their commitment to the program" (Roche & MacKinnon, 1970). In the same vein, Beckhard (1969) and Blake and Mouton (1969) stress that OD must be planned and managed from the top down.

Reprinted by special permission from *The Journal of Applied Behavioral Science*, vol. 8 (1972), no. 1, pp. 79-100, copyright 1972 by NTL Institute for Applied Behavioral Science.

Certainly no one would dispute the proposition that top management commitment to OD is highly valuable and helpful. However, our experience in this study [*Finding 1*] indicates that *a clear-cut commitment at the top of the organizational unit to a particular OD approach is not necessary for a development program to succeed*. Indeed, an attempt to obtain too strong a commitment from top management in the early stages may be threatening enough to cause the withdrawal of any commitment to planned change, especially since the concept of OD and its technologies (e.g., Theory Y, job enrichment, sensitivity training, and the like) are foreign and threatening to the established beliefs of many managers.

Moreover, we found [*Finding 2*] that *total top management understanding of where the OD process will lead and the state of the organization at the end is not necessary for successful programs to take place*. Indeed, given the current state of the art, the OD practitioner himself may not have a clear view of the road ahead, except in very general terms.

What *is* necessary is that someone in a strategic position feel the need for change and improvement. In our plant, that person was the personnel supervisor. Although the plant manager was mildly interested in the initial stages, he was mainly submitting to pressures from the personnel man. Throughout his tenure in the plant, the plant manager's commitment and interest mildly increased, but he was never a strong proponent nor the most skilled manager in some of the new approaches. Futhermore, the plant manager's "boss" never fully knew what was going on in the plant nor did he ever commit himself in any way to the OD program. We now believe that it is possible to change a relatively autonomous unit of a larger organization without the total commitment or understanding of top management in that unit and, in larger and more complex organizations, even without their knowledge.

Initial Commitment to New Approaches

In addition to felt need, the second essential condition is that there be, somewhere in the organization, some initial commitment to experimentation, application, and evaluation of new approaches to present problems. A case study report by the second author (Huse, 1965) describes a successful OD program that took place because a middle manager in a large organization felt the need for change and requested help. He could not have cared less about specific OD principles. He simply wanted help in improving his organization. Davis (1967) points out, in his now classic case study, that top management was not really involved at the beginning and that a majority of the effort was expended in "on-the-job situations, working out real problems with the people who are involved with them."

Of course, it is obvious that top management support of both theory and practice makes it easier for the change agent; conversely, the lack of such support increases the risk involved for consultants and managers, and causes other systems problems, as we shall discuss later in this article. Furthermore, the conditions of a felt need, a strong and self-sufficient commitment to change, and relative unit autonomy are needed. What we *are* saying is that the commonly heard dicta that one must start at the top and that top management must be committed to a set of normative principles are overworked. *Change can and does begin at lower levels in an organization* [*Finding 3*].

A Conceptual Model

If the client system and its management in this case did not (need to) have specific OD concepts in mind, who did? The change agents did.

It is important that the change agent have in mind an organizational model and a flexible set of normative concepts about management with a systems orientation. The organizational model should be general and reflect the complex *interactive* nature of systems variables. The concepts must be updated and changed as new research findings become available and as more is learned about the functioning of the client system, the environment in which the client system operates, and the effects of changes made in the client system. This is, of course, an iterative procedure.

Figure 1 represents the model of organizational change which guided our efforts. This model has some basic characteristics which must be understood if we are to see how it can shape the planning of a change effort. It represents an organization as an open system engaged in a conversion process. Employee needs, expectations, and abilities are among the raw materials (inputs) with which a manager must work to achieve his objectives.

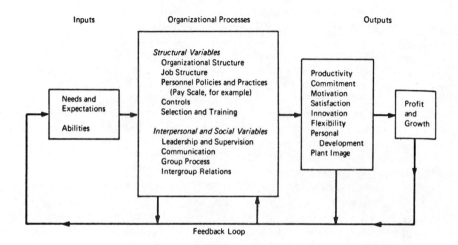

Figure 1. Systems Model of an Organization

Organizations have many processes. Figure 1 includes only the more important ones in general terms, and these exist at both the structural and interpersonal levels. Leadership and communication, for example, are two of the interpersonal dimensions which serve to pull together, integrate, and shape the behavior of organizational members. They convert into effort and attitudes the potential brought to the organization in the form of needs and abilities of individuals. The structure or formalized dimensions of the organization obviously cannot exist independently of the interpersonal variables, but they are different from the interpersonal variables in terms of their susceptibility to managerial control, the means by which they might be changed, and the timing of their change. Previous literature on organizational change has emphasized interpersonal variables; more recent literature (Lawrence & Lorsch, 1969) has emphasized structural variables. It is our opinion, based upon experience, that both interpersonal and structural variables are crucial to effective organizational change. The effects of organizational design or managerial control systems on employees have been researched and documented but are still insufficiently understood. For example, we are convinced that an operant conditioning model can be used to understand the behavior of managers with respect to controls. "Beating" goals and looking good on standard measures are like food pellets to the manager.

In the output column, we have listed multiple outcomes. These are not completely independent, but they are conceptually distinctive enough in their relationship to the organizational process variables that it is useful to think of them individually. It is the optimization of the organizational outputs that leads to long-term profitability and growth for employees and the organization. Other final outcomes could be listed if we were discussing organizations with different objectives.

Inherent in this model are several basic notions: An organization is an open system which, from the human point of view, converts individual needs and expectations into outputs. Organizational outputs can be increased by improving the quality of the input. An example of this would be the selection of people with higher levels of ability and needs. However, because there are costs associated with selecting personnel of higher quality, we might say that efficiency has not increased. The organization may improve its performance, but this gain has been obtained only because the input, i.e., the quality of personnel has improved, not because there has been a change in the manner in which the organization *utilizes* its human resources.

Since organizations are open systems, organizational performance can also improve by unleashing more of the potential inherent in the human resources. If you will, outputs will increase because we have made the conversion process more efficient. This can be done, for example, by designing organizational processes which better fit the organization's environment or by changing organizational processes so that human resources can be fully unleashed and brought to bear on the task and objectives of the organization. The adjustment of organizational processes to reflect more accurately the needs of the environment and of the persons in it is one of the key objectives of our organizational development program.

Figure 1[1] does not cover some of the more traditional but vitally important concepts of an organization as a total system. For example, capital budgets, the R & D thrust of an organization, overhead or indirect budgets, and the marketing direction of an organization are extremely important aspects which need to be considered. Blake and Mouton (1969) have developed the Corporate Excellence Rubric as a means of assessing the health of the organization through a traditional functional framework. Furthermore, current research (Lawrence & Lorsch, 1969) points up the fact that the differentiation of functional units has a tremendous influence upon the effectiveness of an organization. However, for purposes of brevity, these aspects are not covered in this article.

Mechanisms of Change

We chose an eclectic approach to create change in the organizational processes listed in Figure 1, with the basic belief that a variety of approaches to change should be used with the plant in question. The primary mechanism was consulting, counseling, and feedback by a team of four. The primary change agents were the personnel man within the organization (there have been four different ones since the OD effort began); Beer as an external-to-the-plant agent but internal to the organization, and Huse as the outside change agent. The fourth member of the team was a research assistant whose responsibility it was to interview and gather data in the client system for diagnostic and feedback uses by the change agents.[2]

We began a basic strategy of establishing working relationships with individuals at all levels of the organization. We operated as resource persons who could be used to

solve specific problems or initiate small experiments in management; we tried to encourage someone or some organizational component to start implementing the concepts inherent in our model of an organization. Managers gained familiarity with these
ideas through consultation and, to a much lesser extent and without full understanding,
from the initial few seminars that we held. The main ingredients were a problem or a
desire to change and improve, combined with action recommendations from the
change agents. Soon there were a few individuals throughout the organization who
began, with our help, to apply some new approaches. Because most of these approaches were successful, the result was increased motivation to change. To a degree,
nothing succeeds like success!

Models for Learning

There are at least two basic models for learning. The traditional method, that of
the classroom and seminar, stresses theory and cognitive concepts before action. As
Argyris (1967) points out, "The traditional educational models emphasize substance,
rationality. . . ." However, a number of authors (Bartlett, 1967; Bradford, 1964;
Schein & Bennis, 1965) make the point that behavior is another place to start. For
example, Huse (1966) has shown that one's own facts are "much more powerful instruments of change than facts or principles generated and presented by an outside
'expert.' " The process of change in this OD effort started with behavioral recommendations, was followed by appropriate reinforcement and feedback, and then proceeded
to attitudinal and cognitive changes.

Figure 2 summarizes the basic concept from our experience. *Effective and permanent adult learning [Finding 4] comes after the individual has experimented with new
approaches and received appropriate feedback in the on-the-job situation.* This approach is analogous to, but somewhat different from, the here-and-now learning in the
T Group.

In other words, a manager might have a problem. Without discussing theory, the
change agent might make some recommendations relating to the specific situation at
hand. If, in the here-and-now, the manager was successful in the attempt to solve the
problem, this would lead to another try, as well as a change in his attitude toward OD.
This approach capitalizes upon the powerful here-and-now influence which the job and
the organizational climate can have upon the individual. Indeed, such changes can
occur without *any* knowledge of theory.

Either model of learning can probably work to produce change in the individual.
However, if one starts with cognitive facts and theory (as in seminars), this may be
less effective and less authentic than starting with the individual's own here-and-now
behavior in the ongoing job situation. In any case, the process is a cyclic one, involving behavior, attitudes, and cognition, each reinforcing the other. In our case, there
was an early resistance to seminars and the presentation of "Theory." However, after
behavior and attitude changes occurred, there began to be more and more requests for
cognitive inputs through reading, seminars, and the like. It is at this later stage that
seminars and "theory inputs" would seem to be of most value.

That learning starts with behavior and personal experience has been one of the
most important things we have learned as we have worked to effect organizational
change. The process is quite similar to what is intended to happen in laboratory training. What we have found [Finding 5] is that *the operating, ongoing organization may,
indeed, be the best "laboratory" for learning.* This knowledge may save us from an
overreliance upon sensitivity training described by Bennis (1968) when he states that
"when you read the pages of this Journal, you cannot but think that we're a one-

product outfit with a 100 per cent fool-proof patent medicine." This finding may also be the answer in dealing with Campbell and Dunnette's (1968) conclusions that "while T-Group training seems to produce observable changes in behavior, the utility of these changes for the performance of individuals in their organizational roles remains to be demonstrated."

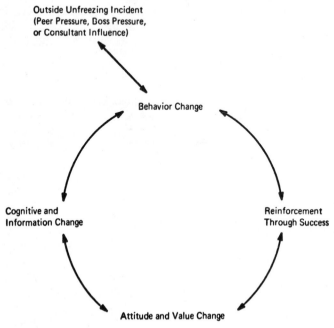

Figure 2. The Learning Process

The unfreezing process. What triggers an individual to unfreeze and to allow the process to begin, if it is not "theory"? First, there are some individuals who are ready to change behavior as soon as the opportunity presents itself in the form of an outside change agent. These are people who seem to be aware of problems and have a desire to work on them. Sometimes all that they need are some suggestions or recommendations as to different approaches or methods they may try. If their experiences are successful, they become change leaders in their own right. *They then [Finding 6] are natural targets for the change agent, since they become opinion leaders that help shape a culture that influences others in the organization to begin to experiment and try out new behaviors.* As Davis (1967) points out, it is necessary to "provide a situation which could initiate the process of freeing up these potential multipliers from the organizational and personal constraints which . . . kept them from responding effectively to their awareness of the problems." Davis used "strangers" and "cousins" laboratories. In our case, the unfreezing process was done almost exclusively in the immediate job context.

An early example of the development of change leaders in our work with this company was the successful joint effort of an engineer and a supervisor to redesign a hotplate assembly operation, which would eliminate an assembly line and give each worker total responsibility for the assembly of a particular product. It resulted in a productivity increase of close to 50 per cent, a drop in rejects from 23 per cent, controllable rejects to close to 1 per cent, and a reduction in absenteeism from about 8 per cent to less than 1 per cent in a few months. Not all the early experiments were successful, but mistakes were treated as part of the experiential learning process.

As some in the organization changed and moved ahead by trying out new behaviors, others watched and waited but were eventually influenced by the culture. An example of late changers so influenced was the supervisor of Materials Control, who watched for two years what was going on in the plant but basically disagreed with the concepts of OD. Then he began to feel pressure to change because his peers were trying new things and he was not. He began by experimenting with enriching his secretary's job and found, in his own words, that "she was doing three times as much, enjoying it more, and giving me more time to manage." When he found that this experiment in managerial behavior had "paid off," he began to take a more active interest in OD. His next step was to completely reorganize his department to push decision making down the ladder, to utilize a team approach, and to enrich jobs. He supervised four sections: purchasing, inventory control, plant scheduling, and expediting. Reorganization of Materials Control was around product line teams. Each group had total project responsibility for their own product lines, including the four functions described above. We moved slowly and discussed with him alternative ways of going about the structural change. When he made the change, his subordinates were prepared and ready. The results were clear: In a three-month period of time (with the volume of business remaining steady), the parts shortage list was reduced from 14 I.B.M. pages to less than a page. In other words, although he was a late-changer in terms of the developing culture, his later actions were highly successful.

The influence of the developing culture was also documented through interviews with new employees coming into the plant. The perception by production employees that this was a "different" place to work occurred almost immediately, and changes in behavior of management personnel were clear by the second month.

In other words, while seminars and survey feedback techniques were used in our work with this plant, the initial and most crucial changes were achieved through a work-centered, consulting-counseling approach, e.g., through discussion with managers and others about work-related problems, following the model of adult learning described earlier.

So much for the manner in which the unfreezing process occurred and some of our learning about this process. What were some of the normative concepts applied and why? A brief overview of our approaches and findings follows.

A Normative Model

Communications

In this phase we attempted to open up communications at all levels. We started monthly meetings at every level of the organization, as well as a weekly meeting between the plant manager and a sample of production and clerical employees. The aim was to institutionalize the meetings to serve as a means for exchanging information and ideas about what had happened and what needed to happen. The meetings, especially between first-line supervisors and production workers, began primarily as one-way communications downward. Little by little, qualitative changes occurred and the meetings shifted to two-way communications about quality, schedules, and production problems. This effort to communicate (which was also extended through many other approaches) was an entire year in attaining success. It was an agonizingly slow process of change. In retrospect, this was a critical period during which trust was building and a culture conducive to further change was developing. Out of this, we concluded [*Finding 7*] that *organizational change occurs in stages: a stage of unfreezing and trust building, a take-off stage when observable change occurs, and a stabilization stage. Then the cycle iterates.* In addition to the communication type of meeting described above, confrontation meetings between departments were also held (Blake, Shepard, & Mouton, 1964). These, too, improved relationships between departments, over time.

Job Enrichment

A second area of change was in job structure, primarily through the use of job enrichment, or, as it has been called in the plant, "the total job concept." We have already discussed the importance of the job for psychological growth and development—our findings in this area parallel those of Ford (1969). Our first experience of tearing down a hotplate assembly line has already been discussed. This was followed by similar job enrichment efforts in other areas. In one department, girls individually assemble instruments containing thousands of parts and costing several thousand dollars. The change here allowed production workers to have greater responsibility for quality checks and calibration (instead of trained technicians). In another case, the changeover involved an instrument which had been produced for several years. Here, production was increased by 17 per cent with a corresponding increase in quality; absenteeism was reduced by more than 50 per cent.

The plant is presently engaged in completely removing quality control inspection from some departments, leaving final inspection to the workers themselves. In other departments, workers have been organized into autonomous workgroups with total responsibility for scheduling, assembly, training, and some quality control inspection. . . . Changes in these areas have evolved out of an attempt to utilize the positive forces of cohesive workgroups. However, like Ford (1969), we have found that not everyone in the assembly workforce responds positively to such changes, although a high majority do so over time.

Mutual goal setting has also been widely adopted. Instead of standards established by engineering (a direction in which the plant was heading when we started), goals for each department are derived from the plant goal, and individual goals for the week or month are developed in individual departments through discussions between the boss and subordinates. Our interview data clearly show that in this way workers understand how their individual goals fit into the plant goal structure and can work on their own without close supervision for long periods of time.

Changes toward a pay process more clearly based on merit (including appraisals for hourly and weekly salaried clerical and technical employees as well as for managerial and professional personnel) were made to reinforce and legitimate an escalating climate of work involvement. More and more employees are now involved in questions of production, quality, department layout, and methods. Assembly workers give department tours to visitors, including vice presidents. Organization-wide technical and product information sessions are held. Concerned more with strategy than with daily problems, the top team has for some time molded itself into a business team, meeting periodically to discuss future plans.

More recently, changes in organizational structure are taking place to move a functionally oriented organization to a matrix organization, using concepts derived directly from Lawrence and Lorsch (1969). This involves, among other approaches, the use of "integrators" at varying levels within the organization.

Systems Interaction

A systems approach requires that mutually consistent changes in *all* subsystems be made in affecting the organizational processes listed in our model. In other words, [*Finding 8*] *multiple changes in the subsystems are needed for the individual employee to change behavior and perceptions of his role.* For example, participative supervision should be accompanied by redesign of jobs to allow more responsibility, by a pay system that recognizes performance, by a communication system that is truly open, and by corresponding changes in other subsystems throughout the organization. Past attempts to change organizations through a nonsystems approach, e.g., through such single media as supervisory training or sensitivity training, have had limited success because other key leverage points have not been changed in the total system. Further, an attempt to change one subsystem too quickly or too drastically can have severely harmful results, as pointed out in the "Hovey and Beard Company" case (Lawrence, Bailey, Katz, Seiler, Orth, Clark, Barnes, & Turner, 1961). Whether structural *or* interpersonal changes should take precedence in a given period of time depends upon the readiness of the system to change and the key leverage points. The key concept [*Finding 9*] is that *structural and interpersonal systems changes must reinforce and legitimate each other.* Figure 3 presents this concept. The change can be in either direction in the model.

We also learned [*Finding 10*] that *systems changes set off additional interactive processes in which changes in organizational functioning increase not only outputs but also develop the latent abilities of people.* We have concluded that the real potential in organizational development lies in setting in motion such a positive snowball of change, growth, and development. For example, as assembly workers took on additional responsibility they became more and more concerned about the total organization and product. "Mini-gripes" turned into "mega-gripes," indicating a change in the maturity of the assembly workers (Huse & Price, 1970). At the same time, this freed up management personnel to be less concerned about daily assignments and more concerned about long-range planning.

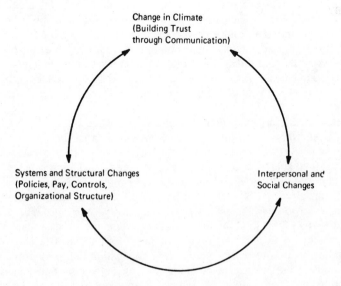

Change in Climate
(Building Trust
through Communication)

Systems and Structural Changes
(Policies, Pay, Controls,
Organizational Structure)

Interpersonal and
Social Changes

Figure 3. The Sequence of Organizational Change

To illustrate this, at the beginning of the OD effort, the organization had a plant manager, a production superintendent, and three first-line supervisors, or a total of five supervisory personnel in the direct manufacturing line. As the assembly line workers took on more responsibility, the five have been reduced to three (the plant manager and two first-line supervisors). The number of inspection and quality control personnel has also been reduced.

A Subsystem Within the Larger Organization

Up to this point in the case study we have been considering the plant as a system in its own right. However, changes set in motion here have also provided the first step in a larger plan for change and development to occur in the parent corporation (consisting of some 50 plants). As a subsystem within the larger system, this plant was to serve as a model for the rest of the corporation—as an example of how change should be planned and implemented. It was our hope that the systems approach to change would create such a clearly different culture in this plant that it would become visible to the rest of the corporation; that people from other segments of the larger organization would visit and become interested in trying similar models and mechanisms of change. Our hopes have been realized. Indeed, both authors are now applying OD concepts to other areas of the organization.

Influence is also exerted upward, with greater acceptance of these concepts by individuals at higher levels in the organization [Finding 11]. It is our perception that changes in organizational subsystems can have strong influences on the larger culture if the change is planned and publicized; if seed personnel are transferred to other parts of the system; if a network of change agents is clearly identified; and if careful planning goes into where and how change resources are to be used. Once again, top management commitment is not a necessary commitment for evolutionary change in a complex, multidivision, multilocation organization. *(Sometimes,* the tail begins to wag the dog.)

Subsystem Difficulties

However, this change process may cause some difficulties in the area of interface between the smaller subsystem and the larger system. For example, the increased responsibilities, commitment, and involvement represented by job enrichment for assembly workers are not adequately represented in the normal job evaluation program for factory workers and are difficult to handle adequately within the larger system. So pay and pay system changes must be modified to fit modern OD concepts. Figure 4 is a model which shows the effects of change in climate on individual model perceptions of equity in pay.

In addition to the larger system difficulties over wage plans, there still exists a great deal of controversy as to the importance of pay as a motivator (or dissatisfier). For example, Walton (1967) takes a basically pessimistic approach about participation through the informal approach, as opposed to the more formal approaches embodied in the Scanlon Plan (Lesieur, 1958), which "stress the economic rewards which can come from [formal] participation." On the other hand, Paul, Robertson, and Herzberg (1969) review a number of job enrichment projects and report: "In no instance did management face a demand of this kind [higher pay or better conditions] as a result of changes made in the studies." In a recent review of the Scanlon Plan (Lesieur & Puckett, 1969), the authors point out that Scanlon's first application did not involve the use of financial incentives but, rather, a common sharing between management and employees of problems, goals, and ideas. Indeed, Ford (1969) reports on the results of a series of job enrichment studies without ever mentioning the words "pay" or "salary." In the plant described in this case, no significant pressures for higher pay have been felt to date. However, there has been sufficient opportunity for promotion of hourly employees to higher level jobs as the plant has grown.

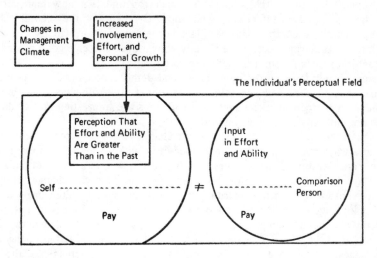

Figure 4. Equity Model

It is certainly not within the scope of this article to handle the controversy regarding the place of pay as a motivator. We do want to make the point that standard corporate job evaluation plans are only one instance of the difficulties of interface between the client plant as a subsystem and the larger system. In our experience, these and other areas have been minor rather than major problems, but they have been problems.

Changes in Consumption of Research Findings

An important by-product of our experience has been [*Finding 12*] that *the client system eventually becomes a sophisticated consumer of new research findings in the behavioral sciences.* As mentioned earlier, there was early resistance to "theory"; but as the program progressed, there was increasing desire for "theory." We also found that a flexible and adaptable organization is more likely to translate theory into new policies and actions. Perhaps this is where behavioral scientists may have gone wrong in the past. We may have saturated our client systems with sophisticated research studies before the culture was ready to absorb them. This would suggest that a more effective approach may be carefully planned stages of evolution from an action orientation to an action-research orientation to a research orientation. This implies a long-range plan for change that we often talk about but rarely execute with respect to the changes in organizations that we seek as behavioral scientists.

Results of The Organizational Development Program

To a great extent we have tried to share with you our results and findings throughout the article. In addition, we are retesting these concepts in several other plants. In retrospect, how much change really occurred at the client plant, and how effective have been the new approaches introduced? We have only partial answers since a control plant did not exist and since the plant was relatively new; no historical data existed against which to compare performance. However, considerable data do exist to support the thesis that change has occurred and that new managerial approaches have created an effective organization. (In addition, the second author is conducting ongoing research in another plant in the organization which has historical data. Before- and aftermeasures have already shown dramatic change: e.g., reduction in manufacturing costs for the plant of 40 to 45 percent.)

Extensive interviews by the researchers and detailed notes and observations by the change agents indicate considerable improvement after our work with this plant. Communication is open, workers feel informed, jobs are interesting and challenging, and goals are mutually set and accomplished.

In each of the output dimensions, positive changes have occurred which we think, but cannot always prove, would not have occurred without the OD effort. Turnover has been considerably reduced; specific changes in job structure, organizational change, or group process have resulted in measurable productivity changes of up to 50 percent. Recent changes in the Instrument Department have resulted in productivity and quality improvements. We have witnessed the significant changes in maturity and motivation which have taken place among the assembly workers. A change to a project team structure in the Materials Control Department led to a reduction of the weekly parts shortages. Following the findings of Lawrence and Lorsch (1969), the use of "integrators" and project teams has significantly reduced the time necessary for new product development, introduction, and manufacture. A fuller evaluation of the integrator role and the project organization as it affects intergroup relations and new product development is reported elsewhere (Beer, Pieters, Marcus, &, Hundert, 1971).

Several recent incidents in the plant are evidence of the effect of the changes and bear repeating. An order called for in seven days and requiring extraordinary cooperation on the part of a temporary team of production workers was completed in fewer than seven days. A threatened layoff was handled with candor and openness and resulted in volunteers among some of the secondary wage earners.

New employees and managers now transferred into the plant are immediately struck by the differences between the "climate" of this plant and other locations. They report more openness, greater involvement by employees, more communication, and more interesting jobs. Even visitors are struck immediately by the differences. For example, one of the authors has on several occasions taken graduate students on field trips to the plant. After the tour, the consensus is, "You've told us about it, but I had to see it for myself before I would believe it." Managers transferred or promoted out of the plant to other locations report "cultural shock."

Summary and Conclusions

The Medfield Project (as it can now be labeled) has been an experiment in a systems approach to organizational development at two systems levels. On the one hand, we have regarded the plant as a system in and of itself. On the other hand, we have regarded the plant as a subsystem within a larger organization. As such a subsystem, we wanted it to serve as a model for the rest of the organization. Indeed, as a result of this study, OD work is going forward elsewhere in the parent company and will be reported [elsewhere].

Although we have shared our findings with you throughout the article, it seems wise now to summarize them for your convenience, so that they may be generalized to other organizations and climates.

Findings

1. A clear-cut commitment to a particular OD approach is not necessary (although desirable) for a successful OD program to succeed.

2. Total top management understanding of where the OD process will lead and the state of the organization at the end is not necessary for organizational change to occur.

3. Change can and does begin at lower levels in the organization.

4. Effective and permanent adult learning comes after the individual has experimented with new approaches and received appropriate feedback in the on-the-job situation.

5. Rather than the T Group, the operating, ongoing organization may be the best "laboratory" for learning, with fewer problems in transfer of training.

6. Internal change leaders are natural targets for the change agent, since they become influence leaders and help to shape the culture.

7. Organizational change occurs in stages: a stage of unfreezing and trust building, a take-off stage when observable change occurs, and a stabilization stage. Then the cycle iterates.

8. Multiple changes in the subsystems are needed for the individual employee to change behavior and perceptions of his role.

9. Structural and interpersonal systems changes must reinforce and legitimate each other.

10. Systems changes set off additional interactive processes in which changes in organizational functioning not only increase outputs but also develop the latent abilities of people.

11. Influence is also exerted upward, with greater acceptance of these concepts by individuals at higher levels in the organization.

12. The client system eventually becomes a sophisticated consumer of new research findings in the behavioral sciences.

Perhaps the most important and far-reaching conclusion is that as organizational psychologists we have viewed our role too narrowly and with an insufficient historical and change perspective. Our research studies tend to be static rather than dynamic. We need to do a better job of developing a theory and technology of changing and to develop a flexible set of concepts which will change as we experiment with and socially engineer organizations. We are suggesting a stronger action orientation for our field and less of a natural science orientation. We must be less timid about helping organizations to change themselves. We must create a positive snowball of organizational change followed by changes in needs and expectations of organizational members, followed again by further organizational change. The objective of change agents should be to develop an evolving system that maintains reasonable internal consistency while staying relevant to and anticipating changes and adaptation to the outside environment. As behavioral scientists and change agents, we must help organizations begin to "become."

Notes

1. Cf. The traditional aspects included in the conceptual model developed by Huse (1969).

2. We should like to acknowledge the help and participation of Mrs. Gloria Gery and Miss Joan Doolittle in the data-gathering phase.

References

Argyris, C. On the future of laboratory training. *J. appl. Behav. Sci.,* 1967, *3* (2), 153-183.

Bartlett, A. C. Changing behavior as a means to increased efficiency. *J. appl. Behav. Sci.,* 1967, *3* (3), 381-403.

Beckhard, R. *Organization development: Strategies and models.* Reading, Mass.: Addison-Wesley, 1969.

Beer, M., Pieters, G. R., Marcus, S. H., & Hundert, A. T. Improving integration between functional groups: A case in organization change and implications for theory and practice. Symposium presented at American Psychological Association Convention, Washington, D.C., September 1971.

Bennis, W. G. The case study—I. Introduction. *J. appl. Behav. Sci.,* 1968, *4* (2), 227-231.

Blake, R. R., & Mouton, J. S. *Building a dynamic corporation through grid organization development.* Reading, Mass.: Addison-Wesley, 1969.

Blake, R. R., Shephard, H. A., & Mouton, J. S. *Managing Intergroup conflict in industry.* Houston, Tex.: Gulf, 1964.

Bradford, L. P. Membership and the learning process. In L. P. Bradford, J. R. Gibb, and K. D. Benne (Eds.), *T-Group theory and laboratory method: Innovation in re-education.* New York: Wiley, 1964.

Campbell, J. P., & Dunnette, M. D. Effectiveness of t-group experiences in managerial training and development. *Psycholog. Bull.,* August 1968, 70, (2), 73-104.

Davis, S. A. An organic problem-solving method of organizational change. *J. appl. Behav. Sci.,* 1967, *3* (1), 3-21.

Ford, R. N. *Motivation through the work itself.* New York: American Management Association, 1969.

Huse, E. F. The behavioral scientist in the shop. *Personnel,* May/June 1965, *42* (3), 50-57.

Huse, E. F. Putting in a management development program that works. *California Mgmt Rev.,* Winter 1966, 73-80.

Huse, E. F., & Price, P. S. The relationship between maturity and motivation in varied work groups. *Proceedings* of the Seventieth Annual Convention of the American Psychological Association, September 1970.

Lawrence, P. R., & Lorsch, J. W. *Organization and environment.* Homewood, Ill.: Richard D. Irwin, 1969.

Lawrence, P. R., Bailey, J. C., Katz, R. L., Seiler, J. A., Orth, C. D. III, Clark, J. V., Barnes, L. B., & Turner, A. N. *Organizational behavior and administration.* Homewood, Ill.: Irwin-Dorsey, 1961.

Lesieur, F. G. (Ed.) *The Scanlon plan: A frontier in labor-management cooperation.* Cambridge, Mass.: M.I.T. Press, 1958.

Lesieur, F. G., & Puckett, E. S. The Scanlon plan has proved itself. *Harvard Bus. Rev.,* Sept./Oct. 1969, *47,* 109-118.

Paul, W. J., Robertson, K. B., & Herzberg, F. Job enrichment pays off. *Harvard Bus. Rev.,* Mar./Apr. 1969, *47* (2) 61-78.

Roche, W. J., & MacKinnon, N. L. Motivating people with meaningful work. *Harvard Bus. Rev.,* May/June 1970, *48* (3), 97-110.

Schein, E. H., & Bennis, W. G. *Personal and organizational change through group methods: The laboratory approach.* New York: Wiley, 1965.

Walton, R. E. Contrasting designs for participative systems. *Personnel Admin.,* Nov./Dec. 1967, *30* (6), 35-41.

CHAPTER 5

Performance Evaluation and Human Resource Accounting

In the first four chapters of this book, two major points have repeatedly been made. First, the federal government requires that selection procedures must be demonstrated to be related to job performance. Generally, the criterion measure used to validate the selection procedure (chap. 2) has not been an objective measure of job performance, but rather a subjective evaluation of job performance in the form of performance ratings by superiors. An important question remains to be answered by industrial psychologists: Are performance appraisals accurate? In the first article in this chapter, Miner examines the relative advantages and disadvantages of appraisals made by superiors, peers, subordinates and the employee himself. He then makes recommendations for improving the accuracy and consistency of managerial appraisals. We have noted a number of points with which we are in disagreement with Miner, but these caveats should simply point out to the reader that much research is needed in this area. One of the things we recommend is that whenever feasible personnel managers continually compare the performance ratings of the employee to some objective measure of performance. Also, it is recommended that training in performance appraisal techniques be made a regular part of any supervisory development program. In an all-white sample, Scott and Hamner ("The Effects of Order and Variance in Performance on Supervisory Ratings of Workers," paper given at 45th annual meeting, American Psychological Association, May 1973) found that supervisory ratings were accurate in the sense that as performance levels increased, the performance ratings of those subjects increased. However, Hamner, *et al.* ("Race and Sex as Determinants of Supervisory Ratings in a Work Sampling Task," Michigan State University, 1974, mimeo) found that males versus females subjects and black versus white subjects were rated differently even when their average performance remained the same.

The second point to be made is that the personnel function is concerned with human resource management. Attainment of any organization's goals requires that the performance of our managers be measured, compared, and recorded. The second reading in this chapter, by Caplan, discusses how we can set organizational objectives and performance criteria in order to evaluate not only individuals, but work groups and divisions as well. He recommends that we use "human-asset" accounting techniques to attach a "price" to the value added to the product by a work unit and use this "price" as a means of feeding back the performance level of the unit being appraised. By incorporating behavioral considerations into management accounting, Caplain maintains you can give a manager credit for increasing his investment in human resources and charge him for using up that investment. The advantage of this approach is that it maybe more objective than the supervisory ratings discussed by Miner and the feedback is given more frequently. Brummet, Pyle, and Flamholtz describe a company's human resource accounting system designed to measure investments in employees and differential returns which may accrue to those investments.

Management Appraisal:
A Review of Procedures and Practices

JOHN B. MINER

Does the supervisor appraise your performance? Is this appraisal written, formal, and permanent? Does it affect your performance? Are you a manager who must appraise subordinates and write up these appraisals? Has the company recently instituted a system of appraisal and development by objectives? The chances are that you answered "yes" to many or all of these questions, for approximately 80 percent of all U. S. companies have a formal management appraisal system (10). I stress management, for the shift is away from appraisal of the rank and file (42).

Many of these companies, and most of the managers being appraised, are unsatisfied with their formal appraisal system. This is a fair conclusion, for the whole concept is in a state of flux—new approaches, new plans, and new methods. With this constant change, where is a manager to turn for guidance?

For most of us, management appraisal is extraordinarily difficult. It is hard to pass judgment on a fellow man, especially if that judgment will become a permanent part of his company record, affecting his future. The procedure is further complicated by the absence of many needed facts and of widely accepted theories. Yet the attainment of any organization's goals requires that the performance of our managers be measured, compared, and recorded. Growth requires that potential be evaluated. These requirements can best be met by a thoughtfully adopted formal appraisal system, one that best conforms to current knowledge and theory.

The purposes of this article are to provide this knowledge and theory in capsule form, and to offer a handy reference to current work. I have done this by asking—and answering—questions, those most frequently asked about the evaluation of executives. . . .

What Are the Relative Merits of Appraisals Made by
Superiors, Peers, Subordinates, and the Man Himself?

Appraisals made by superiors, peers, subordinates, or the man himself all have merit, but for different qualities.

About 98 percent of all evaluation forms are designed to be completed by the immediate superior. Furthermore, this approach appears to have widespread acceptance. Subordinates characteristically prefer to have their work evaluated in this manner (21).

There is ample evidence that ratings made by peers differ considerably from those made by superiors. The results of a study conducted at North American Aviation (39) indicate that two levels of supervision agree reasonably well; superiors and co-workers do not. Co-workers apparently consider somewhat different factors and additionally, on the average, give higher ratings.

Reprinted with the permission of author and publisher from *Managerial Motivation and Compensation* (MSU Business Series), 1972, Tosi, House, and Dunnette, eds. A condensed version of this article appeared in the October 1968 *Business Horizons,* copyright 1968 by the Foundation for the School of Business at Indiana University. Reprinted by permission.

Similar discrepancies occur when self-ratings are compared with those of superiors. While various levels of supervision tend to agree, superior and self-ratings rarely do (34). Self-ratings emphasize getting along with others as important for success, while superiors stress initiative and work knowledge (21). Furthermore, self-ratings are usually inflated: the self-ratings consistently run higher (32).

There is reason to believe that self-interest can exert considerable influence on peer, subordinate, and self-ratings to the point where the evaluations may lack organizational relevance. Where favorable results have been reported with these techniques, it has been almost exclusively in an artificial research setting. It seems likely that their use as the *primary* element of a regular on-going appraisal system would produce somewhat different results, and that mutual- and/or self-protection could well become a more important consideration in the ratings than the profitability of the company (2).

Although the above statements argue strongly for appraisal by superiors, certain additional facts limit this conclusion. For one, many companies use a management-by-objectives approach, which has a considerable participative component. Managers have a say in setting their own objectives and in determining whether their objectives have been met. This is actually self-rating. Experimental evidence from studies done at General Electric indicates that such participation in the appraisal situation can contribute to more effective performance (12). Thus, at least for purposes of management development, self-rating of a kind has some value.

Peer rating also has received significant support from recent research. A study utilizing middle-level managers at IBM indicates quite clearly that those men rated high by other managers at the same level were more likely to be promoted subsequently (36). It seems entirely possible that at the middle and upper levels of management, where organizational commitment is often high, objective peer evaluations that are relatively free of protective bias can be obtained. Such evaluations may well prove particularly valuable in the identification of leadership potential, just as self-evaluations appear to be most useful for developmental purposes. The Air Force currently is experimenting rather extensively with peer ratings, operating on the theory that they are particularly significant in the measurement of potential.

A recent proposal favors a combination appraisal process utilizing superior, peer, and self-ratings (19). The advantages are sizable. The knowledge that superior ratings also are being obtained reduces bias in the peer and self-ratings. At the same time, the latter two techniques capitalize on unique observational opportunities. The match, or correlation, between the different types of ratings provides a measure of integrated perception among different people in the company, and thus of the capacity to concentrate effort behind goals (29). To the extent that peer and self-ratings support superior ratings, acceptance is likely to be at a high level, and personnel actions, such as promotion and firing, can be carried out without resistance. To the extent they do not, resistance is likely to emerge. Furthermore, self-ratings and peer ratings are available for purposes of development and the identification of potential. Finally, special attention can be focused on those individuals whose ratings diverge sharply. An appraisal involving high superior and self-ratings combined with very low peer ratings is clearly not the same as one with high ratings from all three sources. Yet, if only superior evaluations are obtained, significant aspects of the situation may go undetected.

The major advantage of the tripartite approach is that it provides a wealth of information about the individual and the organization. This approach also pulls together a number of schools of thought on appraisals. All in all, it appears to be *the* approach to management appraisal of the future. Development of such complex programs and effective utilization of the information made available, however, will require expertise beyond that currently available in many companies.

Are There Advantages in Using More Than One Rater?

Research consistently shows that using more than one rater is advantageous. The best evidence comes from studies conducted by the U.S. Army (4), which indicate a clear superiority for the average of ratings made by several individuals over those made by only one person. The rationale behind averaging ratings from the same type of source—either superiors, peers, or subordinates—is that an average tends to reduce the impact of any single biased rating. The larger the number of raters, the more diluted the effects of individual bias. In one study, for example, managers who were found to be particularly considerate and kind to their subordinates also gave them very high ratings (17). When averaged with the evaluations of more production-oriented managers, such overly lenient ratings have less impact on the final appraisal. Alone, their impact is complete.

However, the availability of raters with access to a sufficiently large sample of work behaviors can set a limit on the number of raters that should be used. Increasing the size of the rating group by adding people who are not really qualified to evaluate and who, therefore, will give erroneous data defeats the value of the averaging process. One of the potential values of peer and subordinate appraisals is the availability of a large number of individuals who can qualify as raters because of their particularly good opportunities for observation.

What Is the Value of Rating Reviews by a Hierarchical Superior of the Rater?

Various provisions for reviews by the direct-line superior of a rater are a common feature of appraisal systems (21). In the U.S. Army procedure, there are in essence two reviews—one by the indorser, who also makes his own rating, and one by the reviewer, who merely indicates that a review has been made. Thus the original rater has his evaluations scrutinized twice, the indorser once (7). A review procedure may operate in a number of ways. One approach requires the rater to present his evaluations orally to a review board of superiors (37). In other cases, as with the military, only the written forms are reviewed at higher levels. A reviewer may have the authority to change evaluations directly without any consultation, to personally require the rater to make changes, to advise on changes, or merely to indicate disagreement on the rating form.

Under appropriate circumstances, such review does appear to contribute to evaluation quality (2). Ideally, adequate knowledge of a manager's performance exists at several hierarchical levels above him. Given this requirement, the best approach is to pass the appraisals upward so each manager can make his evaluation either independently, as in the case of the immediate superior, or with knowledge only of what those below him think. This chain of evaluation should stop when it reaches a level in the hierarchy where adequate knowledge of performance does not exist. There is little point in including at the top of the chain a reviewer who does not also evaluate. If such an individual does not have any basis for evaluating a man, then there is nothing gained by adding his signature to a form. If he does have such a basis, then his ratings should be averaged with the others.

This rater-indorser chain approach has the advantage that each manager, except the one at the top, knows that his evaluations will be scrutinized. The approach also provides for multiple ratings under conditions that protect against undue influence from a superior who may have the least adequate basis for appraisal. The information flow is upward from what can be presumed to be the most knowledgeable individual to the least, rather than the reverse. The use of such an approach assumes that a superior will not change or influence his subordinate's ratings in any way. Evidence indicates that, when actual changes at higher levels are permitted, they do nothing to improve the evaluation process. However, the superior can disagree in his own ratings and thus mitigate the effects of what he feels is an error.

Should Management Appraisals Be Made at the Same Time As Salary Recommendations?

The real problem is not whether management appraisals and salary recommendations should be done together, although traditionally this is the case, but rather, to find some method of avoiding the common tendency to decide on salary first and then adjust the performance ratings to fit. [Editor's note: See "Using Pay to Motivate Job Performance," by E. E. Lawler, III, in chap. 6 for additional opinions and evidence concerning this topic.] Because salary, in practice, is influenced by many factors other than merit, the ratings frequently are distorted. I cannot locate any research that bears directly on the question. Nonetheless, studies at General Electric clearly indicate that feeding back information on salary actions concomitantly with management appraisal data is not desirable insofar as motivational and developmental goals are concerned (24). Criticism tied directly to pay action produces so much defensiveness that there is little prospect of learning occurring. Energies focus primarily on self-protection rather than self-improvement (33).

Separating appraisals and salary actions in time is one way of reducing distortion. Yet many managers unquestionably do prefer to couple them, which well may lead to biased appraisals. An approach that would overcome bias and still permit a simultaneous dual decision clearly would be helpful. A means of changing perceptions—of both the salary administration and appraisal processes—seems called for. Although evidence is lacking, I believe this change could be achieved through a training program, provided the content of the program truly represented top-management philosophies. The training would consider various factors that inevitably influence salary actions, including the labor market, previous salary history, budgetary limitations, equity considerations, and rate ranges as well as merit. The training also would consider sources of bias in appraisal. With such an approach, pay and performance possibly could be separated in the manager's mind just as, or perhaps more, effectively as through the interposition of time.

What Are the Pros and Cons of Feedback from the Rater to the Man Being Rated?

Usually, the results of appraisals are given to the man who has been evaluated; this may be done in a number of different ways and with varying amounts of detail (21). The question is whether it should be done at all. An adequate answer requires two kinds of information stemming from two sub-questions: (1) how does the feedback requirement affect the ratings, and (2) how does the feedback requirement affect the man who has been rated?

Feedback and Ratings

A Lockheed Aircraft study (40) provides the best example of how the feedback requirement may influence ratings. The regular evaluations, which were not revealed to subordinates, were followed at a two-week interval by a second appraisal, which included discussions of the ratings with the men. The mean score for the 485 men involved rose dramatically, from an initial 60 to 84, out of a possible 100. Apparently, when faced with the prospect of making face-to-face negative comments, many managers avoided the problem by inflating their ratings. Thus almost everyone was placed toward the top of the scale.

This problem of inflation when the man rated has access to the results has plagued the armed forces for years (7). Although direct feedback by the superior is not required by law, the legal structure does indicate that an officer may inspect the evaluations in his file and that under certain conditions he may appeal. Anticipating that efficiency reports might be inspected, raters tend to make favorable statements. A variety of techniques, including forced choice, forced distribution, and critical incidents, have been introduced with little success over the years to deal with this inflation of ratings, which remains the major problem of the armed forces appraisal systems today.

Thus, where valid ratings are necessary for salary administration, promotion, transfer, discharge, and evaluation of selection procedures, feedback is not desirable. [Editor's note: This is a controversial opinion. See "Current Methods of Worker Motivation in Organizations," by W. Clay Hamner, in chap. 6.] It is particularly important to avoid optional feedback, in which a manager does as he pleases. Under such circumstances, managers who plan to discuss their evaluations with subordinates will inflate them; those who do not plan to do so will not inflate them. As a result, the two types of ratings actually will be on different scales. Assuming the existence of a single scale under these circumstances not only will result in injustice to the individual, but also will produce decisions detrimental to the organization as well.

Feedback and the Man Rated

The major source of information on the motivational or developmental effects of feedback is a series of studies conducted at General Electric (12, 16, 24). The findings of this research on the dynamics of the feedback interview are summarized as follows:

1). Criticism tends to have a negative impact on achievement of goals.

2). Praise has little effect, either positive or negative. [Editor's note: A recent study by Daniel Grady and W. Clay Hamner ("Positive Reinforcement at Michigan Bell," Michigan State University, 1974, working paper) has shown that praise, when administered appropriately, has a very positive effect on performance.]

3). Performance tends to improve when specific objectives are established.

4). Defensiveness as a consequence of criticism results in inferior performance.

5). Coaching is best done on a day-to-day basis and in direct association with specific acts, not once a year.

6). Mutual goal setting by superior and subordinate yields positive results.

7). Interviews intended primarily to improve performance should not deal with salary and promotion at the same time.

8). Participation by the subordinate in establishing his own performance goals yields favorable results.

9). Separate performance evaluations are required for different purposes.

On the whole, the results of the General Electric research seem to provide appropriate guides for action. Nonetheless, subsequent research has raised some doubts about the value of goal setting as it actually is done within the context of the management-by-objectives approach (22).

Feedback can be an effective motivational and developmental tool, but often it is not. Whether systematic appraisal interviews should be attempted depends on the approach taken and the skill of the interviewer. Feedback very clearly can do more harm than good.

Ideally, a feedback interview should be goal-oriented and should take a problem-solving approach to make a positive contribution, but this is not easy to do. Getting a manager to agree on a set of objectives and standards is one thing; getting him to recognize where and why he has fallen short in his performance is quite another (25). However, the requisite skill can be developed in many managers through training (23, 31).

Based on the evidence currently available, the appropriate conclusion seems to be that only those ratings made specifically for motivational or developmental purposes should ever be fed back, and then only by a fully trained and skilled interviewer. Feedback has tremendous potential for harm as well as good. It can be a major source of managerial turnover.

On What Types of Characteristics Should Managers Be Rated?

In selecting the types of characteristics on which to rate a manager, it is most important to include only those characteristics which manifest themselves in the work situation. The rating factors should be firmly anchored in behavior manifestations that characteristically occur on the job and that influence performance (10). There is a tendency to include a variety of traits that do not meet these requirements. Often rating scales deal with aspects of "good" and "bad" people that cannot be adequately judged from job contact alone, or that matter little, if at all, in effective performance. In this connection, it is well to note that it is not always the "good" people who do well. One study found that an intense sense of honesty and ethics almost guaranteed failure in a particular type of sales job (26).

Ratings also should deal with characteristics that can be described clearly so that all raters will have the same kinds of behavior in mind (2). Considerable evidence indicates that certain personality traits, such as character and aggressiveness, are viewed so nebulously that agreement on whether people possess them is almost impossible. Such traits should not be included unless qualified in considerable detail. Generally, the closer the factors are to job behavior and results, the more raters will agree in their evaluations of a person.

How Can Ratings Be Spread Out Along a Scale Most Successfully?

One approach to spreading ratings out is the forced distribution technique, which is a variant of ranking. However, rather than having as many categories as there are managers to be rated, the number of categories is predetermined, as is the percentage of the men to be placed in each category. In theory, the technique, like ranking, has considerable appeal. In practice, however, it presents so many difficulties that, at least for *management* appraisal, it cannot be recommended. One problem is that the percentages are meaningless unless the group to be rated by a single manager is large. Where spans of control are limited, this condition is not met. Furthermore, there is the difficulty of combining groups. Is the lower 10 percent of one group likely to be at the same performance level as the lower 10 percent of another? This same problem of combining groups occurs, of course, with ranking also. Furthermore, raters tend to resist the forced distribution (42). The result is a continuing conflict between those responsible for administering the appraisal system and the managers doing the rating. In the end, either the ratings are adjusted to fit the required percentage distribution, with great potential for error (17), or the forced distribution technique is abandoned entirely.

Given the conclusion that forced distribution techniques are not satisfactory for management appraisal, what other procedures are available to produce a meaningful spread of ratings along a scale? The armed services have faced this problem continually over the years. As indicated previously, since the man rated has ready access to the Armed Service Efficiency Reports, scores tend to pile up at the high end of the scales. In the late 1940s and early 1950s, two rather complex procedures were developed to deal with this problem. The forced choice approach was introduced by the Army and then adopted by the Air Force, which subsequently developed the critical incident technique to replace it. Neither approach proved successful (9). Forced choice failed because rating officers resisted a procedure that made it difficult, if not impossible, for them to determine how they actually had rated a man; in addition, leniency was not entirely overcome. The critical incident approach proved too complicated, too time-consuming, resulted in too much concern with the final score, and did not really solve the leniency problem. In both cases, resistance from rating officers in the field eventually was sufficient to terminate use of the technique. Research evidence indicates that graphic rating scales are actually just as valid as these more complex procedures (4).

All this does not mean that steps cannot be taken to produce a satisfactory spread of ratings. The following procedures used in business organizations have proved successful in extending this range:

1). Maintain security so evaluations are not available to the men rated or fed back to them (40).

2). Avoid ambiguous descriptions of the characteristics to be rated and of steps on the scale; the rater must have a clear understanding of exactly what job behavior he is to consider (3).

3). Carry out training aimed at providing an understanding of the desirability of a wide range of scores (20). Particular stress should be placed on getting overly considerate managers, who want more than anything else to help men, to spread their ratings out. These are the raters who typically have the smallest ranges (17).

If these three conditions are met, and an adequate number of steps or levels exist in the scale, the usual graphic rating scale should yield a satisfactory spread of scores and should prove the most generally useful (2).

Does Stress on Recent Events Bias Ratings?

Studies do indicate, as many have hypothesized, that specific instances of effective or ineffective behavior occurring shortly before evaluations unduly affect the ratings (10). Apparently, raters remember recent events more vividly and, therefore, weigh them more heavily. This situation suggests the need for relatively frequent ratings—at least every three to six months. Averaging such evaluations to yield a running appraisal score will minimize the effects of any specific recency bias. Another antidote involves keeping managers aware of the recency problem. Some managers might be induced to keep notes on performance throughout the rating period and then to review these at appraisal time. Even without this technique, however, sensitivity to the fact that recent events can have an excessive effect should make it easier to counteract the tendency. All of this, of course, represents another training area.

Is There a Method That Will Ensure Consistency of Application?

Evidence on the value of introducing an educational process as an integral part of a total appraisal system is consistently positive. Normally, this educational process is based on the spoken word, but, on occasion, it may utilize written materials as well. Some uses of these procedures already have been noted, but additional features of the communication problem should be mentioned. Studies indicate that training can serve to increase the agreement between different raters, reduce bias (40), increase accuracy generally, prevent inflation of scores (5), and spread out the rating distribution (20). The evidence in support of training in the skills required to conduct an effective feedback interview already has been noted. In general, training sessions should be conducted by a person qualified as an expert on management appraisal and familiar with the details of the particular system in use. There should be an opportunity for considerable discussion and some practice with the rating forms. Various sources of error and bias, as well as factors that will make the ratings most useful, need primary attention (41).

In spite of the consistently favorable evidence, a great many companies do not build training procedures into their appraisal systems. In fact, a lack of adequate training is the major problem of most programs (21). In addition, there is reason to believe that many programs that have succumbed to widespread managerial resistance could have survived had they been introduced with adequate training. Although group sessions usually are used, these may be supplemented with some individual assistance at the time the ratings are made. Manuals containing information similar to the training program also have proved useful (5).

What Can Be Done to Overcome the Resistance That Hampers Many Appraisal Systems?

Many people look on the whole process of evaluating performance quite negatively. This feeling appears related to fears of receiving low ratings if an appraisal system is instituted and survives, and to a strong belief in the seniority principle (30). Evidence shows that less effective managers tend to be the ones most opposed to performance appraisal (14). Furthermore, many managers, in addition to rank-and-file employees, strongly believe seniority is the best guide for making personnel decisions. As a result of these factors, and perhaps others, any management appraisal system will encounter some resistance. This resistance may block the initiation of a program entirely, but it is particularly likely to manifest itself once a program is instituted and there is something to shoot at. Resistance will vary, depending on the values predominant in the company, and it may relate rather specifically to certain kinds of approaches.

Obviously, the greater the resistance the more those instituting the program will have to concentrate on those who will do the rating, and the more the management group as a whole will have to be involved in developing the system. These approaches demonstrate the willingness of those who will be using the data to do part of the work to ensure a successful program. The alternative procedure involves inducing the raters to come to the users of the data. This procedure is entirely satisfactory where acceptance is high, but where it is not merely mailing out forms along with directives and follow-up memorandums will only increase negative feeling. In addition to going to the raters, having large numbers of managers participate in the construction of the system itself is another successful approach (2). This can be done extensively if managers are used both as a source for developing items and as judges of proposed items (38).

The need for special procedures to help overcome resistance will vary, depending on the nature of the program. Many managers tend to resist feeding back appraisal results, for instance. Thus, acceptance problems may be anticipated when this is required. Many managers strongly dislike peer and subordinate ratings (2). Thus the use of a tripartite system along the lines noted previously may require special attention. Forced choice and forced distribution procedures are known to be sources of resistance and, accordingly, require more than the usual efforts to develop favorable attitudes.

How Can Potential Be Evaluated and What Factors Are Predictive of Potential?

To determine a method for evaluating potential and the characteristics that are predictive of potential, research must show that some measure did in fact predict success in management over a considerable period of time after the original measurement. The following discussion is restricted entirely to studies of this kind. Predictions made by managers are considered first, then predictions by psychologists.

Managerial Prediction

In connection with managerial appraisal programs, ratings of potential for advancement frequently are obtained. The difficulty with using ratings of this kind for research is that they are available and known and quite obviously can influence a man's career entirely apart from his actual competence. Even with this bias included, results with these potential ratings by superiors are not impressive. Clearly a great many individuals identified in this manner as having high potential do not advance very far (11). In one study, departments within a single company varied considerably in the extent to which potential ratings were even predictive of the first promotion after appraisal (29). Results like these have led some writers to conclude that the evaluation of potential is beyond the scope of the usual management appraisal system and that the matter should be left to specialists in the field (35). Many ratings of potential are believed to be merely the inverse of the manager's age and thus convey little new information.

The armed forces have carried out most of the research on the predictive value of ratings by superiors, usually with relatively short intervals between the initial predictions and the subsequent measurement of success (18). The correlations obtained are not impressive. These findings contrast sharply with those for peer ratings; in the latter case much better predictions of potential are obtained. Why this difference between superior and peer predictions exists is a matter of conjecture at the present time.

Psychological Prediction

A considerable amount of predictive research has used psychological techniques. Some studies utilize separate measures, such as psychological tests or biographical inventories; other use the overall evaluations of psychologists derived from a combination of sources, including interviews, observation of behavior, and tests. In general, tests of intelligence and mental abilities do seem to be predictive of success. However, in many highly selected managerial groups, intelligence tests are not very helpful in identifying potential because all the managers score at such a high level. At the foreman level, intelligence tests are more effective as indicators of subsequent performance (18).

Consistently positive results have been obtained with the Miner Sentence Completion Scale in a series of predictive studies (27). This measure was designed specifically for predicting success in management. Although the test discriminates most effectively at the graduate level, it can identify individuals with managerial potential as early as the third year of college (28).

Psychological tests in the personality area have produced uneven results when used individually. In a number of cases, they have not proved very useful (18). Yet, enough exceptions suggest that some personality tests can yield good potential estimates. In general, measures of characteristics such as dominance, self-confidence, and persuasiveness are most useful (10). A considerable amount of research has used biographical inventories containing questions similar to those found in application blanks. This research has produced sufficiently positive results to recommend the approach (10, 18). However, companies tend to keep the specific results of these studies secret so managerial candidates do not learn the "right" answers. Thus studies aimed at establishing those factors that are predictive in a given company must be carried out individually. Nonetheless, published research does show that a prior pattern of success is likely to be predictive of subsequent success.

Results with comprehensive evaluations by psychologists using a variety of source data also are encouraging. Studies using this approach have predicted success over a period as long as seven years (1, 8). Yet there have been some significant failures also.

A related approach, even more comprehensive in that managers are studied over a period of days with a whole host of techniques, is the assessment center. AT&T has conducted much of the research with this technique under the title of The Management Progress Study. Staff assessments of potential for advancement derived from these assessment situations have consistently proved predictive of promotion and salary progress over periods up to eight years (6). Those assessments were not made available to those making promotion and compensation decisions. Research indicates that those who have moved up most rapidly are more intelligent, more active, control their feelings more, are more noncomforming, exhibit a greater work orientation (6), are more independent, desire more of a leadership role, and have stronger achievement motivation (13). Although this type of approach is extremely expensive relative to the usual psychological evaluation (15), it appears to yield even higher correlations with later success in management jobs.

There is reason to believe that any psychological approach is likely to be effective only to the extent it is attuned to the value and reward structures of the particular organization (29). Thus the development of psychological predictors to identify potential within a given company must involve a complex interaction between analysis of the individual and analysis of the organization. Such an interaction involving both individual assessment and social psychological research seems to provide the best guide for management appraisal systems of the future.

References

(1) Albrecht, P. A.; Glaser, E. M.; and Marks, J. 1964. Validation of a multiple-assessment procedure for managerial personnel. *Journal of Applied Psychology* 48:351-60.

(2) Barrett, R. S. 1966. *Performance rating.* Chicago: Science Research Associates.

(3) —————— et al. 1958. Rating scale content, I: Scale information and supervisory ratings. *Personnel Psychology* II:333-46.

(4) Bayroff, A. G.; Haggerty, H. R.; and Rundquist, E. A. 1954. Validity of ratings as related to rating techniques and conditions. *Personnel Psychology* 7:93-113.

(5) Bittner, R. 1948. Developing an industrial merit rating procedure. *Personnel Psychology* 1:403-32.

(6) Bray, D. W., and Grant, D. L. 1966. The assessment center in the measurement of potential for business management. *Psychological Monographs* 80:1-27.

(7) Brooks, W. W. 1966. An analysis and evaluation of the officer performance appraisal system in the United States army. M. S. thesis, George Washington University.

(8) Dicken, C. F., and Black, J. D. 1965. Predictive validity of psychometric evaluations of supervisors. *Journal of Applied Psychology* 49:34-47.

(9) Druit, C. A. 1964. An analysis of military officer evaluation systems using principles presently advanced by authorities in this field. M. A. thesis, The Ohio State University.

(10) Dunnette, M. D. et al. 1966. Identification and enhancement of managerial effectiveness. Richardson Foundation Survey Report.

(11) Ferguson, L. L. 1966. Better management of managers' careers. *Harvard Business Review* 44:139-52.

(12) French, J. R. P.; Kay, E.; and Meyer, H. H. 1966. Participation and the appraisal system. *Human Relations* 19:3-20.

(13) —————; Katkovsky, W.; and Bray, D. W. 1967. Contributions of projective techniques to assessment of managerial potential. *Journal of Applied Psychology* 51:226-32.

(14) Gruenfeld, L. W., and Weissenberg, P. 1966. Supervisory characteristics and attitudes toward performance appraisals. *Personnel Psychology* 19:143-51.

(15) Hardesty, D. L., and Jones, W. S. 1968. Characteristics of judged high-potential management personnel—The operations of an industrial assessment center. *Personnel Psychology* 21:85-98.

(16) Kay, E.; Meyer, H. H.; and French, J. R. P. 1965. Effects of threat in a performance appraisal interview. *Journal of Applied Psychology* 49:311-17.

(17) Klores, M. S. 1966. Rater bias in forced-distribution performance ratings. *Personnel Psychology* 19:411-21.

(18) Korman, A. K. 1968. The prediction of managerial performance: A review. *Personnel Psychology* 21:295-322.

(19) Lawler III, E. E. 1967. The multitrait-multirater approach to measuring managerial job performance. *Journal of Applied Psychology* 51:369-81.

(20) Levine, J., and Butler, J. 1952. Lecture vs. group decision in changing behavior. *Journal of Applied Psychology* 36:29-33.

(21) Lopez, F. M. In press. *Evaluating employee performance.* Chicago: Public Personnel Association.

(22) Mendleson, J. L. 1967. Manager goal setting: An exploration into its meaning and measurement. D. B. A. thesis, Michigan State University.

(23) Meyer, H. H., and Walker, W. B. 1961. A study of factors relating to the effectiveness of a performance appraisal program. *Personnel Psychology* 14:291-98.

(24) Meyer, H. H.; Kay, E.; and French, J. R. P. 1965. Split roles in performance appraisal. *Harvard Business Review* 43:123-29.

(25) Michael, J. M. 1965. Problem situations in performance counselling. *Personnel* 42:16-22.

(26) Miner, J. B. 1962. Personality and ability factors in sales performance. *Journal of Applied Psychology* 46:6-13.

(27) ——————. 1965. *Studies in management education.* New York: Springer.

(28) ——————. 1968. The early identification of managerial talent. *The Personnel and Guidance Journal* 46:586-91.

(29) ——————. 1968. Bridging the gulf in organizational performance. *Harvard Business Review* 46:102-10.

(30) ——————. 1969. *Personnel and industrial relations—A managerial approach.* New York: Macmillan.

(31) Moon, C. G., and Hariton, T. 1958. Evaluating an appraisal and feedback training program. *Personnel* 35:36-41.

(32) Parker, J. W. et al. 1959. Rating scale content: III. Relationships between supervisory and self-ratings. *Personnel Psychology* 12:49-63.

(33) Patton, A. 1968. Executive motivation: How it is changing. *Management Review* 57:4-20.

(34) Prien, E. P., and Liske, R. E. 1962. Assessments of higher level personnel: III. Rating criteria: A comparative analysis of supervisor ratings and incumbent self-ratings of job performance. *Personnel Psychology* 15:187-94.

(35) Richards, K. E. 1959. A new concept of performance appraisal. *Journal of Business* 32:229-43.

(36) Roadman, H. E. 1964. An industrial use of peer ratings. *Journal of Applied Psychology* 48:211-14.

(37) Rowland, V. K. 1951. Management inventory and development. *Personnel* 28:12-22.

(38) Smith, P. C., and Kendall, L. M. 1963. Retranslation of expectations: An approach to the construction of unambiguous anchors for rating scales. *Journal of Applied Psychology* 47:149-55.

(39) Springer, D. 1953. Ratings of candidates for promotion by co-workers and supervisors. *Journal of Applied Psychology* 37:347-51.

(40) Stockford, L., and Bissell, H. W. 1949. Factors involved in establishing a merit-rating scale. *Personnel* 26:94-116.

(41) Tiffin, J., and McCormick, E. J. 1965. *Industrial Psychology.* 5th ed. Englewood Cliffs, N. J.: Prentice-Hall.

(42) Whisler, T. L., and Harper, S. F. 1962. *Performance appraisal.* New York: Holt, Rinehart and Winston.

A Behavioral View
of Performance and Evaluation

E. H. CAPLAN

Performance Evaluation in Decentralized Organizations

The essential task of corporate management in a decentralized firm is to create an organizational environment which insures that, to the extent possible, those responsible for important decisions will make them in a manner that best contributes to the

Reprinted with permission from E. H. Caplan, *Management Accounting and Behavioral Science,* 1971, Addison-Wesley, Reading, Mass.

accomplishment of the objectives of the firm. In the case of division managers with profit responsibility, this means that there must be consistency between the goals of the manager, the goals of the division, and the goals of the organization. A crucial factor in achieving such goal congruence is the process by which the performance of the division manager is evaluated. Both the philosophy and the procedures of evaluation have a significant influence on behavior. The attitudes of top management with respect to performance measures are as important as the measures themselves. The evaluation process can be viewed as consisting of the following major phases.

1. Specification of organization objectives.

2. Establishment of criteria for relating the performance of division managers to the accomplishment of organization objectives.

3. Development of procedures for measuring operating results in terms of the performance criteria.

4. Communication of organization objectives, performance criteria, and measurement procedures to division managers.

5. Measurement and evaluation of performance.

6. Establishment and use of feedback processes so that division managers are informed of the results of the evaluation process.

At first glance, each of the above steps seems relatively simple and straightforward, but this is not at all the case. Actually, the entire process is tremendously complicated. In order to demonstrate the nature of these complications, we will examine in some detail the problems of defining organization goals and performance criteria, as well as the difficulties associated with the development and use of indexes of performance.

Organization Objectives and Performance Criteria

. . . The goal structure of business organizations is both diverse and complex. Most firms have a number of objectives of differing degrees of importance, and their relative importance changes over time. Moreover, the objectives are often competitive in that the attainment of one can be traded off against the attainment of another; occasionally they are even incompatible, because the attainment of one precludes the attainment of another.[1] In view of the difficulties in identifying a clear-cut and well-ordered array of goals, it can be anticipated that many actions will result in positive contributions to the accomplishment of some objectives and negative contributions to the accomplishment of others. For example, the concentration on short-run profitability may hinder the achievement of longer-range goals, including future profitability. Furthermore, certain goals may be difficult to express in quantitative terms, which means that the measurement of their attainment will be difficult. Yet these nonquantifiable goals may be as important to the organization as objectives that are easier to evaluate. The danger here is that those objectives which lend themselves to relatively easy evaluation may receive a disproportionate share of attention merely because they are easily evaluated. Finally, even if organization objectives could be clearly and uniquely defined, it would still be necessary to identify a set of criteria by which their accomplishment could be judged. This, in itself, is a formidable test.

An illustration of a comparatively sophisticated effort to establish overall performance objectives can be found in General Electric's eight "key result areas." These are: profitability; market position; productivity; product leadership; personnel development; employee attitudes; public responsibility; and balance between short-range and long-range goals. Apparently, each of these areas represents a criterion by which the performance of division managers is evaluated. But it should be evident that this list avoids few of the problems discussed above. In the first place, performance directed at one criterion (e.g., profitability) could conceivably have an unfavorable effect on other criteria (e.g., personnel development, employee attitudes, and public responsibility). This means that some effort must be made to establish guidelines for evaluating decisions which produce conflicting results. But it is certainly not a simple task to devise methods for attaching relative weights and trade-off rules for these criteria, particularly since each of them has already been identified as a *key* result area. Furthermore, it is clear that certain of General Electric's criteria are more easily quantified than others. Assigning a meaningful numerical value to accomplishments regarding public responsibility, for example, would seem to be almost impossible. Thus there is a distinct possibility that a few of the eight criteria may receive substantially more weight in the evaluation process simply because the procedures for measuring them are better developed.

Another problem with the General Electric criteria relates to the different time spans involved in the flow of costs and benefits associated with the various key result areas. An effective personnel development program, for instance, can be very expensive in a particular year—thereby reducing the profits for that period—yet the benefits of such a program, in the form of improved motivation and efficiency, may not be fully realized for several years. As a result of such timing differences, the measurements of any particular period may be seriously distorted.

Each of the difficulties mentioned above is significant in its own right, and when they are all combined, the magnitude of the total problem becomes enormous. Note that although General Electric's attempt to define performance criteria seems to leave a number of issues unresolved, this company nevertheless has devoted considerable talent and effort to the task and is probably farther ahead in this respect than most other business firms. It is not surprising that most organizations have been notably unsuccessful in establishing objectives and criteria which are truly effective for performance evaluation purposes. In many firms of which we are aware, the only criterion that receives any serious attention is profitability. And there are a great many complications even with this apparently precise calculation (see the discussion below). Since there seems to be no simple solution to the problems inherent in establishing goals and performance criteria, business organizations may be well advised to observe two principles. First, every effort should be made to develop the *best possible* set of goals and criteria and, second, the evaluation process should explicitly recognize that the process itself is imperfect. In particular, specific criteria and indexes of performance should be used cautiously and with full awareness of their potential for generating dysfunctional behavior.

Indexes of Performance

Once a set of performance criteria has been formulated, the next step is to develop procedures for evaluating accomplishment in terms of the criteria. In practice, this step almost always includes the establishment of quantitative measures or indexes of performance. While such indexes are certainly useful, they can produce a number of undesirable side effects, and their indiscriminate use can easily do more harm than good.

V. F. Ridgway has provided a valuable analysis concerning the use of three types of quantitative indexes: (1) *single criterion* indexes which involve the measurement of only one quantity; (2) *multiple criteria* indexes in which several quantities are measured simultaneously; and, (3) *composite criteria* indexes involving several separate quantities which are measured, weighted, and then averaged.[2] Empirical research on single criterion measures of performance has demonstrated that such measures result in behavior which over-emphasizes the single factor to the exclusion of other factors which may be equally important to the overall success of the organization. [Editor's note: For a more recent discussion of the multiple vs. composite criterion controversy, see F. L. Schmidt and L. B. Kaplan, "Composite vs. Multiple Criteria: A Review and Resolution of the Controversy," *Personnel Psychology*, 24, 3, 1971, 419-34.] For example, if the single factor being measured is quantity of output, employees may concentrate on quantity and neglect such other major considerations as quality, maintenance of equipment, and costs.

The limitations inherent in single criteria indexes have led to the increased use of multiple measures. Their purpose is to focus attention on a variety of aspects of performance. However, according to Ridgway, multiple measures also have weaknesses.

> The use of multiple criteria assumes that the individual will commit his or the organization's efforts, attention, and resources in greater measure to those activities which promise to contribute the greatest improvement to over-all performance. There must then exist a theoretical condition under which an additional unit of effort or resources would yield equally desirable results in over-all performance, whether applied to production, quality, research, safety, public relations, or any of the other suggested areas. . . .
>
> Without a single over-all composite measure of performance, the individual is forced to rely upon his judgment as to whether increased effort on one criterion improves over-all performance, or whether there may be a reduction in performance on some other criterion which will outweigh the increase in the first. This is quite possible, for in any immediate situation many of these objectives may be contradictory to each other.[3]

Ideally, the "functional fixation" problem associated with single indexes and the weighting problem associated with multiple measures can be solved by the use of composite indexes. Here, each objective is measured and receives a weight according to its relative importance to the organization. Such a weighting system makes it possible to combine the various criteria into a single composite measure of overall performance. But, unfortunately, composite measures raise a new set of problems. When multiple criteria are used, pressure to improve one aspect of performance can be accommodated by reductions in efforts to attain other objectives. With a composite index, however, this is harder to accomplish, since a reduction in any of the variables being measured will reduce the overall index. Therefore, increases in pressure in one area cannot be absorbed throughout the system, and the results of the increased pressure can be a number of unwanted behavioral consequences. Ridgway notes that although evidence concerning the effectiveness of composite measures is limited, "there is still a clear indication that their use may have adverse consequences for the over-all performance of the organization."

In summarizing his analysis of research concerning performance indexes, Ridgway emphasizes the behavioral implications of these measures:

> Quantitative performance measurements—whether single, multiple, or

composite—are seen to have undesirable consequences for over-all organizational performance. The complexity of large organizations requires better knowledge of organizational behavior for managers to make best use of the personnel available to them. Even where performance measures are instituted purely for purposes of information, they are probably interpreted as definitions of the important aspects of that job or activity and hence have important implications for the motivation of behavior. The motivational and behavioral consequences of performance measurements are inadequately understood. Further research in this area is necessary for a better understanding of how behavior may be oriented toward optimum accomplishment of the organization's goals.[4]

The behavioral impact of any index is determined by two factors: (1) the variable that it measures—its content; and (2) the force with which it is applied—the rewards and punishments associated with it. Since the above discussion suggests that the content of most indexes involves a number of complications, it is necessary to avoid applying any particular index with excessive force. The implications of these comments for management accounting need little elaboration. Accountants must continually inquire into the validity and appropriateness of the indexes that are being used for evaluation and control. Moreover, they must be constantly aware of the possibility of unintended and undesired behavioral responses to their performance measures.

Return on Investment

In the preceding discussion of performance criteria and measures, it was mentioned that the most frequently used criterion in business organizations is profitability. There appear to be several reasons for the attention devoted to profits in the evaluation process. First, we live in a society which includes profit as one of its values. Second, some minimum level of profits is required for the survival and growth of business enterprises. Third, profitability has the *appearance* of being easily quantifiable and, therefore, is generally considered to represent a fair and impartial measure of performance. The most common indexes of profitability are "accounting net income," "return on investment," and "residual income." Since accounting net income is involved in the calculation of the other two measures, we need not consider it separately. Return on investment and residual income both relate income to the investment required to earn that income. While there are important differences in the two measures, these differences are not crucial for our purposes.[5] Therefore, we will focus our comments on the more widely used (although not necessarily better) of the two —return on investment. Three points should be emphasized at the outset. First, return on investment can be a worthwhile index of performance. Second, the definition and calculation of this index involve numerous subjective accounting decisions which make the outcome much less precise than it appears to be at first glance. Third, return on investment can be—and often is—overemphasized in the process of performance evaluation.

The computation of return on investment involves dividing "net income" by the "investment" in assets of the organization or subunit being evaluated. Conceptually it is an ideal index, because it relates resources and accomplishments. Further, since return on investment is a ratio measure, it can be used to compare the performance of entities of different sizes. Thus there are several advantages to the use of this index in the evaluation process. There are also several disadvantages. First, and most important, the definitions of "income" and "investment" that are applied in a particular situation can have a significant influence on the behavior of the individuals whose performance is being measured. For example, there are literally an infinite number of combinations of variables that can be used to define "investment." The investment figure can include all assets or only certain selected assets. These assets can be valued using: one of several forms of market value; original cost; or a variety of definitions of net book value. Some or all liabilities may be deducted from total assets. If long-term assets are included net of depreciation, then the depreciation method can significantly affect the values. The foregoing represents just a few of the many possible variations in the definition of "investment," and a similar situation exists with regard to "income." An astute manager whose objective is to maximize return on investment can be expected to identify the specific set of variables involved in the computation of the index and act accordingly. Thus the accounting procedure for defining income and investment will have significant influence on managerial behavior and, even when the index is carefully constructed, there is no reason to assume that it will automatically produce organizationally desirable actions.

A second major problem with the use of return-on-investment indexes is the tendency of business firms to place too much emphasis on them. This tendency is probably due in part to a failure to recognize the subjective nature of the index and, in part, to the difficulties associated with obtaining quantitative measures of performance relative to other important goals. The return-on-investment figure for a given period highlights the accounting view of profitability for that particular period—and very little else! All of the relevant research on motivation indicates that a heavy-handed emphasis on short-run profit maximization can lead to many dysfunctional consequences for the organization. Even though managers may recognize that their actions are inappropriate in terms of the total organization, if their evaluation is primarily dependent on short-run profit measures, they can be expected to make decisions which produce a good showing in terms of short-run profit. It is sometimes claimed that this problem can be avoided by concentrating on *long-range* profits, but this seems to be a spurious argument. If a company uses return on investment intelligently and does not overemphasize its importance as a measure of performance, the resulting influence on behavior need not create major problems. Rather, it is in those firms which place a great deal of reliance on the index that the most serious behavioral problems will arise and, in such firms, it is unlikely that a manager whose performance appears poor in the short run will be around long enough for his contribution to be evaluated in terms of long-run profitability.

As indicated earlier, the influence that a particular performance measure will have on behavior is determined by two factors. First, the nature of the measurement and, second, the strength with which it is applied. The more pressure that is associated with a profitability index, the more likely that managers will concentrate on the index itself instead of making decisions which are best for the organization. Unfortunately, it appears that return-on-investment indexes are in danger of becoming a fad, and that they are being misused by many firms that have adopted them without thoroughly understanding the potential behavioral consequences. Such firms often combine traditional financial accounting concepts with autocratic styles of management in developing and applying short-run profitability measures which focus too much attention on too few variables. Furthermore, the utilization of computers and more powerful data-processing procedures has made it possible to apply these dysfunctional measures with ever increasing efficiency!

A specific example may help to illustrate the nature of the behavioral problems that can arise when short-run indexes of performance are applied too forcefully and without questioning their behavioral consequences. Although the incident reported here involved standard costing, its more general implications should be obvious. We are aware of a company which has introduced a rather sophisticated standard cost system. The principal purpose of the system is to motivate production department foremen to be more efficient. Foremen who are able to operate within the standards are rewarded with quarterly bonuses and substantial praise. Foremen whose departments produce unfavorable variances are penalized, in the short run by criticism and loss of bonus, and in the long run by dismissal. This company is also very proud of the fact that the standards are kept "up-to-date." The quarterly performance reports that we have seen indicate that most of the departments tend to operate just a fraction better than standard. The accountants who developed the system believe it is excellent and, as a matter of fact, it did improve performance. Nevertheless, a little additional thought suggests that the system is not working quite as well as it appears to be at first glance. In actuality, under this system, the foremen are being encouraged *not* to put into effect any cost reduction techniques that they might discover. For if they do, although they may increase their bonus in the current quarter, the standards will immediately be changed and they will have to live with tighter standards in the future. It is much more likely that rather than officially implement cost savings, the foremen will hoard innovations for use whenever they need them to meet their standards. Certainly any management accounting tool which discourages creativity and innovation must be subject to question. But that is precisely what is being accomplished by this company's performance evaluation procedures. Finally, it might be noted that it would hardly require an expert behavioral scientist to identify this kind of problem—all that is necessary is an accountant who is alert to behavioral considerations.

Accounting for Human Assets

We will conclude this [article] on performance measurement with a discussion of "human-asset" accounting. This is appropriate for two reasons. First, the concept of human-asset accounting involves an explicit attempt to incorporate behavioral considerations into management accounting. Second, it is possible that human-asset accounting will represent one of the major innovations in accounting and control during the next decade. This revolutionary proposal has been suggested by Rensis Likert, a social psychologist. Likert and his associates have been engaged in a long-term study of management styles and their effect on the achievement of organization goals. The findings which have resulted from this research have led to the development of a behavioral model of management. In order to understand Likert's view of the role of management accounting, it is first necessary to examine the nature of his model.

Likert has identified four basic systems of management:

System 1—exploitive authoritative
System 2—benevolent authoritative
System 3—consultative
System 4—participative group[6]

The titles of the four systems are self-explanatory. The first three represent varying degrees of authoritarian management. The fourth system, on the other hand, involves the type of supportive and participative management that is recommended by many modern organization theorists. Likert suggests that an organization's management style can be classified into one of these four systems through the observation of certain variables. These variables consist of three broad classes: causal variables such as organization structure, management policies, and leadership strategies; intervening variables involving the attitudes, motivations, perceptions, and performance goals of the members of the organization; and end-result variables which reflect the achievements of the organization such as net income, productivity, and scrap losses.

Likert's basic thesis is that a firm in which the causal variables display the characteristics of System 4 will generate more effective intervening variables and thus more desirable end-result variables. According to Likert, the philosophy and practices of present-day management accounting concentrate on a few end-result variables which are consistent with a System 1 view of management. He argues that by overemphasizing short-run profits and cost savings, management accounting systems may actually penalize the manager who is making the greatest long-run contributions to the organization. For example, a System 1 manager can achieve apparent gains in production volume, cost reduction, and profitability by using up his human assets. Although these human assets—in the form of employee attitudes and customer goodwill—are as important to the success of the organization as any physical assets, their loss may not be immediately noticeable. Therefore, the accounting system will reflect the supposed gains of the System 1 manager but no record exists of the real costs that have been incurred. Eventually, of course, the decrease in human assets will be reflected in the accounting reports as profits begin to fall or costs begin to rise. By then, however, changes in other variables may obscure what has occurred. Furthermore, by the time this happens, the guilty manager may have been promoted on the basis of his apparent short-run success and the person who fills the vacated position will probably be held responsible for the negative results.

Since Likert's research has convinced him that System 4 management is generally more desirable both for the organization and its participants, he is anxious to encourage organizations to adopt this approach. But one of the barriers to more widespread acceptance of participative management is traditional management accounting which highlights performance in terms of System 1 variables. Thus the System 4 manager who attempts to build high morale and motivation will be penalized for his efforts by the short-run profit orientation of the accounting indexes. Likert argues that appropriate performance evaluation for System 4 management must include the identification and measurement of the causal and intervening variables which are emphasized in System 4. These are primarily human variables. Therefore, to be consistent with—and supportive of—System 4 management, accounting must be expanded to include the reporting of estimates of the value of the human organization and of customer goodwill.

Human-asset accounting would, in effect, give a manager credit for increasing his investment in human resources and charge him for using up that investment. In order to accomplish that task, it will be necessary for accountants to assign values to human assets and measure changes in them over time. Certainly, management accounting is not now in a position to undertake such measurements. Before it is possible, accountants and behavioral scientists working together will need to develop a whole range of new measurement techniques based on a substantial amount of research. As a first step in this direction, several researchers are working with a certain firm in an attempt to develop a "human resource accounting system."

> The elements of this system can be outlined briefly. First, an attempt has been made to identify human resource costs and separate them from other costs of the firm. Techniques and procedures have been formulated to distinguish between the asset and expense components of human resource costs. The resulting human assets are then classified into functional categories such as recruiting, hiring, training, development, and familiarization. Amounts in the functional asset accounts are then allocated to "personalized asset accounts" for individual managers.[7]

It is not unreasonable to assume that many important organizational variables which are not now reflected in performance indexes and reports will in the future have to be measured and included as part of the evaluation process. While the development of techniques for the measurement of such variables will not be an easy job, it is certainly not an impossible one. The critical question for accountants is whether these measurements will become part of the management accounting function or whether they will be developed independently of accounting. The ultimate answer to this question will depend largely on the extent to which accountants are willing to accept the responsibility for such measurements.

Conclusion

The principal concern [here] has been to suggest the need for applying behavioral theory to the management accounting function. We have argued that the viewpoint of contemporary management accounting must continue to be expanded from the traditional accounting model to encompass concepts of human behavior in business organizations that have been derived from modern organization theory. In particular accountants should endeavor to develop an increased awareness and understanding of the complex social and psychological forces which motivate organization participants. This does not imply that economic considerations are unimportant—indeed, they are undoubtedly of great significance. Nevertheless, it appears that most attempts to explain, predict, or motivate human behavior on the basis of economic factors alone are likely to be notably unsuccessful.

Present-day management accounting is clearly the single most important formal source of information available to business managers. It is difficult—indeed impossible—to visualize any modern complex business firm functioning at all without the communication, planning, and control aids provided by accountants. Techniques such as budgeting, standard costing, and return-on-investment analysis represent accounting procedures which are virtually indispensable to management. However, it is doubtful that the maximum contribution of accounting will be realized until these technical procedures are applied within the context of an understanding of the behavioral implications of management accounting.

Notes

1. Stanley E. Seashore, "Criteria of Organizational Effectiveness," *Michigan Business Review*, Vol. XVII (July, 1965), p. 26.

2. V. F. Ridgway, "Dysfunctional Consequences of Performance Measurements," *Administrative Science Quarterly*, Vol. I (September, 1956), pp. 240-247.

3. *Ibid.*, p. 245. Reprinted by permission.

4. *Ibid.*, p. 247. Reprinted by permission.

5. For an excellent discussion of the relative merits of these profitability indexes for divisional evaluations, see Solomons, *Divisional Performance: Measurement and Control*, especially Chapters 3 and 5.

6. Rensis Likert, *The Human Organization: Its Management and Value* (New York: McGraw-Hill Book Co., 1967).

7. R. Lee Brummet, Eric G. Flamholtz, and William C. Pyle, "Human Resource Measurement—A Challenge for Accountants," *The Accounting Review*, Vol. XLIII, No. 2 (April, 1968), p. 221. Reprinted by permission.

Human Resource Accounting in Industry

R. LEE BRUMMET
WILLIAM C. PYLE
ERIC G. FLAMHOLTZ

Investments in the Business Enterprise

Investments are expenditures made for the purpose of providing future benefits beyond the current accounting period. If a firm purchases a new plant with an expected useful life of fifty years, it is treated as an investment on the corporate balance sheet, and is depreciated over its useful life. If the structure should be destroyed or become obsolete, it would lose its service potential and be written off the books as a loss which would be reflected as an offset against earnings on the company's statement of income.

Firms also make investment in *human* assets. Costs are incurred in recruiting, hiring, training, and developing people as individual employees and as members of viable interacting organizational groups. Furthermore, investments are made in building favorable relationships with *external* human resources such as customers, suppliers, and creditors. Although such expenditures are made to develop future service potential, conventional accounting practice assigns such costs to the "expense" classification, which, by definition, assumes that they have no value to the firm beyond the current accounting year.

For this reason human assets neither appear on a corporate balance sheet, nor are

From *Personnel Administration,* July-August 1969. Reprinted by permission of the International Personnel Management Association.

changes in these assets reflected on the statement of corporate income. Thus, conventional accounting statements may conceal significant changes in the condition of the firm's unrecognized human assets. In fact, conventional accounting statements may spuriously reflect *favorable* performance when human resources are actually being liquidated.[1] If people are treated abusively in an effort to generate more production, short term profits may be derived through liquidation of the firm's organizational assets. If product quality is reduced, immediate gains may be made at the expense of customer loyalty assets.

A need exists, therefore, to develop an organizational accounting or information system which will reflect the current condition of and changes in the firm's human assets. Some accountants have recognized such a need, but measurement difficulties pose problems for them. As early as 1922, William A. Paton observed:

> In the business enterprise, a well-organized and loyal personnel may be a more important "asset" than a stock of merchandise. . . . At present there seems to be no way of measuring such factors in terms of the dollar; hence, they cannot be recognized as specific economic assets. But let us, accordingly, admit the serious limitations of the conventional balance sheet as a statement of financial condition.[2]

Importance of Human Resources

Why have industry and the accounting profession steadfastly neglected accounting for human resources? Aside from the measurement difficulties, the answer may be found, partly, in the perpetuation of accounting practices which trace their origins to an early period in our industrial history when human resource investments were relatively low. In more recent years, however, those occupational classifications exhibiting the highest rates of growth, such as managerial and technical groupings, are those which require the greatest investment in human resources.[3] In addition, rising organizational complexity has created new demands for developing more sophisticated interaction capabilities and skills within industry.[4] These and other factors, coupled with persistent shortages in highly skilled occupational groupings increase the need for information relevant to the management of human resources.

Resource Management Needs

Although oversimplified, management may be viewed as a process of *acquisition and development, maintenance,* and *utilization* of a "resource mix" to achieve organizational objectives. . . . Accounting and information systems contribute to this process by identifying, measuring, and communicating economic information to permit informed judgments and decisions in the management of the resource mix. Management needs information regarding: (1) resource acquisition and development, (2) resource maintenance or condition, and (3) resource utilization.

Resource Acquisition and Development Information Needs

Organizations acquire a wide variety of resources to achieve their purposes. Investments are undertaken in those resources which offer the greatest potential returns to the enterprise given an acceptable degree of risk. Calculation of resource acquisition and development costs is necessary, therefore, not only for investment planning, but also as a base for determining differential returns which accrue to those investments. The *resource acquisition and development information needs* reflect themselves along two dimensions; (1) the need for measurement of *outlay costs* when assets are actually acquired, and (2) the need for estimating the *replacement cost* of these investments in the event they should expire.

Resource Maintenance or Condition Information

Investments are undertaken in resources with the objective of creating new capabilities, levels of competency, types of behavior, forms of organization, and other conditions which will facilitate achieving organizational objectives. An information need exists, therefore, to ascertain the degree to which investments in resources actually produce and sustain the desired new capabilities, levels of competency, types of behavior, and forms or organization.

Resource Utilization Information

Once new capabilities, levels of competency, and other "system states" are achieved, *resource utilization information* needs become more salient. Management should know the degree to which changes in resource conditions or "system states" are translated into organizational performance. The answer to this question is reflected in the rate of return on the investments which created the new "system state" or resource condition.

Conventional Accounting and Information Needs

Conventional accounting or information systems answer these three basic information needs for *non-human resources*. Measurement of investment in plant and equipment fulfills the "acquisition information need." Over time, these assets are depreciated, and new investments are recorded. The current "book values" of such investments reflect, at least in theory, the "resource condition" of the organization's physical assets. Finally, "utilization information needs" are supplied in the form of return on investment calculations.

Unfortunately, conventional accounting systems do not answer these three basic information needs for human assets. The objective of our research effort, therefore, is to develop a body of human resource accounting theory and techniques which will, at least in part, alleviate these information deficiencies.

Human Resource Accounting Model

The development of human resource accounting in the business enterprise derives from the pioneering work of Rensis Likert and his colleagues at the University of Michigan's Institute for Social Research. For more than two decades, their research studies have revealed that relationships exist between certain variable constructs and organizational performance. "*Causal variables*," such as organizational structure and patterns of management behavior have been shown to affect "*intervening variables*" such as employee loyalties, attitudes, perceptions, and motivations, which in turn have been shown to affect "*end-result variables*" such as productivity, costs, and earnings.[5] Furthermore, research by Likert and Seashore indicates that time lags of two years or more often exist between changes in the "causal variables" and resultant changes in the "end-result variables."[6]

As seen in Figure 1, Likert's three variable models have been adopted into a human resource accounting model with the addition of two variable constructs—*"Investment variables"* and *"return on investment variables."* Why have these new variable classifications been added? All business firms wish to improve organizational performance. In doing so, however, a more crucial question is, *how much* will performance be improved and *what will it cost*. When a firm invests in new capital equipment, the costs of various alternatives are estimated for each along with projected rates of return. For example, one piece of equipment may cost $75,000 and have an estimated rate of return of 20 percent, while another may cost $100,000 with a return estimate of 15 percent.

An important objective of our research is to extend capital budgeting concepts to the firm's human resources. If the company invests $50,000 in a new training program, what is the anticipated return? If the firm invests $75,000 in an organizational development program, what return will accrue to that investment?

Human Resource Variables and Information Needs

Investment Variables

Investments in both human and non-human assets are recorded in dollar units and are measured to fulfill the *"resource acquisition and development information"* needs of management through identification of investment *outlay costs* and *replacement costs*. Conventional accounting practice now identifies *non-human* resource investments, at least on an outlay cost basis. In January 1968, a human resource accounting system was operationalized at the R. G. Barry Corporation to measure "individual employee" investments. Development work is now in progress to provide a system for identifying "organizational investments."

"Causal Variables"

These are independent variables which management may alter to affect the course of developments within the organization. These variables include the type and condition of plant and equipment, and the type and level of employee competency, managerial behavior, organizational structure, and related factors. As suggested by the arrows in Figure 1, the state of the "individual employee causal variables" is more likely to *directly* affect the "end-result variables" (e.g., productivity, costs, and product quality) than the "organizational causal variables," whose effects tend to pass through a series of "intervening variables," which will be discussed shortly.

"Causal variables" are measured to supply the "resource maintenance or condition information" needs of management. Both dollar and socio-psychological based measurements may be employed to reflect the condition of the "causal variables." Conventional accounting practice now provides "non-human causal variable" data in the form of asset book values which, at least in theory, reflect the current state of those assets. A similar system for measuring "individual employee causal variables" has been implemented at the R. G. Barry Corporation. Questionnaire survey techniques developed by the Institute for Social Research are being employed to measure "organizational causal variables."

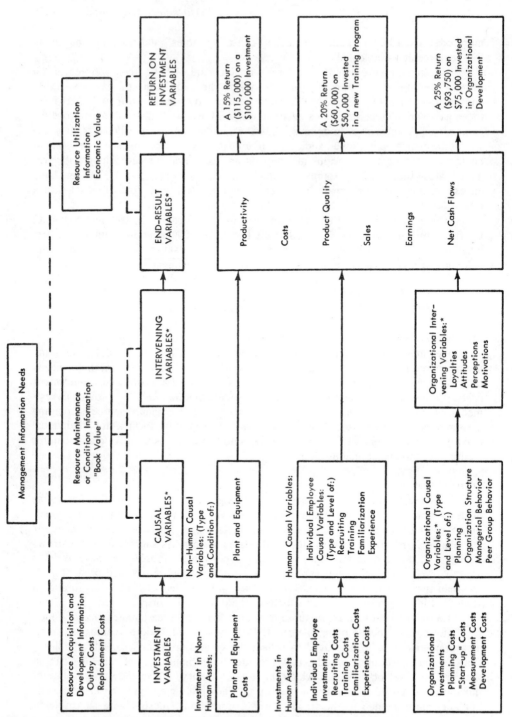

Figure 1. A Human Resource Accounting Model (with Examples of Variables)
   * A more complete listing of variables is found in Rensis Likert, *The Human Organization: Its Management and Value*, Appendix III.

Intervening Variables

As stated above, the effect of "organizational causal variables" may not be directly reflected in the "end-result variables." Time lags of two years or more have been observed between changes in these "causal variables" and resultant changes in the "end-result variables." The effects of changes in "organizational causal variables" have been traced through a series of *"intervening variables,"* which include employee loyalties, attitudes, perceptions, and motivations.

"Intervening variables" are not measured in dollar units, but in terms of a scaling of perceptions derived from a socio-psychological questionnaire. Measurements of the "intervening variables" are directed toward the "resource maintenance or condition information" needs of the organization.

End-result Variables

These are dependent variables which reflect the achievements of the organization. The particular "end-result variables" for a given enterprise are a function of performance objectives which have been defined by that organization. These may include the level of productivity, costs, product quality, sales, earnings, net cash flows, employee health and satisfaction, and related factors.

"End-result variables" are normally measured in monetary terms, but they may also be reflected in socio-psychological units, as in the case of employee satisfaction. Changes in "end-result variables" may be associated with variations in "investment," "causal," and "intervening" variables through multiple correlation analyses of data collected in each of the variable classifications over an extended period of time. In this fashion, "end-result variables" may be expressed in the form of *"return on investment variables"* where a particular change in the "end-result variables" can be significantly associated with a particular "investment variable" change. For example, if $75,000 were invested in an organizational development program, and a $93,750 change in predetermined "end-result variables" was observed, a return of 25 percent would be realized on the investment. Such analyses may be employed to improve the allocation of organizational resources by indicating which investment patterns should be increased, reduced, or maintained at their current level.

Ultimately, it may be possible to place a current valuation on the firm's human resources through a process of discounting estimates of future "end-result variables," using time lags and relationships which have been observed among the variable classifications. The results of this valuation can be cross-checked against the unexpired costs which are recorded in the human asset accounts.

Human Resource Accounting Objectives

The ultimate objective of the research is to develop an integrated accounting function which fulfills basic information needs with respect to physical, financial, and human resources both internal and external to the organization. As an intermediate objective, we are concentrating on the development of an *internal human resource* accounting capability. This research effort divides itself into three functions: (1) *the development of a human resource accounting system oriented to basic managerial information needs,* (2) *the development and refinement of managerial applications of human resource accounting,* and (3) *the analysis of the behavioral impact of human resource accounting on people. . . .*

Research at the R. G. Barry Corporation

Since October 1966, the University of Michigan has been engaged, along with the management of the R. G. Barry Corporation, in development of what is believed to be the first human resource accounting system. The Barry Corporation's 1,300 employees manufacture a variety of personal comfort items including foam-cushioned slippers, chair pads, robes, and other leisure wear, which are marketed in department stores and other retail outlets under brand names such as Angel Treds, Dearfoams, Kush-ons, and Gustave. The corporate headquarters and four production facilities are in Columbus, Ohio. Several other plants, warehouses, and sales offices are located across the country. The firm has expanded from a sales volume of about $5½ million in 1962 to approximately $20 million in 1968.

Implementation of a Human Resource Accounting System

The first phase of a human resource accounting system became operational at the R. G. Barry Corporation during January 1968. This system measures investments which are undertaken in the firm's some 96 members of management, on both *outlay cost* and *replacement cost* bases. An account structure applicable to organizational investments is now being developed. The Barry Corporation is now in the process of extending human resources accounting to other occupational classifications in the firm. In the future, a system will be developed for its customer resources. A model of an outlay cost measurement system for employees is presented in Figure 2.

Historical and Replacement Investments Measured

An Outlay Cost Measurement System

Investments in human resources may be measured in terms of outlay costs. *Outlay costs* are sacrifices incurred by the firm in the form of out-of-pocket expenditures associated with a particular human resource investment. These are measured in terms of *non-salary* and *salary* costs. Examples of the former include travel costs in support of recruiting or training, and tuition charges for management development programs. The latter would include employee salary allocations during an investment period. For example, if an executive attends a two-week management seminar, his salary for this time period should be viewed as part of the investment, in addition to the tuition and travel costs. Similarly, if during the first year of tenure with a firm, 30 percent of a new manager's time is devoted to familiarization with company policy, precedents, organi-zation structure, interaction patterns, and the like, 30 percent of his salary should be recorded as an outlay cost associated with the familiarization investment.

At the R. G. Barry Corporation, instruments have been designed to measure in-vestments undertaken in *individual managers* for each of the functional accounts indi-cated in Figure 2. To qualify as assets, specific expenditures must meet the test of offering service potential beyond the current accounting period in relation to long term written corporate objectives. Charges to the functional accounts are also entered in "individualized accounts" for each manager. With a few modifications the individual manager account structure will also be applied to other occupational groupings within the firm. However, it is not contemplated that "individualized accounts" will be de-veloped for factory and clerical personnel.

Procedures have also been designed to record investment expirations. Asset ac-counts are amortized on two bases: (1) *maximum life* and (2) *expected life*. Functional

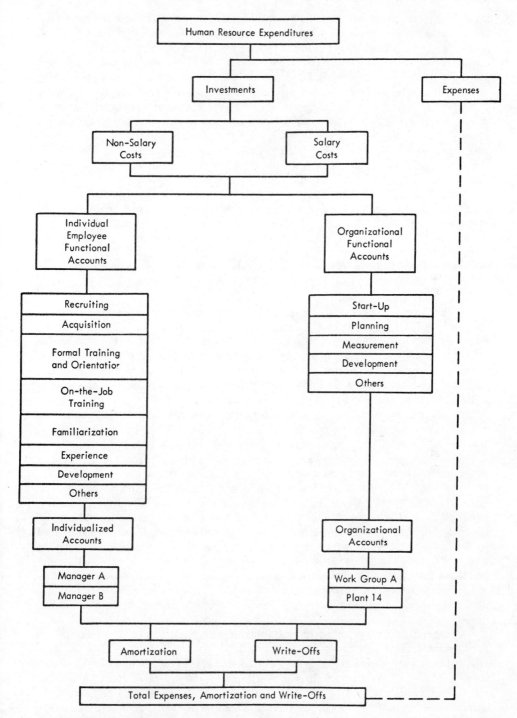

Figure 2. Model of an Outlay Cost Measurement System

investments are separately identified in each manager's account and are amortized according to the *maximum life* of each investment type. For example, recruiting and acquisition costs provide benefits to the firm so long as an employee remains with the organization. The *maximum life* of this investment would be the mandatory retirement age less the employee's age when hired. If *maximum life* were relied on exclusively for amortization, asset accounts would be overstated since employees frequently leave the firm prior to the mandatory retirement age. To assure a more realistic statement of assets, maximum life amortization periods are adjusted to expected life by application of weighted probabilities which reflect a particular individual's likelihood of remaining until mandatory retirement based upon his age, tenure, organizational level, marital status, job satisfaction, and related factors. *Expected life* periods are employed in the amortization of the functional accounts.

The choice between these two bases is essentially a choice between relevance and verifiability. "Maximum life" provides a highly verifiable base, but it is less relevant than "expected life." "Expected life" may, to some degree, be influenced by job satisfaction as well as many other factors. For this reason, a firm may wish to obtain a range of estimates. To be more conservative, "expected life" is employed to calculate the investments shown on the firm's balance sheet and an adjustment to net income based upon changes occurring in those investments. Other estimates may be more useful for planning purposes.

Specific measurement instruments have been designed to record human asset losses resulting from turnover, obsolescence, and health deteriorations. Turnover is immediately identifiable; however, obsolescence is much more elusive. For this reason individual employee asset accounts are reviewed quarterly for obsolescence by each supervisor. Review also occurs when an employee is transferred to a new position. Accounts are also adjusted for known health deteriorations in proportion to the seriousness of the impairment as reflected in actuarial data.

As suggested in Figure 2, an outlay cost measurement system designed to record *organizational investments* is now being developed at the R. G. Barry Corporation. Investments are undertaken in human resources *over and above* those made in *individual employees as individuals*. Organizational "start-up" costs are reflected in heavy individual employee investments and in production below standard during the initial period when the organization is building and developing group interaction patterns for the first time. Additional investments are also made in the form of organizational planning. Furthermore, periodic measurement of organizational causal and intervening variables are in themselves investments in the organization when they lead to development activities which improve the functioning of the enterprise as an interacting system. Finally, investments are undertaken in the organization which cannot be readily traced to individual employees. A portion of the operating costs of the personnel department, company library, health service, safety department, and similar departments may be traced to activities which offer long term benefits to the organization.

Charges made to the "organizational functional accounts" will also be allocated to appropriate entities such as work groups, plants, divisions, or the enterprise as a whole. In addition, a capability is being developed to reflect expirations which occur in these accounts. Many "organizational investments" differ *in kind* from "individual employee investments" which lose their usefulness to the firm when a particular individual leaves the firm. For example, benefits could be derived indefinitely from costs incurred in molding the organization into a system of effective interacting groups despite a moderate level of individual employee turnover within the system. This suggests the possibility that some organizational investments may be non-depreciable.

This would not, however, preclude the possibility of expirations. If for example, an enterprise invests $50,000 in an organizational development program which succeeds in improving employee attitudes and motivations by a measurable amount, subsequent deterioration in those attitudes and motivations could justify a write-off of the original investment.

A Replacement Cost Measurement System

The outlay cost system described above is designed to record human resource investments, obsolescence, and losses as they are actually incurred. These data, however, only partially fulfill the "resource information" needs of the organization. For planning purposes, the *positional replacement cost* of human resources becomes more salient. Positional replacement costs are the outlay costs (recruiting, training, etc.) which would be incurred if an incumbent should leave his position. The human resource accounting system which has been installed at the R. G. Barry Corporation has the capability of supplying average positional replacement cost data for each manager. These positional replacement cost data reflect annual adjustments for price level changes. The system also records "compositional" investment changes since some investments undertaken in the past will not be repeated and, conversely, others not made in the past will be undertaken in the future. For these and other reasons, positional replacement cost may be less than, equal to, or greater than historical outlay cost.

Appropriate Measurement Units

As noted above, "investment variables" are measured exclusively in dollar or socio-psychologically based units. However, "causal variables" may be measured in either dollars on socio-psychological terms. For example, the current condition of the firm's plant and equipment (a "causal variable") should be reflected at its current book value, although other indicators can also be employed. Similarly, the *current condition* of the company's "individual employee investments" (a "causal variable") should be reflected at the book values recorded in the functional asset accounts discussed above. However, other indicators are being developed as cross-checks. Socio-psychological survey questions are now being used to measure employee perceptions of the current condition of "individual employee causal variables" such as the quality of recruiting and training. Trends in these data are being compared with trends in the individual employee asset account balances. These socio-psychological data may suggest more realistic amortization procedures for individual employee investments." The current condition of "organizational causal variables" may also be reflected in the current book value of "organizational investments," recorded in dollar units. However, socio-psychological survey instruments may prove more valid since managerial behavior (a "causal variable") may be altered independently of cost outlays.

"Intervening variable" measurements have been undertaken at the R. G. Barry Corporation and additional surveys are planned. However, an accumulation of several years' data will be required before meaningful "return on investment variables" may be calculated.

Human Resource Accounting Applied

Human resource accounting system applications are oriented toward fulfilling the three basic organizational information needs: (1) resource acquisition and development information, (2) resource maintenance or condition information and (3) resource utilization information. Inasmuch as the human resource accounting system at the R. G. Barry Corporation is in an early stage of development, its potential applications can only be stated in tentative terms at this time.

It is contemplated that the system will generate two types of data: (1) information which is integrated with conventional accounting statements and (2) information which is presented independently of these statements.

Human Resource Data Integrated and Conventional Financial Reports

One of the first reports generated by the system is a *balance sheet* indicating the firm's investment in human resources. The corporate *income statement* is also affected to the degree that there is a net change in the firm's investment in human resources during the reporting period. This situation is illustrated in Figure Three. The two balance sheets indicate that a hypothetical company experienced a *net increase* in its investment in *individual employees* during the period. This change, taken by itself, would result in a

	Dec. 31, 1967	Dec. 31, 1968
ASSETS		
Current Assets (cash, etc.)	$1,000,000	$1,500,000
Plant and Equipment	8,000,000	8,000,000
Investment in Individual Employees		
(recruiting, training, development, etc.)	750,000	850,000
Organizational Investments		
(start-up, planning, development, etc.)	900,000	700,000
TOTAL ASSETS	$10,650,000	$11,050,000
EQUITIES		
Liabilities	$2,000,000	$2,000,000
Owner's Equity:		
Stock	6,000,000	6,000,000
Retained Earnings (including investment		
in human resources)	2,650,000	3,050,000
TOTAL EQUITIES	$10,650,000	$10,050,000

INCOME STATEMENT
Year Ending December 31, 1968

Sales		$2,000,000
Expenses		1,500,000
Net Income		$ 500,000
Adjustment for change in investment in human resources		
—Individual employee adjustment	+$100,000	
—Organizational adjustment	−$200,000	−100,000
Adjusted Net Income		$ 400,000

Figure 3. Balance Sheet

positive adjustment to the firm's net income[9] of $100,000. However, this firm also experienced a *net decline* in its organizational investments during the period. (This could result, for example, from a plant being closed in one location with operations being moved to another state.) This change, taken by itself, would result in a negative net income adjustment of $200,000. When the two changes are taken together, a negative adjustment of $100,000 is reflected in the firm's net income.

Data generated by the human resource accounting system at the R. G. Barry Corporation indicate that the replacement investment of their some 96 managers is approximately $1,000,000, while the current "book value" is about $600,000. The firm invests around $3,000 in a first line supervisor and upwards of $30,000 in a member of top management.

Other Human Resource Accounting Reports

A variety of additional reports are now being generated by a human resource accounting system. Periodic comparative data for different work groups, plants, and divisions contrast human resource investment changes during reporting periods. Turnover losses are also being quantified and analyzed according to such factors as employee job satisfaction, age, occupation, tenure and the like. Special purpose reports are also being prepared to evaluate various organizational alternatives which require investments in human resources. To increase production capacity, for example, should a firm expand its existing plant or construct a new facility? For each alternative these reports indicate projected new investments, write-offs, and the effect on net cash flows. Once a particular alternative is chosen, actual investment, write-offs and cash flows may then be contrasted against projections. As patterns of return on investments in human resources become apparent, the firm will learn which investment types should be increased, reduced, or maintained at their current level.

The ultimate success of any accounting system is determined by its impact on the behavior of people. Where the goals of employees and the organization are reasonably consistent, data may be employed as a problem solving tool to achieve organizational objectives. However, the social science literature is replete with evidence of the distortions which may be introduced into an information system when individual and organizational goals are not congruent.[10] For this reason, an integral part of human resource accounting research will focus on determining the behavioral impact of an operational human resource accounting system on employees. Socio-psychological survey instruments supplemented by personal interviews will be employed to assess the impact. These data will, in turn, be used to design organization development activities which will facilitate installation and sustained operation of the human resource accounting system.

Conclusions

Human resource accounting is now in an early stage, and a host of problems remain to be resolved before a fully developed system can become operational. However, the initial results are encouraging as many beneficial results are being derived prior to full scale operation. Investments in human resources may be determined at a relatively early stage. The techniques developed to measure these assets may also be employed in extended organizational and manpower planning which underlie and sustain corporate growth. Even before return on investment data become available, measurement of trends and rates of change in "causal" and "intervening" variable data may suggest new behaviors and investment routes which will improve organizational effectiveness.

Notes

1. Renis Likert, *The Human Organization: Its Management and Value,* McGraw-Hill, 1967, pp. 101-115.

2. W. A. Paton, *Accounting Theory,* New York: The Ronald Press, 1922, pp. 486-87.

3. U.S. Bureau of the Census, Historical Statistics of the United States, Colonial Times to 1957, Washington, D.C. 1960, pp. 74-75; pp. 202-14.

4. Likert, *op. cit.,* pp. 156-160.

5. *Ibid.*

6. Likert, R. and Seashore, S., "Making Cost Control Work," *Harvard Business Review,* November-December 1963, pp. 96-108.

7. This research will be described in greater depth in a monograph now being prepared by the authors. . . .

8. Where relationships between the level of job satisfaction and expected tenure can be identified, turnover losses may be calculated in dollar terms and predicted for varying levels of job satisfaction, as a function of measured changes in causal and intervening variables.

9. The net income that would be indicated without a human resource accounting system.

10. Argyris, C., "Human Problems with Budgets," *Harvard Business Review,* January-February 1953, pp. 97-110; Whyte, W. F., *Money and Motivation,* New York: Harper & Row, 1955.

CHAPTER 6

Motivating Performance in Organizational Settings

Due to the energy crisis, shortage of materials and increased foreign competition, management and union officials alike are more concerned today than ever before with increased productivity of the work force. To encourage and help employees increase their output, many companies are introducing plans designed to increase the level of motivational involvement of the employees. In the first reading in this chapter, Hamner compares and contrasts three proactive motivational programs which are currently being used by organizations. The *positive reinforcement* program as used by Michigan Bell and Emery Air Freight is based on the theory that behavior is determined by its consequences. The *task structure* (job enrichment) approach as used by AT&T, assumes that making a task intrinsically rewarding will lead to increased output. The *climate* or organizational development (O.D.) approach, as used by General Motors and Saga Industries, is based on the premise that the work climate and attitudes of fellow employees can enhance or be detrimental to employee performance. As noted earlier by Beer and Huse (chap. 4), after the work group has been through a stage of unfreezing and trust building, recommendations made by the groups for improving performance may include rearranging the task or changing the consequences of the task. O.D. then, is designed to change the attitudes of people as well as the task structure and reinforcement consequences, while a positive reinforcement approach is primarily interested in changing the feedback system, and a job enrichment approach is primarily interested in changing the task involvement. Therefore, the three programs reviewed in the Hamner article while not independent approaches, work on different components of the job and involve different levels of intervention by the organization.

In the second reading, Lawler describes how pay can be used to motivate good performance. Following the premise of the positive reinforcement approach, Lawler's point is clear: If pay is not a motivator of performance, it is because it is not tied to performance. In his article he explains under what conditions pay can and cannot be made contingent on performance. Lawler concludes his article by examining the detrimental motivational effect of secret pay plans in organizations.

In the last reading in this chapter, Tosi and Carroll discuss how participation by subordinates in the goal-setting process can increase worker involvement, motivation, and planning behavior—which ultimately increases performance. In addition to involving work groups in goal-setting behavior and self-feedback, a successful Management by Objectives (MBO) Program as discussed by Tosi and Carroll, must reward employees more as their level of performance increases.

279

Worker Motivation Programs: Importance of Climate, Structure, and Performance Consequences

W. CLAY HAMNER

In the past few years, management, unions, and government agencies have joined workers in demanding that changes be made in the work environment in order to improve the quality of work life and to create an atmosphere which would lead to increased productivity. Levitan and Johnston (1973a) say that workers are able to demand more today because of a rise in income which has loosened the economic bond of the work place. Workers are now able to trade marginal boosts in income for more leisure. The work force today is better educated than ever before. The ratio of illiterates has declined from 1 in 5 in 1870 to 1 in 100 today, and the number of college degrees granted yearly has increased from 10,000 to one million. The average manual worker in 1973 had a 12th-grade education, and this formal education was supplemented by the access to newspapers, radio and television which are credited with keeping the workers informed as to changes taking place around them.

Twenty-one percent of the work force in 1972 was under 24 years of age and was concentrated in the lowest-paid and lowest-skilled jobs even though they had the highest level of education (Levitan and Johnston, 1973a). Because of changes in backgrounds, experts warn that unless something is done to improve the quality of work, a crisis of discontent may ensue. The evidence of discontent is abundant: high rates of absenteeism, high turnover rates, strikes, poor worker attitudes, and industrial sabotage (see, e.g., Levitan and Johnston, 1973b, 1973c).

In order to examine the current status of worker discontent, the Secretary of Labor commissioned the Survey Research Center at the University of Michigan to examine the attitudes of workers toward their jobs and the organizations for whom they worked. The results indicated that a significant number of American workers are dissatisfied with the quality of their working lives. Dull, repetitive, seemingly meaningless tasks, offering little challenge or autonomy, are causing discontent among workers at all occupational levels. This discontent has resulted in a restricting of output, poor quality work, and refusal of overtime. It has contributed to high absenteeism and turnover rates and to militant demands for higher wages, more fringe benefits, and greater participation in decision making *(Work in America,* 1973).

Long before this report was completed, management began to examine ways to improve the work environment in order to reverse the trends of higher absenteeism and turnover caused by worker discontent. Management's philosophy seems to be shifting away from the belief that an increase in the rights and benefits of workers leads to a decrease in the rights and benefits of management, and shifting toward a belief that an investment in a program which will benefit the worker will also benefit management. Stephen H. Fuller, Vice-president of Personnel and Organizational Development at General Motors said "We do not view this [worker motivation program] as an either/or situation. Our challenge is *not* people versus profit, it is people *and*

This article was prepared especially for this book.

profit'' (Fuller, 1973). John F. Donnelly, President of Donnelly Mirrors, Inc., con-
curred, saying,

> We continued to invest heavily in consulting services and training in the be-
> havioral sciences because these investments seemed to pay off more consistently
> than investments in equipment. In fact, we began to see that the more effectively
> we used behavioral science to engage our people, the more wisely we made our
> capital investments (Donnelly, 1971, p. 10).

In their attempt to improve the quality of the working experience, workers often
find the union as much of an obstacle as management. When the auto workers in
General Motors' Vega plant in Lordstown, Ohio, struck asking for an improvement in
quality of their work life, the international leaders of the United Automobile Workers
insisted on bargaining for more pay and shorter working hours to take the worker away
from the job (Drucker, 1973). However, there are many indications that unions are
now becoming interested in "people programs" which will improve the quality of the
work environment and increase productivity. The new union attitude favoring increased productivity came about primarily as a result of the pressure of the energy
crisis and foreign competition, rather than from demands of workers, management or
governmental agencies. Unions, like management, appear to accept that an increase in
productivity *and* an increase in the quality of the workers' involvement in the organization are compatible with each other and in the best interest of workers and unions as
well as management. I. W. Abel, President of the United Steel Workers of America,
summarized the changing attitude of unions toward productivity and quality of work
life when he stated:

> I call upon every American to enlist in the crucial battle to improve our lagging
> productivity. Nothing less is at stake than our jobs, the price we pay, the very
> quality of our lives . . . . Things have been so good for so long that we've
> become wasteful and inefficient. So wasteful that, incredibly enough, many firms
> nowadays actually expect to scrap 20 percent of what they produce . . . . How
> can we improve? In these ways:
>
> *By stepping up the efficiency of each worker.* Does this mean work speed-
> ings, job eliminations? Hardly. It does mean cutting down on excessive
> absenteeism, tardiness, turnover, and overtime. It does mean improving the
> morale of workers, more effective work incentive—and really listening to the
> man at the work bench. . . .
>
> *By improving our technology and really using the technology we already
> possess* . . . . The steel industry and the United Steel Workers of America have
> established joint advisory committees on productivity at each plant. This
> cooperative venture is a recognition that workers and employers share a com-
> mon problem. (Abel, 1973)

In response to pressure from these various groups to make the work more challenging and rewarding, many organizations have set up formal motivation programs.
While there are many titles for these programs, most of the innovative programs currently being tried can be classified into one of three categories. The *positive reinforcement* program works on the premise that behavior is determined by its consequences.
The *task structure* or job enrichment program assumes that a job which a worker

finds intrinsically rewarding and challenging will motivate the worker to increase his level of performance. The *climate* or the organizational development program is based on the theory that the organizational climate and the attitudes of fellow employees can enhance or be detrimental to employee performance.

Each of these programs works on the premise that some form of change in the organization can lead to an improvement in employee performance. A climate approach is designed to change the task structure and reinforcing consequences as well as the attitudes of people, while a positive reinforcement approach is primarily interested in the feedback system and a task structure approach is primarily interested in changing the task involvement of the worker. While the three programs reviewed are not independent approaches, they work on different components of the job and involve different levels of intervention by the organization.

Each of these three kinds of worker motivation programs are "proactive" programs in the sense that they are programs which are designed not only to cure current "industrial ills," but are also designed to anticipate and prevent future problems with worker discontent. A fourth approach currently being used by some organizations is a program designed to give workers more time away from the work place and more variety in scheduling their hours of work. The *flexitime* and *four-day-work-week* programs are a reactive approach to the problem of worker alienation which are designed to allow the workers free time away from a negative work atmosphere, rather than designed to change one or more of the components of the work environment.

Each of these approaches will now be examined in relation to its theoretical assumptions and their effectiveness in organizational settings. Since each program has its own group of followers, it is only natural that criticisms for each program have also been generated. These criticism and disadvantages will also be presented along with recommendations for future use of motivation programs.

Positive Reinforcement Program

Theoretical Background

The principles of positive reinforcement are based on the premise that people perform in the way that they find most rewarding to them and that management can improve the worker's performance by providing the proper rewards. The theoretical underpinnings of this program are based on the learning principles described by Thorndike (1911) and Skinner (1953).[1] Thorndike's Law of Effect states simply that behavior which appears to lead to a positive consequence tends to be repeated, while behavior which appears to lead to a neutral or negative consequence tends not to be repeated. Skinner and his followers (see, e.g., Wiard, 1972; Whyte, 1972; Nord, 1969; Hamner, 1974) contend that when workers enter the work place they have developed a sense of right versus wrong and have been thoroughly conditioned by their parents and by society. Therefore, they argue that the only tool needed for worker motivation is the presence or absence of positive reinforcement. In other words, managers do not, as a general rule, need to use avoidance learning or punishment techniques in order to control behavior.

Whyte (1972) says "positive reinforcers generally are more effective than negative reinforcers in the production and maintenance of behavior" (p. 67). Wiard (1972) points out, "there may be cases where the use of punishment has resulted in improved performance, but they are few and far between" (p. 16). Drucker (1973) says "B. F. Skinner's rigorous research on learning theory leaves little room to doubt that rewards, or positive reinforcements, are the efficient way to learn" (p. 92). Skinner best sum-marizes the simplicity of a positive reinforcement program when he says:

> . . . Supervision by positive reinforcement changes the whole atmosphere of the workspace and produces better results. A constantly critical position on the part of the supervisor encourages bad morale, absenteeism and job changing. . . . With positive reinforcement you get at least the same amount of work, and the worker is more likely to show up every day and less likely to change jobs. In the long run, both the company and the worker are better off ("Conversations with B. F. Skinner," 1973, p. 35).

Sorcher and Goldstein (1972) agree with Skinner that one reason organizations fail to motivate workers is that they "turn them off" rather than "turn them on" with their reinforcement practices. They state that a good illustration of this maladaptive be-havior is the manager who attempts to motivate an employee to improve his poor performance, but simply threatens him to the point where the employee becomes less effective and more hostile toward the manager.

A positive reinforcement philosophy of management differs from traditional moti-vational theories (see Hunt and Hill, 1970) in basically two ways. First, as noted above, a positive reinforcement program calls for the maximum use of positive rein-forcement and the minimum use of punishment. Punishment tends to leave the indi-vidual feeling controlled and coerced and leads to immaturity in the individual, and therefore eventually in the organization itself (e.g., see Tannenbaum, 1962, and Ar-gyris, 1964). Second, a positive reinforcement program avoids psychological probing into the worker's attitudes as a possible cause of behavior. Instead, the work situation itself is analyzed, focusing on the reward contingencies which cause a worker to act the way he does.

A positive reinforcement program, therefore, is results-oriented, rather than proc-ess-oriented. Geary A. Rummler, President of Praxis Corporation, a management con-sultant firm, claims that the motivational theories of behavioral scientists such as Herz-berg and Maslow, which stress workers' psychological needs, are impractical. "They can't be made operative. While they help to classify the problem, a positive reinforce-ment program leads to solutions" *(International Management,* 1973, p. 35). Sorcher and Goldstein (1972) agree, stating that a positive reinforcement procedure is quite different from the traditional approach to behavior change in that it does not rely on an approach aimed at first changing attitudes, then hoping that behavior will fall in line with those attitudes. "Instead, this procedure is based on some of the fundamentals of social learning, i.e., imitation (behavioral rehearsal) and reinforcement, and is aimed directly at behavior change without relying on the diversionary tactics of attitude change" (p. 41).

Stages in Program Development

Positive reinforcement programs currently used in industry generally involve at least four stages. The *first step* according to E. J. Feeney, Vice-president of Emery Air Freight Corporation, is to define the *behavioral* aspects of performance and do a performance audit.[2] This step is potentially one of the most difficult, since some com-panies do not have a formal performance evaluation program, especially for the non-managerial employees, and those which do have a program are often rating the em-ployee on nonbehavioral or nonjob-related measures (e.g., friendliness, overall attitude, etc.). But once these behavioral aspects of the job are defined, and managers see how poorly some of these are being performed, the task of convincing managers that improvement is needed and persuading them to cooperate with such a program is simplified. Feeney reports, "Most managers genuinely think that operations in their bailiwick are doing well; a performance audit that proves they're not comes as a real and unpleasant surprise" *(Organizational Dynamics,* 1973b, p. 42).

Not only does the performance audit help the manager accept the program, but it also helps the employees identify themselves as meaningful contributors to the objectives of the organization. Frost (1973) said:

> If the employees are helped to identify "what day it is"—the competitive bid made for the job, the cost of the materials, the cost of the machine, its coolants, and maintenance, the cost of set-up and down time, . . . the employees can perceive the relevance of their contribution and the rationale of management's administration. Everyone in the organization becomes important and an interdependent part. Everyone in the organization comes to play a small part or a big part, but an essential part. Everyone becomes a resource that is available and called upon to perform effectively to achieve the organization's objectives. The personal and professional goals for dignity, recognition and significance become compatible with the organization's need to be fiscally sound and competitive (p. 4).

Defined levels of performance which are specifically determined and clearly stated, therefore, help both the manager and the employee establish a base-line measure against which to measure their future performance (Wiard, 1972; Emery, 1973). Rummler *(International Management,* 1973) says that a person should get all the data that are available about his performance, not selective information. Ideally, it should come from the system, from a computer, so that it appears objective, neutral, and unemotional. In this manner, the employee and the manager are better able to accept the program as one that will mutually benefit them both.

The *second step* in developing a working positive reinforcement program is to develop and set specific and reasonable goals for each worker. Sorcher and Goldstein (1972) suggest that the failure to specify concrete behavioral goals is a major reason many programs do not work. They state, "Goals must be defined in measurable terms—they should be expressed in behavioral terms such as employee turnover or schedules met rather than only in terms of 'better identification with the company' or 'increased job satisfaction'" (p. 36). The goals set, therefore, should be in the same terms as those defined in the performance audit as being specifically related to the task at hand. The goals should be reasonable and set somewhere between "where you are" (as defined in the performance audit) and some ideal.

While goals can be set by the manager, it is important that they are accepted by the employee. An even better approach would be to allow the employees to work with management in the setting of the work goals. By using a participatory management technique to enlist the ideas of those performing the job, you gain not only the acceptance of goals, but also means and ways of obtaining new goals, according to J. C. Emery, President of Emery Air Freight Corporation (1973).

Luthans and White (1971) see the popular management system, management by objectives (MBO)[3] as providing an excellent system for meeting the first two stages of a positive reinforcement program. They state, "Manpower managers can utilize behavior modification[4] techniques to generate direction and self-control among all levels of personnel. . . . Management by objectives provides an opportunity for all personnel to contribute to job goals and encourages the setting of checkpoints to measure progress'' (p. 45). However, both Luthans and White (1971) and Carroll and Tosi (1973) agree that MBO goal setting alone is ineffective without feedback and positive reinforcement.

The *third step* in a positive reinforcement program is to allow the employee to keep a record of his or her own work. This process of self-feedback maintains a continuous schedule of reinforcement (see Ferster and Skinner, 1957) for the worker and permits the worker to gain intrinsic reinforcement from the task itself. Where employees can total their own results, they can see if they are meeting their goals or not and whether they are improving over their previous level of performance (as measured in the performance audit stage). In other words, the worker has two chances of being successful—either by beating his previous record or by beating both his previous record and his established goal. E. D. Grady, Division Traffic Manager for Michigan Bell, says that the manager should set up the work environment in such a way that people have a chance to succeed. One way to do this he says is to "shorten the success interval." Grady says, "If you're looking for success, keep shortening the interval of measurement so you can get a greater chance of success which you can latch on to for positive reinforcements" *(International Management,* 1973, p. 34). For example, rather than set goals in monthly or quarterly terms, set them in weekly or daily terms. This doesn't reduce the level of the goal, but it may reduce the per-ceived difficulty of the goal.

The *fourth step* of providing positive reinforcement for good performance is the most important step in a positive reinforcement program and is one that separates it from all other motivation plans. The supervisor looks at the self-feedback report of the employee and/or other indications of performance (e.g., sales records) and then praises the positive aspects of the employee's performance (as determined by the performance audit and goals set). This extrinsic reinforcement should strengthen the desired performance, while the withholding of praise for the performance which falls below the goal should give the employee incentive to improve that level of perform-ance. Since the worker already knows the areas of his or her deficiencies, there is no reason for the supervisor to criticize the employee. In other words, negative feedback is self-induced, whereas positive feedback comes from both internal and external sources.

As noted previously, this approach to giving feedback follows the teachings of B. F. Skinner, who believes that use of positive reinforcement leads to a greater feeling of self-control, while the avoidance of negative reinforcements keeps the individual from feeling controlled or coerced. Skinner says "You can get the same effect if the super-visor simply discovers things being done right and says something like 'good, I see you're doing it the way that works best'" *(Organization Dynamics,* 1973a). Sorcher and Goldstein (1972) say the reason punishment fails is because of the increased educa-tion level and social status of the employee. Drucker (1973) says, "the stick fails be-cause fear is altogether incompatible with the reliable production of knowledge. It produces efforts and anxieties, but it generally inhibits learning" (p. 92). Rummler says that when a manager has to go into the negative aspect of a workers performance, he should do it in a positive manner—"What can I do to help?" If he accuses the em-ployee, the worker will have a dozen excuses.

While the feedback initially used in step four of the positive reinforcement pro-gram is praise, it is important to note that other forms of reinforcements can have the same effect. M. W. Warren, the Director of Organization and Management Develop-ment at the Questor Corporation, says that the five "reinforcers" that Questor has found to be the most effective are (1) money, but only when it is a consequence of a specific performance, and the relation to the performance is known; (2) praise or recognition; (3) freedom to choose one's own activity; (4) opportunity to see one's self become better, more important, or more useful; and (5) power to influence both co-workers and management. Warren states, "By building these reinforcers into programs at various facilities, Questor is getting results" (1972, p 29). The need for using more than praise after the positive reinforcement program has proved effective is discussed by Skinner.

> It does not cost the company anything to use praise rather than blame, but if the company then makes a great deal more money that way, the worker may seem to be getting gypped. However, the welfare of the worker depends on the welfare of the company, and if the company is smart enough to distribute some of the fruits of positive reinforcement in the form of higher wages and better fringe benefits, everybody gains from the supervisor's use of positive reinforcements (*Organizational Dynamics,* 1973a, p. 35).

Results of Positive Reinforcement Programs

Companies which claim to be implementing and using positive reinforcement programs such as the one described above include Emery Air Freight, Michigan Bell Telephone, Questor Corporation, Cole National Bank in Cleveland, Ford Motor Company, American Can, Upjohn, United Air Lines, Warner-Lambert, Addressograph-Multigraph, Allis-Chalmers, Bethlehem Steel, Chase Manhattan Bank, IBM, IT&T, Proctor and Gamble, PPG Industries, Standard Oil of Ohio, Westinghouse and Wheeling-Pittsburgh Steel Corporation (see *Business Week,* December 18, 1971, and December 2, 1972). In addition, another 200 firms have contacted E. J. Feeney of Emery Air Freight since Emery's success with positive reinforcement was first reported (*Organizational Dynamics,* 1973b). Because the program is relatively new in industrial settings (most have begun since 1968), few statements of their relative effectiveness have been reported. In December, 1972 *Business Week* stated that "there's little objective evidence available, and what evidence there is abounds in caveats—the technique will work under the proper circumstances, the parameters of which are usually not easily apparent" (p. 49).

In the area of employee training, Northern Systems Company (Nord, 1969), General Electric Corporation (Sorcher and Goldstein, 1972) and Emery Air Freight (*Organizational Dynamics,* 1973b) claim that positive reinforcement has improved the speed and efficiency of their training program. In their programmed learning program, the Northern Systems Company says the trainee gains satisfaction only be demonstrated performance at the tool station. Through positive reinforcements, he quickly perceives that correct behaviors obtain for him the satisfaction of his needs, and that incorrect behaviors do not (Nord, 1969). Emery has designed a similar program for sales trainees. *Business Week* (December 18, 1971) reported the success of the program by saying:

> It is a carefully engineered, step-by-step program, with frequent feedback questions and answers to let the salesman know how he is doing. The course contrasts with movies and lectures in which, Feeney says, the salesman is unable to gauge what he has learned. The aim is to get the customer on each sales call to take some kind of action indicating that he will use Emery services. Significantly, in 1968, the first full year after the new course was launched, sales jumped from $62.4 million to $79.8 million, a gain of 27.8 percent compared with an 11.3 percent rise the year before.

Since 1969, Emery has instituted a positive reinforcement program for all of its employees and credits the program with direct savings to the company of over $3 million in the past three years *(Organizational Dynamics,* 1973b) and indirectly with pushing 1973 sales over the $160 million mark. While Emery Air Freight is by far the biggest success story for a positive reinforcement program to date, other companies are also claiming improvements as a result of initiating similar programs. At Michigan Bell's Detroit office, 2,000 employees are now under a positive reinforcement program. Michigan Bell credits the program with reducing absenteeism from 11 percent to 6.5 percent in one group, from 7½ percent to 4½ percent in another group, and from 3.3 percent to 2.6 percent for all employees. In addition, the program has resulted in reports being completed correctly and on time 90 percent of the time as compared to 20 percent of the time prior to the program's implementation *(Business Week,* Dec. 2, 1972; *International Management,* 1973). The Wheeling-Pittsburgh Steel Corporation credits its feedback program with saving $200,000 a month in scrap costs *(Business Week,* Dec. 2, 1972).

In an attempt to reduce the number of employees who constantly violated plant rules, General Motors implemented a plan in one plant that gave employees opportunities to improve or clear their records by going through varying periods of time without committing further shop violations. They credit this positive reinforcement plan with reducing the number of punitive actions for shop rule infractions by two-thirds from 1969 to 1972 and the number of production standard grievances by 70 percent during the same period of time (Schotters, 1973a).

Gamboa and Pedalino (1973) describe a company which used a lottery to solve the problem of employee absenteeism. The company adopted a plan suggested by Skinner when he said:

> . . . Let's take an example of how you could use a lottery to solve the problem of absenteeism. With today's high wages, missing a day's wages doesn't much matter. But suppose you have something like a door prize every day. When you come to work, you get a ticket, and at the end of the day there's a drawing. Then a man will think twice before staying away. If absenteeism is a real problem, a reasonable prize per day might solve it. *(Organizational Dynamics,* 1973a).

In this company, each day an employee came to work and was on time, he was allowed to choose a card from a deck of playing cards. At the end of the five-day week, he had five cards or a normal poker hand. The highest hand in each department won $20.00, and all full-time employees who worked 50 days straight had their names placed in a lottery from which two $50.00 prizes were drawn. Absenteeism dropped from 3.01 percent to 2.46 percent (18.3 percent decrease) until the program was discontinued, at which time the absenteeism jumped to 3.2 percent. Ford Motor Company tried a similar lottery in which all employees within one section of a plant with a perfect attendance record for a month were eligible for a drawing to determine the winner of a prize worth $150.00. After several months the program was dropped because no change in absenteeism took place.

Criticisms of the Program

While critics of Skinner's theory are abundant, critics of a positive reinforcement approach applied to industry are few. Whyte (1972) said while he agreed with the principles of a positive reinforcement approach to management, he criticized the application of the program to the work force on the basis that it is generally developed on an individual feedback basis while many work situations depend on group cooperation. A second major criticism by Whyte is that "at its simplest level, the problem of the prediction and control of behavior involves creating conditions in which the behavior that positively reinforces one person also positively reinforces the other person (in the same group or organization) . . ." (p. 98). Therefore, what one worker finds rewarding, another may not. The design of the rewards are crucial, according to Whyte.

Skinner *(Organizational Dynamics,* 1973) and Whyte (1972) both state that a feedback system alone may not be enough. Skinner recommends that the organization should design feedback and incentive systems in such a way that the dual objective of getting things done and making work enjoyable is met. He states:

> It is important to remember that an incentive system isn't the only factor to take into account. How pleasant work conditions are, how easy or awkward a job is, how good or bad tools are—many things of that sort make an enormous difference in what a worker will do for what he receives. One problem of the production-line worker is that he seldom sees any of the ultimate consequences of his work. He puts on left front wheels day in and day out and he may never see the finished car. . . . (p. 39).

Drucker (1973) worries that perhaps the use of positive reinforcers may be misused by management to the detriment of the economy. "The carrot of material rewards has not, like the stick of fear, lost its potency. On the contrary, it has become so potent that it threatens to destroy the earth's finite resources if it does not first destroy more economies through the inflation that reflects rising expectations" (p. 89). Skinner (1969; 1973) agrees that reinforcers can be misused. He says that what must be accomplished, and what he believes is currently lacking, is an effective training program for managers. "In the not too-distant future, however, a new breed of industrial manager may be able to apply the principles of operant conditioning effectively *(Organizational Dynamics,* 1973a, p. 40)."

Task Structure or Job Enrichment Program

Theoretical Background

Both research and practical experience have indicated that jobs should include opportunities for personal achievement, responsibility, recognition, growth, and achievement in order to provide high levels of employee performance. In other words, work should provide employees with positive satisfaction which is derived from using their individual talents and skills.

One method by which this objective is being achieved in organizations is through job enrichment. Job enrichment is a concerted attempt to stem and even reverse long-term trends among industrial engineering programs toward job simplification and specialization (Hulin and Blood, 1968). In simple terms, job enrichment involves the redefinition or restructuring of jobs so that employees have greater planning and control responsibilities in the execution of their overall assignment. Job enrichment should be distinguished from job enlargement, where workers are given more work to do without any greater planning and control responsibilities.

The theoretical principles on which job enrichment is based are not nearly as clear and straightforward as those of the positive reinforcement program already described. Skinner and his followers (known as *behaviorists*) see job enrichment as being a method of making the task intrinsically reinforcing and, therefore, they describe the enriched job as leading to higher levels of performance because it leads to a positive reward state and the absence of an enriched job leads to a negative or neutral reward state (see *Organizational Dynamics,* 1973a and Nord, 1969). According to Luthans (1973), job enrichment as it is currently practiced in industry is a direct outgrowth of Herzberg's two-factor theory of motivation (see Herzberg, 1968) and is therefore based on the assumption that in order to motivate personnel, the job itself must provide opportunities for achievement, recognition, responsibility, advancement, and growth. The program entails "enriching" the job so that these factors are included.

Scott (1966) offers a third theoretical explanation of why an enriched task design increases the motivation level of the worker. Scott's activation theory explanation is based on physiology. Briefly, this theory holds that cues received from the environment travel to the appropriate cortical projection region of the brain for information purposes and are also diffused over a wide area of the cortex in order to arouse or activate the organism. According to Scott, the more variety and stimulation in an enriched task, the higher is the state of arousal or activation and the more motivated is the worker. In short, with routine, repetitive tasks, after a period of time the "sameness" of the cue received leads to a decrease in arousal level and therefore a decrease in motivation and performance.

Lawler (1969) offers still a fourth theoretical explanation of why an increase in complexity of task design will lead to higher levels of performance. The theory of motivation that best describes "why" job enrichment increases commitment and involvement on the part of the employee is an "internal state" theory called "expectancy theory" (see Vroom, 1964). While the details of this theory are beyond the scope of this paper, this theory basically says that an enriched task is *perceived* by the worker as leading to an intrinsic reward. Lawler (1969) says:

> Thus, it appears that the answer to the *why* question can be found in the ability of job design factors to influence employee's perceptions of the probability that good performance will be intrinsically rewarding. Certain job designs apparently encourage the perception that it will, while others do not. Because of this, job design factors can determine how motivating a job will be (p. 429).

Regardless of their theoretical position, most behavioral scientists (e.g., see Argyris, 1957; Kornhauser, 1965; Likert, 1961; Whyte, 1972) regard extreme division of labor and the resulting job simplification and specialization as leading almost inevitably to monotony, job dissatisfaction, and decreased performance.

Even though there is disagreement as to *why* job enrichment works, the programs being put forth by the various "reformers" can be reduced to a few common elements (Levitan and Johnson, 1973a). The elements are: (1) Individuals should be given maximum freedom to control their work and develop their skills; (2) jobs should be designed to give each person a series of tasks which are varied, challenging, and meaningful in terms of the end product; and (3) the status differential which has separated supervisors and employees should be replaced by a team concept with an emphasis on shared goals.

Stages in Program Development

The leading advocate of job enrichment in the U. S. today is probably Robert Ford, Personnel Director—Work Organizations and Environmental Research at AT&T. From 1965 to 1968, AT&T conducted 19 formal field experiments in job enrichment and has expanded the program today to many other areas of the Bell system. Based on AT&T's

constant reaffirming of their job enrichment program, Ford (1973) sees the job enrichment strategy as involving three stages. The *first step* is designed to improve work through systematic changes in the modules of work. In this stage the worker is given a whole, natural unit of work and specific or specialized tasks are assigned to the individuals which enable them to become experts in this expanded work module. Ford says that in defining modules that give each employee a natural area of responsibility, AT&T tries to accumulate modules of work until one of these three entities has been created for the worker: (1) a customer outside the organization, (2) a client within the organization or (3) a task in the manufacturing end of the business where individuals can produce complete or large portions of the complete product.

AT&T has recently added a "nesting" of jobs together in this stage in order to improve morale and upgrade performance. This method goes beyond enriching *individual* jobs and puts together people whose work modules complement one another. Job nesting, therefore, is the opposite of job pooling (e.g., a secretarial pool) where workers who perform a similar task are located together.

The *second step* enriches the work through systematic changes in the control of the work module. In this stage, as an employee gains experience, the supervisor should continue to turn over responsibility until the employee is handling the work completely. The ultimate goal is to let the worker have complete control over his or her job. This increases the accountability and control of individuals over their own work and indeed makes each employee a manager of his task. Eugene Cafiero, Group Vice-president at Chrysler, sees this as a crucial stage in getting the most out of a job enrichment program. In a recent speech Cafiero discussed the results of Chrysler's recent experience at enriching workers' jobs. He said:

> A man doing a job all day long knows more about that job than anyone else; he knows how to improve it better than anyone else. We want to give our people a chance to speak up. We feel that this program is working through more satisfied employees. We at Chrysler Corporation are trying to avoid the impersonal feelings that are often associated with large corporations . . . (*Detroit Free Press,* July, 25, 1971).

The *third* and *final step* is perhaps the most important to the success of the job enrichment program. In this stage the job is enriched through systematic changes in the feedback that signals whether something has been accomplished. In this stage, periodic reports are made directly available to the worker himself rather than to the supervisor. Just as in the positive reinforcement program, this stage allows the worker to monitor the quality and quantity of his own work in order to make the corrections necessary. Ford (1973) says that "Definition of the module and control of it are futile unless the results of the employee's effort are discernible. Moreover, knowledge of the results should go directly to where it will nurture motivation—that is, to the employee. People have a great capacity for midflight correction when they know where they stand" (p. 99).

Unlike a positive reinforcement program, job enrichment requires a big change in managerial style. A positive reinforcement program, rather than trying to change managerial style, would be designed to increase the behavioral repertoire of a manager in his ability to give varied kinds of feedback as it relates to worker performance (Sorcher and Goldstein, 1972). Job enrichment calls for increasing modules, moving controls downward, and designing effective feedback systems. Therefore, the job enrichment program involves not only changing a worker's task involvement and the feedback he receives, but it also changes the traditional *relationship* of the supervisor with his subordinates.

Results of Job Enrichment Programs

There are literally scores of companies today involved to some extent in job-enrichment programs. These include Texas Instruments, Corning Glass Works, IBM, AT&T, Proctor and Gamble, Bankers Trust, Merrill, Lynch, Pierce, Fenner and Smith, Donnelly Corporation, Imperial Chemical Industry, Ltd., Maytag, Motorola, Gaines Food Company, and Buick.

Just as for positive reinforcement programs, evidence of the effectiveness of job enrichment programs is sketchy, lacks empirical rigor, probably is reported only by companies that have experienced success, and is often qualitative in nature (Hulin, 1971). As Levitan and Johnston (1973a) warn:

> These experiments with job redesign are all "success stories." Indeed, most of the literature on work reform is the product of advocates reporting positive results. But there are major gaps in the case for job reform. Companies which find authoritarian controls and unchanged job rewards to be successful as ever are not included in the surveys. Companies whose enrichment and participation plans turn sour rarely trumpet the news (p. 36).

Nevertheless, many companies are reporting success stories and, as a result other companies are eagerly spending millions of dollars each year trying to duplicate their success.

In 1966, Reif and Schoderbek found that 41 of 210 companies surveyed had used job enrichment. The most popular reasons for undertaking job enrichment were cost reduction, profit increase, and an increase in job satisfaction. As far back as 1950, Walker reported that a job enrichment program at IBM was a success. More recently, Ford (1969) reported that after job enrichment was installed in the Shareholder Relations Department at AT&T there was a 27 percent reduction in the termination rate and an estimated costs savings of $558,000 over a twelve-month period. In twelve districts of AT&T where the program was tried with service representatives, resignations and dismissals dropped by 14 percent, which could mean an annual savings of $10 million in operating costs (Janson, 1970). In the Imperial Chemical Industries, Ltd., salesmen productivity increased by 19 percent a year after job enrichment, whereas in a similar group without job enrichment, sales dropped by 5 percent a year (Janson, 1970).

Motorola found that bench (individual) assembly required 25 percent more workers in addition to increased training time in order to implement a job enrichment program. They report that the higher cost in wages was offset by greater productivity, less need for inspection, a higher quality product and lower work costs (*Business Week*, Sept. 4, 1971). The Maytag Company found that greater flexibility in terms of production scheduling was one of the major advantages of job enrichment over assembly-line production. They reported that they could add or subtract work stations or shifts without affecting production of other workers (Stewart, 1967).

Buick Motor Division has been involved in a substantial job enrichment program in its Product Engineering Area since 1971. Prior to this project, skilled hourly mechanics would work on cars in Buick's engineering fleet and perform assignments based on a work ticket that had been completed by engineering personnel. Now, however, mechanics not only complete the work tickets themselves, but also are encouraged to perform any repair they consider necessary and to inspect their work upon completion. They credit this program with increasing productivity by 13 percent, reducing petty grievances to near zero, and significantly reducing the number of rework cases (Schotters, 1973b).

Texas Instruments gave full responsibility for janitorial services to the worker involved. The men met to decide how the work would be divided and to set up schedules and establish standards. As a result of this job enrichment effort, manpower needs declined from 120 to 71, cleanliness improved, and turnover was reduced from 100 percent to 10 percent quarterly (Herrick, 1971). In 1971, Gaines Food Plant in Topeka, Kansas, attempted to enrich all jobs by organizing workers into teams where they are paid according to their skill level and not according to their position in the hierarchy (supervisor versus worker). Symbols such as assigned parking spaces and separate eating facilities have been eliminated and all decision-making, including goal-setting, has become a team process. They report the program has resulted in a 91 percent reduction in absenteeism over the industry average, 40 fewer employees than predicted necessary, and the best safety record in the General Food Corporation (*American Machinist,* 1973). As a result of the success of the Gaines Food project, similar efforts are being made by the Mead Corporation, Proctor and Gamble, and Scott Paper Company. Scott is building a small plant in Dover, Delaware, which it plans to operate under this new module approach in an attempt to combat production-line boredom (*Detroit Free Press,* October 29, 1973).

Bankers Trust and Merrill, Lynch, Pierce, Fenner and Smith adopted a job enrichment program where work modules were set up by customer or function. In both cases, significant money savings were realized in terms of increased productivity and reduced supervisory time (Rickleffs, 1972). A similar job enrichment program was initiated by Xerox for its technical representatives. Machine servicemen were given more authority to decide expenses, schedule work, order inventories, interview and train new personnel, and determine work loads. They credit this program with leading to increased performance level (Jacobs, 1972).

Other companies which have reported success with a job enrichment program include Monsanto, Weyerhauser, Exxon, Polaroid, and Ampex Tape in the United States; Volvo and Kockums Shipyards in Sweden; Daimler-Benz and Volkswagen in Germany, Renault in France; and Olivetti and Fiat in Italy (*American Machinist,* 1973). Regardless of the criticism leveled against job enrichment, it appears that job enrichment is seen as a success by many companies and cannot be dismissed as a passing fad. The president of Donnelly Mirror said, "If you need proof that involving people in their total job pays off, ask what you got in return for your last labor contract. If you are less than satisfied with the bargain, ask yourself how much it would be worth to get the support of your people in effecting just the cost reductions that your engineers already know about" (Donnelly, 1971, p. 12).

Criticisms of the Program

Criticisms of job enrichment programs have come from all groups, including academicians, managers, workers, union representatives, and industrial engineers. Academicians criticize the success studies as being incomplete and poorly designed and generally hold them to have little empirical validity. Hulin (1971) said, "It is unfortunate that most of these studies provide indirect evidence, at best. . . . Many of these studies have been poorly controlled, and most of the authors have attempted to generalize from severely limited data."

Many groups criticize the job enrichment advocates for pushing job enrichment as a social cure for worker discontent even when their organizations may lose profits as a result of such programs. Recognizing the cost involved in meaningful job reform, some reformers have argued that job enrichment should control the design of the production process, even if productivity is reduced. They suggest that "social efficiency" should be given priority over consideration òf purely economic efficiency *(Work in America,* 1973). Many supporters of job enrichment criticize this stand as being impractical and unnecessary. Levitan and Johnston (1973a, p. 38) say, "If changes in technology and hardware to improve the quality of work are to be made, they must also promise higher profits." Drucker (1973, p. 92) agrees: "The manager who pretends that the personal needs of the worker—for affection, for example—come before the objective needs of the task is indeed a liar or poor manager. The rare worker who believes him is a fool."

Along these same lines, there are some jobs which cannot be enriched beyond a certain point. All the redesign in the world cannot make certain dull tasks exciting. According to Levitan and Johnson (1973a), "The basic limit to work redesign is that society requires that certain tasks be done. . . . The prospects for humanizing work are limited by the realities of the work to be done—realities which are beyond the power of planners to control" (p. 5).

Perhaps the most damaging criticism leveled by many critics is that many workers do not feel alienated from their jobs and do not desire more responsibility or involvement at their workplace. Levitan and Johnston (1973a) ask, "Is the quality of work life the main standard by which they judge the quality of their lives? It appears that for most workers the quality of work is less important than the standard of living" (p. 40). According to the Bureau of Labor Statistics, the predominant issue in collective bargaining is still wages. In 1971, three of every four days lost in strikes were the result of wages or benefit disputes.

Attempts to enrich jobs are often frustrated by union constraints in the form of restrictive job descriptions, tenure requirement, craft jurisdictions, and general mistrust (Myers, 1971). The labor unions tend to oppose job enrichment because they thrive on conflict with management (Gooding, 1970). Leonard Woodcock, President of the United Automobile Workers Union says, "Those who contend that boredom and monotony are the big problems among assembly workers, are writing a lot of nonsense" (Baxter, 1973).

Little and Warr (1971) say that workers on a piece rate oppose job enrichment as an attempt to cut the rate and lower their earnings. Conart and Kilbridge (1965) reported that in one company, about one-third of the workers who had an opportunity to move to enriched jobs expressed a preference for their present jobs because they felt that the existing incentive system maximized their earnings.

According to Reif and Luthans (1972) many groups of workers are not alienated, other groups of workers actually enjoy looking outside the organization for their intrinsic rewards, and still other groups of workers may have a high need for structure. Job enrichment may have a negative effect on each of these groups.

Mitchell Fein's research for the American Institute of Industrial Engineers, claims that a check into many of the job enrichment case histories and studies of workers done over the past 10 years indicates that job enrichment does not work—primarily because workers do not want it (Baxter, 1973).

Despite each of these criticisms, the evidence still shows that job enrichment works for some groups of people. The criticisms point out the necessity of considering individual differences of workers when deciding on a motivation program of job enrichment (Lawler, 1973a). Hulin and Blood (1968, p. 50) emphasize this point when they say:

Specifically, the argument for larger jobs as a means of motivating workers, decreasing boredom and dissatisfaction, and increasing attendance and productivity is valid only when applied to certain segments of the work force—white-collar and supervisory workers and non-alienated blue-collar workers.

Organizational Climate and Development Program

Theoretical Background

Many writers praise the positive reinforcement programs and the job enrichment or task structure programs as being a step in the right direction in the fight against worker discontent. Some of these same writers, however, claim that these programs are not enough. Neither of the previous programs does much to change the hierarchical structure of the organization and neither program examines the interpersonal and attitudinal problems of the worker with the people with whom he comes in contact. Lawler (1973b) suggests that what workers want most, as reflected in more than 100 studies in the past 20 years, is to become masters of their immediate environments and to feel that their work and they themselves are important. While advocates of both positive reinforcement and job enrichment programs would argue that this is one of the purposes of their respective programs, others would say that the worker cannot have high self-esteem unless the climate in which he works is a healthy one. "Climate," as used by these writers, can be defined as a set of properties of the work environment and is assumed to be a major force in influencing the behavior of the employees on the job (Gibson, Ivancevich and Donnelly, 1973). The properties include the size, structure, leadership patterns, interpersonal relationships, systems complexity, goal direction, and communication patterns of the organization (Forehand, 1968). Therefore, an improvement in the organizational climate would involve more than changing the task structure (job enrichment) or the reinforcing consequences (positive reinforcement), but also may involve a change in the organizational climate and structure and the interpersonal support of the employees.

Proponents of an improved climate approach contend that "the traditional hierarchical system of organizations breeds a climate of fear and mistrust, which reduces management effectiveness. Programs in team building, sensitivity training, encounter groups . . . are advocated to unfreeze the climate" *(American Machinist,* 1973, p. 80). Many times the task of building a climate which encourages achievement in an organization is one of changing the concern of management from power-compliance ("Here is what needs to be done, and here is how to do it") to one that offers warmth and support to each individual, communicating organizational goals and standards, but not attempting to control the means of reaching these goals (Kolb, Rubin and McIntyre, 1971, p. 71).

The climate that characterizes the work situation helps to determine the kinds of worker motivation actually aroused. Climates tend to mediate between the task requirements and the needs of the individual. "The capacity to influence the organizational climate is perhaps the most powerful leverage point in the entire management system. Because climates can affect the motivation of organizational members, changes in certain climate properties could have immediate and profound effects on the motivated performance of all employees" (Litwin and Stringer, 1973, p. 539).[5]

A healthy organizational climate, according to Schein (1970, p. 126) involves one that:

1. Takes in and communicates information reliably and validly.

2. Has internal flexibility and creativity to make the changes which are demanded by the information obtained.

3. Gains integration and commitment to the goals of the organization, from which comes the willingness to change.

4. Offers an internal climate of support and freedom from threat, since being threatened undermines good communication, reduces flexibility and stimulates self-protection rather than concern for the total system.

In recent years the term *organizational development,* or OD, has become the recognized classification for the motivation program used to help the organization reach the healthy climate described by Schein. Blake and Mouton (1967) says that "Organizational development deliberately shifts the emphasis away from the organization's structure, from technical skill, from wherewithal and results *per se,* as it diagnoses the organization's ills. Focusing on organization purposes, the human interaction process, and organization culture [climate], it accepts these as the areas in which problems are preventing the fullest possible integration within the organization" (p. 11). French (1969) adds, "Organization Development refers to a long range effort to improve an organization's problem solving capabilities and its ability to cope with changes in its external environment with the help of external or internal behavioral scientist consultants (change agents)" (p. 387).

A successful OD program requires skillful change agent intervention. The change agent's purpose is to affect planned change in the total personnel system both now and in the future (French, 1969). The term OD, therefore, implies a normative re-education strategy intended to affect systems of beliefs, values, and attitudes within the organization so that it can adapt better to the accelerated rate of change in technology in the industrial environment, and in society in general. Later stages in the OD process may include formal organizational restructuring which is frequently initiated, facilitated, and reinforced by the normative and behavioral changes (Winn, 1968).

Organizational development is based more on history and less on theory than the previous two programs discussed. The overall OD approach is an extension of the use of laboratory or sensitivity training methods. Sensitivity or laboratory (T-group) training evolved primarily from the field theory and group dynamics concepts of Lewin (1944, 1951, 1952).[6] In addition, Roger's (1942) client-centered therapy approach had a great impact on the change-agent's behavior in the sensitivity session. Rogers emphasizes the permissive, supportive, but nondirective role of the counselor. In Rogers' therapy, the counselor should not set the goals or the direction of the change but, instead, provide a method by which the client can set these for himself.

Based on the work of Lewin and Rogers, sensitivity training attempts to make the individual within the group more aware of himself and his impact on others. The objective of a sensitivity training session is to provide an environment which produces a learning experience for the group. The role of the trainer or change agent is to facilitate the learning process by encouraging the group to set their own directions and goals (Bradford, Gibb and Benne, 1964). Laboratory training as an organized method of bringing about attitude and behavioral change within groups began in 1947 at the National Training Laboratory in Bethel, Maine, under the direction of Lewin, Benne, Bradford, and Lippitt. Since the beginning at Bethel, sensitivity training has become *one* of the techniques widely used in a formal OD program.

In 1957, McGregor at Union Carbide and Shepard and Blake at Esso began to apply laboratory training systematically to the problems facing these organizations (Luthans, 1973). Based on McGregor's experience in ongoing organizations, he wrote his (1960) exposition of participatory theory "Y" to replace authoritarian theory "X" approaches to management. According to Leavitt (1965), McGregor's development of theory "Y" and Likert's (1961) development of interaction influence theory, which both call for "supportive relationships" by leaders in industry, has contributed a great deal to the usefulness of laboratory training in organizations. Other theorists who have contributed to the introduction of organizational development as we know it today include, among others, Argyris (1962), Bennis (1966), Beckhard (1969), Burke (1971), Blake and Mouton (1967) and Greiner (1967).

Stages in Program Development.

Because OD is an evolving field, it is difficult to describe a "typical" program (Strauss, 1973; Hampton, Summer, and Webber, 1973). Strauss says "as an evolving field, OD presents a moving target, making it difficult to define or criticize" (1973, p. 2). Hampton, et al. (1973) point out that while there are general similarities, "there are almost as many methods of organization development as there are consultants engaging in this kind of work" (p. 857). The general similarities in most approaches to OD has led Strauss (1973), Hampton, et al. (1973), and French (1969), to describe various stages in a "typical" OD program. The reader is reminded, however, that the actual OD program in any one organization may vary from the "typical" program described below.

The *first stage* of the OD program is a diagnostic stage of planned organizational change. This stage involves gathering data about the state of operations in the organization, and the state of interpersonal attitudes and behavior. In this stage, T-group type sessions may be held in order to develop problem solving skills, examine interpersonal relations, and examine basic attitudes. These sessions are generally designed to act as team-building or group problem-solving sessions. During this stage the change agent, who has usually interviewed each participant prior to the session, frequently provides *feedback* to the group in terms of the items or themes which have emerged (French, 1969). One of the purposes of this stage is to improve the way people work together. It involves changing basic attitudes of both supervisors and subordinates and opens up communication channels to allow all employees a larger voice in how they do their jobs.

Many advocates of OD recommend that the first team session should be held by the president of the firm and his staff, and then with groups throughout the organization. Without the support of top management, it is generally felt that the program is probably doomed to failure.[7] William Crockett, Vice-president of Saga Foods, recalls his fears about this first stage: "Do you really want him [the change agent] to dredge into the depths of all our feelings about one another and about you? Isn't it being disloyal for us to tell him our problems and our feelings? Does it serve any purpose for these problems to be brought in the open and exposed?" (Crockett, 1970, p. 295). The fears expressed by Crockett are not uncommon. Schein (1969) and others use the term "unfreezing" to describe this stage because people have a way of becoming "frozen" in their attitudes and relations with other people and often are unaware that they are seen as obstacles in the solving of operational problems.[8]

The *second stage* of the OD program is an *action* stage of planned organizational change. After group and intergroup relationships have been identified and a period of trust and communication has been established within the organization, these work groups begin to establish ways to deal with on-the-job structural and human relations programs. This stage represents the participatory stage of the other two programs discussed. The work team may suggest actual changes in structure and monitoring of the task, interdepartment communication procedures, or other changes they deem necessary to solve the problem they identified in the first stage. This stage may involve all of the steps involved in the positive reinforcement program and the job enrichment program, including team performance appraisal, goal-setting, task redesign, and self-monitoring. Of course the team, group, or department works within the boundaries set up by the organization and must be able to show that their suggested changes will lead to improvements for both the organization and the individuals involved.

The *third* and *final stage* is an extension of the first two stages in the sense that the team evaluates their progress and continues to search for *new problems* and to offer *new solutions*. The third stage is a *proactive* stage, where the purpose is to maintain the healthy climate established in the first two stages by a continual monitoring of the system and examining the team's working relationship to the system.

The OD program differs from the positive reinforcement program and the job enrichment program in that it examines attitudes as well as behavior, it is an organization-wide program as well as a department or team program, and it is a broad-based program which continues to examine the organization climate, the task structure, *and* the reinforcement consequences. Strauss (1973) notes that for OD to have a lasting effect, the participants must (1) move from confrontation to behavior, (2) move from training groups to work problems, (3) move from intent to implementation (including structural change), (4) move from sporadic action to routinization, and (5) widen and make permanent the entire OD effort. The essence of OD, therefore, is the concept of helping the organization to gain insight into its own processes, develop its own diagnostic and coping resources, and improve its own internal relationships with the help of an outside and/or inside consultant who acts as a catalyst (Schein, 1970).

Results of OD Program.

OD has become a big business. In 1969-70, one firm which specializes in OD consulting, Scientific Methods, Inc., numbered among its clients 45 of the top 100 U. S. corporations, conducted courses on every continent, and projected profits of $1.1 million (Strauss, 1973). Examples of companies using OD as a motivation plan include TRW systems, Polaroid, Union Carbide, Royal Dutch/Shell Group, J. Lyons and Company, Esso, Weyerhauser, U. S. Steel, Corning Glass, Clark Equipment Company, and General Motors.

Even though many companies are reportedly using an OD program, research on the effectiveness of OD efforts is as yet sparse, partly because of the great difficulty in defining criteria for organizational effectiveness (Schein, 1970). Strauss (1973) adds, "In the end, OD is likely to be evaluated in terms of gut reactions rather than dispassionate research. After all, OD deals with emotions [attitudes], and it engenders emotional reactions. For some, it is almost a religion" (Strauss, 1973, p. 42).

While most of the evidence is testimonial in nature, there is some evidence that OD has led to improvements in working satisfaction and increased company profits. Schein (1970) credits a team-building program in group dynamics and interpersonal relations for management trainees as resulting in the defeat of a union vote in a large oil refinery. Kaiser Steel Company credits a team effort by workers with increasing productivity by 32 percent and thereby keeping the plant open after it had a scheduled closing due to low productivity and a loss in profits.

Texas Instrument has initiated an OD program which they call a People and Asset Effectiveness Program. Mark Shepard, President of Texas Instruments, said, "We've found that if you get people involved, they'll set tougher goals for themselves than you would dare do, and have fun doing it" *(Business Week,* Sept. 29, 1973, p. 88). After a three-year period, Texas Instruments found that this program resulted in return on assets per person rising from 5.6 percent to 10.1 percent. When asked to what he credited the success of the program, Frederick Ochsner, Vice-president of Personnel at Texas Instruments, said,

> It is a whole bunch of things acting synergistically. It's the attitudes, team improvement programs, the campus involvement, the open-door management policy, the nonstructural pecking order. It's the unified goal-approach—with everybody looking at his own piece of that goal. . . . The key is flexibility. Two things people want in life. They want to achieve and they want to be loved. And if you provide an atmosphere where these things can occur with a minimum amount of structure in the work flow, you are going to get what you want *(Business Week,* Sept. 29, 1973, p. 88, 90).

Saga Administrative Corporation began an OD program in 1971 and today employs six full-time change agents. Saga stresses team building and has developed an overlapping team approach to management. (see Likert, 1961). In 1972, Saga held 225 team building sessions. Although the costs or benefits of Saga's OD program are not measurable, Board Chairman, W. P. Laughlin, claims that profitability is borne out by increased productivity. Saga claims its turnover rate among its 23,000 employees has been reduced to 19 percent annually—compared with 34 percent for the entire food industry—as a result of their OD program.

Donnelly Mirror Company has the longest history of success with an OD program. In the early 1950s Donnelly instituted democratic reforms which sought to humanize assembly-line production. Using the Scanlon plan, a type of OD program (Bennis, 1966; Frost, 1973) Donnelly has been able to show that their "humanistic" approach works. The president of Donnelly says, "We are not talking about a gimmick that someone can install by himself. The company has to change its relationship to its people. The company has to lead, it has to create the climate of trust. This is hard, demanding work that needs the leadership and support of the top people in the company" (Donnelly, 1971, p. 13). While the Scanlon plan is similar to most other OD programs in that it follows the three stages described in a "typical" program, it is unique in that the employees share directly in changes in profits in the form of a monthly bonus plan. All employees receive salaries, rather than hourly wages, and they collectively set the rates at which they would be paid. In return for this, the employees have the responsibility for implementing productivity increases to support pay raises.

As a result of their unique OD program, Donnelly's productivity gains have resulted in an average salary bonus of 12 percent of wages since the changes were instituted. Wages have risen steadily, while unit productivity costs have fallen, enabling the company to decrease prices, expand sales, and increase profits. Scrap losses dropped by 75 percent from their former level and goods returned due to poor workmanship dropped by 90 percent (Gooding, 1970).

While Donnelly Mirror has one of the longest histories with an OD program, the largest OD program is currently being conducted in the General Motors Corporation. Stephen H. Fuller, Vice-president of Personnel and Development, reports that formal OD functions are now operating in 20 major GM organizations. More than 125 OD change agents are working full-time in 55 GM plants in the United States, Canada, and overseas subsidiaries *(National Alliance of Businessmen,* 1973). The OD program used by GM is an eclectic approach where each plant program is designed differently according to the needs of that plant. F. J. Schotters, Director of Personnel Development, describes the OD program at GM as "a long range, planned program to improve the effectiveness of the *total* organization—whether it be a work group, department, plant, or staff. It can involve many types of activities, such as greater involvement and participation by employees with respect to their own jobs and in the particular areas in which they work, better communications, team building and changes in job content, supervisory relations and organizational structure" (Schotters, 1972a).

A survey conducted by the Institute for Social Research of the University of Michigan clearly demonstrated to GM that "the way employees see (and react to) the management climate and organizational structure has a direct, measurable effect on both employee behavior and work performance" (Schotters, 1972b). Landen and Carlson (in progress, 1973) said, "The survey findings clearly indicated sources of motivational potential needed improvement at each of the plant sites. The long-range program designed to bring about needed changes in the organization is now entering its third year [since 1969]. Results to date have been very encouraging."

One of the reasons that GM felt it had to institute some type of motivational program was a dramatic rising absenteeism and turnover rate. In 1972 Schotters reported that "Conservative estimates indicated that the current annual cost of absenteeism—considering only fringe benefits—is about $50 million. The cost of turnover involves another estimated $29 million. Thus, these are areas of major concern for every operation in GM—not only because of the costs involved but also because these trends indicate a serious deterioration of employee attitudes toward their work . . ." (Schotters, 1972c). To combat the high absenteeism rate, one Oldsmobile engine plant put several foremen and their hourly workers through group problem-solving (team-building) programs. As a result of these programs, several suggestions by the group for improving the absenteeism and turnover were accepted by the engine plant management. They credit this program with reducing total absenteeism in the plant during the first five months of 1971 by 6 percent, while absenteeism in the rest of Oldsmobile went up by 11 percent. Turnover in the engine plant was down by 38 percent in the engine plant, while the rest of Oldsmobile was down by 14 percent. Based on the success of this program, the project is now being extended throughout the Oldsmobile Division (Schotters, 1972c).

A full-fledged OD program was begun in 1971 in the Chassis Department of the General Motors Assembly Division (GMAD) at Arlington, Texas. With the help of two change agents, 104 hourly employees and four foremen were involved in a program designed to improve communications and attitudes. General Motors reports that this program resulted in a 50 percent decrease in grievances filed per month, housekeeping improved and foremen became more willing to make decisions on problems as they arose without relying on higher supervision. As a result of this program, similar projects are being inaugurated at GMAD (Schotters, 1972d).

Space does not allow us to give all the results of the OD progress in the 55 GM plants. Landen and Carlson (in progress, 1973) summarize the state of the OD programs in GM when they state "One vital point can be concluded from these and a variety of other programs now underway in the corporation: we are probably only beginning to touch the surface of a deep reservoir of untapped human potential among *all* GM employees. . . . Employee motivation is increasingly regarded as a core issue in the future of General Motors."

Criticisms of the Program

Of the motivational programs currently in use by industry, this is probably the most controversial. Strauss (1973) says:

> For my taste, OD has been plagued by too much evangelical hucksterism. Though considerable thought has been given to professional ethics, there are as yet no generally accepted codes of behavior. OD techniques have been subject to some scientific research, but it is a bit premature to conclude that OD is truly a scientific method or the "science-based" approach. And it is downright misleading to suggest that OD's utility has been proven scientifically valid. . . . OD is a fad and American companies are suckers for gimmicks (p. 14).

The majority of the criticism leveled at the OD program centers around the "unfreezing" stage where attitudes and interpersonal relationships are examined. Whyte (1972) says, "Executives say, 'What we must do is change people's attitudes'; as politely as I can I tell them to forget attitudes. The problem is to change the conditions to which people are responding. If he does that, people will behave differently and he will find that attitudes—if they still interest him—will adjust themselves to the new situation" (p. 67). Sorcher and Goldstein (1972) report that "difficulties encountered by those who try to change behavior by first changing attitudes are well known. Moreover, there is no certainty that attitude change will lead to behavior change on the part of managers or supervisors, since other attitudes may intrude and prevent behavior change" (p. 36).

This criticism of the attitude change process centers around three issues. First, many psychologists believe that attitudes do not cause behavior, but rather behavioral experiences lead to attitude formations (see, e.g., Bem, 1964). Second, many critics feel that changing attitudes in a group setting may do more harm than good because the rewards of the organization will not reinforce the changed attitudes (e.g., see House, 1967). Third, many writers contend that there are many poorly trained change agents and consultants who may cause more harm than good in a team-building session (e.g., see Campbell and Dunnette, 1968; Bennis, 1969).

Maslow (1965) described his experiences with trying to apply theory Y management for Non-Linear Systems of Del Mar, California, and concluded that "The demands of theory Y were far higher than I had recognized and many involve 'inhumanity' to the weak, the vulnerable and the damaged who are unable to take on responsibility and self discipline" (quoted by Drucker, 1973, p. 87). Not only are some employees unable to cope with the OD process, but many managers as well are not willing to accept a different style of management. Andrew Kay, President of Non-Linear Systems, Inc., said that OD programs work fine during good times and periods of economic gains. In fact from 1960-65 production rose 30 percent and customer complaints dropped 70 percent under the OD program set up by Maslow. But when the aereospace industry fell apart in 1970, Kay said he had lost touch with his company and the company was not ready to respond to the changing environment. Vice-president Coombe agreed. "So much emphasis was put on the results of sensitivity sessions—and the long-run planning was not carried on in a businesslike manner" (*Business Week,* September 2, 1972, p. 68). By returning to a more autocratic leadership style, Kay claims to be back on solid financial grounds.

Hampton, et al. (1973) summarize the stage of development of OD by saying that until the advent of OD, nobody made participative management and structural job enlargement operational. They also warn:

> But OD has its limitations; analysis, clarity, reality, openness, and facing up to the truth may be an alternative to closed-system stereotypical thinking, but there is no guarantee that it will work in all organizations. The viewpoint which the modern

manager must take, therefore, is that this method of management has both powerful benefits and powerful limitations. The key is to try to understand when and
under what circumstances such a technique will succeed (p. 870).

Flexitime—Escape or Motivation?

An alternative form of confronting the problem of worker discontent has recently
been introduced in many firms throughout the world. This program is called *flexitime*
and is designed to allow the employee more latitude and freedom in setting up his or her
own schedule. This motivation plan originated in Germany in the late 1960s. The program allows the workers, either as individuals or team, to establish their own starting
times, within limits set by the company (e.g., between 7:30-9:30 A.M.). The worker
must complete 8 hours before closing. In some companies, if the employees like, they
can build up time during the week by reducing their lunch hours and breaks and use the
time to either leave early on Friday afternoon (e.g., at 3:00 P.M.) or else leave earlier in
the day (e.g., at the end of 7½ *work* hours if the lunch hour were reduced by 30 minutes).
The extent of flexibility is related to the degree of interdependence among jobs
(Werther, 1973).

A similar program to the flexitime program is the four-day-week program. Under
this program, each employee has to complete forty hours a week, but has a three-day
weekend, rather than the traditional two-day weekend.

As noted earlier, the positive reinforcement, job enrichment, and organization development programs are *proactive* in nature because they seek to examine the causes of
worker discontent and solve the problems in order to make the workplace a more
stimulating and exciting place to work. The flexitime and four-day-week programs have
been criticized by some as being *reactive* programs which tend to ignore the real problems of worker discontent. These critics claim that rather than facing up to the fact that
high turnover and absenteeism is a symptom of either a poor feedback system, a boring
task, or an unhealthy climate, they reward the workers' discontent by giving them more
time away from the work place. Herzberg (1968) says, "This represents a marvelous
way of motivating people to work—getting them off the job! We have reduced (formally
and informally) the time spent on a job over the last 50 or 60 years until we are finally on
the way to the '6½-day weekend' . . . The fact is that motivated people seek more hours
of work, not fewer" (p. 67). Ford (1973), while not as critical as Herzberg, agrees; "The
growing pressure for a four-day work week is not necessarily evidence that people do
not care about their work: they may be rejecting their work in the form that it confronts
them" (p. 96). Levitan and Johnson (1973b) say, "The easiest way to improve an
unpleasant job is to reduce the working hours."

Counter-arguments against the critics could be made by saying that flexitime and
the four-day-week programs are really considering the "total man" by allowing him the
freedom to schedule, within reason, his work time to better meet his personal and family
needs. Kahn (1973) says that allowing people freedom in choosing the hours they work
and allowing them freedom to bid for the task they wish to perform are natural ways to
recognize the individuality of man. Also, it should be noted that the programs, as
currently designed, do not call for a reduction in hours, but only a rearranging of the
hours. However, the critics feel that this may only be a first step by unions in a reduction
of the number of hours and even number of years a worker would have to work before
being allowed to escape the organization.

Regardless of these arguments, many companies are finding a flexitime program beneficial. Moles (1973) reported that 5,000 companies and 2.5 million workers world-wide are currently on the flexitime working hours plan. In the United States, 100,000 workers are currently on this plan in such companies as Sun Oil, National Bank, the city government of Baltimore, the city government of Washington, D.C., Hewlett-Packard, Samsonite, Nestlé's, and Scott Paper Company. Werther (1973) reviewed the success of these programs and reported that the companies found that worker tardiness decreased, absenteeism due to medical appointments or family commitments were reduced, and better use of parking facilities, cafeterias and locker rooms was possible. The disadvan-tages Werther noted were more time had to be spent on scheduling, and also that flexitime wouldn't work on shift-work and assembly-line operations because of the interdependency of the workers.[9] Sandoz-Wander of East Hanover, New Jersey, im-plemented a flexitime program for a six-month trial period. After the trial period, 88 percent of the supervisory personnel voted to adopt the system permanently, citing better worker morale and increased productivity as the reasons (Cray, 1973). While Hewlett-Packard of Palo Alto, California, did not find an increase in productivity, they did find that their flexitime program led to a significant reduction in absenteeism and turnover *(American Machinist,* 1973).

While the evidence for this program (as for all programs described in this paper) still lacks empirical validity, it appears that flexible working hours may become the way of the future for many workers. Before the program can claim to be a method of reducing worker discontent, however, much more objective research is needed.

Motivation Programs in the Future

The four programs described in this paper represent the most current programs designed to reduce worker discontent and increase productivity in operation today. Many writers believe we have only begun to "scratch the surface," however, and call for more innovative steps to be taken.

Porter (1973) sees the way of the future being through use of more effective positive reinforcement programs. He states:

> Whatever new systems are adopted by organizations, there is sure to be one prominent feature of the work environment in [the year] 2001: work and fun will be combined on the job. . . . The merger of work and enjoyment will not, however, occur at the expense of organizational performance; through the effective restruc-turing of the reward environment, high levels of organizational performance can become the means for direct, personal gratification. Employees of progressive organizations of the future will be eager to perform (p. 131).

The types of rewards Porter sees being used in the future to gain commitment to the organization and/or being made contingent on superior performance in addition to pay, include: (1) opportunity to schedule one's own working hours, (2) a redistribution of job duties, (3) opportunity to create new jobs, (4) opportunity to participate in bonus draw-ings, (5) opportunity to choose any area of the organization in which to work for a limited period of time, (6) on-the-job nonwork activities, (7) new organizational ven-tures, (8) accrual of time off for sabbatical or educational leave, and (9) intercompany exchange of employees (1973, p. 127).

Lawler (1973a) sees the programs being implemented in industry today as being a step in the right direction in the fight to humanize work. Lawler, however, fears that most programs will fail unless we consider the individuality of the worker in the design of our motivational programs. Lawler states:

> When I look at the psychological research on people, I see convincing evidence that individuals differ significantly in their needs, skills and abilities. This is not to say that individuals aren't similar in many ways, for they are; but to be human is to be unique. To be humanized, an organization must recognize the uniqueness and sovereignty of each human being. In practical terms, this means that organizations and jobs must be designed in ways that are responsive to the differences which exist among people. Approaches to organization design and management which recommend standardized jobs, authoritian management, and piece-rate incentive plans for all don't do this, and neither do approaches which recommend enriched jobs, democratic management and MBO plans for all. Therefore, neither of these approaches has produced or is likely to produce a humanized organization (1973, p. 2).

Lawler contends that the place to start in individualizing the work available to people is in the selection and placement process. During the job interview, the applicant should be given information about the situation which exists and the various jobs available for which he is qualified. The interview should include more of a counseling atmosphere in order to allow the applicant to make self-selection decisions. Weitz (1965) and Wanous (in press) both report evidence that when job applicants are given valid information about the job, they will make better choices. In building a selection model (see Korman, 1971), the personnel manager should consider such items as motivation, reactions to different leadership styles, and preferred organizational climate, and attempt therefore to place the employees in those departments and with those leaders where they will have the greatest chance of success (Lawler, 1973a, p. 6).

One company which is currently experimenting with placing people in the department and under the leadership style most appropriate to their personality makeup is Texas Instruments. Charles L. Hughes, Director of Personnel and Organization Development at Texas Instruments, says, Companies must develop existentially managed organizations that truly accept and respect people with differing values" *(Business Week,* Sept. 29, 1973). As a first step, Hughes has classified 600 employees into six work-personality categories according to the way they perceive the world. The six categories include: (1) tribalistic—workers who respond to strong leadership and who are happy and dedicated when shown genuine care and concern; (2) existential—employees willing to do a job only if it is meaningful; (3) egocentric—entreprenuerial workers; (4) conformists—traditional workers; (5) manipulative—achievement-oriented workers; and (6) sociocentric—socially-oriented employees. Hughes hopes this research will influence Texas Instruments' selection and placement procedures, producing a more flexible organization. In the future, for example, Hughes would like to see an existential worker given an existential supervisor.

In order to overcome the deficiencies of the current motivation program, and to make the work place more adaptive to individuality and thereby increase the productivity of the labor force, Jackson Grayson, Dean of the Graduate School of Business at Southern Methodist University recommends we create an American Productivity Institute. Grayson says:·

> The current exploding attention to human factors in the work place is a relatively new Western phenomenon. I believe it will have as profound an impact on our

ways of performing and regarding work and increasing productivity as the phenomenon of capital investment did during the Industrial Revolution. So far, though, it has emerged more extensively abroad than in the U.S. It manifests itself in the groups called Quality Control Circles in Japan, and at Olivetti in Italy, Norsk-Hydro in Norway, ICI in Britain, and in the U.S. in companies such as AT&T, Proctor and Gamble, Corning Glass, and Texas Instruments (*Business Week,* July 14, 1973, p. 16).

By setting up this private institute, Grayson hopes that sociologists, psychologists, labor relations experts, industrial relations officers, union leaders, plant managers, and others could be brought together and share ideas on the ways to solve worker discontent and make the future of worker motivational programs more successful and rewarding for all.

It appears that the organization of the future will truly become a more enjoyable and exciting place to be. What is needed now is more sharing of information and ideas by advocates of various programs and by organizations themselves. In this way, methods of increasing productivity and decreasing worker discontent can be speeded up and we can move into the twenty-first century with a renewed pride in our jobs and the quality of our work life.

Notes

1. For a detailed explanation of the principles of learning theory, see W. Clay Hamner, "Reinforcement Theory and Contingency Management in Organization Settings," in H. Tosi and W. Clay Hamner (eds.) *Organizational Behavior and Management: A Contingency Approach,* St. Clair Press, 1974.

2. A performance audit is a procedure where management determines the behavioral and job-related aspects of a department or a work unit such as a 10 percent rate of absenteeism, a 15 percent scrap rate, a 90 percent of standard production rate, etc. This should be distinguished from a performance evaluation where a manager rates an individual on both behavioral and non-behavioral aspects of his job over a specified period of time.

3. See S. J. Carroll and H. L. Tosi, *Management by Objectives: Application and Research,* Macmillan, 1973.

4. Reinforcement techniques. See A. Bandura, *Principles of Behavior Modification,* Holt, Rinehart and Winston, Inc., New York, 1969.

5. Schneider and Hall (1972) argue that organizational climate is a perceptual variable and therefore cannot be directly manipulated. Because it is an intervening variable, it is harder to influence than inputs (task) or outcome (reinforcement) variables.

6. According to Lewin (1944), to change an individual (or a group) you must change his "life space." The life space consists of the person and the psychological environments as it exists for him at that point in time. Lewin regarded the properties of the "field" of the life space at any given time as the only determinant of behavior. See M. E. Shaw and P. R. Costanzo. *Theories of Social Psychology,* McGraw-Hill, 1970, pp. 117-36.

7. M. Beer and E. F. Huse disagree with this common assumption. See "A Systems Approach to Organizational Development," *Journal of Applied Behavioral Science,* 8, 1972, pp. 79-101.

8. Beer and Huse (*op. cit.*) and others correctly point out that while O.D. evolved out of a T-group background, an O.D. program does not limit itself to climate changes and may not involve any T-group training.

9. It should also be noted that the need for car-pooling due to the energy crisis may be hurt by the flexitime schedule. However, the four-day-week program would lend itself to car-pooling and is proposed by some as a means of conserving energy.

References

Abel, I. W., Advertisement, *Sports Illustrated* 39, 17, October 22, 1973.

"How Industry is Dealing with People Problems on the Line," *American Machinist*, November 12 (1973), 79-91.

Arygris, Chris, *Integrating the individual and the organization*, Wiley, 1964.

Arygris, C. *Interpersonal Competence and Organizational Effectiveness*, Dorsey Press, 1962.

Argyris, C., *Personality and Organization*, Harper, 1957.

Baxter, J. D., "Whatever Happened to Job Enrichment?" *Iron Age*, November 8 (1973), 35-36.

Beckhand, R., *Organizational Development: Strategies and Models*, Addison-Wesley, 1969.

Bem, D. J., *An Experienced Analysis of Beliefs and Attitudes*, unpublished doctoral dissertation, University of Michigan, 1964.

Bennis, W. G., *Organizational Development: Its Nature, Origins, and Prospects*, Addison-Wesley, 1969.

Bennis, W. G., *Changing Organizations*, McGraw-Hill, 1966.

Blake, R. R. and J. S. Mouton, "Grid Organization Development." *Personnel Administration*, January-February, 1967.

Bradford, L. P., Gibb, J. R. and Benne, K. D., *T-group Theory and Laboratory Method*, Wiley, 1964.

Burke, W. W., "Management and Organizational Development: What Is the Target of the Change?" *Personnel Administration*, 34 (1971), 44-56.

"How to make Productivity Grow Faster," *Business Week*, July 14, 1973, 15-16.

"Motorola Creates a More Demanding Job," *Business Week*, September 4, 1971, 32.

"The Humanistic Way of Managing People," *Business Week*, July 22, 1972, 48-49.

"Where Being Nice to Workers Didn't Work," *Business Week*, September 2, 1972.

"How Texas Instruments Turns Its People On," *Business Week*, September 29, 1973, 88, 90.

"The 'Humanistic' Way of Managing People," *Business Week*, July 22, 1972, 48-49.

"New Tool: Reinforcement for Good Work," *Business Week*, December 18, 1971, 68-69.

"Where Skinner's Theories Work," *Business Week*, December 2, 1972, 64-65.

Carroll S. J. and Tosi, H. L. *Management by Objectives*, Macmillan, 1973.

Campbell, J. P. and Dunnette, M. D., "Effectiveness of T-group Exercises in Managerial Training and Development," *Psychological Bulletin*, 70 (1968), 73-104.

Conart, E. H. and Kilbridge, M., "An Interdisciplinary Analysis of Job Enrichment," *Industrial and Labor Relations Review*, April, 1965, 377-395.

Cray, D. W., "Coming to Work Whenever You Want," *The New York Times*, Sunday, Feb. 4, 1973.

Crockett, W. J., "Team Building—One Approach to Organizational Development," *Journal of Applied Behavioral Science*, 6 (1970), 291-306.

"Workers Get a Voice in Chrysler Operations," *Detroit Free Press*, July 25, 1971.

"A New way to Work," *Detroit Free Press*, October 29, 1973, sect. B, 10-11.

Donnelly, J. F., "Increasing Productivity by Involving People in Their Total Jobs," *Personnel Administration*, Sept.-Oct., 1971, 8-13.

Drucker, Peter F., "Beyond the Stick and Carrot: Hysteria over the Work Ethic," *Psychology Today*, Nov. 1973, 87, 89-93.

Emery, J. C., "How to Double your Sales and Profits Every 5 Years," speech before the *Sales Executive Club of New York*, 1973.

Ferster, C. B. and Skinner, B. F., *Schedules of Reinforcement*, Appleton-Century-Crofts, 1957.

Ford, Robert, "Job Enrichment Lessons at AT&T," *Harvard Business Review*, 1973, 96-106.

Ford, Robert, *"Motivation Through the Work Itself,"* American Management Association, 1969.

Forehand, G. A., "On the Interactions of Persons and Organizations," in R. Tagiuri and G. H. Litwin (eds.), *Organizational Climate*, Harvard University, Division of Research, 1968, 65-82.

French, W., "Organizational Development Objectives: Assumptions and Strategies," *California Management Review,* 12 (1969), 23-34.

Frost, Carl F., "A Change Agent's View of the Scanlon Plan," paper presented at the *American Psychological Association,* Montreal, August, 1973.

Fuller, Stephen H., "Employee Development," speech before the *National Alliance of Businessmen,* Detroit, Michigan, September 24, 1973.

Gamboa, V. U. and E. Pedalino, "Behavior Modification and Absenteeism: Intervention in One Industrial Setting," University of Michigan working paper, 1973.

Gibson, J. L., Ivancevich, J. M., and Donnelly, J. H., *Organizations: Structures, Processes, and Behavior,* Business Publications, Inc. 1973.

Greiner, L. E., "Patterns of Organization Change," *Harvard Business Review.* 45 (1967).

Gooding, Judson, "It pays to Wake up the Blue-collar Worker," *Fortune,* September, 1970.

Hamner, W. Clay, Reinforcement Theory and Contingency Management," in H. L. Tosi and W. Clay Hamner (eds.), *Organizational Behavior and Management: A Contingency Approach,* St. Clair Press, 1974.

Hampton, D. R., Summer, C. E., and Webber, R. A., *Organizational Behavior and the Practice of Management,* Scott, Foresmen and Company, 1973.

Herrick, N. Q., "The Other Side of the Coin," paper delivered at the 2oth Anniversary Invitational Seminar of the Profit Sharing Research Foundation, Evanston, Ill., Nov. 17, 1971.

Herzberg, F., "One More Time: How Do You Motivate Employees?" *Harvard Business Review,* 46, (1968), 53-62.

House, R. J., "T-group Education and Leadership Effectiveness: A Review of the Empirical Literature and a Critical Evaluation," *Personnel Psychology,* 20, 1967, 1-32.

Hulin, C. L., and Blood, M. R., "Job Enlargement, Individual Differences and Worker Responses," *Psychological Bulletin,* January, 1968, 41-55.

Hulin, C. L., "Individual Differences and Job Enrichment—The Case Against General Treatments," in J. Maher, *New Perspectives in Job Enrichment,* Van Nostrand Reinhold, 1971, 159-91.

Hunt, J. G. and Hill, J. W. "The New Look in Motivation Theory in Organizational Research," *Human Organizations,* Summer, 1969, 100-109.

"The Power of Praise," *International Management,* October, 1973, 32-35.

Jacobs, C. D., "Job Enrichment at Xerox Corporation," paper presented at the *International Conference on the Quality of Work Life,* Sept. 24-29, 1972, Arden House, New York.

Janson, R., Job enrichment: "Challenge of the 70's," *Training and Development Journal,* June, 1970, 7-9.

Kahn, R. L., "The Work Module—A Tonic for Lunchpail Lassitude," *Psychology Today,* 6, 1973, 35-39, 94-95.

Kolb, D. A., Rubin, I. M. and McIntyre, J. M., *Organizational Psychology: An Experimental Approach,* Prentice-Hall, 1971.

Korman, A. K., *Industrial and Organizational Psychology,* Prentice-Hall, 1971, 178-203.

Kornhauser, A. W., *Mental Health of the Industrial Worker: A Detroit Study,* Wiley, 1965.

Landen, D. L. and Carlson H. C. "Employee Motivation: A Vast Domain of Unrealized Human and Business Potential," chapter to be included in forthcoming book by A. J. Marrow, (Ed.) *American Management Association,* in preparation, 1973.

Lawler, E. E., "Job Design and Employee Motivation," *Personnel Psychology,* 22, 1969.

Lawler, E. E., "Individualizing Organizations: A Needed Emphasis in Organizational Psychology," paper presented at the *American Psychological Association Convention,* Montreal, August, 1973a.

Lawler, E. E., "What Do Employees *Really* Want?" paper presented at the *American Psychological Association Convention,* Montreal, August, 1973b.

Leavitt, H. J., "Applied Organizational change In Industry," in J. G. March (ed.), *Handbook of Organizations,* Rand McNally, 1965, 1144-1170.

Levitan, S. A. and Johnston, W. B., "Job Redesign Enrichment—Exploring the Limitations," *Monthly Labor Review,* July, 1973a, 35-41.

Levitan, S. A. and Johnston, W. B., "Changes in Work: More Evolution than Revolution," *Manpower,* September, 1973b, 3-7.

Levitan, S. A. and Johnston, W. B., *Work Is Here to Stay, Alas,* Olympus, 1973c.

Lewin, K., "Constructs in Psychology and Psychological Ecology," *University of Iowa Studies in Child Welfare,* 1944, 20, 1-29.

Lewin, K., "Group Decision and Social Change," in G. E. Swanson, T. M. Newcomb, and E. L. Hartley (eds.) *Readings in Social Psychology,* Holt, 1952, 459-473.

Lewin, Kurt, *Field Theory in Social Science,* Harper and Brothers, 1951.

Likert, R., *New Patterns of Management,* McGraw-Hill, 1961.

Little, A. and Warr, P., "Who's Afraid of Job Enrichment?" *Personnel Management,* Feb., 1971, 34-37.

Litwin, G. H. and Stringer, R. A., "Motivation and Organizational Climate, in D. R. Hampton, C. F. Summer, and R. A. Webber (eds.), *Organizational Behavior and the Practice of Management,* Scott-Foresman, 1973, 538-550.

Luthans, F., *Organizational Behavior,* McGraw-Hill, 1973.

Luthans, F. and White, D. O., "Behavior Modification: Application to Manpower Management," *Personnel Administrator,* July-August, 1971, 41-47.

McGregor, D., *The Human side of Enterprise,* McGraw-Hill, 1960.

Moles, L., "Workers Decide own Hours," *The State Journal,* Lansing, Mich., Sept. 23, 1973, 10.

Myers, M. S., "Overcoming Union Opposition to Job Enrichment," *Harvard Business Review,* May, 1971.

Nord, W. R., "Beyond the Teaching Machine: The Neglected Area of Operant Conditioning in the Theory and Practice of Management," *Organizational Behavior and Human Performance,* 1969, 375-401.

Conversation with B. F. Skinner, *Organization Dynamics,* 1973a, Winter, 31-40.

"At Emery Air Freight: Positive Reinforcement Boosts Performance," *Organizational Dynamics,* 1, 1973b, 41-50.

Poor, Riva, *4 Days, 40 Hours: Reporting a Revolution in Work and Leisure* (rev. ed.), Bursk and Poor Pub., 1973.

Porter, L. W., "Turning Work into Nonwork: The Rewarding Environment," in M. D. Dunnette (ed.), *Work and Nonwork in the year 2001,* Brooks/Cole, 1973, 113-133.

Reif, W. E. and Luthans, F., "Does Job Enrichment Really Pay Off?," *California Management Review,* Fall, 1972, 34-35.

Reif, W. E. and Schoderbek, P., "Job Enlargement: Antidote to Apathy," *Management of Personnel Quarterly,* Spring, 1966, 16-23.

Rickleffs, R., "The Quality of Work," *The Wall Street Journal,* August 21, 1972, 1.

Rogers, C. R., *Counseling and psychotheraphy,* Houghton Mifflin, 1942.

Schein, E. H., *Process Consultation: Its Role in Organizational Development,* Addison-Wesley, 1969.

Schein, E. H., *Organizational Psychology,* 2nd. edition, Prentice-Hall, 1970.

Schneider, B., and D. T. Hall, "Toward Specifying the Concept of Work Climate," *Journal of Applied Psychology,* 1972, 56, 447-455.

Schotters, F. J., "What Is 'Organizational Development'? Does It Work?," *G.M. Personnel Development Bulletin,* no. 9, August 17, 1972a.

Schotters, F. J., "New Tool to Measure Organizational Effectiveness," *G.M. Personnel Development Bulletin,* no. 5, May 1, 1972b.

Schotters, F. J., "Oldsmobile Action Program on Absenteeism and Turnover," *G.M. Personnel Development Bulletin,* no. 2, Feb. 3, 1972c.

Schotters, F. J., "Organizational Development at GMAD-Arlington," *G.M. Personnel Development Bulletin,* no. 6, May 17, 1972d.

Schotters, F. J., "GMAD Fremont's Absenteeism and Discipline Programs," *G.M. Personnel Development Bulletin,* no. 18, April 2, 1973a.

Schotters, F. J., "Job Enrichment at Buick Products Engineering," *G.M. Personnel Development Bulletin,* no. 22, June 4, 1973b.

Scott, W. E., "Activation Theory and Task Design," *Organizational Behavior and Human Performance,* 1, (1966), 3-30.

Skinner, B. F., *Science and Human Behavior,* Macmillan, 1953.

Skinner, B. F., *Contingencies of Reinforcement,* Appleton-Century-Crofts, 1971.

Sorcher, M. and Goldstein, A. P., "A Behavioral Modeling Approach in Training," *Personnel Administration,* Mar.-April, 1972, 35-41.

Stewart, P. A., *Job Enrichment: In the Shop, in the Management Function,* Center for Labor and Management, University of Iowa, 1967.

Strauss, G., "Organizational Development: Credits and Debits," *Organizational Dynamics,* 1 (1973), 2-18.

Tannenbaum, A. S., Control in Organizations: Individual Adjustment and Organizational Performance," *Administrative Science Quarterly,* 7 (1962), 236-257.

Thorndike, F. L., *Animal Intelligence,* Macmillan, 1911.

Warren, M. W., "Performance Management: A Substitute for Supervision," *Management Review,* October, 1972, 28-42.

Wanous, J. P., "Effect of a Realistic Job Preview on Job Acceptance, Job Survival, and Job Attitudes," *Jounral of Applied Psychology,* in press.

Wiard, H., "Why Manage Behavior? A Case for Positive Reinforcement," *Human Resource Management,* Summer, 1972, 15-20.

Winn, A., "The Laboratory Approach to Organizational Development," paper read at the Annual Conference, *British Psychological Society,* Oxford, September, 1968.

Weitz, J., "Job Expectancy and Survival," *Journal of Applied Psychology,* 1965, 245-247.

Werther, W. B., "The Good News and Bad News of Flexible Hours," *Administrative Management,* November, 1973, 78-79, 96.

Whyte, W. F., "Skinnerian Theory in Organizations," *Psychology Today,* April 1972, 67-68, 96, 98. 100.

Work in America, report of a special Task Force to the Secretary of Health, Education and Welfare, Cambridge, Mass.: The MIT Press, 1973.

Vroom, V., *Work and Motivation,* Wiley, 1964.

Using Pay to Motivate Job Performance

E. E. LAWLER

The research evidence . . . clearly indicates that under certain conditions pay can be used to motivate good performance. The required conditions are deceptively simple. . . . They are deceptively simple in the sense that establishing the conditions is easier said than done. Theory and research suggest that for a pay plan to motivate people, it must (1) create a belief among employees that good performance will lead to high pay, (2) contribute to the importance of pay, (3) minimize the perceived negative consequences of performing well, and (4) create conditions such that positive outcomes other than pay will be seen to be related to good performance. In this [paper], we shall consider some of the problems an organization confronts when it tries to set up a pay system that will satisfy these four conditions. We shall not, however, go into the second condition—the importance of pay—in detail. . . . Of the other three conditions, the first is the most basic; it is the central issue around which any discussion of pay and motivation must revolve. We shall approach this issue by asking the following questions: To what degree is pay actually tied to performance in organizations? Do employees feel that pay should be tied to performance? Which of the various ways of tying pay to performance lead most directly to the establishment of the conditions that must exist if pay is to motivate job performance?

Tying Pay to Performance

One obvious means of creating the perception that pay is tied to performance is actually to relate pay closely to job performance and to make the relationship as visible as possible. Several studies have attempted to determine the degree to which this is done in organizations and have come up with some unexpected results. Their evidence indicates that pay is not very closely related to performance in many organizations that claim to have merit increase salary systems. Lawler and Porter (1966) show that pay is related to job level, seniority, and other non-performance factors. Svetlik, Prien, and Barrett (1964) show that there is a negative relationship between amount of salary and performance as evaluated by superiors. Lawler (1964) shows that managers' pay is relatively unrelated to superiors' performance evaluations. Meyer, Kay, and French (1965) show that managers' raises are not closely related to what occurs in their performance appraisal sessions.

Studies by Haire, Ghiselli, and Gordon (1967) and by Brenner and Lockwood (1965) also indicate that at the managerial level, pay is not always related to performance. The evidence in both these studies consists of salary history data; they point up some interesting tendencies. Haire et al., for example, have established that the raises managers get from one year to another often show no correlation with each other. If the companies were tying pay to performance, the lack of correlation would mean that a manager's performance in one year was quite different from his performance in another year. This assumption simply does not fit with what is known about performance: A manager who is a good performer one year is very likely to be a good performer the next. Thus, we must conclude that the companies studied were not tying pay to performance. Apparently, pay raises were distributed on a random basis, or the criteria for rewarding raises were frequently changed. As a result, recent raises were often not related to past raises or to performance.

Overall, therefore, the studies suggest that many business organizations do not do a very good job of tying pay to performance. This conclusion is rather surprising in light of many companies' very frequent claims that their pay systems are based on merit. It is particularly surprising that pay does not seem to be related to performance at the managerial level. Here there are no unions to contend with, and one would think that if organizations were effectively relating pay to performance for any group of employees, it would be at the managerial level. Admittedly this conclusion is based on sketchy evidence, and future research may prove it to be wrong. It may be, for instance, that pay is indirectly tied to performance and that the tie is obscured by promotion policies. All the studies reviewed here looked at the relationship between pay and performance within one management level. Even though there is no relationship between pay and performance within a level, there may actually be a relationship if the better performing managers are promoted and because of this receive higher pay. There is little evidence, however, to suggest that this is true.

Failure to tie pay closely to performance in many companies could mean that pay is not motivating job performance. In order for pay to motivate performance, it must appear to be related to performance; and employees are not likely to believe that pay is related to performance if it actually is not. Lawler (1967b) has shown that in one instance where pay was not related to performance, managers were aware of this fact and, consequently were not motivated by pay. This study also showed that in a group of organizations where measurements indicated that pay was only marginally tied to performance, managers had a fairly high belief that pay was related to performance. Thus, the data suggest that, given some positive indicators, employees are willing to believe that pay is based upon performance. Often, however, the positive indicators are missing, and as a result, pay does not motivate the employees to perform effectively.

Do Employees Want Pay to Be Based upon Performance?

One reason pay is not closely related to performance in many organizations may simply be that employees object to this way of handling pay. If employees object to seeing their pay tied to their performance, there can be real problems in trying to implement any kind of merit pay system, since it could be and, in fact, would probably be undermined by the employees themselves. One of the clearest findings that comes out of the research on incentive systems like the Scanlon Plan is that these plans work best when the employees want the plan and when they trust management (Whyte, 1955). Thus, the issue of whether employees in general are favorably inclined toward incentive plans is a crucial one when consideration is given to using pay as a motivator.

Two studies have measured managers' attitudes toward how their pay should be determined, and both show that managers prefer to have their pay based upon performance. Lawler (1967b), for example, found that managers believe that performance should be the most important determinant of their pay, but feel that in fact it is not. There was a consistent tendency across all companies for there to be a large gap between how important managers felt performance was in determining pay and how important they felt it should be. This gap between what should be and what was reflects the inability of the companies to develop pay plans that fit the needs of employees. It also indicates that pay could be a much stronger source of motivation in these organizations. In one sense this gap represents a challenge to management to develop a more motivating pay system.

Andrew and Henry (1963) have also presented data to show that managers prefer to have their pay based upon performance. Perhaps the most interesting finding they reported was a tendency for educational level to be related to preferences. Less-educated managers were less in favor of having their pay based upon performance than more highly educated managers. This finding also is congruent with evidence that blue-collar employees are somewhat less enthusiastic about having their pay based upon performance than are managers. But before the studies concerned with blue-collar employees are discussed in detail, a study of salesmen should be mentioned. It shows that they, like the managers, prefer to have their pay based upon general performance and merit rather than upon such factors as seniority and market competition (Research Institute of America, 1965).

Studies done among blue-collar workers to determine their preferences with respect to pay plans, do not show overwhelming acceptance of merit-based plans. The studies are a little difficult to interpret, however, since many of them asked for reactions to specific pay plans, such as piece rate plans, rather than to the general idea of merit-based pay. Workers might, for example, object to piece rate plans but still favor other kinds of merit-based systems. Thus, it is hard to tell if the workers studied objected to the principle of merit pay or to the specific plans queried.

Two studies provide strong evidence that often workers are not favorably inclined toward incentive pay schemes. A large-scale study by the Opinion Research Corporation (1949) found that, although workers felt that incentive plans got the highest output per man, 65 percent of the respondents preferred hourly pay plans. Similarly, a study in Great Britain by Davis (1948) found that 60 percent of the workers sampled were opposed to a system of payment based on results. There is evidence that opposition to incentive plans is lower among workers who have been working on such plans. In the Opinion Research Corporation study (1949), for example, 59 percent of the workers who had been on incentive plans opposed them while 74 percent of the workers who had been on hourly wages opposed incentive plans. Other studies show that incentive plans are usually endorsed by workers already on them, and suggest that in some instances the majority of workers favor them. A study reported by *Factory* (1947), for example, reports that 59 percent of the workers sampled who were not paid on an incentive basis said "they would like to work under such a system if it were fairly run." This finding suggests that employees in general are not against pay based upon performance, although they might be against certain merit pay systems. The results of another study by the Opinion Research Corporation (1946) are presented in Table 1. They show the same pattern: Workers on merit plans prefer such plans, and workers on hourly rates prefer them. The data show, however, that overall only 36 percent of the workers studied prefer piece rate plans. It is possible that a far larger proportion would be in favor of merit pay in principle, but would not prefer the piece rate plan to an hourly pay rate.

TABLE 1

REPLIES TO QUESTION: "ON A JOB WHICH COULD BE PAID BY EITHER PIECE RATE OR HOURLY RATE, WHICH WOULD YOU RATHER WORK ON?"
(OPINION REASEARCH CORPORATION, 1946)

	No. of Mfg. Manual Workers	Percentage Who Prefer		
		Piece Rate	Hourly Rate	Do Not Know
Total	919	36	61	3
Paid by:				
Hourly rate	658	24	73	3
Incentive plan	131	57	39	4
Piece rate	130	75	22	3
Union status:				
No union where work	220	43	53	4
Have union	699	34	63	3
Members	597	33	65	2
Nonmembers	102	35	54	11

Beer and Gery [Editor's note: Michael Beer and Gloria Gery, "Individual and Organizational Correlates of Pay System Preferences", in H. L. Tosi, R. J. House and M. D. Dunnette (eds.), *Managerial Motivation and Compensation*, M.S.U. Press, 1972, pp. 325-49] have carefully analyzed what determines whether an employee will prefer merit-based pay. Their data suggest that individual preferences are influenced by a person's needs and by the situation in which he finds himself. Employees high in advancement and responsibility needs seemed to prefer merit systems; those with strong security needs did not. The more competent the individual, the better his past experience with the system and the better his relationship with his boss, the more he preferred merit-based pay. Jones and Jeffrey (1964) have found that in one plant workers strongly preferred incentive pay schemes while in another they strongly rejected the idea of incentive pay. Considered together, this evidence suggests that workers are not necessarily opposed to incentive schemes, but that the situation in which they work and their work history may lead them to oppose them. Presumably in many situations opposition to incentive pay comes about because the employees feel they cannot trust the company to administer incentive schemes properly.

Over-all, the studies indicate that workers are less favorably disposed toward merit pay plans than are managers; in fact, the majority of the work force in many organizations may be against them. This conclusion has important practical implications for management. Clearly, to install an incentive plan successfully at the worker level will be difficult. A lot of effort may have to be devoted to building up a relationship of trust between management and workers, and to explaining the particular plan to be instituted as well as the whole concept of incentive pay. To install an incentive plan at the management level may be much easier, since the value system of managers appears to be more congruent with the idea of merit pay.

No incentive pay plan will ever work at any level in an organization unless superiors are committed to the plan and are willing to see their subordinates paid different amounts of money based upon their performance. Superiors must provide a large part of the performance information upon which pay decisions are based. If superiors reject systems that reward people according to their performance, then they are unlikely to provide valid performance evaluations and it will be impossible to base pay upon performance. The evidence indicates, however, that, in general, at least in the United States, managers in business organizations are willing to base pay upon performance. There is some evidence to suggest that good managers are much more amenable to the idea than poor managers, but still, the generalization holds (Gruenfeld & Weissenberg, 1966). It is, of course, consistent with the research that shows managers generally in favor of basing pay on merit.

Some preliminary evidence indicates that there may be cross-cultural differences among managers in their attitudes and values concerning pay. My own research shows that English managers are less willing to distribute pay on the basis of performance than American managers. In making pay raise decisions, the English respondents seem to give much greater weight to nonperformance factors, such as seniority and family situation. Similar findings for other European countries have been reported by Bass (1968). If these preliminary findings are confirmed by future studies, the possibility of using pay to motivate people may be more limited than is frequently suggested. To base pay on performance in many countries, an organization would probably have to undertake a tremendous educational program among managers as well as workers. Even then they might find it ineffective because it conflicts with the basic values of the people.

Methods of Relating Pay to Performance

There are virtually as many methods of relating pay to performance as there are organizations, and at times it seems that every organization is in the process of changing its approach. The R.I.A. (1965) study found for example, that one out or every three companies has "recently" changed its method of paying salesmen. Campbell, Dunnette, Lawler, and Weick (1970) report that their survey of company personnel practices showed widespread dissatisfaction with current pay systems. Such dissatisfaction is hardly surprising in light of the previously reported finding that pay is not closely related to performance in many companies. It is doubtful, however, that the problems and the dissatisfaction can be corrected simply by changing the mechanics of the plan already in use. Many plans seem to fail not because they are mechanically defective, but because they were ineffectually introduced, there is a lack of trust between superiors and subordinates, or the quality of supervision is too low. No plan can succeed in the face of low trust and poor supervision, no matter how valid it may be from the point of view of mechanics.

Still, some types of plans clearly are more capable than others of creating the four conditions mentioned at the beginning of [this article]. Some plans certainly do a better job of relating pay to performance than others, and some are better able to minimize the perceived negative consequences of good performance and to maximize the perceived positive consequences. One of the reasons pay often is not actually related to performance is that many organizations simply do not have pay plans that are correctly set up in order to accomplish this. Often this comes about because the particular conditions in

TABLE 2
A CLASSIFICATION OF PAY-INCENTIVE PLANS

	Performance Measure	Reward Offered	
		Salary Increase	Cash Bonus
Individual plans	{ Productivity Cost effectiveness Superiors' ratings	{ Merit rating plan	{ Sales commission Piece rate
Group plans	{ Productivity Cost effectiveness Superiors' rating		Group Incentive
Organizationwide plans	{ Productivity Cost effectiveness Profit	{ Productivity Bargaining	Kaiser, Scanlon Profit Sharing (e.g., American Motors)

the organization itself may not have been taken into account when the plan was developed. No plan is applicable to all situations. In a sense, one may say that a pay plan should be custom-tailored. Companies often try to follow the latest fads and fashion in salary administration, not recognizing that some plans simply do not fit their situation (Dunnette & Bass, 1963). Let us stress again, however, that mechanical faults are by no means the only reason that pay plans fail to relate pay to performance. Many of those which fail are not only well designed mechanically but also appropriate to the situation where they are used.

In looking at the mechanics of various types of pay programs, we shall group them together according to the way they differ on three dimensions. First, pay plans distribute rewards on different bases: individual, group, or organizationwide. Second, they measure performance differently: The measures typically vary from admittedly subjective (i.e., based on superiors' judgments or ratings) to somewhat objective (i.e., based on costs, sales, or profits). Third, plans differ in what they offer as rewards for successful performance: salary increases, bonuses, piece rates, or—in rare cases—fringe benefits. Table 2 presents a breakdown of the various plans, following this classification system. This classification yields some eighteen different types of incentive plans. A more detailed classification system would, of course, yield more. The table shows where the better-known plans fit in. It also shows a number of plans that are seldom used, and thus do not have a commonly known name. For example, companies do not typically base salary increases to individuals on the cost effectiveness of their work group. This does not mean that such a plan is a bad approach to distributing pay; it just means that it is not used very often.

Evaluating the Different Approaches to Merit-based Pay

It is possible to make some general statements about the success of the different merit pay plans. We shall evaluate the plans in terms of how capable they have proved to be in establishing three of the conditions that are necessary if pay is to motivate performance. Such an evaluation must, of course, reflect actual experience with the different approaches in a number of situations. Here we are ignoring for the moment the effect of situational factors on the effectiveness of the plans in order to develop general ratings of the plans.

TABLE 3
RATINGS OF VARIOUS PAY-INCENTIVE PLANS

Type of Plan		Performance Measure	Tie Pay to Performance	Minimize Negative Side Effects	Tie Other Rewards to Performance
SALARY REWARD	Individual plan	Productivity	+2	0	0
		Cost effectiveness	+1	0	0
		Superiors' rating	+1	0	+1
	Group	Productivity	+1	0	+1
		Cost effectiveness	+1	0	+1
		Superiors' rating	+1	0	+1
	Organizationwide	Productivity	+1	0	+1
		Cost effectiveness	+1	0	+1
		Profits	0	0	+1
BONUS	Individual plan	Productivity	+3	−2	0
		Cost effectiveness	+2	−1	0
		Superiors' rating	+2	−1	+1
	Group	Productivity	+2	0	+1
		Cost effectiveness	+2	0	+1
		Superiors' rating	+2	0	+1
	Organizationwide	Productivity	+2	0	+1
		Cost effectiveness	+2	0	+1
		Profit	+1	0	+1

Table 3 lists the different types of incentive plans and provides a general effectiveness rating for each plan on three separate criteria. First, each plan is evaluated in terms of how effective it is in creating the perception that pay is tied to performance. In general, this indicates the degree to which the approach actually ties pay closely to performance, chronologically speaking, and the degree to which employees believe that higher pay will follow good performance. Second, each plan is evaluated in terms of how well it minimizes the perceived negative consequences of good performance. This criterion refers to the extent to which the approach eliminates situations where social ostracism and other negative consequences become associated with good performance. Third, each plan is evaluated in terms of whether it contributes to the perception that important rewards other than pay (e.g., recognition and acceptance) stem from good performance. The ratings range from +3 to —3, with +3 indicating that the plan has generally worked very well in terms of the criterion, while —3 indicates that the plan has not worked well. A 0 rating indicates that the plan has generally been neutral or average.

A number of trends appear in the ratings presented in Table 3. Looking just at the criterion of tying pay to performance, we see that individual plans tend to be rated highest, while group plans are rated next, and organizationwide plans are rated lowest. This reflects the fact that in group plans to some extent and in organizationwide plans to with his most recent performance. This does not usually happen with salary increase programs, since organizations seldom cut anyone's salary; as a result, pay under the salary increase plan reflects not recent performance but performance over a number of years. Consequently, pay is not seen to be closely related to present behavior. Bonuses, on the other hand, typically depend on recent behavior, so that if someone performs poorly, it will show up immediately in his pay. Thus, a person under the bonus plan a great extent, an individual's pay is not directly a function of his *own* behavior. The pay of an individual in these situations is influenced by the behavior of others with whom he works and also, if the payment is based on profits, by external market conditions.

Bonus plans are generally rated higher than pay raise and salary increase plans. Under bonus plans, a person's pay may vary sharply from year to year in accordance cannot coast for a year and still be highly paid, as he can be under the typical salary merit pay program.

Finally, note that approaches which use objective measures of performance are rated higher than those which use subjective measures. In general, objective measures enjoy higher credibility; that is, employees will often grant the validity of an objective measure, such as sales or units produced, when they will not accept a superior's rating. Thus, when pay is tied to objective measures, it is usually clear to employees that pay is determined by their performance. Objective measures such as sales volume and units produced are also often publicly measurable, and when pay is tied to them, the relationship is often much more visible than when it is tied to a subjective, nonverifiable measure, such as a superior's rating. Overall, then, the suggestion is that individually based bonus plans which rely on objective measures produce the strongest perceived connection between pay and performance.

The ratings with respect to the ability of pay programs to minimize the perceived negative consequences of good performance reveal that most plans are regarded as neutral. That is, they neither contribute to the appearance of negative consequences nor help to eliminate any which might be present. The individual bonus plans receive a negative rating on this criterion, however. This negative rating reflects the fact that piece rate plans often lead to situations in which social rejection, firing, and running out of work are perceived by individuals to result from good performance. Under a piece rate system, the perceived negative consequences of good performance may cancel out the positive motivational force that piece rate plans typically generate by tying pay closely to performance.

With respect to the final criterion for pay plans, tying nonpay rewards to performance, the ratings are generally higher for group and organizationwide plans than for individual plans. Under group and organizationwide plans, it is generally to the advantage of everyone for an individual to work effectively. Thus, good performance is much more likely to be seen to result in esteem, respect, and social acceptance, than it is under individual plans. In short, if a person feels he can benefit from another's good performance, he is much more likely to encourage his fellow worker to perform well than if he will not benefit, and might even be harmed.

It should be clear from this short review that no one pay plan presents a panacea for a company's job motivation problems. Unfortunately, no one type of pay program is strong in all areas. Thus, no organization probably ever will be satisfied with its approach, since it will have problems associated with it. It is therefore not surprising to find that companies are usually dissatisfied with their pay programs and are constantly considering changing them. Still, the situation is not completely hopeless. Clearly, some approaches are generally better than others. We know, for example, that many of the approaches not mentioned in the table, such as stock option plans, across-the-board raises, and seniority increases, have no real effect on the performance motivation of most employees. In addition, the evidence indicates that bonus-type plans are generally superior wage increase plans and that individually based plans are generally superior to group and organizationwide plans. This suggests that one widely applicable model for an incentive plan might take the following form.

Each person's pay would be divided into three components. One part would be for the job the employee is doing and everyone who holds a similar job would get the same amount. A second part of the pay package would be determined by seniority and cost-of-living factors; everyone in the company would get this, and the amount would be automatically adjusted each year. The third part of the package, however, would not be automatic; it would be individualized so that the amount paid would be based upon each person's performance during the immediately preceding period. The poor performer in the organization should find that this part of his or her pay package is minimal, while the good performer should find that this part of his or her pay is at least as great as the other two parts combined. This would not be a raise, however, since it could vary from year to year, depending on the individual's performance during the last performance period. Salary increases or raises would come only with changes in responsibility, cost of living, or seniority. The merit portion of the pay package would be highly variable, so that if a person's performance fell off, his or her pay would also be decreased by a cut in the size of the merit pay. The purpose of this kind of system is, of course, to make a large proportion of an individual's pay depend upon performance during the current period. Thus, performance is chronologically closely tied to large changes in pay.

The really difficult problem in any merit pay system, including this one, is how to measure performance. A valid measure of performance must meet several requirements. Not only must it be valid from the point of view of top management, but it must lead to promotion and pay decisions that are accepted by people throughout the organization: Supervisors, subordinates, and peers must all accept the results of the system. Without this wide acceptance, pay raises will not be seen to reflect merit. Employees gain much of their knowledge about how pay systems operate by watching what happens to other people in the organization. If people whom they feel are doing good work get raises, then they accept the fact that a merit pay system exists. On the other hand, if workers they do not respect get raises, their belief in the system breaks down. Obviously the more the appraisal system yields decisions that are congruent with employees' consensus about performance, the more the employees will believe that a merit system exists. The performance measure should also be such that employees feel that their contributions to the organization show up in it very directly. They must feel that they have control over it, rather than feeling that it reflects so many other things that what they do has little weight. . . . Finally, the performance measure or measures should be influenced by all the behaviors that are important for the job holder to perform. People perform those behaviors that are measured, and thus it is important that the measure be sufficiently inclusive.

The performance appraisal systems that are actually used by organizations range all the way from superiors' subjective judgments to the complicated "objective" accounting-based systems that are used to measure managers' effectiveness. The problems with the simple, subjective, superiors' judgments are obvious—the subordinates often see them as arbitrary, based upon inadequate information, and simply unfair. The more objective systems are appealing in many ways. Where they can be installed, they are the best, but even they often fail to reflect individual efforts. Stock option plans are a good example. With these plans, pay is tied to the price of the stock on the market, and this presumably motivates managers to work so that the price of the stock will go up. The problem with this approach is that for most managers the connection between their effort and the price of the stock is very weak.

Plans that base bonuses or pay increases on profit centers or on the effectiveness of certain parts of the business may work, but all too often much of the profitability of one part of the organization is controlled more by outside than inside forces. Another problem with this kind of system is illustrated by the fate of most piece rate incentive plans used at the worker level. They give the false illusion that objective, highly measurable rates can be "scientifically" set and that trust between superiors and subordinates is not necessary, since the system is objective. Experience has shown that effective piece rate systems simply cannot be established where foremen and workers do not trust each other and have a participative relationship. No completely "objective" system has ever been designed, nor will one ever be. Unexpected contingencies will always come up and have to be worked out between superiors and subordinates. Such events can be successfully resolved only when trust based upon mutual influence exists. Where poor relationships exist, workers strive to get rates set low and then they restrict their production, because they do not believe that good performance will in fact lead to higher pay in the long run.

Thus the answer in many organizations must rest in a reasonable combination of the simple, superior-based rating system and a system which uses more objective measures. First, we must accept the fact that no system can ever be 100 percent objective and that subjective judgments will always be important. Second, we must realize that the key to general acceptance of the decisions that the appraisal system yields lies in having as broad as possible participation in the system.

What would such a system look like? It would be based upon superior-subordinate appraisal sessions where subordinates feel that they have a real opportunity to influence their boss. Obviously, such a system cannot operate, nor can any other for that matter, unless superior-subordinate relations are such that mutual influence is possible. In the first appraisal session the superior and subordinate would jointly decide on three things. First, they would decide on the objectives the subordinate should try to achieve during the ensuing time period. This period might last from three months to several years, depending on the level of the job. Second, they would decide on how the subordinate's progress toward these objectives will be measured. Objective measures might be used as well as subjective ratings by peers and others. Third, they would decide what level of reward the subordinate should receive if he accomplishes his objectives. A second meeting would be held at the end of the specified time period in order for the superior and subordinate to jointly assess the progress of the subordinate and decide upon any pay actions. Finally, a few weeks later the whole process would begin again with another objectives-setting session. The advantages of this kind of system extend far beyond pay administration. It can create a situation where superiors and subordinates jointly become much more certain of what the subordinate's actual job duties and responsibilities are. Some recent studies suggest that there is often greater than 70 percent disagreement between superior and subordinate about what constitutes the subordinate's job, so agreement on his score would not be an insignificant step forward. The fact that the subordinate has a chance to set goals and that he commits himself to a certain level of performance may have an impact on his motivation that is independent of rewards like pay. There is evidence that when people commit themselves to challenging goals, needs like esteem and self-realization can come into play and motivate them to achieve the goals. This system also offers the subordinate a chance to become involved in important decisions about his own future and thereby encourages a kind of give and take that seldom exists between superiors and subordinates.

Despite the fact that it is possible to state some general conclusions about the effectiveness of different pay plans, perhaps the most important conclusion arising from the discussion so far is that it is vital to fit the pay plan to the organization. What might be a wonderful plan for one organization may for a whole series of reasons be a bad plan for another. Thus, although it is tempting to say that X approach is always best, it is wiser to turn now to a consideration of the factors that determine which kind of plan is likely to be best in a given situation.

Factors Influencing the Effectiveness of Different Pay Plans

In selecting a plan for a particular organization, what situational factors must be considered? . . . One factor that must be considered when an organization is deciding what type of pay plan to use is the degree of cooperation that is needed among the individuals who are under the plan. When the jobs involved are basically independent from one another, it is perfectly reasonable to use an individual-based plan. Independent jobs are quite common; examples are outside sales jobs and certain kinds of production jobs. In these jobs, employees contribute relatively independently to the effectiveness of the total group or organization, and thus it is appropriate to place them on an incentive scheme that motivates them to perform at their maximum and to pay little attention to cooperative activities.

As organizations become more complex, however, more and more jobs demand that work be done either successively (i.e., work passes from one person to another) or coordinately (i.e., work is a function of the joint effort of all employees) (Ghiselli & Brown, 1955). With successive jobs and especially with coordinate jobs, it is doubtful that individual incentive plans are appropriate. For one thing, on these jobs it is often difficult to measure the contribution of a given individual, and therefore difficult to reward individuals differentially. The organization is almost forced to reward on the basis of group performance. Another problem with individual plans is that they typically do not reward cooperation, since it is difficult to measure and to visibly relate to pay.

Cooperation is essential on successive and coordinate jobs, and it is vital that the pay plan reward it. Thus, the strong suggestion is that group and organizationwide plans may be best in situations where jobs are coordinate or successive.

A related issue has to do with the degree to which appropriate inclusive subgoals or criteria can be created for individuals. An example was cited earlier of an individual pay plan that motivated salesmen to sell but did not motivate them to carry out other necessary job activities such as stocking shelves. The problem was that pay was tied to the most obvious and most measurable goal in the job, and some of the less measurable activities were overlooked and unrewarded. This situation occurs frequently; for many jobs, it is quite difficult to establish criteria that are both measurable quantitatively and inclusive of all the important job behaviors. The solution to the problem with the salesmen was to establish a group incentive plan. Indeed, inclusive criteria may often be possible at the group and organizational level but not at the individual level. It is quite easy to think of jobs for which a criterion like productivity might not be inclusive enough when individuals are looked at, but might be inclusive enough when a number of jobs or employees are grouped together. The point, of course, is that in choosing an incentive plan, an organization must consider whether the performance measures that are related to pay include all the important job activities. One thing is certain: If an employee is not evaluated in terms of an activity, he will not be motivated to perform it.

The point has often been made that, wherever possible, objective performance measures should be used. There are, however, many situations where objective measures do not exist for individual or even group performance. One way of dealing with such situations is to measure performance on the basis of larger and larger groups until some objective measures can be found. Another approach is to measure performance on the individual or small group level and to use admittedly subjective measures. . . .

One further issue must be considered when an organization is installing a pay plan: will the individuals under the plan actually be able to control the criteria on which they will be evaluated? All too often the criteria are unrelated to the individual worker's efforts. A good example of this is the American Motors Corporation profit-sharing plan: The individual worker is not in a position to influence the profits of the company, yet this is a criterion upon which part of his pay is based. If a pay system is going to motivate employees, the criteria must be such that the employees can directly influence them. The criteria must, in short, be within the employees' control. This point, of course, argues for the use of individual criteria where possible, since they best reflect an individual's efforts.

Pay systems may also be results or process-oriented; that is, they may reward employees chiefly for results (e.g. actual production) or for the way the task or job is carried out. There are usually problems with any system that rewards process only, just as there are problems with systems that reward results only. Perhaps the ultimate example of what can happen in the process-oriented system can be seen in the large bureaucracies that grow up in many civil service and other large organizations. In these bureaucracies people seem motivated to follow the rules, and not to accomplish the objectives for which the organization was established. On the other hand, a salesman may be motivated only by a short-term desire to maximize results. His behavior may lead to a sale, but it may be such that his organization never makes another sale to that buyer. A pay system must be designed to reward both process and results. This may be difficult in many situations; process is particularly difficult to measure objectively, and thus subjective measures may have to be used. . . . Subjective measures can only be used effectively where a high degree of trust exists.

Pay Secrecy

Secrecy about pay rates seems to be an accepted practice in organizations, regardless of whether they use individual or group plans, bonus or salary increases, objective or subjective performance measures. Secrecy seems to be particularly prevalent with respect to management pay (Lawler, in press). Some research suggests that one of the effects of secrecy may be to reduce the ability of pay to motivate (Lawler, 1965a; Lawler, 1967c). . . . The argument that has been presented against secrecy is that it makes accurate social comparisons impossible (Festinger, 1954). Secrecy thus makes it difficult to conclusively and visibly establish that pay is tied to performance. Further, it is argued that because social comparisons are difficult, employees often get incorrect feedback about their own performance.

One of the findings that has consistently appeared in the research on pay secrecy is that managers tend to have incorrect information about the pay of other managers in the organization. Specifically, there is a general tendency for them to overestimate the pay of managers around them. For example, in one organization the average raise given was 6 percent, yet the managers believed that it was 8 percent, and the larger their raise was, the larger they believed other people's raises were (Lawler, in press). This had the effect of wiping out much of the motivational force of the differential reward system that was actually operating in the company. Almost regardless of how well the individual manager was performing, he felt that he was getting less than the average raise. This problem was particularly severe among the high performers, since they believed that they were doing well yet receiving a minimal reward. They did not believe that pay was in fact based upon merit. This was ironical, since their pay *did* reflect their performance. What actually existed did not matter as far as the motivation of the managers was concerned; they responded to what they thought existed. Thus, even though pay was tied to performance, these managers were not motivated because they could not see the connection.

There is another way in which pay secrecy may affect motivation. Several studies have shown that accurate feedback about quality of work is a strong stimulus to good performance (Vroom, 1964). People work better when they know how well they are doing in relation to some meaningful standard. For a manager, pay is one of the most meaningful pieces of feedback information. High pay means good performance. Low pay is a signal that he is not doing well and had better improve. The research shows that when managers do not really know what other managers earn, they cannot correctly evaluate their own pay and the feedback implications of it for their own performance. Since they tend to overestimate the pay of subordinates and peers and since they overestimate the raises others get, the majority of them consider their pay low; in effect, they receive negative feedback. Moreover, although this feedback suggests that they should change their work behavior, it does not tell them what type of change to make. When managers are not doing their jobs well, negative feedback is undoubtedly what they need. But it is doubtful that it is what managers who are working effectively need.

Note that one recommendation that appears in the discussion of factors affecting the importance of pay as well as in the discussion of factors affecting the belief that pay depends upon performance is that pay information should be more public. Unless this condition exists, pay is not likely to motivate performance, because it will be seen neither as an important satisfier of higher-order needs nor as something that is obtainable from good performance. Making pay information public will not itself establish the belief that pay is based upon merit or ensure that people will get accurate performance feedback. All it can do is clarify those situations where pay actually *is* based upon merit but where it is not obvious because relative salaries are not accurately known. This point is apparent in some unpublished data collected by the author. An organization was studied that had a merit-based plan and pay secrecy. At the beginning of the study, the data collected showed that the employees saw only a moderate relationship between pay and performance. Data collected after the company became more open about pay showed a significant increase in the employees' perceptions of the degree to which pay and performance were related. The crucial factor in making this change to openness successful was that pay was actually tied to performance. Making pay rates public where pay is not tied to performance will only serve to emphasize more dramatically that it is not, thereby further reducing the power of pay to motivate. . . .

References

Andrews, I. R. & Henry, M. M., Management attitudes toward pay, *Industrial Relations,* 1963, 3, 29-39.

Bass, B. M., Ability values, and concepts of equitable salary increases in exercise compensation, *Journal of Applied Psychology,* 1968, 52, 299-303.

Brenner, M. H. and Lockwood, H. C., Salary as a predictor of salary: A 20-year study, *Journal of Applied Psychology,* 1965, 49, 295-298.

Campbell, J. P., Dunnette, M. D., Lawler, E. E., & Weick, K. E., *Managerial Behavior, Performances and Effectiveness,* New York: McGraw-Hill, 1970.

Davis, N. M., Attitudes to work among building operatives, *Occupational Psychology,* 1948, 22, 56-62.

Dunnette, M. D. & Bass, B. M., Behavioral scientists and personnel management, *Industrial Relations,* 1963, 2, (3), 115-130.

Factory, What the factory worker really thinks about his job, unemployment, and industry's profit, *Factory Management and Maintenance,* 1947, 105 (12), 86-92.

Festinger, L., A theory of social comparison processes, *Human Relations,* 1954, 7, 117-140.

Ghiselli, E. E. & Brown, C. W., *Personnel and Industrial Psychology,* (2d ed.) New York: McGraw-Hill, 1955.

Gruenfeld, L. W. & Weissenberg, P., Supervisory characteristics and attitudes toward performance appraisals, *Personnel Psychology,* 1966, 19, 143-152.

Haire, M., Ghiselli, E. E. & Gordon, M. E., A psychological study of pay, *Journal of Applied Psychology Monograph,* 1967, 51 (4), (Whole No. 636).

Jones, L. V. & Jeffrey, T. E., A quantitative analysis of expressed preferences for compensation plans, *Journal of Applied Psychology,* 1964, 48, 201-210.

Lawler, E. E., Managers' job performance and their attitudes toward their pay, Unpublished doctoral dissertation, Univ. of Calif., Berkeley, 1964.

Lawler, E. E., Managers' perceptions of their subordinates' pay and of their superiors' pay, *Personnel Psychology,* 1965, 18, 413-422.

Lawler, E. E., The multitrait-multirater approach to measuring managerial job performance, *Journal of Applied Psychology,* 1967, 51, 369-381 (b).

Lawler, E. E., Secrecy about management compensation: Are there hidden costs? *Organizational Behavior and Human Performance,* 1967, 2, 182-189 (c).

Lawler, E. E., Secrecy and the need to know, in R. House, M. Dunnette, & H. Tosi (Eds.) *Readings in Managerial Motivation and Compensation,* in press.

Lawler, E. E. & Porter, L. W., Predicting managers' pay and their satisfaction with their pay, *Personnel Psychology,* 1966, 19, 363-373.

Meyer, H. H., Kay, E. & French, J. R. P., Split roles in performance appraisal, *Harvard Business Review,* 1965, 43 (1), 123-129.

Opinion Research Corporation, *Wage Incentives,* Princeton, N.J.: 1946.

Opinion Research Corporation, "Productivity" from the worker's standpoint, Princeton, N.J.: 1949.

R.I.A. Sales compensation practices, an RIA survey, New York: Research Institute of America, File No. 32, 1965.

Svetlik, B. Prien, E. & Barrett, G., Relationships between job difficulty, employee's attitudes toward his job, and supervisory ratings of the employee effectiveness, *Journal of Applied Psychology*, 1964, 48, 320-324.

Vroom, V. H., Work and motivation, New York: Wiley, 1964.

Whyte, W. F., (Ed.) Money and motivation: An analysis of incentives in industry, New York: Harper, 1955.

Management by Objectives

HENRY L. TOSI
STEPHEN CARROLL

Since Drucker (1954) and McGregor (1960) made favorable statements about management by objectives, organizations of all types have made increasing use of this method. While most of the early discussion of MBO emphasized its use as a tool for the development of more objective criteria for performance evaluation, it has become apparent that subordinate participation in goal setting has resulted in greater levels of ego involvement, increased motivation and increased planning behavior, all of which have an effect upon performance.

These advantages stemmed from the process of setting goals and using them, in place of personality traits and characteristics for evaluation of performance. Management by objectives has been described as a general process in which ". . . The superior and the subordinate manager of an organization jointly define its common goals, define each individual's major areas of responsibility in terms of the results expected of him and use these measures as guides for operating the unit and assessing the contribution of each of its members." (Odiorne, 1965).

The logic of MBO is, indeed, attractive. There is an intrinsic desirability to a method which motivates performance and enhances measurement while at the same time it increases the participation and involvement of subordinates.

The Elements of MBO

There are three basic aspects of MBO which will affect its success: goals and goal setting; participation and involvement of subordinates; and, feedback and performance evaluation.

Goals and Goal Setting.

A number of studies[1] have clearly demonstrated that when an individual or group

From *Personnel Administration*, vol. 33 (July-August 1970), pp. 44-49. Reprinted by permission of the International Personnel Management Association.

has a specific goal, there is higher performance than when the goals are general, or have not been set. Generally, high performance can be associated with higher individual or group goals. A number of studies[2] also suggest that performance improvement occurs when an individual is successful in achieving past goals. When there is previous goal success, the individual is more likely to set higher goals in future periods, and he is more likely to attain them.

Participation.

There have been a number of diverse findings about the relationship of participation in decision-making and productivity. These apparently contradictory findings have been resolved by concluding that if the subordinate perceives the participation to be legitimate, it will have positive effects on productivity. In addition, participation does seem to have an effect on the degree of acceptance of decisions reached mutually. There is also evidence[3] that involvement and participation are positively correlated with the level of job satisfaction.

Feedback.

Both laboratory and field research have demonstrated that relatively clear, unambiguous feedback increases problem solving capacities of groups and improves the performance of individuals.[4] Positive attitudes, increased confidence in decisions, and greater certainties of superior's expectations were found to be related to communications which clarified roles and role expectancies with more and better information.

Feedback, in the form of formal appraisal in a work setting, when based on relatively objective performance standards, tends to be related to a more positive orientation by subordinates of the amount of supervision their boss exercises. Positive actions are more likely to be taken by subordinates when feedback is viewed as supportive and is objectively based.

MBO and Employee Motivation

Studies of the MBO process in organizations strongly suggest that changes in performance and attitude, which seem positive and desirable, appear to be associated with how it is formally implemented. The implementation of MBO alters the expectations of organization members about performance appraisal and evaluation. These expectations, if not met, may affect the degree of acceptance of the MBO approach. (See Raia, 1965; and Tosi and Carroll, 1968.)

This problem may be resolved, to some degree, through proper setting of objectives and use of the MBO process. We believe certain minimal conditions must prevail if MBO is to have its motivational effect:

Goal Clarity and Relevance.

Few managers would quarrel with the notion that organizational goals should be made known to the members. Individual perceptions of the goal are important here. Tosi and Carroll (1968) have suggested some dimensions of goals which need to be communicated to members. First, goals should represent the unit's needs. The members must be aware of the importance of the goals. The development of relatively objective criteria increases the perception of goal clarity. If goals have these properties, they are more likely to have effects upon the individual working towards them.

Managerial Use and Support.

"Top management support" is important for the success of any program. The best evidence of support is the use of the technique by the manager himself. Formulating goals, discussing them with subordinates, and providing feedback based on these goals will have substantially greater effect on a subordinate than simply saying "this has the support of top management."

Many managers mistakenly feel the verbalization of support for a policy is adequate enough. They send a memo to subordinates stating that top management wishes a program to be implemented. This, obviously, does not insure compliance. "Do as I say, not as I do" will not work. Verbalized policy support must be reinforced by the individual's perception of the superior's action and behavior in using an objective approach. It is of little or no use to support MBO philosophy orally and not use it!

The Need for Feedback.

While a number of studies have concluded that goals have a greater impact on performance than just feedback alone we do not believe it to be an either/or situation. Feedback about well-developed goals seems a fundamental requirement for behavior change. It may be that the subordinate's perception of the specificity objectivity and frequency of feedback is interpreted as a measure of the superior's support of an objectives approach.

Some Other Cautions.

There are other significant points that cut across those made above: there are personal as well as organization constraints which must be taken into consideration in the development of goals. The organizational unit and the organization level affect the nature of the goals which can, and will, be set. Goals at lower levels may be more precise and probably more objectively measured. The goals of one functional area, engineering for instance, may be much more general than those of another, say the marketing department.

MBO and the Compensation Process

If, as McClelland (1961) suggests, individuals high in need achievement will expend more effort in reaching challenging goals irrespective of external rewards associated with goal accomplishment, MBO may supplement or complement standard compensations procedures. Tying MBO into the financial reward system could have a handsome pay-off. It is for this reason that we suggest how information obtained from MBO can be used in making improved compensation decisions.

Internal Wage Administration.

MBO can be of assistance in developing salary differentials within a particular job class. By assessing the level of difficulty and contribution of the goals for a particular job and comparing them with similar jobs, better determination of the appropriateness of basic compensation differentials may be made.

MBO may be useful in providing information about changes in job requirements which may necessitate re-evaluation and adjustment of compensation levels for different positions. By observing changes in objectives over time, changes in job requirements may be detected which could lead to revisions in compensation schedules.

The objectives approach can aid in determining supplementary compensation levels such as stock options, bonus plans, and administration of profit sharing plans. This type of compensation is usually given when performance exceeds the normal position requirements. A properly developed objectives approach will take into account both normal job duties as well as goals and activities which extend beyond them. The extent to which an incumbent is able to achieve these non-routine objectives should be one, but perhaps not the only, factor in ranking unit members in order of their additional contribution to group effectiveness. It will provide a sound basis for determining what the level of supplemental compensation should be. Needless to say, goals which extend beyond normal job requirements should contribute importantly to organizational success.

A possible problem needs to be noted here. When goals go substantially beyond the current job requirements it may be due to the individual's initiative and aggressiveness. If this happens, it may be more appropriate strategy to change the position of the individual, not to redefine his job and change his compensation levels. A method must be developed which takes this possibility into consideration, as well as the fact that different managers will have different goals. This does not seem to be the appropriate place to detail such a device. A weighing approach which considers the capability of the manager, the difficulty of the goal, and its importance to the unit might resolve this problem.

Performance-linked Rewards.

If goals are developed properly, their achievement may be more readily associated with an individual so that appropriate individual rewards may be given. The *goal statement* is the heart of the "objectives approach." It is a description of the boss's expectancies which will be used in the feedback and evaluation process. It is a communicative artifact which spells out, for both the boss and the subordinate, the objectives *and* the manner in which they will be obtained. It should *contain two elements,* the *desired goal level* and the *activities* required to achieve that level of performance. This permits not only a comparison of performance against some criterion, but also allows determination of whether or not events, which are presumed to lead to goal achievement, have taken place if appropriate criteria are not available.

This has important implications for the problems of assessment, evaluation, and compensation. Some goals may be neither measurable nor adequately verifiable. Yet, intuitively we know what must be done to achieve them. If this is the case, and we have distinguished between goals and activities, we can at least determine whether activities which are presumed to lead to desired ends have taken place.

It is important to recognize the distinction between measuring the achievement of a goal level and determining whether or not an event presumed to lead to goal achievement has taken place. If we are unable to quantify or specify a goal level in a meaningful way, then we must simply assume that the desired level will be achieved if a particular event, or set of activities, has taken place. For example, it is very difficult to find measurable criteria to assess a manager's capability in developing subordinates, yet we can determine if he has provided them with development opportunities. If they have participated in seminars, attending meetings or gone to school it may be *assumed* that the development activities are properly conducted.

Promises and Problems

By its very nature, MBO seems to be a promising vehicle for linking performance to the evaluation process and the reward system in order to encourage both job satisfaction and productivity. It appears that higher performance and motivation is most likely when there is a link between performance and the reward systems (Tosi and Carroll, 1968; Porter and Lawler, 1968). It may be that this link can be achieved through the process of feedback regarding goal achievement and the association of rewards and sanctions to achievement. Goal attainment should be organizationally reinforced, and the reinforcement should be different for individuals, as a function of their own attainment. The use of an "objectives" approach in conjunction with a compensation program may also result in less dissatisfaction with the allocation of compensation increases made. Certainly there is virtually universal agreement among managers that rewards should go for actual accomplishments rather than for irrelevant personal characteristics and political or social standing.

There may be problems arising from the use of MBO and its emphasis on goals and goal achievement. Many organizations have adopted the objectives approach because it seems to be a better appraisal device, and they have used it primarily in this manner. But, an appraisal system should furnish information needed to make other personnel decisions, such as promotion and transfer. Information furnished by the objectives approach may not be adequate for these purposes. Accomplishment of goals at a lower level job may be a good indicator of capability in the current job and/or level of motivation, but not of the individual's abilities to perform at higher levels of responsibility, especially if the requirements on the higher level job are much different from the current position.

Conversely, goals accomplished at a lower level may be indicative of promotability to a particular high level job if there is high goal congruence between the two positions. At any rate, there is certainly no reason to rely strictly upon the objectives approach for these decisions. It can be used along with other criteria, such as assessment of traits, when this is deemed an important dimension by the decision makers. Another potential difficulty should be pointed out. If the objectives approach becomes the basic vehicle for the determination of compensation increases, then managers may quickly learn to "beat the system." Unless higher level managers are skilled in the use of MBO, subordinates may set objectives which have high probabilities of achievement, refraining from setting high risk goals. When any system becomes too formalized, managers learn how to beat it, and those using it become more concerned with simply meeting the formal benefits for both the individual and the organization [and the results] are probably no different from earlier more traditional methods of appraisal.

The "objectives approach" seems to be a practical way of motivating organization members, but it is not an easy path to follow. It requires a considerable amount of time and energy of *all managers,* in addition to extensive organization support to make it work. MBO may lose some of its mystique, value, importance, and significance when it must be translated into a formal policy requirement. It is too easy to consider a formal MBO program as merely another thorn in the manager's side, with no positive gains for implementing it. To succeed, an MBO program must be relevant, applicable, helpful, and receive organization support and reinforcement. One way in which this can be done is to link it to other elements of the structural system which reinforce behavior, such as compensation and reward programs.

References

Drucker, Peter. *The Practice of Management.* New York: Harper and Brothers, 1954.

McClelland, D. C. *The Achieving Society*. Princeton: Van Nostrand, 1961.

McGregor, Douglas. *The Human Side of Enterprise*. New York: McGraw-Hill, 1960.

Odiorne, George. *Management by Objectives*. New York: Pitman, 1965.

Porter, Lyman and Lawler, Edward. *Managerial Attitudes and Performance*. Homewood, Illinois: R. D. Irwin, 1968.

Raia, Anthony. "Goal Setting and Self Control," *Journal of Management Studies,* II-I, February 1965, pp. 34-35.

Tosi, H. and Carroll, S. "Managerial Reactions to Management by Objectives," *Academy of Management Journal*. December 1968, pp. 415-426.

Notes

1. See for instance Bryan, J. F. and Locke, E. A. "Goal Setting as a Means of Increasing Motivation" *Journal of Applied Psychology,* 1967, Vol. 51, pp. 274-277; Locke, E. A. "Motivational Effects of Knowledge of Results: Knowledge of Results: Knowlege or Goal Setting?" *Journal of Applied Psychology,* 1967, Vol. 51, pp. 324-329.

2. See Lockette, R. R., *The Effect of Level of Aspiration Upon the Learning of Skills*. Unpublished doctoral dissertation, University of Illinois, 1956; Yacorzynski, G. K., "Degree of Effort III. Relationship to the Level of Aspiration" *Journal of Experimental Psychology,* 1941, 30 pp. 407-413; Horowitz, M, et. al., *Motivational Effects of Alternative Decision Making Processes in Groups*. Bureau of Education Research, University of Illinois, 1953.

3. Vroom, Victor. *Some Personality Determinants of the Effects of Participation,* Englewood Cliffs: Prentice Hall; Tosi, Henry, "A Reexamination of Some Personality Determinants of the Effects of Participation," *Personnel Psychology* (forthcoming).

4. See Wertz, J. A., Antoinetti, and Wallace, S. R. "The Effect of Home Office Contact on Sales Performance," *Personnel Psychology,* 1954, Vol. 7, pp. 381-384; Smith, E. E. "The Effects of Clear and Unclear Role Expectations on Group Productivity and Effectiveness," *Journal of Abnormal and Social Psychology,* 1957, Vol. 55, pp. 213-217; and, Leavitt; Hand Mueller, A., "Some Effects of Feedback on Communication," *Human Relations,* 1951, Vol. 4, pp. 401-410.

CHAPTER   7

Job and Work Satisfaction

For years many in industrial psychology held to the belief that job satisfaction causes job performance. Now, after decades of research, it is known that this is not generally true. In fact, as Lawler points out in his article in this chapter, the opposite relation may hold: performance may cause satisfaction. Even though they may not cause performance, job satisfaction and job attitudes are important. First, the degree of satisfaction and fulfillment that people derive from their work life is an important consideration in itself. And, as Lawler points out, a theory of job satisfaction is necessary to the understanding of the processes involved in producing satisfaction and dissatisfaction. Secondly, job dissatisfaction is apparently a cause of absenteeism and turnover, as the review of research evidence by Porter and Steer clearly indicates. Finally, Jeswald's article demonstrates just how great the economic impact on the organization of these two personnel behaviors can be. The obvious implication is that increases in employee job satisfaction can lead to important cost savings for the organization.

Satisfaction and Behavior

E. E. Lawler

Compared to what is known about motivation, relatively little is known about the determinants and consequences of satisfaction. Most of the psychological research on motivation simply has not been concerned with the kinds of affective reactions that people experience in association with or as a result of motivated behavior. No well-developed theories of satisfaction have appeared and little theoretically based research has been done on satisfaction. . . . Most of the research on the study of satisfaction has been done by psychologists interested in work organizations. This research dates back to the 1930s. Since that time, the term "job satisfaction" has been used to refer to affective attitudes or orientations on the part of individuals toward jobs. Hoppock published a famous monograph on job satisfaction in 1935, and in 1939 the results of the well-known Western Electric studies were published. The Western Electric studies (Roethlisberger & Dickson, 1939) emphasized the importance of studying the attitudes, feelings, and perceptions employees have about their jobs. Through interviews with over 20,000 workers, these studies graphically made the point that employees have strong affective reactions to what happens to them at work. The Western Electric studies also suggested that affective reactions cause certain kinds of behavior, such as strikes, absenteeism, and turnover. Although the studies failed to show any clear-cut relationship between satisfaction and job performance, the studies did succeed in stimulating a tremendous amount of research on job satisfaction. During the last 30 years, thousands of studies have been done on job satisfaction. Usually, these studies have not been theoretically oriented; instead, researchers have simply looked at the relationship between job satisfaction and factors such as age, education, job level, absenteeism rate, productivity, and so on. Originally, much of the research seemed to be stimulated by a desire to show that job satisfaction is important because it influences productivity. Underlying the earlier articles on job satisfaction was a strong conviction that "happy workers are productive workers." Recently, however, this theme has been disappearing, and many organizational psychologists seem to be studying job satisfaction simply because they are interested in finding its causes. . . .

The recent interest in job satisfaction also ties in directly with the rising concern in many countries about the quality of life. [Editors note: The concept of "quality of work" or "quality of life" is receiving a large amount of emphasis in speeches made by industrial psychologists, labor leaders, and managers. We believe it will become an important issue of concern for personnel managers in the very near future.] There is an increasing acceptance of the view that material possessions and economic growth do not necessarily produce a high quality of life. Recognition is now being given to the importance of the kinds of affective reactions that people experience and to the fact that these are not always tied to economic or material accomplishments. Through the Department of Labor and the Department of Health, Education, and Welfare, the United States government has recently become active in trying to improve the affective quality of work life. Job satisfaction is one measure of the quality of life in organizations and is worth understanding and increasing even if it doesn't relate to performance. This reason for studying satisfaction is likely to be an increasingly prominent one as we begin to worry more about the effects working in organizations has on people and as our humanitarian concern for the kind of psychological experiences people have during their lives increases. What happens to people during the work day has profound effects both on the individual employee's life and on the society as a whole, and thus these events cannot be ignored if the quality of life in a society is to be high. As John Gardner has said,

> Of all the ways in which society serves the individual, few are more meaningful than to provide him with a decent job. . . . It isn't going to be a decent society for any of us until it is for all of us. If our sense of responsibility fails us, our sheer self-interest should come to the rescue [1968, p. 25].

As it turns out, satisfaction is related to absenteeism and turnover, both of which are very costly to organizations. Thus, there is a very "practical" economic reason for organizations to be concerned with job satisfaction, since it can influence organizational effectiveness. However, before any practical use can be made of the finding that job dissatisfaction causes absenteeism and turnover, we must understand what factors cause and influence job satisfaction. Organizations can influence job satisfaction and prevent absenteeism and turnover only if the organizations can pinpoint the factors causing and influencing these affective responses.

Despite the many studies, critics have legitimately complained that our understanding of the causes of job satisfaction has not substantially increased during the last 30 years (for example, see Locke, 1968, 1969) for two main reasons. The research on job satisfaction has typically been atheoretical and has not tested for causal relationships. Since the research has not been guided by theory, a vast array of unorganized, virtually uninterpretable facts have been unearthed. For example, a number of studies have found a positive relationship between productivity and job satisfaction, while other studies have found no evidence of this relationship. Undoubtedly, this disparity can be explained, but the explanation would have to be based on a theory of satisfaction, and at present no such theory exists. One thing the research on job satisfaction has done is to demonstrate the saying that "theory without data is fantasy; but data without theory is chaos!"

Due to the lack of a theory stating causal relationships, the research on job satisfaction has consistently looked simply for relationships among variables. A great deal is known about what factors are related to satisfaction, but very little is known about the causal basis for the relationships. This is a serious problem when one attempts to base change efforts on the research. This problem also increases the difficulty of developing and testing theories of satisfaction. Perhaps the best example of the resulting dilemma concerns the relationship between satisfaction and performance. If satisfaction causes performance, then organizations should try to see that their employees are satisfied; however, if performance causes satisfaction, then high satisfaction is not necessarily a goal but rather a by-product of an effective organization.

Why has the research on job satisfaction developed so slowly and in such an atheoretical way? One important reason seems to be the lack of attention paid to job satisfaction by psychologists interested in learning, development, and other traditional psychological topics. In marked contrast is the area of motivation where . . . a number of theories have been stated. Motivation theories from other areas of psychology have proven very helpful in understanding motivation in organizations and have formed the basis for our approach to thinking about motivation in organizations.

Unfortunately, no similar set of theories exists in the area of satisfaction. What little theory there is comes almost entirely from the research of industrial psychologists. In some cases this theory is not explicit but is implied by the way satisfaction is measured. For example, although Porter (1961) has never presented an actual theory of satisfaction, a particular manner of defining satisfaction is implicit in his approach to measuring need satisfaction. His approach indicates that he sees satisfaction as the difference between what a person thinks he should receive and what he feels he actually does receive. Before examining in detail any of the theories of job satisfaction, it is important to distinguish between the concepts of facet or factor satisfaction and overall job satisfaction. Facet satisfaction refers to people's affective reactions to particular aspects of their job. Pay, supervision, and promotion opportunities are frequently studied facets. Job satisfaction refers to a person's affective reactions to his total work role. . . .

Theories of Job Satisfaction

Four approaches can be identified in the theoretical work on satisfaction. Fulfillment theory was the first approach to develop. Equity theory and discrepancy theory developed later, partially as reactions against the shortcomings of fulfillment theory. Two-factor theory, the fourth approach, represents an attempt to develop a completely new approach to thinking about satisfaction.

Fulfillment Theory

Schaffer (1953) has argued that "job satisfaction will vary directly with the extent to which those needs of an individual which can be satisfied are actually satisfied" (p. 3). Vroom (1964) also sees job satisfaction in terms of the degree to which a job provides the person with positively valued outcomes. He equates satisfaction with valence and adds "If we describe a person as satisfied with an object, we mean that the object has positive valence for him. However, satisfaction has a much more restricted usage. In common parlance, we refer to a person's satisfaction only with reference to objects which he possesses" (p. 100). Researchers who have adopted the fulfillment approach measure people's satisfaction by simply asking how much of a given facet or outcome they are receiving. Thus, these researchers view satisfaction as depending on how much of a given outcome or group of outcomes a person receives. . . .

Discrepancy Theory

Recently, many psychologists have argued for a discrepancy approach to thinking about satisfaction. They maintain that satisfaction is determined by the differences between the actual outcomes a person receives and some other outcome level. The theories differ widely in their definitions of this other outcome level. For some theories it is the outcome level the person feels should be received, and for other theories it is the outcome level the person expects to receive. All of the theoretical approaches argue that what is received should be compared with another outcome level, and when there is a difference—when received outcome is below the other outcome level—dissatisfaction results. Thus, if a person expects or thinks he should receive a salary of $10,000 and he receives one of only $8,000, the prediction is that he will be dissatisfied with his pay. Further, the prediction is that he will be more dissatisfied than the person who receives a salary of $9,000 and expects or thinks he should receive a salary of $10,000. . . .

Equity Theory

Equity theory is primarily a motivation theory, but it has some important things to say about the causes of satisfaction/dissatisfaction. Adams (1963, 1965) argues in his version of equity theory that satisfaction is determined by a person's perceived input-outcome balance in the following manner: the perceived equity of a person's rewards is determined by his input-outcome balance; this perceived equity, in turn, determines satisfaction. Satisfaction results when perceived equity exists, and dissatisfaction results when perceived inequity exists. Thus, satisfaction is determined by the perceived ratio of what a person receives from his job relative to what a person puts into his job. According to equity theory, either under-reward or over-reward can lead to dissatisfaction, although the feelings are somewhat different. The theory emphasizes that over-reward leads to feelings of guilt, while under-reward leads to feelings of unfair treatment. . . .

Two-factor Theory

Modern two-factor theory was originally developed in a book by Herzberg, Mausner, Peterson, and Capwell (1957), in which the authors stated that job factors could be classified according to whether the factors contribute primarily to satisfaction or to dissatisfaction. Two years later, Herzberg, Mausner, and Snyderman (1959) published the results of a research study, which they interpreted as supportive of the theory. Since 1959, much research has been directed toward testing two-factor theory. Two aspects of the theory are unique and account for the attention it has received. First, two-factor theory says that satisfaction and dissatisfaction do not exist on a continuum running from satisfaction through neutral to dissatisfaction. Two independent continua exist, one running from satisfied to neutral, and another running from dissatisfied to neutral (see Figure 1). Second, the theory stresses that different job facets influence feelings of satisfaction and dissatisfaction. Figure 2 presents the results of a study by Herzberg et al., which show that factors such as achievement recognition, work itself, and responsibility are mentioned in connection with satisfying experiences, while working conditions, interpersonal relations, supervision, and company policy are usually mentioned in connection with dissatisfying experiences. The figure shows the frequency with which each factor is mentioned in connection with high (satisfying) and low (dissatisfying) work experiences. As can be seen, achievement was present in over 40 percent of the satisfying experiences and less than 10 percent of the dissatisfying experiences.

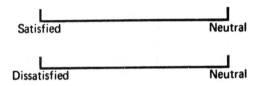

Figure 1. Two-factor Theory: Satisfaction Continued

Perhaps the most interesting aspect of Herzberg's theory is that at the same time a person can be very satisfied and very dissatisfied. Also, the theory implies that factors such as better working conditions cannot increase or cause satisfaction, they can only affect the amount of dissatisfaction that is experienced. The only way satisfaction can be increased is by effecting changes in those factors that are shown in Figure 2 as contributing primarily to satisfaction. . . .

Equity Theory and/or Discrepancy Theory

Equity theory and discrepancy theory are the two strongest theoretical explanations of satisfaction. Either theory could be used as a basis for thinking about the determinants of satisfaction. Fortunately it is not necessary to choose between the theories, since it is possible to build a satisfaction model that capitalizes on the strengths of each theory. . . . We will try to build such a model. In many ways, equity theory and discrepancy theory are quite similar. Both theories stress the importance of a person's perceived outcomes, along with the relationship of these outcomes to a second perception. In discrepancy theory, the second perception is what the outcomes should be or what the person wants the outcomes to be; in equity theory, the second perception is what a person's perceived inputs are in relation to other people's inputs and outcomes. Clearly, it could be argued that the two theories are talking about very similar concepts when they talk about perceived inputs and the subject's feeling about what his outcomes should be. A person's perception of what his outcomes should be is partly determined by what he feels his inputs are. Thus, the "should be" phrase from discrepancy theory and the "perceived inputs relative to other people's inputs and outcomes" phrase from equity theory are very similar.

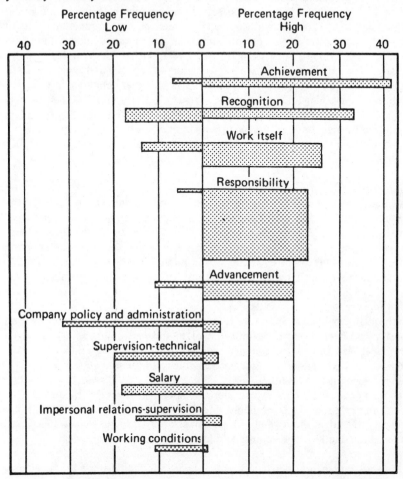

Figure 2. Comparison of Satisfiers and Dissatisfiers (Adapted from Herzberg et al., *The Motivation to Work*, 2nd ed., copyright ©1959 by John Wiley & Sons, Inc., reprinted by permission.)

Determinants of Satisfaction

The research on the determinants of satisfaction has looked primarily at two relationships: (1) the relationship between satisfaction and the characteristics of the job, and (2) the relationship between satisfaction and the characteristics of the person. Not surprisingly, the research shows that satisfaction is a function of both the person and the environment. These results are consistent with our approach to thinking about satisfaction . . . that personal factors influence what people feel they should receive and that job conditions influence both what people perceive they actually receive and what people perceive they should receive. . . .

The evidence on the effects of personal-input factors on satisfaction is voluminous and will be only briefly reviewed. The research clearly shows that personal factors do affect job satisfaction, basically because they influence perceptions of what outcomes should be. . . . The higher a person's perceived personal inputs—that is, the greater his education, skill, and performance—the more he feels he should receive. Thus, unless the high-input person receives more outcomes, he will be dissatisfied with his job and the rewards his job offers. Such straightforward relationships between inputs and satisfaction appear to exist for all personal-input factors except age and seniority. Evidence from the study of age and seniority suggests a curvilinear relationship (that is, high satisfaction among young and old workers, low satisfaction among middle-age workers) or even a relationship of increasing satisfaction with old age and tenure. The tendency of satisfaction to be high among older, long-term employees seems to be produced by the effects of selective turnover and the development of realistic expectations about what the job has to offer.

Consequences of Dissatisfaction

Originally, much of the interest in job satisfaction stemmed from the belief that job satisfaction influenced job performance. Specifically, psychologists thought that high job satisfaction led to high job performance. This view has now been discredited, and most psychologists feel that satisfaction influences absenteeism and turnover but not job performance. However, before looking at the relationship among satisfaction, absenteeism, and turnover, let's review the work on satisfaction and performance.

Job Performance

In the 1950s, two major literature reviews showed that in most studies only a slight relationship had been found between satisfaction and performance. A later review by Vroom (1964) also showed that studies had not found a strong relationship between satisfaction and performance; in fact, most studies had found a very low positive relationship between the two. In other words, better performers did seem to be slightly more satisfied than poor performers. A considerable amount of recent work suggests that the slight existing relationship is probably due to better performance indirectly causing satisfaction rather than the reverse. Lawler and Porter (1967) explained this "performance causes satisfaction" viewpoint as follows:

> If we assume that rewards cause satisfaction, and that in some cases performance produces rewards, then it is possible that the relationship found between satisfaction and performance comes about through the action of a third variable —rewards. Briefly stated, good performance may lead to rewards, which in turn lead to satisfaction; this formulation then would say that satisfaction rather than causing performance, as was previously assumed, is caused by it.

[Figure 3] shows that performance leads to rewards, and it distinguishes between two kinds of rewards and their connection to performance. A wavy line between performance and extrinsic rewards indicates that such rewards are likely to be imperfectly related to performance. By extrinsic rewards is meant such organizationally controlled rewards as pay, promotion, status, and security —rewards that are often referred to as satisfying mainly lower-level needs. The connection is relatively weak because of the difficulty of tying extrinsic rewards directly to performance. Even though an organization may have a policy of rewarding merit, performance is difficult to measure, and in dispensing rewards like pay, many other factors are frequently taken into consideration.

Quite the opposite is likely to be true for intrinsic rewards, however, since they are given to the individual by himself for good performance. Intrinsic or internally mediated rewards are subject to fewer disturbing influences and thus are likely to be more directly related to good performance. This connection is indicated in the model by a semi-wavy line. Probably the best example of an intrinsic reward is the feeling of having accomplished something worthwhile. For that matter any of the rewards that satisfy self-actualization needs or higher-order growth needs are good examples of intrinsic rewards [p. 23-24].[1]

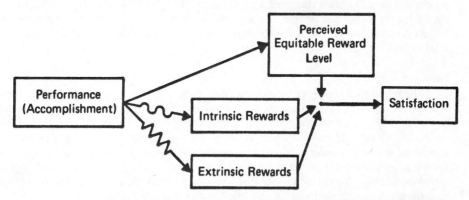

Figure 3. Model of the Relationship of Performance to Satisfaction (From Lawler, E. E., and Porter, L. W., "The Effect of Performance on Job Satisfaction," (in *Industrial Relations,* 1967, 7, 20-28. Reprinted by permission of the publisher, Industrial Relations.)

Figure 3 shows that intrinsic and extrinsic rewards are not directly related to job satisfaction, since the relationship is moderated by perceived equitable rewards (what people think they should receive). The model in Figure 3 . . . shows that satisfaction is a function of the amount of rewards a person receives and the amount of rewards he feels he should receive.

Because of the imperfect relationship between performance and rewards and the important effect of perceived equitable rewards, a low but positive relationship should exist between job satisfaction and job performance in most situations. However, in certain situations, a strong positive relationship may exist; while in other situations, a negative relationship may exist. A negative relationship would be expected where rewards are unrelated to performance or negatively related to performance.

To have the same level of satisfaction for good performers and poor performers, the good performers must receive more rewards than the poor performers. The reason for this, as stressed earlier, is that performance level influences the amount of rewards a person feels she should receive. Thus, when rewards are not based on performance —when poor performers receive equal rewards or a larger amount of rewards than good performers—the best performers will be the least satisfied, and a negative satisfaction-performance relationship will exist. If, on the other hand, the better performers are given significantly more rewards, a positive satisfaction-performance relationship should exist. If it is assumed that most organizations are partially successful in relating rewards to performance, it follows that most studies should find a low but positive relationship between satisfaction and performance. Lawler and Porter's (1967) study was among those that found this relationship; their study also found that, as predicted, intrinsic-need satisfaction was more closely related to performance than was extrinsic-need satisfaction.

In retrospect, it is hard to understand why the belief that high satisfaction causes high performance was so widely accepted. There is nothing in the literature on motivation that suggests this causal relationship. In fact, such a relationship is opposite to the concepts developed by both drive theory and expectancy theory. If anything, these two theories would seem to predict that high satisfaction might reduce motivation because of a consequent reduction in the importance of various rewards that may have provided motivational force. Clearly, a more logical view is that performance is determined by people's efforts to obtain the goals and outcomes they desire, and satisfaction is determined by the outcomes people actually obtain. Yet, for some reason, many people believed—and some people still do believe—that the "satisfaction causes performance" view is best.

Turnover

The relationship between satisfaction and turnover has been studied often. In most studies, researchers have measured the job satisfaction among a number of employees and then waited to see which of the employees studied left during an ensuing time period (typically, a year). The satisfaction scores of the employees who left have then been compared with the remaining employees' scores. Although relationships between satisfaction scores and turnover have not always been very strong, the studies in this area have consistently shown that dissatisfied workers are more likely than satisfied workers to terminate employment; thus, satisfaction scores can predict turnover.

A study by Ross and Zander (1957) is a good example of the kind of research that has been done. Ross and Zander measured the job satisfaction of 2680 female workers in a large company. Four months later, these researchers found that 169 of these employees had resigned; those who left were significantly more dissatisfied with the amount of recognition they received on their jobs, with the amount of achievement they experienced, and with the amount of autonomy they had.

Probably the major reason that turnover and satisfaction are not more strongly related is that turnover is very much influenced by the availability of other positions. Even if a person is very dissatisfied with his job, he is not likely to leave unless more attractive alternatives are available. This observation would suggest that in times of economic prosperity, turnover should be high, and a strong relationship should exist between turnover and satisfaction; but in times of economic hardship, turnover should be low, and little relationship should exist between turnover and satisfaction. There is research evidence to support the argument that voluntary turnover is much lower in periods of economic hardship. However, no study has compared the relationship between satisfaction and turnover under different economic conditions to see if it is stronger under full employment.

Absenteeism

Like turnover, absenteeism has been found to be related to job satisfaction. If anything, the relationship between satisfaction and absenteeism seems to be stronger than the relationship between satisfaction and turnover. However, even in the case of absenteeism, the relationship is far from being isomorphic. Absenteeism is caused by a number of factors other than a person's voluntarily deciding not to come to work; illness, accidents, and so on can prevent someone who wants to come to work from actually coming to work. We would expect satisfaction to affect only voluntary absences; thus, satisfaction can never be strongly related to a measure of overall absence rate. Those studies that have separated voluntary absences from overall absences have, in fact, found that voluntary absence rates are much more closely related to satisfaction than are overall absence rates (Vroom, 1964). Of course, this outcome would be expected if satisfaction does influence people's willingness to come to work.

Organization Effectiveness

The research evidence clearly shows that employees' decisions about whether they will go to work on any given day and whether they will quit are affected by their feelings of job satisfaction. All the literature reviews on the subject have reached this conclusion. The fact that present satisfaction influences future absenteeism and turnover clearly indicates that the causal direction is from satisfaction to behavior. This conclusion is in marked contrast to our conclusion with respect to performance—that is, behavior causes satisfaction. . . .

The research evidence on the determinants of satisfaction suggests that satisfaction is very much influenced by the actual rewards a person receives; of course, the organization has a considerable amount of control over these rewards. The research also shows that, although not all people will react to the same reward level in the same manner, reactions are predictable if something is known about how people perceive their inputs. The implication is that organizations can influence employees' satisfaction levels. Since it is possible to know how employees will react to different outcome levels, organizations can allocate outcomes in ways that will either cause job satisfaction or job dissatisfaction.

Absenteeism and turnover have a very direct influence on organizational effectiveness. Absenteeism is very costly because it interrupts scheduling, creates a need for over-staffing, increases fringe-benefit costs, and so on. Turnover is expensive because of the many costs incurred in recruiting and training replacement employees. For lower-level jobs, the cost of turnover is estimated at $2000 a person; at the managerial level, the cost is at least five to ten times the monthly salary of the job involved. Because satisfaction is manageable and influences absenteeism and turnover, organizations can control absenteeism and turnover. Generally, by keeping satisfaction high and, specifically, by seeing that the best employees are the most satisfied, organizations can retain those employees they need the most. In effect, organizations can manage turnover so that, if it occurs, it will occur among employees the organization can most afford to lose. However, keeping the better performers more satisfied is not easy, since they must be rewarded very well. . . . Although identifying and rewarding the better performers is not always easy, the effort may have significant payoffs in terms of increased organizational effectiveness.

Note

1. Lawler, E. E., and Porter, L. W. The effect of performance on job satisfaction. *Industrial Relations*, 1967, 7, 20-28.

References

Adams, J. S. Toward an understanding of inequity. *Journal of Abnormal Psychology*, 1963, 67, 422-436.

Adams, J. S. Injustice in social exchange. In L. Berkowitz (Ed.), *Advances in experimental social psychology*. Vol. 2. New York: Academic Press, 1965.

Gardner, J. W. *No easy victories*. New York: Harper & Row, 1968.

Herzberg, F., Mausner, B., Peterson, R. O., & Capwell, D. F. *Job attitudes: Review of research and opinion*. Pittsburgh: Psychological Service of Pittsburgh, 1957.

Herzberg, F., Mausner, B., & Snyderman, B. *The motivation to work*. (2nd ed.) New York: John Wiley & Sons, 1959.

Hoppock, R. *Job satisfaction*. New York: Harper & Row, 1935.

Lawler, E. E., & Porter, L. W. The effect of performance on job satisfaction. *Industrial Relations*, 1967, 7, 20-28.

Locke, E. A. What is job satisfaction? Paper presented at the APA Convention, San Francisco, September 1968.

Locke, E. A. What is job satisfaction? *Organizational Behavior and Human Performance*, 1969, 4, 309-336.

Porter, L. W. A study of perceived need satisfactions in bottom and middle management jobs. *Journal of Applied Psychology*, 1961, 45, 1-10.

Roethlisberger, F. J., & Dickson, W. J. *Management and the worker*. Cambridge, Mass.: Harvard University Press, 1939.

Ross, I. E., & Zander, A. F. Need satisfaction and employee turnover. *Personnel Psychology*, 1957, 10, 327-338.

Schaffer, R. H. Job satisfaction as related to need satisfaction in work. *Psychological Monographs*, 1953, 67 (14, Whole No. 364).

Vroom, V. H. *Work and motivation*. New York: John Wiley & Sons, 1964.

Organizational, Work, and Personal Factors in Employee Turnover and Absenteeism

LYMAN W. PORTER
RICHARD M. STEERS

To those concerned with studying the behavior of individuals in organizational settings, employee turnover and absenteeism represent both interesting and important phenomena. They are relatively clear-cut acts of behavior that have potentially critical consequences both for the person and for the organization. It is probably for this reason that turnover and absenteeism have been investigated in a relatively large number of studies to date and are likely to remain a key focus of personnel research by psychologists. . . .

In the past, there have been some four reviews of the literature dealing with turnover and absenteeism. Three of these (Brayfield & Crockett, 1955; Herzberg, Mausner, Peterson, & Capwell, 1957; Vroom, 1964) are now somewhat dated in relation to all of the research carried out during the past decade or so, and the fourth (Schuh,

Reprinted by permission of the author and the publisher from *Psychological Bulletin*, vol. 80 (1973), no. 2, pp. 151-76. The research was supported by a grant from the Office of Naval Research, Contract No. N00014-69-A-0200-9001, NR 151-315.

1967) represents a highly specialized review of only a portion of the available literature. Before proceeding to our own analysis of the recent literature, it will be helpful to summarize briefly what was uncovered by these previous reviews.

Brayfield and Crockett (1955) and Herzberg et al. (1957) both found evidence of a strong relationship between employee dissatisfaction and withdrawal behavior (i.e., both turnover and absenteeism). Brayfield and Crockett went further, however, to point out major methodological weaknesses in a number of the studies, such as the failure to obtain independent measures and the use of weak or ambiguous measurement techniques. In fact, such flaws were so prevalent that they questioned whether methodological changes alone would substantially alter the magnitude of direction of many of the obtained relationships. In general, then, Brayfield and Crockett pointed as much to a need for increased rigor in research techniques as toward the acceptance or rejection of an attitude-withdrawal relationship.

Several years later, Vroom (1964) again reviewed the literature pertaining to job satisfaction and withdrawal. The results of his analysis generally reinforced the earlier conclusions. Vroom reported that the studies he reviewed showed a consistent negative relationship between job satisfaction and the propensity to leave. In addition, he found a somewhat less consistent negative relationship between job satisfaction and absenteeism. Vroom interpreted the findings concerning job satisfaction and withdrawal as being consistent with an expectancy/valence theory of motivation; namely, workers who are highly attracted to their jobs are presumed to be subject to motivational forces to remain in them, with such forces manifesting themselves in increased tenure and higher rates of attendance.

Schuh's (1967) review focused primarily on studies of the prediction of turnover by the means of personality and vocational inventories and biographical information. From his review, he concluded that there was not a consistent relationship between turnover and scores on intelligence, aptitude, and personality tests. On the other hand, some evidence was found that vocational interest inventories and scaled biographical information blanks could be used to fairly accurately predict turnover. Moreover, a very small number of older studies pertaining to job satisfaction were cited in the review, and these too seemed predictive of turnover. . . .

Job Satisfaction and Withdrawal

Subsequent to the publication of the earlier reviews, a number of new investigations have appeared concerning the relationship of overall job satisfaction to turnover and absenteeism. These findings are briefly summarized here in order to determine how they relate to the earlier findings as previously reviewed.

In two related predictive studies of particular merit, Hulin investigated the impact of job satisfaction on turnover among female clerical workers. Using the Job Descriptive Index as a measure of job attitudes, Hulin's (1966) first study matched each subject who subsequently left the company over a 12-month period with two "stayers" along several demographic dimensions. Significant differences were found between the stayer and leaver groups on mean satisfaction scores. Hulin concluded that at least in this sample, subsequent leavers *as a group* could be accurately distinguished from stayers based on a knowledge of the workers' degree of job satisfaction up to 12 months prior to the act of termination.

These findings raised the question as to the possibility of reducing this turnover by increasing a worker's degree of satisfaction on the job. Toward this end, the company instituted new policies in the areas of salary administration and promotional opportunities. Approximately 1-1½ years after these changes, Hulin (1968) again administered the Job Descriptive Index to a sample similar to the previous one. Subsequent leavers were matched with two stayers each, and again it was found that termination decisions were significantly related to the degree of worker satisfaction. Equally important was the finding that satisfaction scores with four of the five Job Descriptive Index scales rose significantly between the first and second studies. Simultaneously, the department's turnover rate between these two periods dropped from 30 percent during the first study period to 12 percent during the second.

Other important studies have yielded essentially the same results among life insurance agents (Weitz & Nuckols, 1955), male and female office workers (Mikes & Hulin, 1968), retail store employees (Taylor & Weiss, 1969a, 1969b), and female operatives (Wild, 1970).

Taking a somewhat different approach to the topic, Katzell (1968) and Dunnette, Arvey, and Banas[1] investigated the role of employee expectations at the time of hire as they related to later job experiences and turnover. In both studies, no significant differences were found to exist at the time of entry between the expectation levels of those who remained and those who later decided to leave. However, as time went on, significant differences did emerge; those who remained generally felt their original expectations were essentially met on the job, while those who left felt their expectations had not been met.

Also relevant to the role of met expectations in the participation decision are the field experiments of Weitz (1956), Youngberg (1963), and Macedonia (1969). These studies (described in greater detail below) found that where individuals were provided with a realistic picture of job environment—including its difficulties—prior to employment, such subjects apparently adjusted their job expectations to more realistic levels. These new levels were then apparently more easily met by the work environment, resulting in reduced turnover.

Many studies, therefore, point to the importance of job satisfaction as a predictor of turnover. However, it appears that expressed intentions concerning future participation may be an even better predictor. In a large scale investigation of managerial personnel, Kraut[2] consistently found significant correlations between expressed intent to stay and subsequent employee participation. Such findings were far stronger than relationships between expressed satisfaction and continued participation. And, in a study of turnover among Air Force pilots, Atchison and Lefferts (1972) found that the frequency with which individuals thought about leaving their job was significantly related to rate termination. Based on these preliminary findings, an argument can be made that an expressed intention to leave may represent the next logical step after experienced dissatisfaction in the withdrawal process.

While considerable investigation has been carried out since the previous reviews concerning the relation of job satisfaction to turnover, only two studies have been found considering such satisfaction as it relates to absenteeism. Talacchi (1960), using the Science Research Associates' Employee Inventory, found a significant inverse relation between job satisfaction and absenteeism among office workers. He did not, however, find such a relation concerning turnover. And Waters and Roach (1971), using the Job Descriptive Index with clerical workers, found significant inverse relations between job satisfaction and both turnover and absenteeism.

In summary, the recent evidence concerning the impact of job satisfaction on withdrawal (especially on turnover) is generally consistent with the findings as reviewed by Brayfield and Crockett (1955), Herzberg et al. (1957), and Vroom (1964). (These new findings are summarized in Table 1.) It appears, however, that the major asset of these more recent findings is not simply their confirming nature but rather their increased methodological rigor over those studies reviewed previously. Most of the earlier studies contained several design weaknesses (see, e.g., the discussion by Brayfield & Crockett) which the more recent studies have overcome to a significant degree. For example, 12 of the 15 new studies reviewed here were predictive in nature. In addition, several of the research instruments used in the more recent studies (e.g., the Job Descriptive Index) appear to be more rigorously designed in terms of validity, reliability, and norms. Thus, these newer studies go a long way in the direction of providing increased confidence in the importance of job satisfaction as a force in the decision to participate.

TABLE 1
STUDIES OF RELATION OF JOB SATISFACTION TO TURNOVER AND ABSENTEEISM

Investigator(s)	Population	n^1	Type of withdrawal studied	Relation to withdrawal
Weitz & Nuckols (1955)	Insurance agents	990	Turnover	Negative
Weitz (1956)	Insurance agents	474	Turnover	Negative
Talacchi (1960)	Departmental workers	NA	{ Turnover	Zero
			Absenteeism	Negative
Youngberg (1963)	Insurance salesmen	NA	Turnover	Negative
Hulin (1966)	Female clerical workers	129	Turnover	Negative
Hulin (1968)	Female clerical workers	298	Turnover	Negative
Katzell (1968)	Student nurses	1852	Turnover	Negative
Mikes & Hulin (1968)	Office workers	660	Turnover	Negative
Dunnette et al.	Lower level managers	1020	Turnover	Negative
Macedonia (1969)	Military academy cadets	1160	Turnover	Negative
Taylor & Weiss (1969a, 1969b)	Retail store employees	475	Turnover	Negative
Kraut	Computer salesmen	Varied	Turnover	Negative
Wild (1970)	Female manual workers	236	Turnover	Negative
Waters & Roach (1971)	Female clerical workers	160	{ Turnover	Negative
			Absenteeism	Negative
Atchison & Lefferts (1972)[2]	Air Force pilots	52	Turnover	Negative

Note. NA = not available.

[1] Sample sizes reported here and on the following tables reflect the actual number of subjects used in the data analysis from which the reported results were derived.

[2] Both Kraut, and Atchison and Lefferts found that an expressed intention to leave represented an even more accurate predictor of turnover than job satisfaction.

Specific Factors Related to Withdrawal

While consideration of the role of overall job satisfaction in the decision to partici-pate is important, it tells us little about the roots of such satisfaction. Knowing that an employee is dissatisfied and about to leave does not help us understand *why* he is dissatisfied, nor does it help us determine what must be changed in an effort to retain him. For the answer to these critical questions, it is necessary to look more closely at the various factors of the work situation as they potentially relate to the propensity to withdraw. We begin our discussion with those factors that are generally organizationwide in their impact on employees and move toward those factors that are more unique to each individual.

Organization-wide Factors

Organization-wide factors for purposes of this discussion can be defined as those variables affecting the individual that are primarily determined by persons or events external to the immediate work group. Under this rubric would fall such factors as pay and promotion policies and organization size. . . .

The results of . . . investigations relating organizational environment factors to withdrawal, are summarized in Table 2.

Pay and promotional considerations often appear to represent significant factors in

TABLE 2
STUDIES OF RELATIONS BETWEEN ORGANIZATION-WIDE FACTORS
AND TURNOVER AND ABSENTEEISM

Factor	Population	*n*	Type of withdrawal studied	Relation to with-drawal
Satisfaction with pay and promotion				
Patchen (1960)	Oil refinery workers	487	Absenteeism	Negative
Friedlander & Walton (1964)	Scientists and engineers	82	Turnover	Negative
Knowles (1964)	Factory workers	56	Turnover	Negative
Saleh et al. (1965)	Nurses	263	Turnover	Negative
Bassett (1967)[1]	Engineers	200	Turnover	Negative
Ronan (1967)	Administrative & professional personnel	91	Turnover	Negative
Hulin (1968)	Female clerical workers	298	Turnover	Negative
Dunnette et al.	Lower level managers	1020	Turnover (pay)	Zero
			Turnover (promotion)	Negative
Kraut	Computer salesmen	Varied	Turnover	Negative
Telly et al. (1971)	Factory workers	900	Turnover	Zero[2]
Conference Board (1972)	Salesmen; management trainees	Varied	Turnover	Negative
Participation in compensation plan design				
Lawler & Hackman (1969)	Custodians	83	Absenteeism	Negative
Scheflen et al. (1971)	Custodians	NA	Absenteeism	Negative
Organization size				
Ingham (1970)	Factory workers	8 units	Turnover	Zero
			Absenteeism	Positive

Note. NA = not available.

[1] Bassett posited such a relationship but did not specifically test for it.

[2] This relation was explained by the nature of the union contract, which standardized pay and promotion procedures based essentially on seniority.

the termination decision. While several of the recent studies reviewed simply confirmed such a conclusion, other studies investigated the reasons behind such a relationship. These studies fairly consistently pointed out the importance of perceived equity and met expectations as important forces in such a decision. The size of the pay raise or the rate of promotion, while important in and of themselves, are, in addition, weighed by an employee in the light of his expectations, given his level of self-perceived contribution. The resulting determination of his degree of satisfaction or dissatisfaction then apparently inputs into his decision to remain or to search for preferable job alternatives.

The results of one study indicated that turnover rates appear to be fairly constant among organizations of varying sizes, while absenteeism is significantly higher in larger firms than in smaller ones. Some theoretical considerations were offered to explain this variance but were not effectively substantiated by empirical data.

Immediate Work Environment Factors

A second set of factors instrumental in the decision to withdraw centers around the immediate work situation in which the employee finds himself. In previous reviews, Brayfield and Crockett (1955) found that negative employee attitudes toward their job context (especially at the lower levels) were significantly related to absenteeism and, to a lesser extent, to turnover. And Herzberg et al. (1957) found that such factors as the nature of the social work group were of particular importance in the decision to participate.

Since these reviews were published, significant research has been carried out which tends to supplement existing knowledge concerning the importance of immediate work environment factors in withdrawal. Factors to be considered here include *(a)* supervisory style, *(b)* work unit size, and *(c)* the nature of peer group interaction. . . .

These findings, summarized in Table 3, provide a relatively clear picture of the relation of at least three immediate work environment factors to an employee's decision to participate or withdraw. Several studies have pointed to the importance of supervisory style as a major factor in turnover. Apparently, when one's expectations concerning what the nature of supervision should be like remain substantially unmet, his propensity to leave increases. No studies, however, have been found relating supervisory style to absenteeism. This neglect of absenteeism studies is rather surprising considering the widely accepted notion of the centrality of the supervisor as a factor in such withdrawal.

The size of the working unit has been shown to be related to both turnover and absenteeism among blue-collar workers; however, insufficient evidence is available to draw conclusions concerning such influence on managerial or clerical personnel.

Finally, most of the research in the area of co-worker satisfaction demonstrates the potential importance of such satisfaction in retention. Such findings, however, are not universal. A possible explanation for the divergent findings is that some people have a lower need for affiliation than others and may place less importance on satisfactory co-worker relations. Alternatively, it is possible that some organizational settings provide for a greater degree of peer group interaction, thereby increasing the probability that one's level of expectations would be met in this area. In either event, co-worker dissatisfaction cannot be overlooked as a possible cause of attrition.

Job Content Factors

It has long been thought that the duties and activities required for the successful performance of an individual's particular job can have a significant impact on his decision to remain with and participate in the employing organization. Such job require-

TABLE 3
STUDIES OF RELATIONS BETWEEN IMMEDIATE WORK ENVIRONMENT FACTORS AND TURNOVER AND ABSENTEEISM

Factor	Population	n	Type of withdrawal studied	Relation to withdrawal
Satisfaction with supervisory relations				
Fleishman & Harris (1962)	Production workers	NA[1]	Turnover	Negative (curvilinear)
Saleh et al. (1965)	Nurses	263	Turnover	Negative
Ley (1966)	Production workers	100	Turnover	Negative
Hulin (1968)	Female clerical workers	298	Turnover	Negative
Skinner (1969)	Production workers	85	Turnover	Negative (curvilinear
Taylor & Weiss (1969a,1969b)	Retail store employees	475	Turnover	Zero
Telly et al. (1971)	Production workers	900	Turnover	Negative
Receipt of recognition and feedback				
Ross & Zander (1957)	Female skilled workers	507	Turnover	Negative
General Electric Company (1964a)	Engineers	36	Turnover	Negative
Supervisory experience				
Bassett (1967)	Technicians and engineers	200	Turnover	Negative
Work unit size				
Kerr et al. (1951)	Production workers	894	Turnover	Positive
			Absenteeism	Positive
Acton Society Trust (1953)	Factory workers	91	Absenteeism	Positive
Hewitt & Parfitt (1953)	Factory workers	179	Absenteeism	Positive
Metzner & Mann (1953)	Blue-Collar workers	251	Absenteeism	Positive
	White-collar workers	375	Absenteeism	Zero
Mandell (1956)	Clerical workers	320	Turnover	Positive
Argyle et al. (1958)	Production departments	86	Turnover	Zero
			Absenteeism	Positive (curvilinear)
Revans (1958)	Factory workers	Varied	Absenteeism	Positive
Baumgartel & Sobol (1959)	Blue- and white-collar workers	3900	Absenteeism	positive
Indik & Seashore (1961)	Factory workers	NA	Turnover	Positive
			Absenteeism	positive
Satisfactory peer group interactions				
Evan (1963)[2]	Management trainees	300	Turnover	Negative
Hulin (1968)	Female clerical workers	298	Turnover	Negative
Taylor & Weiss, (1969a,1969b)	Retail store employees	475	Turnover	Zero
Farris (1971)	Scientists and engineers	395	Turnover	Negative
Telly et al. (1971)	Production workers	900	Turnover	Negative
Waters & Roach (1971)	Clerical workers	160	Turnover	Zero
			Absenteeism	Negative

Note. NA = not available.

[1] A total of 56 foremen plus approximately 3 subordinates of each foreman took part in the study: specific N not reported.

[2] Inference based on study results.

ments are presumed to represent for the individual either a vehicle for personal fulfillment and satisfaction or a continual source of frustration, internal conflict, and dissatisfaction. In recent years, several new investigations have appeared which provide added clarity to the role of such job-related factors in the withdrawal process. Four such factors will be discussed here: (*a*) the overall reaction to job content, (*b*) task repetitiveness, (*c*) job autonomy and responsibility, and (*d*) role clarity. . . .

In general, turnover has been found to be positively related to dissatisfaction with the content of the job among both blue- and white-collar workers. Insufficient evidence

TABLE 4
STUDIES OF RELATIONS BETWEEN JOB CONTENT FACTORS AND
TURNOVER AND ABSENTEEISM

Factor	Population	*n*	Type of withdrawal studied	Relation to withdrawal
Satisfaction with job content				
Saleh et al. (1965)	Nurses	263	Turnover	Negative
Hulin (1968)	Clerical workers	298	Turnover	Zero
Katzell (1968)	Student nurses	1852	Turnover	Negative
Dunnette et al.	Lower-level managers	1020	Turnover	Negative
Taylor & Weiss (1969a, 1969b)	Retail store employees	475	Turnover	Negative
Kraut	Computer salesmen	Varied	Turnover	Negative
Wild (1970)	Female manual workers	236	Turnover	Negative
Telly et al. (1971)	Production workers	900	Turnover	Negative
Waters & Roach (1971)	Clerical workers	160	Turnover	Negative
			Absenteeism	Negative
Task repetitiveness				
Guest (1955)	Automobile assembly line workers	18	Turnover	Positive
Kilbridge (1961)	Production workers	568	Turnover	Zero
		331	Absenteeism	Positive
Lefkowitz & Katz (1969)	Factory workers	80	Turnover	Positive
Taylor & Weiss (1969a, 1969b)	Retail store employees	475	Turnover	Positive
Wild (1970)	Female manual workers	236	Turnover	Positive
Job autonomy and responsibility				
Guest (1955)	Automobile assembly line workers	18	Turnover	Negative
Ross & Zander (1957)	Female skilled workers	507	Turnover	Negative
Turner & Lawrence (1965)	Blue-collar workers	403	Absenteeism	Negative
Taylor & Weiss (1969a, 1969b)	Retail store employees	475	Turnover	Negative
Hackman & Lawler (1971)	Telephone operators and clerks	208	Absenteeism	Negative
Waters & Roach (1971)	Clerical workers	160	Turnover	Negative
Role clarity				
Weitz (1956)	Insurance salesmen	474	Turnover	Negative
Youngberg (1963)	Insurance salesmen	NA	Turnover	Negative
Macedonia (1969)	Military academy cadets	1260	Turnover	Negative
Lyons (1971)	Nurses	156	Turnover	Negative

Note. NA = not available.

is available, however, to draw any such conclusions concerning absenteeism, but initial investigations point to a similar relationship. More specifically, the available data tend to indicate that both absenteeism and turnover are positively associated with task repetitiveness, although such a conclusion may represent an oversimplification of the nature of the relationship (see, e.g., Hulin & Blood, 1968). Finally, a strong positive relation has been found consistently between both forms of withdrawal and a perceived lack of sufficient job autonomy or responsibility.

The degree of role clarity on the part of the individual can apparently affect turnover in two ways. First, an accurate picture of the actual tasks required by the organization can function to select out, prior to employment, those who do not feel the rewards offered justify doing such tasks. And, secondly, accurate role perceptions can serve to adjust the expectations of those already employed to more realistic levels as to what is expected of them in terms of performance. The resulting increased congruence between expectations and actual experience apparently can serve to increase satisfaction and continued participation. No conclusions can be drawn concerning the effect of role clarity on absenteeism due to a lack of investigations on the subject.

The results of those studies relating to job content are summarized in Table 4.

Personal Factors

Factors unique to the individual also appear to have a significant impact on the problems of turnover and absenteeism. Such factors include (a) age, (b) tenure with the organization, (c) similarity of job with vocational interest, (d) personality characteristics, and (e) family considerations. While often overlooked by investigators, the inclusion of such items are central to developing a comprehensive model explaining the dynamics of work participation. . . .

The findings concerning personal factors in withdrawal are summarized in Table 5. Age is strongly and negatively related to turnover, while being somewhat positively (though weakly) related to absenteeism. Similarly, increased tenure appears to be strongly related to propensity to remain. One possible explanation here may be that increases in tenure result in increases in personal investment on the part of the employee in the organization (i.e., after a while, he may not be able to "afford" to quit). No solid conclusions can be drawn concerning the impact of tenure on absenteeism, however, due to conflicting results.

From limited studies, turnover appears to be related positively to the similarity between job requirements and vocational interests. No studies were found that related such interests to absenteeism, however. Predicting turnover or absenteeism from interest inventories (assuming they are properly validated) represents an important possibility for organizations because such data can be collected *prior* to employment. Such an advantage does not exist for most predictors of withdrawal.

The majority of studies investigating the relationship between personality traits and withdrawal center around turnover so no conclusions can be drawn about their relation to absenteeism. Apparently, the possession of more extreme personality traits may lead to an increased tendency to leave the organization. While further investigation is definitely in order here, a tendency exists for employees manifesting very high degrees of anxiety, emotional instability, aggression, independence, self-confidence, and ambition to leave the organization at a higher rate than employees possessing such traits in a more moderate degree. The implications of such a phenomenon, if borne out by further research, need also to be investigated for their effects on organizational efficiency and effectiveness. That is, if such a pattern really exists, research is needed as to the desirability for the organization of accepting a higher turnover rate in exchange for

TABLE 5
STUDIES OF RELATIONS BETWEEN PERSONAL FACTORS
AND TURNOVER AND ABSENTEEISM

Factor	Population	n	Type of withdrawal studied	Relation to withdrawal
Age				
Minor (1958)	Female clerical workers	440	Turnover	Negative
Naylor & Vincent (1959)	Female clerical workers	220	Absenteeism	Zero
Fleishman & Berniger (1960)	Female clerical workers	205	Turnover	Negative
de la Mare & Sergean (1961)	Industrial workers	140	Absenteeism	Positive
Shott et al. (1963)	Male office workers	561	Turnover	Zero
	Female office workers		Tenure	Negative
Cooper & Payne (1965)	Construction workers	392	Absenteeism	Positive
Ley (1966)	Factory workers	100	Turnover	Negative
Bassett (1967)	Technicians and engineers	200	Turnover	Negative
Downs (1967)	Public service organization trainees	1736	Turnover	Positive
	Public service organization employees (after training)		Turnover	Negative
Stone & Athelstan (1969)	Clerical workers	453	Turnover	Negative
Farris (1971)	Scientists and engineers	395	Turnover	Negative
Robinson (1972)	Female clerical workers	200	Turnover	Negative
Tenure				
Hill & Trist (1955)	Factory workers	289	Absenteeism	Zero
Baumgartel & Sobol (1959)	Male blue-collar workers	3900	Absenteeism	Negative
	Female blue-collar, male and female white-collar workers		Absenteeism	Positive
Fleishman & Berniger (1960)	Female clerical workers	205	Turnover	Negative
Shott et al. (1963)	Male and female office workers	561	Turnover	Negative
Knowles (1964)	Factory workers	56	Turnover	Negative
Robinson (1972)	Female clerical workers	200	Turnover	Negative
Congruence of job with vocational interests				
Ferguson (1958)	Insurance salesmen	520	Turnover	Negative
Boyd (1961)	Engineers	326	Turnover	Negative
Mayeske (1964)	Foresters	125	Turnover	Negative
"Extreme" personality characteristics[1]				
Cleland & Peck (1959)	Ward attendants	54	Turnover	Positive
Hakkinen & Toivainen (1960)	Miners	135	Turnover	Positive
MacKinney & Wolins (1960)	Male production foremen	175	Turnover	Positive
Meyer & Cuomo (1962)	Engineers	1360	Turnover	Positive
Sinha (1963)	Industrial workers	110	Absenteeism	Positive
Farris (1971)	Technical personnel	395	Turnover	Positive
Family size				
Naylor & Vincent (1959)	Female clerical workers	220	Absenteeism	Positive
Knowles (1964)	Male factory workers	56	Turnover	Negative
Stone & Athelstan (1969)	Female physical therapists	453	Turnover	Positive
Family responsibilities				
Guest (1955)	Male auto assembly line workers	18	Turnover	Positive
Minor (1958)	Female clerical workers	440	Turnover	Positive
Fleishman & Berniger (1960)	Female clerical workers	205	Turnover	Positive
Saleh et al. (1965)	Nurses	263	Turnover	Positive
Robinson (1972)	Female clerical workers	200	Turnover	Positive

[1] See text for more detailed description.

possible resulting increases in performance from such mobile employees. No research has been found that demonstrates that low-turnover employees (those possessing more moderate personality traits) are in fact better performers. Thus, reduced turnover may be an undesirable goal if it is bought at the price of reduced work-force effectiveness.

Finally, family size and family responsibilities were generally found to be positively related to turnover and absenteeism among women, while their impact on men appears to be mixed.

Summary and Discussion

The foregoing review clearly shows that a multiplicity of organizational, work, and personal factors can be associated with the decision to withdraw. It is possible, however, to summarize briefly those factors for which sufficient evidence exists to draw meaningful conclusions concerning their relation to withdrawal.

In general, very strong evidence has been found in support of the contention that *overall* job satisfaction represents an important force in the individual's participation decision. In addition, based on preliminary evidence, such satisfaction also appears to have a significant impact on absenteeism. These trends have been demonstrated among a diversity of work group populations and in organizations of various types and sizes. Moreover, the methodologies upon which these findings are based are generally of a fairly rigorous nature.

However, as noted earlier, it is not sufficient for our understanding of the withdrawal process to simply point to such a relationship. It is important to consider what constitutes job satisfaction. Under the conceptualization presented here, job satisfaction is viewed as the sum total of an individual's met expectations on the job. The more an individual's expectations are met on the job, the greater his satisfaction. Viewing withdrawal within this framework points to the necessity of focusing on the various factors that make up the employee's expectation set.

We have proposed four general categories, or "levels" in the organization, in which factors can be found that affect withdrawal. Sufficient evidence exists to conclude that important influences on turnover can be found in each of these categories. That is, some of the more central variables related to turnover are organization-wide in their derivation (e.g., pay and promotion policies), while others are to be found in the immediate work group (e.g., unit size, supervision, and co-worker relations). Still others are to be found in the content of the job (e.g., nature of job requirements) and, finally, some are centered around the person himself (e.g., age and tenure). Thus, based on these findings, the major roots of turnover appear to be fairly widespread throughout the various facets of organizational structure, as they interact with particular types of individuals.

On a more tentative level, initial findings indicate that role clarity and the receipt of recognition and feedback are also inversely related to turnover. However, not all of the possible factors reviewed here have been found to be clearly or consistently related to termination. For example, conflicting data exist concerning the influence of task repetitiveness and of family size on such withdrawal.

Much less can be concluded about the impact of these factors on absenteeism due to a general lack of available information. Sufficient evidence does exist, however, to conclude with some degree of confidence that increased unit size is strongly and directly related to absenteeism. In addition, tentative evidence suggests that opportunities for participation in decision making and increased job autonomy are inversely related to such behavior.

One further point warrants emphasis here concerning the turnover studies reviewed above. To a large extent, there is an underlying assumption, often inferred but sometimes stated, that the reduction of all turnover is a desirable goal. Such an assumption may be questioned on several grounds. First, from the individual's point of view, leaving an unrewarding job may result in the procurement of a more satisfying one. Second, from the organization's standpoint, some of those who leave may be quite ineffective performers, and their departure would open positions for (hopefully) better performers. The important point here is that a clear distinction should be made in future research efforts between effective and ineffective leavers. The loss of an effective employee may cost far more than the loss of an ineffective one, and the costs of efforts to retain the latter may well exceed the benefits. Third, given the present state of technological flux, turnover may in some ways be considered a necessary evil. It may be necessary to simply accept certain levels of turnover as the price for rapid change and increased efficiency. . . .

References

Acton Society Trust. *Size and morale.* London: Author, 1953.

Argyle, M., Gardner, G., & Cioffi, I. Supervisory methods related to productivity, absenteeism and labor turnover. *Human Relations,* 1958, 11, 23-40.

Atchison, T. J., & Lefferts, E. A. The prediction of turnover using Herzberg's job satisfaction technique. *Personnel Psychology,* 1972, 25, 53-64.

Bassett, G. A. *A study of factors associated with turnover of exempt personnel.* Crotonville, N.Y.: Behavioral Research Service, General Electric Company, 1967.

Baumgartel, H., & Sobol, R. Background and organizational factors in absenteeism. *Personnel Psychology,* 1959, 12, 431-443.

Boyd, J. B. Interests of engineers related to turnover, selection, and management. *Journal of Applied Psychology,* 1961, 45, 143-149.

Brayfield, A. H., & Crockett, W. H. Employee attitudes and employee performance. *Psychological Bulletin,* 1955, 52, 396-424.

Cleland, C. C., & Peck, R. F. Psychological determinants of tenure in institutional personnel. *American Journal of Mental Deficiency,* 1959, 64, 876-888.

Conference Board. *Salesmen's turnover in early employment.* New York: Author, 1972.

Cooper, R., & Payne, R. Age and absence: A longitudinal study in three firms. *Occupational Psychology,* 1965, 39, 31-43.

de la Mare, G., & Sergean, R. Two methods of studying changes in absence with age. *Occupational Psychology,* 1961, 35, 245-252.

Downs, S. Labour turnover in two public service organizations. *Occupational Psychology,* 1967, 41, 137-142.

Evan, W. M. Peer-group interaction and organizational socialization: A study of employee turnover. *American Sociological Review,* 1963, 28, 436-440.

Farris, G. F. A predictive study of turnover. *Personnel Psychology,* 1971, 24, 311-328.

Ferguson, L. W. Life insurance interest, ability and termination of employment. *Personnel Psychology,* 1958, 11, 189-193.

Fleishman, E. A. A leader behavior description for industry. In R. M. Stogdill & A. E. Coons (Eds.), *Leader behavior: Its description and measurement.* (Ohio Studies in Personnel; Research Monograph No. 88) Columbus: Ohio State University, Bureau of Business Research, 1957. (a)

Fleishman, E. A. The Leadership Opinion Questionnaire. In R. M. Stogdill & A. E. Coons (Eds.), *Leader behavior: Its description and measurement.* (Ohio Studies in Personnel; Research Monograph No. 88) Columbus: Ohio State University, Bureau of Business Research, 1957. (b)

Fleishman, E. A. *Revised manual for Leadership Opinion Questionnaire.* Chicago: Science Research Associates, 1968.

Fleishman, E. A., & Berniger, J. One way to reduce office turnover. *Personnel,* 1960, *37,* 63-69.

Fleishman, E. A., & Harris, E. F. Patterns of leadership behavior related to employee grievances and turnover. *Personnel Psychology,* 1962, *15,* 43-56.

Friedlander, F., & Walton, E. Positive and negative motivations toward work. *Administrative Science Quarterly,* 1964, *9,* 194-207.

General Electric Company, Behavioral Research Service. *Attitudes associated with turnover of highly regarded employees.* Crotonville, N.Y.: Author, 1964. (a)

General Electric Company, Behavioral Research Service. *A comparison of work planning program with the annual performance appraisal interview approach.* Crotonville, N.Y.: Author, 1964. (b)

Guest, R. H. A neglected factor in labour turnover. *Occupational Psychology,* 1955, *29,* 217-231.

Hackman, J. R., & Lawler, E. E., III. Employee reactions to job characteristics. *Journal of Applied Psychology,* 1971, *55,* 259-286.

Hakkinen, S., & Toivainen, Y. Psychological factors causing labour turnover among underground workers. *Occupational Psychology,* 1960, *34,* 15-30.

Herzberg, F., Mausner, B., Peterson, R. O., & Capwell, D. F. *Job Attitudes: Review of research and opinion.* Pittsburgh: Psychological Service of Pittsburgh, 1957.

Hewitt, D., & Parfitt, J. A note on working morale and size of group. *Occupational Psychology,* 1953, *27,* 38-42.

Hill, J. M., & Trist, E. L. Changes in accidents and other absences with length of service. *Human Relations,* 1955, *8,* 121-152.

Hulin, C. L. Job satisfaction and turnover in a female clerical population. *Journal of Applied Psychology,* 1966, *50,* 280-285.

Hulin, C. L. Effects of changes in job-satisfaction levels on employee turnover. *Journal of Applied Psychology,* 1968, *52,* 122-126.

Hulin, C. L., & Blood, M. R. Job enlargement, individual differences, and worker responses. *Psychological Bulletin,* 1968, *69,* 41-55.

Indik, B., & Seashore, S. *Effects of organization size on member attitudes and behavior.* Ann Arbor: University of Michigan, Survey Research Center of the Institute for Social Research, 1961.

Ingham, G. *Size of industrial organization and worker behaviour.* Cambridge: Cambridge University Press, 1970.

Kahn, R., Wolfe, D., Quinn, R., Snoek, J., & Rosenthal, R. *Organizational stress: Studies in role conflict and ambiguity.* New York: Wiley, 1964.

Katz, D., Maccoby, E., Gurin, G., & Floor, L. *Productivity, supervision and morale among railroad workers.* Ann Arbor: University of Michigan, Survey Research Center, 1951.

Katz, D., Maccoby, N., & Morse, N. *Productivity, supervision and morale in an office situation.* Ann Arbor: University of Michigan, Institute for Social Research, 1950.

Katzell, M. E. Expectations and dropouts in schools of nursing. *Journal of Applied Psychology,* 1968, *52,* 154-157.

Kerr, W., Koppelmeier, G., & Sullivan, J. Absenteeism, turnover and morale in a metals fabrication factory. *Occupational Psychology,* 1951, *25,* 50-55.

Kilbridge, M. Turnover, absence, and transfer rates as indicators of employee dissatisfaction with repetitive work. *Industrial and Labor Relations Review,* 1961, *15,* 21-32.

Knowles, M. C. Personal and job factors affecting labour turnover. *Personnel Practice Bulletin,* 1964, *20,* 25-37.

Lawler, E. E., III. *Pay and organizational effectiveness: A psychological view.* New York: Mcgraw-Hill, 1971.

Lawler, E. E., III, & Hackman, J. R. Impact of employee participation in the development of pay incentive plans: A field experiment. *Journal of Applied Psychology,* 1969, *53,* 467-471.

Lefkowitz, J., & Katz, M. Validity of exit interviews. *Personnel Psychology,* 1969, *22,* 445-455.

Ley, R. Labour turnover as a function of worker differences, work environment, and authoritarianism of foremen. *Journal of Applied Psychology,* 1966, *50,* 497-500.

Lyons, T. Role clarity, need for clarity, satisfaction, tension and withdrawal. *Organizational Behavior and Human Performance,* 1971, *6,* 99-110.

Macedonia, R. M. Expectation-press and survival. Unpublished doctoral dissertation, Graduate School of Public Administration, New York University, June 1969.

MacKinney, A. C., & Wolins, L. Validity information exchange. *Personnel Psychology,* 1960, *13,* 443-447.

Mandell, M. *Recruiting and selecting office employees.* New York: American Management Association, 1956.

March, J. G., & Simon, H. A. *Organizations.* New York: Wiley, 1958.

Mayeske, G. W. The validity of Kuder Preference Record scores in predicting forester turnover and advancement. *Personnel Psychology,* 1964, *17,* 207-210.

Metzner, H., & Mann, F. Employee attitudes and absences. *Personnel Psychology,* 1953, *6,* 467-485.

Meyer, H., & Cuomo, S. *Who leaves? A study of background characteristics of engineers associated with turnover.* Crotonville, N.Y.: General Electric Company, Behavioral Science Research, 1962.

Mikes, P. S., & Hulin, C. Use of importance as a weighting component of job satisfaction. *Journal of Applied Psychology,* 1968, *52,* 394-398.

Minor, F. J. The prediction of turnover of clerical employees. *Personnel Psychology,* 1958, *11,* 393-402.

Naylor, J. E., & Vincent, N. L. Predicting female absenteeism. *Personnel Psychology,* 1959, *12,* 81-84.

Patchen, M. Absence and employee feelings about fair treatment. *Personnel Psychology,* 1960, *13,* 349-360.

Porter, L. W., & Lawler, E. E., III. Properties of organization structure in relation to job attitudes and job behavior. *Psychological Bulletin,* 1965, *64,* 23-51.

Porter, L. W., & Lawler, E. E., III. *Managerial attitudes and performance.* Homewood, Ill.: Irwin, 1968.

Revans, R. Human relations, management and size. In E. M. Hugh-Jones (Ed.), *Human relations and modern management.* Amsterdam: North-Holland Publishing, 1958.

Robinson, D. D. Prediction of clerical turnover in banks by means of a weighted application blank. *Journal of Applied Psychology,* 1972, *56,* 282.

Ronan, W. W. A study of some concepts concerning labour turnover. *Occupational Psychology,* 1967, *41,* 193-202.

Ross, I. C., & Zander, A. Need satisfaction and employee turnover. *Personnel Psychology,* 1957, *10,* 327-338.

Saleh, S. D., Lee, R. J., & Prien, E. P. Why nurses leave their jobs—An analysis of female turnover. *Personnel Administration,* 1965, *28,* 25-28.

Scheflen, K. C., Lawler, E. E., III, & Hackman, J. R. Long-term impact of employee participation in the development of pay incentive plans: A field experiment revisited. *Journal of Applied Psychology,* 1971, *55,* 182-186.

Schuh, A. The predictability of employee tenure: A review of the literature. *Personnel Psychology,* 1967, *20,* 133-152.

Shott, G. L., Albright, L. E., & Glennon, J. R. Predicting turnover in an automated office situation. *Personnel Psychology,* 1963, *16,* 213-219.

Sinha, A. K. P. Manifest anxiety affecting industrial absenteeism. *Psychological Reports,* 1963, *13,* 258.

Skinner, E. Relationships between leadership behavior patterns and organizational situational variables. *Personnel Psychology,* 1969, *22,* 489-494.

Stogdill, R., & Coons, A. (Eds.) *Leader behavior: Its description and measurement.* Columbus: Ohio State University, Bureau of Business Research, 1957.

Stone, T. H., & Athelstan, G. T. The SVIB for women and demographic variables in the prediction of occupational tenure. *Journal of Applied Psychology,* 1969, *53,* 408-412.

Talacchi, S. Organization size, individual attitudes and behavior: An empirical study. *Administrative Science Quarterly,* 1960, *5,* 398-420.

Taylor, K., & Weiss, D. Prediction of individual job termination from measured job satisfaction and biographical data. (Research Report No. 30) Minneapolis: University of Minnesota, Work Adjustment Project, October 1969. (a)

Taylor, K., & Weiss, D. Prediction of individual job turnover from measured job satisfaction. (Research Report No. 22) Minneapolis: University of Minnesota, Work Adjustment Project, May 1969. (b)

Telly, C. S., French, W. L., & Scott, W. G. The relationship of inequity to turnover among hourly workers. *Administrative Science Quarterly,* 1971, *16,* 164-172.

Turner, A. N., & Lawrence, P. R. *Industrial jobs and the worker: An investigation of response to task attributes.* Boston: Harvard University Press, Division of Research, 1965.

Vroom, V. *Work and motivation.* New York: Wiley, 1964.

Walker, C. R., & Guest, R. H. *The man on the assembly line.* Cambridge: Harvard University Press, 1952.

Waters, L. K., & Roach, D. Relationship between job attitudes and two forms of withdrawal from the work situation. *Journal of Applied Psychology,* 1971, *55,* 92-94.

Weitz, J. Job expectancy and survival. *Journal of Applied Psychology,* 1956, *40,* 245-247.

Weitz, J., & Nuckols, R. C. Job satisfaction and job survival. *Journal of Applied Psychology,* 1955, *39,* 294-300.

Wild, R. Job needs, job satisfaction, and job behavior of women manual workers. *Jounral of Applied Psychology,* 1970, *54,* 157-162.

Youngberg, C. F. An experimental study of "job satisfaction" and turnover in relation to job expectancies and self expectations. Unpublished doctoral dissertation, New York University, 1963.

The Cost of Absenteeism and Turnover in a Large Organization

THOMAS A. JESWALD

It can be argued that managers should be interested in employee job satisfaction simply on the basis of altruism. But, regardless of the degree of concern for the welfare of others which managers feel, the relationship between employee job satisfaction and the organizations's absenteeism and labor turnover is a more relevant consideration in business. Real costs are associated with both absenteeism and turnover. Although these costs are not generally reported on the balance sheet as the more direct business costs are, they are usually identifiable and often calculable.

Industry has paid relatively little attention to the cost of absenteeism and turnover until recently. Indeed, it was not until 1973 that the Bureau of Labor Statistics began to publish national absenteeism data.[1] Perhaps one reason for this apparent lack of interest was the feeling that some degree of both absenteeism and turnover was "normal," that is, an unavoidable cost of doing business. As both of these indicators moved upward for

This article was prepared especially for this book.

many industries in the late 1960s and early 1970s,[2] more efforts to measure and control related costs were begun. Some large companies found, for example, that the reduction of absenteeism by a single percentage point would result in real cost savings of several millions of dollars annually.

This article describes the types of costs incurred by organizations due to employee absenteeism and turnover. They are presented in order of increasing difficulty of measurement.

Costs of Absenteeism

Fringe Benefits

It is a trend in many industries for fringe benefits to account for an increasing proportion of the total employee compensation package. These benefits include a number of items for which the company incurs expenses, regardless of whether the employee is at work or absent. Fringe benefits are highly visible and their costs are often simple to compute; $10.00 to $20.00 per man day of absence is typical for large, unionized companies. The most important cost items are the following:

1. *Insurance.* Employers may pay for premiums for life, disability, accident, sickness, prescription drug, or dental insurance for employees and their families. For many companies insurance is the most costly fringe benefit, and also the most costly absenteeism expense.

2. *Pensions.* A company's contributions to a pension plan are generally made according to a regular schedule, independent of the employee's absence record.

3. *Vacation and holidays.* Paid time off the job is given with the presumption that the employee will be present each scheduled working day. Thus a portion of all vacation and holiday pay must be considered an expense of absenteeism.

4. *Social Security Tax and Unemployment Compensation Tax.* In theory, these costs should exist only for salaried workers. That is, the amount of the company payment is based upon actual employee earnings, and hourly paid workers earn nothing while absent. However, in many large companies these costs may exist for hourly workers merely because of the accounting procedure. A corporate account might be established from which these taxes will be paid. Forecasted production volume and manpower levels are used to predict the total cost. Each plant then is assessed a share of the cost based on the number of employees on the payroll, rather than actual earnings of individual employees.

Overtime Costs

The absence of a certain critical number of employees may require the company to schedule overtime work. Employees then receive an overtime wage premium for work which is normally done at the standard wage. The excess of the premium over the standard wage must then be considered a cost of absenteeism for hourly employees. For salaried workers, the entire premium amount is the true cost, since the absent employee draws his normal salary. Thus overtime costs may range from $15.00 per man-day for minimum wage hourly employees, to several hundreds of dollars for salaried employees.

Some managers feel that there is also a more subtle cost of overtime due to the "overtime-absenteeism cycle." It is sometimes observed that employees working many overtime hours seem to "reward" themselves with an occasional day of absence. When production schedules are tight, this absenteeism may cause the company to schedule still more overtime work. To break this cycle management may have to consider alternative ways of reducing the pressure on the work force, for example, facilities expansion or short-term subcontracting of work.

Underutilization of Facilities

Absenteeism often leaves idle certain tools, equipment, and work space which depreciate in value during the period of absence. In some instances these properties also must be maintained during the absence. Estimated cost: $25.00 to $100.00 per day.

Loss of Productivity

The effect of absenteeism on productivity is easiest to see for those jobs directly involved with manufacturing. Measures of productivity for service jobs or jobs requiring more abstract reasoning and planning may not be affected by short-term absenteeism. However, certain costs do exist in principle, even if a dollar figure cannot be calculated.

1. *Reduced output due to understaffing.* If an absent employee is not replaced, the total output of the organization is decreased. Also, a burden may be placed on other employees simply due to disruption of a normal routine.

2. *Break-in cost for replacements.* If an absent employee is temporarily replaced by another employee, the company will likely incur costs related to:

- Initial substandard production of the replacement.
- Supervisor time spent orienting or instructing the replacement.
- Time spent by other employees instructing or assisting the replacement.
- Excessive inspection of the replacement's work by the supervisor or quality control personnel.

Costs of Turnover

Many of the types of costs associated with turnover are the same as those associated with absenteeism. There are likely to be differences in the magnitude of those costs, however. Often the higher costs are incurred in the case of turnover.

Fringe Benefits

1. *Social Security Tax and Unemployment Compensation Tax.* These tax rates are not applied to an employee's entire income without restriction. There is a specified maximum annual amount of each tax which can be paid. When an employee separates, the company cannot reclaim the current year's taxes paid by reason of his employment. When a replacement is hired, these taxes are paid, once again, up to the maximum amounts. The company's cost is the difference between the annual maximum tax for one employee and the total annual tax paid in the names of the separated employee and replacement(s). Depending upon the time of year and the federal and state tax laws, this cost may be $50.00 to $100.00 per separation.

2. *Terminal Vacation.* Some companies permit an employee who voluntarily quits to take part or all of the vacation time due him at the end of his tenure.

Severance Pay

In many large companies, the discharge of an employee is accompanied by a terminal payment of a lump sum or the equivalent of several days' wages.

Overtime Costs

If there is a shortage of individuals with appropriate skills in the labor market, the company may be required to schedule overtime work. Unfortunately, this situation may also lead the company into the overtime-absenteeism cycle. As with absenteeism, $15.00 per man-day would be a minimum overtime cost.

Underutilization of Facilities

To the extent that replacement of a separated employee is delayed, expenses of $25.00 to $100.00 per man-day are incurred due to the idle time of capital.

Administrative Costs

The larger the company, the greater the administrative costs are likely to be when an employee separates. This is due to the complexity of record-keeping systems in larger companies. A separation occurring in one plant may set these activities into motion:

- Notification of the plant employment office of the position opening.
- Notification of the State Employment Service of the position opening.
- Removal of the separatee's records from personnel files at the plant, divisional, and corporate levels.
- Notification of the payroll office to pay any terminal wages due the separatee and to remove the name from the active file.

The costs involved in these actions should not include portions of the salaries of clerical and administrative personnel, when those salaries are considered to be part of the company's overhead. True costs, however, lie in the use of computer facilities to alter the various records; $20.00 to $50.00 per separation would be typical.

Employment Costs

As with administrative costs, the costs of employing replacements should not include those expenses which are considered as overhead. Wages of employment office personnel would not be included unless overtime work or new temporary help is required. This situation might occur in periods of layoff or large-scale out-placement due to the closing of a facility. Typical employment costs include the following items:

- Local newspaper advertising.
- Recruiting travel expenses.
- Time of management personnel (outside the employment office) spent interviewing candidates.
- Employment tests.
- Physical examinations.
- Computer expenses for the creation of new records.
- Moving expenses.
- Cash bonus.

The possible range of employment costs is quite large—from $50.00 to $3,000 per accession.

Training Costs

Orientation and formal training expenses for replacement personnel are true turnover costs if they are not considered as overhead. Once again the possible range of expenses is from $50.00 to several thousands of dollars.

Loss of Productivity

1. *Reduced effort between the decision to quit and the actual quitting.* Some employees lose interest in maintaining their job performance upon deciding to quit. Thus the period of time between their decision and their termination may yield substandard quantity or quality of work.

2. *Reduced output due to understaffing.*

3. *Break-in cost for replacements.* The same cost sources apply here as listed in this category for absenteeism costs. Break-in costs due to turnover are likely to be much greater, however. Zimmerer[3] points out that a company does not break even with its investment in a new employee until that employee surpasses the standard level of acceptable performance. The true break-even point is reached when the employee makes a sufficient *extra* contribution to profits to make up for his nonproductive time spent in training.

Establishing Acceptable Levels of Absenteeism and Turnover

Although the costs of each absence and separation may be substantial, most companies are willing to bear those costs to some degree. The decision as to what levels of absenteeism and turnover are acceptable for a company should depend on two considerations. The first of these concerns the dollar savings and other advantages which might accrue in each case. The following are examples of circumstances in which savings are associated with absenteeism:

• A company may maintain a pool of part-time or temporary employees to be used as absentee replacements. These individuals are paid a lower wage and receive fringe benefits worth perhaps 25 percent to 50 percent of regular employee benefits.

• In times of lagging sales or when production is poorly scheduled, the company may accumulate a stockpile of completed units of production. Some managers may actually encourage employees to take brief personal (unpaid) leaves of absence. These absences are less costly than either excessive stockpiling or layoffs.

The advantages of turnover include these:

• Rates of pay for new hires are lower than rates of experienced employees. In unionized companies where rates are fixed by an agreement, turnover results in personnel cost savings. For salaried work groups, these savings may be, in part, passed on to other employees in the form of merit increases in pay.

• Eligibility for some fringe benefits does not occur until seniority is established. Thus the company experiences savings in insurance premiums, vacation pay, etc.

• To the extent that turnover occurs in jobs above the entry level, opportunities for upward mobility are created.

• To the extent that those who terminate are poor performers, turnover presents the opportunity to upgrade the quality of the workforce.[4]

A thorough cost-benefit analysis of absenteeism or turnover will almost certainly demonstrate that only very low rates and temporary periods of either will contribute to profits. Rates of absenteeism and turnover in most large business organizations today are considerably above these optimal low rates. As a result, businesses incur millions of dollars in added costs each year. Nevertheless, the generalization that both absenteeism and turnover are always undesirable is an oversimplification.

The second factor for a company to consider is the turnover and absence experience of similar organizations. Data compiled by the Bureau of Labor Statistics, and published in the *Monthly Labor Review,* provide relevant benchmarks for most industries. For example, in July, 1973, the quit rate experienced by companies manufacturing electrical equipment was 2.1 percent, compared to 5.0 percent for furniture and fixture manufacturers.[5] This type of information gives greater perspective to a single company's analysis of its problems, and can facilitate the planning of more appropriate corrective actions.

Notes

1. Hedges, J. N., "Absence from work—A Look at Some National Data. *Monthly Labor Review,* July, 1973, pp. 24-30.

2. Hedges reports that between 1967 and 1972, the overall proportion of workers reporting part-week absences increased from 3.9 percent to 4.3 percent.

3. Zimmerer, Thomas, the true cost of labor turnover. *Management of Personnel Quarterly, 10,* 2, 1971, pp. 9-12.

4. For a fuller discussion of how turnover can perform this function, see the article by E. E. Lawler in chap 6.

5. *Monthly Labor Review,* November, 1973, p. 97.

CHAPTER   **8**

Union Constraints on Personnel Actions

In the early days, unions capitalized on worker dissatisfaction in order to attract new members. Today a large number of new members join unions automatically as required under a union shop contract. (See article by Hamner in chap. 6.) In the first reading in this chapter Bok and Dunlop examine the history and nature of the bargaining relationship which has resulted from the unionization of employees. Our second reading by Stagner and Rosen examines the types of disputes which generally result between management and organized workers today. These disputes may result in strikes, worker slowdowns and worker grievances. Stagner and Rosen examine the dynamics of labor-management conflicts and offer principles to the personnel or labor relations specialist that can be applied in settling these disputes.

The last reading in this chapter discusses a different constraint placed on management by unions. Vogel maintains that the white-collar work force is becoming ripe for unionism—primarily because management has not learned from the history of the labor movement. White-collar workers in many firms face the same conditions as unionized employers: pay that is not related to performance, rigid working hours, working conditions similar to blue-collar occupations, and no say in the decisions made. Vogel predicts that unless managers learn from their past mistakes, the advantages for white-collar workers of joining the union will increase, primarily because the disadvantages are already present.

Collective Bargaining
in the United States: An Overview

D. C. BOK
J. T. DUNLOP

The democratic character of labor organizations and the nature of their internal operations have aroused particular interest in the United States.[1] If unions were largely devoted to political action or social reform, rather than collective bargaining, their internal affairs might have attracted no more attention than those of the American Medical Association or the National Association of Manufacturers. But unions have traditionally been preoccupied with collective bargaining, and this preoccupation has given labor organizations a significance that has stimulated interest in almost every phase of union activity and has created a series of problems for employers and for the economy as a whole.

Although the practice of collective bargaining has been known for more than one hundred fifty years, the term itself seems to have been first used in 1891 by Mrs. Sidney Webb, the Fabian writer and, in collaboration with her husband, historian of the British labor movement.[2] As the Webbs stated, "In unorganized trades the individual workman, applying for a job, accepts or refuses the terms offered by the employer without communication with his fellow workmen. . . . But if a group of workmen concert together, and send representatives to conduct bargaining on behalf of the whole body, the position is at once changed."[3] Individual bargaining is thus transformed into collective bargaining.

The Special Character of Collective Bargaining
in the United States

Collective bargaining is carried on within a framework of law, custom and institutional structure that varies considerably from one country to another. The framework of bargaining in the United States has certain characteristics that sharply distinguish it from that of most other industrial democracies.

Decentralization
Perhaps the most significant characteristic of the American collective-bargaining system is that it is highly decentralized. There are approximately 150,000 separate union-management agreements now in force in the United States. A majority of union members work under contracts negotiated by their union with a single employer or for a single plant. Only 40 percent of employees covered by collective agreements involve multi-employer negotiations, and the great bulk of these negotiations are confined to single metropolitan areas.

In Europe and Australia, on the other hand, the great majority of union members are covered by general agreements negotiated for large groups of employees on a multi-employer basis. Collective bargaining in Sweden, for example, is normally carried out within the framework of a national agreement negotiated by the central conferedation of labor unions and its counterpart on the management side. Subsidiary agreements then are hammered out in negotiations conducted on an industrywide basis. Additional negotiation takes place at the plant level. Since each of these levels of negotiation may cover some of the same subjects, such as wages, the bargaining arrangements may be said to consist of three tiers, in contrast to the single tier that is more typical in the United States. In Great Britain, there are normally two separate tiers, an industrywide negotiation followed by bargaining at the plant level.[4] In France the dominant pattern of bargaining is initially regional. In the typical case, a general agreement covering a large section of the country is negotiated by an association representing a group of loosely related industries. Thus, a key French negotiation takes place within the greater Paris region involving the metalworks sector—a group which includes a variety of industries ranging from steel plants and automobile factories to jewelry shops and repair establishments. In addition to regional negotiation, bargaining may also take place at the plant level, usually with individual workers but sometimes through regular plantwide negotiations with the unions.

The prevalence of plant and company negotiations in the United States is a natural outgrowth of the patterns of organization among employers and unions, the great size of this country, and the highly competitive character of its economy. National negotiations, along Scandinavian lines, are hardly feasible, since the AFL-CIO has much less authority over its affiliates than the central confederations in most other industrial democracies (with the possible exception of Great Britain), and managements also are less centralized in their decisions on labor-relations issues. The manager in America has been strongly inclined to act independently in working out his labor and personnel policies. To be sure, multi-employer bargaining associations are not unknown; they are quite common on the local level and exist on a nationwide basis in a few industries, as in railroads. Nevertheless, it is difficult to envisage American employers following the example of their Swedish counterparts by forming a single national confederation with power to veto any important bargaining concession by a member firm or to compel any member to join in a lockout. Nor is it likely that American employers will follow the lead of those abroad in forming powerful bargaining associations in virtually all major industries.

Exclusive Jurisdiction

In the United States, unlike most countries in Western Europe, one union serves as the sole representative for all the employees in a plant or other appropriate bargaining unit. [Note: Government employment, however, provides some exceptions to exclusive representation. Executive Order 10988 provided for more than one form of recognition by a government agency, so that two or more unions may legitimately be recognized in federal employment. In New York City government, different unions may represent the same worker for different purposes, one for grievances and another for wages and benefits.] This practice conforms to the American political custom of electing single representatives by majority vote. It also can be traced back to the tradition of conflict among the autonomous international unions. To restrain such conflict, the American Federation of Labor—as far back as the 1880s—developed the concept of exclusive jurisdiction. Under this principle, only one union was authorized to represent employees in a particular occupation, a group of jobs, or, occasionally, an industry. Employers generally accepted exclusivity since it stabilized labor relations by diminishing disputes among competing unions. It was natural, therefore, for the principle to be embodied in public policy when the government began to develop detailed regulation over collective bargaining. Thus, during World War I and under the Railway Labor Act of 1926, a system of elections was adopted to enable groups of employees to select a single representative by majority vote. The same procedures were subsequently carried forward on a broader scale in the National Labor Relations Act of 1935 and its subsequent amendments.

A different system of representation prevails in most other industrial democracies.[5] In a few countries, as in West Germany, the federation is made up of unions neatly divided along industrial lines so that there is less need for an explicit doctrine of exclusive jurisdiction in order to curb union rivalries. There also are a number of nations where the labor movement is split along political or religious lines that reflect fundamental ideological cleavages in the society. Under such circumstances, there are obvious objections to any system that would give one union exclusive rights over its rivals. In France, for example, neither employers nor the political parties in power would accept a system that would allow the Communist-controlled unions to win exclusive bargaining rights wherever they could enlist a majority of employees against the opposing Socialist and Catholic organizations. Instead, each of the rival unions is simply given the right to represent its members, and collective bargaining normally takes place through uneasy coalitions among the three major labor federations.

Individual Bargaining

Under almost any system, collective bargaining leaves room for a degree of individual negotiation over certain terms and conditions of employment. Even in the United States, the law explicitly provides that an employee can discuss individual grievances with representatives of management.[6] And in a few fields—for example, the performing arts—agreements typically leave employees free to bargain individually for salaries above the minimum. For the most part, however, collective agreements in the United States specify the actual wages and terms of employment which in fact govern the workers in the bargaining unit, and individual employees do not negotiate different terms on their own behalf.

In most other industrial democracies, the scope for individual or small-group bargaining is much greater. Collective agreements generally do no more than provide minimum wages and conditions. In the tight labor markets that have prevailed in so many of these countries, actual wages have drifted well above the contract rates in the great majority of plants. As a result, though negotiated pay increases put upward pressure on wage levels, the actual rates of pay are largely fixed by individual bargaining, often initiated by employers seeking to keep their work force from going elsewhere.[7]

Collective agreements in the United States also tend to specify many more conditions of employment than is the case in other countries. In Western Europe, for example, a union contract normally obliges the employer to observe little more than a minimum-wage scale and a few basic provisions relating to working conditions and perhaps a few fringe benefits. In this country, on the other hand, agreements are extremely detailed and far-reaching in their content. Collective bargaining typically regulates standards for discipline, promotion criteria, transfers and layoffs, priorities for determining who will be laid off and recalled, shift schedules, procedures for resolving grievances and a wide variety of other matters.

The decentralized structure of the American industrial-relations system does much to explain the greater reach of the collective agreement and the more restricted role for individual and small-group bargaining and unilateral action by the employer. In Europe, where negotiations normally embrace entire industries or groups of related industries in particular regions and where so many diverse employers participate in the negotiations, it is extremely difficult to write a detailed set of contract rules applicable to each participating firm. As a result, the parties have been content to negotiate contracts containing only a limited number of minimum terms and conditions.

In this country, on the other hand, the pattern of plant and companywide bargaining enables unions to negotiate contracts specifying a detailed system of wages and working conditions to be observed at each workplace. Even in industries where multiemployer bargaining has prevailed, unions have been sufficiently organized at the plant level to negotiate supplementary provisions to take account of special conditions in particular plants. But in most European countries, where plant locals scarcely exist, this process has been much slower to develop. Lacking strong organizations at the workplace, unions have left many terms of employment to be resolved through individual bargaining or by consultation with workers' councils,[8] which often are established by law and are not formally a part of the union hierarchy.

The Role of Law in Fixing Conditions of Employment

Just as individual bargaining plays a part, along with collective negotiations, in setting terms and conditions of employment, so also does the law have a role in the process. In every industrialized country, legislation has been passed to perform such functions as fixing minimum wages or maximum hours, or providing safety requirements, or requiring payroll deductions for social security and other welfare programs. In at least one respect, however, the law performs a broader function abroad than it does in the United States. In other industrial democracies, outside the Scandinavian bloc, legislation has been passed that can be used to extend the terms of collective agreements to nonunion enterprises in the same industry. In a few countries, the extension of the collective agreement is ordered by a labor tribunal or a regular court. More often, either the union or the employers' association can petition a designated public official who has descretion to extend the terms of the agreement throughout the industry in question. In the United States, however, no comparable procedure exists. [Note: One consequence of the arrangements in the United States is that the economically weak—agricultural labor and those employed in small retail establishments, for example—have relatively little protection. They are excluded from much social legislation and do not enjoy the benefits of collective bargaining. The Davis-Bacon Act does, however, specify that the Secretary of Labor shall predetermine the wage rates and benefits to be paid to workers employed on construction projects under federal government contract; and the Walsh-Healy Act empowers the Secretary to prescribe the prevailing minimum wages in connection with the government's purchases. In Great Britain the Wages Councils, and in Australia the arbitration courts, provide more egalitarian conditions of employment for the unorganized without bargaining power; they extend to such workers benefits comparable to those developed by parties to collective bargaining.]

The absence of any authority in law to extend a collective-bargaining contract to others who have not accepted the agreement is rooted in the structure of the American industrial-relations system. It is comparatively easy to extend a contract containing a few minimum terms and conditions, particularly when the contract has been negotiated by an association representing a large and representative group of firms. In the United States, however, where rival unions may coexist in a single industry, where contract terms set actual rather than minimum requirements, and where provisions are highly complex and often vary from one firm to another, it would be very difficult to find a single set of terms that would be suitable for all firms in the industry.

In another respect, the structure of bargaining in this country has caused the law to play a more ambitious role in collective negotiations than it does abroad. Although we rely less heavily on legislation to fix the substantive terms of employment, there is much more regulation in the United States over the tactics and procedures of bargaining.

This difference largely reflects the special tensions and pressures that arise in a highly decentralized system of bargaining. Under plantwide or companywide negotiations, the individual employer must confront the union in his enterprise, instead of leaving negotiations to his employer association to be conducted on a regional or industrywide basis. The bargaining process reaches into the details of his business, seeking to regulate every aspect of working conditions in his plant. The contract terms do not merely set minimum standards but also fix the actual conditions to be observed. Above all, the institution of bargaining threatens to subject him to contract obligations that may put him at a disadvantage with his nonunion competitor or even other organized enterprises. Under these circumstances, the bargaining process is accompanied by greater tension, and the employer often resists the union more strenuously than is common abroad. In turn, the law responds to these strains and seeks to contain antagonisms within reasonable bounds. Thus, law in the United States defines the subjects that must be bargained about. It requires the parties to "bargain in good faith" and clothes this obligation with detailed rules proscribing stalling tactics, withholding of relevant information, and other forms of behavior that are considered unfair. The net result is a complex of regulations that greatly exceeds anything to be found in other industrialized countries.[9]

The Role of the Parties in Determining the Structure of Bargaining

These special characteristics help to define the framework of the American system of collective bargaining. Within these contours, several types of negotiation go on. The most familiar aspect of bargaining involves the discussions between the parties over the terms and conditions of employment for the workers involved. But a vital part of the bargaining process has to do with determining the structure and the procedures through which these discussions will take place.

One question of structure has to do with the level at which different issues should be resolved. This problem is particularly significant in any negotiation that affects more than one place of work. In a situation of this kind, the parties must decide which issues should be agreed upon at the negotiating table and incorporated into a master agreement and which should be left for labor and management representatives to settle at the company, plant, or departmental level.[10] Agreements made at these subsidiary levels are called local supplements. Sometimes the interdependence between the two settlements creates problems. Is one settlement contingent upon the other, and is a failure to conclude one a basis for a strike or lockout in all units? Which settlement will be made first?

These questions are often difficult to resolve. In a multi-plant company, for instance, such matters as the amount of time allowed for wash-up before the end of a shift or the allocation of parking facilities might be best handled at the plant level. But it is also clear that policies or precedents on these matters at one plant may influence decisions elsewhere. Considerations of bargaining power and market competition may also influence the level at which particular issues are treated. As technological and market changes take place, it may be necessary to alter these arrangements and provide for more centralization on some issues, as with the introduction of containers in the East Coast longshore industry, and greater decentralization in other instances, such as the determination of the number of trainmen in a crew on the railroads. Since conditions vary widely from one plant or industry to another, there is little uniformity among collective-bargaining relationships in the pattern of centralization and decentralization in negotiations.

A second problem in arranging negotiation procedures concerns the range of jobs, territory, and employees to be governed by the ensuing agreement. Several illustrations may be helpful. The basic steel companies took major strikes in 1946 in part to achieve separate negotiations for their fabricating facilities from their basic steel operations. As a result, separate agreements with different expiration dates and different wage scales now are negotiated at different times, reflecting the different competitive conditions that affect these two types of operations. In view of differing market conditions for the different products involved, the major rubber companies have on occasion insisted on differential wage increases for tire plants and those plants making rubber shoes and other rubber products. Conversely, twenty-six cooperating international unions sustained an eight-month strike in the copper negotiations of 1967-68 in an effort to obtain collective-bargaining agreements with the same expiration dates and identical wage increases for all employees of a company.

A third set of structural problems has to do with the relations among different craft unions bargaining with a common employer. In recent years, the newspaper printing industry, the West Coast shipbuilding industry, and the construction industry have suffered many strikes growing out of disagreements over the wage pattern or sequence of settlements among a group of interrelated crafts agreements. For example, the 114-day New York newspaper strike of 1962-63 was fought by Bertram Powers, president of Local 6 of the International Typographical Union, largely to change a system of bargaining which had existed since the early 1950s. Under the prior agreement, wage settlements had been made with the Newspaper Guild and then extended to other newspaper unions. As a result of the strike, contract expiration dates were negotiated which removed the five-week lead the Guild had previously held and thus eliminated its ability to impose an industrywide pattern on the other unions before they ever got to the bargaining table. Thus, the strike enabled Powers to put an end to a follow-the-leader pattern that had deprived his union of any real power to negotiate its own wage agreements.[11]

Serious questions may arise also in deciding which subjects should be encompassed within the scope of collective bargaining. The subjects that are dealt with vary widely, reflecting in each contract the problems of the relevant workplace and industry. Some maritime agreements specify the quality of meals and even the number of bars of soap, towels, and sheets that management is to furnish to the crew. Such provisions are natural subjects for negotiation, since they are vital to men at sea, but they would make no sense in a normal manufacturing agreement. In some contracts in the ladies' garment industry, companies agree to be efficient and to allow a union industrial engineer to make studies of company performance. These provisions would be regarded as ludicrous in the automobile industry. Detailed procedures respecting control over hiring are central to collective bargaining in industries with casual employment, where employees shift continually from one employer to another, as in construction and stevedoring; but in factory and office employment, new hiring typically is left to the discretion of management. In this fashion, the topics raised in collective bargaining tend to reflect the problems of the particular workplace and industry.

The law also plays a part in deciding the subjects for negotiation, since the National Labor Relations Act (Section 9a) requires the parties to bargain in good faith over "rates of pay, wages, hours of employment, or other conditions of employment." Pursuant to this Act, the National Labor Relations Board and the courts have decided which subjects are mandatory topics for collective bargaining and which are optional. In some instances, particular subjects or bargaining proposals have been held to be improper or illegal and hence nonnegotiable, such as a union's insistence on a closed shop or an employer's demand that the union bargain through a particular form of negotiating committee or take a secret ballot prior to calling a strike. On the whole, however, the Board and the courts have steadily broadened the scope of mandatory bargaining to include Christmas bonuses, pensions, information on plant shutdowns, subcontracting, provisions for checkoff of union dues, and many other topics.

The provisions of the National Labor Relations Act would appear to make legal rulings decisive as to the scope of bargaining. And on a few issues, such as pension plans, litigation undoubtedly played a significant role. In the main, however, although the law may help to define the outer limits of bargaining, the actual scope of negotiations is largely decided by the parties themselves.

The Process of Bargaining: Negotiation, Administration, and Consultation

In common parlance, "collective bargaining" is used to refer to three separate forms of labor-management activity: negotiations for a new contract, administration of an existing agreement, and informal consultation on matters of common interest to the parties.

Negotiation

The process of negotiating a new agreement varies widely from one firm to another. In a number of industries, for example, the smaller firms will usually follow the pattern set by a larger competitor; bargaining for them will mean little more than seeking to make a few minor adjustments in the pattern-setting agreement to take account of special conditions. In larger firms—and particularly in the pattern-setting companies—bargaining will be a much more elaborate and difficult process.

When bargaining involves more than simply accepting a standard agreement, there will normally be much preparation on both sides. The union will develop a series of demands through local meetings, consultation among officials, and sometimes the use of surveys and questionnaires. Management will likewise develop its position through meetings among its officers and staff. Both parties will normally arm themselves with research data; for example, they may study the nature of prior grievances, draw upon studies of market and employment trends, and analyze the financial and competitive position of the firm itself.

Once these preparations are complete, the process of bargaining often proceeds through a series of stages. At the outset, the union customarily presents a long and extravagant list of demands. In many instances, the company will respond by submitting its own proposals, which are typically far apart from those of the union. Although this exchange may seem as irrelevant and ritualistic as the mating dance of the great crested grebe, it can serve a variety of purposes. By putting forward many exaggerated demands, the parties create trading material for later stages of negotiations. They disguise their real position and thus give themselves room for maneuver as bargaining progresses. They explore a wide range of problems that may have been bothering each side, and they have the opportunity to explain concerns to each other. They manage to satisfy their constituents or principals by seeming to back numerous proposals, only to scale down many of the demands or abandon them altogether later on in the negotiations when it is more expedient to do so. A proposal may be advanced and explored, only to be put aside for more serious negotiation in subsequent years.

After the initial presentations, there normally is a period of exploration in which each side tries to clarify the proposals of the other and marshal arguments against them. At this stage of negotiation, little change can be expected in the positions of the parties. As bargaining progresses, each side will begin to formulate a combination of proposals, or "package," which it considers an appropriate basis for settlement. The package offered by each side gives the other party a clearer sense of the priorities attached to various items and the possible concessions to be gained. In this process, more than one package may be put forward by either side.

Eventually, before or after a stoppage, an agreement will be reached. The meeting of the minds will normally be arrived at first during informal talks between key negotiators, and the proposed settlement will then be discussed before the full negotiating committees on either side. Thereafter, the tentative agreement must be reduced to contract language, usually with the advice of lawyers and after much further discussion over details of wording.

After the agreement is reduced to writing, ordinarily it must be ratified or approved by the principals involved. On the union side, ratification may be required by the membership of the union, by a specified group of elected delegates, or by an elected wage policy committee, as in the case of the basic-steel agreement. Management negotiators in a single company will need the approval of the president or the board of directors. In association bargaining, the approval of the elected directors or the full membership of the association is typically required.

The ratification of settlements by union members serves a variety of purposes. By obtaining an explicit vote of approval for the settlement, subsequent enforcement of the agreement by management, by union officers, or by an arbitrator is made easier. Ratification also requires union negotiators to explain and "sell" the agreement to the membership. In doing so, ratification provides a check to insure that the negotiators keep in touch with the rank and file and reflect their interests in the bargaining process.

The quality of union leadership and its influence on the membership are subtly reflected in collective bargaining and ratification. In many bargaining relationships, ratification on the union side is a formality. The negotiators, by common consent, are in touch with the membership or wage policy committee with power to ratify; the negotiators are highly respected, and their views and recommendations carry great weight. In other instances, the union leaders occupy a more tenuous position; they lack the influence and prestige to guarantee acceptance even of a satisfactory contract.

As previously observed, there has been a marked increase in the proportion of settlements that have been rejected in the ratification process. According to federal mediators, the most common reasons for rejection are dissatisfaction with the size of wage and fringe benefits, lack of understanding by the leaders of the real desires of the members, internal political rivalries, and inadequate ratification procedures that give undue weight to the views of dissident members. At times, however, a rejection can be a deliberate tactic in the bargaining process. Union representatives may take a management offer to the members to demonstrate the unity and the sentiments of the rank and file. They may appear to accept a proposal and later oppose ratification in order to extract further concessions from management. Such stratagems normally are harmful to bargaining relationships. Management is unlikely to make its best offer at the bargaining table once it has been burnt by the use of a rejection as a tactical maneuver; it will save its best offer for a later date, thus causing the agreement-making process to become more difficult.

Administration of The Contract

Although many of the most important issues concerning the terms of employment will be settled explicitly in the collective agreement, controversies will continue to arise over its meaning and application. Such disputes are inevitable. Most collective agreements are highly complex documents covering a multitude of problems Typically, they are negotiated within a limited period of time, often in an atmosphere of rush and crisis. As a result, certain problems are bound to be overlooked. Others arise from changing circumstances that could not possibly have been foreseen when the contract was signed. Still others reflect ambiguities which were deliberately created by the parties with the thought that not every controversy could be settled in negotiations if the agreement was ever to be signed within the time available.

Almost all collective agreements contain procedures to be used in resolving "grievances," or disputes over the application of the contract. In some cases, the procedures are very simple. In the construction industry, for example, where many contractors have a work force that changes constantly from one job to another, it is often not feasible to operate an elaborate grievance machinery. Hence, disputes often are settled at the workplace through informal discussions between the union representative and the employer. Similarly, grievances in small establishments often are resolved by having the aggrieved employee get in touch with the union representative, who then may take up the matter directly with the employer. Where larger numbers of employees are involved, however, the grievance machinery tends to become more elaborate.

Most contracts for larger plants provide several stages at which a grievance can be considered. Typically, the aggrieved employee will first present his complaint to the foreman or supervisor, with or without the assistance of a union representative. The great majority of grievances are settled at this stage; were it otherwise, higher management and union officials could easily become overwhelmed with the task of reviewing complaints. But where an accommodation cannot be reached at this early stage, the contract will provide one or more levels of appeal at which disputes can be considered by progressively higher echelons within the union and management hierarchy. If no settlement can be reached through this process, the agreement will typically provide for presentation to an outside arbitrator, who will issue a final and binding decision following a hearing of the parties.

Today, arbitration procedures can be found in an estimated 94 percent of all collective-bargaining agreements. Nevertheless, not all disputes are made subject to this procedure, even in contracts with fully developed grievance machinery. For example, contracts signed by the major automobile companies expressly provide that the arbitrator shall not decide disputes involving production standards used in the measured day-work system; in some of these firms, matters involving health and safety and rates of new jobs are likewise excluded from arbitration.[12] Despite such exceptions, it is fair to say that arbitration represents the dominant method for resolving grievances that the parties cannot settle by themselves. Through this procedure, a peaceful and impartial resolution of disputes is obtained without the delay and formality that might result from taking such matters to court or making the dispute a test of economic power.

In light of the experience in countless plants, it is clear beyond dispute that an effective, well-administered grievance procedure can play an indispensable role in improving labor relations and providing a measure of industrial due process to the workers involved. The advantages to be gained have been summed up in the following terms by a distinguished panel of labor relations experts:

A major achievement of collective bargaining, perhaps its most important contribution to the American workplace, is the creation of a system of industrial jurisprudence, a system under which employer and employee rights are set forth in contractual form and disputes over the meaning of the contract are settled through a rational grievance process. . . . The gains from this system are especially noteworthy because of their effect on the recognition and dignity of the individual worker. This system helps prevent arbitrary action on questions of discipline, layoff, promotion, and transfer, and sets up orderly procedures for the handling of grievances. Wildcat strikes and other disorderly means of protest have been curtailed and effective work discipline generally established. In many situations, cooperative relationships marked by mutual respect between labor and management stand as an example of what can be done.[13]

Joint Consultation

In many labor-management relationships, the parties have fashioned machinery to consult with one another during the term of the collective agreement. Such arrangements may involve high-level officials from both sides or specialists concerned with particular technical problems. They may or may not include impartial representatives.

Many purposes can be served by discussions of this kind. A study committee may be useful in exploring some special question, such as a pension program or a new job evaluation plan, which is too complex to be handled satisfactorily in the limited time available for regular contract negotiations. In other cases, a committee may be needed to construct and administer special machinery for dealing with a large, continuing problem such as the displacement of personnel through automation or the closing of a plant. Regular consultation may be employed to develop information and exchange ideas with a view to narrowing the range of issues to be taken up in subsequent contract negotiations. In a strike-torn firm or industry, a committee may also be formed to search for ways of resolving underlying problems or redesigning bargaining procedures in order to eliminate the sources of controversy.[14]

These three processes—negotiation, administration, and joint consultation—are not always readily disentangled in practice. Discussions between representatives of the parties may be of a mixed character. They may talk over a particular grievance and in so doing agree to exchange letters which embody the solution of a more general problem. The administrative and the legislative functions are here closely intertwined. A joint study committee may, on occasion, find a resolution for some pending grievances, agree on some new provision in the contract, or simply provide an exchange of information and opinion. Nonetheless, it is helpful to distinguish these three types of interaction between labor and management organizations even though general usage may employ the term "collective bargaining" to describe them all.

The Social and Economic Functions of Collective Bargaining

If society is to evaluate the institution of collective bargaining and compare it with alternative procedures, its social and economic functions must be clearly perceived. Five functions seem particularly important.

Establishing the Rules of the Workplace

Collective bargaining is a mechanism for enabling workers and their representatives to participate in establishing and administering the rules of the workplace. [Note: Some writers have contended that collective bargaining is a process of joint decision making or joint management. It is true that many rules are agreed to by the parties and written into the collective agreement. But many other functions are left exclusively to management. Moreover, labor agreements typically specify areas within which management takes the initiative, with unions being left to file grievances if they feel that management has violated the contract. Although management may consider it wise to consult with the union before taking certain types of action, it is normally not obligated to seek advance consent from the union. It is misleading to equate collective bargaining with joint management by unions and employers.] Bargaining has resulted in the development of arbitration and other safeguards to protect the employee against inequitable treatment and unfair disciplinary action. More important still, the sense of participation through bargaining serves to mitigate the fear of exploitation on the part of the workers. Whether or not wages would be lower in the absence of bargaining, many employees would doubtless feel that their interests would be compromised without the presence of a union or the power to elect a bargaining representative. In view of these sentiments, collective bargaining may well serve as a substitute for sweeping government controls over wages as a device for insuring adequate, visible safeguards to protect the interests of employees.

Choosing the Form of Compensation

Collective bargaining provides a procedure through which employees as a group may affect the distribution of compensation and the choices between money and hours of work. One of the most significant consequences of collective bargaining over the past two decades has been the growth of fringe benefits, such as pensions, paid holidays, health and welfare, and vacations with pay. If unions had not existed, it is unlikely that individual workers would have spent added income in exactly the same way; indeed, it is doubtful whether, in the absence of collective bargaining, health and pension plans at present prices would have grown widespread. Moreover, though speculations of this kind are treacherous, the history of social-insurance legislation in the United States suggests that, under a system where the government was responsible for setting wages and terms of employment, fringe benefits would not have grown to the extent they have.[15]

These fringe benefits have had a significant impact upon the whole economy. There can be little question that collective bargaining played a major role in focusing priorities and attention upon medical care in the past decade. With the growth of health and welfare plans, information about medical care has been widely disseminated and developed; a body of experts in business and labor have arisen, and the pressures for public programs in the medical field have been accelerated. In much the same way, the extent of expansion in vacation-oriented industries—motels, resorts, transportation, boating, and leisure goods—must be partly attributed to the emphasis in collective bargaining on greater vacation benefits for employees.

Standardization of Compensation

Collective bargaining tends to establish a standard rate and standard benefits for enterprises in the same product market, be it local or national. Labor contracts in the ladies' garment industry seek to establish uniform piece rates (and labor costs) for all companies that produce the same item within the same general price brackets; all the firms in the basic steel industry confront virtually the same hourly wage schedule for all production and maintenance occupations; and all construction firms bidding on contracts in a locality confront known and uniform wage schedules.

Such uniformity is naturally sought by unions. As political institutions, they desire "equal pay for equal work" in order to avoid the sense of grievance that results when one group of members discovers that another group is performing the same job in another plant at a higher wage. Thus, unless there are stong economic reasons for maintaining wage differentials, unions will normally push hard for standardization.

From the standpoint of employers, it should be observed that uniform wage rates do not necessarily imply uniform labor costs. Firms paying the same hourly rates may have varying wage costs as a result of differences in equipment and managerial efficiency. But competition tends to remove these differences and promote more uniform labor costs among close rivals. In highly competitive industries, employers often have a keen regard for such standardization; it protects the enterprises from uncertain wage rate competition, at least among firms subject to the collective agreement.

From the standpoint of the economy as a whole, the effects of standardization are mixed. In some instances, wage uniformity may be broadened artificially beyond a product market area, as when the wage rates in a tire company are extended to apply to its rubber-shoe-work. The effect is to produce a less efficient use of economic resources. The resulting premium over the wages paid in other rubber-shoe plants eventually will compel the tire companies to give up doing business in the rubber-shoe field. In a more important sense, however, the effect of uniformity has been positive in that it has favored the expansion of more profitable, more efficient firms. In a country like France, on the other hand, bargaining establishes only minimum rates, so that backward companies can often survive by paying lower wages than their competitors if they can somehow manage to retain the necessary work force.

Determining Priorities on Each Side

A major function of collective bargaining is to induce the parties to determine priorities and resolve differences within their respective organizations. In the clash and controversy between the two sides, it is easy to assume a homogeneous union struggling with a homogeneous management or association of employers. This view is erroneous and mischievous. In an important sense, collective bargaining consists of no less than three separate bargains—the agreement by different groups within the union to abandon certain claims and assign priorities to others; an analogous process of assessing priorities and trade-offs within a single company or association; and the eventual agreement that is made across the bargaining table.

A labor organization is composed of members with a conglomeration of conflicting and common interests. The skilled and the unskilled, the long-service and the junior employees, the pieceworkers and the day-rated workers, and those in expanding and contracting jobs often do not have the same preferences. A gain to one of these groups often will involve a loss to another. Thus, in George W. Taylor's words, "To an increasing extent, the union function involves a mediation between the conflicting interests of its own membership."[16]

Similarly, corporate officials may have differing views about the negotiations, even in a single company. The production department and the sales staff may assess differently the consequences of a strike. The financial officers may see an issue differently from the industrial-relations specialists. These divergences are compounded where an association of companies bargains with a union, for there are often vast differences among the member firms in their financial capacity, vulnerability to a strike, concern over specific issues, and philosophy toward the union.

One of the major reasons that initial demands of both parties often diverge so far from final settlements is that neither side may have yet established its own priorities or preferences, or assessed the priorities of the other side. In many cases, these relative priorities are established and articulated only during the actual bargaining process. (This view of the bargaining process helps to explain the sense of comradeship that labor and management negotiators often develop through the common task of dealing with their respective committees and constituents.)

This process of accommodation within labor and management is central to collective bargaining. It should not be disparaged as merely a matter of internal politics on either side. In working out these internal adjustments in a viable way, collective bargaining serves a social purpose of enormous significance. The effective resolution of these problems is essential to the strength of leadership and to the continued vitality of both the company and the union.

Redesigning The Machinery of Bargaining

A most significant function of collective bargaining in this country is the continuing design and redesign of the institution itself. While it is true that the national labor policy—as reflected in legislation, administrative rulings, and court decisions—has a bearing on some features of collective bargaining, the nature of the institution is chiefly shaped by the parties themselves. As previously noted, the collective-bargaining process largely determines the respective roles of individual bargaining and union-management negotiations. It defines the subjects to be settled by collective bargaining. It determines the structure of bargaining relationships. It establishes the grievance procedures and prescribes the uses of arbitration and economic power in the administration of an agreement. It decides the degree of centralization and decentralization of decision making. It influences the ratification procedures of the parties. The results are seldom fixed. The bargaining parties must reshape their bargaining arrangements from time to time in response to experience and emerging new problems. Thus, the design of collective bargaining and its adaptation to new challenges and opportunities have much to do with its capacity to fulfill its social functions effectively and without undue cost to the public.

Five Major Issues

In certain respects, collective bargaining is being subjected to a closer scrutiny than in the past, because of the special circumstances in which the country now finds itself. On the one hand, it is plain that society is becoming more critical of its institutions and more demanding in the performance it expects of them. Collective bargaining must now be judged in the light of the American position in the world, which has created new demands for economic progress and monetary stability. The consequences of labor negotiations must be viewed in the light of more insistent demands for full employment. And though labor and management have grown more professional in their dealings with each other and more successful in avoiding strikes, Secretary of Labor Willard Wirtz could still observe that ". . . neither the traditional collective-bargaining procedures nor the present labor-dispute laws are working to the public's satisfaction, at least as far as major labor controversies are concerned."[17]

At the same time, the climate in which collective bargaining must operate has also become more trying. In recent years, bargaining has been spreading rapidly into the field of public employment, where the parties are often inexperienced in labor relations and the problems involved are in many respects more difficult than in the private sector. Full employment has also placed new strains upon the bargaining process. With jobs so plentiful employees are less amenable to discipline and control. Their demands have grown larger, particularly in an economy where the cost of living has been creeping upward. Labor shortages have likewise created difficulties by forcing managers to hire less-experienced and less-qualified employees.

From these pressures have emerged five groups of questions that have been debated increasingly in recent years. . . .

1). Economic strife and dispute settlement. What can be done to protect the public
interest when the parties to collective bargaining engage in economic warfare? Is the
exertion of economic and political pressure an appropriate way to resolve bargaining
disputes? Would not compulsory arbitration be a superior procedure, substituting facts
and reason for power? What can the parties themselves and the government do to
improve the performance of collective bargaining?

2). Efficiency and productivity. What is the impact of collective bargaining upon managerial efficiency? How extensive and serious are restrictive work practices, and what
can be done about them? Does the rule-making character of collective bargaining necessarily stifle management in its quest for reductions in labor costs? When is a rule of
collective bargaining an appropriate protection of the health, safety, or convenience of a
worker, and when is it an undue limitation of efficiency? How can uneconomic work
practices be eliminated in the future?

3). Inflation. What are the consequences of collective bargaining for inflation? The
experience of many Western countries since World War II, including our own, raises the
question whether free collective bargaining, continuing high employment, and price
stability are compatible. What can be done to make collective bargaining less conducive
to inflation or to reduce its inflationary bias at high levels of employment?

4). Public employees. In recent years, the process of negotiations has been spreading
rapidly to many sectors of public employment. Are the procedures of private bargaining
appropriate to public employment? Is the strike a suitable means to induce agreement in
the public sector? What is the proper relation between negotiations in the public sector
and legislative bodies and civil service? What machinery is appropriate to resolve disputes in public employment?

5). New opportunities for bargaining. What are likely to be the new subjects of collective bargaining in the private sector in the years ahead? What are the new needs and
opportunities to which collective bargaining procedures can fruitfully be applied?

Notes

1. The literature on the theoretical analysis of collective bargaining includes the following:
Sidney and Beatrice Webb, *Industrial Democracy* (London: Longmans, Green, 1914); Sumner H.
Slichter, *Union Policies and Industrial Management* (Washington, D.C.: Brookings Institution,
1941); Neil W. Chamberlain, *Collective Bargaining* (New York: McGraw-Hill, 1951); Allan Flan-
ders, *Industrial Relations: What Is Wrong with the System?* (London: Faber and Faber, 1965);
Sumner H. Slichter, James J. Healy, and E. Robert Livernash, *The Impact of Collective Bargain-
ing on Management* (Washington, D.C.: Brookings Institution, 1960); John T. Dunlop, *Industrial
Relations Systems* (New York: Henry Holt, 1958).

2. Webb, *op. cit.,* p. 173, n. 1. The reference to the writing of Mrs. Webb, Beatrice Potter, is
The Cooperative Movement in Great Britain (London, 1891), p. 217.

3. Webb, *op. cit.,* p. 173.

4. See *Royal Commission on Trade Unions and Employers' Associations,* Minutes of Evidence 2 and 3, Ministry of Labour (London, Her Majesty's Stationery Office, 1966), "We have to
face that in many areas we have effectively two tiers of negotiation at the present time, the national
bargaining and the bargaining on the factory floor on bonuses and piece rates," p. 47.

5. For a discussion of some other Western industrial-relations arrangements, see *Royal
Commission on Trade Unions and Employers' Associations,* 1965-1968 (London: Her Majesty's

Stationery Office, 1968); Val R. Lorwin, *The French Labor Movement* (Cambridge: Harvard University Press, 1954); J. E. Issac and G. W. Ford, eds., *Australian Labour Relations Readings* (Melbourne: Sun Books, 1966); Adolf Sturmthal, ed., *White-Collar Trade Unions, Contemporary Developments in Industrialized Societies* (Urbana: University of Illinois Press, 1966); *The Trade Union Situation in Sweden,* Report of a Mission from the International Labour Office (Geneva: International Labour Office, 1961); Walter Galenson, *Trade Union Democracy in Western Europe* (Berkeley: University of California Press, 1964).

6. Labor-Management Relations Act, 1947, Section 9 (a).

7. See D. J. Robertson, *Factory Wage Structures and National Agreements* (Cambridge, England: University Press, 1960).

8. See Adolf Sturmthal, *Workers Councils, A Study of Workplace Organization on Both Sides of the Iron Curtain* (Cambridge: Harvard University Press, 1964).

9. See Robben W. Fleming, "The Obligation to Bargain in Good Faith," in *Public Policy and Collective Bargaining,* Joseph Shister, Benjamin Aaron, and Clyde W. Summers, eds. (New York: Harper and Row, 1962), pp. 60-87.

10. E. Robert Livernash, "Special and Local Negotiations," in *Frontiers of Collective Bargaining,* John T. Dunlop and Neil W. Chamberlain, eds. (New York: Harper and Row, 1967), pp. 27-49.

11. See A. H. Raskin, "The Great Manhattan Newspaper Duel," *Saturday Review,* May 8, 1965, p. 8.

12. See John T. Dunlop, "The Function of the Strike," in *Frontiers of Collective Bargaining, op. cit.,* pp. 103-21.

13. *The Public Interest in National Labor Policy* (New York: Committee for Economic Development, 1961), p. 32.

14. H. A. Clegg and T. E. Chester, "Joint Consultation," in *The System of Industrial Relations in Great Britain,* Allan Flanders and H. A. Clegg, eds. (Oxford, England: Basil Blackwell, 1954), pp. 323-64; James J. Healy, ed., *Creative Collective Bargaining: Meeting Today's Challenges to Labor-Management Relations* (Englewood Cliffs, New Jersey: Prentice-Hall, 1965); William Gomberg, "Special Study Committees," in *Frontiers of Collective Bargaining, op. cit.,* pp. 235-51.

15. See *The Princeton Symposium on The American System of Social Insurance* (New York: McGraw-Hill, 1968).

16. "The Public Interest: Variations on an Old Theme," *Proceedings of the Eighteenth Annual Meeting of the National Academy of Arbitrators,* 1965 (Washington, D.C.: B.N.A. Incorporated, 1965), p. 195.

17. W. W. Wirtz, *Labor and the Public Interest* (New York: Harper and Row, 1964), p. 49.

Forms and Methods of Settling Industrial Disputes

R. STAGNER
H. ROSEN

In the coalition that is the industrial enterprise, many kinds of conflicts can and do occur. . . . Disputes occur because of differences in goals or in perceived pathways to goals. Disputes may increase in number and intensity because of organizational structures. They are also profoundly affected by economic influences, an area with which we [will not deal] except to point out that acceptable economic returns to the parties will depend to some extent upon perception—there is no economic formula to determine a "fair day's work" or a "fair day's pay." Controversies are also affected by the supply of alternative jobs (the labor market), by perceived wage levels elsewhere, and by customary profit ratios.

We are concerned with disputes between organized managers (the employer) and organized workers (the union). There are many other kinds of industrial disputes, of interest to various kinds of social scientists, that will not be explored here. However, so that the student can place union-management disputes in a context of other kinds of disputes, we present Table 1 to show the many other possibilities. Some of these other kinds of disputes have little or no impact on union-management controversy and, hence, are dismissed from further examination—particularly the management-government category, which is relevant only when it grows out of a union-management dispute (e.g., when the union charges unfair labor practices and appeals to the National Labor Relations Board). Similarly, the union-government category may grow out of a union-management dispute (e.g., when the union tries to pressure an employer to sign a contract by picketing the stores to which he sells his output or to which his trucks deliver merchandise).

TABLE 1
VARIETIES OF INDUSTRIAL DISPUTES

Parties	Example
Management-Government	Antitrust action
Intermanagement	Price competition between companies; disputes over patents and fulfillment of contracts
Interunion	Jurisdictional disputes, as between carpenters and millwrights over installation of factory equipment
Union-Government	Prosecution for secondary boycotts; collusion with employers against customers
Intramanagement	Factions within management striving for control of company
Intra-union	Factions within union striving for control of union
Union-Management	Union and company debate over division of earnings between wages and profits

Conflicts within management, such as *factionalism,* or between management and a rebel stockholder group usually have no significant tie with labor relations. Occasionally, one faction within management advocates a "tough line" with the union and the other group is more conciliatory; but even this connection is rare. Intramanagement disputes are most often related to the desire for personal power on the part of leaders of factions within the executive organization.

Interunion disputes occasionally cause union-management problems, and the manager is often the innocent victim. If he signs with one union, the other may picket him—even though it has no members on his payroll. During the hectic early days of the national space program, contractors sometimes paid two groups of workers to do the same job, to avoid the delays inherent in jurisdictional disputes.

The major psychological factor involved in jurisdictional disputes is job security. Since workers develop certain expectations about what work is properly theirs, giving this work to another group (brother unionists or not) threatens their job security. A second factor is the desire of union officers for power. If the two competing ship-officers unions were merged into a single organization, many disputes would be eliminated; however, many men would lose prestige and power, as well as their salaries, from the resulting abolition of duplicated offices. Leaders of one union raid another for members because added membership fattens the union treasury and strike fund, raises the bargaining power to a higher level, and inflates the ego of the leader. Jurisdictional disputes may result from the desire of either the leader or the members to protect traditional jobs and perhaps to add new job opportunities.

Intra-union disputes may occasionally precipitate a union-management controversy, because the leaders of union factions vie with each other to demonstrate to the rank-and-file their ability to win concessions from the boss. Thus, a competition arises similar to that in presidential election campaigns in which the major candidates try to outdo each other in boasting of their toughness toward Communists. (Such competition at the national level is far more dangerous, since it exacerbates tensions that could precipitate a nuclear catastrophe; but the intraplant friction caused by union leaders is also an unpleasant reality.)

Management sometimes contributes to union factionalism. Some executives believe—without much evidence—that divided unions are weak unions and therefore less of a threat. Covertly, they may encourage a continuing split; e.g., by making concessions to one side while refusing similar settlements requested by an opposing faction.

Other inter- and intra-union feuds may be based on ideological and other considerations. The Reuther-Addes fight within the UAW, just after World War II, was at least partly motivated by the Reuther group's anticommunist feelings. The conflict between the AFL-CIO and such groups as the Teamsters and the Longshoremen arises in part from the public reaction to reports of racketeering in these two unions, which was hurting honest unions by the association of ideas.

Having mentioned various kinds of industrial disputes that occasionally affect our central interest, let us now turn to disputes between the management of a company and the union that represents a group of employees of that company. This type of dispute probably accounts for over 90 percent of disputes affecting unions, and it is the kind we wish to examine in greater detail.

Union-management disputes may be classified in at least two ways: (a) by the occasion of the dispute, and (b) by the form it takes. By *occasion* we mean whether the dispute occurs in a union-organizing campaign, in negotiating a contract, or in the grievance procedure under an existing contract; and by *form* we mean the use of verbal weapons (such as hearings and table-pounding), of slowdowns and interferences with production, or of picketing and strikes. Our primary interest will be in the interlocking relationship between motivation, perception, organization, and leadership, as basic variables, and in the occasion and form of the overt dispute.

"Dispute" or "Conflict"?

We have rather carefully adhered to the term *industrial dispute* . . . because of the negative emotional tone associated with the word *conflict*. When one reads of a conflict, he thinks of uninhibited violence and bloodshed. Although such manifestations occur (consider the Perfect Circle strike of 1957 or the Essex Wire strike of 1964), this kind of occurrence was much commoner at the turn of the century and in the period of active unionization from 1935 to 1940.

The concept of dispute used here is a generic one, including within its compass both *competitive* behavior (which in our society is approved, at least in fields other than labor relations) and *conflict* behavior. A dispute is said to occur when two or more parties are striving toward goals which are (or are perceived to be) mutually exclusive or when the means used by one party to achieve its goal negate (or are perceived to negate) the goal-directed behavior of the other party. Thus, the desire of workers and management for more money represents mutually exclusive goals, at least in the short run; i.e., if workers get more, managers and stockholders get less. Promotion by seniority is perceived by the unionists as instrumental to a goal of security, but it is perceived by executives as blocking efficiency. Workers and managers agree that security and efficiency are desirable goals, but the tactics they utilize are in opposition (see Fig. 1).

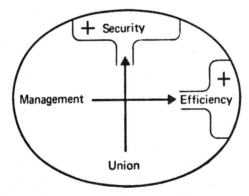

Figure 1. Situation when Worker Goals are Perceived as Blocking Management Goals.

A distinction between competition and conflict may be based on whether *rules* are perceived to be applicable: disputes under agreed-upon rules, as in price competition, would ordinarily not be called conflict; bombing the shop of a competitor, on the other hand, is conflict, not competition. In some cases the rules are ambiguous, and perceptions often differ; what businessmen call "cutthroat competition" and economists call a "game of ruin" occurs when rules are not perceived to be applicable.

It is not always easy to decide which rules apply—or whether any rules apply—to a given dispute. However, the kind of distinction we propose can be made, in most cases. To take a familiar illustration, two heavyweight boxers meet in the ring under clearly defined rules; they have mutually exclusive goals (only one can win); violence and bloodshed are very likely; yet we call this *competition,* not *conflict.* Tactics and circumstances are clearly laid down, and negative sanctions are provided if either breaks the rules. Suppose these same two men get into an argument in a bar and go into the alley to settle their dispute. They may well end up in a police station, charged with disturbing the peace, although their physical behavior is almost identical with that in the prize ring. Their behavior is *conflict,* because it flouts the rules laid down by society.

The rules that govern a dispute define the *expectations* which we discussed earlier. When rules get out of step with established expectations, as in the case of the Prohibition Act, they are difficult to enforce. The Civil Rights Act of 1964 codified expectations about which many people differed, and the enforcement of the act over the next few years will encounter many difficulties. When Congress passed the Wagner Act in 1933, many businessmen found that the rules did not fit their expectations and they rebelled against this law for some years.

Rules governing union-management disputes are laid down in a written contract. As in the instances just cited, such a contract may incorporate rules which do not fit the established expectations; and conflict may result. When a company that has fought unions for years finally signs an agreement with one, many supervisors have trouble adjusting; they go on firing union activists and ignoring seniority clauses until their expectations gradually become modified in conformance with the rules.

The written contract builds upon, but does not eliminate, what we have called the "psychological contract," the relationship of reciprocity in expectations of employer and employee. No contract can spell out just what the executive expects of the worker; job descriptions give only a small portion of the picture. Neither can any contract tell what treatment the employee expects from the company. Nevertheless, putting the contract in writing eliminates some ambiguity, clears up some confusions, and makes possible a gradual adjustment of expectations toward a common set of rules. As both sides agree on these, the relationship moves from conflict to competition, a dispute under rules.

Disputes at Contract Negotiation

The rules under which bargaining takes place are fuzzy and ambiguous. Although the NLRB requires both parties to bargain "in good faith," nobody knows what this means. It clearly does not mean that the union must abandon a claim whenever it is rejected by management, nor does it mean that management must yield when the union persists. The most we can say is that the rules require the parties to keep talking for a "reasonable" period of time; but even the word *reasonable* is subject to wide differences in interpretation. Given these ambiguities, it is not surprising that conflict is more likely to occur at contract-negotiating time than on other occasions.

Both parties bring certain expectations to the negotiations. It is general practice for each group to write its own expectations into proposals for the new contract. Thus management may try to write in that all promotions are based on ability alone. Unionists, knowing how hard it is to define ability with precision, fear discrimination and try to write in that all promotions are based on seniority alone. The likely compromise is one that attempts to incorporate both factors.

Similarly, each side is likely to have, at the beginning of negotiations, an idea of the limit beyond which it will make no concessions. This limit results in a *bargaining zone* for each side, with the preferred solution at one end and the tolerance limit at the other.

On a specific issue, such as union security, the union's desire may be a union shop with dues checkoff and superseniority for officers; the lowest acceptable settlement may be a union shop with an escape clause for a few present employees. The employer's wish may be for no union-security clause at all, and his tolerance limit may be compulsory union membership after a ninety-day probationary period. As the parties bargain, they explore these limits and, hopefully, find an area in which a compromise is possible. For both sides, there is a *bargaining zone* between the employer's tolerance limit and the union's tolerance limit. This conception is diagrammed in Figure 2.

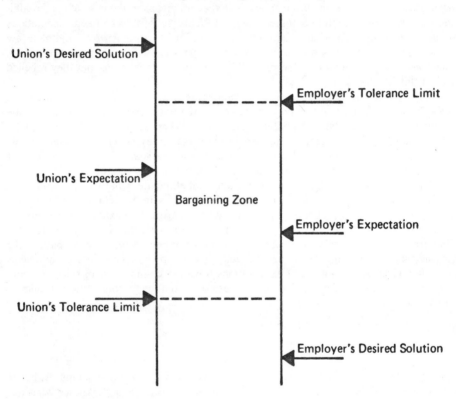

Figure 2. Desires, Expectations, and Tolerance Limits that Determine the Bargaining Zone

What factors determine the bargaining zone? . . . A contract clause that is unprecedented may seem completely unacceptable, whereas a familiar one is easily agreed to. In 1939, when rubber-workers in Akron were earning about 75c per hour, they did not demand an increase to $2.00; they asked for 90c and settled for 80c. Today no employer would resist a wage demand for 90c an hour (if anyone asked for it!). His range of acceptability is far above this point. This illustration shows that what is perceived as an unreasonable demand under one set of circumstances may look quite sensible under other conditions.

Standards of acceptability in bargaining are likely to be anchored to three sets of data: (a) industry practices, (b) community practices, and (c) recent trends. Thus, if one rubber company has granted extra vacations to employees of fifteen years' service, unions expect the same concession to be granted elsewhere in the industry (and executives in other companies are prone to feel that they must match the competition). Wage and other benefits are tied to the community average also. Workers in a low-paying industry who live in a community where wages are high will be keenly discontented, whereas, if they live in a low-income community, they will feel less severely frustrated. Finally, rising or falling trends in prices and wages affect our standards of expectation.

Conflicting parties, however, will select from among the data available only those items that fit their purposes. The union does not cite low-wage companies when making a case for an increase; and the company does not point to competitive practices when these are more generous than what it desires to grant. Each side can always find some instances to support the "wished-for" solution; and each side will tend to ignore the evidence presented by the opposition. Nevertheless, communication does take place; each takes some cognizance of the data, and the level of acceptability shifts. Management moves up a little, and the union down a little, until an acceptable point for both is identified. . . .

Disputes and the Grievance Procedure

Although disputes in contract bargaining draw more public attention, disputes about the behavior of the parties under a contract are more frequent. The *grievance procedure* is written into a contract to provide a set of rules under which such disputes can be settled in an orderly way, without an overt conflict. No contract can be written in such a way that every participant will agree on its meaning; just as contracts between businessmen can be taken to court or to arbitration, so union agreements must have a provision for settling disputes about whether the parties are living up to the contract.

When a worker files a grievance with his union steward, he is simply complaining that he is not receiving his rights (as he sees them) under the contract. Union spokesmen will sometimes heatedly say, "The company has violated this contract five hundred times in the past year," in reference to the number of grievances filed. This emotional way of stating the case implies that the worker is always right and the foreman is always wrong. But this implication is not easy to prove, and, as a rule, the foreman believes just as sincerely that he was interpreting the contract fairly.

In American firms, the grievance procedure usually provides for four steps. At first, the worker simply talks with his foreman. If the foreman modifies the situation to the employee's satisfaction, nothing is put into writing. This is the most efficient way to handle personal-grievance problems.

Second, if the worker is not satisfied, he writes out a grievance and files it with his committeeman or steward. As a result, the two may go together and talk with the foreman. Large numbers of grievances (in the typical company, over half of those written down) are settled at this first session. Often the steward convinces the worker that the contract does not cover the point at issue. However, if the steward wants to be re-elected, he may put up a show of a fight with the foreman and then resignedly say to the worker, "Well, I tried hard but couldn't get him to see reason."

Third, the steward may pass unsettled grievances, which he thinks involve contract violations, to a local committee of the union, which meets with production and labor-relations-staff people. Most of the remaining grievances are settled at this level. Unless arbitration is provided for, this is the final step before a strike. (In a multiplant company there may be one more level, in which the international-union representative sits down with the corporation official in charge of labor relations and tries to negotiate a settlement.)

Fourth, is *arbitration,* the last level for many union-management agreements. . . .

A grievance may be almost anything the employee wants to complain about, though his complaint must be tied to a clause in the contract. Because of the flexibility of the perceptual process, however, tying complaints to contracts is not as difficult as it might seem. For example, the employee who accuses his foreman of favoritism in the assignment of overtime work "sees" the foreman's actions in terms of his own desires. The worker may need the extra money; he may dislike a fellow worker who got the overtime work and extra pay; he may be annoyed with the foreman and want to get him in trouble with his boss by harassing him. But the foreman may "see" someone else as needing the money more; or that seniority should rule; or that an alphabetical procedure is fair; or that he is free to select anyone he wishes. Out of such divergent perceptions it is easy to build an industrial dispute.

Tactics Other Than Strikes

Management is in a position to stand pat on most of these controversies. The decision has been made and the action taken; it is up to the union to protest the unfulfilled conditions.

What shall the union leader do if the union's protest is ignored? There are a number of tactics other than a strike that he may utilize. Of these, we shall consider first some of the tactics used by workers themselves, whether organized or not.

The Slowdown

It is probable that even slaves used the *slowdown* against their masters. As far back as any records go in modern industry, this tactic has been used to pressure the employer to resolve a grievance. Mathewson (6) describes a food-packing plant in which workers learned that they could get some relief from work pressures by jamming the assembly line.

Some workers learn that if they obey all company rules in a blind, routine fashion, it slows down operations tremendously. The transit workers on the New York subway system, for example, can paralyze the system by observing all the obsolete safety rules on the books. Bus and truck drivers frequently take the same opportunity. Workers also make use of the device of reporting in sick. A big metropolitan dairy once had approximately four thousand drivers call in sick on the same day. Without considering the statistical probability that this coincidence represented real illness, we can see that the pressure on the employer was tremendous.

Some observers think that slowdowns will be more difficult for the worker with automated machinery. This does not seem probable. On the contrary, it is safe to predict that if workers have an unresolved grievance, they will find ways to stop the automated production line at irregular intervals and force the employer to act on their complaints.

Sabotage

The term *sabotage* is very instructive, because it is derived from the French *sabot,* meaning a wooden shoe; the term became popular through the practice of French factory workers of allowing a wooden shoe to fall into the machinery when they were discontented about working conditions. Management ultimately found this argument very persuasive in convincing them that they had better listen to worker grievances.

Sabotage is not always organized. One automobile executive told us of an operation in which production had been increased from 2,000 to 3,000 units per day by modification of a drill-press layout. However, the worker on this job resented the fact that he got no pay increase (the change was purely mechanical), and he discovered that by bumping the sheet metal against the drill as he removed the finished piece he would eventually break the drill and have to wait for it to be replaced. By some curious accident, the average production continued around 2,000 units per day. We do not know whether this message got through to top management, but if such breakdowns happen on a whole series of machines, it is understood rather promptly.

Legal Harassment

The union leaders have options such as filing charges against the employer with the NLRB on various disputed issues. Although these charges, in most cases, are eventually rejected by the Board, they require that the employer fill out forms, send witnesses to testify, and hire a lawyer or assign a member of his legal staff. Therefore, the nuisance value of the charges may be considerable, which sometimes contributes to accelerated settlement of disputes. The threat of legal harassment, however, is a two-edged sword. Employers may harass the union by NLRB charges, and they may even sue the union for damages under the Taft-Hartley Act. Few such suits ever come to trial and even fewer lead to collection of damages; usually the employer succeeds in convincing the union that a specific tactic must be abandoned, and when it is, the employer drops the suit.

Group Solidarity

In informal actions, as in the strike, the solidarity of the workers is very important. The sick-call technique depends on its use by a substantial majority of workers. If only a few cooperate in a slowdown, the employer is not under pressure.

We shall have something to say later about the problem of employee loyalty and group allegiance. At this point, the effectiveness of such tactics for putting pressure on the employer depends on the attitudes of the workers and on their willingness to take some individual risks in behalf of group goals.

The Strike

The reader may be perplexed by the fact that strikes, which monopolize newspaper reports on union-management relations, receive so little space here. The explanation is fairly simple. Strikes, like wars and other disastrous social conflicts, are similar to the visible part of an iceberg—they attract our attention to a danger. The vastly more significant portion (about nine-tenths) is hidden from view—yet the damage is done by the hidden portion of the iceberg. Strikes, therefore, serve a useful purpose when they call our attention to the fact that *unresolved industrial disputes* are in progress.

The Strike as Work Stoppage

In its simplest form, the strike is simply a concerted refusal to work. The employer has sales plans (or perhaps sales) that call for a given amount of production; the workers refuse to produce unless their demands are met. This refusal is a straightforward form of economic pressure, like that of a customer who refuses to buy unless the terms of trade are altered or that of a supplier who refuses to deliver raw materials unless the price is raised. The employer has the option of yielding or going—at least temporarily—out of business.

The Strike as an Information Device

The strike may often act primarily as a device to communicate to the public the fact that the workers are discontented and feel maltreated. In Italy and France, for example, many strikes are limited to twenty-four hours or even less. The unions do not have financial resources to help members through a long strike. Thus the strike is a technique for trying to mobilize the sympathy of the public and of the government. This kind of strike happens occasionally in the United States. A union may call a strike, which it has no hope of winning in terms of economic strength, in the hope that (a) it may get support from other unions, (b) it may get support from the public, or (c) it may induce the government to put pressure on the employer to settle.

Picketing is an important aspect of this public-information tactic; it is protected under the free-speech provision of the Bill of Rights. Pickets may succeed not only in communicating issues to the public, they may also embarrass management so that a settlement will be made that the union could not win on economic strength alone.

Public Perception of the Strike

The average citizen gets his information about a strike from newspaper headlines (regrettably, most people never read the stories under the headlines). Thus, the impression is usually one of unleashed violence and aggression. One sees headlines like these: "Union pickets jailed for overturning car"; "Union leader accuses plant guards of brutality"; "National Guard mobilized to keep peace"; "Six injured as shotgun blast cuts into picket line"; "Company guarantees protection to all who want to work"; "Plant damaged from brick-throwing unionists"; "Transportation workers refuse to cross picket line." When the strike involves the public more directly, we find these kinds of headlines: "Food rots as longshoremen refuse to unload"; 'Community terrorized as violence flares"; "Gasoline rationing feared as strike goes into fourth week"; "Strike imperils national security, says high official."

Psychoanalysts argue that most of us have repressed hostilities, which, we are afraid, may erupt if we are off guard; thus, we are intensely stimulated by outbursts of aggressive action in the environment. There seems to be some truth in this observation, as witness the morbid sightseers around a big fire, a catastrophic tornado scene, or a riot. Whether or not this theory is correct, the occurrence of violence in a strike induces anxiety, and people begin to demand government action. Since (on the surface, at least) the union precipitated the strike, the demand is likely to be for action against the union.

Dynamics of the Strike

It is precisely because of the adverse public view of strikes that we have presented our analysis of industrial disputes so methodically. If the reader is conscious of the vast background of motivational and perceptual factors that are involved in the causal process that results in the strike, perhaps he may realize that no simple explanation and no simple placing of blame on either side is going to be adequate.

The strike is inevitably tied in with *collective bargaining*—the attempt of both parties to establish a set of mutually acceptable expectations about each other. Insofar as both parties in bargaining hope to *optimize* (get the most gratification from the other party with the least loss to themselves), the bargaining relationship becomes one where both parties attempt to determine the consequences of various courses of action. [Elsewhere we have] discussed how the SEU model, utilizing motivational and perceptual factors, operated for the single person or group. In collective bargaining, the model applies to a two-group situation.

Collective bargaining is a sort of poker game. If a given course of action is undertaken, the expected utilities of the consequences, and the probability of their occurring, must be determined by a party in the dispute not only for itself but for the opposing party as well. Thus, the parties must attempt to put themselves in the "others' shoes." Interestingly enough, both company and union leadership are aware of a need for such mutual understanding, and have quite recently formalized the procedure both in role-playing and prebargaining approaches. For example, Table 2 indicates that it is essential for the union to make an estimate of whether management considers Alternative 1 or Alternative 2 more acceptable. Union tactics will be governed in considerable degree by the intensity of management opposition anticipated; and the firmness of the company negotiators will depend upon management's estimation of union strength and persistence.

TABLE 2

ILLUSTRATION OF UNION AND COMPANY ALTERNATIVES AND RELATED CONSEQUENCES

Company	*Union*
ALTERNATIVE 1:	**ALTERNATIVE I:**
Giving in to union demands Perceived *Consequences:* 1. Lessening of investor return 2. Loss of competitive standing 3. Setting bad precedent 4. Avoiding costly strike 5. Avoiding government and public ill will	Accepting company counteroffer Perceived *Consequences:* 1. Loss of membership support 2. Loss of status within union movement 3. Setting bad precedent 4. Avoiding costly strike 5. Avoiding government and public ill will
ALTERNATIVE 2:	**ALTERNATIVE 2:**
Refusing to accede to union demands Perceived *Consequences:* 1. Due to potential strike, loss of investor return 2. Due to potential strike, loss of competitive standing 3. Loss of government and public good will 4. Maintenance of company prerogatives 5. Breaking union power	Sticking to original demands Perceived *Consequences:* 1. Prove strength and determination of union to members 2. Due to potential strike, loss of member income 3. Due to potential strike, loss of member support 4. Loss of government and public good will 5. Teach company a "lesson"

In major negotiations, such as those of the UAW with the "Big Three" auto companies, an almost formal ritual has been established. "Trial balloons" are released, either at the bargaining table or in the newspapers, and the vigor of the reaction to these proposals is carefully assessed. Each side asks for considerably more than it expects to get (see Fig. 2) and is constantly on the alert for cues to the issues on which the opponent is willing to fight to the finish. Since both teams are composed of professionals who have dealt with each other for years, the chances steadily improve that this information exchange will be accurate and that a settlement without serious disruption of the economy will result.

The Losses from Strikes

"If man were the rational economic animal postulated by classical economic theory, strikes would long since have disappeared from the American scene" (10, p. 439). Workers as well as employers lose heavily in any kind of extended strike. If both sides calculated long-run gains and injuries realistically, the necessary compromises would be reached without a strike. Note, for example, that the average worker puts in about two thousand hours a year on his job. Thus, a gain of 5c an hour over a prestrike offer gains him $100 a year. At current wage levels, this means that he has to work a year just to recoup the loss of one week on strike; hence, on a five-week strike, it takes five years just to get back even, before any net gain in earnings is experienced. From the union viewpoint, other losses must also be considered. These include the decrease of membership, expenditures for emergency aid to striker families, and possible political backlash in the form of restrictive legislation against unions.

The losses to the employer are harder to determine but substantial. During strikes, white-collar workers are usually kept on salary, and maintenance costs and interest charges continue. Customers may be lured away by competitors who can promise immediate delivery, and the public image of the firm may suffer substantially, especially if trouble occurs during the strike. Considering the sums spent to "improve the image," such losses may be costly to recoup.

Losses to consumers, and to the economy as a whole, are sometimes important. Hardships result from interference with normal marketing procedures; in a transportation tie-up, food may spoil. Thus, when work stoppages occur, there are other losses, beyond the major ones to workers and employers.

Violence in Strikes

Not the least of the costs of strikes is the occurrence of violence. Pickets marching around a plant recite their grievances and reinforce one another's hostilities. They may impulsively block the owner or top executives from getting in, or start throwing rocks to express their feelings. If the employer violates the strikers' expectations by hiring strike-breakers and attempting to operate his plant, he is likely to trigger extreme hostility. In the Essex Wire strike of 1964 nonstrikers' cars were forced off the road and the occupants beaten, plant windows were broken with bricks, and a plant guard was hit by shotgun fire. Although such incidents are rare as compared with the period 1935-1939, they are still deplorably frequent.

How can men who would not dream of beating up another man to take 5c from him beat up strangers in the course of an effort to gain a pay raise of 5c per hour? Several psychological factors operate in such behavior: the feeling of *social approval* for violence (since the other fellows do the same thing, it can't be wrong); reduced fear of punishment, because of *anonymity* (there are so many strikers that the police can't identify anybody to arrest, and witnesses won't testify anyway); the *excitement* of the situation; *displacement* of aggression from other frustrations; and the *stimulation* from belligerent leaders—all these motives contribute to irrational outbursts of violence on the part of strikers.

Whereas violence is rarely initiated by employers, *provocative* actions among them are common. Hiring additional guards, setting up barricades, and displaying armaments are employer actions not conducive to peaceful arbitration. Other employers, in their public comments on a strike, suggest that theirs is a righteous cause, in which they are justified in lashing out with all force available. However, because of a similar self-righteousness, millions of people have been killed in the many religious wars of this planet's history; there is a grave danger when an aggressive man feels that the improper behavior of unionists justifies his resort to uninhibited violence.

Lockouts

The manager also has an outlet for his annoyance, or simply a tool for imposing economic power, in the *lockout*. This outlet takes the form of saying, "If you don't conform to our demands, we'll close the plant." Thus the worker's concern over his job security is mobilized against his other motives, such as the desire for money, or some other goal he was seeking.

The employer may use the threat of a lockout to put the pressure of a majority of workers upon a minority which has a grievance. Where several employers bargain as a group with a single union, the threat of the union to strike a single employer can be countered by the threat of the association to close down every plant. Thus the complaining workers are faced with pressure from their fellow union members, who have no desire to be without paychecks while the dispute is being settled.

Principles of Dispute Settlement

Union-management disputes may be separated into those that arise from negotiations of new contracts and those that arise from disagreements over the meaning of contracts already signed. The latter are usually called *grievance cases,* and the former *contract cases.* Although the basic principles for settling these controversies are the same, some techniques (such as voluntary arbitration) that are widely used for grievance cases are rarely if ever used for contract cases. Despite this technical difference, we shall discuss the psychological principles of dispute settlement as if the two cases were the same—which, for our purposes, is almost always true.

Psychologists find their basic principles for guiding settlement of disputes in the laws of human behavior—specifically in the phenomena of perception, motivation, emotion, and frustration. These principles are the same, whether the disputes are between husband and wife, parent and child, Catholic and Protestant, Jew and anti-Semite, or Negro and white-supremacist.

Group disputes arise for only two reasons. One is that group A prevents group B from obtaining some sort of goal, and the second is that group A is perceived by group B as blocking its goal attainment, even though independent observers may agree that no such blockage occurs. The two reasons thus resolve into one: group A is perceived as threatening the goal achievement of group B.

. . . At this time, we wish to concentrate on the settlement of disputes that have already developed. Let us first identify three basic principles, and then see how they apply to some concrete instances of industrial disputes.

A Higher Loyalty

Parties to a dispute will settle their differences fairly readily if members of both groups acknowledge a *higher loyalty* to some more inclusive group. Unionists and executives share a loyalty to the nation which often plays a significant role in settling controversies. This loyalty was most conspicuously displayed during World War II, when the no-strike pledge of unions cut lost time from work stoppages to a minute fraction of its former total. But it has also operated in many other instances, such as in the acceptance by railroad unions of the compulsory arbitration of work rules, and the submission by employers to governmental orders to cease operations or to rehire discharged unionists. The importance of this psychological factor can best be demonstrated by quarrels between nations, in which case there is no higher loyalty, and in which it is considered a man's patriotic duty to kill off as many of the enemy as possible. Should either management or union lose confidence in the impartiality of the government, a similar kind of open warfare might be resorted to in union-management conflicts.

Superordinate Goals

Disputes may be settled with little difficulty when both parties recognize some goal above the one they are fighting about. In union-management disputes, this common goal is likely to be the necessity to keep the enterprise going, since profits and wages alike depend on production and sales. The goal of "mutual survival" is in the background of all discussions, and neither party—except under extreme emotional pressure—is likely to try to destroy the other. In the 1930s, many corporate executives still thought they could destroy unions, and, consequently, mutual considerations were less effective than they are today; but that particular belief has virtually disappeared.

A Common Frame of Reference

Disputes may be controlled when the parties can come to a reasonable agreement regarding the facts. When the twelve-hour day in industry was standard, managers could not "see" that it placed a heavy strain on workers. Today, there is general agreement that an eight-hour day is the most that should be demanded except under emergency conditions. A common frame of reference means that events in the enterprise will be perceived in a similar way.

We can illustrate in many ways the importance of similarity in perception. For example, the image held of the opposing party is important in dispute settlement. If the executive perceives the union as irresponsible and violent, he will be suspicious of its proffered agreements, and will try to hedge his promises with all kinds of reservations. This action will arouse the suspicions of the union leaders, who will interpret it as evidence that he intends to weaken or nullify the agreement.

Established expectations have their role to play. The manager has the belief that he alone has the right to determine the speed of operation of the machines. If the union challenges this belief, the manager may lose sight of the issue and he becomes more concerned with inroads upon his prerogatives. He may feel personally injured if his freedom of action is restricted beyond what he considers proper.

It has often been urged that negotiators for each side try to state the case for the other side, to be sure they understand it. Thus, the head of the management team would try to verbalize what the union is asking for, to the satisfaction of the union committee; the unionists in turn would have to show that they can put in words what management is asking, to the satisfaction of the management group. Such devices help in developing a common frame of reference; or, more precisely, they help in attaching verbal labels to events in the same pattern, so that communication becomes possible. However, this process does not guarantee that both sides have equal knowledge of the positions taken. Blake and Mouton (1) found that when two teams of managers competed to solve a problem, each group might meet the test of verbalizing the opposed position, although, on a test of information, they still knew more about their own solution than about the competing solution. Thus, this technique, though helpful, is no panacea.

It would probably be beneficial if more managers had work experience at the factory level. Current practice, however, is to hire recent college graduates as junior executives, and the only factory-work experience they get is of an observational variety. This management-hiring trend may make mutual understanding even more difficult in the future.

Applying the Principles

The basic principles for settling disputes operate in various specific devices such as bargaining, mediation, and arbitration. Since, in a sense, all union-management relations begin with the bargaining of a contract to cover the responsibilities of the parties to each other, let us discuss the bargaining process, to see how our basic principles operate in specific areas of disputes.

The Bargaining Process

Bargaining begins when one side attempts to communicate to the other its perception of the work situation and to induce a change in this situation. Bargaining may be directed toward higher wages, toward less loafing on the job, toward elimination of safety hazards, or toward any other goals that either management or union desires.

Bargaining is necessary because the situation as seen by management does not coincide with that seen by workers and union officers. If the two percepts agreed, joint action would be almost automatic. For example, if unionists agreed that workers were taking excessive time off, they would not object to its elimination. The controversy is over what is "excessive." Similarly, if managers saw a four-hour stretch on the assembly line as intolerable, they would quickly change the work rules. In this case, the controversy relates to an operational definition of "intolerable."

The bargaining process is a kind of learning situation for the members of each committee. Percepts of the work situation, expectancies, and levels of aspiration are built up over a period of many years, and the usual work situation tends to reinforce these established images. When managers talk only to managers, they are not contacting other views on any issues. Similarly, when unionists talk only to their fellows, they reinforce one another's version of the facts. The bargaining session is different, in that the union requires managers to take a look at some evidence that they have previously ignored, and management insists that the union representatives examine some information that is not compatible with their fixed opinions.

Over a period of time, the participants begin to see the facts in a slightly different light. Perhaps most of this change is in the estimate of the opponent's bargaining limit. The union spokesmen decide that if they push beyond a certain point, management will take a strike. The company team concludes that if they do not yield up to a specified level, the union will walk out. As each party modifies its demands, the discussion moves into the bargaining zone, and a peaceful settlement becomes possible. Graphic examples of this change will be found in Douglas (3). Although the cases Douglas describes are contract negotiations, the generalizations apply equally well to settling grievances. The only difference is that the written contract provides certain clauses which define the limits of the bargaining zone.

A major change that bargaining may produce is in the frame of reference, or the managers' standards set by "what other firms are doing." The union may bring in evidence—which management has preferred to ignore—to the effect that a certain change in work rules has been accepted by much of the industry. Management may present data on wage scales in the community that vitiate the union plea of inequity. Thus each side is, to some extent, compelled to assess data that it had previously ignored. This process may induce a shift in the bargaining zone.

In bargaining sessions, both sides usually make ritualistic avowals of their desire for mutual survival: the union denies any wish for the ruin of the company, and managers disavow any hope to break the union. Each also proclaims its loyalty to the welfare of the community and the nation. Whether these assertions are more than rituals is not clear. They may serve to remind each group of its dependence upon the other, if only to a limited extent, and this reminder favors peaceful settlement of the dispute. . . .

The Grievance Machinery

Normally, after a contract has been negotiated, procedures are established for settling disputes about the application of the contract. This procedural machinery serves mainly to bring the dispute within rules, so that it can be handled in an orderly fashion (through "competition" rather than "conflict").

Grievance hearings, at the first stage, require that both sides try to get all the relevant facts (but, naturally, each gathers evidence to support its contention). In some cases, it appears that either the worker or the foreman was misinformed, and the grievance is quickly cleared up. In other instances, there is a basic disagreement over the meaning of the contract. Such disputes may result in strikes, if the contract does not provide for arbitration.

We must not be surprised if the foreman (or the worker) is unclear about the interpretation of the union contract. In one study (2), even top union and management officials—those who had negotiated the agreement—gave different answers to questions about contract clauses.

The existence of established grievance machinery is probably the most important single factor for reducing the intensity and frequency of union-management conflicts. It prevents tensions from building up and assures the worker of an orderly procedure for handling his case. Because of the participation of union officials in it, to defend his position, he feels more willing to accept a verdict, even if unfavorable.

The use of bargaining officials, who are somewhat removed from the specific irritation, serves two purposes. First, distance lends perspective; thus, the more emotional elements of the worker-foreman interaction become diluted, or even disappear, at higher levels of the grievance procedure. Second, higher officials are more acutely aware of superordinate goals, which are very important to them. The foreman cannot know much about customer relations, but the vice-president for labor relations may be well aware that labor peace is very important at the moment. Further, he may know that this issue involves others that have implications beyond the ken of the foreman. Likewise, the international-union representative may abandon the worker's grievance, because he sees implications detrimental to union welfare (e.g., when resolving the grievance might arouse factional controversy inside the union).

Machinery for Dispute Settlement

Many controversies go beyond the level of in-plant grievance and the problems of negotiating new contracts. In some disputes, one or both parties may feel that their basic interests have become involved, and in others, emotional intensity may become so high that settlement at lower levels is impossible. We shall consider some of the techniques that are applicable to such disputes.

Government Intervention

When strikes or threats of strikes imply enough violence and hazards to third parties, government intervention may be required. For example, in 1962, after it had installed diesel locomotives and other advanced equipment, railroad management began a campaign to reduce the number of workers in freight service. Because this campaign threatened the jobs of many thousands of *operating* employees, the *operating* brotherhoods threatened a nationwide strike if the freight-service layoffs went into effect. Faced with this frightening possibility, Congress voted its first compulsory-arbitration law. Under this law, a panel was set up to hear the arguments of both sides and to render a verdict that could be enforced by the courts.

Government intervention, however, can be effective only when both sides are convinced of the impartiality of the arbitration panel, and its success depends to some extent on the patriotism of managers and unionists. If a radical union rejects the basic value of national unity, or if the arbitrators appear biased, the arbitration is likely to fail. Open violence, or continued hostility, if violence is suppressed, is likely to follow.

The railroad arbitration of 1962 was government intervention in its extreme form, *compulsory arbitration.* More common is *government mediation,* in which government representatives persuade (or press) both sides to sit down and negotiate when private talks have proved unsuccessful. However, before we explore this kind of settlement, let us consider *private arbitration.*

Private Arbitration

Many union-management contracts include a clause that provides for binding arbitration of disputes that occur over the meaning of the contract's terms. In practice, these disagreements involve different ways of perceiving situations. For example, a contract may list "sleeping on the job" as a ground for discharge. Without visual evidence, however, a foreman may decide that a man who was away from his post for forty-five minutes was sleeping, and fire him. The arbitrator may be required to decide whether the contract has been violated.

Similar ambiguous situations arise in connection with decisions about the proper amount of overtime pay, the pension rights of a retired employee, the right of a worker to refuse to enter a hazardous workplace, and many others. The worker and his representatives "see" the evidence in a way favorable to him; the manager may "see" something quite different. The arbitrator, as an outsider with a specialized knowledge of factory conditions, is asked to decide which percept is justified in terms of the relevant contract clause.

Establishments which have few cases going to arbitration are likely to hire an arbitrator when occasion requires; large corporations, such as the automobile companies, retain a *permanent umpire,* who is always available to hear disputes that cannot be settled at lower levels. In either case, it is customary for the cost to be split equally between management and union, and, after any settlement, either side can terminate the arbitrator's employment. If the arbitrator is a permanent umpire, the terminating party must pay *all* of his salary for the remainder of the year, a requirement that discourages impulsive actions.

Why do most large corporations, jointly with the unions, hire permanent umpires to hear arbitration cases and render decisions? The answer to this goes back to our discussion of perception. There is no way of knowing the "real" facts in any industrial dispute, because they differ according to the observer involved. A worker (and his steward) may honestly assert that he is working at a high output while the foreman alleges, with equal sincerity, that he is slowing production deliberately. A safety hazard that looks trivial to a safety engineer may look quite threatening to the worker who is in the situation for several hours a day. In short, there will always be disagreements about whether the facts support the position of management or the position of the union.

It would be possible to have wildcat strikes over such disagreements and, thus, to settle them by sheer economic force. But wildcat strikes are messy procedures, and they disrupt the activities of people not directly involved. The grievance and arbitration procedures provide an orderly way of handling disputes under an existing contract without resorting to picket lines and sit-downs at every turn. As long as both parties have confidence that the arbitrator is impartial, they will accept his decision as final. Any decision, even an unfavorable one, is often preferred to a continuing state of ambiguity and tension.

Mediation of Disputes

To accelerate the settlement of labor disputes, *outside mediation*—generally from the federal or state mediation service—may be necessary. The mediator may be invited in by the parties, when bargaining seems about to break down, or, more often, he may offer his assistance when a strike is dragging on and the parties have developed so much hostility that they refuse to speak to each other.

Unlike the arbitrator, the mediator has no power to impose a binding solution within an existing contract. He is usually brought in when a new contract is up for discussion and there are no agreed rules to apply. Thus, he is a kind of technical consultant to both sides, helping them find a solution, rather than a judge deciding who is right. He has only such tools as his prestige as an official mediator, his persuasiveness, his knowlege of union contracts, his sense of humor, and his ability to see the facts as they appear to each of the parties.

One of the mediator's main contributions is his opportunity to break the communications barrier between the parties. In a long strike—especially if there is any violence—tempers rise, each side calls the opposing leaders unpleasant names, and the parties may simply refuse to sit down together and bargain. Thus, the request from the mediator, in the name of the federal or state government, that the parties meet with him for talks on the problem is, in many cases, important to industrial peace.

Spokesmen for union or management sometimes become committed to positions from which it is embarrassing to retreat. For instance, a company president may state publicly, "We will never sign a contract with this union." Later he may discover that it will be economically wise to sign the contract. A request from a federal or state mediator to resume negotiations now helps to save face. If the president can point to a request from the White House, or even from the governor of his state, that he resume negotiations, he avoids an appearance of defeat.

The mediator can make other important contributions. He usually has a much wider range of experience with contract clauses than either the local management or the local union have. If he is experienced, he has learned to perceive the issues as they are perceived from both sides of the table. When he finds the parties deadlocked, he may be able to introduce a new way of defining the situation or an alternative way of phrasing a clause that will fall within the "bargaining zone" and, hence, be acceptable to both sides. In some disputes, he may simply keep calling meetings; since neither side is willing to take the public responsibility for breaking off these talks, the negotiators may become worn down to the point where they will reach agreement rather than continue the wearying routine.

Virtually the only sanction that the mediator has is public opinion, and even this weapon is not always reliable. Unless a strike causes great inconvenience, the public pays little attention, so that neither party will anticipate severe public censure if the mediator blames it for breaking off discussions. To a large extent, the mediator must rely upon persuasion and the ultimate operation of economic pressures on both sides to open the road to a settlement.

The Hidden Agenda

A basic requirement for mediating disputes is to find out what the parties *really* want. Unfortunately, their goals are not always discernible in their verbalized demands. We have noted elsewhere that some union demands are primarily punitive in character, as when it is impossible to eliminate unpleasant working conditions but possible to punish the company by demanding higher wages and other concessions. Aside from such cases, we find many examples of poorly verbalized or unstated goals which are sought in the dispute.

Consider the case of an impending reduction in the work force due to automated machinery. The union may demand that the coming layoffs be based solely on seniority, whereas management may demand that only those workers be kept on who have demonstrated their ability to do the new jobs. On the surface, such demands appear irreconcilable. However, closer inspection may indicate that the union is basically concerned with favoritism and bias in layoffs and wants a guarantee that no one will be laid off because of his union activity. It may happen that management wants to keep a few technically trained, valuable men who have not been on the job long enough to meet the standard of seniority that would have to be applied. Under these conditions, the mediator can propose a compromise that gives union officers superseniority as protection or that gives management the right to keep some workers without regard to seniority.

The average person is not always capable of giving an accurate account of his motives. Each of us has many desires that he prefers not to acknowledge even to himself. One role of the professional unionist is to verbalize the desires of workers, who perhaps find self-expression difficult or dangerous; but executives are not exempt from this phenomenon. Observations by McMurry (7), Eliasberg (4), and others indicate that successful industrialists may have unconscious desires for power and unacknowledged aggressive impulses that drastically limit their ability to negotiate intelligently with labor unions. The work of Muench (8, 9) suggests that the methods of clinical psychologists for making unconscious material conscious can make important contributions to mutual understanding—which is the first step in dispute settlement.

The Widened Agenda

Just as unrevealed goals may need to be brought into the open, so unintended consequences or wider implications of the controversy may need consideration. An arbitrator is barred from widening the dispute; he must rule within limits set by a contract. The mediator, however, can ask for a broader frame of reference. He may inquire of the union leaders whether they may not split their union by introducing a new seniority policy; he may call the attention of management to possible public displeasure with a plan to finance "paid" vacations through state unemployment insurance. The mediator can be very flexible; he may seek to rule out discussion of anything but the narrow point at issue, or he may insist on widening the agenda to include unintended consequences of a debated proposal. The skilled mediator is the person who knows when to adopt one tactic or the other.

The Public Interest

It would seem that the superordinate goal or higher good that disputing parties should seek, above their own advantage, is the *public interest*. Unfortunately, objective definitions of the public interest are hard to find. Each partisan sees his own goals as representing "the public welfare." Management spokesmen say, "It is in the public interest to keep prices down and avoid inflation," and union leaders retort, "It is in the public interest to keep purchasing power up and avoid recessions." What is the public interest? Obviously, it includes both of these alternatives, and many others.

Some would argue that the government is in the best position to determine the public interest. But when we observe the regional and interest blocs that exist within Congress, each asserting that his group's welfare is in the public interest, we lose enthusiasm for such a criterion. We are not accusing the labor and management leaders of cynical hypocrisy. Each man can truthfully and honestly say that, *as he sees it,* the national welfare will be best served if his side wins the victory. Perceptual distortions operate so effectively that he cannot see the arguments on the other side.

For the near future, decisions will probably continue to be made on the basis of political or economic strength. If the public sufficiently dislikes such decisions, a new coalition will probably develop enough political power to reverse the policies.

The Role of the Irrational

Executives and workers often hold to certain positions because of emotional involvement rather than "rational" self-interest in the economic sense. For example, an executive may say that he would simply refuse a demand for a profit-sharing clause on the ground that "it is not right." He would consider the probability and cost of a strike, but his decision would not be based on economic grounds. Similarly, workers may strike over excessive and arbitrary controls over workplace behavior, even though they will lose a great deal of money because of their action.

Perhaps it is fortunate that people sometimes act irrationally. Life could become pretty dull if everyone cooly calculated costs and made decisions on a purely economic basis. In evaluating industrial-relations problems, we must avoid the error of assuming that economics has the final or even the larger portion of the answer. A keen awareness of human emotions and of the variety of goals sought is thus important.

It is equally necessary that we recognize the valuable contributions to industrial harmony made by mediators and arbitrators. By their very detachment from the immediate conflict situation, they are able to view the problem in a larger perspective and see it without the distorting influences of personal emotion and motivation. Such perception makes for judicious and realistic problem solutions.

References

1. Blake, Robert R., and Mouton, Jane S. Reactions to intergroup competition under win-lose conditions. *Mgt. Sci.,* 1961, 7, 420-435.

2. Derber, M., Chalmers, W. E., and Stagner, R. The labor contract: Provision and practice. *Personnel,* 1958, 34, 19-30.

3. Douglas, Ann. *Industrial peacemaking.* New York: Columbia Univ. Press, 1962.

4. Eliasberg, W. A study in psychodynamics of the industrial executive. *J. clin. Psychopathol.,* 1949, 10, 276-284.

5. Ford, Henry, II. Bargaining and economic growth. Address to American Society of Corporation Secretaries, June 22, 1964.

6. Mathewson, S. B. *Restriction of output among unorganized workers.* N.Y.: Viking, 1931.

7. McMurry, R. N. The clinical psychology approach. In A. Kornhauser (Ed.), *Psychology of labor-management relations.* Champaign, Ill.: Industrial Relations Research Assn., 1949.

8. Muench, George A. A clinical psychologist's treatment of labor-management conflicts. *Personnel Psychol.*, 1960, 13, 165-172.

9. Muench, George A. A clinical psychologist's treatment of labor-management conflicts: A four-year study. *J. hum. Psychol.*, 1963, I, 92-97.

10. Stagner, R. *Psychology of industrial conflict.* New York: Wiley 1956.

Your Clerical Workers Are Ripe for Unionism

ALFRED VOGEL

. . . There are currently over 13 million clerical workers (i.e., stenographers, secretaries, bookkeepers, business machine operators) in the United States; many are young, many are black, and most are women. The only larger group, with over 14 million members, consists of semi-skilled personnel (i.e., assemblers, machine operators, drivers, etc.), and Census Bureau data indicate that the gap between the two will be even smaller by 1975.

While semiskilled workers are heavily unionized, clerical workers have traditionally resisted union overtures, relying instead on management responsiveness to their problems. But the foundation of this resistance to unions—positive attitudes toward management—is breaking down. The evidence comes from a recent analysis, performed by the Opinion Research Corporation [Editors note: The author is Vice-President of Opinion Research Corporation], where the attitudes of clerical employees toward management during the past 15 years were reviewed. The results indicate that during the last five years there has been a marked and growing dissatisfaction among these workers—to the extent that many may soon turn to unions for a solution to their problems.

Furthermore, the unions are exhibiting an increased interest in wooing clerical and other white-collar workers. For example:

The UAW and the Steelworkers Union have set up white-collar units.

The Office and Professional Employees International Union has launched, with considerable fanfare, a campaign to organize one million bank employees.

The Alliance for Labor Action (a conglomerate of the UAW, Chemical Workers, Distributive Workers, and Teamsters) is embarking on an expanded white-collar organization effort, especially in the South.

Traditionally middle-class, white-collar groups such as teachers, engineers, nurses, and social workers already form a growing percentage of organized labor, and it appears that the large army of clerical employees is becoming ripe for a similar move. Just how ripe, and what management can do about it, is the focus of this article. The conclusions are supported by a wide sample of attitudes from over 25,000 employees in over 90 companies; and the businesses surveyed represent a solid cross section of U.S. industry—banks, insurance companies, manufacturing companies, and utilities. In most cases at least 50 companies are included in the analysis of a single issue.

Beneath the Surface

Numerous observers have pointed out the difficulties that face unions attempting to organize clerical employees. Some of the reasons are structural (e.g., the physical problem of reaching this group with the union message). But the majority of reasons for clerical workers' resistance are sociological: (a) the widespread feeling that unions are beneath their dignity and that they can bargain for themselves, (b) the belief that they, as members of the middle class, are identified with management and therefore should reject unions, and (c) the tendency to think of unions as unseemly, rabble-rousing organizations. . . .

During the past decade, unions have had only modest success at best in organizing clerical workers and other white-collar employees. For example, while over one million nonmanagerial white-collar workers were recruited by unions from 1958 to 1968, the yearly level of this group's union membership has remained at about 11 percent.[1]

At least on the surface, the probability of union success in organizing clerical workers appears to be limited—a slow process of washing away rocks of resistance, winning an election here, losing an election there. Certainly nothing approaching a breakthrough, like the great CIO successes with industrial workers in the 1930's, *seems* to be in order.

But beneath the surface there are signs that attitudes are changing, that clerical employees are becoming sufficiently provoked by management to take a second look at unions. . . .

White-collar Blues

Clerical workers indeed *have* become much less satisfied on most key employee relations issues in recent years (1966 to the present) than in past years (1955 to 1965). *Exhibit I* shows attitude comparisons for these two periods. The vertical line represents clerical employees' average favorable ratings of their company for the base period, 1955 to 1965; the horizontal bars are average percentage increases or decreases in these same ratings since 1966. All three sections of *Exhibit I* (basic employment conditions, personnel practices, and communication) show substantial declines for the recent five-year period and indicate that some fundamental union arguments should have increasing receptivity among clerical workers. For example:

• The contention that unions can guarantee good pay, adequate benefits, and protection of job security. (Employee satisfaction with management on each of these issues has declined considerably.)

• The claim that unions offer protection from arbitrary management decisions and can assure fair treatment for organized workers. (In this connection, note especially the declines in ratings for "Deals fairly with everyone," "Takes employees' interests into account," and "Applies policies consistently.")

Note too that clerical employees feel increasingly remote and shut off from management. Communication has always been a problem; but, according to clerical employees, it has become worse than ever in recent years. Many say they do not know what is going on, cannot get the ear of upper management, and are not even told in advance about changes affecting their own work. In short, clerical employees are beginning to feel like mere cogs in a great impersonal bureaucracy, and there is a growing tendency to see management as a nameless, faceless mask of authority and indifference.

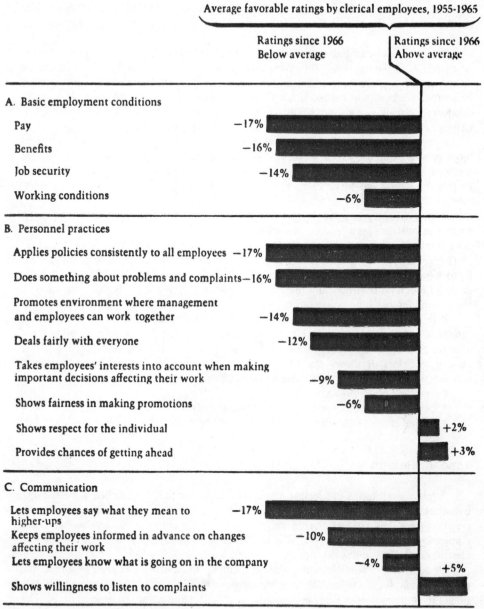

Average favorable ratings by clerical employees, 1955-1965

Ratings since 1966
Below average

Ratings since 1966
Above average

A. Basic employment conditions

Pay   −17%

Benefits   −16%

Job security   −14%

Working conditions   −6%

B. Personnel practices

Applies policies consistently to all employees −17%

Does something about problems and complaints −16%

Promotes environment where management and employees can work together −14%

Deals fairly with everyone −12%

Takes employees' interests into account when making important decisions affecting their work −9%

Shows fairness in making promotions −6%

Shows respect for the individual +2%

Provides chances of getting ahead +3%

C. Communication

Lets employees say what they mean to higher-ups −17%

Keeps employees informed in advance on changes affecting their work −10%

Lets employees know what is going on in the company −4%

Shows willingness to listen to complaints +5%

Note: All figures are percentage points difference.

Exhibit I. Corporate responsiveness: comparative ratings on key employee relations issues

Depth of Decline

One could argue, of course, that not just clerical employees, but employees generally, are more critical of their companies today; everyone is more critical. Students riot, hardhats beat up hippies, and blacks protest and burn down buildings. It is just the times we live in.

Comparisons of attitudes over time for other occupational groups—engineers, managers, and hourly employees, for example—do, in fact, show some decline in favorable ratings and some increase in criticism. But the knowledge that other employees may also be more disturbed than before is not likely to appease clerical employees. It is small comfort for a man with a weak heart to be told that more Americans than ever before are having heart attacks. He wants something done about *his* heart problem.

Moreover, the attitudes of clerical employees have declined more sharply than those of any group for which we have similar comparative information. They have, for instance, sloped down considerably more than those of the heavily unionized blue-collar employees who have historically viewed management far less enthusiastically on a comparative basis.

Exhibit II compares the favorable ratings by both of these groups for the same employee relations issues discussed earlier. Among blue-collar employees the results are a standoff—up on some factors, down on others. The tangible factors (pay, benefits, and job security) show substantial declines in both groups. But on most of the intangible factors (personnel practices and communication), the ratings of clerical workers have declined much more drastically than those of blue-collar workers. In fact, on some of these same factors blue-collar ratings have actually improved.

It is important to point out that I am talking about relative declines in favorable ratings. Clerical employees currently have more favorable opinions of their employers and, on balance, still express less criticism than do blue-collar workers. But the gap is closing, as *Exhibit II* shows, and there are actually some issues where clerical attitudes are already less favorable than those of blue-collar employees. These include:

- Applying policies consistently.
- Letting employees speak up to higher authority.
- Telling employees what is going on in the company.

Time for Reform

While the attitudes of clerical employees in the companies studied have moved, overall, in a more negative direction since 1966 than have the attitudes of hourly workers, this trend has not yet caused an en masse movement to unionization. For most companies, there is still time to act—time to find out how much discontent exists among clerical employees and what their major problems are.

Of course, it is possible that many companies will be lucky (we are presuming that most would prefer not to have their office employees unionized) and will avoid unionization of their clerical work force by ignoring the problem and doing business as usual. The traditional reluctance of office employees to join unions, for whatever reasons, may be a sufficient deterrent.

However, teachers, nurses, and other middle-class groups have already begun to turn toward unions, and, in view of what is happening to employee attitudes, it would be a bad bet, I think, for companies to depend on the historical reluctance of clerical workers to sign up.

Reversing the Trend

There is no pat formula for resolving the problems of clerical employees. Often, however, concerned upper management is prone to rely on individual supervisors as instrumental figures in successful resistance to unionization. It feels that as long as employees respect and admire their supervisor, there is nothing to worry about. And if employees are dissatisfied, this is evidence that their immediate boss is not doing his job.

Although the supervisor is important and sometimes crucial in employee decisions on whether to join a union, companies may be grossly misled if they think good supervision is a sufficient bulwark against discontent. In fact, our studies show that clerical employees normally *do* respect their supervisor. They tend to think he knows his job, treats them with respect, and communicates with them adequately on job-related matters. Furthermore, as is shown in *Exhibit III,* the ratings that office employees give their supervisor have, for the most part, stayed about the same during the periods we have been discussing (changes of one, two, or three percentage points are not really significant). It is the ratings of the companies overall and of their personnel practices that have gone down.

Looking at the data, there are two evident exceptions to the general stability of supervisor ratings. In the more recent period, clerical employees: (a) rate their supervisor significantly less favorably on taking action on their complaints or problems, and (b) rate their supervisor more favorably on his willingness to listen to them. It seems that many of these workers are trying to say that the boss is a nice, sympathetic guy, but he is really powerless to do much about their problems. It is the people upstairs who do not listen or act. . . .

More explicitly, criticism focuses on matters over which the company, not the supervisor, has most control—pay, benefits, job security, various personnel practices, and broad-gauged communications matters. Strong supervisors and good training programs for them, though necessary and laudable, are not by any means the sole answer or a problem panacea. Companies must look deeper—and elsewhere.

Many clerical employees are working under circumstances that differ little from factory conditions. For example, behind the marble facade and Doric columns of almost any bank or insurance company are huge, bullpen areas inhabited by regiments of clerks and paper-pushers. The work itself is fragmented and often experienced as dull and boring. It is small wonder that these clerical employees feel increasingly cut off and expendable. In effect, management's task is threefold:

1. To make the work itself more challenging and interesting. In this respect, job enrichment programs in many instances seem particularly applicable to clerical employees.

2. To become responsive to the underlying needs of clerical employees, i.e., the need to be heard by management, to count in the scheme of things, and to be treated fairly.

3. To be responsive to complaints about tangible matters—pay, benefits, working conditions—whatever they may happen to be in the particular situation.

And action can pay off. We did a survey for a machine company several years ago which revealed intense dissatisfaction in many of these areas. Management then took strong and well-organized steps to improve the situation, including changes in the promotion system, direct access to management, and involvement of employees in planning change. Interviews a year later showed remarkable improvements in employee attitudes. For example, in the first survey, less than one fifth thought their company was a good place to work; in the second survey, two thirds held this opinion.

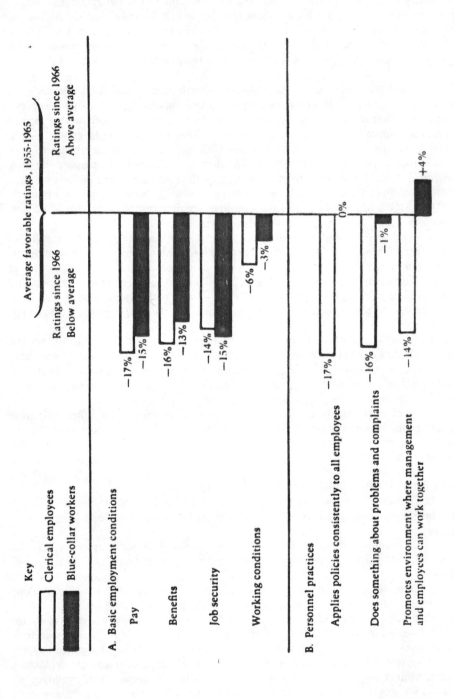

Key

☐ Clerical employees

■ Blue-collar workers

Average favorable ratings, 1955-1965

Ratings since 1966
Above average

Ratings since 1966
Below average

A. Basic employment conditions

Pay — —17% / —15%

Benefits — —16% / —13%

Job security — —14% / —15%

Working conditions — —6% / —3%

B. Personnel practices

Applies policies consistently to all employees — —17% / 0%

Does something about problems and complaints — —16% / —1%

Promotes environment where management and employees can work together — —14% / +4%

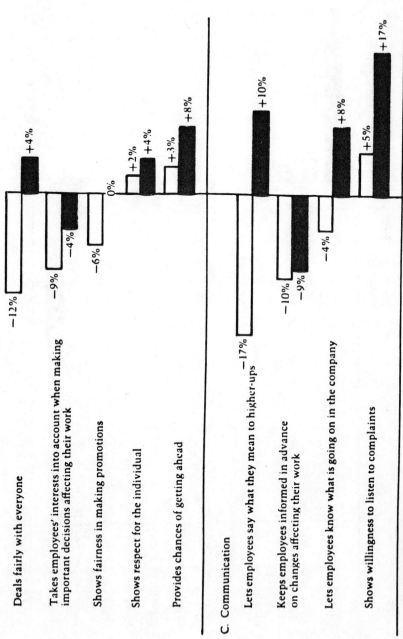

The chart shows percentage point differences with the following categories and values:

Deals fairly with everyone — +4% / −12%

Takes employees' interests into account when making important decisions affecting their work — −9% / −4%

Shows fairness in making promotions — −6%

Shows respect for the individual — +2% / +4%

Provides chances of getting ahead — +3% / +8%

C. Communication

Lets employees say what they mean to higher-ups — +10% / −17%

Keeps employees informed in advance on changes affecting their work — −10% / −9%

Lets employees know what is going on in the company — +8% / −4%

Shows willingness to listen to complaints — +5% / +17%

0%

Note: All figures are percentage points difference.

Exhibit II. Comparison of clerical and blue-collar ratings

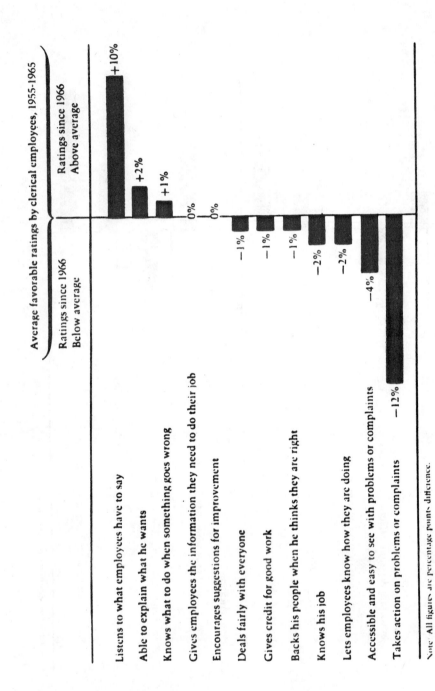

Exhibit III. Comparative ratings of supervisor

Concluding Note

It certainly seems likely that unless management begins to act now, clerical discontent will increase in the future. The attitude comparisons I cited indicate the pervasiveness of this trend.

By and large, management lost out to unions when the discontent of factory workers emerged in the 1930's. Will history repeat itself with office workers? We do not know. But we do know that this time individual companies will not have the excuse that there was no way they could see the threat coming.

Note

1. See Edward R. Curtin, *White-Collar Unionization*, New York, National Industrial Conference Board, Personnel Policy Study #220, 1970), p. 4.

CHAPTER 9

Current Problems in Personnel: Women, Minorities, and the Disadvantaged

Starting a decade ago with the 1964 Civil Rights Act, this nation took upon itself a serious commitment to eliminate job discrimination and to upgrade the economic and employment status of minorities and the disadvantaged.

Much of the responsibility for fulfilling this commitment has fallen upon business and industry. A visit to almost any personnel office today is enough to convince the perceptive individual that the practical and legal problems and difficulties involved in meeting this responsibility are much on the minds of personnel men. Nevertheless, as Silberman points out, much progress has been made during the last decade; both the absolute and relative economic status of blacks has improved. Silberman goes on to describe the role of an expanding economy, more realistic employment standards, and government policies in effecting this change.

Government anti-discrimination efforts—specifically those of the U.S. Equal Employment Opportunity Commission—are the topic of former EEOC Chairman Brown's paper. The 1972 Equal Employment Opportunity Act, which amends the 1964 Civil Rights Act—which established the EEOC—provides the EEOC with the power to take recalcitrant companies to court. This important new power, along with precedents set by recent court decisions and out-of-court settlements, can only mean that government impact on personnel procedures will be even greater in the seventies than it was in the sixties.

Seligman's argument is that although government anti-discrimination efforts have done much to eliminate old-fashioned discrimination, they have sometimes spawned a new, equally undesirable form of discrimination: reverse discrimination or preferential hiring of minorities and women. His article is perhaps the most lucid exploration of this controversial issue available at this time.

Although many minority group members are disadvantaged, the bulk of the disadvantaged and hard-core unemployed are from the nation's majority. Starting in the middle and late 1960s, many companies responded to social and governmental pressures and established special hard-core hiring and training programs. Today, enough information has been gathered and enough research done to make it desirable for us to pause and review the findings. The last article in section A of this chapter accomplishes this task. One conclusion from the Goodman, Salipante, and Paransky review is that organizational and program variables may be more important than his personal and background characteristics in determining whether the hard-core employee is successful.

Personnel departments today are charged with the responsibility of assuring top management that every step possible will be taken to give women employees equitable treatment in *all* job openings, in *all* training and career development programs and in *all* pay decisions. According to the Munts and Rice article, in banning sex discrimination in employment, Title VII of the Civil Rights Act of 1964 posed a serious threat to state legislation designed to protect women workers against long hours and conditions endangering their health and safety. These authors raise the question of whether the position taken by the EEOC (see readings by Dunn and Stephens, chap. 1; Ruch, chap. 2; and Brown, chap. 9) tends to discriminate against, rather than protect, women employees. (Before we are willing to accept the argument by Munts and Rice, however, we would need to see more empirical evidence that women employees actually need differential protection in the area of health and safety. It seems highly unlikely that women who are qualified for a physically challenging job during the first forty hours of a week would suddenly be faced with a threat of reduced safety as a result of overtime, while their male counterparts would not.)

In the second reading in section B of this chapter, Loring and Wells give a woman's point of view on how management can develop an affirmative action program for women. They recommend that management examine its current attitudes about women as managers before starting an affirmative action program. Following this "unfreezing" stage (see Beer and Huse, chap. 4), Loring and Wells recommend a step-by-step program for managers to follow in order to meet the goal of equality between the sexes in all levels in the organization.

Our last reading by Bem and Bem examines a specific problem faced by personnel managers seeking to attract qualified women into an organization: How do job descriptions placed in advertisements affect the sex of the applicants? They report two studies which indicate that both sex-biased wording in job advertisements and the placement of help-wanted ads in sex-segregated newspapers discourage men and women from applying for "opposite-sex" jobs for which they might be qualified. (Because of the findings reported in this article, AT&T has now directed that all of its advertisement and recruiting material be rewritten to remove sex bias.)

Section A
Minorities and Disadvantaged
in Personnel Decisions

Black Economic Gains—Impressive But Precarious

CHARLES E. SILBERMAN

. . . Some students of the racial problem argue that only a relative handful of blacks have been able to move into the economic mainstream. Dr. Andrew Brimmer, the first and only black member of the board of governors of the Federal Reserve System, speaks of a "deepening schism between the able and the less able, between the well prepared and those with few skills" and suggests the schism may be widening.

In fact, job barriers have been coming down for all blacks, not only those with a college degree. The number of Negro families earning less than $3,000 a year decreased by one-third between 1960 and 1968, after adjusting for changes in the purchasing power of the dollar, as high-school graduates—and even "dropouts"—have been able to move into jobs from which Negroes traditionally have been barred, or to which they have had little access. Since 1960 the number of Negroes holding clerical jobs has more than doubled, and the number of Negro sales workers has risen 61 percent. In the blue-collar sector, the number of Negro craftsmen and foremen increased by 70 percent, of semiskilled workers by 41 percent. Equally important, a substantial proportion of the increase in semiskilled jobs occurred in comparatively well-paying durable-goods industries such as autos and steel.

As more Negroes found better-paying and/or higher-status jobs, their numbers decreased in the kinds of low-paying and low-status jobs to which Negroes traditionally have been confined. Thus the number of Negro domestic household workers dropped 28 percent, the number of nonfarm laborers by 8 percent, and the number of farmers and farm laborers by no less than 56 percent. And while the number of Negro service workers did increase, more of them graduated to more prestigious service jobs, such as firemen, policemen, guards, and watchmen.

The consequence of all this has been a rapid increase in the returns Negroes receive from investment in education, an increase already being reflected in the statistics of Negro income. In sharp contrast to the situation of only a few years ago, the gap between median Negro and white incomes is now smaller for Negroes with a year or more of college than it is for those with no more than a high-school education (and smaller for those with a high-school education than for those with only an elementary-school diploma). Actually, current statistics understate the situation, since they take no account of the fact that a large proportion of better-educated Negroes are men and women who got their schooling recently and are just starting out in life.

The discrepancy between blacks and whites is likely to narrow still more in the near future, since the experience of other ethnic groups who have encountered discrimination indicates that there tends to be a lag of one or two decades between gains in educational attainment and their translation into increased income and occupational status. The same thing appears to be happening now to black Americans. And as the returns from education increase, so does the incentive to stay in school longer. The combination of more education and more job experience in turn is laying the base for a new period of catching up.

But Negroes will not be able to catch up unless the economy returns to a rapid rate of growth. Indeed, a rate of growth fast enough to keep the economy at full employment for an extended period of time is a prerequisite for any Negro progress at all. Full employment is the most effective solvent of discrimination in the labor market, because the alchemy of labor shortage turns people previously classified as unemployable into highly desirable employees. Since 1963, when it began intensive recruiting efforts, Chase Manhattan Bank has hired half of its new employees from minority groups. In part, of course, this reflects management's growing social consciousness, in part its desire to avert racial violence, but the overriding reason is that the bank's traditional supply of white clerical help has largely dried up. As one bank officer explains, "We need people. They're people. It's as simple as that."

Moving down the Queue

It is not quite as simple as that. But, allowing for some rhetorical exaggeration, the bank officer has provided a concise explanation of what economists call "the queue theory of the labor market." According to this theory, the available supply of labor is arrayed in order of workers' desirability, and employers choose job candidates from as far up the queue as they can. As aggregate demand for labor increases, employers have to move further and further down the line, taking people they previously had found unacceptable.

Since Negroes are heavily concentrated at the bottom of the queue, it takes a sustained period of expansion before employers begin reaching into the black labor pool. In part, this is because Negroes do have poorer qualifications. But only in part. While employers do move down the queue in an orderly sequence, the criteria for rating workers are highly subjective and frequently quite irrational.

A large element of irrationality is introduced by employers' lack of knowledge about the relation between entrance requirements—amount and quality of education, age, score on qualifying tests, etc.—and actual performance on the job. Since personnel men cannot admit their ignorance, still less admit that hiring is arbitrary and irrational, they feel bound to rest their judgments on such so-called "objective" criteria. Yet there is considerable evidence that the correlation between job performance and length of schooling or grades is quite low for a broad range of occupational categories. In some occupations there may even be an inverse correlation between education and job performance: the more education employees have, the higher their rate of turnover and, in some instances, the lower their productivity.

Just how senseless many "objective" standards really are was revealed during the past few years when, under the pressures of an apparent labor shortage, corporate managers took a hard look at their personnel practices. The experience of New York's First National City Bank is typical of a great many corporations, manufacturers as well as financial companies. Robert Feagles, a senior vice president, recalls that, when he was put in charge of personnel in 1965, turnover was abnormally high, with about 500 jobs going begging in a work force of 12,000. More important, supervisors were hanging on to incompetent people for fear that they would be replaced only by even less competent people—or not at all. Feagles' first move, therefore, was to create a personnel-research group, which proceeded to analyze the nature of the work performed in the job categories that accounted for the largest proportion of new hires.

The results were discomfiting, to say the least. By and large, the researchers found that the qualifications the bank required for a broad range of jobs bore little relationship to the actual requirements of the job. For example, supervisors all over the bank had been complaining that the young people hired as pages rarely stayed more than three months or thereabouts. The reason, Feagles' researchers found, was that the personnel department, which gave a battery of entry tests, had set a score of 130 on the Wonderlic I.Q. test as the minimum for a job as a page. But youths with that degree of intelligence found they could not stand the monotony for more than a few months.

For most entry jobs a high-school diploma was required, yet the jobs could be performed just as well, and in the case of particularly monotonous routine tasks, perhaps better, by people with substantially less education. A high degree of literacy was essential in other jobs, not because of the intrinsic nature of the work but because of the way it had been structured. By breaking the work down in different ways, dropouts could do the job without difficulty.

The labor shortage, in brief, was the product of the bank's unrealistic requirements. By lowering job requirements to those actually needed to perform the work in question, and by substituting a newly created set of aptitude tests for the old ones, First National City was able to tap a completely new source of supply in the city's predominantly black and Puerto Rican neighborhoods. At first, the flow of applicants was small; on the basis of past experience, many blacks and Puerto Ricans did not bother to apply since they took it for granted that they would not be hired. "We had to make ourselves believable in the labor market," Feagles puts it. To do so, the bank began active recruiting in minority neighborhoods, advertising in Negro and Spanish newspapers, contacting church groups and antipoverty agencies, and visiting high schools. As a result, the minority complement went from 12 percent to 24 percent of the work force in four years; it is now above 30 percent.

When the "Hard Core" Softens

Many of the factors corporate managers used to cite as compelling reasons for their inability to find or hire many Negro employees have turned out to be a lot less compelling when the supply of white workers dried up. Many blacks, to be sure, do lack the necessary job skills, but when labor is in short enough supply, it pays employers to incur substantial costs to teach the skills. There is reason to believe, in fact, that a substantial proportion of the "new" jobs which members of the National Alliance of Businessmen claim to have created for the so-called "hard core" unemployed are filled by men the companies would have hired even if there had been no special program.

A prolonged period of full employment softens the hard core in another way. For most jobs the most important kind of intellectual capital is what has been learned on the job rather than what has been learned in school. Negroes have been caught up in a vicious circle; the fact that so many jobs were barred to them in the past left many blacks poorly equipped for the jobs that began to open up in the Sixties. All the more so, since workers need two kinds of knowledge: specific work skills, and social skills—i.e., punctuality, acceptance of discipline and work rules, and so on. Lack of these social skills has constituted the biggest disadvantage of Negroes who previously had been limited to casual labor or other transient jobs. But social skills are learned on the job in much the same way that specific work skills are acquired. Hence the boom of the late Sixties—by providing steady jobs for previously unemployable blacks—equipped them with the social and other skills they need to compete for employment in the future.

The Zero-Sum Game

A further reason why rapid economic growth helps the Negro is that it reduces white resistance to black gains. Some of this resistance stems from deep-rooted racial hatred, but a great deal of it, though cloaked perhaps in anti-Negro rhetoric, grows out of a real conflict of interest. The harsh fact is that if Negroes gain a larger share of the "better" jobs, whites, by definition, will be left with a smaller share. More black foremen will mean proportionately fewer white foremen; more black school principals will mean fewer white principals; more black corporate vice presidents will mean fewer white vice presidents.

What this means is that the struggle to achieve Negro equality is, in the parlance of game theorists, a "zero-sum game," in which one group's gains are offset by another group's losses. Not entirely so; to some degree, whites' losses in terms of jobs and income are offset by less tangible gains—greater social peace (or less social disruption), a sense of satisfaction that justice is being achieved. What a good many civic leaders have sometimes failed to recognize, however—the Urban Coalition is a prime example—is that the people who enjoy the intangible or psychic gains are not necessarily the ones who bear the brunt of the losses, e.g., white blue-collar workers, whose chances of becoming foremen are diminished.

But if job opportunities are growing for everyone, whites are likely to be less resentful of the fact that Negroes are taking a larger share of the better jobs. If the number of foremen, craftsmen, plant managers, corporate executives, and school principals is growing, the absolute *number* of whites holding such jobs can increase even though the white *proportion* declines. Rapid economic growth can reduce white resentment still more, by making it possible for whites to move into other occupations. And if their real income is growing, whites are less likely to object to the fact that their tax dollars are being used, in part, to provide compensatory education and job training for Negroes.

Government has a large role to play, therefore, both in overcoming discrimination and in keeping the economy expanding rapidly. Governmental policy is important, too, as a means of influencing the composition of economic output, since the opportunites for upgrading black occupations and incomes vary widely from industry to industry.

Construction, for example, is a labor-intensive industry with a wage scale well above average, which means that increased employment of Negroes there would have a greater impact on black income than increases in almost any other blue-collar industry. And since the potential demand for construction will grow substantially over the next ten years, the number of blacks employed can be increased without threatening the jobs of whites. The degree to which the industry will be able to meet the projected demand will be strongly influenced by what the government does to stimulate housing and urban renewal. The degree to which that demand leads to greater employment of blacks depends on what government does to break down racial discrimination, which is more intense in construction than in most industries.

While rapid economic growth is a prerequisite for Negro progress, it is not enough; it must be supplemented by a direct attack on all forms of discrimination. The changes of the past five or ten years have reduced and occasionally eliminated some forms of discrimination. As is usually the case, however, solving one set of problems creates another set, or brings old problems into sharper focus. The more that overt discrimination in hiring recedes, the more important other kinds of discrimination become. Eliminating the disparities between blacks and whites is a two-stage process: giving Negroes equal access to initial employment, and giving them an equal crack at advancement. . . .

The Executive as Educator

. . . It is not enough for presidents or executive vice presidents to decree an end to discrimination within the company. Such decrees frequently are nullified by what one black executive calls "the not-in-my-department syndrome," whereby department managers express agreement in principle but find all sorts of reasons to explain why the decree cannot be put into practice "in my department." Hence top executives must act as educators, persuading supervisors—plant managers, foremen, etc., down the line—to change their ways.

Executives will be unable to educate their subordinates, however, unless they first educate themselves. There is no particular reason to assume that managers are any freer from racial prejudice than the rest of us; it is virtually impossible to have grown up in the U.S. without having absorbed *some* sense of superiority or distaste toward blacks. But executives have been quicker than most to recognize the high stakes that are involved for business and for the whole society in overcoming prejudice and discrimination. Businessmen made considerable progress in that direction in the Sixties. There is reason to hope that they will find the courage and strength to do what needs to be done in the Seventies.

The Equal Employment Opportunity Act of 1972

WILLIAM BROWN III

On March 24, 1972, President Nixon signed into law "The Equal Employment Opportunity Act of 1972" (P.L. 92-261), thereby concluding the long drought of a lack of effective Federal enforcement of equal employment opportunity. The 1972 Act, which in effect is a series of major amendments to Title VII of the Civil Rights Act of 1964 (42 U.S.C. § 2000e *et seq*), establishes for the first time in the Federal Government an independent agency which has the power to effectively prohibit all forms of employment discrimination based on race, religion, color, sex or national origin. This agency, the Equal Employment Opportunity Commission (EEOC), has, pursuant to the new law, been given the power to institute civil actions to eliminate violations of the nondiscrimination in employment requirements of Title VII. The adoption of the 1972 law concludes almost seven years of efforts by the EEOC and civil rights groups to enact such enforcement powers for the agency, and promises to usher in a new era of activism in the enforcement of equal employment opportunity in both private and public employment. The effect that this new law will have upon the personnel policies of the Nation's employers is self-evident, and should not be underestimated. The EEOC has been laboring with the handicap of lack of enforcement powers since its inception in 1965, and it is only fair to say that now having been granted that which it has sought for so long, it intends to use it.

The main purpose of the 1972 Act is to amend the existing provisions of Title VII to correct certain deficiencies which were allowed into the original version of Title VII. Of these, the lack of enforcement powers for the EEOC was the most serious.[1] The 1972 Act corrects this deficiency by empowering the EEOC to bring civil actions directly in the Federal courts to enforce violations of Title VII. The new law also expands the coverage of Title VII to encompass employees of state and local governments or governmental organizations, employees of educational institutions, and employers or labor organizations with 15 or more employees or members (the previous coverage had only included employers or labor organizations with 25 or more employees or members). The new law also provides additional protection for Federal employees as regards equal employment opportunity and clarifies certain procedures relating to the Office of Federal Contract Compliance (OFCC) in the Department of Labor.

Enforcement Provision

It was the opinion of both the House Education and Labor Committee and the Senate Committee on Labor and Public Welfare that the major shortcoming of the existing Title VII was its failure to provide the EEOC with direct enforcement powers.[2] As stated by the Committee, the earlier belief that complaints of employment discrimination could be resolved through the voluntary methods of negotiation, persuasion, and conciliation had been shown wrong, and that viable enforcement procedures would be

From *Personnel Administration*, May-June 1972. Reprinted by permission of the International Personnel Management Association.

required in order to insure that the provisions in Title VII were obeyed. Accordingly, both the House and Senate Committees recommended the adoption of proposed legislation which would grant the EEOC the ability to go beyond its voluntary compliance procedure to insure that employers whose employment practices were violating the prohibitions of Title VII would be required to change their practices in accordance with the law.[3] Both House and Senate agreed with the recommendations of the Committees and adopted enforcement procedures allowing the EEOC to bring civil actions directly in the Federal courts.[4]

The impact of this provision is obvious. Where before, employers against whom charges of employment discrimination had been filed could only be required by the EEOC to voluntarily resolve the allegations raised in a charge, with the adoption of the new law, the EEOC may now bring a civil suit against any employer covered by the Act if such voluntary resolution should fail.[5] While under the old law employers could choose to ignore Commission opinions and take a chance that individuals who had been aggrieved would not take the time, or could not afford, to take a case to court, the current provisions allow the EEOC to sue on its own initiative in such situations.

The basic procedures with respect to the enforcement provisions of the new law provide:

1. Existing procedures for filing a charge with the Commission shall remain. However, where before a charge of unlawful employment discrimination had to be filed with the Commission within 90 days after an alleged unlawful employment practice had occurred, that time limit has now been expanded to 180 days.[6] However, in cases where the unlawful employment practice is of a continuing nature, then the last day of the violation and not its inception determines the running of the 180 days;

2. Existing procedures have also been retained as regards deferral to State fair employment practice agencies.[7] In those cases where a charge arises in a jurisdiction to which the Commission normally defers, the time periods for filing a charge with the EEOC have been extended to 300 days after the alleged unlawful employment practice occurred or to 30 days after the State or local agency has terminated its proceedings.[8]

3. A new provision has been added which allows charges to be filed "by or on behalf of" an aggrieved individual.[9]

4. The provisions of the prior law with respect to the Commission's procedures for informal methods of settlement (i.e. conference, conciliation and settlement) have been retained. However, should such procedures fail, the Commission is then authorized to proceed with a lawsuit against the respondent;

5. The Commission may bring a lawsuit at any time after 30 days from the filing of the charge with the Commission.[10] The Commission may also request the court at any time for temporary or preliminary relief, before the final disposition of a charge.[11]

6. The individual complainant may also bring a case to court without recourse to the Commission or, if a charge is dismissed by the Commission or if within 180 days after a charge has been filed with the Commission it has not filed a civil action, the individual may take the case directly to court.[12]

Changes in Jurisdiction

The 1972 law also made some changes in the coverage of the Act. It eliminated the previous exemption for employees of State and local governments and employees of educational institutions.[13] It also expanded the coverage of the law, one year after enactment (i.e. March 24, 1973), to apply to all employers and labor unions with 15 or more full-time employees or members.[14] A specific exception was made with respect to elected officials of State or local governments and their immediate personal staff who would not be covered by the provisions of the Act. This exception, however, has been construed very narrowly in the legislative history and should not provide any major exemptions in this area.

The jurisdiction of Title VII as regards religious institutions was also modified. Where before, religious institutions could grant preference in employment to members of their particular religion only as regards religious activities within such institutions, this exemption has now been expanded to include all functions, giving such institutions the right to grant religious preference in hiring, but still prohibiting them from discriminating in any other of the prohibited categories under Title VII.[15]

State and Local Governments

The role of the Commission in enforcing, by civil action, the provisions has been specifically delimited to exclude the filing of suits against State and local governments or their political subdivision.[16] The role of enforcing violations of Title VII where the respondent is a State or local government has been specifically assigned to the U.S. Department of Justice. Complaints alleging employment discrimination by State or local governments would still be filed with the EEOC in the same manner as by employees of private businesses. The Commission would then investigate the charge and pursue resolution of the complaint through its informal negotiations and conciliation procedures. However, if the Commission is unable to achieve a satisfactory conciliation of the charge, it will then refer the case to the Justice Department which may then bring the case to court. While procedures between the Justice Department and the Commission have not yet been fully worked out at the time of the writing of this article, it is expected that these procedures will provide for close cooperation between the two agencies and a smooth transition from the EEOC to the Justice Department will be assured so that individuals who have charges of discrimination against State and local agencies will be fully protected.

Federal Employees Protection

The 1972 law also contains a new section which deals with the equal employment policies of the Federal Government.[17] This section gives the U.S. Civil Service Commission additional responsibility and greater authority to enforce the equal employment programs within the Federal competitive service. Particularly, it authorizes the Civil Service Commission to grant appropriate remedies for violations of equal employment opportunity including back pay for aggrieved individuals.[18]

The other major change effected by this section is the clear authorization for Federal employees to bring civil actions in the Federal courts for violations of equal employment opportunity. Under the provisions of this section, aggrieved employees are permitted to file a civil action within 30 days of a notice of a final action by an agency or by the Civil Service Commission or an appeal from an agency decision, or after 180 days from the filing of an initial charge with an agency or the Civil Service Commission.[19] This provision lays to rest much of the controversy in recent years regarding the rights of a Federal employee to sue the government for its employment policies.

Effect on Employers

The adoption of the 1972 Act places a greater responsibility than before upon all employers to insure that their employment and personnel policies are fully in accord with the principles of Title VII. The new amendments to Title VII are just that —amendments to the existing law. Most of the new provisions are procedural and do not change existing Title VII principles as developed by the Commission, the Department of Justice and the Courts since the 1964 enactment of the Civil Rights Act. The clear intention of the drafters of the new law was to retain the provisions of the previous law unless inconsistent with the new provisions. As stated by Senator Williams, the Senate sponsor of the legislation:

> In any area where the new law does not address itself, or in any areas where a specific contrary intention is not indicated, it was assumed that the present case law as developed by the courts would continue to govern the applicability and construction of Title VII.[20]

While retaining present interpretations, by the enactment of the new law, Congress strengthened some other areas and clarified some that might have been in question before.

The concept of employment discrimination has come a long way from the naive and simplistic concepts held in 1964 with the adoption of the 1964 Act. At that time, discrimination was thought to be comprised of individual acts of bad faith or distinguishable events, for the most part due to ill-will on the part of some identifiable individual or organization. It was essentially thought to be a "human" problem which could readily be eliminated by conciliatory processes. We now know that employment discrimination is much more than that. More often than not, it is the result of institutional "systems" and "effects" rather than isolated events, and the causes of employment discrimination are usually associated with such personnel systems as seniority, lines of progression, transfer provisions, perpetuation of past practices through present requirements, and testing requirements. All of these areas directly affect any management system in any business, and business administration in all its forms must meet all of these problems. While it is impossible, within the space of this article to explain all of the areas of employment discrimination which bear directly upon personnel administration, there are certain problems which can be pointed out in the space of a few lines.

Perhaps the most fundamental concept which bears directly upon employment practices and policies is that proof of intent to discriminate is not a prerequisite to a finding of an unlawful employment practice. Intent is inferred from the totality of the conduct and a party charged with a violation of the Act may not even be aware of his discriminatory acts. The relevant test for employment discrimination is whether the *effect* of a particular practice serves to exclude a disproportionate number of persons in a protected class.[21] Similarly, an employment practice based in part on unlawful considerations is not saved by the fact that other, non-discriminatory considerations may also have been present.[22]

The importance of careful analysis of personnel systems to determine possible violations of Title VII becomes even more important when read in light of the existing principle that most instances of unlawful discrimination under Title VII are by nature violations affecting an entire *class* and not just the single individual who may have actually brought the charge with the Commission.[23] This factor has led to the acceptance by the courts of the use of statistics to demonstrate existing systems of discrimination.

Statistics showing an underrepresentation of a particular class have been held to establish a *prima facie* case of unlawful exclusion and to infer the existence of discrimination.[24] Based on the foregoing principles, the following kinds of employment practices must be considered as potentially in violation of Title VII unless shown as required by business necessity:

1. All tests, either paper-and-pencil variety or other performance projection type which are used as a measure for employment decisions;

2. Minimum educational requirements (e.g., requirement of a high school diploma);

3. Arrest records as a means of disqualifying applicants for employment;

4. Word-of-mouth referral systems; and

5. Use of a rule permitting discharge when an employee's wages have been garnished.

This is by no means a complete list, but does serve to point out some of the common practices used by employers which have been held to violate Title VII. With the enactment of the new amendments to Title VII, all of these principles have been reaffirmed, and the Commission has been given the authority to pursue eradication of any such unlawful employment practices wherever they may be found.

With the new coverage of Title VII, virtually the entire Nation's labor force has now been placed under the protection of Title VII. This means that almost every business administrator in the country now has responsibility to insure that his company's personnel practices do not violate the principles of Title VII. It is incumbent upon business to familiarize itself with the requirements of Title VII and to establish positive programs to bring minorities and women into the mainstream of employment by establishing programs which will not only eliminate discrimination in the future, but will also correct any discrimination of the past. The Commission's role is clear. By granting it enforcement powers, the Congress has recognized the failure that lack of an overall enforcement of equal employment opportunity has generated. Discrimination in employment continues. The task assigned to this agency is to see that it does not continue and it will do its best to see that the job begun in 1964 with the adoption of the original Civil Rights Act is not left unfinished.

Notes

1. As originally proposed, Title VII did provide the EEOC with enforcement powers but this was deleted from the Act as part of a compromise in order to assure passage of other provisions of the 1964 Act. EEOC, Legislative History of Titles VII and XI of the Civil Rights Act of 1964 (G.P.O. 1967) pp. 3003-08, 3017-21.

2. For the views of the two congressional committees on this issue see the Committee Report issued by each Committee respectively to accompany the recommended adoption of the proposed legislation. H.R. Rep. No. 92nd Cong. 1st Sess. (1971) and S. Rep. No. 92nd Cong. 1st Sess. (1971).

3. The only disagreement in the two Committees as regards the enforcement power issue was which of two types of enforcement to adopt, i.e. the right of the EEOC to issue its own administrative cease-and-desist orders (this was the scheme which had been proposed by H.R. 1746, introduced by Congressman Augustus F. Hawkins (D-Calif.) and S. 2515, introduced by Senator Harrison A. Williams Jr. (D-N.J.)) or whether to allow the EEOC to bring civil actions directly in the Federal courts (this was the scheme proposed in H.R. 6760, introduced by Congressman John N. Erlenborn (R.-Ill.) and as an amendment to S. 2515 by Senator Peter H. Dominick (R.-Colo.). While both Committees recommended the cease-and-desist approach, both House and Senate adopted the direct court enforcement approach.

4. The House passed the legislation on September 16, 1971; the Senate passed its version of

the legislation on February 22, 1972; both Houses adopted the Conference Report resolving the differences between the two bills and establishing the final version of the legislation on March 8, and March 6, respectively.

5. P.L. 92-261, Sec. 4(a); VII, as amended, § 706(f) (1).

6. *Id*. § 706(e).

7. Under the new and the old law, pursuant to Section 706(c), the EEOC will defer charges to a State fair employment agency for 60 days. During this time, the EEOC will not act on the charge and will allow the appropriate State agency a first opportunity to resolve the charge. However, pursuant to a recent decision by the U.S. Supreme Court, a charge may be filed with the Commission before it is filed with a State agency; the EEOC may receive and then defer the charge on behalf of a complainant, *Love v. Pullman Co.*

8. *Op. cit.* § 706(e).

9. *Id*. § 706(b).

10. *Id*. § 706(f) (1).

11. *Id*. § 706(f) (2).

12. *Id*. § 706(f) (1).

13. P.L. 92-261, Sec. 2(1) & 2(2); Title VII, as amended, § 701.

14. *Id*.

15. *Id*. § 702.

16. See generally *id*. § 706(f) (1).

17. Title VII, as amended, § 717(a)-(e).

18. The intention of this particular provision of the new law indicates Congressional affirmation of the recent decision by the U.S. Court of Claims awarding back pay in a situation of employment discrimination in the Federal Government. *Chambers* v. *U.S.*, 451 F. 2d 1045 (U.S. Ct. Ct. 1971).

19. *See*, Section-by-section analysis of Sen. Williams, 118 Cong Rec. § 3463 (daily ed. March 6, 1972).

20. *Id*. at § 3460.

21. *Griggs* v. *Duke Power Co.*, 401 U.S. 424 (1971).

22. *King* v. *Laborers, Local 818*. (6th Cir., 1971).

23. *Jenkins* v. *United Gas Corp.*, 400 F. 2d 28 (5th Cir. 1968); *Sprogis* v. *United Air Lines*, 444 F. 2d 1194 (7th Cir. 1971) *cert. den.*,—U.S.—Dec. 14, 1971); *Bowie* v *Colgate Palmolive Co.*, 416 F. 2d 711 (7th Cir. 1969).

24. *Marquez* v. *Omaha District Sales Office*, 440 F. 2d 1157 (8th Cir. 1971); *Jones* v. *Lee Way Motor Freight*, 431 F. 2d 245 (10th Cir. 1970); *Parham* v. *Southwestern Bell Tel. Co.*, 433 F. 2d 42 (8th Cir. 1970).

How "Equal Opportunity" Turned into Employment Quotas

DANIEL SELIGMAN

Soon after it came into office, the Nixon Administration proposed that critics "watch what we do instead of listening to what we say." By this eminently reasonable standard, the Administration today might be judged to favor quotas in employment. The

President has repeatedly assailed them; in fact, the elimination of quotas was identified in a major campaign statement as one of ten great goals for the nation in his second term. Yet during his years in office, and with some powerful encouragement from the executive branch of the U.S. Government, quotas have taken hold in several areas of American life. The controversies about them have centered on their appearance in the construction industry and on university campuses. Oddly enough, very little attention has been paid to employment quotas in large corporations.

The omission is very odd indeed, for it is in corporate employment that quotas are having their major impact on the American labor force and on relations between the races and sexes. Nowadays there are scarcely any companies among, say, the *Fortune* 500 that are not under pressure from the government to hire and promote more women and minority-group members; and many of these companies have responded to the pressure by installing what are, in effect, quota systems.

In most of the controversy over quotas, there is no real disagreement about ultimate objectives. Most educated Americans today would agree that several minorities, and women, suffer from discrimination in employment, that the discrimination is destructive and irrational, and that working to end it is a proper activity for government. Unfortunately, it is not clear what government should do—and all too clear that wise policies do not flow naturally from good intentions.

In discussions of this issue, people who don't define their terms can dither on for quite a while without getting anywhere. Let us begin, accordingly, with some definitions and distinctions. Among companies that have no intention of discriminating against women or minorities, four different postures may be discerned:

1. *Passive nondiscrimination* involves a willingness, in all decisions about hiring, promotion, and pay, to treat the races and sexes alike. However, this posture may involve a failure to recognize that past discrimination leaves many prospective employees unaware of present opportunities.

2. *Pure affirmative action* involves a concerted effort to expand the pool of applicants so that no one is excluded because of past or present discrimination. At the point of decision, however, the company hires (or promotes) whoever seems most qualified, without regard to race or sex.

3. *Affirmative action with preferential hiring.* In this posture, the company not only ensures that it has a larger labor pool to draw from but systematically favors women and minority groups in the actual decisions about hiring. This might be thought of as a "soft" quota system, i.e., instead of establishing targets that absolutely must be met, the top officers of the company beef up employment of women and minority-group members to some unspecified extent by indicating that they want those groups given a break.

4. *Hard quotas.* No two ways about it—specific numbers or proportions of minority-group members must be hired.

Much of the current confusion about quotas—and the controversy about whether the government is imposing them—derives from a failure to differentiate among several of these postures. The officials who are administering the principal federal programs tend, of course, to bristle at any suggestion that they are imposing quotas; they have been bristling with special vigor ever since the President's campaign statements on the subject. Their formulations tend to be somewhat selfserving, however. The officials turn out, when pressed, to be denying that the government is pushing employers into posture No. 4. The real issue is No. 3, preferential hiring, which many government agencies are indeed promoting. Meanwhile, the President and a few other Administration officials concerned with equal-employment opportunity sound as though the objective of the program is to promote pure affirmative action—posture No. 2.

The Conciliators Have Muscles

The U.S. Government's efforts to end discrimination in employment are carried out through two major programs. One was set in motion by Title VII of the Civil Rights Act of 1964, which forbids discrimination based on race, color, religion, sex, or national origin. The act established an Equal Employment Opportunity Commission, which now has two main functions. The first is enforcement: the commission may sue in a U.S. district court, on its own behalf or for other claimants, when it believes that discrimination has taken place. The EEOC has had the power to sue only since March, 1972 [Editors note: See preceding article by Brown.]—previously it was limited to conciliation efforts—and has filed only about twenty-five suits in that time. Chairman William H. Brown III believes that when the commission gets warmed up it might be filing an average of five suits a week.

In practice, Brown suspects, not many of these are apt to be litigated; the right to go into court is useful to the EEOC mainly for the muscle it provides in conciliation efforts. If the EEOC did get into court, it would have to prove outright discrimination; in principle, that is, an employer might comply with Title VII simply by practicing passive nondiscrimination—posture No. 1. However, the conciliation agreements extracted from those accused of discrimination typically call for more than that. Most of the agreements negotiated thus far involve preferential hiring.

The commission's other main function is information gathering. Every enterprise with 100 or more employees must file annually with the EEOC a form detailing the number of women and members of four different minority groups employed in each of nine different job categories, from laborers to "managers and officials." The minority groups are Negroes; Americans of Mexican, Puerto Rican, Cuban, or Spanish origin; Orientals; and American Indians (who in Alaska are deemed to include Eskimos and Aleuts). With some 260,000 forms a year to process, the EEOC is having some difficulty in staying on top of the data it is collecting. "Obviously, we can't look critically at all the reports," Brown concedes. Eventually, however, he hopes to develop some computerized procedures for finding patterns of discrimination, i.e., procedures somewhat analogous to those employed by the Internal Revenue Service in deciding which tax returns to audit.

Meanwhile, the EEOC is getting a fair amount of help from people who believe they are being discriminated against. When any complaint is received at the commission, even one with no visible substance to it, an EEOC staff member pulls the file on the company in question and looks for patterns of discrimination. In fiscal 1972 more than 30,000 charges were filed.

Special Rules for Contractors

The other major federal program is based on the special obligations incurred by government contractors. This program may be traced all the way back to 1941, when President Franklin D. Roosevelt issued an executive order outlawing racial discrimination by defense contractors. Every President since Roosevelt has issued one or more orders extending the reach of the ban. It applies now to subcontractors as well as primes, to civilian as well as military purchases, and to services as well as goods. It affects every division and every subsidiary of any company with a contract worth $10,000 or more. It covers women as well as racial, religious, and ethnic minorities. And it has entailed increasingly expansive definitions of "nondiscrimination." Right now, about a quarter of a million companies, employing about a third of the U.S. labor force, are covered by the executive orders.

At the time President Nixon took office, most government contractors were operating under Executive Order 11246, which had been issued by President Johnson in September, 1965. The order, as later amended by Johnson, required "affirmative action" by employers—but did not specify what this meant in practice. The Office of Federal Contract Compliance had never developed guidelines for determining whether contractors were in compliance. It was left to the Nixon Administration to make the program operational.

The Administration's first major decision about the program was to make it, in the marvelous label applied by the Labor Department, "result-oriented." Affirmative action could have been defined so that it required companies to incorporate certain procedures into their personnel policies—but did not require that any particular results follow from the procedures. The difficulty with this approach was that companies determined to discriminate might simply go through the motions while continuing to exclude women and minority-group members. "It just would have been too easy for them to make patsies of us," said Laurence Silberman, who was solicitor of the Labor Department at the time, and who participated in the formulation of the program. An alternative approach, which was the one essentially adopted, would require each company to set goals and timetables for hiring specified numbers of women and minority-group members; would allow the government to review the goals to ensure that they were sufficiently ambitious; and, if they were not met, would require the company to prove that it had at least made a "good faith effort" to meet them.

This approach was certainly calculated to produce results. The difficulty was that it also seemed likely to produce *reverse* discrimination by companies fearful of losing their contracts. The Administration recognized this problem from the beginning, and agonized over it quite a lot. "No program has given me greater problems of conscience than this one," said Silberman recently, just before leaving the Labor Department to go into private law practice in the capital. In the end, however, the Administration always came back to the view that a program that didn't achieve results would be a charade —and that the only way to ensure results was to require goals and timetables.

The rules of the new game were first set forth in January, 1970, in the Labor Department's Order No. 4, signed by then-Secretary George P. Schultz. At the time, it seems clear, businessmen did not pay a great deal of attention to Order No. 4. It is perhaps worth noting that the momentous changes signaled by the order had never been debated in Congress, not even during the great outpouring of civil-rights legislation in the 1960's. Anyone looking for examples of the growing autonomy of the executive branch of the federal government could do worse than focus on this quite unheralded administrative regulation.

Trying to Be Reasonable

Specifically, Order No. 4 requires that every contractor have a written affirmative-action program for every one of his establishments. Every program must include a detailed report on the company's utilization of each of the four basic minorities in each of its own job categories. (A "Revised Order No. 4," issued by Secretary of Labor J. D. Hodgson in December, 1971, called for reports on women, too.) Whenever there are job categories with fewer women or minority-group members "than would reasonably be expected by their availability," the contractor must establish goals for increasing their utilization.

Well, how does one determine the appropriate utilization rates? The order makes a great show of being helpful in this regard, listing eight criteria that contractors should consider in trying to answer the question. The first is "the minority population of the labor area surrounding the facility"; others include "the availability of minorities having requisite skills in an area in which the contractor can reasonably recruit," and "the degree of training which the contractor is reasonably able to undertake as a means of making all job classes available to minorities." The criteria certainly give contractors a lot to think about, but they do not, in the end, make clear what would be a reasonable utilization rate for, say, black mechanics. A contractor focusing on this matter might find himself utterly confused about the number of blacks in town who were already trained as mechanics, the number who were "trainable," the amount he was expected to spend on training, the distance he was expected to travel to recruit, etc.

In practice, contractors are encouraged to assume that they are underutilizing women and minorities and, accordingly, they have goals and timetables just about everywhere. For example, International Business Machines Corp., which has long been a model employer so far as fair-employment practices are concerned, has goals and timetables today at every one of its 400-odd establishments in the U.S.

Because the criteria are so vague, the goal-setting procedure often becomes an exercise in collective bargaining, with the outcome dependent on the respective will and resourcefulness of the company's top executives and the government's compliance officers. The government is ordinarily represented in these matters by whichever of its departments is contracting for the company's services; the OFCC does some, but not much, coordinating. On the whole, the enforcement varies considerably in both fairness and effectiveness from one company to another. Furthermore, some companies deal with several different departments; Union Carbide, for example, is monitored by the Atomic Energy Commission and the Departments of Defense, Transportation, Labor, Interior, and Agriculture.

The compliance officers themselves are career civil servants, and they seem to come in all varieties. Two quite different criticisms of them are often heard. One is that they are apt to be knee-jerk liberals, persuaded in advance that the big corporation is guilty. The other is that they have often lazily adopted the position that anything the company proposes is fine with them. Herbert Hill, the labor specialist of the National Association for the Advancement of Colored People, is prepared to regale anyone who wants to listen with tales of compliance officers who have been co-opted by corporate personnel departments. One senior official of the Labor Department who has been in a good position to observe the contract-compliance program was asked recently what he thought of these two criticisms. "They're both true," he answered, adding, after a moment's reflection, that the compliance officers also included many thoughtful and conscientious public servants.

What's Happened to Merit?

There is no doubt that, between them, the EEOC and the contract-compliance program have transformed the way big business in the U.S. hires people. Even allowing for those co-opted compliance officers, the government has gone a long way toward wiping out old-fashioned discrimination in the corporate universe. But it is increasingly evident that, in doing so, the government programs have undermined some other old-fashioned notions about hiring on the basis of merit.

The undermining process can be discerned in the campaigns, waged successfully by EEOC and OFCC, against certain kinds of employment standards. Employers who demand certain skills, education levels, or test-score results are presumed to be discriminating if their standards have the effect of excluding women or minority-group members. To counter this presumption, the employer must demonstrate conclusively that the skills are in fact needed for the job. If test-score results are involved, he must also demonstrate that the tests reliably predict the skills in question and, finally, that "alternative suitable . . . procedures are unavailable for his use." One argument the employer *cannot* make is that he had no discriminatory intent in establishing the requirements. Under Title VII, as administered by the EEOC, the intent is irrelevant; it is only the effect that matters—which represents a major alteration in the law of discrimination. [Editor's note: For a fuller discussion of these requirements, see the article "The Impact on Employment Procedures of the Supreme Court Decision in the Duke Power Case," by Floyd L. Ruch, chap. 2.]

The altered concept became the law of the land in March, 1971, when the U.S. Supreme Court upheld the EEOC's view, and overruled a court of appeals, in *Griggs vs. Duke Power*. The company had required applicants for certain jobs to have a high-school diploma and also to score at certain levels in aptitude tests. There was no contention that Duke Power intended these standards to have a discriminatory effect, and it was agreed that they were applied impartially to blacks and whites alike. It was also agreed that the standards resulted in very few blacks being hired. The company argued that it wanted to use the standards to improve the over-all quality of its labor force; but it could not demonstrate that the standards had a direct relationship to the jobs being performed. In ruling that the standards had to be dropped, Chief Justice Warren E. Burger, who wrote the Court's opinion, upheld the EEOC's contention that Title VII "has placed on the employer the burden of showing that any given requirement must have a manifest relationship to the employment in question."

Anyone pondering the particulars of the Duke Power case would have to feel sympathy for the black workers involved. Growing up in a society that had denied them a decent education, they were unfit for many skilled jobs. When they applied to do some relatively unskilled work that they could perform, they were excluded by educational standards—which, the facts suggest, really were extraneous to the company's needs. Unfortunately, the logic of the Duke Power decision suggests that some perfectly reasonable standards are now in trouble too. Companies that have high standards and want to defend them will immediately perceive that the ground rules, which not only place the burden of proof on the employer but require coping with some formidable-looking validation procedures, are not inviting. Many will obviously conclude that it is simpler to abolish their standards than to try justifying them.

The new law presents special management problems to the numerous companies that have traditionally hired overqualified people at entry-level jobs, expecting them to compete for the better jobs. Dr. Lloyd Cooke, who monitors Union Carbide's equal-employment-opportunity program, suggested recently that most big companies like his own could no longer assume there were a lot of highly qualified people searching out their own paths to the top. "Now we must develop upward mobility models that include training along the way."

In addition to all their problems with tests and formal standards, federal contractors often face a new kind of pressure on the informal standards they may have in mind when they hire and promote people. Revised Order No. 4 specifies: "Neither minority nor female employees should be required to possess higher qualifications than those of the lowest-qualified incumbent." The logic of this rule is inexorable, and it too implies lower standards. In any organization that has a number of people working at different levels of skill and competence—a corporate engineering staff, say, or a university economics department—whoever does the hiring would ordinarily be trying to raise the average level of performance, i.e., to bring in more people at the high end of the range. If the organization must take on applicants who are at the low end or face charges of discrimination, it can only end up lowering the average.

Professor Sidney Hook, the philosopher, has assailed the possibilities of this "fantastic" requirement in universities. "It opens the door," he has written, "to hiring persons who cannot meet *current standards of qualification* because, forsooth, a poorly qualified incumbent was hired by some fluke or perhaps ages ago when the department was struggling for recognition."

What Congress Has Proscribed

For reasons that are certainly understandable, neither the EEOC nor the OFCC has ever said in writing that it believed the law to require some hiring of less-qualified people. To do so would apparently conflict with some of President Nixon's animadversions against quotas. In addition, it would seem to go against the plain language of the laws in question. It is, after all, logically impossible to discriminate in favor of blacks without discriminating against some whites; thus anyone espousing preferential hiring of blacks would be bucking Section 703 (a) of Title VII, in which it is deemed unlawful for an employer "to . . . classify his employees in any way which would deprive or tend to deprive any individual of employment opportunities . . . because of such individual's race, color, religion, sex or national origin." In *Griggs,* Chief Justice Burger reaffirmed the intent of the law in plain terms: "Discriminatory preference for any group, minority or majority, is precisely and only what Congress has proscribed."

In pushing preferences for women and minorities, the government's lawyers and compliance officers repeatedly offer the assurance that "you never have to hire an unqualified person." Since unqualified persons are by definition unable to do the job, the assurance is perhaps less meaningful than it sounds. The real question is whether employers should have to hire women or minority-group members who are less qualified than other available workers.

The answer one gets in conversation with EEOC officials is clear enough. If hiring someone who is less qualified will help an employer to utilize women or minorities at proper levels, then he should do so. Chairman Brown was asked recently what an employer should do if he was presumed to be underutilizing women and there were two applicants for a job: a fairly well qualified woman and a man who was somewhat better qualified. "If it's just a question of 'somewhat better,' you should probably hire the woman," he replied.

The Lawyer's Predicament

How can the lawyers who run the federal programs justify preferences that seem to violate the intent of the basic statutes? Not all the lawyers would respond in the same way, but most of them would point to some court decisions at the appellate level that call for preferential hiring and even hard quotas. They would also note that the Supreme

Court has declined to review these decisions. In one important case, for example, the Alabama state troopers were ordered by a federal judge to hire one black trooper for every white man hired until the over-all ratio was up to 25 percent black. Most of the lawyers would also agree with this formulation by William J. Kilberg, the Labor Department's associate solicitor for labor relations and civil rights: "In situations where there has been a finding of discrimination, and where no other remedy is available, temporary preferential hiring is legal and appropriate."

Kilberg himself believes strongly that preferences should be limited to these special circumstances—in which it is indeed hard to argue against them. But other government lawyers view them as natural and desirable in a wide range of circumstances. They argue, for example, that it is unnecessary to require a finding of discrimination; they contend that companies underutilizing women or minority-group members are per se guilty of discrimination and that it is appropriate, in reviewing their goals and timetables, to push for some preference. Furthermore, the EEOC tends to the view that any past discrimination justifies preferences, i.e., it often fails to consider whether other remedies are available.

Last fall H.E.W.'s Office of Civil Rights made a major, but only partially successful, effort to clarify the ground rules of the contract-compliance program. J. Stanley Pottinger, who has headed the office for most of the past three years (he recently moved over to the Justice Department), put together a volume spelling out some guidelines. At the same time, somewhat confusingly, he issued a covering statement that went beyond anything in the volume. It said, "Nothing in the affirmative-action concept requires a university to employ or promote any faculty member who is less qualified than other applicants competing for that position." That statement was, and indeed still is, the only formal declaration ever issued by any contract-compliance official ruling out a requirement for hiring less-qualified job applicants.

Many contractors who read the statement took it for granted that the same rule would apply to corporate employment. Unfortunately, anyone talking about this matter to officials of the Labor Department soon discovers that they regard university hiring problems as somewhat special. There is a view that faculties have a unique need for "excellence," but that in the business world, and especially at the blue-collar level, most jobs are such that employers suffer no real hardship when "less-qualified" people are hired.

A Message to Jack Anderson

Meanwhile, corporate executives tend to take it for granted that, in practice, reverse discrimination is what affirmative action is all about. Whoever it is at International Telephone & Telegraph Corp. that leaks internal memorandums to columnist Jack Anderson recently sent along one on this subject. In the passage that Anderson published, Senior Vice President John Hanway was proposing to another executive that thirty-four rather high-ranking jobs "lend themselves readily to being filled by affirmative-action candidates," i.e., they should be filled by women or minority-group members.

Companies' public declarations about affirmative action do not ordinarily propose so blatantly to prefer these groups, but the dynamics of the program more or less guarantee that there will be preferences. Revised Order No. 4 says, "Supervisors should be made to understand that their work performance is being evaluated on the basis of their equal employment opportunity efforts and results, as well as other criteria."

Supervisors are indeed getting the message. At I.B.M., for example, *every manager* is told that his annual performance evaluation—on which the prospects for promotions, raises, and bonuses critically depend—includes a report on his success in meeting affirmative-action goals. A memo last July 5, from Chairman C. Peter McColough to all Xerox managers in the U.S. (it was later published by the company), warned that "a key element in each manager's over-all performance appraisal will be his progress in this important area. No manager should expect a satisfactory appraisal if he meets other objectives, but fails here." At Xerox, furthermore, the goals are very ambitious these days. Something like 40 percent of all net additions to the corporate payroll last year were minority-group members.

In principle, of course, a line manager who is not meeting his targets is allowed to argue that he has made a "good faith effort" to do so. But the burden of proof will be on the manager, who knows perfectly well that the only sure-fire way to prove good faith is to meet the targets. If he succeeds, no questions will be asked about reverse discrimination; if he fails, he will automatically stir up questions about the adequacy of his efforts and perhaps about his racial tolerance too (not to mention his bonus). Obviously, then, a manager whose goals call for hiring six black salesmen during the year, and who has hired only one by Labor Day, is feeling a lot of pressure to discriminate against white applicants in the fall. "In this company," said the president of one billion-dollar enterprise recently, "a black has a better chance of being hired than a white, frankly. When he's hired, he has a better chance of being promoted. That's the only way it can be."

Some Kind Words for Ability

The future of the "quotas issue" is hard to predict, for several reasons. One is the continuing blurriness of the Nixon Administration's intentions. For a while, last summer, these appeared to have been clarified. In August, Philip Hoffman, president of the American Jewish Committee, sent identical letters to Nixon and McGovern expressing concern about the spread of quota systems in American education and employment. Both candidates replied with letters assailing quotas. The President wrote to Hoffman: "I share your support of affirmative efforts to ensure that all Americans have an equal chance to compete for employment opportunities, and to do so on the basis of individual ability . . . With respect to these affirmative-action programs, . . . numerical goals . . . must not be allowed to be applied in such a fashion as to, in fact, result in the imposition of quotas."

This declaration was followed by a number of newspaper articles suggesting that the Administration was preparing to gut the affirmative-action program. The articles were wrong however. Before the reply to Hoffman had been drafted, a number of Administration officials—they included White House special consultant (on minorities) Leonard Garment, Silberman, and Pottinger—met to discuss the program and to consider whether the time had come to change it. Specifically, they considered whether to drop the requirement for goals and timetables. And they decided, as they had in earlier reviews, to resolve their doubts in favor of standing pat.

It seems clear that the Nixon letter to Hoffman temporarily shook up some members of the equal-opportunity bureaucracy, but it doesn't seem to have led to any major changes in the way the federal program is implemented. Many executives, including some who are vigorous supporters of the program, confess to being baffled by the contrast between the President's words and the bureaucracy's actions. General Electric's man in charge of equal-employment-opportunity programs, whose name happens to be Jim Nixon, remarked recently that he kept reading in the papers that "the other Nixon" was cutting back on affirmative action, but "around here, all we see is a continuing tightening of the noose."

Perhaps the simplest explanation of that contrast between words and actions lies in the very nature of the program. It is logically possible to have goals and timetables that don't involve preferential hiring—and that happy arrangement is what the Administration keeps saying we have now. But there are built-in pressures that keep leading back to preference: the implicit presumption that employers are "underutilizing" women and minority-group members; the further presumption that this underutilization is essentially the result of discrimination; the extraordinary requirement, quite alien to our usual notions about due process, that unmet goals call for the employer to demonstrate good faith (i.e., instead of calling for the government to prove bad faith). It seems reasonable to speculate that at some point the Administration will abandon goals and timetables, conceding that they lead in practice to preferential hiring and even quotas. Indeed, some of the program's senior officials regard the present format as temporary. Pottinger, who has spent a lot of time in recent years arguing that goals don't mean quotas, nevertheless says, "I sure hope they're not permanent."

In any case, one would have to be skeptical of the long-term future of any program with so many anomalies built into it. For a democratic society to systematically discriminate against "the majority" seems quite without precedent. To do so in the name of nondiscrimination seems mind-boggling. For humane and liberal-minded members of the society to espouse racial discrimination at all seems most remarkable.

The Cruelties of Reverse Discrimination

One immediate threat to the program may be discerned, meanwhile, in a number of suits against corporations and universities, alleging some form of reverse discrimination. H.E.W. now has an "ombudsman" working full-time on such complaints. It seems likely that companies engaged in preferential hiring will be hit by more such suits as the realities of their programs sink in on employees and job applicants.

But even aside from all the large litigious possibilities, there are surely going to be serious problems about morale in these companies. It is very difficult for a large corporation to discriminate in favor of any group without, to some extent, stigmatizing all members of the group who work for it. G.E.'s Nixon, who is himself black, says that talk about hiring less-qualified minority-group members makes him uneasy—that "it puts the 'less-qualified' stamp on the minorities you do hire." In companies where reverse discrimination is the rule, there will be a nagging question about the real capabilities of any black man who gets a good job or promotion. The question will occur to the white applicants who didn't get the job; it will occur to customers who deal with the black man; and, of course, it will occur to the black himself. Perhaps the cruelest aspect of reverse discrimination is that it ultimately denies minority-group members who have made it on their own the satisfaction of knowing that.

In short, businessmen who are opting for preferential hiring, or who are being pushed to it by government pressure, may be deluding themselves if they think they're taking the easy way. It seems safe to say that at some point, even if the government does not abandon its pressures for preference, more businessmen will begin resisting them. It should go without saying that the resistance will be easier, and will come with better grace, if those businessmen have otherwise made clear their opposition to any form of discrimination.

Hiring, Training, and Retaining the Hard-core Unemployed

PAUL S. GOODMAN
HAROLD PARANSKY
PAUL SALIPANTE

Many organizations are involved in programs to hire, train, and retain the so-called hard-core unemployed (HCU),[1] and recent years have seen an increasing amount of research on this problem. The purpose of this paper is (a) to provide a conceptual framework which serves to organize these research studies and (b) to evaluate what has been learned and what directions for future research are needed.

One hundred and ninety-two articles on training or employing the HCU (private sector only) were examined; 28% (54) of these related to firms' experiences in HCU programs. From this group 44% (24) were selected on the basis of an empirical criterion, that is, they presented some systematic analysis between independent variables (e.g., type of training, individual differences) and criterion variables (e.g., turnover).

Conceptual Framework

The HCU worker operates in a complex social system. The focal organization providing the training and job, community organizations, government agencies, informal peer groups, and the HCU worker's family are all components of this social system that bear on the HCU worker's behavior. Within each organization there are role relationships and other structural properties (e.g., type of job available, promotion opportunities, pay level) that directly affect the HCU worker's behavior. Recognition of these multiple factors seems necessary in order to understand the HCU worker. Too often, researchers have defined a very limited social system composed primarily of the HCU worker, trainer, and supervisor (cf. Goodman, 1969a).

A social system implies not only multiple variables, but the interdependence of these variables. Change in one variable has a complex effect on the other dimensions. A major theme in most HCU studies is that change should be focused primarily on the HCU worker—that is, how to change him to fit (i.e., be retained by) the organization. A social system model focuses on a broader perspective—what changes at the individual, organizational, or societal level are necessary to provide employment opportunities for the HCU worker.

An expectancy-performance model may also be used in viewing the HCU literature. Basically, this model holds that behavior is a product of the expectancies about behavior-reward contingencies and the attractiveness of these rewards. High retention rates would occur, then, when workers believe that remaining on the job leads to desired rewards, whereas leaving the job does not. Recent studies (cf. Heneman & Schwab, 1972) on the relationship between expectancies and rewards seem to indicate that these concepts are useful predictors of work behavior and that, therefore, they should be applicable to HCU worker behavior.

The basic thesis of this framework is that the HCU worker operates in a complex social system. The multiple factors in this social system affect his expectancies about behavior-reward contingencies and the relative attractiveness of these rewards. These expectancies and rewards, in turn, combine to determine the propensity of the HCU worker to remain on the job and to produce.

This review is organized around different dimensions of the social system that are arranged in terms of levels of social analysis. First, data relevant to individual factors are examined and then other levels of analysis, such as role and structural characteristics of the organization, are examined. The expectancy-performance component is then employed to explain the findings on the relationships between the individual or structural factors and the behavior of the HCU worker.

Individual Characteristics

Age

In a study of 347 HCUs in a large manufacturing company's program for hiring and retaining the disadvantaged, Quinn, Fine, and Levitin (1970) report that termination after job placement was greater for HCUs under 21 (50%) than for those over 21 (37%); age was not related to turnover during the prejob training. In a study of a similar HCU program, Hinrichs (1970) reports a greater turnover for trainees under 21 during training, after training, and 2 years after the training program. Greenberg (1968), Gurin (1968), Rosen (1969), Shlensky (1970), Lipsky, Drotning, and Fottler (1971), Davis, Doyle, Joseph, Niles, and Perry (1973), and Kirchner and Lucas (1972) report a similar relationship between age and dropouts during a training program. In terms of our model, younger HCU workers probably experience greater feelings of distrust toward the focal organization (Clark, 1968). Accordingly, they would perceive lower expectancies about the likelihood of receiving rewards and would be more likely to leave. Older workers probably have higher expectancies and a greater desire for the rewards (i.e., regular salary) that are contingent on attendance. Only Allerhand, Friedlander, Malone, Medow, and Rosenberg (1969) report no relationship between age and any of the criterion variables. There is not enough information on the comparability of this study with other studies we reviewed to determine why the results of Allerhand et al. differ from the other findings on age.

Sex

The evidence indicates that female job retention is significantly higher than the retention of males (Davis et al., 1973; Greenberg, 1968; Gurin, 1968; Shlensky, 1970). Females are also more likely to have a job at the completion of training (Lipsky et al., 1971). Only Allerhand et al. (1969) does not support these relationships.

Marital Status, Family Responsibilities and the Family Environment

Unmarried HCU workers exhibit higher turnover rates than married HCU workers (Hinrichs, 1970; Lipsky et al., 1971; Quinn et al., 1970). The degree of family responsibilities also seems to affect the HCU's behavior. Quinn et al. (1970) and Gurin (1968) report that male HCUs who are the main breadwinners are less likely to drop out. If HCU workers own or rent their own home or apartment, they are more likely to remain on their job (Hinrichs, 1970) and to earn higher wages (Gurin, 1968). (Gurin's study supported this relationship for males but not for females.) The impact of number of dependents—another measure of family responsibility—is more ambiguous. Gurin

(1968), Rosen (1969), and Shlensky (1970) did not find number of dependents to be a significant predictor of HCU behavior. One study (Hinrichs, 1970) reports that number of dependents was positively related to retention, but since that study did not control other individual characteristic variables (e.g., age), its conclusions must be tentatively accepted.

The findings supporting relationship between family responsibilities (e.g., marital status, owning a home) and retention reflect the greater need for job-related rewards (e.g., money); that is, greater responsibilities demand greater resources which can be attained by job attendance. Following the expectancy model, the greater the attraction of rewards related to holding a job, the higher the retention rates.

Birthplace

The birthplace or the geographical area where the trainee spent his formative years seems related to turnover of HCU workers. Higher retention rates were reported for those born in the rural South (Quinn et al., 1970; Purcell & Cavanagh, 1969) and the West Indies or Latin America (Shlensky, 1970) as opposed to those from the urban North. This relationship seems to parallel findings on rural-urban differences (cf. Hulin & Blood, 1968) which suggest that the value premises of rural-born individuals might be more congruent with organizational requirements.

Education

Evidence on the relationship between education and the criterion variables is mixed. Greenberg (1968) and Shlensky (1970) report significant positive relationships between education and job retention; in the latter study, the finding holds only for the black HCU. Gurin (1968), Quinn et al. (1970), Lipsky et al. (1971), and Davis et al. (1973) report no relationships for education. Unfortunately, there is little information in these studies on the distribution of education or the relationships between educational attainment and job requirements to permit a reconciliation of these findings.

Previous Job History

Present job behavior should reflect, to some extent, the patterns of past job behavior and earnings. Quinn et al. (1970) report that terminations were greater (54%) for those with more than two jobs in the last 2 years as compared with those (25%) who held less than two jobs in the same time period. Many of the other studies (cf. Greenberg, 1968; Hinrichs, 1970) report similar relationships. It seems that the inability to stay on past jobs leads to lower expectancies that rewards will follow from job attendance and to lower expectancies by the individual that he is capable of remaining on jobs. Following our model, these lower expectancies should lead to lower job retention.

Personality and Description of Self

Researchers interested in explaining HCU trainee behavior have examined the role of personality. Some studies have used traditional measures of personality characteristics, while others have employed simple-item scales to tap specific attitudes and values. In general, the results are not encouraging. Quinn et al. (1970) introduced some 21 indexes in their study; only two exhibited significant differences in the criterion variables, of which one was in the direction opposite from the prediction. Frank (1969) used a more extensive battery of tests and also obtained few significant results. Gurin's (1968) analysis of five scales dealing with orientation toward work, personal efficacy, and attitudes about the Protestant Ethic also did not reveal any strong consistent relationships to the criterion.

Research by Allerhand et al. (1969), Hinrichs (1970), and Teahan (1969) indicates that there may be some relationship between personality factors and the criterion variables for HCU trainees. Hinrichs (1970) reports that trainees who rated their own ability as high were more likely to be considered highest in performance during a training program. Allerhand et al. (1969) report that individuals who indicated a strong need to be perceived as smart by their boss and who perceived themselves as having a high level of energy and activity were less likely to drop out of a prejob orientation program. Teahan's (1969) study focused on the time span concept. He indicates that terminators from an HCU training program possessed shorter time spans and were less optimistic about their future than were those who remained in training. Data from each of these studies seem to indicate that a favorable self-image and orientation toward producing positive results are related to successful outcomes in an HCU program.

It is interesting to note two differences between the sets of studies presented above. The first set examined more generalized personality traits, while the second set examined attitudes and beliefs about more specific objects. The first set also relied on more traditional personality batteries, while the second set used single items that are designed for the specific research. Since there seemed to be some relationship between personality type variables and the criterion variables in the second set of studies, it may be that the methodology of this set is more appropriate to an HCU population. That is, given a population with low education and potentially negative attitudes toward test taking, it may be preferable to use a smaller set of specific items instead of the traditional personality batteries. However, before one can weigh the relative importance of personality differences, future research must examine the implications of these different strategies. (See Friedlander, 1970, and Goodman, 1970, for a discussion of methodological issues relevant to research in HCU populations.) Also, there is need for a theoretical perspective to aid in identifying relevant personality variables.

Role Characteristics

Within the organization the trainee interacts with supervisors, peers, counselors, trainers, and other organizational participants. The characteristics of these role relationships have a bearing on the likelihood that the HCU workers will remain in the company. For example, the supervisor can affect the amount of rewards the HCU worker receives. Or he can affect the expectation that certain behaviors are rewarded. The modification of rewards, or of expectations that certain behaviors and rewards are connected, should affect the HCU worker's behavior.

Supervisor Role

A number of studies indicate that the supportiveness of the supervisor affects HCU behavior. Beatty (1971) reports that consideration (measured by the Leadership Behavior Description Questionnaire) was positively correlated with performance ($r = .38$). A further analysis, however, indicated that for those trainees in the extremes of the distribution of performance scores, the relationship with consideration was negative. Another important finding is that only first-level supervisory behavior, and not second-level supervisory behavior, was related to HCU trainees' performances. Friedlander and Greenberg (1971) report a similar positive relationship between supervisory supportiveness and performance. Another interesting finding in their analysis is that significant descrepancies existed between the HCU worker and the supervisor in their perception of the supportiveness of the organization; that is, HCU trainees defined the work climate as much less supportive. Friedlander and Greenberg suggest that this differential perception of work climate increases the chances that some reliable (low-absenteeism) HCU workers will find this work situation intolerable and leave, while others will exhibit withdrawal behaviors such as tardiness or absenteeism. Quinn et al. (1970), using different measures of supervisory style, found that being treated fairly reduced the HCU worker's propensity to terminate. Also, HCU workers with more than one supervisor experienced greater turnover (57%) than those with one supervisor (31%). Davis et al. (1973) find no consistent positive relationships between supervisory behavior and the criterion variables. However, their measures of supervisory behavior (e.g., time spent with the worker) are not very specific in terms of how the supervisor deals with the HCU trainee.

In general, the studies seem to indicate supervisory style does affect HCU worker behavior. Supportiveness from the supervisor probably allays some of the HCU worker's fears about the new work situation and provides feelings of positive reinforcement about the work setting. Having a single supervisor increases the predictability of the job and probably clarifies the expectations about rewards and expected performance. Following our model, these conditions seem to lead to higher retention and performance.

Counselor and Trainer Roles

Unfortunately there are few studies meeting our criteria which deal with the effect of the counselor-trainee role on HCU trainee behavior. Quinn et al. (1970) report findings similar to their analyses of the first-line supervisor—the fairness of treatment by the counselor during training is positively related to job retention.

Gurin (1968) provides a provocative analysis of the sources of attractiveness of counselors and trainers for the HCU trainees. Counselors (versus vocational and basic education teachers) were defined as the most attractive staff members by the HCU trainees. Black counselors, however, were perceived as more attractive than white counselors for male trainees, while race differences did not differentiate the attractiveness of the occupants of the training roles. This difference in preference for black versus white counselors may be attributed to the fact that black counselors expressed values and beliefs more congruent with those of the trainees. However, an analysis of trainees' perceptions indicated that they felt black counselors stressed middle-class values more than white counselors did. This finding would seem to indicate that HCU trainees were more willing to accept middle-class socialization attempts from a black than a white counselor. Gurin confirms this point by indicating that there was a positive association (+.27) between stressing middle-class values and the attractiveness of the counselor for black male counselors but no association (—.04) for white counselors. These findings and others reported by Gurin are important because they indicate that certain combinations of race and sex with specific roles have a more powerful effect on the socialization of the HCU worker. In terms of the model, it suggests that these combination effects will have a greater impact in changing expectancies and the attractiveness of rewards and, thus, on retention and job performance.

Peers in the Work Organization

Friedlander and Greenberg (1971) report that HCU workers' perceptions of the supportiveness of their peers and others in the organization to new workers was related to supervisory ratings of performance. In general, the more supportive the trainee viewed his peers and others in the organization, the more likely he was to be evaluated by his supervisor as competent, congenial, friendly, and conscientious, but not necessarily as more reliable. Case studies by Campbell (1969) and Kirchner and Lucas (1971), as well as an experiment by Baron and Bass (1969), also point to the importance of peer-group relationships.

Morgan, Blonsky, and Rosen (1970) examined the reactions at different levels of the existing work force in the firm to a program for the HCU. They found a shift from positive to neutral feelings at the end of the 12-week program. Differences in attitudes toward the HCU and the program varied in terms of the role distance between the trainee and the respondent. For example, individuals at the vice presidential level showed an increase in positive attitudes. For foremen and the rank-and-file group, there was a tendency for positive attitudes to decrease and for negative attitudes to increase ($p > .01$ for change in overall attitudes). The modification in perceived positive and negative consequences at different levels probably reflects greater realization of problems in dealing with HCU workers. The closer one is to the day-to-day problems, the more likely it is that one's perceptions and attitudes should reflect these problems. There are no data in this study to indicate the consequences of this attitude change on the criterion variables. On one hand, the changes might merely reflect reality testing—actual experiences and expectations are more congruent. On the other hand, especially at the foreman and rank-and-file level, it might lead to less positive relationships with the HCU worker.

Roles Outside the Work Organization

Some researchers have looked at the social context of the HCU's family and peer group. Gurin (1968), for example, found that male HCU trainees in the lowest earning quartile more often came from families (reference is to the household of the trainees' mothers) where a greater percentage of adult males were unemployed. Friends of these HCU trainees also were more likely to be unemployed. Other findings (cf. Quinn et al., 1970) on the characteristics of the HCU worker's family, however, have not supported the relationships between indexes of family disorganization and the criterion variables. Therefore, although there is some indication that external role relationships affect HCU behavior, the process by which they affect expectancies, perceived attractiveness of rewards, retention, and performance is not clearly defined.

Organization Program Characteristics

Organizations involved in hiring and retaining the hard core have adopted a variety of training and counseling programs, as well as other supportive services.

Training

The selection of no training versus some, vestibule versus on-the-job training, and attitudinal versus skill training (general or specific) represent some of the choices in designing the training program portion of a program for the HCU. The Quinn et al. (1970) study permits analysis of a group that was trained and a matched control group of direct hires who received no training. The training program in question was prejob and primarily company oriented in nature. An analysis of individuals on the job who had been trained versus those not trained indicated that there were no significant differences in the perceived levels of competence in job-related skills. Trained individuals were more likely to value work, to exhibit positive attitudes toward time schedules, and to show increased feelings of personal efficacy concerning achievement. Since data for this analysis were collected after the trainee was on the job, it is difficult to separate the effects of training from the effects of successfully completing training on these responses. In either case, the trained individual's sense of personal efficacy about accomplishment did increase.

Training, of course, may have dysfunctional consequences by raising expectations beyond the realities of the work situation. Quinn et al. (1970) indicate that trained individuals preferred more autonomy than they experienced on an entry-level job and they perceived the quality of supervision as lower than did direct hires. That is, training leads to greater expectations than the job situation can fulfill. Hinrichs' (1970) study of 300 trainees in a 17-week vestibule training program also indicates some possible dysfunctional consequences of training. Not only did training not change attitudes in the intended direction, but in some cases it seems to have facilitated a change toward feelings of powerlessness. Unfortunately there are no other data presented on the effects of training that could put this result in a broader perspective.

In Allerhand et al.'s (1969) and Frank's (1969) analyses of the effects of training on certain attitudinal and motivational dimensions, there do not seem to be any significant changes as a result of the training experiences. Similarly, Goodale (1971) found that changes in work values of HCU trainees over 8 weeks of training were not significantly different from those of nonequivalent controls (insurance agents and college students).

The impact of training on job retention or performance seems negligible (Friedlander & Greenberg, 1971; Quinn et al., 1970). A study by Rosen (1969) indicates that company orientation training led to lower termination among HCU workers than did quasi-therapeutic training. However, the retention rate of the company-trained HCU workers did not differ substantially from that of regular new hires. Farr (1969) reports that among HCUs placed under sensitivity-trained supervisors, trained HCUs had lower retention (20%) than did untrained HCUs (55%).

There are many case studies concerned with the effects of turnover and performance training. Some (cf. Gudyer, 1970; Habbe, 1968; Janger, 1969) indicate training affects the HCU's behavior (e.g., turnover); other studies (cf. Saltzman, 1969) do not.

In general, reviewing all the studies and their respective methodologies, it seems unlikely that training itself affects job retention or performance. This conclusion is quite congruent with our model of HCU behavior. Job retention is related to the expectancy that job attendance will lead to desired rewards. Although the training might initially affect these expectations, it is the actual work experiences which determine the HCU behavior; that is, the types and amount of rewards available and the frequency of and criteria for their allocation determine the expectancies and the perceived attractiveness of rewards. These factors are quite independent of the training experience.

Counseling
There are no experimental data on the relative effects of different counseling strategies. The earlier discussion of the counselor role sheds some light on how the demographic characteristics of the counselor may influence his effectiveness. Several studies (cf. Allerhand et al., 1969; Hearns, 1968; Purcell & Webster, 1969; Rutledge & Gass, 1968) indicate that counseling may contribute to lower HCU termination rates. However, it is difficult to evaluate the impact of counseling on retention, since these studies do not separate its effect from other structural dimensions.

Although there is no evidence supporting any significant effects of a particular program characteristic (e.g., training), several studies (Davis et al., 1973; Janger, 1972; Sedgwicks & Bodell, 1972) indicate that the combined effects of many program dimensions (e.g., counseling, training, providing transportation) increase job retention. The problem with this conclusion is that we do not know whether other uncontrolled variables might explain this relationship, nor do we know the nature of the interaction effects. Also, Davis et al. (1973) provide a contrasting finding for those considering formal, elaborate programs—the more visible the program, the higher the absenteeism and turnover.

Organization Structural Characteristics

Job Structure

The nature of the job on which the trainee is placed affects his work attitudes and propensity to remain on the job. Quinn et al. (1970) identified four job characteristics which seem related to negative job attitudes and turnover. The inability to change one's job assignment now or in the future was related to higher termination rates for the HCU worker. Assignment to multiple work stations, or not having an idea what their work routine would be like, was also positively related to turnover. Trainees who did not understand some aspects of their job, or how it fit into the larger picture, were more likely to terminate than those who had a better understanding. When job activities were perceived as boring, turnover was more likely (63%) than when HCU workers did not find their job boring (18%); similarly, involuntary terminations were negatively related to skill level (Davis et al., 1973). In addition, a number of case studies (Bonney, 1971; Campbell, 1969; Goodman, 1969b) indicate that job status and job mobility are positively related to retention rates.

Pay

Another organizational characteristic which bears on HCU workers' behavior is the pay system. Although none of the studies we reviewed examined the effects of different pay systems, a number of studies did examine the effect of pay levels. In Shlensky's (1970) analysis, pay was a major predictor among groups (e.g., blacks, young people, and males) that were more likely to terminate and thus served to reduce the propensity to terminate in these groups. Pay did not seem to relate to turnover for whites and older workers. Other studies (cf. Allerhand, 1969; Davis et al., 1973; Purcell & Cavanagh, 1969) also indicate a positive relationship between pay and job retention and between pay and completion of training (cf. Lipsky et al., 1971).

Organizational Commitment and Change

In a few multifirm studies that were reviewed, there is some indication that higher commitment (Allerhand et al., 1969; Hearns, 1968; Janger, 1972), company willingness to change policies and procedures (Allerhand et al., 1969; Goodman, 1969b; Hearns, 1968; Janger, 1971), and more realistic company expectations of the HCU (Allerhand et al., 1969) are associated with higher retention rates.

Employment Stability, Size, Industry

Companies with lower turnover rates in entry-level jobs seemed to have higher retention rates with HCU workers than did other firms (Allerhand et al., 1969). Medium-sized companies (100-500 employees) seemed to retain more HCU workers than did larger or smaller firms (Allerhand et al., 1969). Using multivariate analysis, Lipsky et al. (1971) found that white-collar versus blue-collar jobs and jobs in manufacturing versus nonmanufacturing industries were two significant predictors of training program completions.

Discussion

The evidence indicates that many factors—individual, role, and structural—affect the behavior of the HCU worker. Age, sex, family responsibilities, and place of birth are associated with termination and subsequent earnings of HCU workers. These variables probably relate to the expectancies that job attendance will lead to certain rewards and to the relative attractiveness of these rewards. The product of expectancies and rewards leads to job retention.

The relationships between these individual differences and the criterion variables are by no means simple. First, the individual-level variables may be interrelated. For example, Shlensky (1970) finds age related to turnover among males, but not among females; further, he finds sex related to turnover among HCU aged 16-20, but not among those over 20. It appears, then, that age, sex, and other individual differences do not have simple effects on the criteria; rather, there is evidence of some fairly strong interactions.

A second problem is the relative independence of the individual-level variables and the organizational-level variables. For example, it may be that HCU workers with certain characteristics (e.g., being older) might be placed in more desirable and higher paying jobs. If such were the case, it would be difficult to assess whether a relationship among the HCU between age and turnover were due to age differences or to the more desirable nature of the jobs in which older workers were placed. The evidence concerning this issue is that the relationships between individual variables and the criteria are reduced, but not eliminated, when organizational variables are entered into a regression analysis (cf. Greenberg, 1968; Shlensky, 1970).

Although the relationships are complex, both between individual and organizational variables and among the individual level variables, a number of observations can be drawn from these studies. First, there are clearly no simple selection rules. Also, selecting out HCU workers based on the individual-difference information would be inappropriate given the purpose of HCU programs. Second, the design of a program should reflect the differences among the HCU work force. If a firm must select HCU workers with heterogeneous characteristics, it would seem important to design the program to reflect differences in their expectations and preferences for rewards. That is, a young unmarried male would receive different program inputs than a married female with two children.

The HCU trainee operates in a large social system with many interconnected role relationships. The degree of conflict between the HCU trainee and his counselor, trainer, supervisor, and peers clearly can affect his behavior. In one study there was some indication of an interaction effect between the counselor-trainer role and the similarity of the background characteristics of the role occupant and the HCU trainee. This finding would seem to have implications for selection of individuals as counselors-trainers in an HCU program. In the area of supervision, the perceived supportiveness of one's supervisor is related to job retention. However, there may be large perceptual discrepancies between supervisors and HCU workers on the degree of supportiveness existing in the organization (cf. Friedlander & Greenberg, 1971). Bridging the gap between the supervisor's and HCU worker's perception of the work climate and increasing the level of supportiveness in the organization may be one strategy to increase performance and job retention. At the same time, it is important to remember that other roles (e.g., peers) bear on HCU worker behavior; attention to only one role is not a useful strategy.

Much of the literature on the HCU worker focuses on the effectiveness of the different training strategies to reorient this individual to the world of work. Unfortunately, in the studies reviewed, there is no clear indication that training significantly affects the turnover or performance of the HCU worker. These results seem consistent with our model; that is, it is unlikely that training would have a major impact on job expectancies and the availability and attractiveness of rewards. Our conclusion is not that training of HCU workers should be discontinued. On the other hand, large investments in intensive training programs may not be warranted. Future studies that examine the effects of different training combinations such as short prejob orientation combined with on-the-job training versus extended vestibule training will provide more definitive answers to this question.

Dimensions of the organization such as the type of job and pay system affect the HCU worker's behavior. The HCU workers were more likely to terminate from jobs that they did not understand or that afforded little opportunity for movement, etc. The implication of these findings is that the trainee's behavior must be understood within the technological system in which he operates and that job redesign may represent a useful strategy in affecting the HCU worker's behavior. The level of pay also affects the HCU worker's behavior. The data seem to indicate that firms with relatively lower wage rates for entry-level jobs should avoid HCU programs. Higher paying firms, on the other hand, are in a position to hire HCU workers who would otherwise be most likely to leave; that is, there is some evidence that higher pay reduces the propensity to terminate for those most likely to leave. . . .

The overall theme of this review is that multiple variables affect the HCU worker as he operates in a complex social system. Changes in the behavior of the HCU worker are related to changes in the role-, organizational-, and societal-level variables. In many studies on the HCU worker, there has been an unfortunate assumption that the worker must be changed to fit the organization. Our concept of the complex social system suggests changes must occur at all the main levels of analysis—that is, individual, role, organizational, and societal. . . .

Notes

1. It is difficult to precisely define the term "HCU" used in these studies because of lack of information. However, a general characterization would be: the HCU is a member of a minority group, not a regular member of the work force, has less than a high school education, is often under 22 and of a poverty level specified by the Department of Labor.

References

Allerhand, M. E., Friedlander, F., Malone, J. E., Medow, H., & Rosenberg, M. *A study of the impact and effectiveness of the comprehensive manpower project of Cleveland* (AIM-JOBS). (Office of Policy, Evaluation and Research, U.S. Department of Labor, Contract No. 41-7-002-37) Cleveland, Ohio: Case Western Reserve University, Cleveland College, AIM Research Project, December 1969.

Baron, R. M., & Bass, A. R. *The role of social reinforcement parameters in improving trainee task performance and self-image.* (Final Report, U.S. Department of Labor, Office of Manpower Administration, Contract No. 81-24-66-04) Detroit, Mich.: Wayne State University, September 1969.

Beatty, R. W. First and second level supervision and the job performance of the hard-core unemployed. Paper presented at the meeting of the American Psychological Association, Washington, D.C., September 1971.

Bonney, N. L. Unwelcome strangers: A study of manpower training programs in the steel industry. Unpublished doctoral dissertation, University of Chicago, 1971.

Campbell, R. Employing the disadvantaged: Inland Steel's experience. *Issues in Industrial Society,* 1969, *1*, 30-42.

Clark, K. No gimmicks please whitey. *Training in Business and Industry,* 1968, 5, 27-30.

Davis, O., Doyle, P., Joseph, M., Niles, J., & Perry, W. An empirical study of the NAB-JOBS Program. *Public Policy,* 1973, in press.

Farr, J. L. Industrial training programs for hard-core unemployed. Paper presented at the Seventeenth Annual Workshop in Industrial Psychology (Division 14, American Psychological Association), Washington, D.C., August 1969.

Frank, H. H. On the job training for minorities. An internal study. Unpublished doctoral dissertation, University of California, Los Angeles, 1969.

Friedlander, F. Emerging blackness in a white research world. *Human Organization,* 1970, *29*, 239-250.

Friedlander, F., & Greenberg, S. Effect of job attitudes, training, and organization climate on performance of the hard-core unemployed. *Journal of Applied Psychology,* 1971, *55*, 287-295.

Goodale, J. G. Background characteristics, orientation, work experience, and work values of employees hired from human resources development applicants by companies affiliated with the National Alliance of Businessmen. Unpublished doctoral dissertation, Bowling Green State University, 1971.

Goodman, P. S. Hiring and training the hard-core unemployed: A problem in system definition. *Human Organization,* 1969, *28*, 259-269. (a)

Goodman, P. S. Hiring, training and retaining the hard core. *Industrial Relations,* 1969, *9*, 54-66. (b)

Goodman, P. S. Methodological issues in conducting research on the disadvantaged. In W. Button (Ed.), *Proceedings of Conference on Rehabilitation, Sheltered Workshops, and the Disadvantaged.* Binghamton, N.Y.: Vail-Ballou Press, 1970.

Greenberg, D. H. *Employers and manpower training programs: Data collection and analysis.* (U.S. Office of Economic Opportunity Memorandum RM-5740-OEO) Santa Monica, Calif.: Rand Corporation, October 1968.

Gudyer, R. H. A corporate experience: American Airlines. In W. D. Drennan (Ed.), *The fourth strike: Hiring and training the disadvantaged.* New York: American Management Association, 1970.

Gurin, G. *Inner city youth in a job training project.* Ann Arbor: University of Michigan, Institute for Social Research, 1968.

Habbe, S. Hiring the hard-core unemployed: Pontiac's operation opportunity. *The Conference Board Record,* 1968, 5, 18-21.

Hearns, J. P. New approaches to meet post-hiring difficulties of disadvantaged workers. In *Proceedings of the Twenty-First Annual Winter Meeting, Industrial Relations Research Association.* Madison, Wisc.: Industrial Relations Research Association, 1968.

Heneman, H. G., III, & Schwab, D. P. Evaluation of research on expectancy theory predictions of employee performance. *Psychological Bulletin,* 1972, *78*, 1-9.

Hinrichs, J. R. *Implementation of manpower training: The private firm experience.* Unpublished paper, IBM Corporation, White Plains, N.Y., 1970.

Hulin, C., & Blood, M. Job enlargement, individual differences and worker responses. *Psychological Bulletin,* 1968, *69*, 41-56.

Janger, A. New start for the harder hard core. *The Conference Board Record,* 1969, *6*, 10-20.

Janger, A. *Employing the disadvantaged: A company perspective.* New York: The Conference Board, 1972.

Kirchner, W., & Lucas, J. Some research on motivating the hard-core. *Training in Business and Industry,* 1971, *8*, 30-31.

Kirchner, W., & Lucas, J. The hard-core in training—who makes it? *Training and Development Journal,* 1972, *26*, 34-38.

Lipsky, D., Drotning, J., & Fottler, M. *The Quarterly Review of Economics and Business,* 1971, *11,* 42-60.

Morgan, B. S., Blonsky, M. R., & Rosen, H. Employee attitudes toward a hard-core hiring program. *Journal of Applied Psychology,* 1970, *54,* 473-478.

Purcell, T. V., & Cavanagh, G. F. Alternative routes to employing the disadvantaged within the enterprise. In, *Proceedings of the Twenty-Second Annual Winter Meeting, Industrial Relations Research Association.* Madison, Wisc.: Industrial Relations Research Association, 1969.

Purcell, T. V., & Webster, R. Window on the hard-core world. *Harvard Business Review,* 1969, *47,* 118-129.

Quinn, R., Fine, B., & Levitin, T. *Turnover and training: A social-psychological study of disadvantaged workers.* Unpublished paper, Survey Research Center, University of Michigan, 1970.

Rosen, H. *A group orientation approach for facilitating the work adjustment of the hard-core unemployed.* (Final Report, U.S. Department of Labor) Washington, D.C.: U.S. Government Printing Office, 1969.

Rutledge, A. L., & Gass, G. Z. *Nineteen Negro men: Personality and manpower retraining.* San Francisco, Calif.: Jossey-Bass, 1968.

Saltzman, A. W. Manpower planning in private industry. In A. Weber, F. H. Cassell, W. L. Ginsberg (Eds.), *Public-private manpower policies.* (IRRA publication No. 35) Madison, Wisc.: Industrial Relations Research Association, 1969.

Sedgwicks, R., & Bodell, D. The hard-core employee—key to high retention. *Personnel Journal,* 1972, *50,* 948-953.

Shlensky, B. Determinants of turnover in NAB-JOBS programs to employ the disadvantaged. Unpublished doctoral dissertation, Massachusetts Institute of Technology, 1970.

Teahan, J. E. Future time perspective and job success. In, *Supplement to H. Rosen, A group orientation approach for facilitating the work adjustment of the hard-core unemployed.* (Final Report, U.S. Department of Labor) Washington, D.C.: U.S. Government Printing Office, 1969.

Section B
Women
and Personnel Decisions

Women Workers:
Protection or Equality?

RAYMOND MUNTS
DAVID C. RICE

During the reform period of the decade preceding World War I, states began enacting protective laws for workers. This was acclaimed widely as a public victory over unchecked industrialization. Some of these laws apply only to women, regulating their hours of work and conditions of employment. Now legislatures and courts are taking a new look at women's protective law at the urging of those who feel such legislation restricts women's access to certain jobs and places women at a disadvantage in competing with men. The Equal Employment Opportunities Commission claims that Title VII of the Civil Rights Act of 1964 invalidates women's protective law because it prohibits employment discrimination based on sex. This amendment was added to the Civil Rights Act during congressional debate and was regarded, at the time, as a mere maneuver intended to block passage of the Act, but the ultimate fate of female protective law may turn on the primacy of this federal statute.

State Laws Regulating Aspects of Women's Employment

With the rapid growth of industry, finance, and commerce at the end of the nineteenth century, women entered the labor force in substantial numbers. By 1900 the five million female employees constituted 18 percent of the labor force. Public attention was directed by the National Consumers' League and others to the long hours, low wages, and miserable conditions of many working women. Immigration and rapid urbanization had provided an overabundance of female "help." With few skills, low mobility, and no union protection, women were easily exploited. In the reform movement which began about 1900 as a response to unchecked industrial expansion, legislative protection for women and children laborers was a prominent theme.

The reformers argued vigorously for laws limiting the hours of employment for women. By 1913, twenty-seven states had created maximum weekly or daily hours to protect the "health and morals" of women.[1] The constitutionality of using state police power in this way was upheld in *Muller v. Oregon* (1908), the case in which Louis Brandeis as counsel for the State of Oregon first introduced the "sociological brief." He built his case almost entirely on the testimony of doctors, sociologists, and economists. Judge Brewer, speaking for the court, acknowledged the "abundant testimony of the medical fraternity" and added,

> History discloses the fact that woman has always depended upon man . . . . Though limitations upon personal and contractual rights be removed by legislation, there is that in her disposition and habits of life which will operate against a full assertion of those rights. She will still be where some legislation to protect her seems necessary to secure a real equality of right. . . . Differentiated by these matters from the other sex, she is properly placed in a class by herself, and legislation designed for her protection may be sustained . . . her physical structure and a proper discharge of her maternal functions—having in view not merely her own health, but the well-being of the race—justify legislation to protect her from the greed as well as the passion of man.[2]

Although today it has a ring of quaint chivalry, this is still the best statement of principle behind standards governing women's hours of employment. At their peak, in 1967, these laws existed in forty-six states, the District of Columbia, and Puerto Rico. Some standards were established by statute; others were the orders of minimum wage or industrial commission boards. The standards apply to maximum daily or weekly hours, days of rest, meal and rest periods, and limitations on night work.

Minimum wage legislation for women has a quite different history. Eight laws were enacted in 1912 and 1913 and eight more in the next ten years, but these efforts came to naught in 1923 when they were declared unconstitutional in *Adkins* v. *Children's Hospital*. The decision in this case provides the best statement of the "equality" argument which always has existed as an antithesis to the "protection" argument. Justice Sutherland's argument in the Adkins case occurred in a climate of significant social change brought by World War I. The end of large-scale immigration and war-time pressures for production had brought higher wages, better conditions, and new jobs for women in both the government and private sectors. In addition to their new economic opportunities, women had won the right to vote.

> The Muller decision proceeded upon the theory that the difference between the sexes may justify a different rule respecting hours in the case of women than in the case of men. . . . In view of the great—not to say revolutionary—changes which have taken place since that utterance, in the contractual, political, and civil status of women, culminating in the 19th Amendment, it is not unreasonable to say that these differences have now come almost, if not quite, to the vanishing point . . . *we cannot accept the doctrine that women of mature age, sui juris, require or may be subjected to restrictions upon their liberty of contract which could not be imposed in the case of men under similar circumstances.* To do so would be to ignore all the implications to be drawn from the present-day trend of legislation, as well as that of common thought and usage, by which woman is accorded emancipation from the old doctrine that she must be given special protection or be subjected to special restraint in her contractual and civil relationships.[3]

Thus began a period of fifteen years of ambivalence in public policy with one set of legal precedents supporting state law limiting women's hours and another group denying women minimum wages. The ambivalence was resolved with the crucial one-vote shift on the Supreme Court which followed the 1936 election and the Court "packing" fight. The case involved a hotel chambermaid, Elsie Parrish, who sued for pay due under a hitherto unenforced Washington state minimum-wage. The argument of the court was an echo of the argument in *Muller v. Oregon:* "What can be closer," said Chief Justice Hughes, "to the public interest than the health of women and their protection from unscrupulous and overreaching employers? . . . how can it be said that the requirement of the payment of a minimum wage fairly fixed in order to meet the very necessities of existence is not an admissible means to that end?"[4] *Adkins v. Children's Hospital* was overthrown, and protection of women's wages took its place alongside protection of their hours. As a result of the Parrish decision and the subsequent enactment of the Fair Labor Standards Act, many states adopted minimum-wage laws. In 1970 forty jurisdictions provide minimum wages, of which seven apply to women (or women and minors) only and seven others have some provisions applying to women only. Twenty six of the minimum wage laws have premium-pay-for-overtime provisions, four of which apply to women only; there are other states in which the premium pay for women is found in separate statutes which limit hours of work for women.[5]

In addition to hours and minimum-wage laws, protection for women workers has found expression in statutes governing industrial homework, regulating employment before and after childbirth, prohibiting female workers from entering some occupations, establishing requirements for seating, and imposing restrictions on weight-lifting.[6]

The critics of this legislative history argue that such laws, by making a distinction based on sex, open the door to discrimination. They point out that the Fourteenth Amendment to the U.S. Constitution guarantees equal protection of the laws, but if sex is a valid basis for classification, the meaning of equal protection of the laws for women is defeated.[7]

Title VII and the Equal Rights Movement

The sixty-year tradition of protective laws for women is being challenged by Title VII of the Civil Rights Act of 1964. The Civil Rights bill was introduced in the House of Representatives without any mention of "sex." While the bill was before the House Judiciary Committee, Howard Smith of Virginia decided to add an amendment which would assure its defeat—equal rights for women. His strategy backfired—both the amendment and the bill passed—and the law became effective July 2, 1965. It is interesting that no women's group petitioned for or supported the sex amendment to Title VII.[8]

The trivial circumstances leading to enactment of the sex provision of Title VII and the profound changes it eventually may bring appear to qualify as historical accident. Such a conclusion, however, would overlook a tradition of "equal rights" which has long been a counterpoint to the prevailing protectionist policy. Every year since 1923 an "Equal Rights Amendment" has been proposed to the federal Constitution. This amendment covers the ground of Title VII but goes beyond, providing that "Equality of rights under law shall not be denied or abridged by the United States or by any state on account of sex." Its proponents have argued that economic progress has made protective legislation for women obsolete and that the real effect of such law now is to disadvantage women by providing a basis for discrimination under the guise of safety and welfare legislation.

Although the amendment has not been enacted, interest has continued, and in 1961 a Presidential Commission on the Status of Women further investigated these questions. The Commission recommended that minimum-wage and working standards be extended to men as well as women and emphasized premium overtime pay as the way of limiting hours. Until universally applicable standards could come into being, the Commission urged retention of present laws. It also asked for greater flexibility in regard to weight-lifting restrictions, night work, and occupational limitations.[9]

The Commission endorsed the idea of an equal pay law, an objective long sought by the labor movement, women's groups, and the U.S. Department of Labor. The Equal Pay Act was enacted in 1963. It amended the Fair Labor Standards Act to require that each covered employer pay equal wage rates to men and women doing equal work.[10] At the state level, some dozen states and the District of Columbia now include clauses prohibiting sex discrimination in their fair employment practice statutes (only two of which were enacted prior to the Civil Rights Act), and twenty-nine states have equal pay laws.[11]

However, it is the amended Civil Rights Act of 1964 which is doing most to bring the equal rights philosophy to bear on labor legislation. Coverage of Title VII, which deals with discrimination in employment, is extended to four major groups: (1) employers of twenty-five or more persons, (2) public and private employment agencies dealing with employers of twenty-five or more persons, (3) labor unions with twenty-five or more members or which operate hiring halls, and (4) joint labor-management apprenticeship programs.

The specifications directly applicable to women are those which prohibit any employer, union, or employment agency from discriminating in hiring or firing; wages, terms, conditions, or privileges of employment; classifying, assigning, or promoting employees; extending or assigning use of facilities; and training, retraining, and apprenticeships.

The most important issue in administering the sex discrimination provision of Title VII has been the interpretation of the "bona fide occupation qualification" exception which provides exceptions to Title VII where the employment of members of only one sex is reasonably necessary for the normal operation of a particular business or enterprise. Immediately after passage, this exception assumed great importance as the only meaningful defense to a sex discrimination complaint and it was interpreted by some to be a "saving exception."[12] In fact, however, the Equal Employment Opportunity Commission (EEOC), established by Title VII to interpret and apply its provisions, has construed the bona fide occupational qualification very restrictively. As with the rest of the problems created by Title VII, it " . . . remains for the judiciary to set a final standard for the scope of the exemption, and to pass on the problem of what types of evidence will be relevant in establishing a bona fide occupational qualification."[13]

Enforcement by the EEOC

In an attempt to end some of the confusion arising from the interaction of Title VII and state laws, the EEOC has issued guidelines for compliance with Title VII. These guidelines have gone through several stages. The EEOC began (on December 2, 1965) with a position relative to state protective legislation as follows:

The Commission will not find an unlawful employment practice where an employer's refusal to hire women for certain work is based on a State law which precludes the employment of women for such work: *Provided,* that the employer is acting in good faith and that the effect of the law in question is to protect women rather than subject them to discrimination. However, an employer may not refuse to hire women because State law requires that certain conditions of employment such as minimum wages, overtime pay, rest periods, or physical facilities be provided.[14]

On August 19, 1966 the EEOC changed its position and adopted a new policy stating that it " . . . would not make determinations on the merits in cases which present a conflict between the Act and State protective legislation . . . that in such cases the Commission would advise the charging parties of their right to bring suit. . . ."[15] But in February 1968 the Commission rescinded this policy and reaffirmed the earlier one.[16]

In August 1969 the EEOC went further and declared that state laws prohibiting women from certain occupations or limiting their hours of work "have ceased to be relevant to our technology or the expanding role of the female worker in our economy . . . such laws and regulations do not take into account the capacities, preferences, and abilities of individual females and tend to discriminate rather than protect. . . ." In this, its strongest statement, the Commission asserts that all such laws are in conflict with Title VII "and will not be considered a defense to an otherwise unlawful employment practice or as the basis for the application of the bona fide occupational qualification exemption."[17]

The importance of the EEOC guidelines does not lie in enforcement powers of the Commission but in its role as the administrative agency which interprets the law. It has no power to issue cease-and-desist orders nor to go to court to enforce its recommendations. It can only investigate, recommend, and attempt to conciliate; and when that fails, the original complainant is entitled to go to court. Here the EEOC guidelines become significant: the EEOC may file *amicus curiae* briefs in these cases, and the courts give the Commission's views great weight on the ground that the EEOC has responsibility to interpret and apply the statute.[18]

Accommodation by States

Since 1965 a pressing question has been how states could reconcile their protective laws with Title VII. A Task Force on Labor Standards was created in the federal government to study the issues. It recommended that states with minimum wage and prescribed rest period laws extend the same privileges to men as well as women, and that states incorporate their statutes pertaining to lunch periods, weight-lifting limits, and occupational hazards into a comprehensive safety and health program applicable to men and women alike. The Task Force urged removal of current restrictions, including prohibition on night work. Lastly, it recommended hour limits be replaced with overtime provisions when agreed to by employees. The AFL-CIO representative on the Task Force, Ann Draper, dissented on the grounds that past experience showed voluntarism would not work and that the premium pay provisions are insufficient leverage against excessive weekly hours.[19]

There now exists a clear trend in the states toward eliminating and changing women's hours and weight-lifting restrictions.[20] Delaware has repealed all its women's protective laws, and Nebraska repealed its maximum hours law in the 1969 legislative session. Also in 1969, the legislatures of New Mexico, New York, Puerto Rico, Massachusetts, Connecticut, and Maryland amended their hours laws, allowing more flexibility for women to work longer hours or to work at times previously forbidden. Since 1965, nine states have eliminated or diminished restrictions on women's hours where the women workers are subject to the standards of the federal Fair Labor Standards Act. Many states have considered bills which were not enacted. Some proposals have been made to apply hours legislation to men as well as women, but the direction of most bills is toward diminishing or abolishing restrictions on women. More states probably will take such action during the odd-year state legislative sessions of 1971.

Meanwhile, decisions by state law enforcement officials also are undermining the state statutes.[21] In February 1969 the South Dakota attorney general held that a state law limiting the hours of women was superseded by Title VII. The North Dakota attorney general made a similar decision the next month. In December, following the new EEOC guidelines of August, the attorney generals of Michigan and Oklahoma ruled their laws invalid because of conflict with Title VII. In January 1970 the Department of Industrial Relations in Ohio stated it would no longer enforce its law as did the Corporation Council of the District of Columbia in April—both because of Title VII. The Wisconsin attorney general ruled in July that the state hours law is superseded by Title VII with respect to employers covered by the Act.

Intense feelings are generated about the questions involved. These can be found on opposite sides of the issue even within the same organization. An example is the United Automobile Workers union. The general counsel of the UAW has called protective state laws "undesirable relics of the past. . . . Only a square confrontation with these so-called protective state laws can do the job. The point is, very simply, they do not protect women, they injure them."[22] However, when the issue came up in Michigan, an Ad Hoc Committee Against Repeal of Protective Legislation, led by representatives of the Hotel and Restaurant Workers' union, sought to prevent termination of the hours limitations. Among the witnesses were women members of the UAW who worked in a Chrysler plant.[23]

The Michigan experience is of interest because it produced evidence of what can occur in some companies when hours limitations are suspended. The Michigan law limiting hours to fifty-four a week and ten a day was repealed in 1967 and almost immediately reinstated; the legislature decided instead of repeal to establish an Occupational Safety Standards Commission which was empowered to make an administrative decision on women's hours limitations. In the confusion created, it appears that a Chrysler plant demanded considerable overtime from its employees. A female employee of Chrysler testified before the Commission that she had to work sixty-nine hours a week—six days at ten hours and nine on Sunday. She further testified that women dropped over from fatigue and exhaustion daily and had to be removed by stretcher. Other Chrysler female employees corroborated her testimony. Another witness from a packing company reported, "my boss ordered us to work 12 hours a day, seven days a week."[24]

The dangers of too much overtime also were described by telephone operators who were members of the Communications Workers of America. Expert medical testimony was presented, recalling many of the same issues which arose in the *Muller* case of 1908.[25] An Ad Hoc Committee Against Repeal of Protective Legislation issued a statement saying

Exemptions can be made for executive, administrative and professional women since they frequently find that limitations on hours adversely effect their opportunities for employment and advancement. But the overwhelming majority of the women working in this state need and demand the freedom from forced overtime.[26]

The Occupational Safety Standards Commission chose nevertheless to remove any limit on daily hours. Later, its ruling was successfully challenged in court by the Chrysler women.[27] Still later the attorney general of Michigan declared that state's law invalid, as noted above.

The Michigan experience may or may not be the only instance of a "grass roots" revolt against repeal of a protective hours law, but it indicates that long hours on a compulsory basis still can occur. Since overtime is rarely subject to the controls of collective bargaining, protective law is the main preventive constraint against excessive work demands.

Reaction of the Courts

Three separate cases appear, at this writing, to be headed for eventual resolution by the Supreme Court.

In the *Mengelkoch* case,[28] three female plaintiffs, all heads of families, alleged that the California maximum-hours law conflicts with Title VII and the Fourteenth Amendment. The defendant corporation admitted the women were denied overtime and promotions to positions requiring overtime but urged as justification the state's maximum-hours law, under which no administrative exceptions are available. There is no suggestion that the health or welfare of the charging parties would be affected adversely. The case is now pending in the Court of Appeals.

Another case in the Central District of California, *Rosenfeld v. Southern Pacific Company*,[29] also involved the question of whether a company discriminated against a woman on the basis of her sex. The court held that the "bona fide occupational qualification" clause of Title VII could not be applied in this case. It further held that the California hours and weights legislation discriminates against women on the basis of sex and is therefore void because of the supremacy of the federal law. A summary judgment was granted ordering the company to consider the employee for any position sought —without regard to her sex and without regard to the California law. This case also has gone to the Court of Appeals.

Perhaps the case most likely to reach the Supreme Court is *Weeks v. Southern Bell.*[30] The District Court had held that Southern Bell had not violated Title VII of the Civil Rights Act when it refused to promote Mrs. Weeks to a job which required lifting thirty-one pounds. At the time of this ruling, Georgia had a regulation prohibiting women from lifting more than thirty pounds. By the time the case was heard by the Circuit Court of Appeals, the regulation had been restated more generally: no weight limit was specified, and weights were to be limited "so as to avoid strain or undue fatigue." Furthermore, the regulation applied equally to men and women.

The Circuit Court of Appeals, therefore, based its ruling entirely on whether the company could refuse to assign Mrs. Weeks on the basis that there was here a "bona fide occupational qualification" under Title VII. In interpreting this clause, the court said

. . . that in order to rely on the bona fide occupational qualification exception, an employer has the burden of proving that he had reasonable cause to believe, that is, a factual basis for believing, that all or substantially all women would be unable to perform safely and efficiently the duties of the job involved.[31]

This goes far toward plugging any major exception.

Understandably, the EEOC is pleased with the *Rosenfeld* and *Weeks* cases as well as with the general drift of state legislative and executive decisions. The embattled posture of the EEOC is impressive, and its effectiveness beyond question. We are assured there is much more to come. In a recent weight case[32] which did not involve a state protective law, the chairman of the EEOC stated that this case

> . . . will simplify the law concerning discrimination based on sex, making it easier for employers to understand their obligations under the law, and the court's decision regarding back pay relief should result in substantial encouragement for potential discriminators to obey the law.[33]

Comment and Conclusion

In his study of the legal status of women, Leo Kanowitz has concluded that there has been improvement. Some of the common law doctrine that disparages married women relative to their husbands has been abrogated by statutes; unmarried women also have made legal gains. "The legal status of American women," he says, "has risen to the point that it is not now far below that of the American men."[34] But he notes that discrimination continues flagrantly in law regulating sexual conduct and in the employment area. The authors agree that much needs to be done in the world of work to assure equality of treatment for women. We question whether eliminating all protective legislation for women is either a necessary or proper means to that end.

A suspicion persists that the more ardent advocates of "equal rights" care nothing for protective labor legislation, for either men or women. For example, this language of the court in the *Weeks* case has been cited jubilantly by equal rights advocates:

> Moreover, Title VII rejects just this type of romantic paternalism as unduly Victorian and instead vests individual women with the power to decide whether or not to take on unromantic tasks. Men have always had the right to determine whether the incremental increase in remuneration for strenuous, dangerous, obnoxious, boring or unromantic tasks is worth the candle. The promise of Title VII is that women are now to be on equal footing. . . .[35]

This is exactly the argument which was advanced earlier against workmen's compensation and other labor legislation. It is a statement of Adam Smith's principle of "equal net advantages," which Smith himself pointed out could function only in the theory of a free market.[36] The notion that any intervention by the state distorts the unfettered interplay of supply and demand factors has been used improperly against labor legislation from the beginning. The recurrence now of such an argument, even in vestigial form, carries the discussion beyond the issue of equal treatment of women to the heart of protective legislation itself. The point that equal rights advocates are overlooking is that under many circumstances employers can and do exercise controls over the labor market, particularly in the lesser skilled factory and service employments.

The origins of protective legislation are rooted in the recurring crises which have characterized the growth of industrialization. What was required was use of state police power to assure degrees of freedom for employees through minimum wages, maximum hours, safety codes, and social insurance.[37]

The idea of balance and mutuality in the employer-employee relationship still remains an important objective. The search for equality among employees—particularly women and racial minorities—should be sought within this framework and not at its expense. Nevertheless, a noteworthy aspect of the current situation is that instead of protectionist legislation being extended to include men, it is being rooted out altogether.

It is possible unwittingly to destroy the foundations of protective legislation. There seems to be little awareness of this risk, probably because the tight labor markets of the last eight years have diminished public sensitivity to the multiplicity of interests operating. The danger of depending solely on economic forces is obscured while the opportunities are emphasized. It is not coincidental that employer groups have encouraged the repeal of women's protective legislation and opposed its extension to men.[38] The issue is now maximum hours; will it be minimum wages next?[39]

The hours question is more complex than equal rights advocates paint it. Overtime work is attractive for men and women alike as a way of solving pressing financial problems, but prolonged compulsory overtime usually brings a reaction as the family, social, and psychic cost becomes clear.[40] When one is exhausted with compulsory overtime, he or she is of course free to quit, but this cannot by itself be an argument against protective legislation. The availability of alternative employment must be a consideration. At this time it is premature indeed to base a policy on the assumption that future labor markets always will be tight. Furthermore, a new phenomenon in recent history is the high cost of hiring, due in part to health and welfare programs and other fringe benefits which are employee-related rather than hours-related.[41] It also has been noted that finding, interviewing, processing, and training people often cost several hundred dollars per employee and that labor layoffs and downgrading through seniority systems can cost additional amounts in lost time and training.[42] Under these conditions overtime even at premium rates is cheaper for employers than hiring new employees. Employers have a heavy stake in unilateral control of overtime policy.

In the current discussions one is struck by the abstract nature of the arguments and the paucity of information on possible effects of rooting out protectionist law. This is somewhat ironic, since the legal precedent for women's hours law was the *Muller* case in which Brandeis filed the brief which attempted to bring the realities of economic life into the apparatus of legal thought. If the courts have erred in the past in not being sensitive to discriminatory aspects of protectionist law, it is equally dangerous to block one's vision to the dangers of compulsory overtime. It does not appear that enough attention is being directed toward legislation requiring that overtime must be voluntary for *both* men and women. If hours limitations for women are to be repealed rather than extended to men, the only remaining way to achieve both equality and protection is through laws which require the employee's consent in assigning overtime work. However, as a remedy for the all-at-one-blow extirpation of protective hours law by Title VII, the enactment of voluntary overtime law state-by-state is a difficult and therefore unlikely remedy.

Although further research is required in those states where women's protective law has been repealed, the Michigan experience indicates that some women may still fall victim to compulsory overtime. Such women should not be denied hours protection until voluntary overtime statutes are enacted. On the other hand, there are some women who are qualified to perform jobs requiring lifting weight or working hours beyond the statutory limits. These women should not be denied the opportunity to fill such positions in reliance on state protective laws.

Thus, the question is whether state law which protects some women from the hardships of compulsory overtime must fall under Title VII in order to provide equal employment opportunity for other female workers. It is suggested that until voluntary overtime laws are enacted or until protective legislation is extended to cover men equally, protective laws be retained with administrative exemptions for women desiring positions requiring more overtime. In this way, women desiring protection would be covered while women desiring more strenuous positions would not be denied such employment because of their sex.

However, in light of cases currently pending, the Supreme Court may have to determine whether the abolition of female protective legislation is, as the EEOC contends, a *sine qua non* for eliminating discrimination and whether equality for some women must necessarily entail misery for others.

Notes

1. The most complete account of this activity is still Elizabeth Brandeis' "Women's Hours Law," in John R. Commons, *et al.*, *History of Labor in the United States, Vol. III* (New York: Macmillan, 1935), pp. 457-500.

2. Muller v. Oregon, 208 U.S. 412 (1908).

3. Adkins v. Children's Hospital, 261 U.S. 525 (1923). (Italics added.)

4. West Coast Hotel Company v. Parrish, 300 U.S. 379 (1937).

5. U.S. Bureau of Labor Standards, *State Minimum Wage Laws*, Feb. 1, 1970 (Washington: G.P.O.).

6. U.S. Department of Labor, *Summary of State Labor Laws for Women* (Washington, D.C., March 1969).

7. Pauli Murray and Mary O. Eastwood, "Jane Crow and the Law: Sex Discrimination and Title VII," *The George Washington Law Review*, Vol. 34, No. 2 (December 1965), p.238.

8. The House debate on Smith's amendment turned "ladies afternoon" into a comic discussion. Smith read a letter from a woman constituent decrying the excess of two million [sic] more males than females. Congressman Tuten argued that no southern gentleman would support legislation discriminating against women. Congresswoman St. George spoke in support of the amendment, "We outlast you, we outlive you, we nag you to death. So why should we want special privileges? . . . We are entitled to this crumb of equality." This debate suggests the difficulties the courts have since had in discovering the legislative intent behind the sex discrimination provision. See United States Equal Employment Opportunity Commission, *Legislative History of Titles VII and XI of the Civil Rights Act of 1964* (Washington: G.P.O., 1968), 3213 ff.

9. President's Commission on the Status of Women, *American Woman* (Washington: G.P.O., 1963), pp. 35-38.

10. The Equal Pay Act was a major step forward in ending sex discrimination in employment. The most obvious limitation of the act is the fact that a guarantee of equal pay is of little value to a woman who cannot get the job in the first place due to sex discrimination.

11. Demands for government action for equal pay date back to the Knights of Labor Convention in Philadelphia in 1868, where a resolution was passed urging federal and state governments "to pass laws securing equal salaries for equal work to all women employed under the various departments of government." Public attention was focused on the problem of equal pay for women during World War I when large numbers of women were employed in war industries on the same jobs as men. The National War Labor Board enforced the policy of "no wage discrimination against women on the grounds of sex." In 1919, two states—Michigan and Montana—enacted equal pay legislation. For nearly 25 years, these were the only states with statutes providing for equal pay for women. However, stimulated by the Second World War, 10 additional states passed similar laws. Seventeen others have acted since World War II.

12. Anthony R. Mansfield, "Sex Discrimination in Employment under Title VII of the Civil Rights Act of 1964," *Vanderbilt Law Review*, Vol. 21, No. 4 (May 1968), p. 495.

13. *Ibid.*, p. 496.

14. 21 *Fed. Reg.*, p. 1 (1968).

15. *Ibid.*

16. *Ibid.*

17. 34 *Fed. Reg.*, p. 11,367 (1969).

18. See Weeks v. Southern Bell Telephone and Telegraph Co., cited in fn. 30, below.

19. Task Force on Labor Standards, *Report* (Washington: G.P.O., 1968).

20. Ora G. Mitchell and Clara T. Sorenson, "State Labor Legislation Enacted in 1969," *Monthly Labor Review*, Vol. 93, No. 1 (January 1970), pp. 48-56.

21. Bureau of National Affairs, *State Labor Law Reporter*, 1.32-1.34, March 16, 1970.

22. United Automobile Workers Women's Department, *Statement of Stephen Schlossberg, General Counsel, International Union, UAW, to the EEOC at the Public Hearing* (May 2, 1967), Washington, D.C.

23. Other persons associated with the Ad Hoc Committee came from such groups as the American Federation of State, County, and Municipal Employees, Amalgamated Clothing Workers, Building Service Employees, Council of Catholic Women, Council of Jewish Women, Michigan Credit Union League, YWCA State Council, Musicians Union Local 5, and some 13 other groups.

24. *Detroit Free Press*, Jan. 21, 1969.

25. Testimony of Dr. E. R. Tichauer, professor of biomechanics, Institute of Rehabilitation Medicine, New York University Medical Center.

26. "Statement of Policy of the Ad Hoc Committee Against the Repeal of Protective Labor Legislation for Women Workers in Michigan," mimeo, undated.

27. This decision was based primarily on the court's estimate of the powers of the commission. It argued that the commission did not have the power to rescind the act, and that furthermore it was an employment safety body and did not deal with the field of discrimination. But the decision also ranged over the basic issues of whether women's health and safety required differential treatment, and noted that the commission could have, within its powers, offered some compromise such as "allowance of excess overtime by consent of the woman worker," an approach, the court noted, that seemed to find favor among women who testified in the trial. Stephanie Prociuk v. Occupational Safety Standards Commission. 3rd Circuit Court of Michigan, Wayne County, Michigan, June 20, 1969.

28. Mengelkoch, *et al.* v. Industrial Welfare Commission of California and North American Aviation, Inc. (C.D., California, 1968).

29. 293 F. Supp. 1219 (C.D., California, 1968).

30. Weeks v. Southern Bell Telephone and Telegraph Co., 408 F. 2d 228 (C.A. 5, 1969) *reversed* 279 F. Supp. 117 (S.D. Ga., 1967).

31. *Ibid.*

32. Bowie v. Colgate Palmolive Co., 408 F. 2d 711 (7th Cir., 1969) *reversed*, 272 F. Supp. 332 (S.D. Ind., 1967).

33. Bureau of National Affairs, *Labor Relations Reporter*, 72 Analysis 25, Oct. 13, 1969, pp. 227-228.

34. Leo Kanowitz, *Women and the Law, the Unfinished Revolution* (Albuquerque: University of New Mexico Press, 1969), p. 197.

35. Cited in fn. 30, above.

36. Adam Smith, *Wealth of Nations* (New York: Random House, Modern Library, 1937), p. 99 ff.

37. See John R. Commons and John B. Andrews, *Principles of Labor Legislation* (New York: Harper, 1927).

38. In the 1969 session of the Wisconsin legislature, for example, two bills were considered. the one extending hours limitation to men, the other removing hours limitations for female employees. Employers strongly opposed the first and favored the latter.

39. The recent EEOC guideline abolishes the former specific distinction made between laws which require "benefits" for women (such as minimum wages, premium pay for overtime, rest periods, or physical facilities) and laws which "prohibit" the employment of women. There is in

the guideline no longer a specific direction that an employer may not refuse to employ or promote in order to avoid providing a "benefit" for a woman as required by law.

40. This generalization is based on experience of one of the authors (Munts) in the Textile Workers Union of America.

41. Joseph W. Garbarino, "Fringe Benefits and Overtime as Barriers to Expanding Employment," *Industrial and Labor Relations Review,* Vol 17, No. 3 (April 1964), pp. 426-430.

42. Herbert R. Northrup, "Reduction in Hours," in Clyde E. Dankert, Floyd C. Mann, and Herbert R. Northrup, eds., *Hours of Work* (New York: Harper, 1965), chap. 1, p. 14.

Guidelines for Immediate Action

ROSALIND LORING
THEODORE WELLS

To this end, I am now directing that you take the following actions:

—Develop and put into action a plan for attracting more qualified women to top appointive positions . . . this plan should be submitted to me by May 15.

—Develop and put into action by May 15 a plan for significantly increasing the number of women . . . in mid-level positions. . . This plan should directly involve your top personnel official.

—Ensure that substantial numbers of vacancies on your Advisory Boards and Committees are filled with well-qualified women.

—Designate an overall coordinator who will be held responsible for the success of this project. Please provide this name to me by May 15.

Richard Nixon
April 26, 1971

Top Policy Statement Is Formulated and Announced Throughout the Organization

This is a policy statement from the top, essential to launching a program as pervasive as affirmative action for women, whether within the Federal government or in some other organization. It is also an example of initial goals with a timetable—the parameters within which expected action is to take place.

Developing a climate for change of policies and practices in order to accept women as managers usually means revising some organization-wide procedures and many attitudes and relationships. So radical will these changes seem to some that little progress will be made without consistent committed leadership from top management.

Even with strong support from executives and trainers, this kind of organizational change requires a person near the top—a new manager, consultant or staff officer—to give it concentrated attention. A fresh way of looking at the familiar scene is essential. Analysis, identification, possible solution, collaboration . . . all will be parts of the puzzle for both the line and staff as more people become involved in the processes of change.

The puzzle, of course, is the design of an affirmative action program relating to women. The structure of the program will be variously designed depending upon the applicable compliance agency and the magnitude of the effort being applied. Guidance for planning and implementation, growing out of experience with other projects of organizational change, generally applies to affirmative action programs.

We are assuming that the mechanics and problems of spelling out the specifics of the plan in each organization are available most precisely in the local area and in working with compliance officers having jurisdiction. Developing timetables also entails estimating some elements on which there may be insufficient information at the start, or which are difficult to estimate on any other basis than a well-educated guess. We want to raise a number of considerations and ideas here that we feel need to be part of the thinking and approach in developing affirmative action programs for women, taking such factors and difficulties into account. We are using Revised Order 4 as a basic model. [Editor's note: Revised Order 4 refers to Executive Order 11246, which requires federal contractors to set up affirmative action programs for women and minorities.]

Affirmative Action Officers Need a Wide Range of Responsibility; Should Report to Top Management

The sheer size of the task of turning around an organization, its people and procedures means selecting an affirmative action officer who reports directly to the top management level. The position needs to include responsibility to . . .

• Review and approve: provisions and goals of the program; job opening announcements and ads; job descriptions and requisite qualifications; application forms; tests and other screening devices; other related areas where sex bias may occur in the selection and placement process.

• Review, report and recommend actions for on-going follow-through based on: personnel records; affirmative action files for promotion; reasons for termination, discipline, and rejected promotions of women.

• Review and recommend changes in: personnel policies to assure equitable treatment for women and men; insurance, health and retirement programs to equalize benefits for both sexes and their dependents; other fringe benefit and incentive programs; informal practices and stated policy about leaves, absences, and other time off; other support services such as child care, counseling, etc.

• Review and recommend changes in: training and development programs re: selection, content, results, and rates of job progress subsequent to training.[1]

Selecting the Affirmative Action Officer; Support Groups for Affirmative Action

The logical choice for the women's affirmative action officer is a woman. Why not put a man in charge of affirmative action for women? First, because of the credibility factor. Such a position usually pays well and carries some power in the organization. To select a man could be seen by women employees as meaning that top management intends to continue giving important positions to men. Second, it could appear that a male affirmative action officer is hired to whitewash sex discrimination, not eliminate it. Selecting a woman is *prima facie* good faith. Third, few men are fully aware of the subtleties of discrimination and how it has affected women's lives. Those men sensitive enough to sex discrimination to function effectively as affirmative action officers would well understand that most men in that position would have considerable difficulty in establishing credibility with some women, especially the more aware ones.

How should the affirmative action officer be selected? Requirements might include in-depth knowledge of women's needs, roles, attitudes; what's happening in women's rights activities; current psychological and achievement motivation research on women; organization and management skills; management by objectives; and government regulatory requirements. Experience as a manager, a change-agent or community development expert should be among the other qualifications.

To separate the unaware from the knowledgeable applicant, questions could well include . . .

• How do you recognize "non-conscious sexism" in action?

• How would you select a woman to become a manager with some prediction of her success?

• What work, if any, needs to be done with men managers to make a woman's affirmative action program effective?

• What problems are "women's" problems, "men's" problems, or just human problems?

Applicants will reveal many unconscious as well as conscious attitudes during the interview. Notice what she (he) thinks women are like. Does she (he) stereotype either men or women in her (his) discussion? Can you sense an attitude of vengeance, "getting back" at society in her (his) conversation? What jokes are made, and does hostility underlie them? Vengeance could be a problem but anger may be useful. Try to sense the quality of it. Or is she (he) somewhat anxious to please, looking for how she (he) is expected to respond? "Nice person," deferring qualities may be far less than helpful in this sensitive position. Openness, directness, honesty and self-confidence are vital. So is support for expressing these qualities.

One important caution. Many firms already have affirmative action officers who are minority men, due to the emphasis on minority affirmative action in the past decade. Minority women also hold many similarly visible positions. But problems arising from discriminatory practices against minorities are different from those women experience. Minority women experience both.

Second caution. It must be clear in policy and action that advancement of minority men will not be at the expense of women's advancement nor that women advance at the expense of minority men. This is one sensitive area that can be a key to management's good faith. To pit one group against the other is to undermine the objectives of both. One way to avoid such problems is to select an aware woman who can work with the minority man who is now in affirmative action work. Equal status between them eliminates possible conflicts of interest and makes visible management's equal commitment to both groups. This delicate social balance in black/white, male/female advancement must be weighed in the final selection and placement of affirmative action officers as well as in implementing the program.

Additional people on the affirmative action teams could well include:

• An advisory committee, made up of women and minorities to solicit community and employees' views, to review and comment on policies, grievances, and the administration of the affirmative action program, to propose programs and procedures, and to consider special problems of minority women.

• Personnel staff who have sensitivity and commitment to affirmative action purposes, as evidenced by their work in feminist organizations, and minority communities.

• Supervisors and employees trained to have sensitivity to different attitudes, self-concepts, traditional social roles, and cultural differences among men and women of different ethnic groups.[2]

Responsibility for the success of the program must rest with top management on down through line supervision. Managers and supervisors should be held responsible through their performance reviews for meeting goals and timetables. If they have not met them, the reasons should be made clear. Eventually this information will be requested by compliance officers. Even without that pressure, the realistic problems and needed changes in plans are important for future planning.

Determining the Present Status of Women in the Organization

A survey to determine the practices, policies and attitudes which affect women should also canvas the experiences women have had in the organization and the ambitions they hold.

First, the survey should determine where women are in the organization by work-unit and by levels. When the search turns to women in management it will be necessary to *define a manager* for the purpose of the count. Without a precise definition, some departments may try to appear more progressive to higher management by including doubtful positions as management roles. In fact some organizations, straining hard, have even included executive secretaries as managers. Some include first-line supervision in management, others start at first-line management, which differs according to the size of the organization.

What defines management will have to be determined by each organization individually. The Department of Health, Education and Welfare bases management on pay-grade level. A major banking operation does not include first-line supervisors in its classifications of officials and managers. Their managers include those who supervise other officers, or are responsible for lending, managing and operations functions.

The basis for defining management—whether by pay-level, function, or numbers of people supervised—must be consistently applied by all managers and supervisors. The survey should include questions covering requirements of the guidelines of Revised Order 4 which call for analysis of:

• The composition of the work force and applicant flow by minority group status and sex;

• The total selection process—position descriptions and titles, worker specifications, application forms, interviews, tests, referrals, transfer and promotion practices;

• Seniority;

• Facilities and company-sponsored recreation;

• Special programs including educational assistance;

• All company training programs;

• Work force attitude; and

• Under-utilization of women in specific classifications.

Lateral or vertical movements should occur at similar time rates for women and men. Position descriptions should accurately describe all actual functions and duties.

Tests for selecting women should be validated, or be clearly capable of being validated should they be questioned for sex bias. Women should be participating in company activities and programs and be proportionately represented in training and development programs. A well-designed survey will reveal how men and women are experiencing the prevailing policies, practices and attitudes which affect their progress.

Written policies of the organization should be analyzed for sex bias by the affirmative action officer. Unwritten policies are more subtle and may be discovered via the survey which can include questions that focus on some of the old discriminatory practices of differential interview questions, pay, expectations, promotional opportunity, eligibility for further training among others.

More information can be gotten from observing the results of prior bias, such as the invisible ceiling, assumed responsibilities in housekeeping functions, and what positions are most sex-typed. These evidences can be traced back to how they started. This "audit trail" points back to a source of discrimination where differential ways of treating women from men is evident at the interface with the external market. For example, observe the double message in the employment ad that talks about looking for a man to head up a department, and which also states at the bottom of the ad, "an equal opportunity employer."

Another useful means for locating descriminatory practices is to ask the same questions of men and women, tabulating different patterns of answers. Also, when sex reversal questions are asked (those where the customary sex is replaced with the other sex) any absurdity is a solid clue that sex discrimination is present. Using sex reversal is most revealing of old habits of thinking, and brings the habit into conscious awareness.

Interviews and group sessions, as well as casual conversations can also be a rich source of information about how women feel. Care must be used, however, in interpreting these comments, as well as survey results. They reflect attitudes as of the time expressed, which may change, sometimes very rapidly. In general, most women tend to say what is expected of them, especially to men to whom they have been socialized to defer. It's part of being nice. However, as women become more aware that the price of being nice may be high, they may become more open with their formerly unexpressed viewpoints and experiences. This is the first move toward stepping out of some self-limiting behavior and can identify a potential candidate for career development. New awareness in women may be difficult to understand in comparison to former behavior, but it is a strength that is being released. Once released, it tends to grow.

Finding and Recruiting Women to Fill New Positions

Once the status of women within the organization has been determined, a plan for increasing the number of women and minorities at all levels is set up. Specific targets within definite times are part of this plan. Sometimes there is a point of "operational discrimination"—where the necessary changes seem impossible. If this happens, try making a parallel with other "impossible" situations. Usually they just take a little longer! When you decide "We'll find a way," new possibilities begin to open up. This is "good faith." Finding women who are capable of becoming managers may be somewhat easier than it seems. Thus some thoughts on how "good faith" works . . .

Colleges and Universities
Recruitment from colleges and universities is a major source for potential managers

who are men. Women graduates typically have been avoided by the campus recruiter. Even women with Harvard MBA's have had this experience.[3] The fact that 30 percent of recruiting companies went to women's colleges while 60 percent went to men's colleges[4] is a sure indicator of intent not to recruit women. Women's colleges as well as coeducational institutions are the primary source for recruiting women for entry-level management positions. They are also the place to find well prepared professional and technical women.

Now that the demand for educated women for higher-level positions is increasing, more effective recruiting practices are necessary. What changes can improve the effectiveness of recruiting? In the past, women have been formally recruited but informally excluded. They have been sought as "tokens," recruited on a basis different from men.

Briefly, here's what has been happening. Recruiters may perform formal interviews to give the appearance of active interest, knowing that an "out" will be available. They avoid the possibility of the woman student suspecting sex discrimination. This works well if the men and women students do not exchange information after their respective interviews. Many do. Even if recruiters are careful to ask the same questions and give the same explanations to both women and men students, it is becoming easier to spot lack of seriousness. Women graduates are learning what to look for. The most difficult position for a recruiter is to be seeking a qualified person for a position where the department head refuses to hire women. The recruiter is put in a personal double-bind and a long-term result may be that women graduates learn of this company's poor reputation and avoid interviews.

Recruiting a token woman is usually discovered by the woman graduate who is likely to ask about the invisible ceiling in that company. This is an excellent indicator of how serious the company is in integrating women into the managerial ranks. Some women don't want to be the token, fearing it may be another terminal position. Their concern is with being used to conceal exclusionary practices.

Equal pay for equal work is not yet a reality in campus recruiting policies. The U.S. Department of Labor reports that women are consistently offered lower starting salaries for the same job than are men. In 1970 men received offers averaging $86 a month more than women. In 1971 the difference averaged $68 a month.[5]

Some recruiters are still asking biased interview questions such as the old saws, "How will you be able to combine marriage and a career?" (as though men did not combine then all the time) and, "What will your husband say if you don't get his dinner ready by 6 p.m.?" To ask such questions of women concentrates more on her personal situation than on her capabilities. It implies that her skills are of minor importance to the job and devalues her educational achievements.

Finally, some companies do actively recruit women on the same bases and qualifications as men. We predict this practice will increase sharply, stimulated by Revised Order 4. Personnel managers and recruiters can do a major turn around in their recruiting work when they are backed by solid policy and follow-through. It is vital to establish credibility of serious intent and action over a long period of time. One way to start is by offering equal beginning salaries. The word spreads among students and certain firms will be avoided if actual experience of graduates differs from that represented. Young women are more aware of the sex bias they face. They are not gullible when they feel a solid personal commitment to actively use their education for achievement and advancement in their chosen profession.

Executive Search and Placement Agencies

Next, executive search and placement agencies and consulting firms are a rich source for management men, but not for management women. There are few, if any, who will handle women even though this is in violation of Title XII. Head-hunters are caught in the middle: the law requires them to handle persons for whom there has been no market. It's an open invitation to pass the buck.

In Atlanta, for example, the local NOW chapter undertook to disexigrate want ads. In the process they were successful in persuading personnel and executive agencies to insist on sending women applicants for all openings formerly designated as "male" positions. As these agencies made their client companies aware of the legal requirements to do this, more women were considered for higher positions.

Search practices can be reversed. Organizations can easily require their recruitment agencies to search and send women on all job openings they place. When it's necessary for earning their fees, agencies will become primary sources for higher-qualified women of all kinds. They have proselyted before and possess considerable creative talent in generating new sources when they apply their minds to it. Without question, the agency deciding to develop this market will find itself an innovator with a rich potential for new income. . . .

Some other sources for management women are such organizations as the American Association of University Women, the Business and Professional Women's Talent Bank, National Organization for Women, Federally Employed Women, Women's Equity Action League and the Women's Bureau. In Washington, D.C., Washington Opportunities for Women, a private, non-profit organization provides job matchmaking for people in that area. Other large cities have new agencies forming for this purpose, as well as local chapters of women's organizations.

Recruiting from Within

Probably the best source is women currently employed in the organization, especially those who are bumping their heads against the invisible ceiling. Although there may be no *formal* restrictions to keep women from advancing, practice demonstrates clearly that they will go no higher. The rationale for the ceiling goes, "It's never been done before," and "This is not a good time to try it," or "Our customers wouldn't accept it; they expect to do business with a man."[6]

Women at the invisible ceiling may be in executive assistantships, staff or administrative capacities or in various supervisory positions. Many have trained one or more male bosses for the next-level position for which they may be well qualified themselves, but have not been considered for promotion. Not uncommonly, a less qualified man will be given the promotion and a woman asked to "show him the ropes." Even if a woman holds a position in an acting capacity and is rated excellent in her performance, she seldom gets the promotion permanently. Such women represent a valuable pool of under-used, well-trained, and proven, high-potential management talent.[7]

Problems in Assessing and Selecting Women for Management Positions

Many men may find it difficult to evaluate the technical and professional competence of women. They may feel they can spot these capabilities and potentials in another man, but doubt their judgment about them in a woman. If the woman is attractive, sexy or appealing, how can he be sure he's evaluating her professional and intellectual capabilities rather than being swayed by her physical appearance? Further, when he is used to women performing only as secretaries or perhaps executive assistants, how can he visualize any woman as a manager? On what basis can he choose a woman over a man with sufficient certainty that he is willing to withstand expected pressures from other men? It may even seem like too much trouble, especially if he suspects this is only the beginning of similar problems.

To mitigate this difficulty, male managers may want to consider thinking through the kind of managerial job to be done and what it takes to do it *before* thinking about the sex of the person to fill it. To be fruitful this process will have to explicitly include envisioning a woman filling the job. Most managers are so used to looking for "the best man for the job" that they rarely hear their own assumption that only a man can qualify. This sex-linked assumption must be questioned each time it appears. For some time to come, it may be necessary to seek "the best woman for the job." Whether it is a woman or a man who is finally selected, this way of thinking the matter through will be more thorough, more certain to make the best selection, as well as helping to minimize sex bias.

Almost no woman would want to be selected for promotion solely because she is a woman. Similarly, it is hard to believe any man would want to be selected solely because he is a man. On the other side of the coin, it's frustrating for any woman to realize she is *not* being promoted solely because she is a woman. Yet many a woman has been forced to that realization and to the realization that men do not have parallel experiences.

Not all women employees with the requisite capabilities are good candidates for managerial positions. Many women are conditioned to think of themselves as wives and mothers first and only secondarily as employees. Those women may not be ready to become managers. There are ways, however, of spotting woman with a primary, long-range interest in her career. She is an achieving woman who has:

- A high level of motivation and achievement need
- An identification with a field or profession
- A high degree of individuality
- A strong self-esteem[8]

Recent studies have shown that career-oriented women, more than traditional women, have an experience history and background that contains:

- A working mother who served as a role model
- Strong influence by teachers, professors and people in the chosen profession
- As high school girls, infrequent dating and enjoyment from studying and reading, but dating as much as others in college
- Professionally educated parents with a high socio-economic status from a metropolitan area
- Experience of being out-of-phase; late physical maturity, not belonging to high school cliques, moving frequently.[9]

An achieving woman has more commonly developed from such a background, but this background does not guarantee the development of achievement motivation nor is it the only background in which such motivation can develop. Thus, the sociological factors found in these studies should not be used as selection criteria. Rather, a direct assessment is needed of her character, high tolerance for ambiguity, and plenty of energy and endurance, which she'll need!

Unfortunately, individuality, energy and an outside identification can be seen by an interviewer as indicating a nonconformist and potential trouble-maker. Such a woman does not fit "feminine" expectations. Yet the qualities for managerial functions are not standard female role expectations. Fear of a "trouble-maker" may be fear of an independent thinker. The interviewer's bias, if any, must be compensated for by using another interviewer who does not share a similar bias.

Assessment Centers Need to Include Women Among the Managerial Candidates

Some large companies such as Standard Oil and the Bell System have been using assessment centers for several years to identify men as candidates for management positions. [Editor's note: See the articles on assessment centers by William Byham and Allen I. Kraut in chap. 2.] Some of the methods being developed are proving successful in predicting future success among men over a long period of time. Longitudinal studies are being done.[10] The programs had no women involved at their inception. Therefore, there is no assessment center information available today for predicting the success of women in managerial roles. Where there are early identification plans and assessment center programs, it is urgent that women be included now to start building data for identifying future women managers.

One of the key innovators in this field, Douglas Bray, quickly recognizes the difficulty managers have in identifying unrealized potential in men, and how much more difficult it is for women. He comments that "even her own boss may be skeptical about advancing her, since the undemanding nature of many entry jobs for women does not allow for a real demonstration of ability."[11] This is organizational bias, structured into the entry level position system.

Clearly, an objective assessment of ability is needed, not only to persuade men supervising new women managers, but to determine that she actually has the required capabilities. Considerable new work may be needed in this assessment process to take into account the effects of cultural sex bias. The final selection criteria must, of course, be the same for both men and women. But the means to getting there may be quite different. Substantial changes in self-concept can and do take place in many achieving women. Such changes are less centrally important for men. Cultural expectations for each sex create these differences.

Sponsorship as a Means of Preparing Women for Managerial Responsibilities

In deciding how to move women ahead in management, employers might examine how men get ahead and compare this with how women are advanced. Social psychologist Dr. Martha White has found one such difference for women in science. Women are left out of the informal sponsorship system through which a young man advances by virtue of being the protege of an older, established person.

"Unfortunately, a man may be hesitant about encouraging a woman as a protege," Dr. White says. "He may be delighted to have her as an assistant, but he may not see her as a colleague. He may believe that she is less likely to be a good gamble, that she is financially less dependent upon a job. Because of subtle pressure from his wife, he may temper his publicly expressed enthusiasm or interest. Furthermore, he may fail to introduce her to colleagues or sponser her for jobs."[12]

Management-directed women find few women mentors available and it is rare for a man to chose a woman as a protege. This sets up an insidious cycle: women do not advance rapidly in part because they lack the insights and contacts women managers could give them, resulting in very few women managers to serve as mentors for younger aspiring women.

Women executives and managers should be encouraged to take on such a role, *but* it must not be women alone who are made responsible for women.[13] That would insure the future numbers of women in management would remain almost as low as today. Men managers, too, must identify women subordinates who have potential as managers and sponsor them as they would men. In fact, men managers should be expected by their superiors to coach aspiring women toward managerial preparation, and later sponsor them.

Re-examining Relevancy of Past Experience Can Prove Fruitful

For the mature woman with some relevant experience, the career ladder should be open for entry or re-entry at the most appropriate rung instead of automatically starting at the bottom. Positions which provide equivalent development experience but are not now considered part of the management development sequence should be reconsidered for their relevant value. For example, a mature woman's community experience may have been extensive in budget and finance, personnel, coordination and planning. Some few organizations now recognize such experience on their personnel forms, and in hiring, placement and training decisions. Indeed, social agency experience at the board or committee chairman level is highly comparable to some middle and upper management positions of small and medium-size profit organizations. Or, complex political campaign administration can require similar capabilities as are needed for certain middle management and staff positions. Finally, most difficult to subjectively identify are latent "natural" capabilities that come into use in the challenge of increased responsibilities. Objective assessment methods are needed to assist managers in these choices.

Because most women's life-styles are different from most men's does not automatically make them less valuable—only different. Relevant experience can be garnered from many sources. Any other assumption could produce biased effects.

Awareness Training Is a New Idea in Changing the Climate

Awareness training is a new concept developing with women's affirmative action programs. There are at least three kinds worth considering:

1. Management awareness of cultural bias and sex-role expectations that prevail in the organization and in attitudes of managers at all levels.

2. Women's awareness of their perception of themselves in their career development objectives and considering many new alternatives. For those women who are already aware, the next phase is coping with change in reaching their new objectives, including their part in changing the stereotypic expectations they may face and their responses to them.

3. Men's awareness of what it means to them to be involved in many new working relationships with women as colleagues and sometimes superiors. Changes in women's roles as they move up in managerial expertise will certainly impact men's roles and responses as managers.

Among management training and development people, there is considerable interest as well as concern about such programs and how they should be conducted. Without question, the subject of sex factors in employment, especially management, is potentially volatile in today's climate of active feminism. Polarization between the sexes is just one of many long-buried attitudes that may surface with some intensity as these changes are explored. Objective recognition of the sub-rosa attitudes can greatly facilitate their being handled or resolved. While certain behaviors are now illegal, attitudes are personal even though some may be less than generally acceptable. In awareness training, changing standards of acceptability are also explored.

Films, Discussion, Role-reversal Are Tools for Awareness Training

Many new tools for conducting awareness training are currently being developed. Films, discussions, experiences in role-reversal situations are among the early developments. One film, *51 percent* is valuable in opening up discussion and awareness in managements where the subject is new. It presents three women from different experiential and educational backgrounds, through whom the changing roles of women are played. Viewers see how their attitudes and actions can change the work situation to help reduce barriers to using women's potential for management. It treats the subject generally and is useful as an opener to awareness.

A new film, *Women: Up the Career Ladder,* which this [article's] authors cooperatively designed and produced, goes into work patterns and feelings more deeply. Eight women discuss and cope with their own real problems and possible solutions. Employee follow-up discussion of the various issues in the film usually brings to the surface responses which reveal more underlying expectations that men and women have for each other. It has been used variously: with groups of women only, with mixed groups, with management levels, or with only middle and lower supervision levels.

The Civil Service Commission has an excellent film, *What's the Matter with Alice?* that focuses on those attitudes around a minority woman that can limit her advancement and full use of her education. The process of non-conscious discouragement and non-communication is clearly portrayed and insightfully done.

A variety of pencil-paper tools and awareness readings are also being developed which bring to the surface some of the attitudes that carry a double standard or reflect cultural expectations.

Self-concept inventories are being developed to give persons taking them some insights on how they see themselves and their aspirations in a context of sex-roles. Some of these may develop into new selection tools for management development.

It is our feeling that management awareness training of the first type should be done with all managers and supervisors as one of the first implementation steps of an affirmative action program. The other two types can best be handled as a part of the regular management development program, first on a separate-sex basis, then together. Various task exercises can be used that involve a "trading of expectations" between groups. Many such training tools have already been developed for use in minority awareness programs, as well as in resolving interdepartmental conflicts. With appropriate modifications to fit the subject of sex-role bias, there are a number of useful communication exercises and team-task projects that can be adapted. Care needs to be taken that they accomplish the purpose intended. Review by the women's affirmative action officer is vital before using them in training situations.

This initial awareness training attempts to activate required behavior changes and begins to develop an awareness of attitudes that take longer to perceive.

Management Development Implications for Women—and Men

A woman can't become a good manager without appropriate training any more than a man can. She must develop her skills by moving into progressively more responsible positions where she can use her capabilities and be held accountable for the results. She also needs to attend the same management and supervisory training programs available to similarly qualified men. In addition, some women working in a male-valued environment may need training programs that deal with new working relationships with men. And certainly men may need to reconsider their old attitudes about a woman when she, formerly a subordinate, becomes a peer.

As noted above, a good assessment program is essential to be able to objectively measure both women and men in their management capability, progress and advancement potential. Objectivity needs to prevail, whether it's a small-scale program, or a major management assessment center program.

In the first phase of management development, basic managerial skills need to be emphasized and provision made for advance preparation in weak areas. Key processes, that all managers must have a good grasp of, should be defined by the organization and would include such items as:

- Having the ability to develop goals and objectives
- Being able to build a plan to implement these goals interrelating them with others
- Capable of effective communications, especially with people but also written and formal presentations
- Able to resolve or balance conflicts between work, interests and people
- Good at problem solving in all its phases, with work processes and people problems
- Balanced decision-making, carefully weighing the important elements and generally using good judgment
- Able to determine priorities with flexibility, to change as needed, and stick with them when necessary

Undoubtedly there are others considered essential in some places and not in others. In addition to this general managerial ability list, there usually are further areas that the new woman manager may want or need in her personal development. Moving from subordinancy and relative powerlessness into a position of a different kind of subordinancy with possession of some power can present a woman manager with many new questions. The initial bridge, with open discussion of concerns and alternatives, can be critical at this stage of development for some women. Certainly not all will find this change difficult.

It is later, when moving from middle management into higher management that many successful women have experienced some identity crises and have broken through the competence-femininity conflict into a "fully-functioning person" self-concept.[14] Early awareness of these double-binds can help resolve them before they reach high conflict proportions.

The focus here is on some of the male-female dimensions of management development. It is assumed that the qualifications educationally and technically are present, or being developed in preparation for management development. If the organization is under pressure to have more women in management training, they may feel a need to select a woman who is not ready for such training. If this is the case, it is essential that she be given sufficient preparatory training to give her a basis for additional management training work. When both are done simultaneously, the added pressure on the woman must be taken into consideration when evaluating her achievements.

To knowingly select a person who is underqualified without giving the essential support for probable success is a waste of time and effort on the part of the organization and the woman trainee. It will be better to take more preparatory time and adjust the timetable for accomplishing an increase in the number of women in management training. However, it will be necessary to convince most compliance officers that any delay is not, in fact, lack of good faith. Objective evidence of the need to delay management training pending further preparatory training may be required. Surely some indication that such training is in process is essential. The pressures for promotion will undoubtedly increase as affirmative action programs are implemented.

Promotion Is Where the Barriers Based on Sex Become Most Apparent

Often the very structure of an organization makes it almost impossible for a woman to be promoted. Male managers may be quite willing to promote women, yet find it impossible as long as they follow company rules and policies. Sex-segregated jobs make it difficult for women to achieve promotion because managerial positions in such an organization typically require "male" jobs as prerequisites. The EEOC's investigators have found this to be the case in several companies.[15]

Seniority, in some companies, may be a barrier to women's advancement. When seniority is considered to be total time spent working for the company, women are considered equally. But when seniority is based on time spent in a department and potential managers come only from male-dominated departments, it works against women. Further, if women lose seniority because of maternity breaks in employment, they suffer a sex-linked, discriminatory disadvantage. Seniority rules of that kind are now in violation of the law. Career ladders with vertical and lateral transfers must be developed to provide ways for women to move out of the traditional pattern of dominating the lower job categories. Long-term improvement hinges on there being known ways to advance within the organization. This fact must be made credible by evidence of women having been promoted from within.

Where women are being introduced for the first time into a particular management level or into an all-male work-unit, consideration must be given to the best way to introduce such change. Tokenism with its deleterious effects should be avoided if at all possible. One way to avoid it is to bring more than one woman into previously all-male positions or work units. Women coming into higher responsibilities may need some preparation for coping with being pioneers. Certainly the men in the all-male climate may need some preparation for coping with this change.

As one training officer of a major electrical company said, "Our men have gotten their early education in all-male classes, often studied at male institutions, have worked in and been promoted to positions where only men work, and now our management is all male. They just don't know what to do with the idea of working with women as co-professionals." Too often this is the stark reality of long-standing cultural bias. This group will need awareness training, probably of the introductory kind as well as in more operational depth. . . .

Notes

1. Excerpted from "Affirmative Action Programs for Women: Requirements and Recommendations," Womanpower Consultants, Berkeley, CA 94703. October 1, 1971, p. 3.

2. *Ibid.,* pp. 3-4.

3. Bird, Caroline, *Born Female: The High Cost of Keeping Women Down,* New York: Pocket Books, 1st printing, May, 1969, pp. 43-44.

4. Orth, Charles D., and Frederick Jacobs, "Women in Management: Pattern for Change," *Harvard Business Review,* July-August, 1971, p. 144.

5. *Fact Sheet on the Earnings Gap,* U.S. Department of Labor, Employment Standards Administration, Women's Bureau, December, 1971 (rev.), p. 5.

6. Wells, Theodora, "Woman's Self-Concept: Implications for Management Development," Chapter in Gordon L. Lippitt, Leslie E. This, and Robert G. Bidwell, Jr. (Eds), *Optimizing Human Resources,* Reading, Mass.: Addison-Wesley Publishing Co., 1971, p. 303.

7. *Ibid.* p. 304.

8. Summarized from McCord, Bird, "Identifying and Developing Woman for Management Position," *Training and Development Journal,* November, 1971, p. 4.

9. "How Are Career-Oriented Women Different," *Capsule* (published by ERIC Counseling and Personnel Services Information Center, Ann Arbor, Michigan 48104). Spring, 1971, p. 10.

The article is a summary of three recent research studies comparing "college women who chose conventional career goals with those who chose unconventional career goals (an occupation which is now dominated by men)." The studies are:

(1) Almquist, Elizabeth M., and Angrist, Shirley I., "Career Choice Salience and Atypicality of Occupational Choice Among College Women, *Journal of Marriage and the Family,* 1970, 32(2), pp. 242-248.

(2) Tangri, Florence S., "Role Innovation in Occupational Choice Among College Women," Michigan University, 1969.

(3) Walshok, Mary L., "The Social Correlated and Sexual Consequences of Variations in Gender Role Orientation: A National Study of College Students," Indiana University, 1969.

10. Byham, William C., "Assessment Centers for Spotting Future Managers," *Harvard Business Review,* July-August, 1970, pp. 150-160.

11. Bray, Douglas M., "The Assessment Center: Opportunities for Women," *Personnel,* Sept.-Oct., 1971, p 31.

12. White, Martha S., "Psychological and Social Barriers to Women in Science," *Science,* October 23, 1970, p. 414.

13. Orth and Jacobs, *op. cit.,* pp. 145-146.

14. Hennig, Margaret, "What Happens on the Way Up," *The MBA,* March, 1971, p. 10. This article is a summary of her dissertation research for her DBA from Harvard, entitled "Career Development for Women Executives."

15. For an example of a thorough analysis of how this allegedly operates in the Bell System, see "A Unique Competence," Equal Employment Opportunity Commission, Washington, D.C.

Does Sex-biased Job Advertising "Aid and Abet" Sex Discrimination?

SANDRA L. BEM
DARYL J. BEM

Title VII of the 1964 Civil Rights Act forbids discrimination in employment on the basis of race, color, religion, national origin—and sex. Although the sex provision was treated as a joke at the time . . . the Equal Employment Opportunities Commission (EEOC)—charged with enforcing the Act—discovered in its first year of operation that 40 percent or more of the complaints warranting investigation charged discrimination on the basis of sex. According to a report by the EEOC, nearly 6,000 charges of sex discrimination were filed with that agency in 1971 alone, a 62 percent increase over the previous year.

Title VII extends as well to practices which aid and abet discrimination. For example, the Act forbids job advertisements from indicating a preference for one sex or the other unless sex is a bona fide occupational qualification for employment. In interpreting this provision, the EEOC has ruled that even the practice of labeling help-wanted columns as "Male" or "Female" should be considered a violation of the law.

Nevertheless, a large number of employers continue to write advertisements which specify a sex preference, and many more write advertising copy clearly intended to appeal to one sex only. Moreover, many newspapers continue to divide their help-wanted advertisements into sex-segregated columns. [Editor's note: Ms. Carmen R. Mayni, Director of the Women's Bureau of the U.S. Census Bureau ordered in November 1973 that all job title listings be "de-sexed"; e.g., "fireman" to "firefighter," in "Job Titles De-sexed," *The State Journal*, Lansing, Mich., Sunday, Nov. 25, 1973, p. E7.]

Do these advertising practices aid and abet discrimination in employment by actually discouraging applicants of one sex or the other from applying for jobs for which they are otherwise well qualified? The two studies reported in this article sought to answer this question empirically. Both were conducted and presented as part of legal testimony, the first in a suit filed by the EEOC against American Telephone and Telegraph Company, the second in a suit filed by the National Organization for Women against *The Pittsburgh Press*.

Experiment I

As part of an investigation into sex and race discrimination at the American Telephone and Telegraph Company, the EEOC discovered a pervasive sex bias in AT&T's job advertisements and recruiting brochures. For example, advertisements for the jobs of lineman and frameman were clearly written to appeal only to men (even the job titles are male), whereas advertisements for the jobs of operator and service representative were written to appeal only to women. The EEOC therefore asked us to conduct a study

Reprinted with permission from the *Journal of Applied Psychology*, vol. 3 (1973), no. 1, pp. 6-18.

to determine whether or not this sex bias acts to discourage applicants of the opposite sex. Accordingly, Experiment I was designed to answer the following three questions:

1. Do sex-biased job advertisements discourage men and women from applying for "opposite-sex" jobs?

2. Would more men and women be interested in applying for such "opposite-sex" jobs if the advertisements were unbiased; that is, if the advertisements did not seem to prefer one sex or the other either in their job titles, pronouns, or overall tone?

3. Would even more men and women be willing to apply for such "opposite-sex" jobs, if sex-reversed, "affirmative-action" advertisements were specifically written to appeal to them?

Method

Subjects

One-hundred twenty seniors from a racially integrated high school in the San Francisco Bay area served as subjects. Half were male and half were female. Few planned to go on to any 4-year college. Students who were not planning to go on to college were purposely sought as subjects so that they might be both appropriate for and interested in jobs like those advertised by the telephone company. (As seniors, many would even be preparing for jobs like these in the near future.)

Procedure

Each student was given a booklet containing 12 job advertisements and was asked to indicate on a 6-point scale how interested he or she would be in applying for each job. The scale ranged from "very uninterested" to "very interested" and was labeled at each point. The 12 advertisements included four telephone jobs and eight nontelephone jobs. In order of appearance, the jobs were: appliance sales, telephone operator, photographer, travel agent, telephone frameman, dental assistant, taxicab driver, telephone service representative, assistant buyer, keypunch operator, telephone lineman, and public relations/advertising.

The cover sheet introduced all 12 jobs as follows: "All of the jobs have a starting salary of between $100 and $120 per week with regular raises after that. None of the jobs require any previous training or experience beyond high school graduation; all of them provide paid on-the-job training." The phrase, "An Equal Opportunity Employer m/f," appeared at the end of every job advertisement.

Sex-biased job advertisements. One-third of the booklets advertised the telephone jobs in the sex-biased format used by AT&T. In other words, these ads were copied verbatim from AT&T ads and brochures furnished to us by the EEOC. The four sex-biased telephone advertisements were worded as follows:

Telephone Operator:
WHO SAYS IT'S A MAN'S WORLD?
Behind every man's telephone call, there is a woman. She's a smart woman. She's efficient. She has to be. She places the complex long distance calls people cannot place themselves or helps them locate telephone numbers.

Hers is a demanding job. But we make it worth her while. We can make it worth your while too. Not only do we pay a good salary to start, but also offer group life insurance, group medical coverage, good vacations with pay and free pensions.

A stepping stone to management positions.
Pacific Telephone
An Equal Opportunity Employer m/f

Telephone Service Representative:
IF WE WERE AN AIRLINE, SHE'D BE OUR STEWARDESS!

She is the telephone company. At least to most of our customers, she is. When someone wants a special service, an extra phone, or if there's been a billing problem—this is the girl they talk to.

Her job is to help them.

That's why she sits at a desk. Her own desk. And that's why she doesn't have to type or take shorthand. It's a lot easier to be helpful when you have good working conditions.

She's been to our special Service Representative School. Seven weeks' worth. So she knows her job. And she knows how to handle people. Which is why we need her.

Is it any wonder we think she's special?
Pacific Telephone
An Equal Opportunity Employer m/f

Telephone Frameman:
The telephone frameman plays a vital role in telephone communications. This skilled craftsman connects cables and wires with equipment in our central office in order to provide telephone service. He also works with other craftsmen to correct troubles in wiring.

A frameman should have mechanical aptitude, a liking for technical study, and an interest in electrical circuitry.

Receive full pay during your full-time classroom training.
Pacific Telephone
An Equal Opportunity Employer m/f

Telephone Lineman:
WE'RE LOOKING FOR OUTDOOR MEN!

If sitting at a desk or working indoors is not for you, Pacific Telephone will train you as a lineman, and we'll pay you while you learn.

This job requires manual dexterity, pole-climbing ability, and the desire to work outdoors.

It's smart to look into this opportunity because we are offering more than ever in pay and benefits to get linemen. And we will give raises and chances for promotion to keep you.
Pacific Telephone
An Equal Opportunity Employer m/f

Unbiased job advertisements. One-third of the booklets advertised the telephone jobs in sex-unbiased form, that is, in a form which did not seem to prefer one sex more than the other. This involved altering the tone of the advertisements, as well as eliminating all sex-related job titles and pronouns. However, in all other respects, these unbiased advertisements match AT&T job descriptions exactly. The four unbiased telephone advertisements were worded as follows:

Telephone Operator:
We need calm, coolheaded men and women with clear friendly voices to do that important job of helping our customers. They must be capable of handling emergency calls quickly and competently. They also place the complex long distance calls people cannot place themselves or help them locate hard-to-find telephone numbers.

Theirs is a demanding job. But we make it worth their while. We can make it worth your while too. Not only do we pay a good salary to start, but also offer group life insurance, group medical coverage, good vacations with pay and free pensions.

A stepping stone to management positions.
Pacific Telephone
An Equal Opportunity Employer m/f

Telephone Service Representative:
BE OUR AMBASSADOR TO THE PUBLIC!
You are the telephone company. At least to most of our customers, you would be. When someone wants a special service, an extra phone, or if there's been a billing problem—you are the man or woman they talk to.

Your job is to help them.

You're cool. You know how to handle people in a variety of situations. Yours is a key customer relations job with great opportunities for raises and promotions into management.

Start right off earning a full salary while you attend our special Service Representative School for seven weeks.
Pacific Telephone
An Equal Opportunity Employer m/f

Telephone Frameworker:
WHERE A JOB MEANS MORE
THAN JUST GOING TO WORK!
Just ask frameworkers Susan Frey or Roger Dowling: "We've got a good supervisor. If we run into problems, we can always expect a helping hand. Our supervisor will spend a couple of hours showing us something we don't understand sometimes. We help each other around here.

It's as good an outfit as there is around. If we've got to work for a living, this is the place."

The frameworker plays a vital role in telephone communications. Working in our central office, this skilled craftsperson connects cables and wires with equipment in order to provide telephone service for our customers. The frameworker also works with other craftspeople to correct troubles in wiring.

Receive full pay during your full-time classroom training.
Pacific Telephone
An Equal Opportunity Employer m/f

Telephone Lineworker:
WE'RE LOOKING FOR OUTDOOR PEOPLE!

Are you a man or woman who likes fresh air and exercise? If sitting behind a desk isn't for you, stay physically fit as a lineworker working in the great outdoors for Pacific Telephone.

You can start right off earning a full salary while we train you to do the job.

The lineworker's job requires manual dexterity, pole-climbing, and the desire to work outdoors. Modern power tools and efficient machines help the lineworker do the job, but his or her primary aids are intelligence and a pair of good hands.

It's smart to look into this opportunity because we are offering more than ever in pay and benefits to get lineworkers. And we will give raises and chances for promotion to keep you.

Pacific Telephone
An Equal Opportunity Employer m/f

Sex-reversed "affirmative-action" advertisements. One-third of the booklets advertised the telephone jobs in sex-reversed format. In other words, these ads were worded so as to appeal specifically to that sex not normally recruited for these jobs. Once again, however, the advertisements remained true to AT&T job descriptions. The four sex-reversed advertisements were worded as follows:

Telephone Operator:

We need calm, coolheaded men with clear masculine voices to do that important job of helping our customers. He must be capable of handling emergency calls quickly and competently. He also places the complex long distance calls people cannot place themselves or helps them locate hard-to-find telephone numbers.

His is a demanding job. But we make it worth his while. We can make it worth your while too. Not only do we pay a good salary to start, but also offer group life insurance, group medical coverage, good vacations with pay and free pensions,

A stepping stone to management positions.

Pacific Telephone
An Equal Opportunity Employer m/f

Telephone Service Representative:
IF WE WERE A GOVERNMENT,
HE'D BE OUR AMBASSADOR!

He is the telephone company. At least to most of our customers, he is. When someone wants a special service, an extra phone, or if there's been a billing problem—this is the man they talk to.

His job is to help them.

He's cool. He knows how to handle people in a variety of situations. His is a key customer relations job with great opportunities for raises and promotions into management.

Start right off earning a full salary while you attend our special Service Representative School for seven weeks.

Pacific Telephone
An Equal Opportunity Employer m/f

Telephone Framewoman:
WHERE A JOB MEANS MORE
THAN JUST GOING TO WORK!

Just ask framewoman Susan Frey: "I've got a good supervisor. If I run into problems, I can always expect a helping hand. My supervisor will spend a couple of hours showing me something I don't understand sometimes. We help each other around here.

It's as good an outfit as there is around. If I've got to work for a living, this is the place."

The framewoman plays a vital role in telephone communications. Working in our central office, this skilled craftswoman connects cables and wires with equipment in order to provide telephone service for our customers. She also works with other craftspeople to correct troubles in wiring.

Receive full pay during your full-time classroom training.
Pacific Telephone
An Equal Opportunity Employer m/f

Telephone Linewoman:
WE'RE LOOKING FOR OUTDOOR WOMEN!

Do you like fresh air and exercise? If sitting behind a desk isn't for you, stay slim and trim as a linewoman working in the great outdoors for Pacific Telephone.

You can start right off earning a full salary while we train you to do the job.

The linewoman's job requires manual dexterity, pole-climbing, and the desire to work outdoors. Modern power tools and efficient machines help the linewoman do her job, but her primary aids are her intelligence and her own two hands.

It's smart to look into this opportunity because we are offering more than ever in pay and benefits to get linewomen. And we will give raises and chances for promotion to keep you.
Pacific Telephone
An Equal Opportunity Employer m/f

Summary of procedure. The same four telephone jobs were thus presented in three different formats: the sex-biased format used by AT&T, a sex-unbiased format, and a sex-reversed "affirmative-action" format. All 8 nontelephone ads were worded in sex-unbiased fashion and remained constant in all booklets. In other words, only the wording of the telephone jobs changed from condition to condition. For purposes of analysis, a subject was defined as "interested in applying" for a job if he or she checked any of the following three categories: "slightly interested," "moderately interested," "very interested." A subject was defined as "not interested" if he or she checked "slightly uninterested," "moderately uninterested," or "very uninterested."

Results

Do sex-biased job advertisements discourage men and women from applying for "opposite-sex" jobs? As shown in Figure 1, our results clearly suggest this to be the case.

Consider first the results for women. When the jobs of lineman and frameman were advertised in a sex-biased format, no more than 5 percent of the women were interested. When these same jobs were advertised in a sex-unbiased format, 25 percent of the women were interested. And when the ads for lineman and frameman were specifically written to appeal to women, nearly half (45%) of the women in our sample were interested in applying for one or the other of these two jobs ($X^2 = 8.53, p < .01$, one-tailed). In other words, sex-biased advertisements do discourage women from applying for so-called male jobs; more women would be interested in applying for such jobs if the ad's sex bias were removed; and even more women would be interested if affirmative-action ads were specifically written to recruit them.

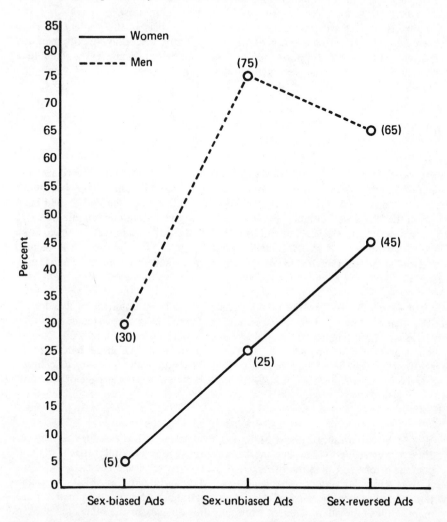

Figure 1. Percent of men and women who were interested in applying for either of the "opposite-sex" jobs. (Each data point represents 20 subjects.)

The results for men show a similar, but not identical, pattern. As can be seen in Figure 1, men are generally more interested in the jobs of operator and service representative than women are in the jobs of lineman and frameman. (This difference may be due, in part, to the fact that Pacific Telephone does employ male operators in the Bay Area.) Despite this fact, the results clearly indicate that sex-biased job advertisements still tend to discourage men from applying for jobs as operator and service representative ($X^2 = 9.09, p < .01$, one-tailed). For when the sex bias is removed, the percentage of men interested in applying for one or the other of these jobs jumps from 30 percent to 75 percent. Wording these ads in sex-reversed "affirmative-action" format does not further increase the percentage of men who are interested. [Neither does it significantly reduce it, however ($X^2 < 1$, n.s.)]. It may be that 75 percent is the maximum one can expect for any particular job and that a sex-reversed format *would* serve to further increase male interest for "female" jobs with lesser initial interest.[2]

The results of Experiment I thus indicate that sex bias in the content of a job advertisement does serve to aid and abet discrimination by discouraging both men and women from applying for "opposite-sex" jobs. Experiment II addresses itself to a second form of sex bias: the segregation of job advertisements into "Male" and "Female" columns.

Experiment II

Method

Fifty-two women attending Carnegie-Mellon University in Pittsburgh were asked to rate each of 32 jobs which had been advertised in Sunday editions of *The Pittsburgh Press*. Sixteen of the ads had been drawn from the "Male" column and 16 had been drawn from the "Female" column. Each woman was given a booklet containing all 32 ads. She was asked to read each ad and to rate it on a 6-point scale which ranged from "definitely unwilling . . ." to "definitely willing—to apply for the job." The women were told to assume that they had the necessary prerequisites for each job: "We are only interested in your preferences, not your skills."

Segregated want ads. Half of the booklets listed the ads in a sex-segregated format identical to that used by *The Pittsburgh Press*. The 16 male jobs were listed in alphabetical order in a column labeled "Jobs-Male Interest." The 16 female jobs were listed in alphabetical order in a column labeled "Jobs-Female Interest." Of these, half listed the male jobs first and half listed the female jobs first. In addition, the following disclaimer, quoted verbatim from *The Pittsburgh Press*, appeared on every other page of the booklet:

NOTICE TO JOB SEEKERS

"Jobs are arranged under Male and Female classifications for the convenience of our readers. This is done because most jobs generally appeal more to persons of one sex than the other.

"Various laws and ordinances—local, state and federal, prohibit discrimination in employment because of sex unless sex is a bona fide occupational requirement. Unless the advertisement itself specifies one sex or the other, job seekers should assume that the advertiser will consider applicants of either sex in compliance with the laws against discrimination.

Integrated want ads. Half of the booklets listed the identical 32 ads in alphabetical order with no sex labeling. The disclaimer again appeared on every other page of the booklet, but with its first paragraph deleted.

Results

Do sex-segregated want ads discourage women from seriously considering those jobs which appear in a "male interest" column? The results show this to be the case. When jobs were segregated and labeled on the basis of sex, as they are in many newspapers, only 46 percent of the women in this study were as likely to apply for "male interest" jobs as for "female interest" jobs. In other words, a majority of the women did prefer "female interest" jobs. But does this really reflect a true preference on the part of women for so-called "female interest" jobs? No, it does not. For when these same jobs appeared in an integrated alphabetical listing with no reference to sex, fully 81 percent of the women preferred the "male interest" jobs to the "female interest" jobs ($X^2 = 6.60$, $p < .02$, two-tailed).[2]

For example, the job of newspaper reporter fell in popularity from 7th place when it appeared in the integrated listing to 19th place when it was segregated and labeled as a "male interest" job. It seems clear that the newspaper editor who wishes to hire only male reporters—in violation of the law—can place his ad in the "Male Interest" column, secure in the knowledge that this will effectively discourage female applicants. It is in this way that sex-segregated want ads can "aid and abet" discrimination in employment on the basis of sex.

Discussion

What can we infer from these studies about the effects of sex-biased advertising on actual job applicants? Can we generalize these results to the actual job-seeking situation? It is our view that, if anything, these studies actually *under*estimate the extent to which sex-biased job advertisements discourage both men and women applicants from applying for jobs for which they are otherwise qualified.

First, we required the men and women in our studies to rate *every* ad regardless of how it was worded. Despite the fact that the instructions on the cover of the booklets stated this specifically and despite the fact that we emphasized the point verbally, spontaneous comments and questions indicated that both the men and the women were highly resistant to reading and rating job advertisements obviously biased as appropriate for the opposite sex. We therefore suspect that most men and women never even bother to read, let alone seriously consider, "opposite-sex" advertisements.

Second, we asked the men and women in our study only to indicate whether or not they would be interested in applying for each job. They did not, in fact, have to expose themselves to the risk of encountering discrimination—or ridicule—by actually applying for jobs which had already been designated by an employer as inappropriate for their sex. Clearly it is easier to say you will apply for a job than to actually apply.

Third, the newspaper study employed the relatively benign form of sex-segregated want ads used by *The Pittsburgh Press*. But most newspapers do not contain the disclaimer and they adhere to the more explicit headings of "Male Help Wanted" and "Female Help Wanted."

In sum, one cannot justify sex-biased advertising on the grounds that men and women have different job preferences. These studies clearly show that sex-biased advertising helps to create and to perpetuate those preferences and, furthermore, that unbiased advertising can serve to alter those preferences. Thus, for an employer to advertise as if there were "male" jobs and "female" jobs is to produce a self-fulfilling prophecy.

Postscript

As noted earlier, the two studies presented here were conducted and presented as part of legal testimony, the first in a suit filed by the Equal Employment Opportunities Commission (EEOC) against AT&T, the second in a complaint filed by the National Organization for Women (NOW) with the Pittsburgh Human Relations Commission against *The Pittsburgh Press*.

When it first became clear to *The Pittsburgh Press* that the pressures from NOW were serious and might lead to successful legal action, the newspaper changed the format of its classified advertising headings from the more blatant "Male Help Wanted" and "Female Help Wanted" to the more benign "Jobs—Male Interest" and "Jobs—Female Interest." In addition, they added the disclaimer reproduced earlier. This alteration of format did not succeed, and the Commission still ruled against them, agreeing with the contention of NOW that sex-segregated advertising columns did, in fact, aid and abet discrimination in employment. Since then the *Press* has lost appeals in the lower courts and the United States Supreme Court has now agreed to hear the case.

The EEOC action against AT&T was filed with the Federal Communications Commission, one of the few federal regulatory agencies with antidescrimination provisions in its guidelines. The occasion for the complaint was a request from AT&T to the FCC for a rate increase. The EEOC investigation of AT&T was a massive one and resulted in their conclusion that AT&T was the country's "greatest oppressor of women." The case has now been settled, and in a letter to us, William H. Brown III, Chairman of the EEOC, stated:

> The agreement which we reached with AT&T was a milestone in the history of civil rights. In addition to an unprecedented back pay award and greatly increased job mobility for women and minorities throughout the Bell System, the companies are committed to recruit and hire or promote females until they hold at least 38 percent of the inside craft jobs and 19 percent of the outside craft jobs. Males will have to be recruited and hired into at least 10 percent of the operator jobs and 25 percent of the other clerical jobs. In the long run, this means that about 100,000 or more persons will be in jobs traditionally held by the opposite sex. These commitments go well beyond any current or previous programs by any company and they have been obtained largely because of your work. . . . Since AT&T's principal justification for its sex-segregation of jobs was lack of interest by females, your experiment provided the spearhead of our argument on that issue.

In addition, AT&T has now directed that all of its advertising and recruiting materials be rewritten to remove sex bias, and a nationwide advertising campaign has been launched in the mass media featuring sex-reversed "affirmative-action" ads for traditionally sex-typed telephone jobs.

For example, an ad has recently appeared in *Life, Newsweek,* and other national magazines which shows an attractive young woman atop a telephone pole. The accompanying text reads:

THE PHONE COMPANY WANTS MORE INSTALLERS
LIKE ALANA MACFARLANE

Alana MacFarlane is a 20-year-old from San Rafael, California. She's one of our first women telephone installers. She won't be the last.

We also have several hundred male telephone operators. And a policy that there are no all-male or all-female jobs at the phone company.

We want the men and women of the telephone company to do what they want to do, and do best.

For example, Alana likes working outdoors. "I don't go for office routine," she said. "But as an installer, I get plenty of variety and a chance to move around."

Some people like to work with their hands, or, like Alana, get a kick out of working 20 feet up in the air.

Others like to drive trucks. Some we're helping to develop into good managers.

Today, when openings exist, local Bell Companies are offering applicants and present employees some jobs they may never have thought about before. We want to help all advance to the best of their abilities.

AT&T and your local Bell Company are equal opportunity employers.

A similar ad is now recruiting male telephone operators. It shows a young man, blonde, casually dressed, sitting at a switchboard, wearing a headset.

THE PHONE COMPANY WANTS MORE OPERATORS
LIKE RICK WEHMHOEFER

Rick Wehmhoefer of Denver, Colorado, is one of several hundred male telephone operators in the Bell System.

Currently, Rick is a directory assistance operator. "So far, my job has been pleasant and worthwhile," he says. "I enjoy assisting people."

We have men like Rick in a lot of different telephone jobs. Both men and women work as Bell System mechanics, truck drivers, installers and engineers.

We want the men and women of the telephone company to do what they want to do, and do best.

Today, when openings exist, local Bell Companies are offering applicants and present employees some jobs they may never have thought about before. We want to help all advance to the best of their abilities.

AT&T and your local Bell Company are equal opportunity employers.

When we were being cross-examined at the FCC hearings, our sex-reversed "affirmative-action" ads were criticized and ridiculed by AT&T attorneys. We leave it as an exercise for the reader to compare our ads with those now appearing in the mass media. (Perhaps we should sue for plagiarism.)

Notes

1. Parametric analyses based on subjects' numerical ratings yield the same conclusions reported here.

2. Surveys have shown that jobs listed in "male interest" columns are preferable in terms of objective features like salary, fringe benefits, opportunity for advancement, etc.

CHAPTER 10

Current Problems in Personnel:
Employee Well-Being in the Work Place

Many studies have been reported that have shown that the work environment can affect worker fatigue and productivity. [See for example J. W. Griffith, W. A. Kerr, T. B. Mayo, and J. R. Topal, "Changes in Subjective Fatigue and Readiness for Work During the Eight-Hour Shift," *Journal of Applied Psychology,* 1950, 34, 163-66.] Behavioral scientists are currently raising questions about the potential effect of the work environment on drug abuse rates, injury rates, alcoholism, and employee mental health.

Union and management alike are deeply concerned over the serious and growing problems of illegal drug abuse and alcoholism among employees at all levels in the organization. Chambers and Heckman discuss the concern of unions about drug abuse among workers in organizations today. The authors propose a program of joint union-management effort to create a rehabilitation center and a drug education center for workers.

The second reading in this chapter, by Trice, examines the major drug abuse problem in industry today: alcoholism. Trice examines the work world behavior of alcoholics and demonstrates how the work setting can contribute to alcoholism or lead to a truly effective means of identifying and treating the problem.

In our third reading, Simonds points out that the Occupational Safety and Health Act (see Dunn and Stephens, chap. 1) has forced organizations to modify the work environment so that an effective accident control program can be maintained. Simonds examines the physical and human conditions which lead to a lack of safety in most firms and concludes that no outside governmental pressure or assistance can substitute for an interested management and an effective safety manager in the organization.

Our last reading by Kornhauser examines a question often ignored by management: Can the task itself, especially when regimented and repetitive, produce poor mental health? Kornhauser focuses on the mental health of occupational groups in the Detroit automobile industry and concludes that mental health may be dependent on factors associated with the job.

Drug Abuse: An Avocation Ends

CARL D. CHAMBERS
RICHARD D. HECKMAN

For years, employee drug abuse was one of many topics discussed superficially by managers during lunch; it competed with the latest ballgame scores, the weather, and company politics. It was not sufficiently detrimental to warrant more than a passing mention between dessert and coffee. It was a minor aggravation that popped up now and then in the shipping department or the mail room.

Today, however, the problem of employee drug abuse is the topic of seminars, workshops, and planning meetings. Company legal departments are immersed in the subject. Supervisors, labor relations people, and the personnel and medical departments are busy trying to understand how the problem affects them. What was an avocation has quickly become a full-time job for many company specialists.

Actually, employee drug abuse is an all-company problem. Labor relations people will have to deal with the unions' growing involvement in drug abuse; security people must cope with a skyrocketing theft rate, much of which points to drug abuse; company lawyers must understand the pitfalls of the law as it pertains to drugs and company liability; and personnel people are being asked to understand the often confusing ethical and discriminatory aspects of preemployment screening. All of this can directly affect a company's profit and loss statement. As one company president put it, "This is no joke, and damn it, my people better get with it."

So your company specialists have their work cut out for them. In order to put their problems in better perspective for managers who are sure to be involved peripherally in discussions about numerous aspects of employee drug abuse, the following sections offer a summary of labor's aims and goals, preemployment screening techniques, and some advice about the legal considerations of drug abuse.

Labor's Concern

Labor unions, like most companies, have no ready answers to the drug problem. But they are now beginning to search for some. Like a good many organizations, they have in the past been extremely silent about the situation, preferring to let management cope with the few instances of employee drug abuse that came to light. In most cases, unions have gone along with the dismissal of drug abusers for other reasons (the effects of drug abuse—absenteeism, chronic lateness, and so forth) and they have been conspicuously absent when some firms have talked about rehabilitation programs for drug-dependent employees.

In all fairness to labor, it has been honest about its tardiness in developing antidrug and rehabilitation programs, admitting that until recently the problem has had a low priority. But as research has revealed the rapid growth and potential extent of the drug problem, several union officials have spoken out, indicating some of the cooperative steps labor may soon ask management to take.

Reprinted with permission of the publisher, Cahners Books, from *Employee Drug Abuse: A Manager's Guide for Action* (1972), by C. D. Chambers and R. D. Heckman.

During the last year, many large unions have been trying to determine the extent of the problem vis-à-vis their members, formulating general position statements, and deciding how best to work with management in minimizing drug abuse. For example, the United Auto Workers was one of the first unions to request major corporations with whom it has contracts to join in cooperative efforts to deal constructively with employee drug abuse.

The UAW's International Executive Board also has called on federal, state, and local governments in the U. S. and Canada to intensify their efforts to develop new knowledge of causes and methods of treatment of drug addiction and to augment support "for the pitifully limited treatment resources available."

After considerable study, the UAW Board said that there are indications in plants of widespread drug abuse which significantly contributes to increased absenteeism and tardiness with resultant disruption of work assignments. At this writing, the UAW plans to propose joint efforts to secure expansion of referral and treatment services, greater research efforts in the development of cures for drug addiction, education programs for nonusers on the dangers of narcotics, and prevention of drug sales on plant property. Agreement on joint efforts to seek solutions to drug problems has already been reached with some companies under UAW contract.

The following statement, issued by the UAW's Board on June 8, 1971, is the base from which the union begins its attack on drug abuse as well as its discussions with management about cooperative approaches:

> The UAW is deeply concerned over the serious and growing problems of drug abuse and narcotic addiction in our society. We believe the spread of these "illnesses" is a reflection of the alienation of many, particularly the young, from our society; it is a reaction to the tensions and pressures of the harsh, real world, feelings of inadequacy and social conflicts which come from a value system which gives higher priority to material achievement than to people; it is an unhappy attempt to find "fantasy" solutions to gnawing personal and family problems; it is often a reflection of the dissatisfactions with the school, the home and the workplace.
>
> We see what we believe to be widespread use and abuse of drugs by workers in the plants, with resultant adverse effects on their ability to function. Drug use contributes to increased absenteeism and tardiness. This in turn disrupts work assignments, with consequent dissatisfaction among the majority of workers who are sincerely trying to do conscientious jobs. The combination of factors has a potentially damaging effect on plant efficiency.
>
> The community at large, including our members, is disturbed by the close relationship of the drug "culture" to crime and violence, and bewildered at these spreading sicknesses in our country.
>
> We recognize that there are no easy solutions, no well-accepted cures for these sicknesses which are social, personal and medical in causation. We have no ready answers to these problems, but we have the conviction that answers must be found if the health of the society and of the work place is to be preserved.
>
> Accordingly, we call upon the federal, state, provincial and local governments to intensify their efforts to develop new knowledge of the causes and methods of treatment of drug addiction and to augment support for the pitifully limited treatment resources now available.
>
> These problems, however, cannot be solved by government alone, or by industry alone, or by the trade union movement. The UAW has already made

provisions with some employers for union and management jointly to seek solutions to the drug problem in the plants.

Such joint activities at a minimum should develop new efforts to:

a. Discourage the use of drugs among those who are not users.

b. Apprehend the narcotics "pushers" in an intensive effort to prevent the sale of drugs in plants and on plant property.

c. Work with the community to provide meaningful referral and treatment resources to rehabilitate drug users.

d. Develop new knowledge and understanding in depth of the causes and cures of narcotics dependence among workers.

We shall call upon managements in the major corporations where our members work to join with us in developing cooperative efforts to deal constructively with these great problems.

Many other unions will soon "call upon" management with specific suggestions for the prevention and treatment of drug abuse among their members. While most unions think that their suggestions for a cooperative antidrug campaign will not be a part of collective bargaining, they are not ruling this out; and it may be that some unions will ask that certain aspects of an antidrug program be part of a union contract.

While labor as well as management suffers from a lack of substantial research, which hinders the creation of specific proposals, union officials have talked enough about the subject of late to indicate the types of steps they will probably ask management to consider:

1. Reversing past experience, unions will advise that any company procedures adopted to combat drug abuse be the result of joint union-management efforts. Success of any drug program, labor will contend, depends on a union's active involvement in a worker's problem. This involvement will be achieved through newly created union-management committees on drug abuse.

2. Many unions are thinking seriously about advocating in-plant union manpower for overseeing the drug problem. They will ask that these people be trained, union counselors who will function on company time much like shop stewards.

3. It may be that additional health insurance benefits will be proposed, including new programs for the coverage of in-patient and out-patient rehabilitation of drug-dependent union members. This issue, of course, will confront squarely the question about whether drug abuse is a crime or a sickness. (This point, however, may be academic, since most medical claims are not made for drug use; rather they are reported as hepatitis and other drug-related illnesses that usually are covered.)

4. Unions will take a harder look at management's policy of immediate dismissal of all employee drug abusers. Questions will be raised concerning development of specific policy as it pertains to rehabilitation vis-à-vis tenure, with emphasis on in-patient leaves-of-absence.

5. With this in mind, joint union-management efforts will be encouraged, aimed toward the creation of residential rehabilitation centers for drug-dependent employees. These will include both out-patient and in-patient facilities, the latter of which is opposite to industry's present view that employees may be offered help only on their own time and if they can continue to perform.

Evident in all this is the fact that unions are finally becoming more interested and involved in the drug problem. Little else is clear now, except that management can expect to be hearing from labor about the problem and it should be ready to evaluate the proposals.

Preemployment Screening

The value of preemployment screening by itself is seriously questioned as a long-term solution to a company's problem of employee drug abuse. You simply cannot keep all drug abusers out of your company, nor can you insure that "clean" applicants will not begin using drugs once on the job. Yet preemployment screening is and probably will continue to be part of policy for a majority of companies; it is a worthwhile adjunct to a comprehensive antidrug program.

According to all experience, however, there really is no foolproof method for screening out drug abusers in preemployment testing.[1] The best one can do is to instruct employment interviewers to look for and question certain warning signs, prior to requesting a physical examination. In addition to the usual observance of the stigmata of needle marks on the inner surface of the forearm (although most addicts wear long sleeves), there should be careful scrutiny of the employment application for evidence of unexplained gaps in the work record, frequent job turnover, reasons for quitting previous jobs, and reference checks.

Reference checks, however, seem not to be working very well when it comes to suspected drug abuse. The reason is that seldom is drug abuse listed as a cause for termination on an individual's personnel record; instead, improper performance usually is recorded, which, of course, is only a by-product of the cause. This same sort of evasion has been used in other sensitive dismissals, such as homosexuality.

It has been said that this really is not an issue because personnel people can talk with each other indirectly, and somehow each gets the proper message. But this does not pertain to drug abuse. Although it is the responsibility of businesses to provide factual and truthful referential reports—or reports that are guarded but understood such as in the case of dismissal for theft—companies truly hedge about the subject of drug abuse for reasons of liability. Too many firms have been stung too many times. It is virtually impossible to prove that a person has used drugs in the past, and some companies that have dismissed a suspected drug user and recorded drug use as the reason for termination on the employee's personnel record have lived to regret it; they have been sued by ex-employees when they found out that possible drug use was the reason they failed to secure another job. It has been claimed in some circles that a few employees have actually planned such a tactic with the hopeful, specific intent of being able to sue a company for libel or defamation of character later.

Hence, in many companies, when an employee is dismissed for drug use it is not recorded as such on his personnel record. Other more traditional reasons are listed. So reference checks can be unreliable and also misleading. If there is no indication on a personnel record that an ex-employee was dismissed for using drugs, a new man in the personnel department may answer a reference question with, "No, he was not using drugs; he was dismissed for excessive absenteeism." This is the only reason the new man knows about. Also, the new man may have been instructed to be tight-lipped when it comes to answering questions about drugs. So while it is good practice to check with employers about whether an applicant has used drugs, beware of the information you receive.

Incidentally, colleges and universities generally will not divulge information concerning drug use of students. Students have the right to request of colleges and universities that information of this kind be withheld or deleted from their files, and schools usually comply. Generally, this type of information includes arrests in connection with drugs, and, in most cases, colleges and universities go along with student requests not to record or divulge information of this kind. In most instances, colleges would not divulge this type of information even if the student did not request that they not do so. As one personnel man puts it, "No wonder the kids raise hell in school, they know they can apply for a job without a blemish on their record; this is a lot of crap and only serves to encourage kids to experiment with drugs." Whether it does or not is a question that is unclear; what is clear is that college reference checks about drug use are a waste of time.

One new procedure may help to enhance the value of reference checks concerning applicants who are suspected of drug use. In some states, companies are being asked to report all employees terminated for drug use to the appropriate city health department. The reason is both for valuable research and to assist in possible follow-up rehabilitation. But this is an extremely controversial topic. Listen to one New York City businessman:

> When we discharge an employee for abusing drugs, I've long had the feeling that the company has a responsibility to report that person to some sort of public health agency, for help. We don't have to report them to any law enforcement agency, but I think we have a moral obligation to try to help them, not just heave them out on the street.
>
> In New York City, there is a strong appeal from the people in the health department that companies be made to report cases of dismissal for drug use for epidemiologic purposes. Right now, it is voluntary, and the health department has assured us that all the information will be confidential. But I know that in the past there have been several attempts on the part of law enforcement agencies to use the health department's records for their own purposes. The police know that the health department's records would contribute toward finding sources of drug sales. I think this is fine, but I also think it would have a negative impact on the rehabilitation efforts of a health department. It is that old bugaboo again about drug use being a crime or a sickness, and I am not about to get into the middle of that argument.

If it ever became mandatory for companies to report employees who have been dismissed for drug abuse to health departments, chances are the health departments would not share the information with other companies anyway. Yet it *is* a possibility —the only one that seems to make sense as far as reference checks of drug abusers are concerned.

Applicants who are suspected of drug use by employment interviewers, yet in all other ways appear to be a suitable potential employee, should be and usually are referred to the medical department for a physical examination. Although there is no known medical test to detect the use of marihuana, recent use of other drugs usually can be detected by chromatography, which finds the presence of drugs in body fluids.

In the New York area, for example, these types of tests are performed for industry by the Laboratory of Chromatography in Bayside. Addressing the American Management Association, Dr. David Sohn, Medical Director of the Laboratory, reported that the biological fluid used in detecting all of the drugs except LSD and marihuana is urine.

> Most drugs are excreted via the urine which provides the greatest amount and concentration of material for study. Obviously, no special techniques, technicians, or sterile materials are needed to obtain the specimen and there is no discomfort to the contributor, as might be the case with blood samples. There is also no serious difficulty or discomfort in obtaining multiple, sequential specimens on the same or subsequent days, as might be the case were blood to be used.

LSD can be detected only from blood serum. It is metabolized too rapidly to be retrieved. The normal dose is so small that it cannot be found subsequently. Marihuana, at present, cannot be detected in any body fluid.

Urine tests can pick up recent use of heroin. But some addicts simply refrain from using it for a few days before their physical examination. Others bring in hidden vials of "clean" urine and substitute it for their own. Yet, on the whole, urinalysis is a worthwhile screening technique.

Several questions are now being raised by many companies anticipating extensive use of chromatography and other preemployment medical tests. Are these tests ethical? And unless all applicants are tested, are they discriminatory? The director of industrial relations for a large utility sums up the beliefs of many of his counterparts:

> I don't believe these tests are either unethical or discriminatory. Our applicants are made to understand that they must take a preemployment physical exam before they can be hired. The results of this exam are evaluated both by the medical department and the personnel department. The applicant is told this, and he is also told that if he doesn't measure up in all preemployment tests, including the medical exam, he cannot be hired. I think this is being honest and ethical. As far as medical tests being discriminatory, I say this: I don't believe that they are discriminatory or not discriminatory. You have to think in terms of the type of job to be done. If we are testing someone for a job involving some of the secrets on which this country's security is based, I think that applicant would receive a different kind of scrutiny than someone else. There are many types of preemployment tests for many types of jobs in many different companies. A clerk typist may not get the same type of examination as an applicant who will be required to lift 75 to 100 pounds every day. If a person is going to be a cable splicer, for example, he gets more than an ordinary color test. Different tests are designed to determine whether applicants are capable of doing different jobs. And there aren't too many jobs you can do well if you are abusing drugs.

A Word to the Wise, about the Law

With the problem of drug abuse in business and industry comes a paper problem —the understanding of a host of statutes, regulations, and court decisions concerning the legal aspects of drug abuse. This is a continuing challenge for your company's legal department or outside counsel because of the newness and complexity of the subject, and because federal and state laws that affect drug abuse are changing constantly.

Employee drug abuse can present legal problems in just about every segment of your company, including security, medical, personnel, and production. Beginning with the illegal possession and sale of narcotics and dangerous drugs on company premises, drug-related activities requiring expert legal advice can range through theft of company property, product liability, false claims for workmen's compensation, union arbitration, equal employment opportunity charges, occupational safety and health, surveillance of suspected employees, suits by employees for slander, libel, and defamation of character, death benefits as they relate to drug abuse, privileged communication between doctor and employee, and many more.

The point is that drug abuse is indeed a legal threat to every company, and while managers and supervisors should be briefed by the company's legal people during regular training sessions about the possible legal ramifications and risks in their dealings with employees, it should be made absolutely clear at the outset that this is an area in which supervisors should rely totally on legal specialists.

The realities and responsibilities of the legal department vis-à-vis drug abuse and its mélange of possible legal problems are beyond the ken of supervisors, and this should be strongly suggested to them. A little knowledge is extremely dangerous, and supervisors who are given a superficial understanding of the legal considerations of drug abuse might cause irreparable harm by thinking they can cope with incidents or situations that could lead to possible litigation.

What then do you tell your supervisors? You tell them first that they are not lawyers and are not expected to be. You tell them that in every instance where there is a question about the legality of a situation, they should do nothing before checking with higher supervision, who, in turn, will check with the company's legal specialists. Impress them most forcefully with this point. Apprehending a thief is one thing, apprehending a suspected thief is quite another.

Because business and industry's experience is still limited, a suitable training session for supervisors designed and implemented by your legal department may be difficult to create. An excellent source for research, however, is a book titled *Legal Considerations: Drug Abuse in Industry and Business,* by Sidney H. Willig, Professor of Law and Director of Drug Law Unit, Temple University. The book is published by Symposium Enterprises, 1460 N.E. 129th Street, P. O. Box 356, North Miami, Florida 33161.

While most of today's legal questions about drug abuse deal with unsettled areas of the law, and varying interpretations may be possible in various jurisdictions, Mr. Willig's book provides a fine base on which one can begin to build an individual company's supervisor training meeting.

That there are numerous interpretations of the law in various jurisdictions is easily shown when one looks at the penalties now on the federal and state books for illegal manufacture, possession, and sale of narcotics and dangerous drugs. They not only vary widely, but they could soon change. While managers probably will have little direct experience with the implementation of these laws, their diversity serves to show current inconsistencies and underscores why supervisors should refer all legal questions to specialists.

At this writing, for example, state laws for the possession, sale or manufacture of marihuana vary widely. In Nebraska, a conviction of first offense possession of marihuana can mean only seven days in jail and a course in drug education. On the other hand, in Texas you can receive up to life imprisonment for possession and sale. In California, conviction of possession can bring one-to-ten years; in Ohio it brings two-to-twenty-five years and a $10,000 fine.

Aside from this type of diversity, there are also the differences in certain types of drug penalties:

Opiates (Opium, Heroin, Morphine)
The illegal manufacture, sale, and possession of opiates is a felony and, upon conviction, sentences range from 2-to-10 years imprisonment for first-offense possession to 10-to-40 years for second offense sale. In all but first-offense possession, suspension of sentence, probation or parole are prohibited. These are federal penalties; state laws vary and in most instances they are more severe than federal law. . . .

[Editor's note: While Chambers and Heckman do an excellent job of discussing a potential drug abuse program, they do not address themselves in this article to the problem of the fatiguing job itself in contributing to drug addiction.]

Note

1. Many people are feverishly working on the problem, hoping to develop a foolproof method. The most recent example is a study of fingerprint patterns by a Massachusetts deputy sheriff who believes that drug addicts might have similar fingerprints. Louis Cataldo of Barnstable, Massachusetts, began noticing the similarity of print patterns among drug offenders arrested in his county. Discussing his theory in an article in the Boston *Globe,* Cataldo said, "My study involving drug addicts shows that their prints are similar, favoring arch, tented arch and radial fingerprint patterns. Considering that arch and tented arch patterns have always been the lowest percentage (six or seven percent) of all fingerprint patterns, the information is of great interest. This is not to say that everyone with this type of fingerprint is a drug or potential drug user; but it is unusual that so many drug addicts have the pattern. Most addicts with this fingerprint pattern range in age from 17 to 21 years." Cataldo says a member of the Pittsburgh police department said he likewise noted similar observations.

Alcoholism and the Work World

HARRISON M. TRICE

In the United States, the relationship of alcoholism to the work world has received increasing attention over the past decade. Government and voluntary groups have been encouraging the cooperation of management and labor in the development of programs to fight this difficult health problem. The Federal government has begun serious work on a program to aid employees who suffer from alcoholism. Even labor unions, which understandably view such programs as anti-labor in character, are showing a willingness to deal openly with the problem. The advances, however, are slow.

The question is often asked: Why should management and labor be concerned about alcoholism? First, there can be a direct increase in operating costs as a result of the alcoholic's inefficiency and absenteeism. Second, alcoholics can generate personnel problems such as lowered worker morale or employer involvement in family problems. Third, the expedient solution of discharge can both deprive the employer of needed experience and aggravate the alcoholic's drinking problem. Fourth, alcoholism is a disease, and each member of society, even business, has an obligation to fight any disease when he can.

The work world has the potential to do something truly effective about alcoholism. Based on a summary of available data concerning alcoholism and the job, I will set forth

Reprinted with permission from *Sloan Management Review,* Fall, 1970, no. 2, pp. 67-75.

several reasons for increasing the effort devoted toward stimulating management and labor to constructive action. I will also discuss the major problems encountered in any preventive program and the unique potential of the work world for recognizing the problem drinker, the first step toward prevention or cure.

Prevention programs must be aimed at the three general development stages of alcoholism. In the early development stage, symptoms are almost nonexistent. The prevention strategy is to eliminate the forces leading to alcoholism before it fully develops. The second stage can be called "disrupted but normal." Symptoms start becoming visible. Early recognition, however, can still prevent alcoholism from developing completely. The third stage is fully developed alcoholism. The only action now possible is to provide treatment that will stop or cure the physical and psychological damage caused by the disease.

Who Is the Alcoholic?

Many people have a preconceived image of the "average alcoholic" as a sloppy, staggering drunk with no visible means of support. This inaccurate image suggests the need for a working definition of alcoholism. Problem drinking and alcoholism are behavioral disorders centered around the employee's family and job which cause him to deviate from his expected role. From the standpoint of the work world, alcoholism can be defined as repeated disruption of job performance due to the consumption of alcohol which impairs the expected role.

The alcoholic is generally a man. Available statistics show the male to female ratio of alcoholics to be five to one over recent years; it should be noted, however, that the female alcoholic is more difficult to identify. The alcoholic is generally middle aged. Studies repeatedly show alcoholism to be concentrated in the mature years of the forties and early fifties, when work productivity is at a peak, when experience and judgment have matured, and when there is still energy for sustained contributions to the organization. Were alcoholism spread more evenly over the age groups, its impact on productivity would clearly be lessened.

The alcoholic is most likely to be recognized in lower-status occupations, although present research suggests that the distribution remains much the same throughout the entire industrial complex. Alcoholism appears among professional, managerial, and white collar employees in proportions roughly similar to those in blue collar and operative jobs. Thus, the risk of losing managerial and professional employees through alcoholism is equal to the risk of losing workers in the lower ranks.

Specific Job Behaviors

Both the quality and quantity of work decline sharply as alcoholism progresses. One study, conducted over a three-year period, compared the work performance of employees who had been diagnosed as alcoholic, psychoneurotic, or psychotic. The results showed the alcoholic employee to be the most impaired.[1] Another study indicated that the "manner" in which the work efficiency declined varies with the occupational type. Higher status employees, such as professionals and managers, tend to appear consistently on the job in spite of the ill effects of drinking.[2] They seem to rationalize their drinking by proving they can continue to work, although in fact their work suffers. A form of on-the-job absenteeism occurs as efficiency declines. Freedom from supervision allows them to continue unchallenged for a relatively long time. In contrast, lower status employees who are more closely supervised engage in much stay-away absenteeism, but do a substantial day's work when on the job. Poor work and absenteeism constitute two of the main impacts of the problem drinker on the organization.

The typical problem drinker continues to work at a full-time job during most of his developing alcoholism, with about 3 percent of a normal work force probably affected. Among higher status employees, the figure is closer to 5 percent. These percentages fluctuate with sex, age, ethnic makeup, and locality.

On-the-job accidents are not significantly characteristic of the alcoholic employee. Studies of both A.A. members and of accident records kept by specific companies deny the popular notion that the alcoholic on the job is accident prone. Four factors seem to account for this finding. First, the developing alcoholic becomes extra cautious, thereby reducing both his effectiveness and his risk of accident. Second, when accident risk runs high, the alcoholic resorts to absenteeism, leading to accidents off the job rather than at work. Third, alcoholics generally work out a routine for controlling the effects of alcohol. Finally, the cooperation of fellow workers, and occasionally supervisors, helps protect a drinker from accident exposure.

The off-the-job accident rate of alcoholics, on the other hand, is three to four times higher than that of non-alcoholics. This increases the cost of stay-away absenteeism as well as the direct cost of sick pay and other employee benefits. There is some evidence to suggest that persons with other behavioral disorders also show high off-the-job accidents rates, but not in such a chronic pattern. Therefore, the amount of sick pay due to absenteeism is probably higher for alcoholics than for employees with other emotional disturbances.[3]

Available evidence indicates that problem drinkers do not show an unusual turnover rate. Following the same pattern as non-alcoholics, they change jobs frequently in lower status occupations, and remain relatively longer in professional and managerial positions. The job-hopper stereotype of the alcoholic is generally untrue, especially in high status occupations.

The alcoholic actively works to conceal his problem, frequently with aid from work associates, subordinates, and occasionally the supervisor. About 20 percent experience little or no help in concealing their drinking. Here again, occupational status governs, with more help being offered to the higher ranks. Lower status workers often receive no aid from either supervisors or fellow workers. Camouflage efforts in any rank are only temporarily successful, but are more successful in the higher positions where freedom from visibility and supervision conceals the problem for much of the development process. In the final stage, the alcoholic can no longer remain hidden from his associates, subordinates, or supervisors.

The effect of the alcoholic on the morale of other employees gives cause for concern to both union and management. In the lower ranks, the alcoholic's fellow workers become disgusted and concerned when forced to pick up part of his work. Supervisors faced with unpredictable scheduling must allot extra time to the problem. The union shop steward must cope with grievances which are likely to embarrass the union. In managerial and responsible professional positions, the alcoholic can clearly lower the morale of all employees on his level and below. It is difficult to respect and follow a leader driven toward incompetence by alcoholism.

Recognizing Alcoholism on the Job: The Problems

Motivating people to recognize alcoholics and insuring accurate identification are the major problems. The motivation problem is the less obvious and the more interesting of the two. The immediate supervisor of the developing alcoholic is often deeply disturbed by the need to work in direct contact with him. As one supervisor reported painfully, "If I had two like *him* in this group of machinists, I'd apply for early retirement." Presently, there are only two studies of supervisor reaction to the problem drinker. Both rate alcoholics as greater supervisory problems than employees with other emotional difficulties.[4] However, even when the supervisor can identify an employee as being an alcoholic, he is hesitant to take action. This reflects the general cultural ambivalence about alcoholism in the United States. Several forces cause the supervisor to vacillate between taking action and treating the problem as part of his normal duties. Among the forces pushing him toward action are the unpredictable performance and the absenteeism of the alcoholic. In addition, the supervisor's work record suffers when the alcoholic does not produce his share or when worker morale deteriorates, reducing production efficiency.

Acting against these forces is the difficulty of recognizing the problem drinker. The early symptoms are characteristic of several other problems and are thus difficult to classify. The supervisor is not a professional psychiatrist or social worker. Without some training, attempts at early classification would be of questionable value due to the risk of premature labeling and the concurrent danger of establishing a self-fulfilling prophecy.

There is also the supervisor's fear that passing his problems to someone else will reflect poorly on his own ability as a supervisor. In addition, such an action can create a form of credibility gap between himself and the employee. Should his action result in the firing of that employee, the supervisor is faced with the more difficult problem of replacing an experienced worker. His reluctance to take action is intensified when he knows the alcoholic's family or has worked closely with the alcoholic for several years. Finally, the supervisor runs some risk of not being supported "upstairs" or of creating a union problem greater than a mere grievance.

In dealing with white collar employees another factor becomes apparent. Warkov and Bacon have shown that supervisors of white collar workers seem unwilling to make the same connection between poor worker performance and alcoholism which they make with lower status employees. Supervisors are less prone to recognize problem drinking among members of their own class. However, the study concludes that once the white collar deviant drinker is recognized, the supervisor is less tolerant of him than those of lower status.[5]

A unique problem exists within a union shop situation. Union officials are reluctant to participate with management in joint prevention programs, regardless of the potential benefits for the alcoholic and for improved union-management relations through cooperation on such programs. Cooperation could lead to charges of collusion from the membership or build conflicts within the union. Moreover, the union has a legal obligation to represent its members in challenging any policy by management, which could include programs aimed at alcoholism.

Recognizing Alcoholism on the Job: The Potential

To demonstrate the superiority of the work place as a setting for preventive and therapeutic action against alcoholism, it is necessary to consider the obstacles which any such program must hurdle. First, the lack of a satisfactory definition of alcoholism tends to make the disease seem unreal. In the work world, however, a definition such as the one presented earlier is more obvious. Second, established social values recognize alcohol as an integral part of everyday life, a symbol of sophistication, a social facilitator.[6] The work world can help keep the use of alcohol in proper perspective by confronting the potential alcoholic with the effects his drinking has on job performance. Third, prevention programs inevitably invade the personal life of the individual. Observing and helping the individual in the work environment could eliminate the need for a social worker, for example, to visit the individual's home. Fourth, premature labeling of an alcoholic may tend to drive him further into the disease. Training supervisors to recognize symptoms and to provide some counseling would allow close observation without labeling the individual or sending him to a clinic. Fifth, rehabilitation processes regarding alcoholism are not yet sufficiently understood. Treatment in the third stage of development is not always effective. Recognition of the problem in the second stage or early in the third stage can eliminate the need for intensive treatment. Sixth, preventive schemes are difficult to integrate into the pivotal institutions of society such as business, the professions, the church, and the family. Yet, preventive efforts cannot remain outside these institutions and be effective. Since the job is one of the pivotal institutions in the employee's life, efforts in this environment are a necessary part of any preventive scheme.

The work world has a greater potential than the family, or even the clergyman or doctor, for overcoming these obstacles. Supervisors, unlike wives and relatives, are not emotionally involved with the problem drinker. Supervisors work under pressure to produce and are therefore more objective about the alcoholic's behavior. They have the highest readiness to act of any of the people close to the alcoholic and have the potential for action. It is they who must cope with the problems of poor job performance, absenteeism, and perhaps eventual replacement.

Potentials for genuine social controls exist in the job situation. The job becomes the key factor in the life of most workers and in this the alcoholic is no exception. For him the job is often his last bastion, and so long as it is intact he sees nothing wrong with his drinking. Consequently, a confrontation for poor job performance may well create the crisis that will open the door for therapy and prevent further development of the disorder. Only the work world has this potential for constructive confrontation.

Management Action

What specific actions can management take to fight alcoholism? The answer lies in supervisor training and realistic company policies. Training of supervisory personnel within a supportive company policy can provide a means of speeding up the recognition process. Four criteria for an effective training program have been suggested.[7] First, training must be relevant to the work world of the supervisor. Specific symptoms should be examined in the order of their appearance. These symptoms include hand tremors, intense nervousness, mood changes, avoidance of associates, and absenteeism. Learning to recognize the symptoms will increase the supervisor's ability to identify an incipient alcoholic. Second, the training should point out the work problems created by the alcoholic. Recognition of such problems as poor morale, lowered efficiency, and increased need of supervision will decrease the tolerance level of the supervisor and result in earlier referral and treatment of the disease. Third, to increase their receptiveness, supervisors should be introduced to the subject prior to formal training. Last, a variety of training techniques, such as films, lectures, case work, and reading, should be employed. This will ensure that at least one method meets with success.

Employers should establish an explicit company policy incorporating the following points: alcoholism is a health problem; the company health plan will include those addicted to the use of alcohol without discrimination; alcoholism is recognized as a unique health disorder which must be confronted with a crisis to effect either prevention or treatment. The policy should call for such confrontation whenever poor performance occurs. If the condition continues, the drinker should be offered unhesitating support in seeking rehabilitation on condition of cooperation. Finally, if the preliminary steps fail, stringent disciplinary methods should be used such as curtailment of fringe benefits, layoffs, and finally discharge. Unless the threat of final separation remains real, the alcoholic will discount the danger and any therapy will fail. Such action removes his last defense, that of an intact job, and acts to offset the emotional rewards of drinking. The confrontation thus reduces the value of alcohol to the alcoholic. Policies based on this approach produce high rehabilitation rates.

Union Action

What specific action can the union take? Early recognition of the problem opens many ways in which the alcoholic can be helped by the union before company discipline becomes necessary. The union can communicate to the worker information about company programs or policies. Coming from a union source, such information is more likely to be believed than if it comes from management. If the drinker has gone beyond the first stages and nears confrontation with the company for his unsatisfactory work, the union can help convince the alcoholic that the company is serious and can suggest that he attend the clinic regularly. The steward can provide aid and counsel to both the alcoholic and his family, helping them through the crisis and back into the work world. He can also persuade fellow workers to welcome the alcoholic back into the old groups.

If the problems of union-management cooperation can be overcome, a joint program against alcoholism can be established. Stewards could be trained along with supervisory personnel to recognize the problems and behaviors of alcoholic workers. Joint observations will help to avoid premature labeling of employees as problem drinkers. The steward should be closely tied to the overall program by making him the link between the alcoholic and his family and job. He should also maintain clear lines of communication with management and higher union officials to simplify joint action. With the union handling most of the personal contact with the member, a joint program should prove possible.

If union-management cooperation is difficult to establish, the union can run its own program on alcoholism. It could: enlist the aid of various community facilities such as A.A., AFL-CIO community service organizations, or information seminars; set up an effective training program for stewards and other union officials; and work toward obtaining management cooperation. Nevertheless, a unilateral program staged by either management or labor will be less effective than a jointly sponsored program.

Conclusion

The greatest possibilities for preventing alcoholism lie in the crisis confrontation strategy growing from natural forces surrounding the job. Unfortunately, this avenue is not yet sufficiently traveled and is often neglected for less promising ways. Management and unions are two pivotal institutions in American life which can be more potent in an enlightened community effort against alcoholism than welfare agencies, medical facilities, or jails. Most alcoholics do belong to the work world and when lost through alcoholism deprive the organization and society of an investment in training, experience, and special knowledge. By recognizing the alcoholic's existence in their own world and treating him there, unions and management can insure a high recovery rate. When business acts on the assumption that alcoholism is a treatable disease and follows through with carefully considered programs, the potential success of constructive programs outside, as well as within, the work world is increased. The strategy is to attack the problem where and when there is a reasonable chance of success, that is, on the job.

Notes

1. See Trice (5).
2. See Trice (4).
3. See Maxwell (3).
4. See Trice (5) and Warkov and Bacon (6).
5. See Warkov and Bacon (6).
6. See Lemert (2), pp. 18-21.
7. See Belasco and Trice (1).

References

1. Belasco, J., and Trice, H. M. *The Assessment of Change in Training and Therapy.* New York, McGraw-Hill, 1969.
2. Lemert, E. *Human Deviance, Social Problems and Social Control.* Englewood Cliffs, N.J., Prentice-Hall, 1967.
3. Maxwell, M. "A Study of Absenteeism, Accidents, and Sickness Payments in Problem Drinkers in One Industry," *Quarterly Journal of Studies on Alcohol,* Vol. 20 (1959), pp. 302-308.
4. Trice, H. M. "The Job Behavior of Problem Drinkers." In: D. Pittman and C. Snyder (eds.), *Society, Culture and Drinking Patterns.* New York, Wiley, 1962.
5. Trice, H. M. "Reaction of Supervisors to Emotionally Disturbed Employees," *Journal of Occupational Medicine,* Vol. 7 (1965), pp. 177-189.
6. Warkov, S., and Bacon, S. "Social Correlates of Industrial Problem Drinking," *Quarterly Journal of Studies on Alcohol,* Vol. 26 (1965), pp. 58-71.

OSHA Compliance: "Safety Is Good Business"

ROLLIN H. SIMONDS

The Occupational Safety and Health Act (OSHA) is beginning to force tens of thousands of businesses to do what many of the larger companies have been doing for years—that is, carry on effective accident control programs. While larger companies are not necessarily better managed than smaller ones, their size makes it practical to employ many staff specialists that smaller firms cannot afford. These staff specialists have the knowledge, time, and facilities to prepare reports that help make higher levels of management cognizant of the impact of many facets of operation on their cost and profit structure. Thus, a former vice-president of General Motors could make an often-quoted comment that "safety is good business."

One can have some sympathy for the managers now almost frantically concerned to find out what OSHA or a state safety inspection force is requiring. It is true that in the tremendous task of determining a myriad of standards for many different industries in a short time, OSHA has established some that appear to need added flexibility to meet certain situations. The worried managements might take some comfort, however, from three facts:

● First, even though the highest purpose of safety is the minimizing of human injuries and deaths, records show that accident reduction is generally accompanied by cost savings greater than the safety expenditures, including, of course, workmen's compensation insurance and statistically measurable uninsured costs, as well as many intangibles.

● Second, the basic purpose of both OSHA and state safety bureaus is the prevention of injuries. Inspectors do not normally try to levy maximum fines for the least infraction of standards. When inspectors find management cooperative in correcting unsafe physical conditions and unsafe acts, they are inclined to try to give the company time to put things in order, even though violations except those of a "de minimus" character must be prominently cited. It is the imminently dangerous situation that they cannot allow to continue even temporarily, and it is failure to make corrections in such a situation that is likely to draw significant penalties.

● Third, it is highly unlikely that a particular company will be inspected by OSHA for a long time. For the fiscal year ending June 30, 1973, 110,000 compliance inspections were proposed and funded, but the number actually made is far short of that—probably 55,000 or less. For this fiscal year 80,000 inspections are budgeted. When one recognizes that more than 5,000,000 workplaces are covered by the Act, it is apparent that less than one in 60 is scheduled for an OSHA inspection this year.

As for the last two points, a system of priorities has been established for inspections, which will be made first where fatalities have occurred, in industries that are known to have bad injury records, and where employees have requested inspection. This means that most companies have considerable time to put their houses in order, particularly very small firms and those in industries where the severity of injuries is low. Furthermore, the fines for violations discovered by inspectors and then corrected are quite small—fines of $25 to $1,000 are not really great enough to have very serious effects. On the other hand, however, failure to correct violations for which citations have been issued can, after administrative review, result in penalties of up to $1,000 a day.

Complying with Federal and State Standards

What should a company do to keep out of trouble with OSHA or a state inspection and enforcement agency? First, depending on the size and nature of the company, someone should be assigned full-time or part-time to develop or carry on a safety program. This person should obtain from the *Federal Register* statements of standards applicable to the industry in question. He should then be sure to include compliance with these in his overall program and should also set up procedures for reporting work injury data as required by OSHA. The U.S. Government Printing Office has a series of self-inspection guides and a kind of index or subject locator that facilitates use of the *Federal Register*. Still another source of information is the OSHA monthly publication, *Job Safety and Health*.

Generally, the OSHA requirements will be approximately paralleled by state standards if the state has been authorized to carry out inspections and enforcement within its borders. But meeting these standards is only a part of a total activity for accident control; indeed, a well-conceived and well-run program for injury control would include a great part of what have become OSHA standards even if there were no such federal law.

The *Federal Register* does not provide full instructions for the operation of a safety program; it is only a source for current legal standards, so the person who has been assigned general safety responsibility will need a basic textbook and might benefit from other materials, such as those that can be obtained from the National Safety Council. Another source of guidance is the advisory service of the insurance company carrying a company's workmen's compensation insurance. Since the amount insurance companies spend on this service is likely to be in the neighborhood of one or two percent of premiums, however, it is clear that unlimited help cannot be expected here.

Some state safety bureaus also provide assistance. One of the most useful of these is the safety education and training division of the Michigan Department of Labor Bureau of Safety. This unit makes available a consultant who will show the economics of accident control through cost estimates, work with management to establish an overall program, and point out some of the correctable conditions or practices. While most of these activities are in greatest demand by small companies, the division also provides training courses used by some industrial giants.

Main Concern: Physical Conditions, Human Conduct

No outside assistance can substitute for an interested management and an effective safety manager inside. Basically, two activities are necessary to control work accidents—correcting accident-producing physical conditions and minimizing unsafe acts. Avoiding the establishment of unsafe physical conditions or correcting any already in existence is the preferable procedure for several reasons:

Frequently, sound engineering or construction will completely preclude the possibility of a particular kind of accident. For example, if the hazard involves a point of operation where hands could be mangled, the equipment may be designed or guarded in such a way that it is impossible for a worker's hands to get into the space where they could be cut or pinched. If the hazard is an open fly-wheel or belt, it can be enclosed so that a break will not send parts flying free. If it is a process releasing toxic vapors, a change in chemicals or an operational design that removes the vapors and then renders them harmless is better than requiring personal protective equipment for workers. Masks, gloves, safety glasses, ear muffs, and so forth are essential in some situations, but elimination of the danger is not only more comfortable for the worker, but a more certain control. The control of human behavior is never absolute.

To take a less humanitarian view and consider legal risks, unsafe physical conditions are likely to be more easily spotted by government inspectors and more specifically detailed in federal or state standards than unsafe acts. The construction of new facilities always affords opportunity either to build in safety or to create long-run, costly problems for accident control, but the present legislation largely cancels the option of taking a calculated risk in erecting structures with accident-producing features. To illustrate, a new power plant now being constructed in Michigan is expected to cost something in the neighborhood of $2 million more to meet the federal safety standards than it would have cost otherwise. Still, the total construction cost of that plant will probably be around $200 million, so, although OSHA is adding significantly to the construction cost, if the safety features do avoid accidents, 1 percent of building cost will not add exorbitantly to power costs.

What Factors Determine Injury Frequency?

Obviously, the primary goal of all the safety efforts is the minimizing of occupational deaths and injuries. Since 1912, accidental work deaths per 100,000 population in the United States have been reduced more than 65 percent, but the annual toll of occupational accidents still includes around 14,000 deaths and two million injuries.

The average injury frequency (number of disabling injuries per million manhours worked) for all industry is usually in the neighborhood of six for National Safety Council members and 13 as estimated by the Bureau of Labor Statistics; however, there are thousands of business organizations with frequencies of 50, 100, 150, and even higher. What are the factors that make one company much more effective than another in controlling injuries when inherent industrial hazards are the same?

First, the writer's studies have indicated that the company with a full-time safety director has a big edge in safety. When companywide safety supervision is a part-time duty of a person, it often becomes secondary to other matters for which he is being pressured. Making safety the one responsibility of one person ensures that he will be constantly alert to hazards and will continually remind, persuade, and prod others about them. Of course, as has been said, it is not practical in many small companies to have a full-time safety specialist; concerns with fewer than two or three hundred employees typically do not even have a full-time personnel manager. Perhaps this failure to have one person with safety as his full assignment is a major reason the worst accident records are most often found in small firms.

Foremost among the others with safety responsibilities are the first-line supervisors. They are really the key people in accident control: They are on the spot when most accidents occur; the actual operations are under their direction; and they know the workers, the equipment, and the materials. It is neither fair nor very efficient, however, to delegate accident control solely to the foreman and blame him when things go wrong. For one thing, local union practice can help or hamper the foreman.

Generally, officials of the big unions are safety-conscious, because they can see the "big picture" of thousands of members and can pretty accurately predict about how many will be killed or injured in the coming year. Locals, on the other hand, in their desire aggressively to support all close-to-home grievances and in their zeal to get high wages and comfort for workers (whom they sometimes know personally) can make it very difficult for foremen to enforce safety rules. For example, at a training program for 40 foremen from scattered plants of a large company, the writer was urgently requested by the participants to use whatever influence he might have to push legislation that would mandate union, as well as management, support for accident control.

Pinpointing Injury Frequency in Small Companies

In an effort to identify other characteristics that lead to better or worse accident records, Iranian Colonel Yaghoub Shafai-Sahrai made an intensive study of 22 American firms of small or relatively small size. This study was carried out with the assistance and direction of the writer, in fulfillment of the doctoral dissertation requirement at Michigan State University. (The Bureau of Business Research of the Graduate School of Business of Michigan State University plans to publish this dissertation in book form in the near future.)

The study covered 11 pairs of companies in 11 different industries in Michigan, with each pair of approximately the same size carrying out similar work, but with a major difference in work-injury experience. In size, they ranged from 80 to 650 employees. The 11 industries were meat products, dairy products, canning and preserving, household furniture, containers and boxes, iron and steel foundries, nonferrous metal-rolling, other primary metal products, metal stampings, metal-working machinery, and motor vehicles and equipment.

Originally, 26 firms were selected on an essentially random basis (except for getting two of similar size in each industry). The Michigan Bureau of Safety could not release injury records for companies by name until authorized by the company in question, but it was inferred from the variety of injury experience reported to the bureau that wide variation could be expected from the sample. The fact that 22 of the 26 companies readily authorized full disclosure of their injury records not only argued against bias in selection, but also indicated widespread interest in the problem of accident control. (In fact, four of the companies tried to hire Dr. Shafai-Sahrai.)

Injury frequencies of the companies ranged from 12 to 173. The average difference in frequency rate between each two pair members was 50, the median 43, the lowest 11, and the highest 129. The ratio of frequency rates between pair members averaged 3.05 to 1, with a median of 3.1 to 1, a low of 1.3 to 1, and a high of 4.6 to 1. Thus, the "twin" companies varied tremendously in accident experience. The rates as a whole were very high compared with national averages, but, as was mentioned earlier, this experience is common among firms in this size range.

The investigative procedure used was plant visits and inspection; analysis of company injury records, both on the site and, after authorization, at the Michigan Bureau of Safety; and executive interviews, which included both a structured part alike for all and an unstructured part. Methods were developed for assigning numbers to indicate relative degrees of elements such as management support, width of span of control, safety devices, and so on. Then the Wilcoxon matched-pairs signed rank test was used to test significance; for other factors, such as percent of workers who were married and whether accident costs were included in the records, only the sign test was used.

The findings indicate that no one factor is the sole key to fewer or more injuries. Eight factors correlated highly with the better injury record within the pairs—in only one instance was there a negative correlation among these. Thus, it is not possible to determine which were the more controlling variables or if certain variables caused the other variables.

The one variable that perhaps had a double effect—a direct one and also indirect by its influence on other conditions favorable to accident control—was top-management interest and involvement in safety. One hypothesis checked was that "in the firms with lower work injury frequency and severity rates, top management is highly interested and involved in the company's overall safety programs and actively participates in and supports safety activity." Statistically, this was strongly supported to a significance level of .05.

Table 1 shows the kinds of top-management activities evaluated and how many were found in the high versus the low injury frequency company in each pair.

TABLE 1

DIFFERENCES BETWEEN TOP MANAGEMENT'S INVOLVEMENT IN SAFETY
IN FIRMS WITH LOW AND HIGH INJURY RATES

Top Management's Activity with Regard to Safety	*Firms with Low Accident Frequency Rates (N=11)*		*Firms with High Accident Frequency Rates (N=11)*	
	Yes	*No*	*Yes*	*No*
Does he attend any safety meetings in the company?	8	3	6	5
Does he chair any of these meetings?	3	8	2	9
Does he regularly receive safety reports?	11	0	11	0
Does he personally conduct any safety audit or inspection?	9	2	4	7
Is he a member of any safety organization?	0	11	0	11
Does he regularly attend any safety meetings or conferences outside the company?	2	9	0	11
Does he emphasize plans for achieving certain safety objectives?	10	1	8	3
Does he actively participate in execution of safety plans?	10	1	7	4
Does he hold review and analysis sessions to compare the results of carrying out safety plans with projected objectives?	9	2	3	8
Are safety figures, reports, and achievements included on the agenda of company board meetings?	8	3	3	8
Total scores	70	40	44	66

It is evident that in the firms with the better safety records, the chief executives put more emphasis on personal audit and inspection than did those in firms with the poorer records. Top management in the former firms also showed more interest in plans to achieve specific safety objectives and held review and analysis meetings to evaluate progress. In eight out of 11 of the better-record companies, safety figures, reports, and achievements were included on the agenda of company board meetings, whereas this was true of only three out of 11 of the firms with poorer experience. Probably the most important reason for the effectiveness of these top-management activities is that they show other members of management, and ultimately all employees, that the boss is genuinely concerned about controlling accidents.

In all instances where accident cost analysis was included in the records in one company of a pair and not in the other, the accident experience of the organization with cost analysis was significantly better. In fact, the frequency rates of the "cost conscious" companies in the five pairs that differed in this regard averaged only about one-third as high as the rates of their "twins."

To turn to another aspect of the study, findings supported to the high significance level of .01 attested to the fact that the percentage of employees who were married was higher in the firms with better accident records. Although in most pairs the percentage of employees married was not greatly different between the two companies, in the three where the difference was marked, the difference in injury experience was also great, as is shown in Table 2. This study corroborated many others that have found a negative correlation between employee age and accident experience, but the striking difference in percentage of employees married and in injury records in two of the above companies cannot be accounted for on the basis of average employee age.

TABLE 2

MARITAL STATUS AND AGE AS FACTORS IN INJURY FREQUENCY

	Percent of Married Employees	Accident Frequency Rate	Average Age
Pair 1 Co. A	85	25	37
Co. B	32	89.4	20
Pair 2 Co. A	90	14.5	37
Co. B	65	45.1	32
Pair 3 Co. A	90	4.17	43
Co. B	35	71.1	37

Space does not permit reporting here the full findings of the study, but another relevant factor over which management has control is the span of control at the level of first-line supervision, usually the foreman. The hypothesis that relative span of control for first-line supervisors is wider in the firms with the higher injury rates within the pairs was strongly supported, to a significance level of .05. Span of control is, of course, dictated in considerable measure by the nature of the work to be done and the layout of a plant or other facility. Some of these differences were offset, however, by the use of the matched pairs in this study. The average span of control among the companies with better records was 16, while the average among the others was 21.

Probably more meaningful is the fact that in only two of the 11 pairs did the larger span of control go with the lower injury frequency. In all four pairs where the high frequency was four or more times as high as the low one, the span of control was greater in the company with more injuries. The average span for the four better-record concerns was 18.5, compared with 26.5 for their counterparts. That this is not an overriding factor is apparent, however, in the fact that in one pair the company with a frequency of 18.8 had a control span of 18, while the other, with a frequency of 61.9, had a span of only 13. In the other pair that was completely contrary to the general result in this respect, a frequency of 34.1 went with a span of 23, while a frequency of 45 accompanied a control span of 18.

An unfortunate difficulty of research in the social science area, including business, is, of course, that "all other things being equal" is generally impossible—one can seldom find situations where only one element is the variable. Therefore, this use of matched pairs only reduces the variability of other factors of possibly important influence. Still, the study adds strong support to the premise that there are factors subject to managerial control that can have a strong impact on the incidence of employee injuries.

Toward an Assessment of the Mental Health of Factory Workers: A Detroit Study

ARTHUR KORNHAUSER

Industrial psychology in America has been most concerned with productivity and organizational effectiveness. Working people are studied primarily as means to the ends of efficiency, whether of the single enterprise or of the larger society. Even when attention is directed to attitudes, feelings, and morale, interest usually centers on how these subjective states affect performance.

An alternative orientation focuses upon working people as themselves the significant ends. Interest attaches to the personal development and well-being of the men and women in industry, the improvement of their individual and social health—especially their "mental health." The present study belongs to this second category. It inquires about the impact of modern economic organization, particularly the demands of mass production manufacturing, on the people involved. What does the industrial way of life do to, and for, the men who man the machines? What does their work mean to them and what are the effects of their factory occupations on their spirit and their life adjustments?

Are factory workers—specifically Detroit auto-workers—happy and well-adjusted in the main? Or are they predominantly bitter or depressed or anxious or apathetic? Are they enthusiastic, idealistic, self-reliant, zestful? Or cynical, alienated, dispirited? One can find assertions that they are all these contradictory things and many more. Evidence to support the assertions is scarce indeed. Even less is known about subgroups, for example by job levels, age, income, and education. Are assembly line jobs peculiarly monotonous, frustrating, deadening—and hated? Does work on the line produce poor mental health? On this question, too, violent disagreement continues despite the debates which go on decade after decade.

Reprinted by permission of the Society for Applied Anthropology from *Human Organization*, vol. 21 (1962), no. 1, pp. 43-46.

In this article I shall sketch a few partial results from a study which attempted to secure evidence bearing on these issues. Along with the findings I shall briefly mention some possible implications and interpretations—and unanswered questions.

The research focuses on comparisons of the mental health of occupational groups in the Detroit automobile industry. The factory workers studied were selected by a systematic sampling procedure from the personnel files of 13 large and medium-sized automotive manufacturing plants. The sample includes only white, American-born men who had been with their present employer three years or more.

In reaching for methods to assess the mental health of these people we adopted two guiding principles: (1) We would begin with a variety of simple, commonly accepted ideas as to what constitutes good versus poor mental health and would proceed in subsequent steps to interrelate, test, and in some sense "validate" these ideas; and (2) we would rely primarily on data obtainable by means of interviews with the working people themselves, supplementing these findings by reports from interviewers, wives of respondents, and company records of absenteeism and medical department visits. Accordingly, several hundred detailed interviews were completed with workers and their wives, all at the homes of the interviewees.

The rationale of our mental health measures is this: We conceptualize mental health not as representing any psychodynamic unity but as a loose descriptive designation for an overall level of success, effectiveness, or excellence of the individual's functioning as a person. The emphasis is on mental health in a "normal" and positive sense; the inquiry does not deal with mental disease or illness. We proceed on the assumption that mental health is multi-dimensional—although this is not at all to imply that there are not certain dimensions of especially great importance relative to others. On the side of practical procedures, our search is not for any peculiarly crucial key measures of mental health but for useful indicators chosen from innumerable possible ones.

More specifically, the study relies upon reports by working men and their wives in regard to the workers' feelings of satisfaction and happiness; their attitudes and sentiments toward themselves, other persons, their world, and their future; their personal and social activities (at work, at home, and in the community); and their psychological and bodily manifestations of disturbing stress or tensions. The interviews also included responses to lists of selected personality inventory items.

A number of indexes were derived from the interview responses. Those which enter into our general measure of mental health are indexes of:

Anxiety and emotional tension
Hostility versus trust in, and acceptance of, people
Sociability and friendship versus withdrawal
Self-esteem versus negative self-feelings
Personal morale versus anomie or social alienation
Overall satisfaction with life

"Validity" of the Mental Health Index

These component indexes were combined to form a total index of mental health. We then classified workers according to their scores on this general index. Although I shall freely refer to the "better" or "poorer" mental health of the men so classified, the statements are necessarily limited by the particular way in which the assessments are made. The meaning and justification of the appraisals must rest largely upon the "face validity" of the indexes—that is, upon the apparent reasonableness of the response material as indicative of what is ordinarily believed to characterize mental health in our culture (positive self-feelings, relative freedom from anxiety symptoms and hostile attitudes, and other qualities suggested by the above list of indexes).

An important additional type of evidence was obtained, however, as a check on whether our measure of mental health does in fact correspond with evaluations used and accepted by professional persons directly concerned with mental health in our society. Does the proposed index of mental health actually measure what the "experts" mean by mental health? Before proceeding to use the index we set up a small-scale "validation" study to answer this question. We arranged to have six experienced, highly qualified clinical psychologists and psychiatrists read the complete interview records of 40 cases and give their overall evaluation of each individual's mental health. Comparison of our quantitative indexes with these independent global ratings reveals that the indexes do, in fact, agree decidedly well with the clinicians' judgments. The tetrachoric correlation is .84; the Pearson coefficient is .76. It is thus apparent that the meaning of mental health represented by our index corresponds closely to what the clinicians also conceive to be better or poorer mental health.

A different type of validity check compared workers' responses with reports by their wives. These comparisons justify the further conclusion that the interview content represents behavior and attitudes possessing some reality in the eyes of another observer. When wives' estimates of whether their spouses are nervous, well satisfied with life, etc. are compared with adjustment-indexes based on the man's own replies, the median correlations are above .50. When these several findings are taken together, they appear to offer considerable justification for employing our indexes for present purposes as presumptive measures, albeit crude ones, of mental health.

Mental Health Differences by Factory Occupational Categories

Our first question here is whether there are, in fact, differences of mental health associated with different types of factory jobs. If it is established that such differences exist, the next task is to search for explanations. As to the occurrence of significant differences our results are clear and unambiguous. When workers are classified by skill level and variety of work operations, mental health scores do show consistent correlation with the occupational hierarchy. The higher the occupational level the better the mental health.

One simple set of figures will suffice to make this more concrete. Let us compare occupations by the percentage of workers enjoying "good" mental health—i.e., having "high" mental health scores (the cutting point for "high" is, of course, arbitrary). We have two age groups—men in their 20's and those in their 40's. (See Table 1.)

A vital next question is whether these occupational differences are due to *effects of the jobs* and their associated conditions, or alternatively, do the differences result from *selection of certain kinds of persons* who go into and remain in the several types of work. Before I consider a little of our evidence on this second question, I wish to emphasize the importance of the first results themselves. If more thorough studies confirm the findings I have reported, the social knowledge thus established may have large consequences. The poorer mental health of workers in lower level occupations cannot fail to affect not only their industrial behavior, as employees and labor unionists, but likewise their roles as citizens and as family and community members. As the knowledge of such differences becomes known (and again I repeat, if confirmed by additional studies), one may anticipate intensified efforts by the lower-placed groups, their leaders, and agencies concerned with their welfare to bring about social and industrial changes intended to eradicate the condition. Such social action programs will sorely need expanded research knowledge regarding crucial determining conditions and promising correctives. But demonstration of the existence of the problem is the first requirement.

TABLE 1
COMPARISON OF OCCUPATIONS BY THE PERCENTAGE OF
WORKERS ENJOYING "GOOD" MENTAL HEALTH

	Percentages with scores indicating "good" mental health	No. of workers
298 men in their 40's		
Skilled workers	56	45
High semi-skilled	41	98
Ordinary semi-skilled	38	82
Repetitive semi-skilled	26	73
Repetitive, machine-paced only (subdivision of preceding category)	16	32
109 men in their 20's		
Skilled and high semi-skilled*	58	33
Ordinary semi-skilled	35	46
Repetitive semi-skilled	10	30
Repetitive, machine-paced only (subdivision of preceding category)	7	15

*The two categories are combined here because of small numbers.

These last comments are in no way intended to minimize the importance of the second question—the issue of whether and to what extent the observed occupational differences are attributable to the influence of the work and its correlates. We now turn to a brief analysis of this question. If the mental health differences are due to the type of persons in the occupations, differences among these people ought to be detectable in the pre-job period of their lives. A first suspicion that crosses one's mind, for example, is that the mental health results may all be "explained away" as due to educational differences. This could occur by reason of the direct association of schooling with both occupational level and good mental health scores (the latter possibly meaning merely greater sophistication and self-protection in answering questions, thus giving the *appearance* of mental health).

Amount of schooling, then, affords one good test of the *selection* explanation of occupational mental health differences. Since substantial educational differences do occur between occupations and since education is also associated with better mental health, the possibility has to be examined whether this association is sufficient to produce the obtained results. Conversely, do occupational mental health differences persist apart from the influence of education—i.e., when only persons of like amounts of education are compared? Our findings strongly suggest that the latter is true. Proportions of workers having good mental health consistently decrease from higher to lower level occupations *for each of three educational categories separately*. Moreover, the magnitude of the differences is very nearly the same as when education is not controlled but is permitted to add its influence (see Table 2).

TABLE 2
Percentage of High Mental Health Scores by Groups Having Specified Occupation and Education
A. Middle-Age Factory Workers

	Education			
Occupation	Grade School	Some H.S.	H.S. Grad.	Total
Skilled	43%(7)	45%(20)	72%(18)	56%(45)
High semi-skilled	33 (46)	45 (33)	53 (19)	41 (98)
Ordinary semi-skilled	31 (35)	39 (36)	55 (11)	38 (82)
Repetitive semi-skilled	24 (46)	29 (21)	33 (6)	26 (73)
Total	30%(134)	40%(110)	57%(54)	39%(298)

Figures in parentheses show the number of cases in each cell on which the accompanying percentage is based.

B. Young Factory Workers

	Education		
Occupation	Some H.S. or Less	H.S. Grad	Total
Skilled and high semi-skilled	57%(14)	58%(19)	58%(33)
Ordinary semi-skilled	33 (36)	40 (10)	35 (46)
Repetitive semi-skilled	10 (21)	11 (9)	10 (30)
Total	31%(71)	42%(38)	35%(109)

Because of small numbers, we here combine the two lower educational groups and the two upper occupational groups.

For the middle-age group (in which there are enough cases to permit more adequate analysis) occupation and education show a small additive effect on mental health as may be noted in Table 2A. Mental health is best among those high in education *and* occupation, poorest for those low in both education and occupation. This is contrary, of course, to the psychologically plausible hypothesis that mental health is adversely affected by lack of congruency between educational status and occupational status—the view that poorest mental health occurs among persons of better education in low-level jobs (and perhaps also among those of low education in high-level jobs). This hypothesis receives no support at all from our data, either for the middle-age group or the younger workers. In fact, the percentage of "good" mental health in lower-level jobs is *greater* for persons having more schooling.

Conclusions

The analysis of our data as a whole leads to the conclusion that educational differences, either by themselves or in interaction with job level, do not account for the observed mental health variation by occupation. To the extent that this conclusion is confirmed and to the extent that other pre-job personal characteristics (possible job *selection* factors) yield similar negative findings, it would indicate that the influences determining occupational mental health differences among factory workers are to be found in the jobs themselves and their associated life conditions.

We have analyzed a few other pre-job characteristics of workers in a manner parallel to that employed in respect to education. The material consists of responses to an extensive series of questions about the workers' boyhood conditions, behavior, attitudes, and aspirations. In a word, the findings are similar to those for schooling though less clear-cut. That is to say, the occupational groups do differ by childhood characteristics (such as reported anxiety symptoms, success in school, self-confidence, economic deprivations, degree of happiness) but when occupations are compared for individuals having the same degree of these pre-job characteristics, occupational mental health differences persist even if somewhat reduced. In respect to childhood goals and values, the occupational groups show only minor differences and there is no evidence that these differences are responsible for any large part of the observed mental health variations.

In sum, then, the indications from our present data are: (a) that mental health (as here assessed) is poorer among factory workers as we move from more skilled, responsible, varied types of work to jobs lower in these respects, and (b) that the relationship is not due in any large degree to differences of pre-job background or personality of the men who enter and remain in the several types of work. The relationship of mental health to occupation, in other words, appears to be "genuine"; mental health is dependent on factors associated with the job. . . .

CHAPTER 11

A Look into the Future

No one who has witnessed the momentous social, organizational, and work-life changes of the last ten years can doubt that rapid change will be the rule of the last decades of this century. It is a truism that the future is capricious and that it delights in defying would-be prophets. But predictions and projections must be made if intelligent planning is to be carried out. Our final articles attempt to extrapolate present trends into the future to provide a glimpse of some of the major changes that may take place. The authors' conclusion is that an increased emphasis on education, social service occupations and highly sophisticated attempts to integrate the poor and the disadvantaged into the American work-life will be the three major developments to come.

Can We Legislate the Humanization of Work?

WILLIAM A. STEIGER

No politician worth his salt gives a speech that doesn't contain a caveat in it somewhere. To be fair, I'm going to begin with mine.

It must be noted that concerns with the quality of work are somewhat cyclical. In times of high employment, we turn to considering the value and meaning of our jobs. In times of employment crisis we turn most of our attention simply to *jobs*, to finding employment.

In the field of employment it is the creation of jobs, the effort to maintain high employment, which has always been our major governmental concern. It will continue to be so. It is fair to say that if we in government don't bend our greatest efforts to improving the economy, and thus the job market, we not only can't humanize work, we can't even assist our citizens to maintain a humanized existence.

I put this sense of priority to you so strongly, not because I do not feel there is a role for government in the humanization of work, but because it must be understood that given a financial choice, government must and will first spend to assist employment. Priorities are a pain maybe, but they are real.

To begin with, I find I must redefine the topic given to me. The question is clearly not, "Can we legislate the humanization of work?" In the broad sense of humanization, the government has been active for years. The question rather is to what extent and in what directions can and should government become involved in this issue?

For the most part, government has historically affected the work place by the passage of broad, philosophical measures, and has left the details of work modes, methods, and various technicalities to labor and business. For this reason I will leave the questions of improvement of assembly lines, etc., to the experts—since for the most part this has not been government's historic role, nor do I believe it should be.

Past examples of government efforts are well known but worth noting. Child labor laws in the early twentieth century clearly affected the work place, the workers, and the community in a positive and long-range fashion. The Fair Labor Standards Act in the '30s established our current pattern of an 8-hour work day, 40-hour week, cutting down abuses of health and safety.

The Walsh-Healy Act in 1936 imposed restrictions on government contractors in terms of hours, wages, and working conditions.

These are examples of direct impact legislation in the field of work condition improvement. In a real sense, they are only the tip of the iceberg. Other legislative measures have had indirect byproducts of tremendous importance to the work force.

Standards for interstate trade, such as the many laws involving food processing and handling, the tough federal meat law of the '60s is one example, clearly were aimed at consumer protection. But surely the inevitable improvement in plant conditions brought the side benefit of improved humanized working conditions.

In the same way various state and local laws for health checks of employees, again designed to protect the consumer, have had the secondary benefit of safeguarding the health of the worker.

Workmen's Compensation, clearly a work humanizer in its efforts to protect the job-injured employee, has had enormous impact in the identification and improvement of conditions leading to such injury or illness. Once such problems must be reported, a part of the battle is over.

These are only a few examples of what we can call the spin-off effect of legislative programs on the work force. One more recent piece of legislation will have a great effect in years to come.

Women's Rights, opening up countless job categories for women, is bound to result in changes in the work place, work conditions, and hours. Whether its effect will be to reverse completely past protective efforts remains to be seen. But change the work place it will!

It must be noted that in two specific areas in the past ten years, government has gone directly and in detail into the work place.

The Williams-Steiger Occupation Health and Safety Act of 1970 is the single most important step by government to deal with the work environment beyond wages and hours. It is a qualitative, not quantitative, bill in that it concerns upgrading work conditions by promulgation of standards for machinery, noise levels, toxic materials and general job safety and health.

It is aimed at insuring every worker a safer and, therefore, in my opinion, more humane place of work.

OSHA covers 57 million workers, 4.1 million places of business and coupled with the Coal Mine Safety Bill of '69, the Metal and Nonmetallic Mine Act passed earlier, and the Longshoreman's Act, covers almost every worker in the United States.

The need was indisputable. According to the Survey of Working Conditions (August 1971, U.S. Dept. of Labor), "the labor's standards problems against which most workers wanted protection were first, work-related illness or injury." . . . . and for good reason.

Such injuries and illness cost the U.S. economy in 1970 9.1 billion dollars in lost wages, hospital insurance costs, workmen's compensation, and the like. Most important, 14,200 lives were lost.

While OSHA has only been in existence one year, it is, I believe, already having an impact on the work place. While its major impact at the moment is in the area of job safety, the long-range significance of OSHA will be, in my judgment, in the health field. This problem is more complex than safety because it does not deal with immediate and visible problems—a lost life, or limb—but with the insidious diminution of a life—the slow creeping, often unknown and unnoticed degeneration of the health of a worker who handles various materials over a span of time. Hopefully, the establishment of standards and revision of these standards based on new and constantly gathered data for the use of such materials will protect the current work force far better than we have ever done before.

For the first time, through the Department of Labor, we hope to have: first, accurate data on work place accidents and deaths, and second, an ability to measure previously little noticed dangers.

(Coal Mine Safety Director says, "No black lung—humanization at the most basic level!")

The second area of direct impact legislation is the field of manpower. Here government again went into the work place, not to affect work conditions, but to affect training, retraining, and job availability.

Manpower training legislation was born in response to the worker's fear of automation. The federal government became an active partner in answering the need for retraining the man replaced by machine. A further step followed later as the fear of automation receded. The federal government began an effort to train or retrain the so-called underemployed or unemployed, to assist the man or woman at the lowest rungs of the employment ladder to move upward to more rewarding and meaningful work. The intent was clearly the humanizing of labor for those in the least rewarding, most monotonous jobs.

Since the passage of the Manpower Development and Training Act in 1962 (MDTA), the concept has broadened significantly to include programs for the disadvantaged, public service employment, and the new careers program. New careers is perhaps the program most directed toward work humanization since it seeks to break down artificial barriers to upward mobility in a variety of public sector employment areas such as health, recreation, police and fire protection, parks, sanitation; the intent is to provide more meaningful work.

So far our efforts in the field of upward mobility have been limited for the most part to the public sector. The federal government has not, as yet, done a good job in attempting to expand this concept of upward mobility to the private sector. A few surveys and some demonstration projects are about the extent of our efforts to date.

Today we spend 3.6 billion dollars on various manpower programs. This is likely to be expanded. The future, in my judgment, will bring an even greater emphasis on the upgrading of those currently employed and will contribute to an acceleration of the growth of public employment.

Where does the federal government's future role lie in the humanization of work?

Every study of work problems has a common thread. There is the constant refrain of the meaningless quality of much employment and the workers' dissatisfaction with it. Improvement is imperative.

As President Nixon noted in his Labor Day [1971] speech, . . . "the work ethic in America is undergoing some changes.

"It means that business, labor, and government should explore the new needs of today's wage earners: We must give the individual worker more responsibility—more of the feeling that his opinion counts.

"We must find ways to better recognize and reward the extra effort a worker puts into his job.

"We must open up new and equal opportunities to allow a person to grow in his job.

"In our quest for a better environment, we must always remember that the most important part of the quality of life is the quality of work. And the new need for job satisfaction is the key to the quality of work."

Let me suggest a few potential areas for the government to assist in this quest for job satisfaction.

Direct impact efforts are easiest to define and some are already in the works. Continuing education and career education together offer one of the best hopes for increasing work opportunities and a satisfied work force.

Career education in the form of vocational technical education has expanded and will continue to do so.

Youngsters must have more options than they do today. In part it is a question of emphases. We must have elementary and secondary counseling in career choices. No child in the United States should ever feel that a college education is the only way to meaningful work and status. Over 40 percent of high school graduates enter colleges and less than half of those ever earn a 4-year degree. Yet in 1970 the federal government spent approximately 14 dollars for college and university education for every dollar spent for vocational technical education. Something is seriously out of balance about this, and every parent in this country should be up in arms.

And so should you. Because until all of us take note of occupational education needs, and support them, we will never impart to employment in technical fields the very status necessary to give it meaning and dignity.

Vocational Education Amendments of 1968 and the unpassed Career Education Act of 1970 are both aimed at giving new life to this educational stepchild. Specifically, the effort is to: *one,* provide guidance counselors in career education starting in 4th, 5th, and 6th grades; *second,* to expand career education in the high school in an effort to change, if not abolish, what has normally been called general education; *third,* to recognize that one does not teach in secondary school a specific skill since evidence indicates a man changes his job many times in a work lifetime. What is needed is a *foundation* for learning specific skills and undertaking future retraining.

If we don't succeed in this effort, I have little hope for work humanization.

A second direct impact effort is in the field of government-funded research. We could and probably should do more.

Neal Herrick has proposed joint government-foundation research into "the identification of bad jobs and the application of technology to eliminate or improve them." Such an effort could supplement the work already started in the private sector in this field and the results of the research should be disseminated.

This suggests a related direct effect approach in the form of tax incentives. We could assist those using newly discovered methods to improve work by granting tax benefits.

Granted, there is a real hesitancy about using this incentive approach insofar as the worker is concerned. We seem to have little problem in giving tax breaks for capital investment and machine depreciation, but meet great resistance at suggestions of tax incentives for employee training and job upgrading. It is, however, an option which should be explored.

Indirect efforts can also have significant impact, as legislative history shows. It is my assumption that almost any effort which increases a worker's positive options humanizes his work. On this assumption, let me suggest some federal legislation which could so increase options.

First and perhaps most significant is any of a variety of federally funded day-care center plans—one of which is sure to pass in the near future. Clearly this vastly increases options for two-job families, and will have tremendous impact on the labor force. Whether we have sufficiently considered the social implications of such centers is another question. However, the potential for job choice clearly increases if two parents can work. One wage earner might, for example, elect to work at less wages temporarily in order to pursue further education and thus attain better employment. Mobility becomes easier.

Tax write-offs for child care for working parents, recently passed, will also clearly increase the chances for mothers to work.

We can also push for upgraded employment services. Jerome Rosow, former Assistant Secretary of Labor, suggests such a simple measure as keeping employment service offices open evenings and Saturdays would greatly improve the opportunities for job hunting for those workers seeking other employment options.

We can remove various legislative and administrative barriers which now exist to experimentation in work hours and schedules.

For example, the Walsh-Healy Act and Contract Work Hours Standards Act of 1962, both of which regulate firms with government contracts over $10,000, prevent such firms from going to a 4-day, 40-hour work week because they require overtime pay for hours worked in excess of 8 hours in one day.

I've introduced legislation which would amend these acts so as not to inhibit those who wish to try a new workweek concept.

It may or may not be viable, but it is an option, and a potentially life-enriching one for the work force.

Finally, maybe business, labor and government should join in a continuing education effort. It is not just the quality of work itself which grows meaningless in our society. We also face grave problems with the satisfying and meaningful use of leisure time which is bound to grow.

Our local schools are under-used and in financial difficulties. They close for summer months and stand empty in the evening. Why not identify first, the schools' capacities to offer a variety of adult educational programs, and second, survey the communities' labor force to determine their interest not just singly, but as family units in such offerings; thirdly, with the help of federal and private business funds on a percentage basis, offer courses to the community's work force.

It would seem to me that the business which enriches the general life of its worker's family in such a way would take a giant step toward humanizing his work life as well.

I suggest the last possibility because I wonder in part if we are not missing the forest for the trees. Indeed much can be done to humanize work. Our society is surely capable of countless technical achievements to eradicate the most objectionable features of almost any work.

But it seems to me that even if we succeed in that area, we have not answered the need that lies behind job dissatisfaction. As our society has advanced, it has become nearly impossible for the individual to see his single small efforts as significant and meaningful to our society. It is not simply work which needs humanizing, but our very lives.

I believe in education, and in its power to enrich man's existence. No man has too much of it, and the society which offers such enrichment must offer, too, hope of an increase in the meaning of each individual life.

Work and Nonwork: Merging Human and Societal Needs

MARVIN D. DUNNETTE
LEAETTA HOUGH
HENRY ROSETT
EMILY MUMFORD
SIDNEY A. FINE

Merging Work and Nonwork

Is it too much to expect that in the future man's capacity for work will be fully integrated with his capacity for pleasure? [Here we will trace] the meager beginnings, the feeble first steps man has taken toward that goal and offer some thoughts on further actions to speed the process.

Perhaps in the year 2001 we will no longer suffer from alienation and apathy; quality of life rather than a sense of needing to belong will provide unity of purpose, and we will have learned to build constructively on our differences rather than waste our efforts in group conflict. Human values and organizational goals in the world of tomorrow will stress autonomy, diversity, and acceptance. Achievement, though still important, no longer will be Western man's central aim. Production of goods and services will be planned toward the broad goal of providing pleasure and improving the quality of each person's life. The worlds of work and nonwork will have merged. Man's capacity for joy and his search for self-actualization will find easy and open expression.

A big order? Yes. Even so, its realization seems within reach, though far from easy to attain. So far, society's maladaptive use of its human and natural resources has been counter to the hope of providing a better life for all. Future efforts to improve the physical and environmental well-being of people, however, will yield millions of new job opportunities—new careers to use fully the human resources available in society.

A Resource Conservation Industry

Technology

In the broadest sense, the age of technology has generated new needs, needs so great and so important that already a new industry—the resource conservation industry—is developing to meet them. Consider, for example, the needs created by just one segment of technology, the invention and mass production of the automobile. Vast numbers of cars and drivers have led to new jobs in driver education, automobile inspection, traffic control, building and maintenance of roads, air pollution control, noise pollution control, recycling junked automobiles, and so on. Other areas affected by the technological revolution are education, urban and rural development, recreation, community services, health care, and pollution control. Needs for improving the quality of our environment and the quality of life create countless new job opportunities.

Education

Only 50 percent of American high schools today provide professional counseling and vocational guidance to students. Increasing the number of counselors—through para-professional training, which will provide new careers—can result in bringing resource conservation job opportunities to the attention of more high school students, encouraging them to enter this field. Better utilization of human resources requires such earlier and greater emphasis on how those resources may be best utilized and directed in the world of tomorrow.

Urban and rural development

Urban-development legislation has a long history; yet, it is estimated that over eight million substandard housing units still exist in the United States. These must be replaced or rehabilitated at prices people can afford. Such work will help to provide jobs and incomes for the unemployed and may also serve as excellent training for such skilled trades as carpentry, plastering, painting, papering, masonry, and glazing.

Rural America also faces the severe problems of low income, few jobs, and substandard education. Extension agents who understand both administrative problems and agricultural development and marketing must train local people. Experts in technical and leadership training could begin to develop the resources of particular rural areas, and trained aides could make significant strides toward improving rural educational systems.

Recreation

Recreational services provide stimulating activities in all phases of human living —educational, social, cultural, and physical—and many new jobs in recreation are created each year. Total employment in the management of public and private recreation areas is expected to reach 1.4 million by 1980. For young people in rural areas, the creation of recreational services provides job opportunities in their own communities.

Within both urban and rural communities, there is already a demand for recreation workers who can perform in many capacities. More personnel are needed to organize and supervise individual and group activities and to direct physical, social, and cultural programs for all ages at hospitals, community centers, and playgrounds. Para-professionals can easily supervise special activities such as tennis, basketball, and even arts and crafts. Many recreational workers today are para-professionals who assist social workers in correctional and welfare institutions as well as in schools and hospitals. Opportunities exist also in industrial settings where recreational activities are provided for company employees. There are shortages of trained recreation workers in hospitals, local government projects, and youth organizations throughout the country. Employment opportunities in these fields grow each year.

Community services

Modern cities demand broader and more comprehensive community services, including law enforcement, day care centers, employment services, and family guidance and counseling services. For example, in the United States today, nearly 400,000 children under 12 are unsupervised during their working mothers' absence from their homes. As more women move into the labor force in the years ahead, these numbers will increase. The establishment of day-care centers will create new jobs as well as answer the direct need for child supervision. The personnel working in these centers may also be able to teach children about such things as home management, nutrition, textiles, clothing, furnishings, buying goods and services, use of leisure time, and economic responsibility.

Health

Cities and rural areas are in serious need of trained medical personnel. Many people do not go to clinics or hospitals for care because of family responsibilities, the lack of accessible facilities, or simply fear of institutional complexities. Para-professional medical workers are needed to teach out-patients to recognize symptoms of common disorders, do follow-up studies on patients, provide transportation to and from clinics, care for children and older people, allay patients' anxieties, and to listen to complaints. And these medical workers need to be in accessible locations. Hospitals, also, need more personnel to orient and interview incoming patients and, in general to give patients more attention.

Pollution control and conservation

Nearly every major river system is polluted. Air in urban areas is contaminated. Man's natural environment needs immediate attention to remain habitable.

Yet pollution is as complex as it is widespread. Smog and soot make our cities dirty but also irritate our eyes, injure our lungs, and affect paint, metals, and even the stone of our buildings. Insecticides and fungicides can contaminate both crops and soils and, eventually, the waterways. The environmental crisis demands intensive efforts to combat and control pollution; thousands of workers are needed to help reverse the ecocidal process. For example, sanitation and health workers, testers, inspectors, environmental educators, research personnel, demonstration agents, and people who function as agents for change are desperately needed.

New Careers for the Poor

Clearly, society's needs dictate an increase in job and career opportunities in education, health care, environmental renewal, personnel services, and recreational activities. These new careers can provide greater personal fulfillment for the nearly 21 million poor people in the United States while also leading to improvement in the overall quality of life for everyone. In a word, wisdom in using the forces and innovations of technology to create a resource conservation industry should reduce the waste and destructive exploitation of human and natural resources.

Job training programs have been tried in the past, but unfortunately they have not been uniformly successful.

Man-job Adaptation: Organizational Accommodation

To make good use of his functional skills in meeting the specific demands of any job, adaptation and accommodation must take place between an individual and the work organization. An individual's functional skills will ordinarily be most efficiently applied and utilized when his adaptive skills are closely attuned to specific organizational conditions and requirements; they will be least effective when his adaptive skills are incompatible with specific organizational demands. Hence effective worker performance and good job training and career development demand an alert organizational system sensitive to the adaptive as well as functional and specific content skills of employees and, most important, a readiness to accommodate its own nature and functioning to the adaptive capabilities and/or potentials of its employees.

Sociologists, child development specialists, and educators have studied the influence of family, social class, and early childhood experiences in school on the acquisition of adaptive skills. Findings from research in all of these areas indicate that differential socialization yields differential adaptive skills, or that differential adaptive skills are a result of the social class, and early childhood and family experiences of individuals.

Successful adaptation seems to require not only conformity to, or the acceptance of, societal norms but also positive and flexible interaction with the environment. Moreover, successful adaptation implies responsiveness not only to society's expectations and rules but also to its novel demands. A person may fit into a particular environment—that is, conform—but when he moves to a different environment, his previously adaptive behaviors may be maladaptive. Consequently, successful adaptation demands behavioral change even though the new behavior is contrary to previous values and attitudes.

Difficulties encountered by most new careers programs flow directly from their unfortunate attachment to bureaucracies. Complex bureaucracies have usually been rigid rather than accommodative, and they have demanded of target participants behaviors that ignore the participants' generally very limited adaptive skills. Program courses have been designed to teach mainly functional skills and impart information about things, data, people, and information processing. Even the on-the-job training and apprenticeships have dealt mainly with specific content. Stresses induced by adaptive breakdowns are regarded frequently as sources of personal and value conflict, not as stimuli for creating adaptive skill training procedures. Program directors are not entirely at fault; their negligence is due in part to the absence of available adaptive skills training methods.

Considerations for Teaching Adaptive Skills

Adaptive skills training is likely to be complex and costly; it cannot be implemented successfully in a series of one- or two-week orientation programs. If adaptive skills are to be learned by adults whose present skills are maladaptive to technological situations, the problem will require nothing less than a total approach. In a sense, society must be willing to make the effort similar to that used in some institutions with persons with mental and emotional problems who are dealt with intensively in a program combining hospitalization and treatment in a normal environment setting.

First, new methods must be developed to assess systematically the level of a person's adaptive skills and, in particular, the relevance of those skills to different job or career assignments. Second, current training and development programs, such as the Job Corps and residential halfway houses, should be evaluated to ascertain what conditions are more or less suitable for different types of persons. Learning conditions simulating early childhood, family, and peer group situations may prove most effective for altering adaptive skill levels to fit specific social and technological conditions. Third, it will be necessary to learn the best way for reinforcing positive adaptive skills in young adults. Can adaptive skills be taught apart from functional and specific content work skills? What is the proper mix and/or emphasis in a work situation? If adaptive skills training is to lead to competence in specific content skills, specific skill training probably should be integrated from the beginning with the more basic skills training.

The emphasis in vocational training should be shifted from teaching a specific skill to teaching functional abilities useful in a variety of settings. Learners should be exposed to a variety of contexts in which they can try out their newly acquired skills and knowledges. This can be done by providing relevant shop or laboratory work situations supplemented by field trips and demonstrations. Company training should, of course, not be the only agency for imparting adaptive skills; schools should continue as important training sites. Curricula should focus not only on subject matter and work-relevant knowledge and skills but also on such adaptive dimensions as attitudes, values, and work habits. Teaching methods should include field trips to places of work, films depicting work and nonwork activities, visits, talks, demonstrations, and role playing. Such activities would allow the students to explore different styles of successful work adaptation. Both teachers and vocational counselors need to be aware of and reinforce a variety of adaptive behavior and attitudes that will be needed in work situations.

Costs of adaptive skills training programs will often exceed the costs of broad content-oriented educational programs. Nonetheless, it is crucial to undertake such training if we are to follow the technological imperative for improving the quality of life through broadening the scope of job and career possibilities. On the other hand, the costs of neglecting such teaching programs would certainly be very high if measured in terms of continued financial dependency, delinquency, criminality, and similar social upheaval for increasing segments of our society.

Prognosis and Hope

Highly efficient and accurate communication between individuals and organizations will be the critical glue in the merged worlds of work and nonwork in the year 2001. Through better communication, adaptation and accommodation will be assured and sustained, and the role conflict and role ambiguity so prevalent in current job training and career programming will have long since disappeared. Ambiguity and conflict in work settings have inevitably led to emotional tension, anxiety, fear, anger, hostility, and finally apathy. But the emergence of new careers is now fully conceded to be a complex social process involving massive change in social arrangements and redefinitions of existing occupations. Creating each new job category means an emergence of a new group, shifts in relationships between colleagues, patterns of economic rewards, and redistribution of autonomy, power, and prestige. It is our hope that the adaptive skills of our present industrial and educational institutions are sufficient to allow them to move flexibly and creatively toward the adaptive skill training programs such as we have discussed above. Only then can the development of a great new industry—a resource conservation industry devoted to giving men and women full opportunities for pleasurable self expression in the world of tomorrow—be certain. . . .

New Approaches for New Careers—Strategic and Technical Considerations

How have poor planning, faulty coordination, and role definition problems affected most new career program efforts? An examination of the basic conditions of difficulty is essential if society is to move beyond the present shambles by the year 2001. Broadly speaking, there are two points of view—strategic and technical.

From a strategic point of view, it must first be ascertained how new careers can fit into existing personnel structures. Such structures are arenas of individual aggrandizement for status, power, or careerism. These structures do, therefore, reflect the basic needs of people for recognition, response, and self-realization, as well as their ability, or inability, to exercise good will and good intentions.

Most present career employees have, over the course of time, worked out personal strategies for getting ahead. They are obviously not willing to step aside for incoming new careerists who operate under different sets of rules. If new rules are indeed more advantageous, they should be administered for the existing work force either before or at least at the same time as their introduction for new careerists. For example, if performance standards are going to be changed for new careerists, they should also be changed for present career employees. If new careerists are to receive transportation assistance, special training courses, or other support services, these same benefits should accrue to present employees, too. Although the need for such equal treatment may seem obvious, it has been, surprisingly, widely ignored.

On the technical level, the implementation of new policies must be examined. In general, persons in charge of public service agencies, especially those agencies concerned with human services, are ignorant of specific role requirements. They know little of how an employee's actions may or may not contribute to specific goals, or how to achieve certain standards of performance; they know little of the technology of the work or how the work should be supervised. Managers at all levels, from the lowest to the highest, must thus learn to define their job goals. Though under constant review, the goals at any time must be firm and explicit. They must, of course, reflect the values and beliefs of the organization but state them explicitly in terms of time, cost, manpower, location, and user (consumer or client). This explicitness is essential for assessing work performance, especially in human service organizations, where bureaucracies tend to shift their focus to record keeping and maintenance activities and away from their essential service roles. Employees can easily outguess the bureaucratic mechanism to learn exactly how to beat the system—to catch on to where the payoff is and then respond accordingly.

Second, task behaviors must accomplish the objectives of the organization. Each employee must know exactly how his contribution relates to overall objectives. In addition, specific job behavior must be explicitly defined; words such as "assists," "prepares," "develops," and "directs" are too general to have effective operational meaning. Job descriptions must outline in specific detail the sources of information, nature of instruction, tools, equipment, methods, and guidelines so that for any job one can draw reliable inferences about the degree of complexity of the task, its relation to things, data, and people, the relevant performance standards, and the general education and specific training required to perform according to standard. Not until these conditions, attainable through existing knowledge, are implemented can an effective personnel management base be laid for the year 2001.

What will happen if these conditions for improving job analyses and job descriptions are met? Four valuable outcomes are likely: accountability, self-selection, team identification, and payment according to achievement and usefulness to the team. All four outcomes have favorable implications for both productivity and personal growth.

Accountability means that every task performance will be capable of evaluation, both intrinsically, according to an employee's behavior, and organizationally, according to the relative contribution toward achieving objectives. Both descriptive standards for the whole performance and numerical standards for specific service or behavioral output will be useful. Given the setting, organization, and resource limitations, it will be possible to trace failure in achieving objectives back to the constituent tasks themselves; thus it can be determined whether failure is due to the objectives set, the methods available, the state of the art, the skills and training applied, or to some combination of these.

Self-selection may be the most important and powerful force in bringing worker and work together. It is certainly the most widely ignored and distrusted, but need it be? Is it possible that self-selection hasn't worked only because of inadequate and imprecise job information, as described above? For example, it has been my experience in the recruitment and promotion situations where task information, delineated in terms of the dimensions described above, was presented to potential candidates, that most of them eliminated themselves for one reason or another. When adaptive skill requirements were also provided, further self-selection took place. Why not learn to control the process of self-selection, a process that passes the option to the workers and makes self-selection part of their own growth? It should be emphasized that every aspect of self-selection as described here is job related.

Team identification is an alternative to job identification. Instead of filling job slots, people would participate in fulfilling overall organizational objectives. Objectives would be the responsibility of teams of workers. A team leader would fulfill several managerial functions such as serving as a channel of communications between team members and higher levels of management for routine organizational information, providing training support for new team members, and acting as a major source of technological and methodological information relevant to objectives and an arbiter in coordinating assignments to team members.

Workers would enter the team largely through self-selection and team acceptance and be taught the more elementary tasks by team members. Workers could progress at their own speed and in accordance with the availability of other team members to train and give support for more and more difficult tasks. They could choose to specialize in some tasks, share obligations for others, or learn all the tasks necessary to achieve the objective. Teams would rotate tasks, including technical and janitorial maintenance. With the learning of each task, the worker would grow in flexibility and in functional capability. Training support would take place both on and off the job. Two observations are in order: (a) much work is now done this way, but not properly acknowledged and rewarded as such, and (b) teamwork is not appropriate for really creative (not innovative) work, nor are really creative individuals usually good team members.

Although lip service is often given to the idea that pay scales are based on merit, they rarely are. For the most part, people are paid on the bases of formally negotiated or informal arrangements (collective bargaining, salary surveys, labor market agreements), seniority, status, and monopolistic practices. Even within a single labor market area, there exist wide pay discrepancies for any given job. Collective agreements tend to establish employment uniformity for those workers included in the agreements, but, even when quality of performance is accounted for, there is still considerable discrepancy between workers inside and those outside the agreement. Too often, workers must bargain for salaries on the basis of their position in the organization or their title, rather than on the basis of job performance. A homemaker is one of the most notorious examples of unfair practices. Well-organized assembly line workers and semi-automatic machine workers performing work that could easily and possibly be performed better (as the work is designed) by a robot are paid three or four times as much as the workers to whom they entrust the care and well-being of their children and who must exercise considerably more discretion and perform a much greater variety of tasks.

Workers employed in the year 2001 would be paid a basic rate for performing a basic core of entry tasks. Then, following a reasonable period of probation, they would receive additional increments. From the start, they would be assigned to a team and allowed to learn additional tasks as they became ready for them until they had learned all the tasks relating to the objectives of the team. They would then earn a team rate. They would carry no job titles, but would be identified with the team and the particular job to be done. There would be no specific educational requirements for achieving pay rates, although functional and specific training would be available and encouraged to enhance the worker's ability. There would be additional increments within pay rates for achieving higher standards. Team leaders and team members would determine who deserved such special merit increases on the basis of task performance standards. However, special merit increases should be quite exceptional, since team participation would recognize a wide range of effective performance.

References

Fine, S. A. *Guidelines for the employment of the culturally disadvantaged*. Washington, D.C.: The Upjohn Institute for Employment Research, September 1969.

Hallowitz, E., & Riessman, F. The role of the indigenous nonprofessional in a community mental health neighborhood service center program. *American Journal of Orthopsychiatry*, 1967, *37*, 766-788.

Roman, M. Community control and the community mental health center: A view from Lincoln Bridge. In *Community Control: Realities and Possibilities*. New Haven: Yale University Press, 1971.

74 75 76 77 78 10 9 8 7 6 5 4 3 2